Adolescence:
A Developmental Transition

◆

SECOND EDITION

DOUGLAS C. KIMMEL
City College of the City University of New York

IRVING B. WEINER
University of South Florida

JOHN WILEY & SONS, INC.
New York / Chichester / Brisbane / Toronto / Singapore

ACQUISITIONS EDITOR   *Karen Dubno*
MARKETING MANAGER   *Catherine Faduska*
SENIOR PRODUCTION EDITOR   *Bonnie Cabot*
DESIGNER   *Ann Marie Renzi*
MANUFACTURING MANAGER   *Susan Stetzer*
PHOTO RESEARCHER   *Mary Ann Price*
ILLUSTRATION   *Jaime Perea*

This book was set in New Times Roman by Digitype

Recognizing the importance of preserving what has been written, it is a
policy of John Wiley & Sons, Inc. to have books of enduring value published
in the United States printed on acid-free paper, and we exert our best
efforts to that end.

Library of Congress Cataloging in Publication Data:
Kimmel, Douglas C.
    Adolescence : a developmental transition / Douglas C. Kimmel,
  Irving B. Weiner. — 2nd ed.
      p.   cm.
    Includes bibliographical reference and indexes.

    1. Adolescence. 2. Adolescent psychology. 3. Puberty.
  I. Weiner, Irving B.   II. Title.
  HQ796.K47 1995
  305.23′6—dc20
                                            94-28382
                                            CIP

Printed in Singapore
10 9 8 7 6 5 4 3 2 1

♦ Preface

This book describes how adolescents grow and develop during the transitional years from childhood to adulthood. Its purpose is to convey to readers what is known about adolescent development, how the behavior of young people can best be understood, and what the experience of adolescence is like for teenagers and those around them.

To achieve these ends, the characteristic individual, interpersonal, and social events of adolescence are discussed with careful attention given to current research findings and influential theoretical perspectives. Available empirical evidence is cited wherever relevant, and selected studies of special significance are described in detail. Alternative interpretations of these data as proposed within various theoretical frames of reference are identified, sometimes leading to conclusions that the weight of evidence points in one direction or another and at other times encouraging the reader to ponder which explanation appears most accurate or useful. Attention is drawn as much as possible to where the current frontiers of knowledge lie and what territory remains to be explored. As for the experience of adolescence, individual examples and first-person accounts are used extensively to convey the flavor as well as the facts of what it means to be an adolescent.

The book consists of 13 chapters organized to provide integrated discussions of the central topics in adolescent psychology. Chapter 1 introduces the transitional formulation of adolescent development—no longer a child, not yet an adult—and describes research methods used in studying adolescence. Chapter 2 then summarizes the major theoretical themes in adolescent psychology. The sequential importance of certain developmental tasks at various stages of adolescence provides an outline for the subsequent chapters.

In Chapter 3 the discussion turns to biological development during adolescence, including the endocrinology of puberty and psychological reactions to physical change. Chapter 4 addresses adolescent cognitive development, with special attention given to information processing and the maturation of thinking capacities, following which Chapter 5 considers maturational aspects of social cognition during the teenage years.

Chapter 6 provides an overview of the outer physical dimension in Riegel's analysis by discussing the social ecology of middle adolescence, with particular reference to how young people cope with and are influenced by five features of the world around them: population demographics, the nature of schools, the world of work, the impact of the media, and bicultural environments.

Chapter 7 explores the family relationships of adolescents, including the impact of nontraditional types of family organization, the influence of personal and societal factors on relationships between the adult and adolescent generations, and autonomy. Chapter 8 turns to the peer relationships of adolescents as expressed in friendship patterns, group membership, heterosocial activities, and the experience of being lonely and shy. Chapter 9 extends the discussion of interpersonal relationships to describe how young people approach sexuality and romance and deal with concerns about such matters as masturbation, homosexuality, contraception, pregnancy, and sexually transmitted diseases. This chapter provides a bridge from middle adolescence to late adolescent issues.

Chapter 10 discusses the culmination of adolescent physical, cognitive, interpersonal, and social maturation in the formation of a sense of identity. Included in this chapter are discussions of how the process of identity formation bears on gender-role influences, vocational choice, and the normatively adaptive nature of adolescent development.

Chapter 11 considers problems that young people sometimes have in adjusting to their school and community and presents information concerning the two problems of this kind that are most likely to interfere with normal adolescent development: academic underachievement and delinquency. Chapter 12 then discusses several other developmental pitfalls and challenges that may undermine the well-being of adolescents and require special help to overcome: drug abuse, running away, suicidal behavior, adjusting to chronic illness and physical disability, and coping with death and dying. Finally, Chapter 13 reviews the nature and treatment of three types of psychological disturbance that often begin during the adolescent years: schizophrenia, affective disorder, and eating disorders, including obesity, anorexia nervosa, and bulimia.

PEDAGOGICAL FEATURES

To help readers study the material and grasp the nature of adolescent development, each chapter begins with a detailed outline and concludes with a summary of its central points. Key words are printed in boldface in the text and listed in a Glossary that provides definitions of them. These key words are also listed at the end of each chapter, along with a series of review questions. Students who are able to answer these review questions will have attained a thorough mastery of the subject of adolescent development.

To enrich the material in the text further, detailed first-person accounts of the experience of adolescence appear in the form of five "Interludes" following Chapters 5, 7, 8, 10, and 11 in which young people comment on their lives and capture various themes discussed in the text.

The first interlude, Sarah, age 13, follows Chapter 5 and is an interview with a normal young adolescent girl who lives in an affluent suburb. Cesar (following Chapter 7) is an American-born 16-year-old boy whose parents immigrated from Ecuador and who lives in New York City. Linda (following Chapter 8) is a middle-class 15-year-old African-American girl living in New York City and attending a private, church-related school. Carol (following Chapter 10) is a white 17-year-old girl living in a medium-sized Southern city. Brad (following Chapter 11) lives in a small town in a rural area. These interludes are transcripts of interviews that lasted 1–2 hours each; they have been edited as little as possible in order to convey the ideas and feelings in the person's own words.

The interviews were designed to explore the major issues faced by adolescents: puberty, relations with parents and family members, friendships and peer relations, sexuality, dating, identity, and goals for the future. The interviewer's questions are indicated by italics in the text. All of the personal names and basic identifying place names have been changed to ensure anonymity. One important characteristic of the five adolescent interviews is that the respondents knew how the interviews were going to be used. Thus, the information is censored by the respondent to the extent that each tended to present his or her life in a relatively positive light. Thus one should read these cases with a healthy mixture of skepticism and openness. In short, these are *developmental* interviews that are exploring the transition of adolescence.

These interludes provide an opportunity to bridge the gap between theoretical concepts and real persons living their complex lives. We feel that the challenge of interpreting these cases in terms of the themes discussed within the chapters is an important part of the learning process, and so we wish to share this task with the student and the classroom instructor. Thus, each interlude is preceded by a brief introduction and several questions to consider while reading, thinking about, and discussing the individual case example.

NEW TO THE SECOND EDITION

For readers familiar with the first edition of this text, several features of the book new to this second edition can be noted. Research methods, previously discussed in an Appendix, now receive special attention in Chapter 1, and an expanded discussion of theories of adolescence constitute a new Chapter 2. The discussion of cognitive development in Chapter 4 is expanded with the addition of a section on information processing and a separate new chapter (Chapter 5) on social cognition. More specific attention than before is paid to the school, both as a social environment (Chapter 6) and in relation to problems of school learning and attendance (Chapter 11). New discussions of the media, of physical and sexual abuse, and of bulimia have been added in Chapters 6, 8, and 13, respectively. There are two new interludes, and the list of key words and review questions following each chapter are new features in this edition. Finally, the biographies of leading figures in the history of adolescent psychology (Anna Freud, Piaget, Erikson, and Sullivan) are supplemented with informational boxes concerning the contributions of leading current researchers in the field (Baumrind, Berndt, Brook, Goldstein, Kohlberg, Money, Paster, Quay, and Riegel).

The text is designed for use in adolescent psychology courses offered in psychology, education, human development, social work, nursing, and medical programs. Its 13-chapter format lends itself well to presentation in a typical semester course. Instructors teaching in a quarter system can readily adapt the text to a 10-unit presentation by combining Chapters 1 and 2 (concerned with history, research, and theory) and Chapters 11–13 (concerned with developmental problems) into single units. An *Instructor's Manual* consisting of teaching suggestions for each chapter, Key Words in order of appearance, Review Questions, multiple-choice questions, and media sources is available.

The following reviewers were especially helpful in preparing this second edition:

Jennifer Connolly
York University

William Gray
University of Toledo

William Hall
University of Maryland

Yvette Harris
Miami University

William Hauck
Bucknell University

Daniel Houlihan
Mankato State University

June Irving
Ball State University

Dolores Jenerson-Madden
Southern California College

Matthijs Koopmans
Adelphi University

James Link
Housatonic Community College

Laddie Lollar
Bethel College

John McManus
Eastern Michigan University

Dennis Papini
Western Illinois University

George Rebok
Johns Hopkins University

Kathleen Ross-Kidder
George Washington University

Robert Rycek
University of Nebraska

Toni Santmire
University of Nebraska

Robert Schell
SUNY-Oswego

Larry Shelton
University of Vermont

We especially thank the five adolescents who shared their feelings and experiences with us in the interludes. Alexandra Woods, Andrea Mowatt, Linda I. Livesy, and Karen Dubno provided valuable assistance in contacting and interviewing them. Ronald W. Schwizer and Frances Weiner helped on various tasks in preparing the manuscript and index. The editorial, photo research, design, and production staff at John Wiley were superb and are listed on the copyright page. Finally, we thank the students and colleagues who gave us comments on the first edition and the students at City College who used a prepublication manuscript of this second edition. We are happy to hear comments on this book, which may be sent to us at our universities, or in care of the publisher.

Douglas C. Kimmel
Irving B. Weiner

◆ Contents

Chapter 5   *Social Cognition: Thinking About Social Topics*   145

Interlude: Sarah, Age 12   171

Chapter 6   *The Social Ecology of Adolescence*   181

Chapter 11   *Problems in School and the Community*   433

Chapter 12   *Pitfalls and Challenges*   471

Chapter 1

◆

The Developmental Transition of Adolescence

◆

Like the horseshoe crab that has outgrown one shell but has not yet produced a new one, adolescence in the human lifespan is a time of transition. It may also be a time of greater vulnerability and stress; but just as surely, it may be a time of wonder, change, and positive growth. Some find it overwhelming; others move through it with relative calm.

Adolescence can be a lonely, troubled period or one of too-rapid growth into parenthood and total independence. Sometimes it is marked by running away; trouble with family, school, or police; delinquency; drug abuse; or reaching out for help and finding no one cares. Oftentimes, however, adolescence is a period of new developments and greater excitement—a time of searching, discovering, and living from day to day to the best of one's ability in a complicated social world of new friendships, new feelings, and different responsibilities and expectations. Occasionally there are unpredictable reactions and strong feelings; sometimes a poetic sensitivity; perhaps ups and downs that are hard to understand. But also there are calm times, periods of boredom, and plain ordinary living and working.

For all, adolescence is a period of transition—a time of change from one phase of life to another. The immaturity of childhood is being left behind; the challenges and potentials of adulthood have not yet been adopted. One is no longer a child, but not yet an adult.

This theme and the idea of transitions are the topics of the first two sections of this chapter. The chapter concludes with a discussion of research methods that are used in psychological studies of adolescence that we draw upon throughout the book.

NO LONGER A CHILD; NOT YET AN ADULT

The word **adolescence** comes from the Latin word (adolescere) meaning "to grow up" or "to grow into maturity" (Muuss, 1982, p. 4). As it is generally used today, adolescence refers to the period of life between childhood and adulthood—roughly corresponding to the teenage years. However, the meaning of adolescence, and the ages at which it begins and ends, differ from one part of the world to another and differ, also, between our 20th century ideas and those of earlier historical periods.

WHEN DOES ADOLESCENCE BEGIN AND END?

Is a 15-year-old boy an adolescent if he has not yet begun to show any of the physical changes of puberty? What about an 11-year-old girl who has already begun menstruation? If we were to visit any sixth-, seventh-, or eighth-grade class, we would find a wide variation in physical, social, and intellectual maturity. A few would have developed almost to their adult height, body hair, and sexual maturity, whereas others would not have begun these changes. Some would have begun dating; others would not. Some would be studying industriously for an adult career, whereas others would be primarily interested in being accepted by their group of friends. Some might act as if they were "grown up" in one way or another, whereas others would appear to be content to retain their childlike mannerisms. One group might seek to act "cool"; another might be smoking or drinking because they feel this is a sign of being grown up; others might avoid all these behaviors because they feel they are signs of immaturity. Can we decide which of these teenagers would be considered to be an adolescent? Or perhaps they all would be adolescents—each unique.

Currently in the United States, the period of adolescence is usually defined by what it is not: when one is too old to be a child, but too young to be an adult. It is a peculiar kind of definition in a way, but is really not that different from the definitions of other stages of the lifespan. When is one "middle-aged"? When is one "old"? Certainly there is great variation among individuals in these periods of adulthood, and the precise ages at which they begin and end are no less ambiguous than the beginning and ending of adolescence.

Consider also the conclusion of adolescence. Is a 14-year-old "prodigy" who has completed her doctorate and is working in nuclear physics an adolescent? What about the 18-year-old father of two children who works for the corner gasoline station, or the 25-year-old medical student who has not yet married or begun to work for a living? Stretching the idea a bit, we might even consider the 35-year-old who is still "searching for himself" to be at least somewhat adolescent.

Rather than setting clear definitions of the beginning or ending of adolescence, we would prefer to accept the ambiguity about the ages at the boundaries of adolescence. However, we can offer two helpful guidelines. First, the *beginning* of adolescence tends to be defined primarily by the individual's biological age. Second, the *ending* of adolescence is most readily defined by the person's social age (Schlegel & Barry, 1991, p. 10).

Biological Age

There are many ways to measure the age or the maturity of an organism. Of course, the most common one for humans is *chronological age*; that is, the amount of time since the person was born. However, as the earlier examples indicated, the mere passage of time does not produce all of the changes that occur at the beginning of adolescence. In addition, as we discuss in Chapter 3, the age of puberty, when measured by the chronological age of a girl's first menstruation, varies by as much as 6.5 years (Tanner, 1971, p. 923).

Another way to measure age is by biological signs, such as the number of teeth that have developed (known as "dental maturity") or the development of bones in the hand and wrist or in other parts of the body (known as "skeletal maturity"). Because every child experiences this biological growth, it is possible to create a scale of development that we may think of as **biological age**. According to Tanner (1971), such an "age" based on skeletal maturity is fairly closely related to the age of a girl's first menstruation (within 2.5 years). Other measures of biological age reflect stages in development of pubic hair, breast development in girls, or genital growth in boys (see Chapter 3). These measures of biological age are closely related to hormone changes and are more accurate markers of the beginning of adolescence than is chronological age.

Social Age

A concept similar to biological age is the social maturity of an individual. Many social institutions have clearly defined the beginning of adolescence, but the age varies greatly. For example, schools mark the beginning of adolescence by graduation from elementary school; in some communities, this occurs at the end of the sixth grade, but in others it is the end of the seventh or eighth grade (ages 12, 13, and 14, respectively). Religious institutions often mark the beginning of adolescence with bar mitzvah, bat mitzvah, or confirmation around age 13. The family, as an institution, also sets the beginning of adolescence when dating is permitted, late night restrictions are relaxed, new freedoms are given, and greater responsibility is expected.

These socially defined measures of maturity are obviously not very exact determinants of the beginning of adolescence. However, regardless of an individual's chronological age, most people in the United States would probably agree that someone who is dating, is in junior high school, and can stay out late only one night a month is clearly an adolescent in terms of *social age*.

It is not possible to determine the conclusion of adolescence in terms of biological age, for there are no biological or physiological changes that mark the late teenage years and early 20s. However, state legislatures have decided the social definitions of the beginning of adulthood and have therefore provided one definition of the social age boundary for adolescence. That is, the age at which one can legally marry without parental consent, engage in any form of sexual behavior with a consenting partner in private, make binding legal contracts, drive a car, drink alcohol, vote, and be tried as an adult for criminal offenses all represent social definitions of the beginning of adulthood. Obviously, these differences between minors and adults vary from state to state, and many of the ages have been lowered (and some raised) in recent years. Also, the age that has been defined for one characteristic often differs for other characteristics: one may be able to marry, vote, and drive at 18, but not drink alcohol. Thus, these legally defined social criteria do not really mark a clear boundary between adolescence and adulthood (and the chronological age for these criteria varies from about 14 to 21).

Similarly, other social institutions have defined criteria for the transition from adolescence to adulthood. These include, in the family, leaving one's parents' home, marriage, and parenthood; in the schools, graduation from high school, college, or ending formal academic studies; and, in the economy, joining the labor force as a full-time worker, or caring for a home and children full-time and perhaps also working part-time.

Taken together, the measures of social maturity mark as clearly as we can the upper boundary of adolescence. Changes in social *roles* (from child to parent; from student to worker), the formal *age grading* in the social structure that changes one from a "minor" to a legally responsible "adult," and the social expectations that we have about how people of any particular age should behave are important indicators of **social age**. Therefore, when one is primarily involved in adult roles, is legally regarded as an adult, and is seen by oneself and by others as an adult, we would regard that person as no longer an adolescent in terms of social age.

CROSS-CULTURAL PERSPECTIVES

The meaning that various cultures give to adolescence differs greatly (Schlegel & Barry, 1991). For example, adolescence is marked by **initiation rites** in some cultures. These ceremonies publicly celebrate the transition of the individual from childhood to adulthood; before the event, the person is regarded as a child, but afterward he or she is given adult status. These rites can be severe trials for males, as recorded among the Thonga tribe of Africa by an anthropologist in 1927:

When a boy is somewhere between ten and sixteen years of age, he is sent by his parents to a "circumcision school" which is held every four or five years. Here in company with his age-mates he undergoes severe hazing by the adult males of the society. The initiation begins when each boy runs the gauntlet between two rows of men who beat him with clubs. At the end of this

Initiation rites in some cultures publicly celebrate the transition from childhood to adulthood.

experience, he is stripped of his clothes and his hair is cut. He is next met by a man covered with lion manes and is seated upon a stone facing this "lion man." Someone then strikes him from behind and when he turns his head to see who has struck him, his foreskin is seized and in two movements cut off by the "lion man." Afterwards he is secluded for three months in the "yards of mysteries," where he can be seen only by the initiated. It is especially taboo for a woman to approach these boys during their seclusion, and if a woman should glance at the leaves with which the circumcised covers his wound and which form his only clothing, she must be killed.

During the course of his initiation, the boy undergoes six major trials: beatings, exposure to cold, thirst, eating of unsavory foods, punishment, and threat of death. On the slightest pretext he may be severely beaten by one of the newly initiated men who is assigned to the task by the older men of the tribe. [Junod, 1927]

Initiation rites for girls serve a similar function of marking the transition from childhood to adulthood, as in this account from the Cheyenne tribe of North American Indians:

The passage of a girl from childhood to young womanhood was considered as hardly less important to the tribe than to her own family. She was now to become the mother of children and thus to contribute her part toward adding to the number of the tribe and so to its power and importance.

When a young girl reached the age of puberty and had her first menstrual period, she, of course, told her mother, who in turn informed the father. Such an important family event was not kept secret. It was the custom among well-to-do people for the father of the girl publicly to announce from the lodge door what had happened and as an evidence of his satisfaction to give away a horse.

The girl unbraided her hair and bathed, and afterward older women painted her whole body with red. Then, with a robe about her naked body, she sat near the fire, a coal was drawn from it and put before her, and sweet grass, juniper needles, and white sage were sprinkled on it. The girl bent forward over the coal and held her robe about it, so that the smoke rising from the incense was confined and passed about her and over her whole body. Then she and her grandmother left the home lodge, and went into another small one near by, where she remained for four days. [Grinnell, 1923, p. 129]

Although these two examples are not typical of modern adolescent initiation rites, they do contain same typical elements (Brown, 1963). That is, severe male initiation rites tend to occur in cultures that value strong bonds among adult males, and it may be that these rites serve to establish those bonds (Young, 1962). Similarly, female initiation rites often involve announcement of her status as a woman and instruction about women's tasks in that society, including rituals about menstruation, contraception, and pregnancy (Brown, 1963).

In cultures where such initiation rites exist, adolescence may be a very short period, lasting perhaps only for the duration of the ceremony, until the training period is completed, or until the boy returns with the proper trophies from his first extended hunt alone. Although these initiation rites must be seen in the context of the whole culture, they provide some clues about the variety of adolescent experiences around the world. We may see some similar initiation rites in our society, but they seldom serve this same function of transforming the child into an adult. Religious ceremonies, such as bar mitzvah or bat mitzvah, initiation into fraternities or sororities, and endurance experiences such as an "Outward Bound" program of survival among a group of young people in the wilderness may each contain some elements of initiation rites (Raphael, 1988). However, in our culture, by themselves they do not make a person into a socially accepted adult.

Earlier in this century, American psychologists regarded adolescence as a period of storm and stress for young people in all cultures. In 1928, Margaret Mead refuted this idea in her anthropological study of girls and young women in Samoa. She reported that adolescence in that South Sea island was a period of calm, gradual shift from the joyful roles of childhood to the joyful roles of adulthood. This implied that some cultures do not give much attention to adolescence at all.

The adolescent girl in Samoa differed from her sister who had not reached puberty in one chief respect, that in the older girl certain bodily changes were present which were absent in the younger girl. There were no other great differences to set off the group passing through adolescence from the group which would become adolescent in two years or the group which had become adolescent two years before. [Mead, 1928/1961, p. 196]

Anthropologists have debated the validity of Mead's observations. Some have claimed that she was biased or misled by her informants, while others have supported her report (Coté, 1992; Levy, 1983; Marshall, 1983). In any event, this study altered the understanding of adolescence and focused attention on variations among adolescents in different cultures.

Today it is recognized that there are a great variety of ways in which adolescence is experienced throughout the world, and our society is neither typical nor unique in its particular style of adolescence. Consider how very different the experience of adolescence must be in the diverse range of social, political, and economic situations around the world. Imagine growing to adulthood in the midst of civil war, or poverty and hunger, or great affluence, or rapid change from one type of society to another. In the 1990s there are adolescents experiencing each of these situations, and yet there are also some nearly universal experiences shared among adolescents in most countries including transistor radios, rock music, jeans, and electronic games. As Mead (1970) pointed out, historical changes such as World War II, the atomic bomb, and transistorized telecommunications have had a profound effect on the lives of nearly all adolescents around the world. More recently, the dramatic changes in Eastern Europe and the former U.S.S.R. will have profound effects on adolescents in those countries. Thus, we must also view adolescence in terms of historical changes.

HISTORICAL PERSPECTIVE

The experience of adolescence not only varies from one culture to another, but also varies throughout historical time in any culture. One may argue that adolescence, as a concept of a stage in human development, is a relatively recent discovery in Western history. Of course, there have always been young people, and a period of youth between childhood and adulthood is reported among all known societies throughout history (Eisenstadt, 1956). But several studies of historical records suggest that in America the concept of adolescence as we know it today appears to have emerged in the late nineteenth century (Elder, 1980; Modell & Goodman, 1990) .

Before the industrial revolution, during the 17th and 18th centuries, young people in the United States and Canada generally lived with their parents and did not gain adult independence until the family land was divided among the children when the parents were ready to relinquish control over the family holdings. Marriage was delayed until the man was able to support a wife, and his life was essentially controlled by his father. After several generations, this pattern began to change as the parcels of land became smaller, and some young people moved to more remote parts of the country or into the growing towns to establish their independence and raise families or seek their fortune. Many of these young people entered a period of semiautonomy by living with the household for which they worked as servants, laborers, or apprentices; some boarded with a family in town while they worked at a job nearby (Katz, 1975).

The growth of commerce and industry during the 19th century, plus the expansion of educational opportunities, greatly reduced the number of idle youth (Elder, 1980). Adolescents lived at home, by and large, thus reversing the trend toward earlier independence begun a few decades earlier. Upper socioeconomic status adolescents were likely to go on to secondary school, and they tended to postpone marriage and work until their schooling was finished. Lower socioeconomic status youth found work, probably helped support their parents' families, and attended school irregularly, if at all. Many worked in hazardous mines, factories and textile "sweat shops."

It was about this time that adolescence, as a clear stage in the lifespan, began to emerge in social thinking. The first textbook on adolescence, written by G. Stanley Hall, was published in 1904. It was his concept of "storm and stress" as a natural part of adolescence that Margaret Mead's 1928 research in Samoa so clearly challenged.

During the 19th century, some children and adolescents worked in textile mills and other jobs to help support the family.

Greater attention has been given to adolescence during the 20th century, especially since the 1950s, as a result of two major historical changes. First was the dramatic increase in school enrollment: in 1890, only 1 out of every 18 young people between ages 14 and 17 was in school; by 1920 it was 1 out of 3; and by 1950 it was 4 out of 5 (Figure 1.1). Although junior high schools existed by 1918, not until the 1950s was that type of school arrangement more prevalent than the structure of 8 years in elementary school followed by 4 years in high school. According to Elder (1980), this growth in school attendance and the creation of junior high schools led to greater emphasis on age (and grade) during the adolescent period, a shift in the control over the training of youth from the family to the school, and a clearer standard for the beginning of adolescence (that is, junior high school).

The second major change was the extraordinary growth in the number of young people, marked particularly by the "baby boom" that followed the end of World War II. The number of people between the ages of 14 and 24 increased by an incredible 52% between 1960 and 1970. Not surprisingly, the number of studies on adolescents grew tremendously during the 1960s, focusing on alienation among youth, student political activism, teenage pregnancy, and delinquency. By the 1970s, the large number of college students received so much attention among social scientists that the early years of adolescence were largely being ignored by researchers. During the 1980s, a renewed focus on early adolescence emerged (Lerner, 1993).

Currently the relative number of adolescents has declined somewhat since the "baby boom" generation has moved into their 40s and the lower birth rate has led to a reduced pro-

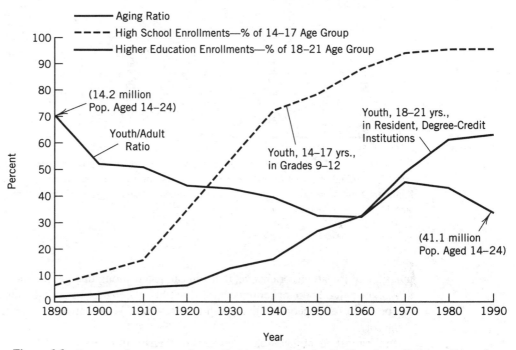

Figure 1.1 Percent of young people enrolled in school grades 9–12 and enrolled in college, from 1890 to 1990. Also shown is the ratio of young people (aged 14–24) compared with older people (aged 25–64), called the youth/adult ratio; the baby boom generation may be seen reflected in the increase in this ratio during the 1960s. [*Source:* G.H. Elder, Jr. Adolescence in Historical Perspective. In J. Adelson (Ed.), *Handbook of Adolescent Psychology.* © 1980 John Wiley & Sons. Figure 1, p. 13. Reprinted with permission.]

portion of young people, while, at the same time, the number of older people has increased. This change has led to the relatively recent emphasis on middle age and aging among social scientists and the public in general. Thus, in our society now, adolescence is generally seen as one of several important periods in the continuous process of lifespan human development—a period uniquely characterized by the transition from childhood to adulthood.

TRANSITIONS IN HUMAN DEVELOPMENT

A central concept for the study of adolescence, and for this book, is the idea of transitions during the human lifespan. If we think of the lifespan of an individual as stretching through time from birth to death, it might look like Figure 1.2. You could place yourself along that line either on the basis of chronological age, or on the basis of the various "milestones" you may have passed (such as puberty, voting, or marriage). You could also note the period we think of as childhood, and the period we consider to be adulthood, with adolescence as a *transition* in between the two. In addition, you may be able to think of a particularly impor-

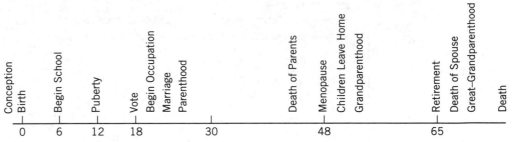

Figure 1.2   The human lifeline. Ages of important events are approximate because there are considerable individual and gender differences in the ages and the order of these milestones. [*Source:* D.C. Kimmel. *Adulthood and Aging.* © 1990 John Wiley & Sons. Figure 1.1, p. 8. Reprinted with permission.]

tant time of transition, or change, that you can locate along this life line; it might be entering school, or parenthood, or retirement; or it might be a change in an individual's life that may not occur in other peoples' lives such as a serious disease, divorce, or a personal crisis of some sort.

In the most general sense, the concept of **transition** refers to a period of change, growth, and disequilibrium that serves as a kind of bridge between one relatively stable point in life and another relatively stable, but different, point. In that sense, adolescence represents the transition between the physical, social, and sexual immaturity of childhood to the physical, social, and sexual maturity of adulthood. Thus, adolescence is a period of change, growth, and disequilibrium in terms of physical, social, and sexual maturity. In addition, the concept of transition implies that the period of life is defined in the culture as an in-between period: one is not a child, but is also not an adult. Kurt Lewin referred to this characteristic of the transitional status by the term "marginal" person: "They are people who belong neither here nor there, standing 'between' the groups" (Lewin, 1948, p. 179). This may be represented graphically by the two drawings in Figure 1.3.

Recent studies of lifespan human development have refined this concept of transition into more specific types of transitions (cf. Kimmel, 1990). One important distinction is between *internal* and *external* causes of transitions. The transition of adolescence is caused by internal biological changes; in contrast, the transition of retirement in later life is caused by external factors such as Social Security regulations. Thus, these two transitions are very different, although each involves the ambiguous social status of a marginal person who is in between two well-defined periods of life—childhood and adulthood for the adolescent, adulthood and old age for the retiree. Other examples of transitions that may be caused primarily by internal changes include falling in love, chronic disease, mental or emotional disorder, psychological maturation, and cognitive development. Other examples of externally caused transitions include graduation from high school or college, marriage, becoming a basketball star, or winning a lottery.

Another important distinction that is helpful for understanding transitions is between those that are *normative* and those that are *idiosyncratic*. Normative transitions are those that are expected to occur, usually at a particular age, as prescribed by the social traditions

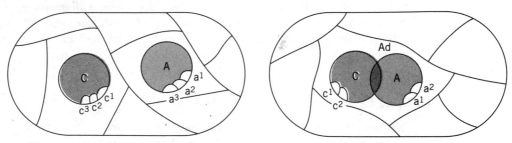

Figure 1.3 The adolescent as a marginal person. In the left drawing, during childhood and adulthood the adults (A) and children (C) are viewed as relatively separated groups. The individual children (c^1, c^2, c^3) and the individual adults (a^1, a^2, a^3) are sure of their belonging to their respective groups. In the right drawing, the adolescent belongs to a group (Ad) that is an overlapping region of the children's (C) and the adults' (A) group; this group may be viewed as belonging to both of them, or as standing between them, not belonging to either one. [*Source:* K. Lewin. The Field Theory Approach to Adolescence. *American Journal of Sociology*, 44, Figure 4, p. 882. © 1939 University of Chicago. Reprinted with permission.]

in the culture. Puberty, marriage, parenthood, and retirement would all be normative transitions in the United States. In contrast, some major transitions are idiosyncratic because they occur to only a few individuals, or occur in unpredictable ways. Examples would include "coming out" as a gay man or lesbian, getting divorced, winning a lottery, discovering one has cancer, saving a life and becoming a national hero, or experiencing the death of one's child.

One additional distinction is between those transitions that are "on time" and those transitions that are "off time" (Neugarten, 1968). For example, puberty can occur either early or late, or it can occur "on time" at the normative, or expected age. Its effects may be different if it occurs off time, rather than on time (see Chapter 3). Similarly, graduating from high school, marriage, parenthood, or retirement may each occur on time or off time and therefore have different effects on the individual.

Those transitions that are on time are also likely to be anticipated or expected, but that is not necessarily always the case. A girl's first menstruation may occur at the normal time, but if she does not know it is going to occur, she may be very upset at the blood flowing from her body and fear that she has some sort of serious problem. Conversely, a person may graduate from high school 2 years ahead of time, but anticipate this transition.

In general, those transitions that are *expected* are less upsetting than those that are *unexpected*. Similarly, those transitions that occur *on time* are likely to be less upsetting than those that occur *off time*.

In summary, we see that developmental transitions may involve relatively long periods of life—such as adolescence. Or they may involve relatively short periods of time—such as graduation from high school. They may be happy moments, or they may be tragic. They may be memorable and perhaps celebrated milestones, or they may be relatively unimportant events that are hardly worth mentioning. Some may involve a long period of self-examination; some bring a major change to one's lifestyle; and some are gone through with almost no reflection. Also, one general transition may contain a number of more s transitions; this is clearly the case with adolescence as a developmental transition, as we will see that it involves many specific transitions. These will include both idiosyncratic and normative (which may be on time or off time), both anticipated and unanticipated, as well as those caused by internal factors and those caused by external factors.

DIALECTICAL ANALYSIS OF TRANSITIONS

The study of a transition, such as adolescence, involves an examination of the process of change in human development. One approach to this is to think of the major dimensions that may cause change during the lifespan and the ways in which these changes interact with each other.

For example, social change in a nation—such as the growing acceptance of nonmarital sexual behavior in the United States—affects all persons in that country to some extent. Similarly, biological change—such as puberty—affects all individuals who experience it. Let us use these two dimensions and consider one aspect of the transition of adolescence, emerging sexual behavior. As a result of hormone changes (an increase in androgens for both boys and girls), sexual interest is greater after puberty (Udry, 1990). This greater sexual interest after puberty, in interaction with greater social tolerance of earlier sexual experience, has produced the contemporary patterns of adolescent sexual behavior: today more adolescents in the United States experience sexual intercourse at earlier ages than in the past. Thus, an individual adolescent's transition from childhood to adulthood sexuality is influenced by the interaction of biological and social forces.

It is important to note that the **interaction** of these forces is not necessarily the simple addition of one force to the other; instead, their result is likely to be different from the sum of the parts. In that sense, the term *interaction* is similar to a chemical reaction where the final result of several chemicals interacting may be quite unlike any of the chemicals separately. In our example, biological maturation does not produce increased sexual behavior, nor does more tolerant social attitudes; instead, increased sexual behavior results from the interaction of these two variables. Likewise, the interaction of biological maturation and social attitudes also has resulted in a variety of other effects: on one hand, increased rates of adolescent pregnancy and sexually transmitted diseases, and on the other hand, increased sex education and greater knowledge about contraceptives (e.g., condoms). Thus, interacting forces may have a broad range of effects not directly related to the changes that began the process.

A **dialectical interaction** is a particular type of interaction in which there is a tension between two or more opposing forces; the result of that interaction is a new synthesis that reflects, not the sum of the forces, but a resolution of them in a way that is different from the original separate forces. To return to the example of the emergence of adolescent sexual behavior, one dialectical interaction today is between the adolescent's growing sexual interest and opportunity at a time in history when the epidemic of acquired immune deficiency syndrome (AIDS) has emerged. The resulting dialectical tension is between risking infection or abstaining from sexual intercourse. The synthesis that is emerging out of these opposing alternatives consists of adherence to safer-sex guidelines, use of a condom, discussing with one's partner the best ways to prevent possible infection, and testing for the virus associated with AIDS. The individual resolution of these dialectical struggles becomes the temporary

Attitudes about abortion confront adolescents with a dialectial tension between opposing points of view.

synthesis that is involved in the dialectic tension the next time sexual intercourse is antici-pated. Likewise, a dialectical tension is faced when an adolescent becomes pregnant and must decide between abortion or childbirth and faces the ethical issues involving the "right to life" or the "right to choice."

An approach to understanding transitions in human development from this dialectical perspective was developed by Klaus Riegel (1976). He proposed that there are four major dimensions of human development: inner-biological, individual-psychological, cultural-so-ciological, and outer-physical (Box 1.1). Each of these dimensions is constantly interacting with others and with other elements within the same dimension. Therefore, each may bring change, create problems, raise questions, or bring transitions in the life cycle.

Because this fourfold progression is obviously complex and changes in one dimension are not always synchronized with the changes in other dimensions, there is usually some de-gree of conflict between the dimensions. In addition, major changes in any of the dimen-sions will bring a confrontation between that dimension and the other dimensions. If this confrontation brings a major reorganization of the other dimensions, then this may be seen as a period of developmental transition.

Thus, a period of relative synchronization across the four dimensions may be upset by a significant change in one or more of the dimensions. For example, the relative synchroniza-tion of the dimensions during late childhood is upset by the change in the inner-biological dimension at puberty, leading to a major reorganization of the other dimensions and the

◆ *Profile*

KLAUS F. RIEGEL

Born in Germany, Klaus Riegel earned his master's degree from the University of Minnesota and his doctorate from the University of Hamburg. He joined the faculty of the University of Michigan in 1959 after a postdoctoral year as a visiting scientist at the National Institutes of Health. He was interested in several aspects of human development including gerontology (the study of aging) and received the Robert W. Kleemeier Award in 1976 from the Gerontological Society of America. He was editor of the international journal *Human Development* from 1970 until his death in 1977 at the age of 51.

His major contribution was in the formulation of a dialectical psychology that focused on activities and changes instead of on stable traits or balanced states. It also recognized the interdependence of historical and individual development. Moreover, he felt that dialectics should be applied to understanding the discipline of psychology or human development itself. Thus, all formulations are subject to new and unpredictable challenges and interpretations.

"Students . . . remember him as a kind, patient, and generous teacher, always willing to listen and encourage. His office, as well as his home, were havens for several generations of students, who found their widely divergent ideas not only tolerated but also clarified and strengthened. . . . [Colleagues] recall his unrelenting energy in contributing to the growth of developmental psychology and in motivating others with his enthusiasm and insights."

[*Source*: In memoriam: Klaus F. Riegel, November 6, 1925–July 3, 1977, *Human Development*, *20*, 1977, 317–325.]

transition of adolescence (cf. Adams, Day, Dyk, Frede, & Rogers, 1992). Throughout the period of adolescence, changes in each of the dimensions produce additional reorganizations in this complex pattern of dialectical interactions. Moreover, each period of relative synchronization of the four dimensions sets the stage for the next reorganization. Referring once more to the example of adolescent sexuality, increased sexual interest (individual-biological dimension), growing acceptance of nonmarital sexual behavior (cultural-sociological dimension), AIDS (outer-physical dimension), and personal beliefs and values about sexual behavior (individual-psychological dimension) all interact in this dialectical manner.

This view sees human development as a process of ceaseless change and is therefore especially appropriate for the study of the transition of adolescence. However, it is also fairly

♦ BOX 1.1 EXAMPLES OF THE FOUR MAJOR DIMENSIONS OF DEVELOPMENT THAT PRODUCE TRANSITIONS THROUGH THE PROCESS OF DIALECTICAL INTERACTION

Individual Psychological	Individual Biological	Cultural Sociological	Outer Physical
Maturity	Puberty	Social attitudes	Economic conditions
Emotional feelings	Health	Social expectations	War
Independence	Pregnancy	Opportunities	Urban or rural life

abstract, so it will be helpful to consider the specific developmental tasks that are involved in this transition.

DEVELOPMENTAL TASKS IN ADOLESCENCE

A useful way to view the transition of adolescence is to think of the specific **developmental tasks** that young people are normally expected to accomplish during the teenage years. Such a list would undoubtedly differ among various cultures and historical periods, but there would also be some generally accepted expectations among most societies. Based on our previous discussion of transitions, such tasks would be considered *normative* (rather than idiosyncratic); the achievement of the task would be expected to occur *on time* (neither too early nor too late); and the tasks would be known and anticipated by the individual (they would not be surprised by unexpected changes or demands). Moreover, such a list of tasks would tap each of the four dimensions of human development proposed by Riegel: individual-biological, individual-psychological, socio-cultural, and outer-physical.

In his book, *Developmental Tasks and Education* (first published in 1951), Robert Havighurst, one of the pioneers in the study of lifespan human development, proposed such a series of *developmental tasks* for individuals at various points in the life cycle. He regarded these tasks as specific knowledge, skills, attitudes, or functions that individuals are expected to acquire or develop at particular points in their lives. They result from a combination of personal effort, physical maturation, and social pressure. Educators can also play a part in helping a person to achieve these tasks, but their influence is most significant at the "teachable moment" when the person is developmentally ready for the task. Havighurst also felt that each task needed to be accomplished in sequence, and so each task depends on the successful achievement of earlier tasks. If a task is not achieved at the appropriate time, it may be difficult or impossible to master it later or to progress on successfully to subsequent tasks.

Each period of life has developmental tasks, according to Havighurst (1972, pp. 45–75). The tasks in adolescence follow the tasks in middle childhood; in turn, they set the stage for the tasks of young adulthood. He specified eight tasks during the adolescent period:

1. Achieving new and more mature relations with age-mates of both sexes.
2. Achieving a masculine or feminine social role.

3. Accepting one's physique and using one's body effectively.
4. Achieving emotional independence of parents and other adults.
5. Preparing for marriage and family life.
6. Preparing for an economic career.
7. Acquiring a set of values and an ethical system as a guide to behavior; developing an ideology.
8. Desiring and achieving socially responsible behavior.

Some may wish to modify the wording of these tasks to reflect recent changes in social expectations about, for example, masculine and feminine roles or marriage and family life; but, in general, these tasks still reflect the tasks one is usually expected to achieve during the adolescent transition in our society.

Can we see the four dimensions proposed by Riegel in these developmental tasks? Biological change would seem to be the basis for the first six tasks. Psychological change is certainly involved in tasks 1, 2, and 4. Cultural-sociological forces are reflected in all of the tasks because they involve social expectations and definitions. The most difficult dimension to understand is the outer-physical one, but it would clearly affect tasks 4, 5, and 6. Economic conditions, school systems, civil war, occupational requirements, and availability of marriage partners are some of these external factors that would affect the achievement of these developmental tasks.

Young people ordinarily accomplish the developmental tasks of adolescence in a sequence of three stages. The first stage is generally referred to as *early adolescence* and coincides roughly with the junior high or middle school years. This is a time when young people are growing rapidly, both physically and in their intellectual capacities, and are beginning to take on adult sexual characteristics. The primary developmental task during early adolescence involves adapting to these biological and mental changes and, as indicated in Havighurst's task 3, accepting how one looks and learning to use one's body and mind effectively.

The second stage is called *middle adolescence* and coincides roughly with the high school years. The primary developmental tasks facing middle adolescents are becoming physically self-reliant and achieving psychological autonomy from their parents; becoming comfortably involved in expanding peer relationships and achieving the capacity for intimate friendships; and learning to handle heterosocial relationships, dating, and sexuality. High school students may carry over from early adolescence some lingering concerns about their physical appearance and capacities; however, their attention focuses mainly on establishing themselves as not only autonomous but also interdependent individuals who are able to get along well with their parents, peers, and dating companions.

The third stage, *late adolescence*, usually begins around the last year of high school and continues until young people have formed a reasonably clear, consistent sense of their personal identity in relation to others, and have begun to form some fairly definite social roles, value systems, and life goals. Late adolescents continue to work on issues of independence and interpersonal relatedness, but the learning of self-reliance and social skills now becomes less important than making decisions about how all of one's capabilities, previously learned skills, important relationships, and already formed attitudes can be meaningfully combined to answer such questions as "What kind of a person am I?" and "What do I want to do with my life?" Late adolescent development thus revolves around tasks 5, 6, 7, and 8 in Havighurst's list.

In the first two sections of this chapter we discussed adolescence as a period of transition from one phase of life to another: from childhood to adulthood. The beginning of adolescence is brought about by changes in the individual-biological dimension. The form it takes reflects the cultural-sociological dimension—as shown by social age expectations and by cross-cultural differences. It also reflects the outer-physical dimension—as shown by the effects of historical forces such as the AIDS epidemic or changes in Eastern Europe and the former Soviet Union. In the next section of this chapter we focus on ways in which psychologists and other social scientists study adolescents in order to separate fact from fiction about this developmental period of adolescence.

RESEARCH METHODS IN THE STUDY OF ADOLESCENCE

Empirical research is vital to contemporary social science. It is not adequate only to hypothesize about the characteristics of adolescents based on one's experience or on a particular theory. We must also study adolescents through **empirical methods**: observation, inquiry about their experience, and carefully designed experiments. These methods produce data that may be *quantitative* (i.e., numerical or able to be structured into categories such as age or height). Alternatively, these methods may produce *qualitative* data that provide information about the detail of individual variation and cannot be categorized without considerable analysis. For example, the question "How often have you had sexual relations in the past 6 months?" would produce quantitative data; the question "Why did you or did you not use contraception?" would produce qualitative data.

The forms of research are limited only by the creativity of the scientist and ethical standards and principles. Among the most common studies are those using questionnaires, interviews, observations, or experiments. Each of these may take place in the adolescent's normal surroundings (such as the school, home, playground, or neighborhood), or in an atypical setting such as the scientist's office or laboratory. They may involve a standard form that the respondent, interviewer, observer, or experimenter uses to record the information in preestablished categories, or they may involve unstructured notes, videotapes, or audiotapes of the person's responses or behavior. The person who is participating in the study is entitled to protection from any possible harm or from any use of the information that might affect the individual, and must consent to participate in the study with sufficient knowledge about the study to make an informed decision to participate. The person has the right to refuse to be tape-recorded, or to any other procedure, and may end participation in the study at any time. The research must comply with ethical standards of the researcher's profession, and the ethical aspects of research must be approved by the organization sponsoring the research.

Because the surroundings are likely to have some effect on the persons who participate in the study, it is important to pay attention to the conditions under which the research is conducted. These are known as *demand characteristics* of the study because they tend to "demand" a particular response. For example, if the interviewer or experimenter is wearing a doctor's white coat, or if the interview takes place in a hospital setting, we would expect adolescents to answer questions about marijuana differently than they would if the interview took place at a rally to legalize marijuana and the interviewer was dressed like other participants. Thus, we should imagine ourselves in the place of the research participant and think what an ordinary cooperative person would be likely to do or say in that situation; only after these demand characteristics have been set aside can we begin to focus on what the study has found and how it compares to other studies on the same topic. A carefully designed study avoids as many of these demand characteristics as possible and, returning to the earlier example, one should not inquire about attitudes toward marijuana use in either a doctor's coat or at a promarijuana rally.

Choice of the **sample** is also very important to note. Because it is usually not possible to study all of the individuals in the world who are of interest for a given study, a researcher typically selects a sample of the total population of individuals of interest. Ideally, the sample is not *biased* in any way that would affect the study. If one wanted to determine the use of marijuana, sampling persons at a rally to legalize marijuana would obviously be a biased sample. However, if one wanted to study the effects of marijuana on sexual behavior, that sample would not necessarily be biased, but one would need to determine the amount of marijuana used by each participant and then compare the amount and frequency of use with sexual behavior. Nonetheless, it would be good to *replicate* the study by repeating it with a different sample of marijuana users to be sure that the sample was not biased in some way. In addition, one would want a *control sample* of nonusers of marijuana to compare with the sample of users. Moreover, one would want the control sample and the user sample to be *matched* in terms of obvious characteristics that might affect the outcome, such as gender, age, marital status, and so on.

The results of a study can be *generalized* only to the population that is represented by the sample. Thus, a sample of eighth-grade students in rural Maine would not produce results that could be generalized to adolescents in urban Atlanta or rural California. However, the results might be applicable to those adolescents if one carefully noted the similarities and differences between the populations. Replication of studies with different samples helps to demonstrate that the results are applicable to populations other than the one studied. But, in general, one must carefully evaluate the research study in order to interpret it correctly. It is incorrect to believe a statement that begins "studies have shown . . ." without asking questions such as: Which studies? On what populations? Conducted in what manner? Was there any bias in sampling or in the researcher's approach? To what degree is the study applicable to other adolescents?

Studies in social science very rarely "prove" some point or other; usually there are enough questions raised by the study to lead one to be cautious about accepting a conclusion as truth with a capital T. Truth is very elusive in social science. Is the response of adolescents to a telephone interview about their relationship with their parents truly accurate? Even if the adolescent tried sincerely to be honest, would not the adolescent's mother, father, or sisters and brothers see it differently? And would one necessarily be candidly honest to a telephone interviewer—even if a parent or friend was not in the same room listening to one's response? It is questions such as these that make the pursuit of knowledge a fascinating project in social science. We are not really searching for Truth, as much as we are attempting to gain a greater understanding of adolescence. It is this purpose that leads social scientists to conduct empirical research.

Two general types of research are useful for understanding adolescence. Developmental research studies those characteristics that change within individuals over time. Nondevelopmental research studies those characteristics that differ between adolescents, or apply to individuals regardless of age.

DEVELOPMENTAL RESEARCH

Studies of adolescence from a developmental perspective have one central concern in common: understanding the changes within individuals that occur with increasing age. However, age is merely a measure of the number of revolutions that the earth has made around the sun since the person's birth. Thus, as noted earlier, chronological age by itself may not be a very meaningful indicator of development. At best, age provides a convenient index of the passage of *time*. Age does not cause change to occur; it merely measures how long change takes and which change happens first in a sequence of developmental changes.

Because some developmental events are time dependent (such as biological maturation), these changes correspond fairly well to the index of age. But other developmental events may be time independent (such as becoming pregnant or moving away from the parental home) and can occur for the first time at any age during adolescence, or not at all. Thus, the goal of developmental research is to replace "age" with an understanding of the time-dependent and time-independent processes that bring about the changes that take place through the course of the human life cycle (Birren & Renner, 1977).

Cross-Sectional, Longitudinal, and Sequential Research Methods

In order to investigate the processes that cause change to occur with age, it is obviously important to identify differences between persons of different ages. The most apparent—and the easiest—way to find age differences is to gather a sample of persons of differing ages, give them questionnaires, tests, or interviews that are appropriate for the question being studied, and compare the results. Such studies are called **cross-sectional** studies because they are based on a cross-section of ages at one point in time.

A second approach to studying the index of age is a **longitudinal study**. In this strategy, a group of subjects is selected, appropriate for the question being studied, and is given a series of questionnaires, tests, or interviews *periodically over several years* (an easy way to remember this is that longitudinal studies take a *long* time). For example, the Fels study began in 1929 studying children from birth until they reached age 18, and in the late 1950s some subjects were restudied when they were between 20 and 29 years of age (Kagan & Moss, 1962). Results of longitudinal studies are called *age changes* because they represent changes within the same individuals over time.

Sequential studies involve a combination of cross-sectional and longitudinal strategies and require a sophisticated statistical procedure to analyze those factors that change with age, those that reflect the year the study was conducted, and those that reflect the year the person was born (Schaie, 1977). This is important because we would expect that young adolescents are different from older adolescents (age), young adolescents are different today from those a decade ago (time of the study), and adolescents born in the 1980s are different from those born in the 1960s (year of birth).

There are disadvantages to each type of study. Among the problems in a longitudinal study is that participants may drop out during the course of the study and possibly distort the representativeness of the sample; also these studies take a long time and it is very expensive to contact and study the participants over a number of years. Sequential studies have these same problems, although they do not necessarily require as long a period of study as longitudinal studies, which may last several decades. Cross-sectional studies do not measure age-related changes in the same individuals, they only measure age differences between groups of people. Thus, they cannot separate the effects of age differences from changes caused by social and historical changes during the individuals' lives; these changes are known as "cohort effects" and are described in the next section.

Age, Time of Study, and Year of Birth (Cohort)

A **cohort** is a group of people born at about the same time—for instance, in 1970, or between 1970 and 1979. Because this group of people grows older together, the cohort moves through the lifespan together. As a result, each cohort experiences somewhat similar historical influences. Also, different cohorts of individuals are affected by historical experiences in

A cohort is a group of people, born at about the same time, who move through the lifespan and experience similar historical influences.

different ways because each cohort of persons is a different age at the time. For example, the invention of television, the civil rights movement, the Vietnam war, and the development of home computers had important effects on young people in our society, but their effects were different if one was born in the 1940s, 1960s, or 1980s.

Obviously, if we know the year someone was born and the date the study was conducted we also know the person's age. Thus, a cross-sectional study conducted in 1995 with a sample of 11-, 15-, and 19-year-olds has a sample of persons born in 1984, 1980, and 1976. Do the differences that may be found reflect normal age changes, or the impact of historical events during the person's life (cohort effects)? Likewise, a longitudinal study in 1995 of persons born in 1980 would be studying developmental changes in adolescents who are 15 years old. But are these 15-year-olds the same as a group of 15-year-olds studied in 1985? It is impossible to separate age from cohort in *cross-sectional* studies and to separate age from time of the study in *longitudinal* studies.

A *sequential* study does allow these different effects to be separated, however. It would, for example, obtain a sample of adolescents born in 1954, 1955, 1956, and 1957; if it studied them three times (in 1970, 1971, and 1972), then it would be able to compare cross-sectional data with longitudinal data and would also have time-lag data representing three groups of 15-year-olds, three groups of 14-year-olds, and two groups of 13-year-olds and 16-year-olds at different times of measurement (Table 1.1). These time-lag data would provide information about changes that may have occurred in the society that affected persons of a particular age.

Nesselroade and Baltes (1974) conducted a study using this sequential design focusing on personality development among about 1,800 male and female adolescents. They found that historical factors between 1970 and 1972 (possibly including the anti-Vietnam-war movement, the resignation of President Nixon, and other events) had a significant effect on the level of independence of all cohorts of adolescents in the study (Figure 1.4). It may be seen that the 1954 cohort was more independent at all three testing times; that generally adolescents became more independent as they grew older; and that 14- and 15-year-olds were more independent in 1972 than adolescents of the same age were in 1971. On other personality dimensions (not shown) they found that adolescents actually decreased during

Table 1.1 ILLUSTRATION OF A SEQUENTIAL STUDY SHOWING THAT CHRONOLOGICAL AGE REFLECTS THE INTERACTION OF YEAR OF BIRTH AND YEAR OF MEASUREMENT[a]

Birth cohort	Time of measurement		
	1970	1971	1972
1954	15 yr	16 yr	17 yr
1955	14 yr	15 yr	16 yr
1956	13 yr	14 yr	15 yr
1957	12 yr	13 yr	14 yr

[a]Vertical columns represent cross-sectional samples; horizontal columns represent longitudinal samples; diagonals of same-aged subjects represent time lag samples.

Source: Based on Nesselroade & Baltes, 1974.

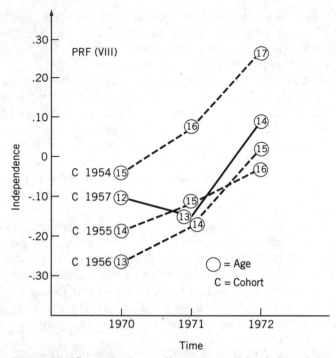

Figure 1.4 Scores on personality tests measuring independence for adolescents born in the years of 1954–1957, measured in 1970–1972; high scores indicate greater independence. The age of adolescent groups is shown in circles. The figure demonstrates the importance of sequential research because cohort, age, and time of measurement each affect level of independence. [*Source:* J.R. Nesselroade & P.B. Baltes. Adolescent Personality Development and Historical Change: 1970–1972. *Monographs of the Society for Research in Child Development*, *39* (1, Ser. No. 154), p. 36. © 1974 Society for Research in Child Development. Reprinted with permission.]

this historical period on characteristics we would expect to increase with age, such as achievement motivation. Overall, the statistical analysis indicated that "time of the study" effects were more important than the age changes, emphasizing the influence of sociocultural environmental factors on development.

Thus, in developmental studies it is important to consider whether the changes we find between adolescents of different ages are, in fact, a result of age-related developmental changes or of historical-cultural factors, or—most likely—the interaction of both. Moreover, we should take care in interpreting developmental data to ensure that possible cohort differences and time of measurement effects do not lead us to generalize the findings inappropriately. In addition, it is important to be cautious of *correlational* studies in which one variable (such as age) is statistically related to another, but the cause-and-effect relationship of the variables is unclear. Simply because two variables (such as blue eyes and blond hair, or age and independence) are statistically correlated does not mean that one causes the other.

NONDEVELOPMENTAL STUDIES

Research on adolescents that does not focus on age-related changes or that examines some phenomenon that has nothing in particular to do with adolescence, but which uses adolescents as participants or respondents in the study, would be considered to be a nondevelopmental study. For example, studies in social psychology on topics such as the attraction between two people, or aggressiveness, or gender roles often use adolescents because they are a convenient sample. Because a great deal of social science research is conducted in colleges and universities, the most readily available pool of potential subjects are college students—often college sophomores in introductory social science classes. Thus without intending to study adolescence specifically, much of the data on human behavior are actually data on adolescents. For example, the study of lifespan human development has called attention to the lack of information about topics such as dating after divorce or after the death of a spouse in old age; nearly all studies of dating are actually studies of adolescent dating. Therefore, it is important to consider the age of the respondents, even in nondevelopmental studies, and to consider the possible effects of cohort and time of measurement effects on these studies, just as we do in developmental studies.

Other studies, although they may consider age, are not developmental in the sense that they are not seeking to understand the causes of time-dependent or time-independent changes. Age is considered only as one of the factors that may help to generalize the data to other samples. Thus, age is treated in the same manner as socioeducational status, gender, ethnicity, or urban/rural residence may be treated in a study of pregnancy rates, voting behavior, or soft-drink preference. Nonetheless, some of these age-related data may be relevant for helping us to understand adolescents.

Because more and more studies are being reported in both scientific journals and popular media that are relevant to adolescence, as well as to lifespan human development, it is important that we learn to pay attention to the issues we have discussed here so that these data may be interpreted in meaningful ways. Among the most important are issues of sampling, possible bias in the study, cohort effects, the confusion of correlation with cause, and limitations in the generalizability of the findings.

In the next chapter theoretical approaches in the study of adolescent development will be presented.

CHAPTER SUMMARY

1. The period of life known as adolescence generally refers to the transition between childhood and adulthood. In our society it corresponds approximately to the teenage years.

2. The beginning of adolescence is best defined by biological age—the physical changes of puberty, such as the rapid increase in height, development of breasts in girls, and growth of the testes and penis in boys. The conclusion of adolescence is best defined by social age—the social roles and behaviors that are regarded as adult.

3. The experience of adolescence differs in various cultures. Anthropologists have reported a variety of patterns ranging from severe initiation rites to a smooth transition from childhood to adulthood. Today adolescents in different countries are growing to adulthood in such diverse conditions as civil war, poverty, hunger, great affluence, and the rapid change from a tribal to a technological society.

4. The nature of adolescence varies in different historical periods. The concept of adolescence as we know it today appears to have emerged in America in the late 19th century. Greater attention has been given to adolescence during the 20th century because of the dramatic increase in school enrollment of 14- to 17-year-old adolescents and the extraordinary growth in the number of young people during the "baby boom" of the 1960s and 1970s.

5. A transition is a period of change, growth, and disequilibrium that serves as a kind of bridge between one relatively stable point in life and another relatively stable, but different, point.

6. Transitions may be caused by internal changes (puberty, falling in love, psychological maturation) or by external changes (graduating from high school, marriage, winning a lottery). Normative transitions (like puberty or marriage) are expected to occur but may be on time or off time. Idiosyncratic transitions (such as winning a lottery) do not happen to most people.

7. Riegel's dialectical analysis of transitions involves the interaction between four major dimensions of development: inner-biological, individual-psychological, cultural-sociological, and outer-physical. Major changes in any of these dimensions bring a reorganization of the other dimensions that may produce a period of developmental transition.

8. Adolescents are normally expected to accom-plish a number of developmental tasks. This process may be divided into three stages: adapting to physical and mental changes (early adolescence); developing independence, peer relationships, and dating (middle adolescence); and establishing a sense of identity (late adolescence).

9. Empirical research is necessary to test ideas and speculations about adolescents with data from actual observations, interviews, questionnaires, and experiments. The method the study used, the characteristics of the sample studied, and possible bias in the study need to be examined carefully.

10. Developmental research focuses on changes that are related to age. Cross-sectional studies use adolescents of different ages at one point in time. Longitudinal studies follow a group of persons over a long period of time. Sequential studies involve a combination of these strategies and provide a means to distinguish those changes that occur with age from those that reflect historical and social changes.

11. A cohort is a group of people born at about the same time (e.g., 1980 or 1979–1981). Such a group have some experiences in common because of the historical period they lived through together. These historical and social experiences may affect patterns of developmental change.

12. Nondevelopmental research often uses adolescent college students as participants in studies on a variety of topics. These findings shed light on adolescent characteristics, but do not necessarily generalize to older adults.

KEY WORDS

adolescence	developmental tasks	interaction	sequential studies
biological age	dialectical interaction	longitudinal studies	social age
cohort	empirical methods	sample	transition
cross-sectional studies	initiation rites		

REVIEW QUESTIONS

1. The book begins with the idea that adolescence is a period of transition. What other words or phrases can you think of that convey the idea of a *transition* (e.g., crossing over a bridge; going through some changes)?

NO LONGER A CHILD; NOT YET AN ADULT

2. At what age did you begin adolescence? Are you still an adolescent today? Why or why not?

3. What is the difference between being an adolescent and being a teenager?

4. What would be a better predictor of a girl's first menstruation: an x-ray of the bones in the hand to measure skeletal maturity, or her chronological age? Why?

5. What age(s) mark the end of adolescence and the beginning of legal adulthood in your state?

6. Are there any events in your community that serve as *initiation rites* into adolescence or adulthood? What are they?

7. If *adolescence*, as we know the concept today, did not emerge until the late 1800s, what did young people do during their teenage years before then?

8. Why has greater attention been given by social scientists to adolescents since the 1950s in the United States?

TRANSITIONS IN HUMAN DEVELOPMENT

9. Describe Figure 1.3 (Lewin's depiction of adolescents) in your own words.

10. Compare and contrast *external* and *internal* causes of transitions; also *normative, idiosyncratic, on-time expected, off-time,* and *unexpected* types of transitions.

11. What does it mean that the interaction of forces is not usually the simple addition of one force to the other?

12. How does a *dialectical interaction* differ from other types of interactions of forces?

13. Explain why transitions occur from the perspective of the dialectical interaction model proposed by Riegel.

14. Review the eight developmental tasks described by Havighurst by reorganizing them according to the early, middle, and late stages of adolescence.

RESEARCH METHODS IN THE STUDY OF ADOLESCENCE

15. What protection must be provided to participants in a research project?

16. Describe the *demand characteristics* of a situation where a suspect is being interrogated by the police. Why is this the opposite of what is desired in empirical research?

17. How would you obtain a nonbiased sample of students at your college? Why could you not use only the students taking a course in adolescent psychology? Once you obtain the sample, could you generalize the results of your study to students of another university? If not, of what value is your study?

18. What does the statement "age does not cause change to occur" mean? What, then, is the goal of developmental research?

19. How do cross-sectional, longitudinal, and sequential studies differ?

20. What is a *cohort*, in terms of social science research? Why is it important to consider cohorts when conducting a cross-sectional study?

21. Why is it necessary to be cautious about all *correlational* studies?

22. Why is a study of dating that is conducted with a sample of college students called nondevelopmental? How could it be made a developmental study?

Chapter 2

◆

Theories of Adolescent Development

◆

BIOLOGICAL MODELS AND THE EFFECTS OF PUBERTY

COGNITIVE AND INTELLECTUAL DEVELOPMENT

CONTEXTUAL PERSPECTIVE ON ADOLESCENT DEVELOPMENT

PERSONALITY DEVELOPMENT
CLASSICAL PSYCHOANALYTIC THEMES
Sigmund Freud / Anna Freud / Peter Blos
THE INTERPERSONAL APPROACH
Preadolescence / Early Adolescence / Late Adolescence
THE EPIGENETIC APPROACH
Identity Versus Identity (Role) Confusion / Intimacy Versus Isolation
RELATIONAL DEVELOPMENT IN ADOLESCENCE
BEHAVIORAL THEMES: THE SOCIAL LEARNING APPROACH
INTERACTION OF THEORETICAL PERSPECTIVES

CHAPTER SUMMARY
KEY WORDS
REVIEW QUESTIONS

Many different theories have been advanced to account for the developmental changes that occur during adolescence. We will not be concerned with detailed discussion of these theories in this chapter. Nevertheless, it is important to identify certain theoretical themes with which students of adolescence should be familiar and on which we draw frequently in later chapters.

These major themes range from primarily *biogenetic* to primarily *sociocultural* conceptions of human development, both of which have their origins in the philosophical speculations that preceded the emergence of scientific psychology. Biogenetic theories of development were influenced by the *predeterministic* philosophy of Jean Jacques Rousseau (1762). According to Rousseau, development from birth to adulthood consists of a series of inborn, internally regulated sequential changes; in unusual circumstances the environment can affect how these changes occur, but it rarely does.

Sociocultural theories of development stem from the *empiricist* philosophy of John Locke (1690). Locke put forward a *tabula rasa* (meaning "clean slate") view in which it is life experience that determines human nature. Biogenetic factors may account for some of a person's dispositions, but a *tabula rasa* means that individual potentialities, personality patterns, and developmental changes result mainly from environmental factors.

These two very different conceptions of development—predeterministic/biogenetic on the one hand and empiricist/sociocultural on the other—are reflected in a *nature–nurture controversy* that has run throughout the modern psychological history of efforts to unravel the origins of human behavior. We touch on this controversy at various points in this book when we consider the determinants of such characteristics as sexual orientation (Chapter 9) and schizophrenic disorder (Chapter 13). In this chapter we will examine how these two concepts relate to central theoretical themes in adolescent psychology.

As noted in the previous chapter, the first textbook of adolescent psychology was published by G. Stanley Hall in 1904. Having been influenced by Charles Darwin's work on biological evolution as well as by Rousseau, Hall added an evolutionary theme to his theory. In his massive, two-volume work Hall argued that psychological development is directed by genetically determined physiological factors that are inevitable, unchangeable, universal, and unaffected by environmental influences. Today Hall's views are of more historical than scientific interest, although his biological and genetic emphasis—as contrasted with sociocultural conceptions of human development—is reflected in some of the theories of adolescent development that we discuss in this chapter. In general, however, contemporary perspectives usually emphasize the interaction of nature and nurture, or biological–genetic and sociocultural influences.

BIOLOGICAL MODELS AND THE EFFECTS OF PUBERTY

At a common-sense level, the biological theory of adolescence has considerable appeal. We all know that hormones increase greatly during the emergence of the physical changes of puberty (see Chapter 3). We also noted in the last chapter that the increased levels of hormones lead to greater sexual desire for both boys and girls. Thus, it would seem that these sweeping biological changes—involving bodily growth, sexual maturation, ejaculation in boys, breast growth and menstruation in girls—would lead to a period of significant transition and change. It would seem that Hall's theory of "storm and stress" during adolescence would be true because of these major physical changes. Moreover, the relatively rapid increase in certain hormone levels would be thought capable of disrupting one's emotional balance and leading to unpredictable behavior, a lack of control, and a general psychological state of being out of balance. Thus, we would expect adolescents to be especially vulnerable to stress, difficult to live with, and generally unstable. This picture is consistent with the view that many adults have about adolescents. It has affected social attitudes about adolescents and has played a role in creating the kind of schools and other institutions in which adolescents spend their time.

Much of this picture about hormone-ravished adolescents is an inaccurate myth, and we will attempt to disprove various aspects of it based on empirical research throughout this book. At this point, however, we need to focus on this implicit theory of adolescence in general. We note that it contains two different ideas. First, this view of adolescence assumes that changes in hormone levels during adolescence have a direct effect on the adolescent's behavior, personality, or adjustment. This model is known as the **direct effects model**. Second, this view implies that the broader physical changes of adolescence, such as increased height or sexual maturation, may affect the nature of the adolescents' interactions with others and thus cause stress or distress to the adolescent. This view is called the **mediated effects model** (Petersen & Taylor, 1980). It may be noted that a *model* is an explanatory device that may be found to be more or less useful. In contrast, a *theory* is stated in a way that allows it to be proven or disproven by evidence.

Since the mid-1980s, advances in research technology have made it possible to study the effects of specific hormones on adolescents, and a variety of studies have been reported (Richards, Abell, & Petersen, 1993). In general, the findings with regard to the direct effects model have been mixed because the various hormones that are affected during puberty seem to have different effects. For example, increased levels of one group (testosterone and estrogen) are related to positive features (such as fewer behavior problems); but another group (gonadotropins and adrenal androgens) appear to bring more problem behaviors. In reviewing the research on this direct effects model, Richards et al. (1993) concluded:

> In trying to sort out the findings emerging from the literature, it appears that it is not increasing or fluctuating hormones alone that affect the emotional states of adolescents. Instead, the interaction of the hormone with a more socially based aspect of change, such as pubertal stage or chronological age, may contribute to teenagers' behavior problems. For example, a very young adolescent boy with high hormone levels or an older adolescent boy with low hormone levels may experience more rebelliousness or aggression. [p. 29]

The second model focuses on *mediating* and *moderator* variables that link biological and psychological changes, or that affect the link between these changes (Figure 2.1). There is considerable support for this model, and we discuss it in detail in the next chapter on puberty. For example, the physical changes at puberty may have negative effects if they occur earlier than average for the girls' peer group; for boys, early maturation may be an advantage (Figure 2.2). To take another example, girls whose breasts develop at the average age were found to have more positive self-image, better peer relations, and higher levels of adjustment than girls whose breast development was not as advanced (Brooks-Gunn & Warren, 1988). Mediating variables differ for each individual and affect the impact of the influence; moderator variables do not differ for the individuals, but affect both the mediating

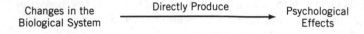

DIRECT EFFECTS MODEL

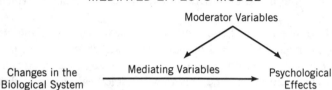

Changes in the   Directly Produce   Psychological
Biological System   ————————————→   Effects

MEDIATED EFFECTS MODEL

Moderator Variables

Changes in the   Mediating Variables   Psychological
Biological System   ————————————→   Effects

Figure 2.1 The direct effects and mediated effects models. [*Source:* M. Richards & A.C. Petersen. Biological Theoretical Models of Adolescent Development. In V.B. Van Hasselt & M. Hersen (Eds.), *Handbook of Adolescent Psychology.* © 1983 Pergamon Press. Reprinted with permission.]

variable and the outcome. In these examples, level of development would be the mediating variable; cultural attitudes about physical maturation would be the moderator variable. Similarly, if one is advanced in physical development, adults may expect greater maturity than would be expected of one's age-mates who are less physically developed. Again, level of development is the mediating variable; social attitudes about expected behavior based on physical appearance would be the moderator variable.

The significance of this model of adolescent development is that it calls attention to the variety of mediating and moderator variables that may affect the impact of biological changes of puberty. Consider the fact that usually adolescents are moving from an elementary school to a larger and different school at about the same time as they are experiencing puberty. This change may produce more stress if it coincides with puberty than if it does not. Likewise, within the family, adolescents often are expected to act more grown up and to take greater responsibility at the same time they are experiencing the physical changes of puberty.

Thus, biological changes associated with puberty may be potentially significant influ-

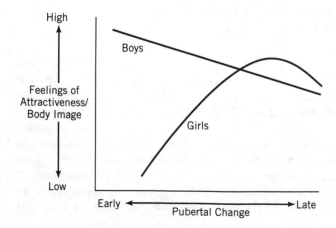

Figure 2.2 The relationship of pubertal change to body image and feelings of attractiveness. [*Source:* M.H. Tobin-Richards, A.M. Boxer, & A.C. Petersen. The Psychological Significance of Pubertal Change: Sex Differences in Perception of Self During Early Adolescence. In J. Brooks-Gunn & A.C. Petersen (Eds.), *Girls at Puberty: Biological and Psychosocial Perspectives.* © 1983 Plenum Press. Reprinted with permission.]

ences on the psychological development of adolescents. The specific nature of their influence, however, is determined less by the biochemical changes within the adolescent than by the sociocultural environment in which the adolescent lives. In particular, the timing of the changes relative to the adolescent's peers and the meaning that is attached to those changes is especially important. Other changes that occur at about the same time, such as moving from one city to another, or from elementary to middle school, can amplify the impact of the changes. These points are discussed in detail in Chapter 3.

It may be noted that these changes in the *individual-biological* dimension of Riegel's model, discussed in Chapter 1, provide a good example of his concept of dialectical interaction. That is, as this dimension changes, the relative balance among the four dimensions shifts to some degree of disequilibrium. The adolescent then seeks to bring the other three dimensions into synchronization with this changed biological dimension. As Riegel's model predicts, as soon as a new synthesis or synchronization is established, it is likely that something else will change, and the system will again be in disequilibrium. When there is also a change in the *cultural-sociological* dimension, such as entering middle school, additional disequilibrium results. If there is simultaneously a disruption in one's *outer-physical* dimension (such as moving to a different city) or in one's *individual-psychological* dimension (perhaps a death or divorce in the family), the adolescent may find that the level of disequilibrium is excessive.

The dialectical interaction between the physical changes in the adolescent's body, perception of those changes by others, and the congruence or incongruence of those perceptions is another way in which Riegel's model can be applied to understanding the impact of puberty on adolescents (Adams, Day, Dyk, Frede, & Rogers, 1992; Adams, Gullota, & Markstron-Adams, 1994).

Thus, the dialectical perspective calls attention to the adolescents' ability to understand, conceptualize, and analyze the changing social situation that is brought about by the physical growth of their bodies. We turn next to considering the effect on adolescent development of the development of these cognitive abilities.

COGNITIVE AND INTELLECTUAL DEVELOPMENT

Not only is the adolescent's body developing, but there is also greater intellectual power emerging during this transition. As is the case with physical development, the pattern of change is not simple to describe; we focus on this topic in detail in Chapter 4, where we discuss Piaget's theory and the information processing model of cognitive development.

Unlike physical development, the changes in cognitive development are not visible, and their manifestation is not the same in all adolescents. One individual may show advances on specific topics or areas of expertise, whereas another adolescent may show advanced development on different topics. Also, the adolescent who is skilled in thinking on abstract or scientific tasks may not show that same level of skill on problems that are personally relevant. Moreover, intellectual ability on school topics may not apply to social skills, and vice versa. Thus, we suggest that a *mediated effects model* similar to the one discussed above may apply also to the link between intellectual development and psychological effects.

Keating (1990) noted that, in general, adolescent thinking tends to use abstract ideas (instead of being limited to concrete reality), to be multidimensional (instead of limited to a single idea), to be relative (instead of absolute), and to become self-reflective.

> Across a wide range of content areas, from logical and mathematical topics, to moral reasoning, to interpersonal understanding, to social and political issues, to the nature of knowledge itself, there is substantial consistency in the ways in which adolescents, compared to children, respond to problems posed to them. [Keating, 1990, p. 64]

These greater capacities do not necessarily apply to ordinary daily problem solving, but are potential abilities that emerge in environments that encourage their development.

The cause of this development in thinking ability is not fully understood, but it is not the simple result of maturation or growth of the brain. Case (1985) suggested that it results from some combination of several interrelated developments: greater automatic processing of basic information, increased capacity of working memory, and greater familiarity with specific knowledge. As a result, thinking becomes more efficient, more dimensions can be kept in mind at one time, and ideas can be organized and reorganized in broad conceptual patterns.

Education obviously plays some role in this development. Keating (1990) suggested that a solid base of fundamental skills needs to be established in childhood, and there needs to be some basic level of knowledge in central domains of information. This base allows an opening up of possibilities for thinking during adolescence in ways that are more advanced than those of childhood.

The development of thinking abilities does not advance all at once during adolescence. In particular, there is often a period of **relativism** in which the adolescent appears to be unsure of the solution to a problem when, in fact, enough information is available to make a decision. Thus, they may have gained a broader perspective, but lost the certainty of childhood; as a result they perform some decision-making tasks less well than either younger children or than older adolescents.

An understanding of the importance of this intellectual development during adolescence sheds light on a variety of other issues in adolescent development. For example, the complexity with which an individual thinks affects the complexity of their self-image, sense of identity, and ability to understand interpersonal relationships. Thus, this perspective on adolescent development calls attention to the adolescents' growing ability to think about and organize their particular situation within the environmental context in which they live. That is, the ways in which they think about their family, their friends, their school, and their own future goals affect their perception of basic elements within their unique life space.

CONTEXTUAL PERSPECTIVE ON ADOLESCENT DEVELOPMENT

The dialectical model discussed above emphasizes the interrelation of individuals with their social and physical environment. The adolescent's growing ability to think about this complex environment is an important aspect of the transition of adolescence. Likewise, in order to understand adolescent development, we must take a broad and complex view of the social environment of adolescent life. This perspective is known as **contextualism** and is an emerging perspective in the study of adolescence (Lerner, 1991).

An adolescent's social-cultural context affects the meaning of physical development, expectations for oneself, and important themes in life.

From the contextual point of view, it is not appropriate to study the adolescent in isolation from his or her environment. The sociocultural context affects the meaning of physical development, the expectations for one's gender, and the important themes of life. The physical environment also plays a part in the lives of adolescents; consider, for example, the differences between life in an urban, suburban, or rural community; or between a low-income and an affluent neighborhood. Size of school, race or ethnic background, religion, and fluency in the language of one's surroundings each play an important part in an adolescent's life, a part that varies from one individual to another. Each of these aspects interacts with the others in the adolescent's pattern of development. This complex interaction may be viewed from the perspective of a dialectical interaction, as described above. It may also be viewed as a network of mutually interacting dimensions of an adolescent's lifespace that is moving through time (Figure 2.3). This model, developed by Lerner, illustrates the relationship between individual adolescents and the social institutions within their unique ecological setting. He noted:

We must as a field conduct our research with considerably greater sensitivity to issues of scontextual variability and diversity in human life and development. Such sensitivity will allow our scientific data base to more adequately reflect, first, the vast array of individual differences in developmental patterns that exist across all of the human life span and, second, the contextual variation (in, for instance, families, communities, societies, cultures, and historical periods) that is both a product and a producer of human diversity across life. [Lerner, 1991, pp. 27–28]

Only through scholarship and application that are sensitive to diversity and context can the richness and complexity of the adolescent period be best appreciated and best used to enhance development during this period. [Lerner, 1993, p. 2]

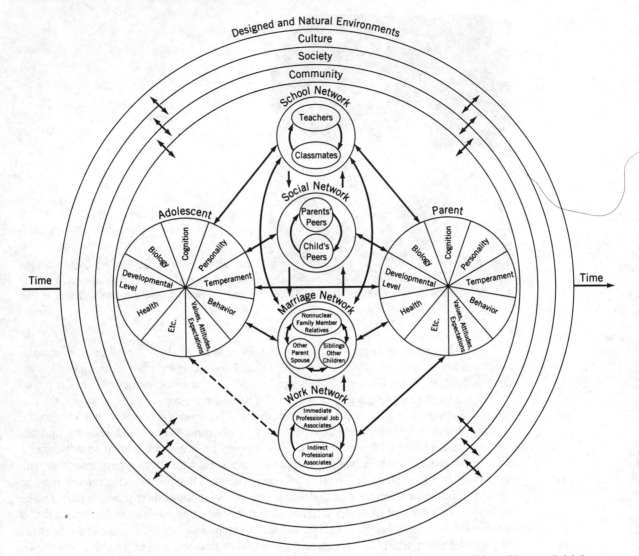

Figure 2.3 A developmental contextual model of adolescent-context relations. [*Source:* R.M. Lerner. Changing Organism-Context Relations as the Basic Process of Development: A Developmental Contextual Perspective. *Developmental Psychology*, *27*, Figure 1, p. 30. © 1991 American Psychological Association. Reprinted with permission.]

In the next section we focus on one key aspect of adolescent development that has received a great deal of attention—the individual's personality development. Although this involves a shift in focus from the complex social environment to the unique individual, we need to keep this broader perspective in mind as we introduce the major personality theories relevant to the study of adolescence.

PERSONALITY DEVELOPMENT

In this section we focus on five theoretical perspectives on the adolescent's personal development: classical psychoanalytic theory; the interpersonal theory proposed by Sullivan; the epigenetic model of eight successive periods of life proposed by Erikson; the relational perspective on adolescent development; and social learning theory.

CLASSICAL PSYCHOANALYTIC THEMES

Like Hall's theory, classical psychoanalytic views of childhood development reflect a strong biogenetic emphasis. Personality is regarded as being formed during the first 5 or 6 years of life under the direction of innate drives or sources of energy (*libido*) that unfold in predetermined ways. By focusing in set order on different zones of the body, these drives produce a universal sequence of *psychosexual* stages known as the *oral*, *anal*, *phallic*, and *genital* stages. Each of these stages is associated with certain personality characteristics, and individual differences among people result from aspects of their development becoming arrested or *fixated* at different stages. For example, being a dependent person is assumed to reflect an oral fixation, and being compulsively neat is regarded as indicating an anal fixation (Fenichel, 1945, Chapter 5; Holzman, 1970).

Although experiential factors can affect when and if developmental arrest occurs, they are much less important in human development than the early childhood focusing of innate drives. From a classical psychoanalytic point of view, adolescence contributes little that is new in personality development. However, it does constitute a distinct phase of adjustment caused by biologically increased sexual drives during puberty. When individual differences appear among adolescents, they are interpretable largely in terms of how young people are reacting to these biological changes.

Another important theme in classical psychoanalytic theory is the concept of **regression**. When people are confronted with situations that are difficult for them to handle, they sometimes resort to coping styles that worked successfully for them earlier in life; this involves *regressing* to a psychologically less mature mode of functioning. Moments of regression are a common occurrence in most people's lives. For example, such often-heard admonitions as "Act your age!" or "Don't be such a baby!" or "Let's handle this in a grown-up way!" are appeals from one person to another to stop behaving in a regressive manner.

When people under stress begin to act in uncharacteristic ways, their changed behavior can often be understood as a regression to some earlier point of fixation. A person with oral fixations may become more dependent than usual as a way of coping with an anxiety-provoking situation, and a person with anal fixations may become more compulsively neat than usual. As another example, children entering adolescence with great anticipations usually have times when they wish they were children again.

This kind of regressive pull accounts for many instances of childish behavior in otherwise well-adjusted teenagers. Regressive pulls also tug at adolescents' parents, giving them mixed feelings about how ready they are to see their children become teenagers and then adults (we discuss these issues in Chapter 7). Not uncommonly, entire families with adolescent children will share periods of regression that constitute a normal variation in human development (Ravenscroft, 1974). Several other classical psychoanalytic themes relevant to our later discussions are found in the individual writings of Sigmund Freud, Anna Freud, and Peter Blos.

Sigmund Freud

Sigmund Freud, the originator of psychoanalytic theory, did not have much to say about the adolescent years. Classical psychoanalytic interest in developmental events, as we have already noted, was vested mainly in early childhood. Nevertheless, in one of his most famous papers, "Three Essays on the Theory of Sexuality," published in 1905, Freud introduced a notion that has considerable bearing on understanding adolescent behavior: the *oedipus complex*.

Freud theorized that all children go through a developmental phase during the preschool years in which they feel strongly attracted to the parent of the other gender—boys to their mothers and girls to their fathers. This attraction, which includes a wish to have an exclusive claim on the affection of the parent of the other gender, inevitably produces feelings of competition with the parent of the same gender. Boys and their fathers now become rivals for the love of the mother in the family, while girls and their mothers become rivals for the love of the father. Most parents have occasion to see this rivalry reflected in what their young children say and do. One common example is a 4- or 5-year-old boy who says to his mother, "If Daddy didn't come home any more, then just you and I could live together."

Oedipal rivalry makes children very anxious, Freud's theory continues, because they fear being severely punished by the same-gender parent for coming between this parent and his or her spouse. In the course of normal personality development, the motive to avoid oedipal anxiety eventually becomes stronger than the motive to possess the parent of the other gender. This leads children, usually by age 6, first to *repress* their oedipal longing (which involves pushing it out of their conscious awareness), and then to ally themselves strongly with their same-gender parent, whom they now seek to model themselves after (instead of compete with). Within the psychoanalytic perspective, this process of resolving oedipal conflicts helps children overcome infantile anxieties and form a gender-appropriate identification—boys with their fathers and girls with their mothers.

These notions about the emergence and influence of an oedipus complex in all children are by no means universally accepted. Even among psychoanalytically oriented clinicians and researchers, there are many who conceptualize family rivalries, anxiety, repression, and identification without focusing specifically, as Freud did, on sexual urges. The notion of an oedipus complex is also difficult to measure for research purposes. The theory attributes some complex emotions to young children who are not yet capable of putting them into words, and the only way of determining whether these feelings really exist is by measuring them indirectly from behaviors that presumably result from them.

These issues aside, Freud (1905/1953) concluded his essay with a section on the "transformations of puberty," in which he suggested that the increased sexual drives of adolescents require them to work through for a second time many of the psychosexual concerns they had previously experienced as young children. What this means specifically, in Freud's theory, is that the oedipus complex is reawakened by puberty and generates a new cycle of feeling attracted to the parent of the other gender, becoming anxious about having these feelings, and resolving the matter by turning away from that parent and toward the same-gender parent. In this view, reemerging oedipal concerns may help to explain many kinds of interactions observed between adolescents and their parents.

Anna Freud

Anna Freud, the daughter of Sigmund Freud, was a distinguished psychoanalyst in her own right. She was one of the first clinicians to write specifically about adolescent behavior, beginning with a very influential book she wrote in 1936 called *The Ego and the Mechanisms of Defense*. Here and in later work she discussed how adolescents use certain kinds of *defense mechanisms* to protect themselves against the special anxieties generated by the onset of puberty (A. Freud, 1936/1946, 1958).

The concept of **defense mechanisms** figures prominently in psychoanalytic interpretations of behavior. When people are confronted with threatening situations or anxiety-provoking impulses, the theory goes, they are motivated to defend themselves against feeling threatened or anxious by calling upon various psychological mechanisms of defense that reinterpret the situation in ways that reduce their level of felt distress.

The *repression* of oedipal longings we mentioned previously, in which anxiety is minimized by pushing a troubling thought or feeling out of one's conscious awareness, illustrates one such defense mechanism at work; a more everyday example of repression may be "forgetting" to keep a dental appointment. Other commonly observed defense mechanisms are *denial*, in which people convince themselves that bad things never really happened; *projection*, in which people seek to avoid responsibility for bad thoughts or feelings by attributing them unjustly to others ("I'm not the one who's being unreasonable, you are"); and *reaction formation*, in which a directly opposite view is taken from the one really held, as when a person who feels guilty over being intolerant of some group abruptly becomes enthusiastically supportive of it and uncritically accepting of whatever it does.

Anna Freud argued that these and other defense mechanisms people learn as children often prove inadequate for curbing postpubertal anxieties associated with increased sexual drives, including the reawakened oedipal attractions. Two additional mechanisms are thus likely to appear during adolescence and influence how some young people behave. One of these is **asceticism**, which involves minimizing anxiety by turning away from temptations and denying oneself the normal pleasures of human life. Ascetic youngsters mistrust enjoyment and avoid any risk of their impulses getting out of control:

> Their safest policy appears to be simply to counter more urgent desires with more stringent prohibitions. . . . We have all met young people who severely renounced any impulses which savoured of sexuality and who avoided the society of those of their own age, declined to join in any entertainment, and, in true puritanical fashion, refused to have anything to do with the theater, music or dancing. [A. Freud, 1936/1946, p. 154]

The other newly appearing defense mechanism that Anna Freud described also consists of minimizing anxiety by being impersonal and is called **intellectualization**. Intellectualization involves thinking about ideas, taking up causes, and debating ethical and moral issues in a manner that avoids or at least minimizes their specific psychological importance or threatening nature to the individual. By *intellectualizing*, people can cast their conflicts and uncertainties in abstract perspectives that keep conflict and uncertainty at a

◆ *Profile*

ANNA FREUD

In March of 1938, in Vienna, Austria, the Nazis came to arrest Sigmund Freud, then 82 years old and terminally ill with cancer. At the Freud home, his daughter Anna pleaded to be taken in his place to Gestapo headquarters, and she was. Fortunately for her and for countless others who have benefited from her contributions to knowledge and to humanity during a long life, she was released frightened but unharmed the next day. For her father, who had been determined that Hitler would never drive him from his lifelong home, this threat to Anna was more than he could bear. Soon after this event the Freuds emigrated to London, where Anna Freud's work over the next four decades earned her worldwide admiration and respect.

Ms. Freud was already a well-established professional person by the time she reached London. Born in 1895 as the youngest of six children of Martha and Sigmund Freud, the founder of psychoanalysis, she grew up in a devoted and intellectually stimulating family environment and studied to be a teacher. After teaching school for a while, she decided to become trained as a psychoanalyst and began her clinical practice in 1922. Although following her father's footsteps and working closely with him—they had adjacent offices and shared the same waiting room for their patients—she was from the beginning of her career a person and a thinker in her own right. During the 1920s and 1930s she was a pioneer in developing psychoanalytic techniques for use with children and adolescents, and a book she wrote in 1936, *The Ego and the Mechanisms of Defense*, constituted the first substantial clinical contribution to the developmental psychology of adolescence.

distance. For example, adolescents struggling with feelings of resentment toward their parents' authority may content themselves with denouncing dictatorships around the world.

Peter Blos

Peter Blos (1962, 1967) has written about adolescent development in much more detail than either Sigmund or Anna Freud. While keeping within the classical psychoanalytic focus on reemerging oedipal concerns, he distinguished several stages of adaptation to the psychological stresses these concerns produce. In the evolutionary tradition of Hall and the psychosexual tradition of the Freuds, these stages describe an unfolding progression that takes young people from childhood to adulthood through six phases of development.

The first of these phases is a period of *latency*, which occurs during the elementary school years. This is a time when no new instinctual drives appear, according to Blos, and

In London, Ms. Freud responded to the outbreak of World War II by starting the Hampstead Wartime Nurseries, which cared for infants and young children whose parents were not available. The nurseries were staffed with child-care workers and child therapists who learned a great deal from Ms. Freud's supervision and expressed interest in receiving continued training after the war. Hence in 1947 she established the Hampstead Child-Therapy Course as a training program in child therapy and later, in 1952, expanded it with a clinical facility into the Hampstead Child-Therapy Course and Clinic. Over time, the Hampstead Clinic became a psychoanalytic center offering the most comprehensive child therapy training, services, and research facilities to be found anywhere in the world. Child and adolescent specialists flocked from all over to spend from one to several years of advanced study there.

During these years Anna Freud published numerous books and articles, the most important of which was *Normality and Pathology in Childhood*. Published in 1965, this book conceptualizes similarities and differences between healthy and deviant development in ways that have had enormous influence on building important bridges between developmental psychology and developmental psychopathology. Later, she turned the full light of her attention from theoretical to practical matters in a 1973 book, *Beyond the Best Interests of the Child*, in which, with coauthors Joseph Goldstein and Albert Solnit, she concerned herself with custodial arrangements for abused children and children of divorce.

World-renowned, the recipient of honorary degrees from eight major universities in the United States and Europe, Anna Freud died in 1982, shortly before her 89th birthday.

[*Sources*: Anna Freud Memorial Issue, *Bulletin of the Hampstead Clinic*, 1986, 6, 1–140; Solnit, A. J., Anna Freud's contributions to child and applied analysis, *International Journal of Psycho-Analysis*, 1983, 64, 379–390; Young-Bruehl, E., *Anna Freud: A biography*. New York: Summit Books, 1988.]

when children expand their mental and emotional capacities in ways that prepare them to deal with the increased drives they will experience during puberty. Next comes *preadolescence*, during which there is a quantitative increase in instinctual drives that is reflected in many sexual fantasies and a high susceptibility to becoming erotically stimulated, but does not involve directing sexual aims toward any particular person.

The third phase, *early adolescence*, is marked by reawakened attraction to the parent of the other gender, followed by a turning away from this parent as a love object and toward close friendships with same-gender peers who are greatly admired. *Adolescence proper* begins when attachments to same-gender friends start to be replaced by heterosexual love objects, and this marks the final break from childish oedipal attachments to the parents, according to Blos.

The fifth phase is *late adolescence*, which is a period of consolidating one's sexual identity and becoming positively aware of and accepting of one's·self. This is followed by *post-adolescence*, an early adult period of implementing life goals established during adolescence in terms of permanent relationships, roles, and choices.

Subdividing adolescence into distinct developmental phases of its own has become a generally accepted theme in adolescent psychology. Blos' observations on identity consolidation and goal implementation in late adolescence and postadolescence are also noteworthy but have been pursued more fully by Erikson, whose contributions we discuss shortly.

Blos contributed another important concept by identifying a theme of **separation-individuation** during adolescence. Especially as middle adolescents, he observed, young people typically feel a little uneasy about separating themselves from their parents and becoming self-reliant individuals in their own right:

> Adolescent individuation is accompanied by feelings of isolation, loneliness, and confusion. . . . The realization of the finality of the end of childhood, of the binding nature of commitments, of the definite limitation to individual existence itself—this realization creates a sense of urgency, fear, and panic. [Blos, 1962, p. 12]

Concerns about separation-individuation account for mixed feelings that most young people have about growing up, which is a theme that reappears in our discussion of family relationships in Chapter 7. It is also a theme that has been criticized by recent studies on women's development, which we discuss later in this chapter.

Blos is nonetheless noteworthy for his attention to both male and female adolescent development, including ways in which boys and girls are similar as well as different. One of his books is in fact evenly divided into two parts, one probing issues faced by early adolescent girls, the other, issues faced by early adolescent boys (Blos, 1970). With this and only a few other exceptions, psychoanalytic formulations have dealt mainly with male development.

Because they see adolescence as a time when strong instinctual drives threaten to overwhelm the young persons' coping capacities, classical psychoanalytic views share Hall's emphasis on the stormy and difficult nature of this time of life. As we have mentioned, we turn in Chapter 10 to evidence that contradicts such a gloomy view of adolescence. Even though psychoanalytic hypotheses about inevitable adolescent turmoil were derived from observational data, they were seriously flawed by the fact that they came from patients in psychoanalytic therapy who were being treated for adjustment difficulties. It has been widely noted that such patient data do not accurately represent the developmental experiences of most adolescents, who do not require mental health care (Adelson & Doehrman, 1980; Offer, Ostrov, & Howard, 1981; Weiner, 1985, 1992, Chapter 1).

THE INTERPERSONAL APPROACH

Harry Stack Sullivan was the most influential of a group of theorists who took issue with the biogenetic determinism of classical psychoanalysis (see the biographical sketch in Chapter 9). He rejected the view that personality is formed primarily by modes of adapting to basic drives. Sullivan argued instead that people are social beings shaped by their cultural and interpersonal environment, and that personality accordingly evolves largely from the manner in which individuals learn to adapt to their sociocultural context.

Sullivan formulated his approach in a series of lectures that were published after his death in a book called *The Interpersonal Theory of Psychiatry* (Sullivan, 1953). These lectures presented a detailed analysis of human development from birth through adolescence that focused on how interactions with other people affect an individual's development. For example, Sullivan believed that infants begin to experience primitive kinds of anxieties not as an experience arising from within themselves, in relation to their innate drives, but as an experience communicated to them from their mothers. Similarly, during preadolescence, he emphasized the important effect of the interaction with a close friend.

Following the tradition of stages, Sullivan's view of development divides the developmental years into several periods, each of which is marked by a major change in an individual's interpersonal relationships. Three of these periods pertain to our concern with adolescent development: preadolescence, early adolescence, and late adolescence.

Preadolescence

Young children typically have many different friends and playmates with whom they share activities and learn to cooperate. When they near the end of elementary school, however, they often develop a very close relationship with just one particular friend, almost always of the same gender, and this, according to Sullivan, is when the period of preadolescence begins. Preadolescent friendships were for Sullivan an important way of preparing for mature and rewarding interpersonal relationships with people of both genders, as friends or lovers, and they precede the onset of puberty. Sullivan called this special new kind of friend a *chum*, and he described the emergence of chumships in these words:

> This change represents the beginning of something very like full-blown, psychiatrically defined *love*. In other words, the other fellow takes on a perfectly novel relationship with the person concerned: he becomes of practically equal importance in all fields of value. Nothing remotely like that has ever appeared before. All of you who have children are sure that your children love you; when you say that, you are expressing a pleasant illusion. But if you will look very closely at one of your children when he finally finds a chum—somewhere between eight-and-a-half and ten—you will discover something very different in the relationship—namely, that your child begins to develop a real sensitivity to what matters to another person. And this is not in the sense of "what should I do to get what I want," but instead "what should I do to contribute to the happiness or to support the prestige and feeling of worth-whileness of my chum." [Sullivan, 1953, p. 245]

This chum relationship, which does not always occur, can be of great significance. Sullivan regarded the chum relationship as the beginning of the capacity for intimacy and love; as providing valuable experience with leading and being led in interpersonal relationships; and as giving young people an opportunity to be accepted and valued by someone very important to them. Two chums getting to know essentially everything about each other—all the secrets and feelings too sensitive to trust with others—leads to "consensual validation of personal worth" (Sullivan, 1953, p. 251). This sharing promotes greater acceptance of oneself and, as Sullivan phrased it, "remedies a good deal of the often illusory, usually morbid, feeling of being different" (p. 256). Thus a relationship with a chum may be very therapeutic and help to remove the "warps" from one's earlier development. It also allows one to *collaborate* with others on mutual projects with a sense of "we" in

A chum is often important during preadolescence.

contrast to the cooperation of earlier childhood where the agreed-upon rules were followed, but "my" prestige was most important. The effects of not having a chum may include unresolved feelings of being different or unacceptable to others of one's own gender, which may affect relationships with others during adolescence and adulthood, according to Sullivan.

Another theme that emerges during this period is *loneliness*. Because of the need young people feel for an intimate relationship with a chum, the lack of such a relationship during preadolescence may be acutely and painfully felt. At the same time, there may be acute fears of becoming involved in this new, close, and demanding kind of relationship. Intense anxiety about becoming close to others can lead young people to avoid companionship, and thereby prevent them from learning about establishing friendships. Yet loneliness is a terrible experience, according to Sullivan, and it can drive a person to seek friendship even though anxiety makes the experience unpleasant. Thus loneliness, which may also be experienced in infancy or childhood, reaches its adult significance in this preadolescent period; not until preadolescence is there such a driving force to escape loneliness (Sullivan, 1953, p. 262).

We elaborate on these themes in discussing friendship formation, loneliness, and romantic attachments in Chapters 8 and 9.

Early Adolescence

Along with his emphasis on sociocultural influences on development, Sullivan also emphasized certain basic needs and tensions that he considered common to all people. He defined the beginning of adolescence as marked by the increased sexual tensions that result from puberty. Adolescence, in his theory, involves dealing with the implications of sexuality and is divided into two periods: early adolescence and late adolescence. The theory appears to apply to both women and men, but his focus was explicitly on male development.

The period of early adolescence begins with the emergence of sexual interest, which he called *lust*. This represents a basic theme in human development that he described as the "lust dynamism." A *dynamism* for Sullivan is a pattern that involves recurring tension or a particular bodily zone of interaction with others. For example, fear is a dynamism that involves a recurring tension; the *oral dynamism* is an example of a dynamism that involves a particular bodily zone. The lust dynamism involves both a recurring tension and a particular bodily zone, that is, the genitals. Thus, when sexual tensions attain significant proportions at puberty and become associated with the genitals as organs of expression, the **lust dynamism** comes into being.

> There are very significant differences, in the physiological substrate connected with the beginning of adolescence, between men and women; but in either case there is a rather abrupt change, relatively unparalleled in development, by which a zone of interaction with the environment which had been concerned with excreting waste becomes newly and rapidly significant as a zone of interaction in physical interpersonal intimacy. . . . The change, from the psychological standpoint, pertains to new needs which have their culmination in the experience of sexual orgasm; the felt tensions associated with this need are traditionally and quite properly identified as *lust*. [Sullivan, 1953, p. 263]

In Sullivan's view, this need for the satisfaction of lust is added to two other basic needs that have emerged earlier: a need for *security*, which refers to freedom from anxiety, and a need for *intimacy*, which refers to close collaborative relationships such as preadolescents have with a chum. In what may have been his most meaningful contribution to understanding personality development in adolescence, Sullivan described how these three basic human needs may interfere or collide with each other.

The need to express themselves sexually often puts young people in situations that make them anxious and thus interferes with their need for security. The need for intimacy may sometimes collide with the need for security and the need for lustful satisfaction. The overriding developmental task of adolescence, as far as Sullivan was concerned, was to get on as good terms with a person toward whom one feels lust as with a person with whom one has an intimate relationship, without being unduly paralyzed by anxiety in the process. This integration of needs is a rich explanatory concept that we elaborate on in the discussion of sexuality and romance in Chapter 9.

Late Adolescence

Late adolescence begins when young people have achieved some reasonable integration of the needs for security, intimacy, and lust in their interpersonal relations, or, in Sullivan's words, "when he discovers what he likes in the way of genital behavior and how to fit it into the rest of life" (1953, p. 297). The late adolescent period then continues through various kinds of broadening and instructive interpersonal encounters leading to "the establishment of a fully human or mature repertory of interpersonal relations, as permitted by available opportunity, personal and cultural" (p. 297).

In this reference to "available opportunity," Sullivan parts company with biogenetic stage theorists and asserts his sociocultural emphasis. As far as he is concerned, late adolescence is not an inevitable phase of development through which all people pass as part of their predetermined destiny. Some people fail to achieve late adolescence, no matter how old they get, because they never find a comfortable integration of security, intimacy, and lust. This he regarded as "the last blow to a great many warped, inadequately developed personalities" (p. 297), and it is a theme we consider in terms of friendship in Chapter 8, in the discussion of aborted identity formation in Chapter 10, and with regard to various other problems and pitfalls of adolescent development (Chapters 11, 12, and 13).

Other people, having achieved late adolescence in good fashion, encounter socioeconomic and cultural obstacles to further growth that restrict their opportunities to develop their potential as fully mature adults. This important theme is reflected in our consideration in Chapter 11 of experiential factors that foster or inhibit academic and vocational fulfillment.

Along with restricted opportunities, Sullivan stressed the possible role of anxiety and negative self-evaluations as impediments to maturation during late adolescence. He regarded *anxiety* as a highly unpleasant experience that is similar to other "uncanny" emotions such as terror or dread, in that one does not know exactly what happened to cause it. Because anxiety is such a terrible feeling, people seek to avoid it whenever possible. Among late adolescents, as in preadolescents approaching chumships, learning new ways of relating to others may be anxiety provoking, and severe anxiety can interfere with or even defeat efforts to establish a mature range of interpersonal relations.

Sullivan also emphasized self-evaluations and noted that young people usually enter late adolescence with some negative or inaccurate views of themselves. Some may feel that they are unworthy of being loved, he said, whereas others feel that they are better than most people. Such views are likely to interfere with interpersonal relations, in the first case by producing anxiety whenever someone begins to show love toward the person, and in the second case by making the person anxious in situations in which others might excel. Unless these inappropriate images are changed, situations that would help correct them may be avoided. In viewing other people, adolescents tend similarly to form inadequate or inappropriate conclusions, which include interpersonal stereotypes of various kinds.

Some of these "inadequate and inappropriate personifications of the self and others" (Sullivan, 1953, p. 300) may be overcome by situations that minimize the anxiety while mildly challenging such views. This process can occur in psychotherapy, as well as in other educative and supportive interactions. In the absence of such helpful experiences, some of these anxieties lead to problem behaviors or psychological disorders, as discussed in Chapters 11, 12, and 13.

In contrast, if the anxieties of the late adolescent period are worked through fairly well, Sullivan concluded, then the mature person will emerge in whom "nothing of great importance collides" and who is "sympathetically understanding of the limitations, interests, possibilities, anxieties, and so on of those among whom they move or with whom they deal. . . . The greater the degree of maturity, the less will be the interference of anxiety with living" (Sullivan, 1953, p. 310).

◆ **BOX 2.1   ERIKSON'S EIGHT STAGES OF HUMAN LIFE**

Opposing Issues of Each Stage	Emerging Value	Period of Life
1. Basic Trust versus Mistrust	Hope	Infancy
2. Autonomy versus Shame and Doubt	Will	Early Childhood
3. Initiative versus Guilt	Purpose	Play age
4. Industry versus Inferiority	Competence	School age
5. Identity versus Identity (Role) Confusion	Fidelity	Adolescence
6. Intimacy versus Isolation	Love	Young adulthood
7. Generativity versus Stagnation (Self-Absorption)	Care	Maturity
8. Integrity versus Despair (and Disgust)	Wisdom	Old age

Source: Based on Erikson (1963, 1976).

THE EPIGENETIC APPROACH

Erik Erikson is the best known and most influential proponent of a theoretical formulation known as *psychoanalytic ego psychology* (see the biographical sketch in Chapter 10). Like Sullivan's theory, this approach includes the sociocultural perspective. It also incorporates many ideas from classical psychoanalysis, but differs from it in three major respects: it emphasizes adaptive rather than instinctual strivings in people—how they cope, in other words, rather than what drives them; it pays more equal attention to the role of environmental influences as well as to intrapsychic events in molding and modifying behavior; and it identifies and addresses a lifelong cycle of personality development, as opposed to an early childhood crystallization of personality characteristics.

Erikson (1963, 1968, 1976) outlined eight ages of life stretching from birth to death. Each age represents a crucial turning point in which certain psychological issues are faced and resolved for better or worse. A central theme in Erikson's presentation of these stages of development is his emphasis on their **epigenesis**. In an *epigenetic* approach, sequential stages are viewed not as *independent* events, in which the accrued learning and maturation of one stage is merely added to the developmental accomplishments of earlier stages, but as interactive events, in which developments during one stage become building blocks on which later stages depend. Fundamental in Erikson's approach, then, is the expectation that how people resolve developmental issues at one age will have considerable bearing on their success in coping with issues of subsequent ages.

Each stage in Erikson's conception of the life cycle represents the kind of dialectical struggle between two opposing tendencies we mentioned in Chapter 1. As shown in Box 2.1, stages of development can thus be represented by two opposite qualities, linked by the word *versus*:

> "Versus" is an interesting little word. . . . Developmentally, it suggests a dialectic dynamics, in that the final strength postulated could not emerge without either of the contending qualities; yet, to assure growth, the syntonic, the one more intent on adaptation, must absorb the dystonic. [Erikson, 1976, p. 23]

Each dialectical conflict between the two extremes is eventually resolved by a synthesis that represents one of the basic human strengths: hope, will, purpose, competence, fidelity, love, care, and wisdom. The struggle involves both inner (psychological) processes and outer (social) processes. The psychosocial strengths that result are "an active adaptation rather than a passive adjustment" of the individual in a social environment, so that individuals "change the environment even as they make selective use of its opportunities" (Erikson, 1976, p. 25).

Each of the eight periods of the life cycle "has its stage of ascendence when physical, cognitive, emotional, and social developments permits its coming to a crisis" (Erikson, 1976, p. 24). However, this sequential progression through the stages involves considerable overlap between them.

> Nobody . . . in life is neatly "located" in one stage; rather, all persons can be seen to oscillate between at least two stages and move more definitely into a higher one only when an even higher one begins to determine the interplay. [Erikson, 1976, pp. 24–25]

For the final stage, death itself functions as a kind of higher stage.

Because our concern is with adolescence, we will briefly discuss just the fifth and sixth stages in Erikson's scheme, although each involves the issues, and builds on the strengths, of the earlier stages and prepares the person for later stages during adulthood.

Identity Versus Identity (Role) Confusion

Erikson's fifth stage arises with the beginning of puberty and the increasing social need to find one's role in life as a sexual, productive, responsible adult with a reasonably consistent set of attitudes and values about oneself. It may also reflect the adolescent's newly acquired ability to think abstractly (the stage of "formal operations" in Piaget's scheme of cognitive development; this will be discussed in Chapter 4). The positive (or syntonic) side of the struggle is a sense of identity: a sense of continuity and consistency of the self over time. The negative (or dystonic) side is a sense of confusion about one's identity or role—a lack of certainty about who one is, or about the part one is playing in the scheme of life. The resolution of this stage involves experiencing each of these opposing tendencies within oneself and in relation to one's social environment. From that dialectical struggle emerges the psychosocial strength of *fidelity*—"the ability to sustain loyalties freely pledged in spite of the inevitable contradictions and confusions of value systems" (Erikson, 1976, p. 25).

During this stage Erikson notes a period of **moratorium**, a kind of psychological pause in development. It may be a time of apprenticeship or adventure; self-discipline or troublesome pranks; academic study or aimlessness and wandering.

> A moratorium is a period of delay granted to somebody who is not ready to meet an obligation or forced on somebody who should give himself time. By psychosocial moratorium, then, we mean a delay of adult commitments, and yet it is not only a delay. It is a period that is characterized by a selective permissiveness on the part of society and of provocative playfulness on the part of youth, and yet it also often leads to deep, if often transitory, commitment on the part of youth, and ends in a more or less ceremonial confirmation of commitment on the part of society. [Erikson, 1968, p. 157]

The early period of this stage involves the overlap between Identity versus Identity Confusion and Industry versus Inferiority (Erikson's stage 4, where the issues involve learning the skills and roles suitable for adult life). The search for one's sense of identity is the crucial issue during the moratorium phase of this stage. It is the time of searching for a sense of identity and a quest for the answer to the question "Who am I?" The later period within this stage involves the overlap between Identity versus Identity Confusion and the next stage, Intimacy versus Isolation.

Intimacy Versus Isolation

Although the capacity for sexual intimacy begins during adolescence, according to Erikson, the individual does not become capable of a fully intimate relationship until one's sense of personal identity is fairly well established. That is, one must have a sense of who one is before one can fuse that identity with another in full appreciation of the other's uniqueness and separateness; earlier attempts at intimacy are frequently attempts to try to define oneself through a romantic relationship with another person.

> Sexual intimacy is only part of what I have in mind, for it is obvious that sexual intimacies often precede the capacity to develop a true and mutual psychosocial intimacy with another person, be it in friendship, in erotic encounters, or in joint inspiration. The youth who is not sure of his identity shies away from interpersonal intimacy or throws himself into acts of intimacy which are "promiscuous" without true fusion or real self-abandon.
>
> Where a youth does not accomplish such intimate relationships with others—and, I would add, with his own inner resources—in late adolescence or early adulthood, he may settle for highly stereotyped interpersonal relations and come to retain a deep *sense of isolation*. [Erikson, 1968, pp. 135–136]

The resolution of this stage involves the dialectical struggle between the opposing tendencies of intimacy and isolation. The psychosocial strength that emerges from this struggle is *love*. The early period of this stage involves the overlap between Identity versus Identity Confusion and Intimacy versus Isolation (as when one attempts to define one's sense of identity through relationships with others); the later period involves the overlap with Generativity versus Stagnation, the stage that refers to producing something that will outlive oneself.

We discuss these two relevant stages in Erikson's theory for the study of adolescence in detail in Chapters 9 and 10. Erikson's views have been criticized as applying primarily to male development and overlooking variations between women and men. For example, the pattern of development in women tends to combine intimacy with identity and generativity. We discuss this view in detail in the next section.

RELATIONAL DEVELOPMENT IN ADOLESCENCE

Carol Gilligan (1982, 1987) questioned the adequacy of most theories of adolescent personality development because, in her view, they are based on and refer to the development of boys and men and are not accurate descriptions of the development of girls and women. She noted that women's characteristics usually have been ignored by these theories, even when the observations on which they were based included women. Moreover, women often have been seen as deviant from normal development when that development is defined on the basis of male patterns.

In particular, each of the theories of personality development discussed up to this point has assumed that the adolescent is a separate and relatively autonomous individual. Indeed, the viewpoint of Blos is that one primary aim of development is "separation-individuation." Even Sullivan's interpersonal theory tends to portray the adolescent as a relatively autonomous person.

A different perspective was proposed by Gilligan (1982, 1987) and by the women at the Stone Center at Wellesley College (Jordan et al., 1991). This perspective focuses on a *relational approach to psychological understanding* that emphasizes the importance of the self in relation with others, empathy or mutual responsiveness in relationships, and the significance of a relational view of development. Although this perspective has been proposed by women to describe women's development, it is both a critique and expansion of other theories that describe human development.

Specifically, Gilligan (1982) critiqued the theory developed by Erikson, described earlier in this chapter.

> The problem that female adolescence poses for theorists of human development is apparent in Erikson's scheme. . . . The preparation for the successful resolution of the adolescent identity crisis is delineated in Erikson's description of the crises that characterize the preceding four stages. Although the initial crisis in infancy of "trust versus mistrust" anchors development in the experience of relationship, the task then clearly becomes one of individuation . . . separateness . . . autonomy . . . [and in] adolescence, the celebration of the autonomous, initiating, industrious self through the forging of an identity based on an ideology that can support and justify adult commitments. But about whom is Erikson talking?
>
> Once again it turns out to be the male child. For the female, Erikson (1968) says, the sequence is a bit different. . . . While for men, identity precedes intimacy and generativity in the optimal cycle of human separation and attachment, for women these tasks seem instead to be fused. Intimacy goes along with identity, as the female comes to know herself as she is known, through her relationships with others.
>
> Yet despite Erikson's observation of sex differences, his chart of life-cycle stages remains unchanged: identity continues to precede intimacy as male experience continues to define his life-cycle conception. [Gilligan, 1982, pp. 11–12]

In contrast to the emphasis on separateness, the **relational viewpoint** emphasizes the importance of dynamic interaction for the development of the self, attending to the feelings of others, and focusing on the "interaction between" as a way of being and acting (Miller, 1981/1991, p. 15). Likewise, one's sense of self-esteem is based on being a part of relationships and taking care of relationships; one's sense of effectiveness comes from emotional connections with others (p. 16). One's identity is as a "being-in-relation," which involves the development of oneself within a complex network of relationships (p. 21). One's sense of morality involves an ethic of care and responsibility for others (Gilligan, 1982). One's sense of power reflects the strength to care for and give to others (McClelland, 1979).

Nancy Chodorow (1974) also noted that women tend to define themselves through relationships with other people and suggested that this may reflect the pattern of continuity in the relationship between the girl and her mother from early infancy through the process of developing her identity as female similar to the mother. Thus, unlike boys who must separate their identity from the mother and define themselves as masculine, girls do not define their identity by separation and individuation, but instead by attachment and empathy with others.

Surrey (1983/1991) summarized several key components of the relational perspective:

1. The primary experience of oneself is relational—organized and developed in the context of relationships (p. 52).

2. Empathy—the cognitive and affective ability to assimilate the experience of another—is a central aspect that requires practice, modeling, and feedback in relationships (p. 54).

3. The mother–daughter relationship for women is a beginning and a model of important relationships with other significant people (p. 55).

4. The process of development involves "relationship-differentiation" that leads to greater levels of complex human relationships. For example, adolescents do not necessarily "separate" from their parents, but want to change the relationship in a way that affirms their developmental changes (p. 60).

5. A relationship involves the subjective experience of others, the expectation of mutuality, and a sense of motivation to care for the other person (p. 61); thus, one is a part of a unit larger than oneself, and the self is more vital and enhanced by these connections with others (p. 62).

This perspective is proposed as an alternate model to the dominant (male) model in our culture for understanding human development, especially for women.

> We were troubled not only by the obvious misunderstandings such as "penis envy," but also by the more pervasive and insidious application to women of models of development inspired by a male culture; these theories consistently mislabeled women as deficient. Thus theories of "human development" which espoused increasing capacity for separation, autonomy, mastery, independence, and self-sufficiency as indications of health and maturity consistently portrayed women as too emotional, too dependent, lacking clear boundaries, and so forth. [Jordan et al., 1991, p. v]

The traditional model of separation and individuation involves an emphasis on independence, self-reliance, individuality, and autonomy. Similar gender differences may also be reflected in the "rules of the game" boys and men learn to play in our society. Janet Lever (1976) observed fifth-grade children playing and noted that boys played competitive games more often than girls did. In such games, boys were better able to settle disputes because they adopted a set of rules to resolve disputes and seemed to enjoy the debates about the rules.

> During the course of this study, boys were seen quarrelling all the time, but not once was a game terminated because of a quarrel and no game was interrupted for more than seven minutes. In the gravest debates, the final word was always to "repeat the play," generally followed by a chorus of "cheater's proof." [Lever, 1976, p. 482]

For girls, disputes tended to end the game. They appeared to feel that continuing a relationship with the other players was more important than continuing the game. Similarly Miller (1982/1991) noted: "Trying to beat the other, hitting as hard as you can, and the like does not mean you are hurting anyone personally; you are just playing the game" (p. 191). Competition, expression of anger, defending one's own territory and dominance, avoiding

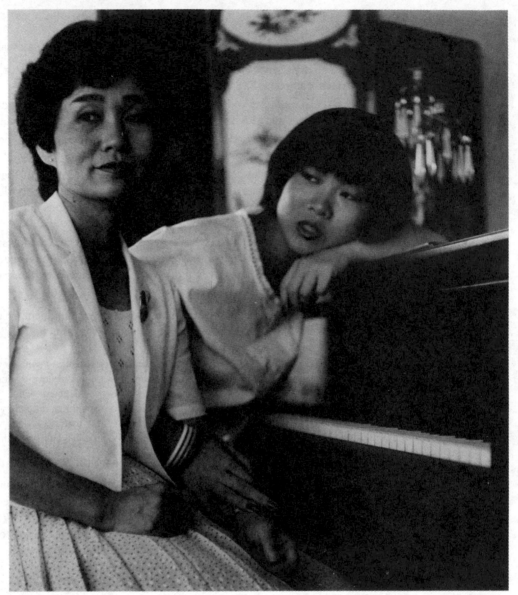

For girls, the mother—daughter relationship is a model of important relationships with other women.

dependency, and a willingness to fight for one's rights are in contrast with the relational idea that one is "in a profound and real sense, responsible for each other" (p. 187).

Other studies have noted the significance of interpersonal relationships for understanding women's development (e.g., Josselson, 1987; Mercer, Nichols, & Doyle, 1989). Gilligan's (1982, 1987) research also suggests that these differences are important for understanding the ways women and men make ethical judgments. She found that women, when they make moral judgments, tend to emphasize responsibility to others, seek to avoid hurting others, focus on maintaining relationships, think in contextual ways (rather than in the abstract), and center their concerns on care about and for others. Men, in contrast, tend to focus on individual rights and obligations in a formal and abstract social system. She has found similar differences among both educationally advantaged adolescents and adults and inner-city teenagers (Gilligan, 1987). However, she also noted that although most respondents tend to focus on either one perspective (justice) or the other (care), about one-third—equally divided between women and men—were able to use either perspective (Gilligan & Attanucci, 1985). Thus, it appears "that loss of perspective is a liability that both sexes share" (Gilligan, 1987, p. 73).

The perspective of Gilligan and her colleagues has begun to focus attention on the diversity of developmental themes during adolescence. There appear to be at least two paths that diverge, with some able to follow both at once. However, although our culture tends to encourage women to follow one path and men to follow the other, other cultures seem not to diverge at this same theme, but probably diverge elsewhere. For example, Lebra (1976) described Japanese behavior as emphasizing belongingness, empathy, dependency, and reciprocity for both men and women. She noted:

> For the Japanese, empathy (*omoiyari*) ranks high among the virtues considered indispensable for one to be really human, morally mature, and deserving of respect. [p. 38]

Moreover, the relational model has been criticized for stressing the virtues of interconnection with others as opposed to independence and autonomy; in reality, one must have some degree of skill in both styles in order to function in our society (Sang, 1992).

In general, data supporting this perspective have been difficult to interpret because they are very complex and because expected differences between the groups have not been clear-cut, a situation not very different from that of the other theories presented in this chapter. Undoubtedly, this perspective will stimulate continued research and may provide not only better understanding of female development, but also greater understanding of male development.

Gender differences are discussed throughout this book in terms of a variety of topics; also, several interludes between the chapters are interviews with women. Many of the themes discussed here may be observed in the interludes as well.

BEHAVIORAL THEMES: THE SOCIAL LEARNING APPROACH

Social learning theory differs from the theoretical perspectives presented so far in two major ways. First, learning theory stresses objective, observable processes rather than such abstract, inferred processes as oedipal conflicts and lust dynamisms. Accordingly, learning theory is based largely on research, often conducted in carefully controlled laboratory conditions. Unlike theories that are derived from clinical observation and intuition and are sometimes difficult to validate, learning theory is based on experiments and involves predictions that can usually be tested experimentally.

Second, the other perspectives assume that physical, sexual, and psychological maturation of puberty determines the central issues of adolescence in certain unique ways. The basic assumption in social learning theory, by contrast, is that the same principles of learning shape development at all ages. Previous experience and current circumstances are relevant to what young people learn, but there is no unique theory of adolescent learning. Adolescents are influenced by their experience in the same way as children or adults, even though they may be learning different kinds of things. In this vein, instead of depicting adolescence as an unusually stormy period, social learning theory emphasizes the similarity of adolescence to other periods of life. Likewise, both men and women learn behavior in similar ways; also, gender differences are largely the result of learning.

Central to behavioral themes in developmental psychology, then, is how people learn. One important form of learning is **conditioning**, which occurs when a reinforcement is linked to a specific behavior. Life is full of conditioned behaviors; repetitive routine behaviors such as getting dressed to start the day's activities and answering the telephone to stop its ringing are learned from prior reinforcement of these actions as ways of accomplishing a desired goal. More complicated behavior may also result from conditioning, such as heading the other way when a person who has previously proved disagreeable comes into sight. Following similar principles, a parent who praises an adolescent for high grades—and a high grade itself—reinforces academic achievement. In addition to providing *external motivation* to achieve, such reinforcement builds in standards of achievement that become *self-reinforcing* and serve as internal criteria for evaluating one's success and accomplishments.

Along with learning that results from the pairing of behavior with some subsequent rewards, another important form of learning is **observational learning**. Many of the complex tasks of life could not be learned simply by trying various behaviors to see which ones are positively reinforced. For instance, driving a car or performing surgery are learned through observing and imitating various models, not by trial and error. Once skills are learned through observation, however, the responses they involve can become conditioned through practice: An experienced driver riding as a passenger in a car may find his or her foot moving automatically as if to press on the brake pedal when danger looms.

Among the major proponents of social learning theory, one whose work bears most closely on adolescent development is Albert Bandura (1969a, 1977, 1986). Bandura advocates a *sociobehavioristic* approach to development that emphasizes observational learning. The key feature of such learning is that it allows a person to learn a wide variety of behaviors that are likely to succeed the first time they are tried, and therefore to be powerfully reinforced. A four-step sequence is necessary for this kind of learning to occur and be translated into behavior:

1. The model to be observed and imitated, and thereby learned from, must first receive the person's attention.

2. The person must remember what the model has done; often this is facilitated by describing the behavior to oneself in words and rehearsing the actions in words.

3. The person must have the requisite skills to reproduce the behavior; sometimes these skills must be developed through practice or await physical maturation.

4. To perform the behavior, once it has been learned and the necessary skills are available, the person must anticipate some reward for its performance. For example, an adolescent boy may have observed his mother smoking cigarettes, but he is not likely to do so himself unless there is some reinforcement for the behavior, such as being accepted by her, or by his friends.

Vicarious reinforcement can motivate long periods of practice to develop skills.

The rewards that translate learned skills into behavior may be direct and external, in the form of praise, admiration, or popularity granted by others. They may be direct but self-reinforcing, as in the case of satisfying internal standards of achievement. Or they can be *vicarious reinforcements*, in which one has observed other people being rewarded for a particular behavior. Vicarious reinforcement means that people can be motivated to learn and perform many behaviors without any direct reinforcement from others or themselves; instead, they may, for example, spend hours practicing basketball, ballet, or mathematics motivated by the hope of receiving the rewards they have seen come to others for proficiency in these skills.

Having been trained originally as a clinician, Bandura has derived some distinctive principles of psychological treatment from his approach (Bandura, 1969b). In addition, he has conducted extensive research on sociobehavioral learning, especially with respect to aggression (Bandura, 1973, 1976). These classic studies have shown clearly how parental behaviors can reinforce aggressiveness by rewarding socially appropriate forms of aggression. Yet, punishing a child for being aggressive can also teach aggression through observational learning, he found. For example, telling children that hitting a younger sibling is bad while also spanking them for it may have the undesired effect of modeling rather than discouraging aggressive behavior. Although this does not mean that parents should avoid exerting control over their children—a theme we elaborate in Chapter 7—it does mean that the models parents present for adolescents to imitate are often more powerful than the values they preach.

General implications of Bandura's observational learning theme are noted throughout our discussions, especially in Chapters 11, 12, and 13 because problem behavior of most kinds run in families. To an unclear, but nevertheless unquestionable extent, this family incidence of developmental variations and disturbances derives from young people modeling themselves after the behavior of their parents and other significant adults in their lives.

One of the strengths of the social learning approach is that it is based on experimental results. However, experiments, like clinical observations, do not automatically reveal the nature of human behavior. For example, it is not necessarily clear that behavior in a laboratory setting applies directly to daily life any more than the concerns of patients in psychotherapy necessarily represent the concerns of people in general. In addition, because there are many models that an adolescent may observe and imitate, determining which models have the greatest influence on which individuals remains a complex question in social learning theory. Moreover, many observed behaviors are not expressed immediately, but may be learned and exhibited much later, or not at all, depending on the situation. What social learning theory does is call attention to the importance of the social environment—both as the arena for learning through observation and as the situation that elicits the performance of behaviors that have been learned.

INTERACTION OF THEORETICAL PERSPECTIVES

It is probably apparent that the several theoretical approaches we have examined overlap each other in various ways and are not incompatible. As we have noted, we draw on ideas from each of these theories in different chapters as they seem particularly helpful in understanding certain aspects of adolescent behavior.

Our point in this approach—and our conviction—is that there is no single "correct" theory of adolescent development. Students of adolescence should compare and contrast different approaches to determine (perhaps not always in agreement with us) which are most useful in studying a particular topic. In this regard, we rarely limit ourselves to just one or another theoretical approach at a time. Instead, we present alternative formulations of the research findings on various subjects to allow readers to make judgments of their own about which theories seem most sensible in accounting for what is known about adolescent behavior.

We also need to keep in mind that these theoretical formulations sometimes appear to contradict each other, or to use the same terms in different ways. For example, Sullivan, Erikson, and Gilligan have a lot to say about *intimacy*. For Sullivan it refers to a quality of preadolescent relationships beginning with chumships; for Erikson it refers to a quality of later adolescent or early adult relationships that is possible only after identity has been formed; and for Gilligan it is often fused with identity issues for women, but is usually separate for men. However, each perspective is useful for understanding adolescents' experience of intimacy.

Similarly, various theorists label the same stages of adolescence with different terms, or different stages with the same term. Sullivan's "early adolescence," for example, includes most of the developmental events that occur in both early and middle adolescence in Blos' scheme. Although such differences in labeling may be confusing, they are not necessarily an important concern. Consider the matter similar to dividing an automobile journey into two long days of driving or into three shorter days—it makes some difference because some places may be passed at dusk in one trip and in full sunlight in another, but it is not a major disagreement because the same ground is covered, just as the same developmental transition is being described in all theories of adolescence. However, if the transition is different for women than for men, the ways that adolescence is described may be significant if some patterns apply to women and others to men, or if the sequence differs for men and women.

This chapter has surveyed theoretical models and perspectives of the developmental transition of adolescence from four major vantage points. We examined the influences of biological changes that begin the period of adolescence. Then we examined the nature of cognitive changes during adolescence. Next we noted the importance of understanding the individual adolescent within his or her social and physical context. We concluded the chapter with an overview of five major perspectives on adolescent personality development. Each of these themes provides a perspective for understanding adolescents and their behavior as they navigate the transition from childhood to adulthood. The next chapter focuses on the biological changes of puberty and their effects during the period of adolescence.

CHAPTER SUMMARY

1. Opposing conceptions of human development are based on: 1) the predeterministic theory that inborn traits determine development—this view is similar to the biogenetic emphasis of Hall's early theory of adolescence; and 2) the *tabula rasa* view that environmental factors are all important—this view is reflected in sociocultural theories of development. Contemporary theories usually emphasize an interaction between these influences.

2. Biological changes associated with puberty may be potentially significant; however, the specific nature of their influence is determined less by the biochemical changes within the adolescent than by the sociocultural environment in which the adolescent lives. In particular, the timing of the changes relative to the adolescent's peers and the meaning that is attached to those changes is especially important.

3. Cognitive development has important effects on adolescent development. In general, thinking becomes more efficient, more dimensions can be kept in mind at one time, and ideas can be organized and reorganized in broad conceptual patterns. This perspective on adolescent development calls attention to the adolescents' growing ability to think about themselves and their particular situation within the environmental context in which they live.

4. The adolescent's social-cultural context reflects a network of mutually interacting dimensions of their life space that is moving through time. Sensitivity to the diversity and context of adolescent lives is important for understanding the interaction between adolescents and their unique environmental setting.

5. Classical psychoanalytic theory traced personality development to the early life emergence of innate drives that become focused on different zones of the body to produce *psychosexual* stages. Adolescence is regarded primarily as a period of adaptation to increased sexual drives during puberty, and *regression* at this time to childish ways of behaving is seen as a common occurrence.

6. Sigmund Freud stressed the importance of childhood *oedipal* attractions to the parent of the other gender. These attractions are reawakened in adolescence, and the conflicts they produce influence a sequence of changing relationships with parents and peers of both genders.

7. Anna Freud described how adolescents often defend themselves against anxiety caused by their increased sexual drives through the mechanisms of *asceticism* and *intellectualization*.

8. Peter Blos subdivided adolescence into several stages in which young people adapt in different and increasingly mature ways to the psychological stresses of this age. Going beyond the traditional psychoanalytic focus on sexual drives, he described an important theme of *separation-individuation* in adolescent–parent relationships.

9. Harry Stack Sullivan emphasized the importance of certain interpersonal events during three adolescent stages of development: forming a very close relationship with a *chum* during preadolescence; the emergence and channeling of sexual feelings—described as the *lust dynamism*—during early adolescence; and the establishment of a full range of interpersonal relationships—integrating needs for security, intimacy, and lust—during late adolescence.

10. Erik Erikson viewed human development as a series of eight stages, each involving a dialectical struggle between two opposing tendencies. The development tasks of the two stages most relevant to adolescence are a sense of *identity*, as opposed to identity (or role) confusion, and a sense of *intimacy*, as opposed to isolation.

11. Carol Gilligan and others studying women's development noted that most theories are male oriented and ignore the importance of relationships with others, especially for women. The relational perspective focuses on development of interpersonal relationships, empathy, the process of relationship differentiation, and a motivation to care for others.

12. Social learning theories of development reflect a *behavioral emphasis* on the role of experience in shaping individual characteristics, skills, and knowledge. People of all ages learn the behaviors they manifest through the learning processes of *conditioning* and *observation*. Albert Bandura has made especially important contributions in applying principles of observational learning to the understanding of adolescent behavior.

KEY WORDS

asceticism	direct effects model	mediated effects model	relational viewpoint
conditioning	epigenesis	moratorium	relativism
contextualism	intellectualization	observational learning	separation-individuation
defense mechanisms	lust dynamism	regression	

REVIEW QUESTIONS

1. What is the nature–nurture controversy about? Can you think of examples from contemporary life that reflect this issue?

BIOLOGICAL MODELS AND THE EFFECTS OF PUBERTY

2. Contrast the *direct effects* and the *mediated effects* models. What are *mediating* and *moderating* variables?

3. Give some examples of the interaction between experiencing puberty and other changes in the adolescent's life.

4. Recall the four dimensions in Riegel's dialectical model (Box 1.1) and consider the interaction of puberty (individual-biological dimension) with changes in other dimensions that might be brought about by: 1) moving to a new city; 2) parents divorcing.

COGNITIVE AND INTELLECTUAL DEVELOPMENT

5. How does increased efficiency of thinking, the ability to hold more than one dimension in mind, and the ability to organize or reorganize ideas into broad conceptual patterns affect an adolescent in school? At home? In interpersonal relationships?

6. Often the adolescent seems overwhelmed by information and takes a relativistic point of view: "I don't know" or "It depends." Why is this?

7. What effect does an adolescent's cognitive development have on his or her self-image and sense of identity?

CONTEXTUAL PERSPECTIVE ON ADOLESCENT DEVELOPMENT

8. Why does adolescent development require attention to the context of that development?

9. How does Figure 2.3 apply to your individual life?

PERSONALITY DEVELOPMENT

10. How are examples of childish behavior in otherwise well-adjusted teenagers explained by psychoanalytic theory?

11. What role do *defense mechanisms* play for well-adjusted people? Give examples of how the ones described by Anna Freud are used by adolescents. Have you used them?

12. Describe Blos' concept of *separation-individuation* and give a few examples from your own relationship with your parents.

13. What are the potential beneficial effects of having a *chum*, according to Sullivan? Did you have one?

14. Give some examples of the "collisions" and "integration" of the adolescent's *lust dynamism* with the need for *security* and *intimacy* during early and late adolescence, respectively.

15. Describe the dialectical tension between the opposing issues of Erikson's stages of identity versus identity (role) confusion and intimacy versus isolation. What is the synthesis he suggested for each of these stages?

16. What is the critique of Erikson's view of development from the perspective of relational models proposed by Gilligan and others?

17. How does the relational view differ from the idea of separation-individuation? Which approach, or both, makes sense to you based on your experience?

18. How does learning theory differ from other models of personality development presented in this chapter?

19. Think of some examples of how you have followed the four-step sequence Bandura described for learning complex behavior.

20. Give some examples of how the differing theoretical approaches discussed in the chapter overlap with each other and are not incompatible with one another. The dialectical model described by Riegel in Chapter 1 may help you to organize your answer to this question.

Chapter 3

◆

Puberty: Inside and Outside

◆

Acne, jeans that seem to get shorter at a rapid rate, growing breasts and genitals, voice changes, pubic hair: you cannot hide the changes of puberty; and you cannot pretend they are happening if they are not. At times it seems everyone is watching you develop. The attention and the changes are sometimes embarrassing. Sometimes they are exciting. Sometimes they are perplexing. Sometimes even frightening.

Puberty may be defined as the process of becoming physically and sexually mature and developing the characteristics of one's gender—female or male—such as physical build, genitals, and body hair. It is dramatic because the changes are so rapid and affect so much of the body. Only the growth in infancy is as rapid; but we were not conscious of our growth then, as we certainly are during adolescence.

Surprisingly, the "clock" that sets the changes of puberty in motion remains a mystery. Occasionally it begins so early that the person is otherwise still a child, or so late that it seems that it will never start. Generally, however, most of the dramatic changes of puberty occur during early adolescence—between the ages of 12 and 16 (Tanner, 1971, 1978). Hormonal changes occur earlier, between ages 7 and 11 in girls and 8 and 12 in boys (Money, 1980); they produce the physical changes that together produce adult sexuality.

In order to understand puberty, we need to begin at the very beginning of life—in prenatal development. We discuss the origins of the hormonal processes that are set in motion by some unknown "biological clock" at puberty. Then, in the next section, we examine the hormonal changes that result from this biological clock and the effects they have on the body. In the third section of the chapter we focus on the physical and genital development that results from these hormonal changes.

The final two sections use a biopsychosocial perspective to discuss the effect of puberty on the individual. How do adolescents respond to these internal and external changes? How does the response of others affect the adolescent? What effect does maturing early or late have on a person? What causes puberty that begins very early or very late? Each of these topics is central to an understanding of the effects of puberty.

ORIGINS OF PUBERTY

The changes experienced at puberty have their origins at the moment of conception. Usually, the father's sperm carries either an X or a Y chromosome to the union with the mother's egg, which carries an X chromosome. If all goes well, the presence or absence of that Y chromosome has dramatic effects during puberty. Let us briefly review this process.

PRENATAL BEGINNINGS: THE ADAM AND EVE PRINCIPLES

The difference between males and females results from the prenatal effects of a few strategically timed biochemicals. That is, the male form is a differentiation that results only in the presence of biochemical substances produced as a result of the Y chromosome. Money (1980) refers to the principle of "adding something to differentiate a male" as the *Adam principle*. If the body does not respond to one or more of these biochemical substances—or if they are not present—then the female form results: the *Eve principle*.

Although the process by which the genes produce an embryo is still largely a mystery, the Adam and Eve principles help us to understand the development of internal reproductive or-

External Genital Differentiation In The Human Fetus

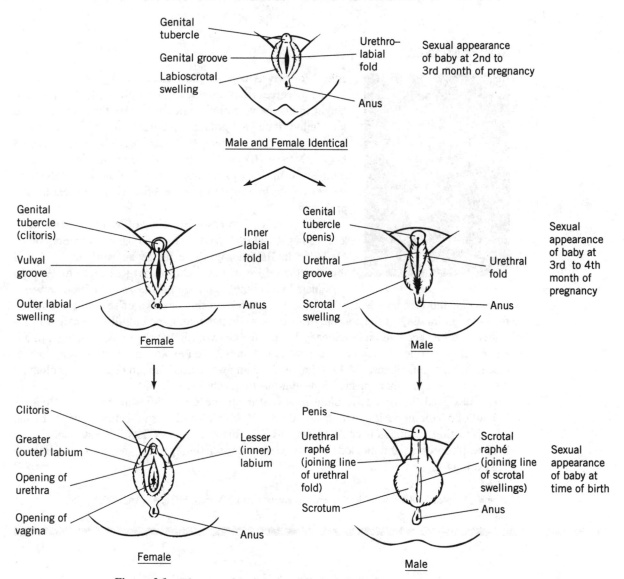

Figure 3.1   Diagram showing the differentiation of external reproductive anatomy in female and male humans. [*Source:* J. Money. *Love and Love Sickness.* © 1980 Johns Hopkins Press. Figure 3–3, p. 20. Reprinted with permission.]

gans. In males, a gene initiates the undifferentiated gonadal cells to develop into testes. Then, about the 12th week after conception, the testes begin producing **testosterone**, a hormone that is one of the group of chemical substances known as *androgens*. The testes also produce a substance called Müllerian duct inhibitory substance (sometimes called MIS). MIS prevents one set of internal ducts (Müllerian) from developing; androgens cause an-

♦ *Profile*

JOHN MONEY

John Money was born in New Zealand in 1921. He earned Master's degrees in psychology/philosophy and education and taught in his native country until 1947. He then emigrated to the United States for graduate study, having been influenced by the cultural anthropologist Ernest Beaglehole. He received his Ph.D. from Harvard in 1952, where he developed a commitment to medical psychology, focusing on birth defects of the sex organs and related genetic, endocrine, and sexological problems.

He is currently Professor Emeritus of Medical Psychology and Pediatrics at the Johns Hopkins University School of Medicine in Baltimore, where he began work in 1951 and founded the Office of Psychohormonal Research. In 1955 he formulated and coined the term *gender role*. In 1966 he was a founder of the Gender Identity Clinic. His research on the varieties of sexuality led to the formulation in 1983 of the concept of *lovemaps*. He has maintained a full-time career in research and has become internationally known for his work in psychoendocrinology and developmental sexology. He also has a worldwide reputation as an expert in gender science, research, and clinical care. In 1986 he received an award from the American Psychological Association for his distinguished contributions to psychology.

He designed the first curriculum in sexual medicine for students at the Johns Hopkins School of Medicine in 1969 and taught it until 1984. He continues to lecture widely. His list of publications contains over 34 books and 346 scientific papers. His interests include the history, philosophy, and methodology of science, especially regarding the study and practice of sexology.

[*Source:* Adapted from a biographical statement prepared by John Money, Ph.D., August, 1992.]

other set of internal ducts (Wolffian) to develop into a system of sperm ducts. Thus, the Adam principle describes the fact that the male gonads and internal organs are produced only if testosterone and MIS are present (Bardin & Paulsen, 1981; Money, 1980; Sanders & Reinisch, 1990).

In females, where none of these biochemical substances is present, the Eve principle operates. Ovaries develop about 3 months after conception. The Müllerian ducts develop into the oviducts, uterus, and vagina; and the Wolffian ducts degenerate (Money, 1980; Ross & Vande Wiele, 1981; Sanders & Reinisch, 1990).

Similarly, the Adam and Eve principles also describe the development of the external genital organs. In males, androgens cause the penis and scrotum to form from the same embryonic material that would otherwise become the female clitoris and outer and inner labia (Figure 3.1). If the androgens are not present, then the external female genital organs form (Money, 1980).

The effects of puberty reflect these events that differentiate male from female during prenatal development. In the next section we focus on the development of the endocrine system that controls the production of the hormones that produce the masculinizing and feminizing changes at puberty. This system also begins functioning before birth.

HORMONAL FEEDBACK SYSTEMS AND PUBERTY

The gonads (ovaries in women and testes in men) produce hormones that circulate in the bloodstream and, due to their effects on reproductive cycles and sexual maturation, are called *sex hormones*. The release of sex hormones from the gonads is controlled by another group of hormones, the **gonadotropic hormones**, produced by the *pituitary gland*, which is a lobe-like organ projecting down from the base of the brain above the roof of the mouth. These gonadotropic hormones are **follicle stimulating hormone** (FSH) and **luteinizing hormone** (LH). The pituitary gland is stimulated to produce gonadotropic hormones by the hypothalamus (a part of the brain located above the pituitary). Through a complex feedback system, these tissues send messages back and forth to stimulate or inhibit the production of sex hormones by the gonads.

The hypothalamus and pituitary continually monitor the level of hormones circulating in the blood. The hypothalamus sends a hormonal message to the pituitary to produce a particular gonadotropic hormone through pulses of a substance known as *GnRH* (gonadotropin releasing hormone). The pituitary may or may not respond to this sex hormone, depending on the level of other hormones. If it does respond, it produces gonadotropic hormones that act on the gonads to stimulate production of the appropriate sex hormone.

Negative Feedback System

Sex hormones are regulated by a *negative feedback system*. If the level of sex hormone is high, the interaction of the hypothalamus and pituitary reduces stimulation to the gonads and thereby decreases production of the hormone. If it is low, greater production is triggered (Figure 3.2). A simple parallel would be a thermostat that signals a furnace to produce more heat when the temperature falls below a certain level, or to shut off when the temperature rises to a certain level.

This negative feedback system is the means by which contraceptive pills work in females. That is, the hormones contained in the pill signal the hypothalamus–pituitary to inhibit production of the hormones that lead to ovulation. In males, a substance called *inhibin* has been identified that is produced by the testes and also plays a role in inhibiting production of at least one of the gonadotropic hormones (Bardin & Paulsen, 1981).

About 80 days after conception, two gonadotropins (FSH and LH) begin to be produced by the fetal pituitary. By 150 days' gestation, the negative feedback system begins functioning. Except for a brief period after birth, this negative feedback system is "set" at a low level during childhood, maintaining secretion of sex hormones at low levels (Grumbach, Roth, Kaplan, & Kelch, 1974, p. 159).

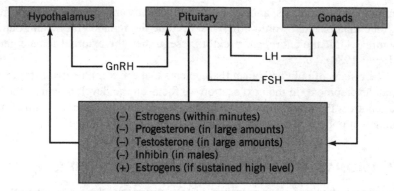

Figure 3.2 Diagram of the negative (−) and positive (+) feedback systems involving the hypothalamus, pituitary, and gonads. Luteinizing hormone (LH) and follicle stimulating hormone (FSH) are known as gonadotropic hormones; estrogens and progesterone are female sex hormones; testosterone is a male sex hormone. [*Source:* Based on Bardin & Paulsen, 1981; Ross & Vande Wiele, 1981, p. 369.]

Changes at Puberty

The "biological clock" that regulates the beginning of puberty has not been firmly identified, although it has been suggested that the pineal gland may play this role. Low levels of sex hormones and gonadotropic hormones during childhood appear to be related to a biochemical substance, *melatonin*, which is produced by the *pineal gland*. This small gland, resembling the shape of a pine cone (hence its name), lies near the center of the head, above and behind the pituitary. It is stimulated by nerve input from the retina of the eye, and its activity is regulated by the external cycle of light and dark. Secretion of melatonin begins almost immediately after exposure to darkness and stops after exposure to light (although persons who sleep during the day apparently shift their melatonin cycle). When injected into humans, melatonin lowers secretion of LH, suppresses secretion of sex hormones, and produces sleepiness (Reichlin, 1981, pp. 625–628).

One study suggested that melatonin may maintain the low levels of gonadotropic and sex hormones during childhood and regulate the increasing levels of these hormones at puberty (Waldhauser et al., 1984). This study found that the level of melatonin in the blood, when measured at night (but not daytime levels), was higher for children 1 to 5 years old than for children 5 to 11 years old; low levels were characteristic of teenagers over age 13 and adults. Moreover, the concentration of melatonin was inversely related to the concentration of LH, and both were related to the degree of sexual maturation during puberty. That is, prepubertal children had relatively high levels of melatonin and relatively low levels of LH; children who were more sexually mature had lower levels of melatonin and higher levels of LH in direct relation to their stage of maturation (Figure 3.3). Similar patterns have been found in children with precocious puberty (i.e., puberty that begins abnormally early); even when the precocious puberty was treated, and the sex hormone levels returned to normally low levels, melatonin levels did not rise, suggesting that melatonin may be the cause, not the result, of pubertal maturation (Waldhauser, Boepple, Schemper, Mansfield, & Crowley, 1991). Although these studies do not prove that the pineal gland, which might be "programmed" to

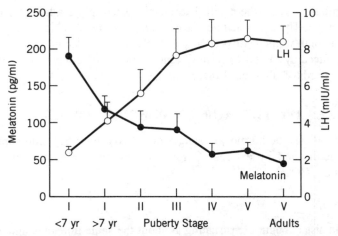

Figure 3.3 Nighttime mean levels of melatonin and LH in blood samples for 58 children and adolescents and 31 young adults, grouped according to stage of sexual maturation based on Tanner's scales (see Figures 2.11, 2.12, and 2.13). Bar represents the standard error of the mean. [*Source:* F. Waldhauser et al. Fall in Nocturnal Serum Melatonin During Prepuberty and Pubescence. *The Lancet, I*, 1984, Figure 3, p. 364. Reprinted with permission.]

release an inhibition of puberty after a certain number of dark–light cycles, is the "clock" that triggers puberty, it is a very interesting possibility. Other factors related to the beginning of puberty clearly are involved and will be discussed in the next section.

Shortly before puberty begins, pulses of GnRH are produced by the hypothalamus at higher levels than previously, and at about 2-hour intervals. These pulses appear to stimulate the pituitary to secrete higher levels of FSH and LH. In turn, the gonads secrete greater amounts of sex hormones. The adrenal gland also begins secreting greater amounts of androgens, which stimulate growth of pubic hair in both boys and girls. These hormonal changes stimulate physical growth and the development of breasts, genitals, and body hair during puberty. However, the exact nature of these hormonal changes is not fully understood (Cameron, 1990; González, 1982; Hopwood et al., 1990).

If these changes begin too early (i.e., precocious puberty), they may be largely stopped and reversed by administering a chemical substance similar to GnRH at a *constant* level (Comite, 1981; Johnson, 1983; Hopwood et al., 1990). If the changes do not begin at the usual time (i.e., delayed puberty), they may be produced by administering GnRH in doses at 2-hour intervals using a timed, portable pump (Hoffman & Crowley, 1982).

Positive Feedback System

About midway through puberty, the hypothalamus–pituitary interaction begins to function also as a *positive feedback system* so that an increase in one sex hormone leads to the stimulation of another sex hormone (Grumbach, Roth, Kaplan, & Kelch, 1974, p. 159). In females this positive feedback results in a surge in LH by the pituitary in response to a rapid rise, and then a sustained high level of estrogen, one of the types of hormones produced by the ovaries. This occurs at the time the ovary is ready to release an egg, and the LH surge results in ovulation. Thus, the positive feedback system plays a key role in **menarche**, the first menstruation. The combined negative and positive feedback systems regulate the menstrual cycle in adult women (Ross & Vande Wiele, 1981). In adult males, the level of the sex hormone produced by the testes (testosterone) is primarily controlled by the negative feedback system (Bardin & Paulsen, 1981, p. 305).

INFLUENCES ON THE AGE OF PUBERTY ONSET

Whatever initiates the hormonal changes of puberty, their beginning appears to be influenced by heredity and by external factors such as body weight, exercise, and nutrition (Hopwood et al., 1990).

Heredity

Identical twin sisters begin menstruating at about the same time, averaging 2 months apart; in contrast, nonidentical twins average 10 months apart in their first menses. Also, the relationship between the age of mothers' and daughters' first menstruation is just slightly less than the correlations of their physical height in adulthood. These examples suggest the importance of genetics in the onset of menstruation. It is thought that the inherited characteristics that influence the timing of puberty are as much from the father's genes as from the mother's, similar to the inheritance of other physical characteristics (Harrison, Weiner, Tanner, & Barnicot, 1964, p. 345).

Body Weight and Exercise

There is considerable evidence that body weight is related to the onset of pubertal changes. It is not clear, however, whether some critical weight is necessary to begin puberty, or whether this weight results from the changes at puberty. For example, whether the girl matures early or late, the average body weight at the beginning of the adolescent growth spurt does not differ; the same is true for the age of first menstruation. A similar relationship between body weight and puberty is also found for boys, although the latest maturing boys differed from the general relationship (Frisch, 1974).

A series of studies by Frisch and her coworkers have found that female competitive athletes in training have a later age of menarche than the general population; they also are more likely to have irregular menstrual cycles or no menses if they had begun menstruating earlier. When athletes (swimmers and runners) who began training before menarche were compared with those who began their athletic training after menarche, athletic training was found to delay menarche by 5 months for each year of training (Frisch et al., 1981). The average age of menarche for those who began training earlier was 15.1 years of age, compared with 12.8 years of age for those who began training after menarche; similar women who had no athletic training reported experiencing menarche at the same age as the latter group, 12.7 years. Also, the premenarche-trained women were more likely to have irregular or no menses compared with the postmenarche trained. The researchers concluded that intense physical activity delays menarche, but it is not clear whether this resulted from the lower ratio of body fat to body weight or the tension and stress of training and competition. They did note that reduced intensity of training or increased nutrition can induce menstrual cycles

Intense physical activity may delay menarche, but it may be caused partly by the tension and stress of performance.

in those women whose cycles had stopped, and there is no reason to expect long-term negative effects (Frisch et al., 1981).

Another study, of ballet dancers between the ages of 13 and 15 observed over a period of 4 years, found similar effects on menarche and the menstrual cycle (Warren, 1980). In this sample of 15 girls, the average age of menarche was 15.4, compared with 12.9 in a control sample of music students. The dancers had less body fat than the music students, and both groups had a sizable height and weight gain before menarche. Breast development was markedly delayed in the dancers, but was greater during periods of less frequent practice. However, pubic hair appeared at the normal age. In many of the women, menarche occurred during periods of little exercise, often while recovering from an injury that prevented practicing, and often in the absence of any weight or body fat increase. Similarly, in those women who had begun menstruating and then stopped, a time of inactivity often reestablished the menstrual cycle. Warren (1980) concluded that the large amount of energy required by training to be a dancer, combined with the low amount of average body fat, may be responsible for the absence of menstrual cycles (*amenorrhea*). She also speculated about the biological reason this might occur.

> The delay in menarche and the amenorrheic state may be an appropriate adaptation of the body to large metabolic demands and may represent a natural form of reversible fertility control, which has been reported in some primitive cultures whose life styles show cyclic changes in nutrition, weight, and activity. [Warren, 1980, p. 1156]

Could it be that the female body does not produce menstrual cycles when there is an excessive drain on the low reserves of body fat? Some researchers think this is the case; others feel body fat is not very important. Also, it is not known how such information might be conveyed to the hypothalamus and pituitary. However, as we have discussed, it appears that the biochemical processes that initiate puberty, whatever they may be, are able to be influenced by factors related to body weight and exercise. In the next section we see that nutrition also seems to play a role.

Nutrition and the Declining Age of Menarche

Interesting historical and world-wide data on the age of menarche are also relevant to the biological clock that triggers puberty. The age of menarche declined at about 2 months each decade between 1900 and the mid-1940s in the United States; it changed from an average age of about 14 years to 12.8 years and leveled off at that age around 1947 (Wyshak & Frisch, 1982). The rate of decline was greater in the Scandinavian countries and less in France, among the European countries where data were available during the period from 1795 to 1981 (Figure 3.4). This long-term, consistent change resulting from external factors is called a *secular trend*.

Tanner (1971) argued that this secular trend toward earlier maturity is largely a result of improved nutrition from conception on through puberty. To support this view, he noted that there are marked variations among countries, paralleling nutritional differences.

> The well-nourished Western populations have median menarcheal ages of about 12.8 to 13.2 years; the latest recorded ages, by contrast, are 18 years in the Highlands of New Guinea, 17 years in Central Africa, and 15.5 years in poorly-off Bantu in the South African Transkei. Well-nourished Africans have a median age of 13.4 (Kampala upper classes) or less, comparable with Europeans. Asians at the same nutritional level as Europeans probably have an earlier menarche, the figure for well-off Chinese in Hong Kong being 12.5 years. [Tanner, 1971, pp. 928–929]

Similarly, a study comparing puberty among two groups of boys whose grandparents were from the same region of Italy, but where one group grew up in the United States and the other in Italy, found that the Italian-American boys reached puberty earlier (and also showed more rapid physical growth) than the Italian boys (Young & Ferguson, 1981, p. 91). This difference was attributed to a nutritional advantage, especially protein intake, in the United States.

It now appears that the well-nourished populations have reached the lower limit in the age at puberty that can be induced by good nutrition. With increased nutrition there is an increase in body weight, so perhaps the level of nutrition influences the age of puberty through processes similar to those that are involved in general body weight. However, just as

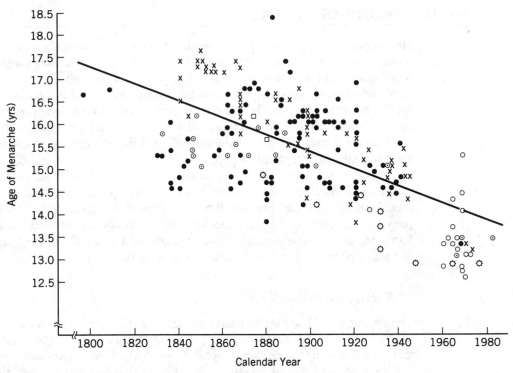

Figure 3.4 The age of menarche has been declining in Western Europe and the United States at the rate of about two months each decade. However, it is no longer declining in the United States and in some European countries. The symbols refer to England (⊙); France (●); Germany (⊗); Holland (□); Scandinavia (X, Denmark, Finland, Norway, and Sweden); Belgium, Czechoslovakia, Hungary, Italy, Poland, Romania, Russia, Spain, and Switzerland (all labeled ○); and the United States (✿, data not included in the regression line). The regression line cannot, of course, be extended indefinitely. [*Source:* G. Wyshak & R.E. Frisch. Evidence for a Secular Trend in Age of Menarche. *New England Journal of Medicine, 306,* 1982, Figure 1, p. 1034. Reprinted with permission.]

we do not know how body weight affects the age at which puberty occurs, so also we do not know the process by which nutrition affects the age of puberty (Hopwood et al., 1990).

In this section we have traced the origin of puberty from the beginnings of femaleness and maleness at conception. The sex hormones produced by the gonads, as well as the hormonal feedback system that regulates the production of these sex hormones, begin functioning before birth and play major roles in the changes that occur at puberty. Although the precise causes of puberty are not known, we have been able to describe the important hormonal changes that take place at the beginning of puberty. We have also identified additional factors—heredity, body weight, exercise, and nutrition—that affect the age at which puberty occurs, even though the processes by which they affect puberty are not known. This discussion has left many questions unanswered because the human body is a very complex network of biochemical interactions that are not yet well understood. But it has also provided the background for understanding the hormonal and physical changes that take place during puberty, which we discuss in the next two sections of this chapter.

HORMONAL ASPECTS OF PUBERTY

Hormones are chemical substances that send a powerful and highly specialized message to particular cells and tissues in the body. They are produced by endocrine glands, which use blood vessels to carry their hormonal products to the target cells. There are several interrelated endocrine systems. One is the gonadal system that includes the testes in males or the ovaries in females. Another is the adrenal system. A third is the hypothalamus and pituitary system. Hormones may also be produced by other body tissues, or they may be created by biochemical transformations within the body and thereby change from one hormone into another (Petersen & Taylor, 1980, pp. 118–119).

Endocrinology is very complex. Similar hormones may have slightly different biochemical forms so that there are several androgens and estrogens. In addition, some hormones inhibit the action of other hormones if both are present at the same time; for example, the effects of androgens or estrogens can be counteracted by the presence of the other. Also, hormones can fluctuate monthly, daily, or hourly; and stress, food, sleep, and drugs can affect hormone levels (Petersen & Taylor, 1980, p. 119).

SEX HORMONES

The sex hormones that play such an important role in differentiating male and female bodies before birth also play a major part in producing mature genital organs and other distinctly male and female bodily characteristics during puberty. If those hormones are not present in sufficient amounts during puberty, or if the body is insensitive to them, the changes produced by those hormones do not occur. Usually, the dramatically increased production of these hormones during puberty, and the difference between the hormone production in females and males, produces sexual maturation and the familiar differences between adult women and men.

There are three groups of sex hormones that are produced in both male and female bodies: **androgens**, **estrogens**, and **progestins**. They are biochemically related, can be transformed from one into another within the body, and can be synthetically produced in a laboratory. Although chiefly produced by the gonads, they are also produced by the adrenal gland.

Androgens are commonly referred to as the male sex hormones; their most important form is *testosterone*. Estrogens and progestins are commonly known as the female sex hormones; *progesterone* is the most important form of the progestins. Males and females have different amounts of each of these hormones, but all three hormones circulate in the bloodstreams of both genders. Because the hormones' level varies by time of the day, and throughout the female sex hormone cycle, it is difficult to compare the levels in men and women. The levels of *estrogens* in adults vary during the monthly female cycle from approximately 3 times as much in women as in men (after menstruation) to 50 times as much (at ovulation); levels of *progesterone* vary from equal amounts to 17 times as much in women, compared with men (depending on the female cycle). Conversely, the levels of *androgens* average about 17 times higher in men, compared with women; but it has been found to be as little as 5 times greater (Money, 1980, pp. 137–138).

As noted earlier, these hormones are circulating in the bodies of infants at birth and are maintained at relatively low levels during childhood by a negative hormonal feedback system. There appears to be very little difference between males and females in these hormones until the pubertal changes begin.

At about age 10 in girls and age 12 in boys, the levels of FSH and LH produced by the pituitary begin to rise; the increase in LH during sleep is especially dramatic and is associated with greater frequency and amplitude in pulses of GnRH secretion (Hopwood et al., 1990; Villee, 1975, p. 357). The increased levels of these gonadotropins stimulate the growth of the gonads (ovaries in females, testes in males), formation of spermatozoa (in males) and ova, or eggs (in females), and the synthesis of the sex hormones. In the ovaries, FSH promotes the development of *follicles*, in which the ova mature, and prepares the follicle to produce estrogens; LH stimulates the production of estrogens (Villee, 1975, pp. 357–359). In the testes, FSH stimulates growth of the seminiferous tubules that produce sperm; LH stimulates the production of testosterone; both LH and FSH are required for sperm production (Bardin & Paulsen, 1981, p. 311).

In males, androgens, in the form of *testosterone* or its related hormone dihydrotestosterone, promote the growth of the testes, penis, prostate (which produces seminal fluid), seminal vesicles (the tubes that temporarily store semen), vas deferens (the duct that transmits sperm from the testes to the ejaculatory duct), and the epididymis (tubes for collecting sperm in the scrotum). Androgens also play a role in the growth of the larynx (which lowers the voice pitch), bone, kidney, and muscle. In addition, they promote sebaceous gland secretion in the skin (sometimes resulting in acne), and recession of the scalp line (Bardin & Paulsen, 1981, p. 303; Villee, 1975, pp. 369, 396).

In both males and females, androgens secreted by the adrenal gland begin to rise at about age 7 and rapidly increase at adolescence. This promotes growth of body hair, which is thought to be greater in males than females because of the additional secretion of androgens by the testes (Villee, 1975, p. 364). Tanner (1962, p. 195) speculated that the gender-related distribution of body hair reflects greater sensitivity of the pubic hair to androgen stimulation; higher levels of androgens are required to stimulate growth of underarm hair, and still higher levels are required for facial hair.

Progesterone can be secreted by the gonads or adrenal gland in males and females and can be converted to estrogens or testosterone. In females, it is primarily secreted by the ovaries under the influence of LH and generally acts on tissues that have been prepared by estrogens (Villee, 1975, pp. 357–363).

In females, production of estrogens and progesterone increases throughout the pubertal stages (Petersen & Taylor, 1980). Both play a major role in pubertal development. Progesterone plays a vital role in the development of the mammary gland during puberty. Estrogens must prepare the mammary gland before progesterone can have its effect, however. Progesterone also appears to be involved in the cyclic temperature changes and the secretion of LH during the menstrual cycle (Ross & Vande Wiele, 1981, p. 378; Villee, 1975, p. 363). Estrogens stimulate breast development, feminizing of body contours, and, together with progesterone, FSH, and LH, begin the functioning of the reproductive system, including the first menstruation, or menarche. Estrogens also affect other parts of the body, including the liver, blood plasma (giving women lower hemoglobin levels than men), and bones (Villee, 1975, p. 380).

On one hand, the powerful feminizing influence of estrogens is apparent when they are used therapeutically with a male, in treatment for cancer of the prostate, for example, or as a part of the treatment of a male-to-female transsexual (a man who seeks to become a woman). Of course, the estrogens must also inhibit the effects of the androgens produced by the testes. Money and Ehrhardt (1972) summarized the effects of estrogens on men:

> The visible effects are enlargement of the breasts; a tendency to feminine deposition of subcutaneous fat; reduced oiliness of the skin; reduced facial acne, if present; and an arrest of masculine balding, if it has begun. Beard and body hair do not disappear, but the hairs tend to be less wiry, and more slow growing. [p. 208]

On the other hand, the powerful masculinizing influence of testosterone is shown when it is used therapeutically on genetically female children with adrenogenital syndrome who appeared male at birth and have been raised as males, but who begin menstruating and showing other feminine changes at puberty. Again, quoting Money and Ehrhardt (1972):

> When testosterone therapy is undertaken at puberty, it arrests feminine enlargement of the pelvis, prevents feminine deposition of fat, and induces masculine muscular development. Breast growth is arrested, though such glandular tissue as may have already developed does not totally regress: it needs to be removed surgically (mastectomy). Body hair grows in masculine distribution, including a beard. The voice deepens as the larynx enlarges to form an Adam's apple. [p. 210]

MENARCHE AND THE MENSTRUAL CYCLE

As noted earlier, *menarche* is the first menstruation the girl experiences; it is a distinct sign of puberty. We also have already discussed the feedback system between the hypothalamus–pituitary and the gonads. It regulates the production of hormones in the gonads by monitoring the level of hormones circulating in the blood. In females, FSH and LH are produced in cycles so that the production of estrogens and progesterone rise and fall during each menstrual cycle (Figure 3.5).

Following menstruation, when the level of both estrogens and progesterone are low, the pituitary increases the secretion of FSH; this stimulates the ovaries to produce more estrogens, and one follicle in the ovary begins to grow to maturity. As the level of estrogens rises, the negative feedback system reduces the amount of FSH, but the sustained high level of estrogens also causes the *positive* feedback system to stimulate the production of LH in a surge that brings the follicle to maturity, triggers the release of the ovum (egg), and stimulates an increased production of progesterone. It also leads to a sharp drop in production of estrogens that is followed by a second rise in the level of estrogens at about the time progesterone levels are high. Ovulation, if it occurs during that particular cycle, happens 16–24 hours after the LH surge begins (Villee, 1975, pp. 379–380).

Progesterone plays an important role in preparing the uterus for pregnancy and, if the egg is fertilized, the levels of progesterone and estrogens are maintained at high levels by secretions from the placenta (Villee, 1975, p. 98). If there is no pregnancy, the high levels of progesterone lead to a drop in LH secretion through negative feedback. Both estrogens and progesterone decline, and the beginning of menstruation follows. Once the cycle becomes stabilized, it repeats approximately every 28 days until it begins to cease at menopause.

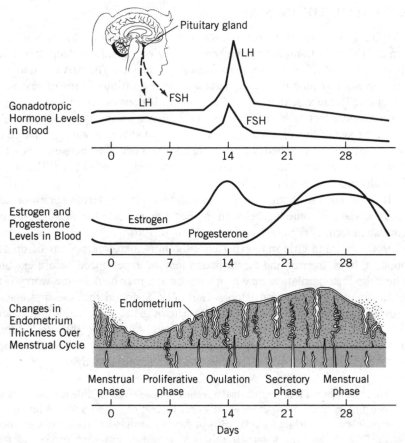

Figure 3.5 Diagram illustrating the concentrations of gonadotropic hormones, estrogens, and progesterone in the blood plasma during a single human menstrual cycle. The changes in thickness of the lining of the uterus are also shown. [*Source:* E.R. Allgeier & A.R. Allgeier. *Sexual Interactions* (3 ed). © 1991 by D.C. Heath and Company. Figure 5.11, p. 155, adapted. Reprinted with permission.]

Contraceptive pills, through hormonal influences, interfere with the cycle by suppressing secretion of FSH and LH because they contain small amounts of estrogens or estrogens and progesterone; thus they prevent ovulation, although menstruation occurs when no pills are taken, or if inert pills are included for 7 of the 28-day cycle of pills.

During the first year or two after menarche, menstrual cycles without ovulation are frequent. One study of 200 adolescent girls in Finland found that 55% of the cycles during the first 2 years did not involve ovulation; by 5 years after menarche, fewer than 20% were anovulatory (Apter & Vihko, 1977). However, it is likely that some of the early menstrual cycles do involve ovulation while others do not. Thus, it is important to note that fertility is possible and unpredictable even before a regular menstrual cycle is established (Petersen & Taylor, 1980, p. 126). We discuss the psychological effects of menarche and girls' reactions to it later in this chapter.

SPERMARCHE IN MEN

The first production of sperm in boys is known as **spermarche**. A boy's first ejaculation of semen, the fluid transporting the semen, may occur during sleep and is known as a "wet dream"; however, not all boys experience wet dreams. The first ejaculation may also occur through masturbation or sexual contact involving various forms of sex play (petting) or intercourse. Because sexual contact and masturbation are usually voluntary acts, social and psychological factors have an important influence on the age at which they begin and thus affect the age of first ejaculation. Age of onset of sperm production, based on a longitudinal study that involved analysis of urine, found that it occurred between ages 12 and 14, usually at a relatively early stage compared with other signs of puberty (Laron, Arad, Gurewitz, Grunebaum, & Dickerman, 1980).

It is not known whether the first ejaculation releases fertile sperm or not. Perhaps, as in females, there is some lag between the beginning of adult sexual functioning and relatively consistent fertility (Petersen & Taylor, 1980, p. 126).

Both boys and girls may experience the muscular contractions of orgasm during childhood; in boys, orgasm and masturbation may be experienced before ejaculation has begun. Thus, the first ejaculation may be a surprise and may cause some worry if the boy does not know about it. Gaddis and Brooks-Gunn (1985) found that the first ejaculation generally provoked positive reactions, but it often caused the boys to feel a little scared. In a study of first sperm emission among 188 Nigerian boys, Adegoke (1993) found that 60% said they had not been prepared for the experience. Although the boys reported both positive and negative reactions, generally the reaction was not strongly negative.

> About 64% of the total sample had a feeling ranging from "a little happy" to "a lot happy" after their first ejaculation experience. Fifty-four percent of the boys felt "a lot" grown-up after the experience . . ., while less than 50% of the total sample had their feelings ranging between "a little" to "a lot" upset, embarrassed, and ashamed. Fifty-five percent of the total sample recorded being "a little scared" to "a lot scared." About 60% expressed that their feelings ranged between "a little surprised" to "a lot surprised." [pp. 206–207]

Over half of the boys (58%) told someone of the experience, most often a friend.

PHYSICAL CHANGES DURING PUBERTY

While the hormones are changing inside the body, dramatic changes are taking place on the outside of the body during puberty. Growth of pubic hair, development of the breasts, and growth of the penis and testes are obvious aspects of these bodily changes. But they are only a part of the total pattern of development that is involved in producing physically mature female and male human beings. Increased strength, height, weight, and ability to perform strenuous tasks characterize the physical changes for both men and women. At the same time, differences between women and men become clearly apparent and important.

Using the information on endocrine changes discussed in the previous section, we describe the process of physical development during puberty. We begin with an overview of the whole process. Then we focus on growth of the body, and, in turn, on the appearance of pubic and body hair, the development of breasts in females, the development of the penis and testes in males, and changes in the skin.

OVERVIEW

J. M. Tanner, an English biologist, studied the patterns and variations in physical growth during puberty. His work was based largely on the Harpenden Growth Study, which involved white British boys and girls who were living in a group home; although the care was excellent, according to Tanner, the participants in the study were "mainly from the lower socioeconomic sector of the population, and some may not have received optimal physical care before entering the home (usually between age 3 and 6 years)" (Marshall & Tanner, 1970, p. 14). Despite the fact that this sample was not representative of all adolescents, it allowed Tanner to study the sequence and timing of development in a large group of girls and boys over a period of several years. In addition, studies on different groups were also included in his report. Except for some variation in the ages at which growth stages are reached in different populations, his data on the sequence and pattern of adolescent growth are generally accepted. Of course, as noted earlier, the age of menarche—and hence the age of puberty—varies in different parts of the world. In the United States, theaverage age at which the growth spurt begins is about 6 months later than in the Tanner sample—11.03 years in females and 13.07 years in males (Petersen & Taylor, 1980, p. 128).

The most significant characteristic of physical development during adolescence is that it may begin several years earlier for some persons than for others, both of whom are normal. Figure 3.6 summarizes all of the physical changes based on Tanner's studies. The ages shown across the bottom of the diagram represent the *average* ages at which the event occurred in his British sample. A similar pattern has been found for American adolescents (Lee, 1980). The numbers beneath some of the bars or boxes in the diagram represent the *range* in age for the event. Thus, the rapid increase in height, known as the **height spurt**, began and ended anywhere between 9.5 and 14.5 years in the girls. In boys, it began anywhere between 10.5 and 16 years of age, and ended anywhere between 13.5 and 17.5 years of age. Thus, one "early maturing" boy or girl may have completed adolescent growth and the other changes of puberty before a person of the same age and gender has begun the height spurt and other changes.

It is not possible to predict the physical maturity of girls between the ages of 11 and 13, or of boys between the ages of 13 and 15, based on age alone (Tanner, 1971, 1978). This point is obvious from Figure 3.7. All of the boys in this Figure are age 14.75; all of the girls are age 12.75; yet their physical development ranges from preadolescent to postadolescent.

Although the age at which the changes of puberty occur varies greatly, the *sequence* of the changes is much more predictable. We note that, in girls, the height spurt occurs first, followed by breast and pubic hair development; menarche is a relatively late event during the pubertal process. In boys, growth of the testes is the first event, followed by the growth of visible pubic hairs (slight growth of pubic hairs may actually coincide with testis growth), and, later, growth of the penis coinciding with the beginning of the height spurt. Thus, while the height spurt occurs *2 years* later in boys than in girls, the first events of puberty are only about *1 year* apart (height spurt in girls and testis growth in boys). In the following section we discuss each of these aspects of adolescent development in detail.

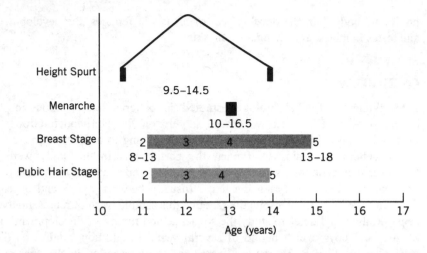

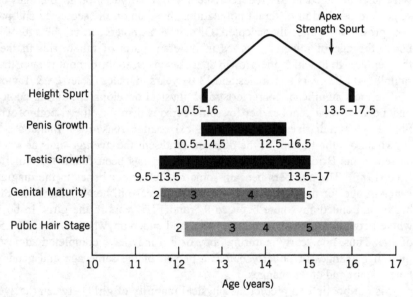

Figure 3.6 Diagram of sequence of events at adolescence in girls and boys. The average girl and boy are represented. The range of ages within which each event charted may begin and end is given by the figures placed directly below its start and finish. [*Source:* W.A. Marshall & J.M. Tanner. Variations in the Pattern of Pubertal Changes in Boys. *Archives of Diseases in Childhood*, *45*, 1970, Figure 8, p. 22. Reprinted with permission.]

GROWTH OF THE BODY

The **adolescent growth spurt** (or height spurt) defines the main characteristic of bodily growth during puberty. Children grow very rapidly in earliest infancy, but growth slows until about age 10 or 11 in girls and 12 or 13 in boys; then the rate of growth increases dramatically (Figure 3.8). For example, a typical boy who has been growing at the rate of 5 cm (2

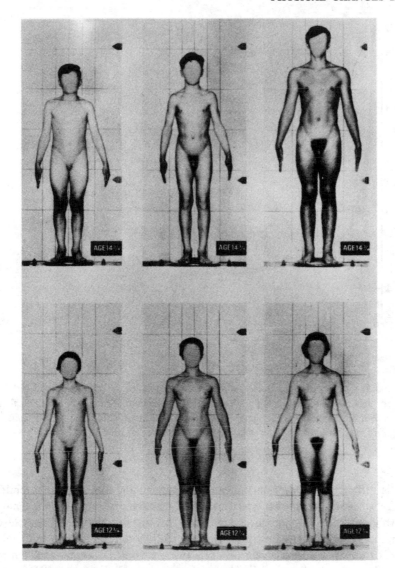

Figure 3.7 Differing degrees of pubertal development at the same chronological age. In the upper row are three boys all aged 14.75 years. In the lower row are three girls all aged 12.75 years. [*Source:* J.M. Tanner, *Growth at Adolescence*. Oxford: Blackwell Scientific Publications, Ltd., 1962, Figures 13 and 14. Reprinted with permission.]

inches) per year suddenly grows about 10 cm (4 inches) in 1 year; he has not grown that rapidly since the age of two. From birth through adulthood, girls mature more rapidly than boys, at least in terms of skeleton growth. A typical girl begins her growth spurt about *2 years earlier* than the typical boy; thus, the boy has more time to grow before the growth spurt than the girl. In addition, during the growth spurt girls grow somewhat less rapidly than boys. As a result of both differences, adult men are generally taller than adult women (Harrison et al., 1964, p. 321; Petersen & Taylor, 1980; Tanner, 1962, pp. 1–3).

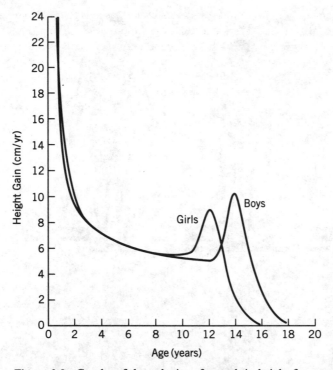

Figure 3.8 Graphs of the velocity of growth in height for a typical boy and girl at any given age. [*Source:* J.M. Tanner, R.H. Whitehouse, and M. Takaishi. Standards from Birth to Maturity for Height, Weight, Height Velocity and Weight Velocity: British Children, 1965. *Archives of Diseases in Childhood, 41*, 1966, Figure 8, p. 466. Reprinted with permission.]

It is difficult to predict an individual's adult height from height in childhood because the age at which the growth spurt occurs is a major influence on the final height attained. Although there is generally a significant relationship between preadolescent and adult stature, a girl or boy may be tall (or short) in childhood, but average in height after adolescence; or the reverse may occur (Tanner, 1971, p. 909). This phenomenon results because the adolescent growth spurt involves not only growth hormone (GH), which is important for body growth during childhood, but also sex hormones, which increase during puberty.

Although the endocrine processes that influence growth during adolescence are not fully understood, it is known that androgens, estrogens, and GH are involved (Underwood & Van Wyk, 1981, pp. 1152, 1156). Androgens interact with GH to promote growth in both genders; they have been shown to increase the effect of GH, and the presence of GH is required for androgens to promote growth. In addition, there is some evidence that androgens stimulate secretion of GH by the pituitary. In males, testosterone is a powerful growth-inducing androgen. The process is less well understood in females because high levels of estrogens terminate growth, although lower levels may stimulate it.

Both estrogens and androgens stimulate epiphyseal maturation (the sealing off of bone growth), so that they produce the concluding process in the growth of the skeleton. In the absence of sufficient levels of androgens or estrogens produced by the gonads, bone growth continues longer than usual. Thus, androgens are thought to be important in producing the adolescent growth spurt in women and men; and androgens and estrogens play a major role in terminating physical growth. For this reason, menarche always occurs after the peak in the growth spurt has been passed, so growth slows down after the first menstruation (Marshall & Tanner, 1969, p. 298; Tanner, 1971, p. 919).

The order in which growth occurs, according to Tanner (1962), is fairly regular. Usually the legs begin growing fastest first; then hip width and chest breadth reach their peak rate of growth. Length of the body trunk and the depth of the chest are the last to reach their peak rate of growth. "Thus a boy stops growing out of his trousers (at least in length) a year before he stops growing out of his jackets" (Tanner, 1971, p. 911).

The hands, head, and feet are the first body parts to stop growing, so they may seem relatively large for the body at first (Tanner, 1971, p. 911). Physical growth is essentially concluded at an average age of 17 or 18 for boys and 15.5 to 16.5 for girls, according to a study in an English school; however, some slight bone growth may continue until the 20s (Tanner, 1962, p. 27).

A spurt in muscle growth coincides with the general growth spurt (Tanner, 1971, p. 911). It is also influenced by the presence of androgens, especially testosterone. Heart muscle, as well as muscles on the limbs, grows rapidly, leading to a marked increase in strength and physical ability. Because girls begin the growth spurt first, they are often stronger than boys of the same age for a time.

> Before adolescence, boys and girls are similar in strength for a given body size and shape; after, boys are much stronger, probably due to developing more force per gram of muscle as well as absolutely larger muscles. They also develop larger hearts and lungs relative to their size, a higher systolic blood pressure, a lower resting heart rate, a greater capacity for carrying oxygen in the blood, and a greater power for neutralizing the chemical products of muscular exercise such as lactic acid. [Tanner, 1971, p. 911]

In addition, the amount of hemoglobin and red blood cells also increase more for boys than for girls (Tanner, 1971, 1978). How much of these differences between typical males and females result from hormonal influences, such as the effect of testosterone, and how much from social factors, such as the difference in amount and kind of physical exercise during puberty, is not known.

At the same time as the height spurt and the spurt in muscle growth, there is also a loss of fat. In boys there is an actual decline in the amount of fat, especially on the arms and legs; in girls there is a decline in the rate at which fat is accumulated on the body, but no actual loss of fat (Tanner, 1971, 1978). This period of decreased fat accumulation follows a period of increased fat about 2 years before the growth spurt begins in all boys, but is readily apparent in only about two out of three. Girls have somewhat more fat than boys from birth on, and this gradual accumulation of fat is less affected by puberty in girls than in boys (Tanner, 1962, pp. 22–24).

Body shape also changes, maturing into the adult female or male pattern. Hips and shoulders grow in both genders, but hips grow more than shoulders in females and shoulders more than hips in males (Petersen & Taylor, 1980). Facial features change as well, more in males than in females, according to Tanner (1962).

Since girls begin the physical growth spurt first, they are often stronger than boys of the same age for a time.

BODY HAIR

Human bodies are covered with three types of hair. (1) *Nonsexual hair* includes eyebrows, eyelashes, and hair on lower legs and forearms. Both men and women, children and adults have this type of hair. (2) *Ambosexual hair* changes from finely textured, unpigmented hair to coarse, thick, heavily pigmented hair during puberty in both females and males; it includes pubic and underarm hair. Also, both genders show some recession of the frontal hairline during puberty; it occurs in 80% of women and in all men. (3) *Male sexual hair* appears in the beard, ears, tip of nose, chest, abdomen, and neck during and after puberty (Parker, 1981, p. 1092).

As noted earlier, pubic hair growth is thought to be produced by androgens from the adrenal glands in both genders. The androgens act on the follicles that produce hair, stimulating hair growth. Male sexual hairs may require the stimulation of higher levels of androgen, compared with ambosexual hairs.

Male pattern baldness is also thought to be influenced by both androgens and age. It is genetically transmitted and occasionally occurs in women. Excessive body hair in women can result from disorders of the adrenal gland or ovary because androgens are also produced by the ovaries (Villee, 1975, p. 365). However, in most cases there is no endocrine abnormality and the hair growth reflects hereditary factors; also standards of how much hair is cosmetically acceptable vary in different cultures (Parker, 1981, p. 1094).

In order to study the development of pubic hair and its relation to other events during puberty, Tanner defined five stages of pubic hair growth (Figure 3.9). They are as follows (Tanner, 1962, pp. 32–33):

> Stage 1: Preadolescent—no pubic hair; any hair growth is the same as on the rest of the abdomen.
>
> Stage 2: Slightly pigmented, downy, straight or slightly curled hair is appearing, mainly along the labia or at the base of the penis.
>
> Stage 3: Hair is much darker, coarser, and more curled; it spreads sparsely across the midsection of the pubic region.
>
> Stage 4: Hair resembles adult in type, but covers a much smaller area; no spread to adjacent areas of thighs.
>
> Stage 5: Adult in type and quantity; distribution shape forms an inverted triangle with a horizontal top; no spread along the midline of the abdomen; may be spread to adjacent areas of the thighs. (In males, additional hair growth up the abdomen may occur after stage 5 is reached.)

Because his studies relied on nude photographs of the participants, the hair had to be more highly visible to be recorded as stage 2 than would be the case if the participants had been rated by first-hand examination; this implies that stage 2 data are not as reliable as the data for the other stages, and stage 2 may, in fact, occur earlier than is reported (Marshall & Tanner, 1969, 1970).

Growth of pubic hair usually takes about 4 years, but it may occur within 2 years, or take as long as 6 years. Underarm hair generally occurs during pubic hair stage 4, about 2 years after pubic hair begins to grow, although it may occur earlier. Hair around the anus appears shortly before the underarm hair (Tanner, 1962, 1971).

The development of male sexual hair also follows a general sequence. The beard begins to grow at about the same time as the underarm hair (i.e., pubic hair stage 4). Tanner (1971) noted: "There is a definite order in which the hairs of moustache and beard appear; first at the corners of the upper lip, then over all the upper lip, then at the upper part of the cheeks in the mid-line below the lower lip, and finally along the sides and lower border of the chin" (p. 917). Additional male body hair, if it develops, may begin at the time of the underarm hair, or during late adolescence. Hair growth on the chest and upper arms usually occurs after hair

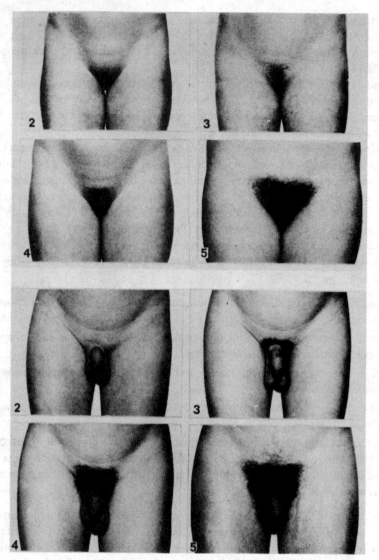

Figure 3.9   Standards for rating five stages of pubic hair development in boys and girls; it may be noted that the boy's penis is uncircumcised. [*Source:* J.M. Tanner, *Growth at Adolescence*. Oxford: Blackwell Scientific Publications, Ltd., 1962, plate 6, facing p. 33. Reprinted with permission.]

develops on the abdomen, calf, and thigh. Of course, some ethnic groups have less or more male sexual hair than others, and family patterns also differ.

BREAST DEVELOPMENT

As shown earlier in Figure 3.6, female breasts begin developing shortly after the height spurt begins, and about the time pubic hair appears. Usually the "breast bud" occurs first, although pubic hair occurs first for about one girl in three (Tanner, 1971, p. 918). Stages of breast development are shown in Figure 3.10. They are defined as follows (Tanner, 1962, p. 37):

Stage 1: Preadolescent—elevation of nipple (papilla) only.

Stage 2: Breast bud stage—elevation of breast and nipple as small mound; enlargement of area surrounding the nipple (areola).

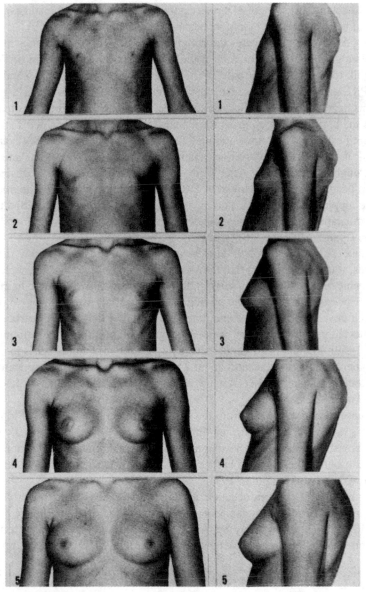

Figure 3.10 Standards for rating five stages of breast development. [*Source:* J.M. Tanner, *Growth at Adolescence*. Oxford: Blackwell Scientific Publications, Ltd., 1962, plate 7, facing page 37. Reprinted with permission.]

Stage 3: Further enlargement and elevation of breast and areola; no difference in the curvature of the areola from that of the breast.

Stage 4: Areola and papilla rise to form a mound above the level of the breast.

Stage 5: Mature stage; papilla projects, but areola recesses to conform to the general contour of the breast.

Usually, development progresses through all the stages, although a few of the participants returned to stage 4 after reaching stage 5. On the average, it took 4 years to progress from stage 2 to stage 5; the length of time required to pass through the stages did not depend on the age at which breast development began (Marshall & Tanner, 1969).

Breast development indicates the complex interplay of the hormones involved during puberty. Estrogens play a major role in the lengthening and branching of the ducts that will carry milk to the nipple, but only in the presence of prolactin (PRL) and growth hormone (GH). PRL and progesterone foster development of the milk-producing glands, but only if estrogens have stimulated and prepared the tissues. When the breast has matured, PRL functions as the hormone that controls the actual formation of milk proteins and the secretion of milk. Both estrogens and progesterone inhibit the production of milk (lactation); the reason that milk is not produced during pregnancy is because both estrogens and progesterone are high throughout pregnancy. After birth, levels of estrogens and progesterone decline and lactation becomes possible. However, lactation requires suckling by the infant, which stimulates the nipple, releasing PRL and oxytocin (OT) via stimuli transmitted through nerves to the hypothalamus. OT causes expulsion of the milk from the breast, while PRL maintains lactation (Frantz, 1981, pp. 401–402).

Because pubic hair growth and breast development result from different hormonal processes, it is not surprising that they sometimes do not occur at the same time. There was considerable variation between girls in the relationship between pubic hair and breast development. For example, half of the participants in the study were in stage 3 of both breast and pubic hair development at the same time, and the other half were in earlier or later stages of breast development when they were in stage 3 of pubic hair development (Marshall & Tanner, 1969). Marshall and Tanner also noted a study of Chinese girls that found pubic hair development did not appear until about 2 years after the breast bud appeared and only a few months before menarche (Lee, Chang, & Chan, 1963); the reason for this ethnic difference is not known.

Likewise, the span of time from the first appearance of a breast bud to menarche may be as long as 5.5 years, or as short as 6 months. Although menarche usually occurs in stage 4 of both breast and pubic hair development, it may take place at any stage of pubic hair development; but it rarely occurs before breast stage 3. It also marks the end of the period of rapid growth in height (Tanner, 1971, p. 919).

Some breast enlargement occurs in about 70% of males during puberty as a result of hormones probably produced by the testes. Usually it is a temporary change and needs no treatment, although some boys may be troubled by it. Similar breast growth may also occur in adult men, especially after a prolonged illness (Bardin & Paulsen, 1981, pp. 339–341).

GENITAL DEVELOPMENT

Growth of the testes is usually the first sign of puberty in males. These two organs are supported by a skin-covered pouch known as the scrotum, which also encloses the epididymis

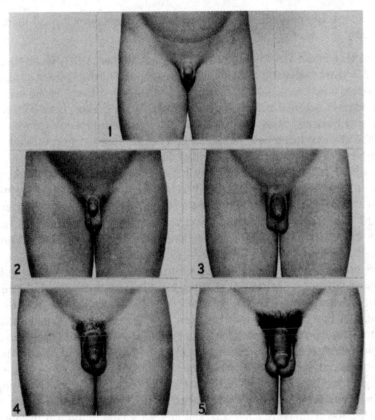

Figure 3.11 Standards for rating five stages of genital maturity in boys. [*Source:* J.M. Tanner, *Growth at Adolescence*. Oxford: Blackwell Scientific Publications, Ltd., 1962, plate 3, facing page 32. Reprinted with permission.]

and vas deferens that store and carry mature sperm to the ejaculatory duct. As noted earlier, the testes are the male gonads, parallel to the female ovaries. They are located outside the body wall because sperm production requires a temperature that is slightly lower than the body. The interaction of hormones to produce maturation of the testes and production of testosterone and sperm was discussed earlier in this chapter.

Tanner (1962, p. 32) has defined five stages of male genital development (Figure 3.11). These stages are:

Stage 1: Preadolescent—penis, scrotum, and testes are about the same size and proportion as in early childhood.

Stage 2: Enlargement of scrotum and testes. Little or no enlargement of the penis. Darkening and change in texture of skin of the scrotum.

Stage 3: Enlargement of the penis, mainly in length; further growth of testes and scrotum.

Stage 4: Continued growth of penis, with greater breadth and development of the glans. Further growth of testes and scrotum; increased darkening of the scrotal skin.

Stage 5: Adult size and shape of genitals; no further growth, and there may be a slight decrease in size of the penis.

In the Harpenden Growth Study, Marshall and Tanner (1970) found that the average boy required 3 years to develop through these five stages. However, some completed them in 1.8 years, while others took 4.7 years. Growth of the testes began, on the average, at age 11.6; but for some it began as early as 9.5 and as late as 13.5. Thus, boys between the ages of 13 and 15 may be at any stage of genital development from preadolescent to adult. The age at which the changes begin does not affect how long it takes to pass through the stages; those who begin early or late may progress either quickly or slowly.

Growth of pubic hair in males may begin at the same time as testis growth, but it is usually slightly later. It is not necessarily related to development of the genitals. About one-third of the boys in genital stage 4 had pubic hair development characteristic of stage 2; one-third were in pubic hair stage 3; and the rest were in either stage 1 or 4. However, by stage 5 of genital development, pubic hair had appeared for all the boys in the study (Marshall & Tanner, 1970).

Penis growth usually begins about the same time as the growth spurt in height—about 1 year after testis growth begins. Androgens, especially testosterone produced by the developing testes, is responsible for the growth of the penis, as well as of the seminal vesicles, prostate, and other male genital structures. First ejaculation is thought to occur about one year after the spurt in penis growth begins (Laron et al., 1980; Tanner, 1971, 1978). Erections of the penis, first occurring at birth, are common during childhood, but become more obvious as the penis becomes larger. With the increase in sexual arousal, resulting from higher levels of androgens, erections may become more frequent after puberty and can occur in circumstances the boy finds embarrassing. However, erections do not always mean that the person is thinking about sex and are, for example, typical during sleep and when awakening in the morning. Complete absence of any erections of the penis may be a sign of endocrine or neurological disorder requiring medical attention.

In females, the uterus and vagina, as well as the clitoris and labia, enlarge and become more sexually responsive during the period of breast development (Tanner, 1971, 1978). The interaction of hormones in the female body prepares her genital organs and the tissues that are involved in her sexual stimulation and orgasm, as well as preparing her breasts, ovaries, and uterus for childbearing.

SKIN: ACNE AND PHEROMONES

During puberty, androgens produced by the testes and ovaries stimulate the development and secretion of sebaceous glands in the skin that can produce oiliness of the skin and acne. **Acne** involves inflammation of the hair follicles and skin glands, often leading to pimples. It may occur on the face, upper back, and chest.

Because androgens are produced in much larger amounts in males and estrogens inhibit the action of the sebaceous glands, acne is more common in boys than girls. Different areas of the body vary in the reaction of these skin glands to androgens. Also, some individuals react to the androgens more than others. Thus, the severity of acne varies from one person to another. It can be very severe in some women, even with low levels of androgens (Parker, 1981, p. 1091).

Apocrine sweat glands also develop rapidly during puberty, especially in the genital, anal, and underarm areas. These glands, in conjunction with the sebaceous glands, produce the characteristic odor of adult men or women; the changes are greater in men (Tanner, 1971, p. 918). These odors, sometimes called *pheromones*, may play a role in sexual attraction or sexual bonding among humans. Such pheromones are very important among other mammals because they signal sexual receptivity during periods of "heat" at ovulation. Whether they play any part in human sexual behavior or development is not clear (Money, 1980, p. 74; Sanders & Reinisch, 1990).

Let us summarize briefly. Female and male physical growth during puberty has several components that develop at different rates. The growth spurt in height occurs about 2 years earlier in females than in males. However, breast development in girls occurs only about 6 months before testis growth in boys, on the average. Differences between the genders in pubic hair growth average about 1.5 years, with earlier development in females. In addition, for girls, the peak of the growth spurt usually occurs *before* breast growth is advanced (stage 4); in boys, the growth spurt peak almost always occurs *after* genital growth is well along (stage 4). Thus, girls are nearly fully grown when their breasts have developed, but boys are just beginning to grow when their genitals begin to develop (Marshall & Tanner, 1970).

The broader issues of the psychological effects of puberty and the effects of early and late maturation are the focus of the final two sections of this chapter.

EFFECTS OF PUBERTY ON THE INDIVIDUAL ADOLESCENT

The hormonal changes during puberty are dramatic, and it would seem likely that they would have important effects on adolescents' emotions and behavior. However, as discussed in Chapter 2, the *direct effects* of hormone changes at puberty are mixed. On one hand, there is some evidence that the increases in testosterone and estrogen are related to fewer behavior problems, higher self-image, and more sexuality. On the other hand, increases in different hormones with puberty (gonadotropins and androgens secreted by the adrenal glands) are associated with more behavior and psychological problems. In contrast, the *mediated effects model* emphasizes the fact that increased levels of hormones interact with social influences that are related to the physical changes and with chronological age to determine the impact of puberty on behavior (Richards, Abell, & Petersen, 1993, p. 29).

Thus, to understand the effect of puberty we need to employ a **biopsychosocial model** that considers the interaction of biological, psychological, and social influences. For example, breast development is an important aspect of the physical changes during puberty for girls. Larger breasts are seen as a sign of maturity, in contrast to the smaller prepubertal breasts; in our culture they are also associated with positive physical attractiveness in both popular and pornographic media. Not surprisingly, Brooks-Gunn and Warren (1988) found that breast growth was positively associated with body image, peer relations, and adjustment. However, too early breast development may cause embarrassment and teasing (Petersen, 1983). Likewise, puberty brings increased weight that our culture views as less attractive than the slim prepubertal body, which may be related to an overconcern with body weight and eating disorders (see Chapter 13). Thus, the effects of hormone changes cannot be separated from the social meaning of the physical changes that result. Finally, the individual psychological impact of those changes reflects the age at which they occur, relative to one's peers.

The interaction of these several different factors is an example of the *dialectical interaction* described in Chapter 1. Adams, Day, Dyk, Frede, and Rogers (1992) suggested the following examples of the dialectical interactions of puberty:

1.   Family and others are likely to expect behavior that is consistent with one's physical maturity, rather than with one's chronological age. Stature, breast growth, and body maturity are readily apparent, but other signs of puberty (such as pubic hair) are not. Thus, the psychological impact of adrenal androgens that produce pubic hair growth may differ from that of other hormones.

2.   In a study of early maturing girls Magnusson, Stattin, and Allen (1985) found that they tended to make friends with older peers; this pattern was associated with more frequent deviant behavior such as playing truant, smoking hashish, getting drunk, pilfering, and ignoring parental prohibitions.

3.   As the hormonal changes of puberty progress, boys tend to become more assertive with their mothers, leading to increased family conflict. Similar patterns are found for girls, especially focused on concerns regarding sexual development and behavior. In turn, fathers respond with increased assertiveness on their part. The typical result of this action is less assertiveness by the adolescent and reduced tension in family relations. Similarly, a study of 51 families by Papini and Sebby (1987) found that the "transpuberty" period was the most stressful, compared with either before or after puberty. They concluded that "Adolescent pubertal maturation changes the family context" (p. 13). Additional findings of increased parent–child conflict and less warm relationships between parents and children during puberty were reported in a review of research by Paikoff and Brooks-Gunn (1991). We discuss these points in detail in Chapter 7, on the family.

Two implications of this dialectical perspective are important. First, development that is out of synchrony with chronological age, or with that of one's age mates, creates a dialectical imbalance that can be problematic. We focus on this "off-time" puberty in the final section of the chapter. Second, the biological changes of puberty interact in dialectical ways with physical and interpersonal changes to produce a variety of effects in the adolescent's life and social relationships. In the next section we focus on one example of this complex dialectic of puberty: menarche for girls.

EFFECTS OF MENARCHE

Empirical studies of menarche indicate that it is a memorable and significant event, that the experience differs considerably from one individual to another, and that a number of influences affect the nature of the girl's reaction to it.

One theme in these studies has been whether menarche is a positive or negative experience. Greif and Ulman (1982) reviewed data from four studies: three found that girls had more negative attitudes toward menstruation after menarche than girls had before menarche; the fourth study found no difference. Also, the girls experienced more negative emotions after menarche than premenarcheal girls expected to experience.

In another study of 639 public school girls, Ruble and Brooks-Gunn (1982) found a variety of reactions to menarche, but most of the reactions were quite mild: "a little bit" negative or upset and "a little bit" positive or excited; many also reported being "a little bit" surprised. In addition, when a sample of 120 fifth and sixth grade girls was interviewed by telephone shortly after they experienced menarche, only 19% volunteered positive reactions (happy, excited), and only 18% mentioned negative feelings (scared, bothered, upset). In contrast, 64% offered neither positive nor negative reactions, but said things like "felt the same," or "felt funny," including 36% who said they were not upset or scared and 19% who expressed mixed feelings. Later the girls were asked specifically what they found positive and negative about the experience:

> The most frequent positive item was sign of maturity (72%). Other positive aspects included: ability to have children (30%), part of being a woman (26%), and being like friends (22%). The most frequent negative aspect was the hassle (46%), for example, carrying supplies or messiness. Other negative aspects included: physical discomfort (30%), behavioral limitations (20%), and emotional changes (17%). Another type of direct question about the meaning of menarche and menstruation concerned menstrual-related "worries." Most girls (70%) referred to at least one worry, which most frequently (89%) concerned uncertainty or possible embarrassment. [Ruble & Brooks-Gunn, 1982, pp. 1560–1561]

Half of these girls reported some physical symptom during the first period (and half did not). The most common symptom was cramps or nausea; others mentioned moodiness or fatigue during or before their period. Generally they did not feel their behavior was restricted, but almost half mentioned something they could not do during their periods, usually swimming or other athletic activity. Nearly all told their mother immediately, but most did not tell anyone else, and only one in five told a friend. Thus the experience was kept secret at first. But after two or three periods, most had begun talking with their girlfriends about menstruation. Girls who were unprepared for menarche expressed more negative feelings about menstruation, and also were more surprised by it than girls who were "at least a little prepared" for it; however, there were no differences in symptoms at the first period between these two groups (but the unprepared girls reported more symptoms later). There was some indication that girls who matured earlier than average had more negative reactions than average or late maturing girls; we discuss this point in more detail later. In summary the authors concluded: "while menarche may be initially disruptive, particularly for early-maturing and unprepared girls, it typically does not seem to be a traumatic experience" (Ruble & Brooks-Gunn, 1982, p. 1565).

Stubbs, Rierdan, and Koff (1989) found two differing sets of attitudes about menstruation among a sample of 11–15-year-old girls: *affirmation* and *worry*. There were no age differences in the positive affirmation attitudes, but early maturers and older girls who had not experienced menarche showed greater worry about menstruation. The authors concluded that more frequent and extensive education about menarche may help foster greater attitudes of affirmation and reduce the extent of worry that is present among some, but not all, girls.

In an earlier study of adolescent girls, Gisela Konopka (1976) noted some of the worry and the affirmation about menarche. One urban Chicana girl expressed worry:

I didn't know about it. She [mother] never told me anything like that. I was scared, I just started washing all my underclothing hoping that my mother won't find out but she came in and caught me, she caught me washing it, and she started laughing at me. I was in the 5th grade, maybe 4th grade. But she never did tell me what it was. You learn more of that from the Girl Scouts. I mean she told me it wasn't anything to worry about, it's something that happens, you know, but she didn't tell me what it meant and stuff like that. [Konopka, 1976, pp. 47–48]

In contrast, an urban African-American girl expressed affirmation:

I had my first period at twelve, knew about it before and wasn't scared. I thought I was feeling pretty good. Cause then I would know I was growing up to be a lady, you know. And I really had a nice feeling. [Konopka, 1976, p. 48]

In summary, based on the evidence available from the adolescent girls' self-reports, menarche generally seems to have subtle and important effects on their feelings about themselves. Although she tends to keep it secret from her friends for a few months, soon she shares the information with friends who probably provide social support for the transition. If the girl expects menstruation and it happens approximately on time—that is, when it is a normative transition—we would not expect any dramatic effect. Of course, if it occurs unusually early—an off-time transition—the effects may be more significant; we discuss this topic in the final section of this chapter. In the next section we discuss more general effects of puberty on adolescent girls and boys in terms of their self-concept and level of self esteem.

PUBERTY, SELF-CONCEPT, AND SELF-ESTEEM

One's sense of oneself involves the **self-concept**, which is the group of ideas and feelings one has about oneself, and **self-esteem**, which is the emotional evaluation one has of oneself, ranging from high self-esteem (positive evaluation) to low self-esteem (negative evaluation). Several studies with college-age persons have found that the self-concept is related to attitudes about one's body and that the more attractive or effective individuals believe their bodies to be, the more positive their self-esteem (Lerner & Spanier, 1980). This finding appears to hold for both males and females, and there are few differences in self-concepts according to gender. Thus we might expect adolescents to change their self-concepts and to grow in self-esteem as their bodies become stronger, more effective, and more attractive by adult standards.

However, studies of adolescents' self-concepts and level of self-esteem do not find much evidence of change during the adolescent years. Offer, Ostrov, and Howard (1981) studied 212 young (age 13–15) males, 373 young females, 276 older males (age 16–18), and 524 older females from a variety of communities in the United States. They found that girls have less positive feelings about their bodies than boys during adolescence, but that there were no statistically significant differences between the younger and older age groups (pp. 47–48). They concluded:

The results reveal that normal adolescents are not in the throes of turmoil. The vast majority function well, enjoy good relationships with their families and friends, and accept the values of the larger society. In addition, most report having adapted without undue conflict to the bodily changes and emerging sexuality brought on by puberty. The only notable symptom among the normals was a situation-specific anxiety, which normal adolescents can handle without undue trauma. [Offer et al., 1981, pp. 116–117]

Similarly, Monge (1973) studied the self-concept of 1,035 males and 1,025 females in grades 6–12. He concluded that there were only minor differences in the self-concepts of adolescents from one age to another and that the data did not support the idea of a "considerable reorganization of the self-concept through pubescence" (p. 391). His study also found that boys had more positive concepts of themselves than girls did on three of the four self-concept factors he identified.

The difference between self-reported levels of self-esteem for adolescent boys and girls was also found in a study by Jaquish and Savin-Williams (1981). However, when behavioral measures of self-esteem were used, instead of self-report measures, there were no gender differences. They argued that girls may be more critical or more sensitive than boys in reporting feelings about themselves. In addition, they identified certain behavioral settings (home and school) in which girls reported lower self-esteem than boys, suggesting that external factors, instead of biological or hormonal factors, may lower girls' self-esteem in some settings but not in others. For example, Richards, Boxer, Petersen, and Albrecht (1990) found that girls in one community where they were likely to be involved in activities after school, such as sports, were more satisfied with their bodies than girls in another school in a different part of the same metropolitan area; boys in both schools had greater levels of satisfaction with their bodies than girls did. Moreover, Petersen (1988) noted that certain subgroups of adolescents, such as unusually attractive girls and adolescents who aspire to be dancers or athletes, may be disturbed when the changes of puberty do not produce their ideal physical characteristics. Thus, we conclude that gender differences in self-esteem are complex and that the influence of an individual's situation is often more important than one's gender.

Another study of adolescent self-concepts and self-esteem focused on cultural differences by studying 796 Japanese boys and girls who were in grades 7–12 or college students (most were in their first year). Lerner, Iwawaki, Chihara, and Sorell (1980) asked the adolescents to rate their bodies' physical attractiveness, physical effectiveness, and self-concept; their responses were compared with similar studies of college students in the United States. As in the other studies noted earlier, there was little evidence of any effect of age on level of self-esteem, except for the college students (who were lower). Thus, the authors concluded:

No interrelation among self-esteem and body attitudes existed across the Japanese noncollege grade cohorts. As such, this data set does not support theories stressing the necessary linkage between self-appraisals and body variables. [Lerner et al., 1980, p. 854]

Also, as in the other studies, gender differences were noted (with males higher in self-esteem). When the Japanese college sample was compared with U.S. college samples, level of self-esteem and ratings of body attractiveness and effectiveness were lower for the Japanese adolescents. Because the cultures represented by these two groups differ in many ways, it is hard to interpret this finding, except to note that self-reported level of self-esteem appears to be affected by sociocultural factors. This is not surprising and parallels the earlier point about gender differences.

In summary, the data suggest that there is relatively little change in adolescents' self-concepts or level of self-esteem from early to late adolescence. Moreover, there is no clear evidence that the physical changes during puberty have an effect on psychological adjustment (Petersen, 1988). Thus, puberty is similar to other normative transitions in development: in general, when it is expected and essentially on time, there are few signs of dramatic change in self-esteem or self-concept for most people. In the next section, we focus on the consequences of puberty being off time.

VARIATIONS IN PUBERTAL DEVELOPMENT

The effects of puberty are best understood based on their biopsychosocial interaction. An example of this interaction is seen in the effects of variation from individual to individual in the chronological age at which puberty occurs. As noted earlier in this chapter, some girls or boys may complete their pubertal development before others of the same age and gender have begun their development, but both are within the normal range of the age for puberty. In addition, the ages at which these changes occur are affected by heredity, nutrition, exer-

Some boys and girls may complete their physical development at puberty before others of the same age and gender have begun theirs.

cise, and stress. These physical changes also give guidelines for defining those cases where puberty occurs unusually early (precocious puberty) or unusually late (delayed puberty).

THE EFFECT OF EARLY AND LATE MATURATION

We consider precocious and delayed puberty in the final sections of this chapter. In this section, we focus on those who experience puberty during the normal ages, but before or after most of their age-mates.

There are two differing ways of thinking about this off-time puberty. First, one may consider it as causing a person to be socially "deviant" because one is different from the statistical average. Such deviance may be an advantage because the person is more grown up (if puberty comes early and the culture values growing up); or it may be a disadvantage because the person is different from one's age-mates. Second, one might think of it as shifting the developmental timetable so that one has less time in childhood, but more time in adolescence if puberty occurs early; and the reverse if it occurs late (Petersen & Taylor, 1980, p. 143). Thus, there can be social and psychological gains and losses either way. The effects also depend on the individual's culture and on whether one is female or male (Richards, Abell, & Petersen, 1993).

Most studies in the United States find that early maturation is generally an advantage for boys. Summarizing several longitudinal studies, Petersen and Taylor (1980) noted that early maturing boys compared with late maturing boys were found to be more relaxed, more attractive to peers and adults, more popular with peers, more self-confident, less dependent, and, especially for middle-class boys, more likely to be leaders. The positive effects seem to persist to age 30, but were not very important by age 38 (Clausen, 1975). Similarly, Nottelmann et al. (1990) reported that later maturation as well as a slower rate of maturation were associated with more adjustment and behavior problems for boys.

The influence of culture is clear in a study that compared Italian boys growing up in Italy and Italian-American boys growing up in Boston. Early maturation was related to more favorable self-concepts only in the Boston sample. The researchers suggested that "reaching maximal physical growth and sexual maturity at an early age does not confer the same social advantages in Italian as in American culture" (Mussen & Young, cited in Young & Ferguson, 1981, p. 163). Thus, the positive influence of early maturation for males appears to result from increased social prestige in some cultures.

The picture is less clear for girls, with some studies finding early maturation to be more problematic than on-time or late maturation (Brooks-Gunn, 1988). For example, a study of girls in West Berlin (Silbereisen, Petersen, Albrecht, & Kracke, 1989) found that early maturation was associated with both better self-esteem and also with greater contact with "deviant" peers (those who "lie to their parents," have "stolen something without being caught," or are "often in trouble with adults"). Socioeconomic status also seems to make some difference, with middle-class girls who mature early showing more self-confidence, whereas working-class girls who mature early show less self-confidence (Clausen, 1975).

Several problems in these studies further confuse this issue. These include the fact that early maturing girls may also be unprepared for menarche. In addition, there are difficulties in measuring early maturation and late maturation (Dorn, Susman, Nottelman, Jnoff-Germain, & Chrouses, 1990); also, different measures of the effect of maturation on personality, the self-concept, and self-esteem are commonly used (Greif & Ulman, 1982).

Although there is some indication that maturing on time is more positive than either late or early maturation for girls, and that early, unprepared menarche may be problematic, one should interpret these conclusions with care. For example, Caspi and Moffitt (1991) suggested that early maturing girls may be experiencing a period of uncertainty, novelty, and ambiguity that characterizes any significant transitional period. As a result, their unique behavioral predispositions may be expressed so that there is more individual variation than usual in the group of early maturing girls. In particular, in a longitudinal study, they found that those girls who matured early and also had behavior problems earlier in childhood showed a greater increase in behavior problems than girls who matured on time or late (Figure 3.12). Early maturing girls who had low levels of behavior problems in childhood showed only a slightly greater increase in problems than on-time girls; later maturing girls showed no increase in behavior problems as a group. Likewise, girls with behavior problems had more difficulty adjusting to early menarche than girls who did not have behavior problems. Thus, early maturation "appears to have accentuated the pre-menarcheal behavioral problems of girls" (Caspi & Moffitt, 1991, p. 164).

Inherent in research on early or late maturation is the problem of defining the meaning of "early" or "late." Should the researcher divide the sample into thirds: early, on time, and late; or should the earliest 15% be compared with the latest 15%, with 70% on time, for example? In addition, should an individual be compared with his or her chronological age-mates, with school classmates, or with friends, who may be older or younger in terms of

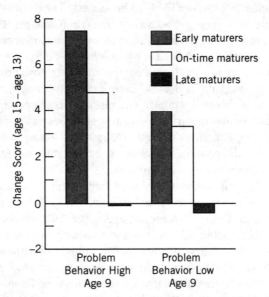

Figure 3.12 Changes in behavioral problems from age 13 to age 15 among early, on-time, and late-maturing girls stratified by their premenarcheal behavior problems (high and low at age 9). [*Source:* A. Caspi & T.E. Moffitt. Individual Differences are Accentuated During Periods of Social Change: The Sample Case of Girls at Puberty. *Journal of Personality and Social Psychology*, *61*, 157–168, Figure 4. © 1991 American Psychological Association. Reprinted with permission.]

chronological age? The difficulties in this research are similar to studies on the effects of early or later retirement from work (Kimmel, 1990). Multiple social and personal factors are involved in one's reaction to these developmental events, and what is "early" or "late" for one person may be on time for another. Moreover, the individual's perception of being early or late may be more important than objective reality, especially with regard to menarche, which may be kept secret (Rierdan, Koff, & Stubs, 1989). Therefore, a biopsychosocial model is necessary to understand the impact of early or late puberty.

PRECOCIOUS PUBERTY

When the physical and endocrine changes of puberty occur much earlier than is average—earlier than 95% of adolescents in Tanner's and other studies—this is known as **precocious puberty**.

In females, precocious puberty involves the beginning of the cyclic hypothalamus–pituitary functioning, secretion of sex hormones, ovulation, and the development of estrogen-dependent physical characteristics before the age of 8 or 9 years. About 10% of these cases are caused by serious illnesses, such as tumors. In some cases, it is caused by medications or cosmetic creams that contain estrogens. Although most cases are not the result of endocrine abnormalities, a thorough clinical examination should be sought (Hopwood et al., 1990; Ross & Vande Wiele, 1981, pp. 379–381).

In males, precocious puberty is defined by androgen secretion and sperm production before the age of 9 or 10 (Reichlin, 1981, p. 632). Early puberty is more frequently caused by a tumor in boys than in girls (Odell, 1979, p. 1376).

In some cases, only one of the pubertal changes occurs early, such as the growth of pubic hair. Because this is caused by androgens produced by the adrenal glands, the possibility of a tumor of the adrenal glands is suggested. Other unusual variations from the typical sequence of physical changes can imply other possible endocrine abnormalities.

Drug therapy to inhibit pubertal development (and ovulation in females) was not often used in the past because it did not prevent the premature termination of physical growth and the resulting short height (Reichlin, 1981, p. 635). However, as noted earlier, providing steady levels of GnRH is now being used as a treatment for precocious puberty (Hopwood et al., 1990; Johnson, 1983; Waldhauser et al., 1991).

Sexual activity does not begin as early as physical development, because sexuality is highly dependent on social development and skills (Meyer-Bahlburg et al., 1985; Rose & Sachar, 1981, p. 649). Money (1980) noted that these "children may be able to procreate by age eight or nine, but they do not establish procreative relationships nor fall in love with older teenagers for whom they are socially too inexperienced and immature. In content, the erotic behavior and imagery of the somatically precocious child parallels social age, which in turn parallels chronologic age more closely than hormonal age" (p. 36).

The experience of too-early puberty may be difficult for the individual to cope with (Eichorn, 1975; Money & Walker, 1971; Stattin & Magnusson, 1990). Such persons are physically more mature than their age-mates, but social and psychological development is usually similar to their friends of the same age. It may seem to the individuals that they are too old for some things, but too young for everything else. The people they feel sexual attraction toward may find them immature and silly; the kids their own age have very different sexual feelings than they do. Also, adults do not know quite how to react to them—as children, or as adolescents. It can be a lonely and frustrating experience. And then, finally, when their age-mates begin to catch up with their physical and sexual development, the others become much taller. That is because individuals whose growth begins very early do not grow as tall before the growth spurt begins, so they wind up shorter in adulthood than people whose adolescent growth spurt occurred at the usual time. In addition, Money and Lamacz (1987) noted that medical examination and exposure of the genitals may be experienced as sexual abuse and have negative effects later in life.

DELAYED PUBERTY

Although the causes of delayed puberty are not known, hereditary factors may be involved because sometimes it is a family pattern. However, it can be caused by too low levels of gonadotropic hormones, and therapeutic replacement of hormones may be necessary. Also, for social or psychological reasons, hormones may be given to begin the pubertal changes if necessary (Bardin & Paulsen, 1981, p. 335). Periodic administration of GnRH by a programmable pump can trigger pubertal changes and fertility in men and women whose puberty is severely delayed (González, 1982, pp. 1155–1158; Styne, 1988).

Medical evaluation for delayed puberty is usually not appropriate before age 13 for girls or age 14 for boys (Styne, 1988). If there are no endocrine abnormalities, puberty eventually occurs in boys without treatment, usually by age 20–22 (Bardin & Paulsen, 1981, p. 335). However, if a boy's puberty is significantly delayed, counseling to reassure him that he will go through a normal puberty and become as mature as his age-mates would be important. In addition, if the boy is showing signs of withdrawal from peers and social contact, health complaints with no physical cause, poor school performance, dropping out of sports, or absenteeism from school, counseling and hormonal treatment may be necessary (Ehrhardt & Meyer-Bahlburg, 1975; Styne, 1988).

In girls, when menarche has not occurred by age 15 or 16, or if breast and pubic hair development has not begun by that age, the cause of the delay should be identified. Errors in the sexual differentiation process before birth are frequently the cause of delayed puberty; other causes include very low levels of gonadotropic hormones, follicles that are insensitive to FSH and LH, and disease of the ovaries (Ross & Vande Wiele, 1981, p. 382). A tumor of the pituitary gland may also be responsible (Dumont, personal communication, 1994).

As noted earlier, physical exercise and training, especially if it involves tension and competition, can cause the menses to be delayed or to cease temporarily (Hopwood et al., 1990; Warren, 1980). Of course, if the menses cease after once beginning, pregnancy is an obvious possibility; but there are other causes that should be explored if pregnancy is not the reason (Ross & Vande Wiele, 1981, pp. 382–383).

In our society, where so much emphasis is placed on being "grown up," sexually attractive, physically strong, and generally "fitting in" with everyone else—especially during adolescence—delayed puberty can be a major personal burden. The loneliness of being physically immature, last to be chosen for competitive sports, never asked out for dates, scared to ask anyone to go on a date, and ashamed of not having pubic hair or physical development like others one's age could make a person angry, hurt, withdrawn, and depressed. Surprisingly, however, delayed sexual development without delayed physical growth may not have a significant effect on the adolescents' self-image; but when there is delayed physical growth, either alone or in combination with delayed sexual maturity, the self-image of both male and female adolescents can be negatively affected (Apter, Galatzer, Beth-Halachmi, & Laron, 1981). Therefore, hormonal treatment may be more important when there is a delay in the adolescent growth spurt, compared with a delay only in sexual maturation. Clearly, each case of delayed puberty needs to be evaluated on an individual basis.

In conclusion, the effects of puberty are diverse and multifaceted and involve biopsychosocial influences in combination. Thus, puberty may be seen as an example of a dialectical interaction in which different aspects of hormonal, physical, and social changes affect each other. Hormone changes may have some direct effects, but are best viewed as mediated by other social and cultural factors. For example, the age at which puberty occurs—early, on time, or late—has some impact. Timing of breast development and increased weight associated with maturation are particularly significant aspects of puberty for girls in our culture. Increased stature and body build are likewise emphasized for boys.

Adolescent boys and girls may need to discuss their fears, anxieties, feelings, and desires related to their sexual and physical changes, but our culture almost pretends that puberty is not important and sometimes increases its effects by requiring multiple social changes at the same time (Richards et al., 1993, p. 39).

We discuss the effects of puberty on the transition from elementary to middle or junior high school in Chapter 6. We note its effects on family relations in Chapter 7. In Chapter 8 we examine the impact of puberty on dating and social relationships.

CHAPTER SUMMARY

1. The physical and hormonal changes of puberty reflect events that differentiate males from females during prenatal development.

2. Under the Adam principle, a male is produced if the Y chromosome is present, androgens, and Müllerian duct inhibitory susbstance (MIS) each does its task, and the tissues are not insensitive to androgen. Then, if all goes well, at puberty a massive increase in androgens produces adult male characteristics.

3. Under the Eve principle, a female is produced if androgens and MIS are not present. Then, at puberty, feminizing hormones, primarily estrogens, produce adult female characteristics.

4. Through complex feedback systems, the hypothalamus, pituitary, and gonads send messages back and forth by hormones to stimulate or inhibit production of sex hormones.

5. During childhood the level of sex hormones

(androgens, estrogens, and progestins) is maintained at a low level that is similar for females and males. For reasons not fully understood, these hormones increase late in childhood and stimulate the changes of puberty. Body weight, athletic training and exercise, heredity, and nutrition appear to affect the age at which puberty occurs.

6. During puberty androgens promote the growth of body hair in both genders; they also are involved in producing oiliness of the skin and acne. In males androgens promote the growth of the penis, testes, prostate, and other tissues and organs. In females estrogens and progestins stimulate development of the breasts, mammary glands, and functioning of the reproductive system, and also affect other tissues and organs.

7. Menarche is the first menstruation for girls. The menstrual cycle involves negative and positive hormonal feedback between the ovaries, which produce estrogens and progestins, and the pituitary, which produces luteinizing hormone (LH) and follicle stimulating hormone (FSH).

8.   The production of sperm (spermarche) is a relatively early event in male pubertal development. The first ejaculation may occur in a "wet dream" or through masturbation. Boys' reactions are generally positive, although some are frightened, especially if they were not informed about it ahead of time.

9.   Physical growth and development of the body during puberty may begin several years earlier for some persons than for others, both of whom are normal. Some adolescents may have completed these physical changes before other adolescents of the same age have begun these changes.

10.   The adolescent growth spurt in stature begins 2 years earlier for girls than for boys, on the average. Androgens are thought to be important in producing the adolescent growth spurt in girls and boys; and androgens and estrogens play a major role in terminating physical growth.

11.   The sequence of physical development is a fairly regular pattern for each gender. Testis growth is the first obvious physical event for boys. Growth of facial hair in boys is a relatively late event; it usually begins during the fourth stage of pubic hair growth, and about the time underarm hair begins to appear. The beginning of the growth spurt in height is the first physical event for girls. Menarche is a relatively late event for girls, usually marking the end of the period of rapid growth in height. Development of the breasts in girls and penis growth in boys also follows a regular pattern, usually beginning within a year after the adolescent growth spurt starts.

12.   The effects of puberty may be seen as dialectical interactions in which a change in physical characteristics such as breast or body development brings changes in other aspects of the adolescent's life space, such as with the family, peers, and self-perceptions. Thus, a biopsychosocial model is useful to understand the impact of puberty.

13.   Menarche generally does not appear to have much effect on adolescent girls' feelings about themselves. This is especially true when the girl expects menstruation and it happens approximately on time.

14.   Coping with simultaneous transitions in several aspects of life may be difficult. However, most adolescents show little change in self-esteem or self-concept as a result of puberty.

15.   Early maturation seems to have positive effects for boys in our culture because of increased social prestige associated with a more mature body build. Early maturing girls appear to be what more vulnerable to deviant behavior, especially if they had behavior problems before puberty.

16.   Precocious puberty occurs if the hormonal and physical changes occur before the age of 9 in girls or the age of 9 or 10 in boys. Physical abnormalities (such as tumors) are frequently a cause of precocious puberty for boys and sometimes for girls.

17.   Delayed puberty may involve endocrine abnormality. Social and psychological difficulties can result if physical growth is delayed too late.

KEY WORDS

acne	estrogens	hormones	puberty
adolescent growth spurt	follicle stimulating hormone	luteinizing hormone	self-esteem
androgens	gonadotropic hormones	menarche	self-concept
biopsychosocial model	height spurt	precocious puberty	spermarche
		progestins	testosterone

REVIEW QUESTIONS

1. What memories do you have of experiencing puberty? What was the best thing about it? What was the worst aspect?

ORIGINS OF PUBERTY

2. Describe the Adam and Eve principles. Give several examples of how they describe the development of male and female genital anatomy.

3. Describe the negative feedback system that involves the hypothalamus, pituitary, and gonads.

4. What are FSH, LH, melatonin, and GnRH? How are they involved with the onset of puberty?

5. Review the evidence that the following influence the age at which puberty occurs: heredity, weight, exercise, and nutrition.

6. Why has the age of puberty declined in many countries during the past 100 years? What does this change imply about the age of puberty in the next century?

HORMONAL ASPECTS OF PUBERTY

7. What are hormones and how do they send a powerful and highly specialized message to a specific organ?

8. List the major effects of androgens (testosterone) on males at puberty. What role do androgens play in female puberty?

9. List the effects of estrogens and progestins on females at puberty.

10. Review the positive and negative feedback systems as they affect the menstrual cycle in women (Figure 3.2).

11. What is the name for the first menstruation for girls? What is the name of the first production of sperm in boys? How are these events similar and different from each other?

PHYSICAL CHANGES DURING PUBERTY

12. Describe Figure 3.6 in your own words. Explain the fact that onse adolescent may have completed the physical changes before another adolescent of the same age has begun them.

13. Why does the growth in height slow down for girls after they begin menstruation?

14. Which stops growing first for boys: leg or arm length?

15. Why are girls often stronger than boys of the same age early in adolescence, but boys are stronger later in adolescence?

16. When does a boy's beard begin to grow, in relation to pubic hair and underarm hair? What is the sequence of moustache and beard development?

17. How long does a girl's breast development take, on average? What factors are involved in breast development?

18. Which characteristic of genital development is usually the first sign of puberty in males?

19. Why is acne usually less common in girls than in boys?

EFFECTS OF PUBERTY ON THE INDIVIDUAL ADOLESCENT

20. Describe the biopsychosocial approach. Discuss how it is similar to the mediated effects model (Chapter 2) and the dialectical interaction model (Chapter 1).

21. Give some examples of dialectical interaction effects of puberty with regard to the family.

22. What are the effects of menarche for adolescent girls in general?

23. Explain the statement: "The influence of an individual's situation is often more important than gender in terms of an adolescent's level of self-esteem."

24. What is the effect of puberty on adolescents' self-concept and level of self-esteem according to research cited in the book? Do you agree?

VARIATIONS IN PUBERTAL DEVELOPMENT

25. Why does early maturation generally have positive effects on boys in the United States?

26. Explain the statement: "Early maturation appears to have accentuated the premenarcheal behavior problems of girls" (refer to Figure 3.12).

27. What is the definition of precocious puberty? What are the causes of it? Can it be treated?

28. Describe the effects of delayed puberty. At what age is it appropriate to seek a medical evaluation for this condition?

29. Why does delayed physical growth have greater impact than delayed sexual development alone?

Chapter 4

◆

Thinking Makes It So: Cognitive Development

◆

The principal idea underlying this chapter is the important role cognition plays in human life. **Cognition** may be defined as the way we think about and know things. **Cognitive processes** include paying attention to particular stimuli, recalling previous experiences from memory, solving problems, and understanding the physical and social world, including one-self. To illustrate this simply, examine Figure 4.1—a square frame that contains two dashes and a dot—and note the caption, "Two elephants sniffing a grapefruit." Next, examine Figure 4.2. This is an example of an assessment procedure developed by Chandler and Helm (1980) for use in the study of cognitive development in children; it is based on a cartooning technique known as "droodles" (Price, 1953). The experimental task is for a child who has seen the complete drawing to guess how a child who had seen only the first figure would in-terpret it. Children cannot solve this task until middle childhood.

This simple illustration points out that the cognitive interpretation of the picture changes its meaning from a design to an idea. As Chandler and Boyes (1982) phrased it:

> Given the tunnel vision imposed, it is ludicrous to imagine that anyone could ever anticipate the larger scene of which the droodle is only a part. Once oriented by the caption, however, the fragments of the original drawing fall into place, and it becomes possible to imagine—even dif-ficult not to imagine—that the drawing is the leading edge of what it is claimed to be. [Chandler & Boyes, 1982, p. 395]

For our purposes, the point of this example is that the way in which we think about some-thing—whether a physical object, a person, or an idea—affects the meaning it has for us. Thus, as noted in Chapter 2, an understanding of the ways in which adolescents think about themselves, other people, and ideas of all kinds provide a central unifying perspective for viewing adolescent personal and social development.

In this chapter we explore this process of cognitive development, especially in terms of adolescent thinking abilities, from two complementary perspectives: the information pro-cessing perspective and Piaget's theory. The next chapter focuses on the important implica-tions of cognitive development for psychosocial aspects of adolescence, including per-ception of others, perception of oneself, identity, friendship, political attitudes, and moral thinking. As may be obvious, cognitive development also affects thinking about par-ents, school, careers, and essentially every topic we will discuss in later chapters. Thus, this chapter discusses the thinking processes that organize all of the adolescent's experi-ences.

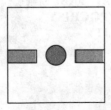

Figure 4.1   Two elephants sniffing a grapefruit. See also Figure 4.2. [*Source:* M.J. Chandler & M.C. Boyes. Social Cognitive Development. In B.B. Wolman (Ed.), *Handbook of Developmental Psychology.* © 1982 Prentice-Hall. Figure 22.2, p. 395. Reprinted with permission.]

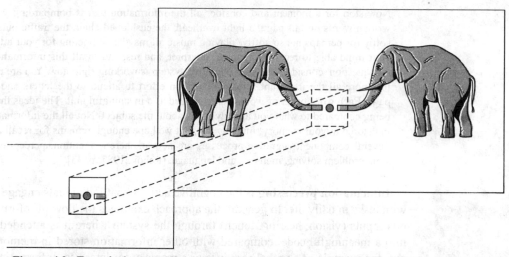

Figure 4.2 Two elephants sniffing a grapefruit. [*Source:* M.J. Chandler & M.C. Boyes. Social Cognitive Development. In B.B. Wolman (Ed.), *Handbook of Developmental Psychology*. © 1982 Prentice-Hall. Figure 22.2, p. 395. Reprinted with permission.]

INFORMATION PROCESSING MODEL OF COGNITIVE DEVELOPMENT

Consider for a moment the complex process that your mind engages in as you make ordinary decisions of everyday life. You arise in the morning and rely on memory to reach out and turn off the alarm, find your way to the shower, and recall the events you must prepare for during the upcoming day. Perhaps you process the information from the mass media about recent news and today's weather forecast as you choose what you will wear and what you will eat or drink. You select your path to the college, based on memory, and if you drive, you recall how to operate your car, attend to any relevant input from traffic, and search for parking. You determine which classroom to enter based on the day of the week, following cues that may be automatic because you have taken the same path so many times. Friends greet you and you recognize each one, by face if not always by name. You take a seat that is, more often than not, in the same place each time, and open your notebook. The instructor begins class and you recognize the words, even though you may never have heard the ideas before. You listen, attempt to understand the concepts, and write the central points in your notebook. You hear a question and an answer or a response occurs to you, so you raise your hand as a signal for permission to talk. When called upon, you speak, and words express an idea that you may never have thought before. Another student responds likewise and you sense that you were understood, but one point needs to be clarified, so you speak again. Then, you write another thought in your notebook, while listening to the next point being made.

From the moment you awoke, your mind was processing information in complex and highly efficient ways, often without your conscious awareness.

Now stop for a moment and consider all the information that is bombarding your senses: the written words on this page, a light overhead, the cushioned chair, the traffic outside, and some softly (or perhaps not so softly) playing music all may be competing for your attention. How is your mind able to receive, organize, interpret, and respond to all this information? To answer this question, consider how your cognitive system is working right now. You are probably trying to ignore all the irrelevant information in an effort to attend to the letters and words on this page. Each word or set of words is recognized as a meaningful unit. The ideas that you read are being compared to what you already know about the subject. Not all the information here is being stored in your memory; much is lost, but we hope enough remains for recall at a later point. Several component cognitive processes are at work here—attention, perception, comprehension, problem solving, memory, and language. [Rebok, 1987, p. 43]

Information processing is the cognitive activity that individuals engage in when dealing with tasks in daily life. In general, the approach examines the flow of information from various inputs (vision, hearing, touch) through the system where it is attended to, transformed into a meaningful code, compared with other information stored in memory, and then output, for example as a verbal response or a memory for later use. Information processing involves solving problems, making decisions, organizing activities, and coping with everyday situations.

The origin of the information processing model has been traced back to the work of the mathematician Allen Turing (1936, 1963), who created the basis on which the modern computer is built. During the 1960s, the study of cognitive processes emerged, and some psychologists began to think of the digital computer as a metaphor for human thought and began to create actual computer models. Although computer-based models have been criticized as too rigid to compare with human thinking, a variety of computational concepts such as encoding, search, and retrieval are common in current theories of cognition (Dellarosa, 1988). The computer model provides a frame of reference for a wide range of studies of human information processing and reasoning; it also recognizes the importance of pattern recognition, a system of logic, and the formation of analogies. In essence, it explains that the human mind relies on a large memory capacity to compensate for relatively limited computing capacities (Hunt, 1989, pp. 624–625). That is, the focus is on what is stored in memory and how is it organized; how this information affects new information processing and behavior; and how the stored information is changed by new information, reflection, and reappraisal (Sherman, Judd, & Park, 1989).

Information processing is an important aspect of cognitive functioning. It may be thought of as consisting of two parts: *structural* aspects of the brain that are neurologically based; and *functional* aspects that depend on external factors such as practice, familiarity, learned strategies, and computational aids. Flavell (1985) noted that adolescents have greater functional capacities than do younger children and that these greater skills clearly explain much of their superior cognitive abilities; it is not clear whether there are age-related increases in the neurological structural aspect that might also account for improved performance. Keating (1990) concluded that brain maturation does not appear to be clearly related to increased cognitive abilities during adolescence and argued that the available data do not support the idea that educators should wait for brain development before presenting adolescents with cognitive challenges. Thus, he felt that links between puberty and growth spurts in the brain, or between advanced physical development of girls as compared with boys and cognitive development, do not seem to be warranted.

Instead, functional aspects, especially cognitive functioning in areas of one's *expertise* and the growth of information in specific *domains* of knowledge, clearly increase during adolescence and thereby improve ability to process relevant information on topics of expertise. **Expertise** refers to systematic knowledge in which some underlying organizing structure provides keys to perception, procedure, and response; examples of possible areas of expertise include auto mechanics, chess, mathematics, music, physics, or sports information. One classic example of expertise (which we refer to later in this chapter) is that expert chess players, when presented with 25 chess pieces from actual games for 5 to 10 seconds were able to remember 90% of the positions of the chess pieces, but novices could remember only 20% of the positions (Chase & Simon, 1973). Further studies have shown that the experts find patterns in the arrangement of the pieces, each containing 4 or 5 pieces; thus, the experts are remembering 5 patterns instead of 25 individual chess pieces. The novices do not recognize these patterns and so they remember only 5 individual pieces, thus accounting for the difference in memory (Bruer, 1993).

As implied, expertise is developed in some specialty. This content area of specialization is referred to as the **domain** of expertise or knowledge. Thus, an adolescent may develop considerable expertise in popular music, baseball, or computer use, but be a relative novice in other areas.

This point about domains of expertise is of considerable importance for understanding cognitive development in adolescence because some theories of development claim that adolescents gain greater cognitive skills across all domains, whereas others argue that individual differences in expertise are more important. Moreover, common-sense observations suggest that adolescents are often quite inept in decision-making skills, even when they have considerable knowledge. For example, despite having driver training, adolescents still have a higher proportion of accidents than older drivers. Likewise, high rates of pregnancy, dropping out of school, and cigarette smoking among adolescents do not appear to reflect high levels of knowledge, despite educational efforts. Thus, cognitive development and knowledge alone are not adequate to explain behavior; sociocultural and individual aspects of development appear to interact with cognition.

Because the cognitive processes involved are complex, the information processing system is usually thought of as consisting of several interacting components such as *processing capacity*, *knowledge base*, and *cognitive self-regulation* (Keating, 1990). That is, a variety of sensory inputs are attended to, perceived, and comprehended by the basic processing capacity. Those areas of lesser or greater knowledge are processed differently, with the latter being more likely to involve automatic responses. Self-regulating processes oversee this information processing and are able to think about thinking and thus to regulate it when necessary, seeking more information, or countering automatic responses that are inappropriate, for example. These three aspects of information processing parallel three components in Sternberg's triarchic view of human intelligence: performance components, knowledge-acquisition components, and meta components.

Consider the example of a typical academic requirement—writing a term paper. Metacomponents are used to decide on a topic, plan the paper, monitor the writing, and to evaluate how well the finished product succeeds in accomplishing its goals. Knowledge-acquisition components are used for research. Performance components are used for the actual writing. But the three could never function in isolation. Before actually writing the paper, you would first have to decide on a topic and then do some research. Similarly, your plans for writing the paper might change as you gather new information. It may turn out that there just isn't enough information on certain aspects of the chosen topic, and you are forced to shift your emphasis. Your plans may also change if certain aspects of the writing go more smoothly than others. (Sternberg, 1988b, p. 59)

We examine these components in detail in the next three sections.

PROCESSING CAPACITY

As noted above, processing capacity may be thought of in terms of structural (neurological) and functional (learned) aspects. Because there is no compelling evidence that puberty brings advances to the *structural* aspects of cognitive processing, we focus our attention on the *functional* aspects that develop during adolescence. These changes include increased efficiency and skill based on learning and experience. That is, many tasks become *automaticized* or automatic, so that when the problem is presented an adolescent can recall the way to solve it, instead of having to discover the path to the solution each time. This ability reflects the growth of memories from past experience from which one can draw to find solutions to similar problems. It also reflects the ability to recognize that the problems are similar to past ones. Thus, the adolescent learns what factors are relevant for the solution, attends to those factors, and ignores irrelevant factors. An example might be that student who can reduce a science problem to a diagram or to a mathematical equation that allows the solution to be recognized readily. This process is similar to the ability of expert chess players to recognize patterns of chess pieces and reflects the concept of *expertise* described above.

According to Sternberg's triarchic theory, the processing component includes five distinct skills (Sternberg, 1988b, pp. 116–147):

1. *Encoding*—identifying each attribute that may be relevant to a solution.

2. *Inference*—discovering relationships between objects or events; for example, *yellow* and *lemon* (the color of fruit).

3. *Mapping*—recognizing a relationship between two relationships; for example, *yellow* and *lemon*, *green* and *lime*.

4. *Application*—generating or choosing the correct response; for example, *yellow is to lemon as* _____ *is to plum*.

5. *Justification*—choosing which of the options provides the best, if not the ideal, solution.

Processing skill also involves increased *memory capacity* such that there is more information available to draw upon to seek appropriate strategies for solving problems. An important process that is involved in this increased memory capacity is called **chunking**, which is the process of combining complex bits of data into meaningful patterns. By using chunking, the chess experts discussed above combined chess pieces into recognizable patterns.

It is important to note that people can extend the limited capacity of short-term memory through *chunking*. Try to encode and rehearse the following digit string. . . :

1 4 9 2 1 7 7 6 1 9 8 4 2 0 0 1

You probably were unable to rehearse this entire string, unless you noted that it contained four famous years (1492, 1776, 1984, 2001). Once you are aware of this, it becomes easy to remember the 16 digits as 4 years. Well-established chunks of knowledge in long-term memory enable you to recode the digits in this manner. [Barsalou, 1992, pp. 96–97]

The development of more powerful processing capacity is not inherently linked to age or to the adolescent period, however. Individuals may develop these abilities based on interest, experience, teaching, and a variety of environmental influences. For example, parental encouragement to think for oneself, to explore, and to experiment would stimulate the development of greater cognitive processing ability. In contrast, peer pressure to avoid intellectual stimulation, autocratic teaching methods, or an excessive fear of failure in school could lead to an impairment in the development of these thinking skills (Keating, 1990).

The skill to solve problems can be taught so that one has an array of strategies for solving different kinds of problems (Bransford & Stein, 1984; Sternberg, 1986a). Moreover, cognitive processing ability may be much greater in certain kinds of problems or topics than in other areas. That is, an individual may show a high degree of skill in areas of expertise, but be relatively inept, or only average, in other areas. We examine this point in the next section.

KNOWLEDGE BASE

As one gains greater knowledge about a particular domain of information (such as chess, crossword puzzles, physics, or baseball), one discovers a variety of intellectual shortcuts that allow thinking to become more automatic in that area. This process does not necessarily lead to *better* problem-solving skills, however. Instead, it may lead one to jump to conclusions that ignore relevant but unexpected information. Thus, increased knowledge can in some cases lead to automatic responses that are incorrect or stereotypic. In this way, misconceptions may persist because we think we know the answer and do not seek or pay attention to new information. Therefore, it is very difficult and perhaps misguided to try to separate the level of processing capacity from the areas of expertise (Keating, 1990).

Knowledge acquisition involves three types of insightful performance: (1) selective encoding—sorting out relevant from irrelevant information; (2) selective combination—linking unrelated, or previously not related, elements; (3) selective comparison—discovery of a nonobvious relationship between old and new information, sometimes using an analogy, metaphor, or model (Sternberg, 1988b, pp. 177–179).

Often, adolescents learn enough to think they do not know the answer, when in fact they do have enough information to solve the problem. That is, they may acquire the idea that some problems involve the complex interplay of several variables and stop at the point they recognize that the answer "depends"; they do not proceed further to the separation of various influences of these variables as each affects the outcome (Keating, 1990). This type of thinking has been described as *relativistic* (Haviland & Kramer, 1991).

Sometimes, adolescents acquire only *pieces of knowledge* but are not able to develop a synthetic or coherent understanding of the ways in which these pieces fit together. Thus, they grasp the basic idea, but cannot shift perspective in order to fit one relevant idea together with another relevant idea to form a more complete understanding.

These mixed gains and losses that result from the growth of knowledge among adolescents lead to difficult educational issues. For example, memorizing information may increase the amount of knowledge, but an uncritical reliance on memory can lead to inaccurate or inappropriate solving of new problems. Moreover, jumping to a conclusion based on one piece of knowledge may be incorrect because other important information is ignored. An easy solution is to say, "I can't tell which is correct"; but this may also ignore the search for relevant information that does solve the problem.

Higher levels of cognitive processing are required that include critical thinking, examining one's thinking for logical flaws or for gaps in information, and questioning the relevance and adequacy of information. For example, often advertising and political campaigns focus on presenting pieces of knowledge in an attempt to convince the viewer that those pieces are the whole story. Another ploy is to present irrelevant information in a way that makes it appear that it is relevant. Thus, social influences may be seen as reinforcing the difficulty of teaching adolescents to develop the highest levels of cognitive processing. These higher level processes are known as cognitive self-regulation.

COGNITIVE SELF-REGULATION

The third component of information processing is the ability to think about one's thinking. **Metacognition** is cognition about cognition; it involves monitoring, reflecting upon, and critiquing one's thoughts. Sternberg (1988b) described the relationship of metacomponents, performance components, and knowledge-acquisition components as a process of feedback (Figure 4.3). That is, metacomponents work together with the performance and knowledge-

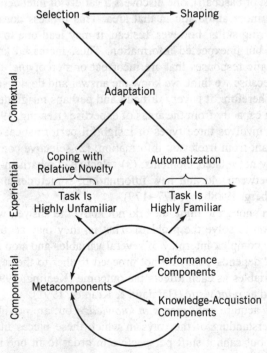

Figure 4.3 Relationship among the various aspects of Sternberg's triarchic theory of human intelligence. [*Source*: R.J. Sternberg, *The Triarchic Mind: A New Theory of Human Intelligence*. © 1988 Robert J. Sternberg. Figure 4, p. 68. Reprinted with permission.]

acquisition components in an integrated fashion. Their interaction leads to adaptation to one's context, selection of a new context, or shaping of the context in new ways.

Metacognition may involve self-reflection, as in the keeping of a diary. It may be seen when one revises a draft of a paper for class, searching for sections that do not make sense or that need more logical justification. It is the skill required to examine the ideas present-ed in a book or a lecture to find flaws or inconsistencies or stereotypes that distort or misrep-resent the facts. Many college teachers seek to teach students to acquire these skills (Box 4.1).

The task of metacognition requires a great deal of knowledge and may be seen as "a luxury of the expert" (Keating, 1990). In this sense, metacognition involves both gains and losses. The gain is in greater mastery of the area of expertise, but the loss is in effi-ciency and automatic responses. One begins checking and rechecking and may end up un-sure and conclude, "I don't know," when in fact, one does know, or could know. Gains and losses are often simultaneously involved in the course of human development; the cause of the gains may be similar to or different from the cause of the losses (Uttal & Perlmutter, 1989).

Moreover, the goals of the student's metacognition—for example, to figure out how to get a high grade from this instructor—may differ from the goals of the instructor (e.g., to teach critical thinking). Similarly, parents may conclude that their adolescents "can't think" when the adolescents are acting upon decisions that differ from those their parents would make. In fact, the adolescents may be thinking based on different metacognitive principles from those of their parents. For example, the parents may fail to understand why their ado-lescent wants to work at a low-paying, unskilled job in order to own a car instead of devot-ing that time to studying.

DEVELOPMENT IN ADOLESCENCE

The information processing perspective allows us to see the complexity of human thought and problem solving. The three-part view presented here summarized key components in cognition. In general, information processing abilities grow at differing rates in different do-mains of knowledge based on the individual's talents, experience, and practice. Moreover, some individuals may have developed a high level of skill in one or two, but not in all three components. Thus, there may be variations in performance between individuals of the same age in their knowledge acquisition, performance, and metacognition skills, and among each individual's domains of knowledge or expertise.

For the most part, however, the changes suggested by the information processing model have not been examined from a developmental perspective, and therefore it is not possible to link them with a precise age period such as adolescence. Rebok (1987) noted that, unlike developmental theories:

> Most information-processing analyses have been based on narrow age ranges; and despite their detailed descriptions of problem solving, they do not form a coherent framework for explaining age changes in performance across a variety of tasks. [p. 294]

In contrast, developmental psychology focuses on finding patterns of change that are re-lated to the level of development. For example, Sternberg and Rifkin (1979) noted that chil-

♦ BOX 4.1   SKILLS AND STRATEGIES THAT ILLUSTRATE METACOMPONENTS OF INFORMATION PROCESSING

Recognizing the Existence of a Problem

Be receptive rather than resistant to adverse feedback.
Seek out criticism as well as praise.
Be on the lookout for strategies that no longer work.

Defining the Nature of a Problem

Ask yourself whether the problem you are addressing is really the one you want to solve.
Redefine an insoluble problem to make it soluble.
Consider whether the goal toward which you are striving is really the one you want to reach.

Generating the Set of Steps Needed to Solve the Problem

Budget the time necessary to decide upon a sequence of steps.
Make the first step an easy one.
Choose steps that are the right size for solving the problem, neither too small nor too large.
Consider alternative steps to a solution before choosing any one set of them.

Strategy Selection: Ordering the Steps for Problem Solution

Don't immediately assume the "obvious."
Make sure that your sequencing of steps follows a natural progression toward the goal you wish to reach.
Don't "self-terminate" prematurely (e.g., stop before the problem has been solved).

Deciding How to Represent Information About the Problem

Know your pattern of abilities for representing information.
Use multiple representations whenever possible.
Use external representations (e.g., draw a diagram).

Allocating Mental and Physical Resources to Solving the Problem

Be willing to spend relatively large amounts of time on global, high-level planning.
Make full use of your prior knowledge in planning and in allocating your resources.
Be flexible and willing to change your plans.
Be on the lookout for new kinds of resources.

Monitoring the Solution to the Problem

Be aware of the need for solution monitoring and act upon this need.
Beware of "justification of effort" (e.g., the greater the investment, the harder it is to write off).
Avoid impulsiveness in solution monitoring (e.g., changing an answer in a multiple-choice exam impulsively; the error may be in the solution monitoring process, not in the original solution).
Be open to but evaluative of external feedback.
Actively seek external feedback.

Source: Adapted from Sternberg (1988b), pp. 79–114.

dren in second grade (approximately age 7) could perform *inferences* in problems involving analogies, but they could not *map* relations until fourth grade (approximately age 9).

Keating (1990) noted four key cognitive achievements that suggest adolescence is a crucial transition in the development of critical thinking: (1) increased automaticity and functional capacity; (2) greater knowledge in a variety of domains of content; (3) wider range and better use of strategies for applying or gaining knowledge; (4) recognition of the relativity and uncertainty of knowledge. These advances are based on fundamental skills such as literacy and basic knowledge in a variety of domains. He concluded:

The transition to adolescence can be characterized as the opening up of possibilities for thinking about the world in a more fundamental way, which also involves yielding the certainty of childhood. This process of differentiation can be seen in many domains beyond the academic, including thinking about the self, relationships to others, and society. [Keating, 1990, pp. 83–84]

In the next section we focus on Piaget's developmental model of cognitive development during late childhood and adolescence; we then compare that developmental model with the information processing model presented here.

PIAGET'S THEORY OF COGNITIVE DEVELOPMENT

Jean Piaget studied qualitative differences in intelligence among children of varying ages, noting how cognitive abilities develop as the children grew older. This approach is very different from the quantitative approach that focuses on differences among individual children of the same age, as in studies of IQ. In addition, Piaget did not place much importance on the child's chronological age because children differ in the age at which they reach various periods of development. Instead, he stressed the *invariant sequence* of the periods, such that each period is reached in its turn, none is ever skipped, and none occurs out of order.

Although Piaget's work did not have a significant effect on the study of children in the United States until the 1960s, it has had a profound influence since then. Contemporary studies of child development not only debate, refine, and expand his work, but also propose alternative models; still, it is not possible to discuss cognitive development in children and adolescents without referring to Piaget's ideas.

We begin this section with a brief overview of Piaget's general theory and then focus on two of the major periods of cognitive development. We conclude with a discussion of variations among adolescents in their level of everyday thinking.

OVERVIEW OF THE THEORY

Piaget stressed the *logical structures* or organizational qualities that define each of the periods of cognitive development. He described two general processes that are involved in the progression from each logical structure to the next. **Assimilation** involves incorporating experience into the existing mental structures. **Accommodation** involves modifying these structures as a result of experience. This integration and modification occurs in a succession of stages that is the same for all children, although the ages at which each is attained may vary. The sequence of periods in cognitive development is shown in Box 4.2.

Four general factors are involved in this progressive sequence of cognitive development, according to Piaget. (1) Maturation of the nervous system creates opportunities for mental growth, but is not sufficient to cause it. (2) Exercise through physical practice and mental experience involves the child actively in the development of understanding of the external world. (3) Social interaction and teaching is necessary, but is insufficient by itself to cause cognitive development. (4) An internal process of self-regulation, called *equilibration*, functions as a kind of feedback system of active adjustment to new information (Piaget & Inhelder, 1969).

Because our goal is to understand adolescent thinking, we focus our discussion on the periods of concrete operations and formal operations.

◆ *Profile*

JEAN PIAGET

Jean Piaget was born in 1896 in a small university town in Switzerland. By the time he was an adolescent he had already published an article on his observations of an albino sparrow he had seen in a park, and he was studying mollusks, a species of shellfish. He then spent a vacation with his godfather who, feeling Piaget's intellectual life should not be limited to natural science, introduced him to philosophy; his readings then broadened to include logic and religion as well. As a result, Piaget developed a life-long interest in *epistemology*, the study of knowledge. But he retained his commitment to science, as well, and sought to find a way to use the observational framework of biology to answer the epistemological questions about the nature, acquisition, and development of knowledge. At the age of 21, he received his Ph.D., based on his study of mollusks, and then began to explore psychology.

When he was 24, he published an article on child psychology and psychoanalysis and then moved to Paris to study psychology and philosophy. He also worked in the laboratory of Alfred Binet, who had constructed a test of intelligence. Piaget began to discover that the child's wrong answers on this test were more interesting than the correct answers. He noted that similar incorrect answers occurred in children of the same age, and that younger and older children had different patterns of incorrect answers to the questions. He concluded that younger children thought in ways that were different from the ways that older children thought. As a result, he rejected a quantitative definition of intelligence that measured "how much" in favor of a qualitative definition that reflected the method of thinking used by children of different ages (Ginsburg & Opper, 1988, pp. 1–3).

This discovery led him to develop a method of interviewing children and to spend a great deal of time observing children engaged in their own activities. He returned to Switzerland the next year, 1921, as Director of Research at the Rousseau Institute in Geneva, and continued his study of children, primarily between the ages of 4 and 12. This confirmed his belief that children under the age of 7 or so think in very different ways than older children. Between 1923 and 1932 he published a series of articles and five books on children focusing on language, reasoning, dreams, natural phenomena, and moral judgment. The birth of the first of his three children in 1925 allowed him to observe the development of thinking in his own children, using the painstaking method of a biologist observing and classifying mollusks. This observation led to a two-volume study of development during the first two years of life, published in 1936. In the 1940s, Piaget focused on children's thinking about scientific and mathematical concepts, which he continued to study until his death in 1980. By the 1950s he had also returned to his earlier interest in epistemology, attempting to link the development of knowledge in society to the development of cognition he had observed in children and adolescents.

[*Source:* Crain, 1992, pp. 100–101; Ginsburg & Opper, 1988.]

♦ **BOX 4.2 PERIODS OF DEVELOPMENT IN PIAGET'S THEORY OF COGNITIVE DEVELOPMENT**

Period I.   **Sensori-Motor Intelligence:** Intelligence of action, consisting of six stages beginning with the use of reflexes at birth and concluding with the understanding of object permanence (at approximately age 2).

Period II. **Preoperational Thought:** Begins with the advent of thought, using mental symbols. Thinking differs from adult thinking and is a period of organization and preparation for concrete operations (extends approximately from ages 2 to 7).

Period III. **Concrete Operations:** Logical and systematic thought about concrete, physical objects and activities (approximately from ages 7 to 11).

Period IV. **Formal Operations:** Ability to think about thinking and other abstract and hypothetical ideas (begins about age 11).

CONCRETE OPERATIONS

The term **operation** refers to those actions that a person performs mentally that form a coherent and reversible system. For example, the mental combination of two classes into a superordinate class (mothers and fathers are parents), or mental addition or subtraction of two numbers are each considered to be operations. All operations are mentally reversible; that is, the combination of two classes can be separated again, or numbers added together can be subtracted. In the stage of **concrete operations** the child is able to perform a variety of operations on objects that are physically present, on thoughts about such objects, and on the results of previous experience with the physical world. The operations in this stage are called "concrete" because they involve objects; they do not involve hypotheses or reasoning about possibilities or the future. Most adolescents can use concrete operations easily and usually rely on them for daily problem solving.

Let us take one example from Piaget's classic studies on the conservation of liquids to illustrate these concrete operations. Of course, when a liquid is poured from one container to another there is essentially the same amount of liquid in the second container as there was in the first. There are a number of ways to prove this: pouring the liquid back into the first container and noting that it reaches the original level, pouring each into a standard measuring glass, and so on. However, the young child does not know this and cannot understand it, according to Piaget (Figure 4.4).

To provide a sample of the way Piaget and his collaborator, Bärbel Inhelder, described these concepts, we quote their summary (Piaget & Inhelder, 1969):

The clearest indication of the existence of a preoperational period . . . is the absence of notions of conservation until about the age of seven or eight. Let us reexamine the experiment relating to the conservation of liquids in which the contents of glass *A* were poured into a narrower glass *B* or a wider glass *C*. Two facts are particularly noteworthy in the judgments of four- to six-year-olds who think that the liquid increases or decreases in quantity. First, the young subjects seem to reason only about states or static configurations, overlooking transformations: the water in *B* is higher than it was in *A*; therefore it has increased in quantity, regardless of the fact that it is the same water that has merely been poured from one container to another. Second, the transformation, although the child is perfectly well aware of it, is not conceived as a re-

Figure 4.4 Conservation of liquid experiment. Child sees that beakers A1 and A2 contain the same amount of liquid. He then pours A2 into a wider glass, and claims that now A1 has more because it is taller. [*Source:* Photo courtesy of William C. Crain.]

versible movement from one state to another, changing the form but leaving the quantity constant. It is viewed as a particular action, a "pouring," situated on a level other than that of physical phenomena and assumed to have results that are literally incalculable, that is, non-deductive in their external application. However, at the level of concrete operations, after seven or eight, the child says: "It is the same water," "It has only been poured," "Nothing has been taken away or added" (simple or additive identities)[;] "You can put the water in *B* back into *A* where it was before" (reversibility by inversion); or, particularly, "The water is higher, but the glass is narrower, so it's the same amount" (compensation or reversibility by reciprocal relationship). [pp. 97–98]

In this example, the term *conservation* refers to the fact that the amount of liquid does not change when it is poured from one glass to the other (i.e., the quantity is conserved). Matter is neither added nor destroyed by changing its shape. The term *reversible* refers to the fact that conservation may be demonstrated by reversing the transformation—by pouring the liquid back into the original container.

Similar studies on other forms of conservation have been conducted. For example, conservation of substance involves a lump of clay that is rolled into a sausage shape or into a pancake shape. Because no clay is added or taken away, the same amount of clay exists in both of these forms. This can be demonstrated by reversing the transformation. In Piaget's experiments children usually achieve this understanding by age 7 or 8. Another example is conservation of volume in which an object is dropped into water and the amount the water level rises is equal to the volume of the object regardless of how much the object weighs. Again, this can be tested by reversing the transformation. Piaget reported that this understanding is achieved by around age 11 or 12.

The fact that different types of conservation tasks are not solved at the same age is an example of Piaget's concept of *horizontal déclage*, which means that the child cannot generalize the understanding from one area to another. This indicates how the concrete operational thinker is bound by the concrete task at hand; however, it raises questions about the uncertainty of conservation skills in general (Winer & McGlone, 1993).

Each of these tasks indicates that before developing concrete operations children rely too much on appearances, are deceived by their perception, and do not have the cognitive ability to analyze the problem presented correctly. At first, one might think that the children are capable of being taught to use concrete operations. However, investigators have found it surprisingly difficult to teach conservation, and once a child does seem to have learned it, he or she does not always apply the same skill to similar tasks. Moreover, the very difficulty of teaching the cognitive skills indicates that they are not likely to be developed ordinarily by teaching (Crain, 1992, pp. 129–130). Instead, Piaget argued, children develop these thinking abilities on their own as a result of actively exploring their environment. Of course, teaching may play a role, especially if the child is at the point of almost developing the ability, but it cannot replace this process of self-directed cognitive development.

Piaget tried to be more specific about how children develop by introducing the concept of *equilibration*. By this Piaget referred to the individual striving for a state of harmony and balance between the ability to understand the environment and the problems the environment poses. Not being able to be certain of the correct solution to a problem creates conflict for the child, and there may also be conflict between competing solutions as the child considers the problem. For example, in the conservation of liquids problem, the young child focuses attention primarily on the height of the liquid in the glass. However, if the liquid is poured into a very wide glass, its low level and the width of the glass is likely to capture the child's attention. The child may then be uncertain whether to continue focusing only on the height of the liquid, or to shift to the width of the glass. If attention shifts to width, this, too, is not a certain solution to the problem, and the child then oscillates between width and height. But by paying attention to both height and width, the child notices that a change in one results in a change in the other; at this point, the child may relate the change in height to the transformation of pouring, which leads to an understanding of conservation. This process of development may require several months or years. Once the concrete operations problems can be solved, the preadolescent's thinking is flexible and effective when based on physical experience.

The concept of *decentering* is also involved in solving concrete operations problems. It refers to the child's evolving ability to take more than one perspective on a problem at a time. At birth the infant is centered entirely on itself and does not separate self from the environment. The process of development is generally one of decentration. This process may be defined as the gradual evolution of the objective relationships between one's body and actions and all of the other events and objects in the universe. This includes not only the physical universe, but also the social world of interpersonal relations (Piaget & Inhelder, 1969, pp. 94–95). At the end of the period of concrete operations, the preadolescent's thinking processes are able to focus on two or three relevant dimensions of the concrete physical problem in search of the solution.

This concrete operational level of cognitive development is potentially very powerful. One is able to use logical ways of thinking about the concrete physical world. One also looks for facts to prove or to disprove one's views. This level of thinking is characteristic of young adolescents; older adolescents and adults use it for everyday problem solving of concrete tasks. The thinking is limited to the real concrete physical facts, however.

> Concrete operations are adult-like adaptations with a focus on the empirically real, both in what has been traditionally considered the "real" aspects of the acknowledged "physical" environment and the "real" aspects of the acknowledged social or interpersonal environment. This orientation to "real" characteristics of the acknowledged environment(s) produces an emphasis on "the real facts" and nothing but the facts. Whatever is being reasoned about must be real, even if what is being reasoned about is abstract. Nonreal abstract possibilities and nonexperientially based aspects of physical reality are transformed into, and treated as if they were, an extension of one's own experientially based adaptations. [Gray, 1990, p. 232]

This type of thinking has also been termed *absolute* and is typical of early adolescence (Haviland & Kramer, 1991).

FORMAL OPERATIONS

The period of **formal operations** involves an even higher degree of equilibrium than is achieved in concrete operations. This level of equilibrium allows thought to be effective and flexible even when dealing with hypothetical and abstract ideas. The adolescent with formal operational thinking can imagine the possibilities in a situation and can compensate mentally for changes in reality (Ginsburg & Opper, 1988, p. 180). One can think about nonpresent objects, the future, possibilities, and hypotheses that are not concrete and real. One is able to think about abstract ideas that one does not believe in, or to draw conclusions from things that are only possible. It marks the beginning of the sort of logic that is involved in scientific experimentation.

Formal operations represents the mental ability to perform logical operations on the operations of the concrete period. Piaget interpreted these formal operations as a set of 4 logical transformations and 16 binary operations. Although these are too complex for brief discussion here, detailed summaries are readily available elsewhere (e.g., Ginsburg & Opper, 1988; Gray, 1990; Neimark, 1982).

Three classic science problems illustrate the shift in cognitive ability from concrete to formal operations: the balance beam, the pendulum, and the combination of liquids.

The Balance Beam

A beam, supported at the center, is shown to the children, and various weights are available. Obviously, two equal weights placed on the beam at equal distances from the center pivot are in balance (Figure 4.5). The children are then asked where a heavier weight should be placed to balance the original weight. A child may discover that the heavy weight must be

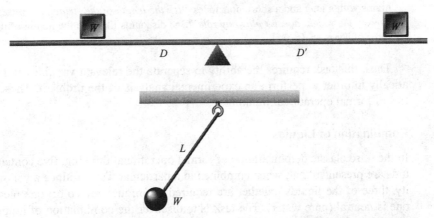

Figure 4.5   Illustration of balance beam (above) and pendulum problem (below).

placed closer to the pivot in order to balance the lighter weight. From this, the child may hypothesize that the weight (W) is inversely proportional to the distance (D) from the pivot. That is, $W/D = W'/D'$. This is not simple reversibility, however; it is a mental operation on reversibility, namely, an inverse relationship. It is no longer one transformation that is involved, but two: increasing one (weight) in the exact proportion the other is decreased (length) that is required for the beam to remain in balance. This kind of *proportional* reasoning is characteristic of formal operational thinking (Piaget & Inhelder, 1969).

The Pendulum Problem

A pendulum, consisting of a weight hanging on a string, is shown to the children and they are asked to determine what affects how rapidly the pendulum swings from one side of its arc to the other. They are shown how to vary the weight (W), change the length (L) of the string, release it from different heights, and push it with different amounts of force. The children are allowed to experiment with the pendulum in any way they please.

Concrete operational children approach the problem in a haphazard manner, varying several factors at once. They use no pattern to test the influence of weight, length of the string, height from which it is released, or force of the push that may be given to start the swing. Thus, young children's conclusions are not accurate; for example, they may conclude that weight influences the rate of swinging because a heavy weight on a short string swings faster than a light weight on a long string.

To solve this problem, children need to be able to perform the mental processes involved in conducting a scientific experiment. They must separate each variable from the others— weight, length, height of the swing, and force of the push. Then they must hold all possible factors constant while they change one variable at a time. Consider the following observations by Inhelder and Piaget (1958):

EME [child's code name, aged 15 years, 1 month], after having selected 100 grams with a long string and a medium length string, then 20 grams with a long and a short string, and finally 200 grams with a long and a short, concludes: "*It's the length of the string that makes it go faster or slower; the weight doesn't play any role.*" She discounts likewise the height of the drop and the force of her push. [p. 75]

Thus, this task requires the ability to separate the relevant variables and to think systematically in order to perform an experimental analysis of the problem. These are characteristics of formal operational thinking.

Combination of Liquids

In the third classic demonstration of formal operational thinking, five containers of clear liquids are presented that, when combined in a particular way, produce a yellow liquid. In reality, three of the liquids together are required to produce the color; one bleaches it out; and one is neutral (pure water). The task is to discover the combination of liquids that produces the color and the roles of the other two. The younger child (approximately age 7 to 11) usually combines the liquids two at a time and then puts all five together, neither producing the appropriate color nor determining the influence of each. However, "after the age of twelve he proceeds methodically, testing all possible combinations of one, two, three, four, and five elements, and thus solves the problem" (Piaget & Inhelder, 1969, p. 134).

Thus, the adolescent is able to imagine all of the possible combinations and then systematically proceeds to test all of these possibilities. That is, chemicals 1 and 2 are combined, then 1 and 3, and so on; then 1, 2, and 3, and so on; then 1, 2, 3, and 4; and eventually all five in a well-planned series of all possible combinations. This mental process of considering, in the abstract, all conceivable combinations is a demonstration of the formal operational ability to think about possibilities in a way that younger children do not.

To summarize, the adolescent begins in the realm of the hypothetical and imagines all the possible determinants of the results. To test hypotheses, the adolescent devises experiments which are well ordered and designed to isolate the critical factors by systematically holding all factors but one constant. She observes the results correctly, and from them proceeds to draw conclusions. Since the experiments have been designed properly, the adolescent's conclusions are certain and necessary. [Ginsburg & Opper, 1988, p. 187]

As we discuss in the next chapter, Piaget believed that this change in perspective from focusing on reality in concrete operations to focusing on possibilities in formal operations is important for emotional and interpersonal ideas as well as for the kind of examples described here. However, it is important to note that these changes do not occur all at once; instead, adolescents gradually apply these cognitive abilities to a greater range of thoughts and situations.

INDIVIDUAL VARIATIONS DURING ADOLESCENCE

There is a curious finding: not all adolescents, or even adults, seem to reach the more advanced stages of formal operations (Neimark, 1982). For instance, Blasi and Hoeffel (1974) concluded that "a rather large percentage of individuals of normal intelligence and of average social background, not only at the age of adolescence but also in adulthood, do not seem to function at the formal operational stage" (p. 348). This finding raises the question of why some adolescents do reach (or use) formal operations while others do not. Piaget (1972) suggested that it might be a question of interest and ability. Some persons might use formal operations in their area of expertise; for example, a boy or girl who does not demonstrate formal operations on the standard tasks might do so when working on a car or discussing a favorite topic. However, Kuhn (1986) explored this possibility using a study that required participants to evaluate evidence on the relationship of specific foods to catching a cold. She found that formal operations were not shown by a substantial number of the participants in this study that used a real-life problem. Thus, the reason not all adolescents show formal operations is not known.

Gray (1990) suggested the key is that the sophistication of concrete operations, and of formal operations, has been underestimated. That is, concrete operations may provide successful cognitive strategies for the solution of most problems as long as the person is not overwhelmed by the facts. Moreover, formal operations require a great deal of effort, energy, and perhaps also knowledge. At this level, according to Gray (1990), knowledge is not just "something that I know"; it is something that I "know how to do" (p. 249).

Concrete operations may be adequate for most daily problem-solving as long as the facts are not too complex.

If formal operational adaptations are not necessary for the existence and/or enhancement of the person with(in) the acknowledged environment, then they will probably not be constructed. It is clear that the acknowledged environment of most individuals, including school for those in school, work places for those who work, and the general environmental milieu does not require formal operations for successful psychological functioning. [Gray, 1990, p. 247]

We conclude that there is a range of performance among adolescents when they solve cognitive problems. Some, typically the youngest, are consolidating their ability to use concrete operations; others are using concrete operations in sophisticated ways, focusing on facts and concrete information. Some older adolescents, especially in areas of their expertise or where the environment clearly demands abstract thought, may be beginning the difficult construction of formal operational adaptations.

COMPARISON WITH THE INFORMATION PROCESSING MODEL

A major difference between information processing and Piaget's theory is that from the former perspective, no stages necessarily exist, and development may proceed at different rates in different domains of knowledge (Smith, Sera, & Gattuso, 1988). That is, while there is greater information and domain-specific knowledge acquired between childhood and adolescence, the change depends as much on experiences, opportunities, and skills as it does on development per se. Thus, whereas Piaget's theory is developmental and generally related to age, information processing theory is not primarily a developmental theory.

There are some parallel concepts between these two views of cognitive development, however. For example, both structural and functional components in the information processing system can increase over time. Moreover, greater knowledge and expertise in domains of experience can lead to cognitive growth as the gaps in understanding are filled in; at the concrete operations level, this concept parallels Piaget's notion of *equilibration*, discussed earlier (Siegler, 1989).

Likewise, the concepts of assimilation and accommodation, as Piaget described, may be seen in the information processing model. *Assimilation* would be the process by which information relevant to the growth of expertise is input to the system and stored for future use. *Accommodation* would involve a restructuring of one's way of thinking, which may be termed a "paradigm shift" in information processing (Torney-Purta, 1989).

In addition, the concept of *domains of expertise* may explain why Piaget's stage of formal operations is not used by all adolescents, as noted above. That is, those adolescents who have greater expertise in some specific domains will be able to rely on automatic responses, knowledge of what information to search for, and memory of previous relevant experiences to solve the problem. For example, expertise in science would lead one to perform better on the Piaget tasks described earlier in this chapter; in contrast, another adolescent might not do as well on the science tasks, but have expertise in music or the game of chess. Likewise, tasks that are easy for some adolescents because of their cultural or experiential background may be quite novel and difficult for other adolescents of equal cognitive ability because the tasks are part of one's domain of competence for the former group, but not for the latter group. Ginsburg and Opper (1988), writing from Piaget's perspective, reached a similar conclusion:

Some adolescents and adults fail to show evidence of the ability to use formal operations on some tasks. This may be due to a lack of environmental stimulation which results in a slowing down or stoppage of development. Or it may be due to the use of limited testing procedures which are biased in favor of adolescents from particular backgrounds. Perhaps all adolescents can use formal operations in situations of interest to them. Piaget leans toward this last interpretation. [p. 205]

POST-FORMAL OPERATIONAL THOUGHT

There is speculation about levels of thinking that are even more advanced than formal operations. One such style of thought is called **dialectical thinking** (Riegel, 1973). As suggested by the discussion in Chapter 1, this type of thinking involves recognizing the conflict between interacting forces that are always changing. Riegel (1977) described dialectical thinking as thought that includes but transcends formal logic:

Dialectical logic recognizes that it cannot exist without formal logic. This recognition provides a more general basis to dialectical logic than is available to formal logic. Formal logic fails to recognize such mutuality and is bound to consider itself immutable. Dialectical logic represents an open system of thinking that can always be extended to incorporate more restricted systems. Formal logic aims at a single universal analysis. As a consequence it is inflexible and primarily concerned with static conditions. Formal logic cannot apprehend itself. In particular, it cannot apprehend itself in the developmental and historical process. [p. 41]

There is evidence that this style of thinking is more frequently found among college faculty than among undergraduate freshmen; undergraduate seniors use it less than the faculty, but more than the freshmen (Basseches, 1980). Perhaps its use reflects level of education, but it might also reflect level of maturation. Kramer and Woodruff (1986) found that older adults showed higher levels of dialectical thinking than younger adults. They also concluded that dialectical reasoning requires formal operations, but involves development beyond that level.

EMOTIONS AND COGNITIVE DEVELOPMENT

Level of thinking may also be affected by the extent of *emotional involvement* in the topic. A study by Blanchard-Fields (1986) selected three dilemmas to be solved by "college-track" high school students, undergraduate college students, and highly educated adults. One dilemma was designed to have a low degree of emotional involvement: conflicting accounts of a war between two fictitious countries, North and South Livia, each written by a partisan of one country. Two dilemmas were designed to have high emotional involvement for the respondents:

The first of these tasks was the *visit to the grandparents conflict*. Again, two conflicting perspectives, that of the parents and that of their adolescent son, were presented, describing a trip to the grandparents' house. The adolescent was unwilling to attend, and the resolution that followed was described from the differing perspectives of coercion and compromise. . . . The final task consisted of the *pregnancy dilemma*, involving the decisions of a man and a woman about an unintentional pregnancy. Again, differing perspectives were presented: a woman's proabortion stance and a man's antiabortion stance. [Blanchard-Fields, 1986, p. 326]

The high school students did not differ from the college students on the dilemma involving the fictitious war between North and South Livia, but they were significantly lower in reasoning level on the visit to the grandparents and the pregnancy dilemmas. This suggested that adolescents (and perhaps others as well) reason at less advanced levels when the topic is especially emotionally salient to them. The highly educated adult group performed at higher reasoning levels for all three dilemmas (Figure 4.6).

Conversely, Haviland and Kramer (1991), using the famous diary of Anne Frank, proposed that emotional expression and normal developmental issues such as menarche or achieving autonomy from parents can be associated with increased levels of cognitive reasoning (Figure 4.7). The types of thinking examined were *absolute*, which is typical of early adolescence, *relativistic*, which emerges during early or middle adolescence, and *dialectical*. For example, in Anne Frank's diary, a peak of emotional expression at menarche was associated with an increase in all three types of thinking, with relativistic thought reaching its highest level up to that time (at page 120 in the diary).

As noted in Chapter 2, cognitive perspectives are an important approach for understanding adolescent development. The complex topic of the interaction of emotion and cognition during adolescence is one important area for continued research. There also are alternative

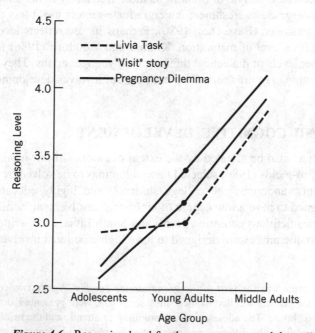

Figure 4.6 Reasoning level for three age groups and three different dilemmas. [*Source:* F. Blanchard-Fields. Reasoning on Social Dilemmas Varying in Emotional Saliency, *Psychology and Aging, 1,* 325–333, Figure 1. © 1986, American Psychological Association. Reprinted with permission.]

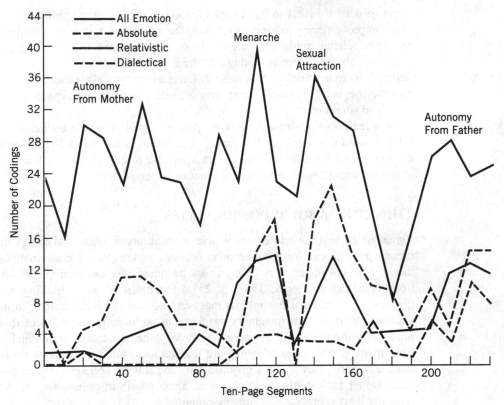

Figure 4.7 Incidence of cognition and emotion throughout the course of Anne Frank's diary. [*Source:* J.M. Haviland, & D.A. Kramer. Affect-Cognition Relationships in Adolescent Diaries: The Case of Anne Frank. *Human Development*, *34*, 143–159, Figure 1. © 1991 S. Karger AG, Basel. Reprinted with permission.]

models emerging to describe cognitive development. Obviously, this is an active area of research and theory development (Case, 1991; Chandler & Boutilier, 1992; Demetriou, Efklides, Papadaki, Papantoniou, & Economou, 1993).

In the next section we summarize the major characteristics of adolescent thinking reflecting the confluence of the information processing perspective and Piaget's view of cognition.

ADOLESCENT THINKING ABILITIES

Flavell (1985) noted that a variety of factors may be responsible for age-related changes at adolescence. Qualitative thinking and greater mathematical skills allow adolescents to approach problems with a different perspective than is true of younger children. Likewise, greater skill in the capacities Sternberg (1990) termed "higher-order processes"—such as a sense of what it means to think well instead of poorly and the ability to think about thinking—improve during adolescence. Also, the adolescent's specific competencies grow and are more reliably applied to relevant tasks. Although the reasons for these differences in cognitive ability between young children, older children, and adolescents have been debated, there is no debate that these differences are typically observed. This does not imply that they begin all at once; instead, they gradually develop and expand to more and different ideas and situations.

In a review of adolescent thinking abilities based primarily on Piaget's theory, Keating (1980) noted that there are five major characteristics that mark the difference between the thinking of adolescents and younger children. We briefly discuss each and then suggest five characteristics from the information processing perspective.

THINKING ABOUT POSSIBILITIES

Piaget noted that the adolescent is able to think about ideas and things that are not concretely present, can form connections between various possible alternatives, and can even think about the impossible. Thus, reality becomes only one example of all possible situations (Inhelder & Piaget, 1958, p. 251). Examples of such thinking might include, in physics, a particle that has infinite mass and no size (a "black hole"); in mathematics, the square root of -1 (an imaginary number); in philosophy, the concept that consciousness precedes self-consciousness; and in psychology, the idea that an individual's personality can have many facets, some of which are unconscious. Of course, adolescents do not always think abstractly; they spend a great deal of time solving concrete, day-to-day problems. The point is that adolescents are able to think about possibilities in a way that younger children typically do not, or, as Piaget argued, cannot.

This ability to think about possibilities affects many areas of the adolescent's life. As we discuss in the next chapter, it affects thinking about oneself, one's sense of identity, political ideals, and moral issues; in later chapters we will note how it affects relations with parents and peers, and vocational choice.

THINKING THROUGH HYPOTHESES

Closely related to thinking about possibilities is the ability to develop hypotheses, and to test them. However, hypotheses are possibilities that may turn out to be *impossibilities*. Testing hypotheses is the basis of the scientific method. To conduct an experiment one must hypothesize not only what will confirm one's predictions, but also what will disconfirm them and then design an experiment to test the predictions. The observations that are made must be accurate, and the hypotheses must be tested systematically if the findings are to be valid.

Like the scientific method, this cognitive skill involves discarding hypotheses that turn out to be incorrect, accepting hypotheses that are confirmed, and developing additional hypotheses to be tested. It provides adolescents with the ability to make predictions, act on those predictions, and modify their expectations based on empirical evidence. Of course, this does not imply that adolescents actually do function this way in their social and personal lives, even most of the time. The point is that their cognitive abilities allow them the possibility of applying these skills in a wide variety of areas in their lives.

Forming a hypothesis and testing it with accurate observations in a systematic manner are characteristics of adolescent thinking abilities.

THINKING AHEAD

The sign "PLAN AHEA$_D$" where the last letter does not quite fit, is a common example of another difference between the thinking of adolescents and younger children. Children begin tasks without first considering what the outcome will be and without systematically developing a strategy for achieving the task successfully. Planning involves the cognitive ability to think about all of the steps that are required and to think these steps through, in sequence, in the abstract before beginning the task. Thus, in the combination of liquids problem described earlier, one must not only understand all of the possible combinations, but be able to list them and plan to carry out each combination. Likewise, one must plan the appropriate test for each hypothesis that one is exploring in the bending of the rods problem. In general, thinking ahead is an important component in scientific reasoning.

This ability to plan may also be important for understanding a wide range of adolescent behaviors. For example, Dembo and Lundel (1979) reviewed the many factors that are involved in adolescents' use of contraception. Among those that are important is the ability to anticipate the possible outcome of sexual intercourse and to plan the appropriate steps to prevent a possible unwanted pregnancy. Similarly, Peterson and Murphy (1990) found that higher levels of cognitive reasoning are associated with greater knowledge about AIDS and also with sexual knowledge. Other factors involved in thinking about sex will be discussed later in this chapter and in Chapter 9.

THINKING ABOUT THOUGHTS

The ability to think about thinking also characterizes adolescent cognitive skills. For example, *introspection*, or thoughts about one's own thoughts and feelings, is frequently noted among adolescents (Elkind, 1974). Activities such as keeping a diary, writing poetry, spending time alone thinking about oneself, and long "deep" discussions with friends all indicate the fascination that adolescents sometimes find in thinking about thoughts.

Another aspect of this ability to think about thoughts is the adolescents' growing skill in finding ways to improve study skills, memory, and problem-solving ability. This *metacognition*, or the ability to think about cognition and the awareness of knowledge, increases with age during adolescence and becomes more sophisticated as well (Flavell, 1985).

In addition, Piaget called attention to the characteristic of formal operations that defines this stage of cognitive development in his scheme, namely, the ability to perform *operations on operations*. This process involves using logic to analyze logic, formulating rules about rules, and comparing and contrasting ideas using more abstract, higher-order, ideas.

THINKING BEYOND OLD LIMITS

Once the adolescent's thinking ability is freed from concrete reality and able to consider all manner of abstract possibilities, its scope increases greatly in the breadth of topics that are thought about. No longer bound by things as they are, the adolescent can question reality and the way social, physical, and emotional issues have been seen before. Thus, political questions, religious beliefs, moral issues, and personal relationships may be evaluated, questioned, and debated. This new ability can be a source of excitement and pleasure, so that the act of challenging old ideas can be stimulating and occasionally enjoyed for the newness of the skill itself. This ability may also provide an important source of intellectual ferment and even political change as young people think about important social issues. As Piaget and Inhelder noted:

> The same unity of behavior encountered earlier in the various stages is found again between eleven or twelve and fourteen or fifteen, when the subject succeeds in freeing himself from the concrete and in locating reality within a group of possible transformations. This final fundamental decentering, which occurs at the end of childhood, prepares for adolescence, whose principal characteristic is a similar liberation from the concrete in favor of interest oriented toward the non-present and the future. This is the age of great ideals and of the beginning of theories, as well as the time of simple present adaptation to reality. This affective and social impulse of adolescence has often been described. But it has not always been understood that this impulse is dependent upon a transformation of thought that permits the handling of hypotheses and reasoning with regard to propositions removed from concrete and present observation. [Piaget & Inhelder, 1969, pp. 130–131]

In addition to these five typical changes in adolescent thinking from the perspective of Piaget's theory, there are five typical changes that may be identified from the information processing perspective.

THINKING BASED ON EXPERIENCE

As a result of greater experience and skill in selected domains, adolescents are able to solve problems similar to those they have dealt with in these domains previously. For example, we described earlier the studies of chess experts who are able to remember the positions of chess pieces by recalling the patterns formed by the pieces. Likewise, the ability to solve the science-like problems Piaget used may reflect similar types of experience in the past.

One benefit of experience is that it provides different strategies for solving problems. Consider the "tower of Hanoi" problem, where the person is asked to move three concentric disks from one pole to another, with the same order at the end as at the beginning (Figure 4.8). One strategy is to use a *random search strategy* in which trial and error is used until the problem is solved. Even an ability to calculate the possible combinations and to try each might show formal operations but would still use the random search strategy. Another approach is to use the *means-end analysis* in which the goal state is compared with the initial state and the steps to reduce the difference are identified. For example, a subgoal is to move

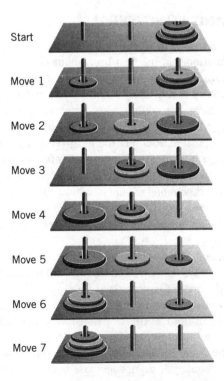

Start

Move 1

Move 2

Move 3

Move 4

Move 5

Move 6

Move 7

Figure 4.8   The three-disk tower of Hanoi problem.

the large disk to the first pole; this can be accomplished by moving the small disk to pole 1, the medium disk to pole 2, and then moving the small disk back to pole 2.

For other types of problems, it may be possible to visualize the steps that are required if one uses the strategy of *working backward* from the goal state to the initial state. When solving a maze, for example, working backward would be a good strategy because there are many dead ends when one begins at the initial state. Working from the end state and drawing a line back to the beginning will solve it more efficiently.

> What determines which of several alternative strategies will be used in a problem situation? One major factor is a person's prior knowledge of the problem or similar set of problems. Perhaps a child who has a toy peg-and-disk set would perform differently on the tower of Hanoi problem than a child who has never seen such a toy. [Rebok, 1987, p. 293]

Consider also the cognitive skill of **mapping** that involves recognizing a relationship between objects or events, discussed above. As noted, children are capable of inference, but not of mapping until about the fourth grade. The ability to perform *second order mapping* that involves recognizing a functional relationship between a relationship and an object or event does not occur until adolescence, however. That is, the analogy: *yellow* . . . *lemon/red* . . . *apple*, a first-order mapping that involves physical characteristics, would be solved at an earlier age; but *electrician* . . . *wire/plumber* . . . *pipe*, which involves functional relationships, would typically not be solved until adolescence (Sternberg, 1988b).

MEMORY: SHORT-TERM AND LONG-TERM

Remembering information involves *retrieval* of information that has been stored after it has been perceived and encoded. Information that has just been input is thought of as being in **short-term memory**. Unless the information is manipulated in some way (such as being written down or rehearsed), the memory is not likely to be easy to recall in a few hours or days. The student who reads the textbook but neither takes notes nor discusses the material with a classmate will have difficulty remembering what was read by the time of the exam a week later. If the information is manipulated, it enters the **long-term memory** where it can be recalled at a later time. Long-term memory is the store of information that is remembered after a few minutes, such as information for the next exam, shopping lists, and directions to the campus. It also consists of *remote memory*, where information has been rehearsed so thoroughly that it is very resistant to forgetting. Memorized lines of a poem, one's address when a child, and recollections of life years ago are examples of remote long-term memory.

Two methods for manipulating memories so that they are more likely to be remembered are *chunking* and *mnemonic strategies*. We described chunking earlier, when the memory of chess pieces was described. The information is organized into groups (called chunks) that are remembered. Thus, while the ordinary person's memory span is about seven items (plus or minus two), chunking several items into a single pattern will markedly increase the amount of items that can be remembered (Rebok, 1987).

Mnemonic skills can increase the usual memory span for specific tasks more than tenfold (Chase & Ericsson, 1981). Such strategies do not increase overall memory capacity for unrelated information, however. One such strategy is to organize a list of digits into a meaningful pattern. For example, 4 9 2 7 7 6 9 4 1 could become 1492, 1776, 1941 by adding a 1 before each group of three digits; the meaningless list now can be remembered as a series of historical dates. Similarly, most arithmetic classes taught some variation of the mnemonic "Please Remember My Dear Aunt Sally" to remember the order of mathematical operations when solving an equation (powers, roots, multiplication, division, addition, subtraction). Likewise, medical students have a variety of mnemonics they employ when memorizing the names of bones and other parts of human anatomy.

As a result of experience that allows chunking, practice using mnemonic skills, and the development of study skills, adolescents can show high levels of memory ability. Motivation to remember is probably the most important factor that limits or enhances an adolescent's memory functioning, however.

ATTENTION

Imagine that you are listening to a recording of two different spoken messages played simultaneously in each ear, or that you are watching two different television programs at the same time. If one is instructed to listen to only one message and to repeat it out loud, very little is remembered about the unattended message (Cherry, 1953). Older children and adults are generally better able to pay attention in spite of competing voices than younger children (Doyle, 1973; Sexton & Geffen, 1979).

Most adolescents attempt to divide their attention between different tasks, such as reading a textbook and listening to music, or watching television and cooking. If one of the tasks is familiar and has become automatic, then little attention is directed at it unless something unexpected occurs. The divided attention may affect memory storage, however, by interfering with the rehearsal or manipulation of the information in short-term memory. Thus the student who "reads" the textbook, but was somewhat distracted by television at the same time, may not recall much information from the textbook.

During adolescence and adulthood, attention and the ability to ignore irrelevant information is affected by memory, learning, and intelligence. In general, adolescents become more skilled at selective attention than children; that is, they are better able to focus on the relevant aspects for the solution of the problem (Miller & Weiss, 1981). Moreover, adolescents typically find different aspects of stimuli *perceptually salient*, and they are better able to ignore irrelevant stimuli and focus on the most relevant information compared with younger children. Such skill is important, for example, in driving a car through city traffic (Rebok, 1987).

STRATEGIC PROCESSING

It is usually assumed that people have limited capacity to process information, and the more complex the task, the more of this capacity is used.

Reading a new recipe may require so much of this limited strategic resource, for example, that a cook is unable to do anything else simultaneously, and would be unable to follow a piece of music in the background. However, strategic tasks vary in the amount of strategic resource that they require, with some tasks requiring less than others. . . . Some tasks may demand more of the strategic resource than exists. Playing a new video game may overwhelm novices because they can't process all of the relevant stimuli simultaneously. [Barsalou, 1992, p. 79]

To compensate for this limited resource, a variety of strategies are possible. One, noted above, is selective attention. Another is skill, which leads to *automatic processing* of information, requiring less attention or less of the strategic resource. Another strategy is divided processing in which multiple processors, each designed for different cognitive tasks, are working at the same time. It may be that there is an "executive" function that schedules, monitors for high-level goals, and looks for problems, but most basic information processing is managed by various automatic processes and by various multiple processors. "Consequently, control of information processing is distributed over a variety of control mechanisms, with the executive system providing just one type of control that may be essential for human intelligence" (Barsalou, 1992, p. 91).

Although the model of different levels of processing functions is speculative, it is likely that adolescents are more advanced in strategic processing abilities than younger children. In addition, deficits in executive functioning ability have been proposed to underlie many forms of adolescent maladaptive behavior such as delinquency (Moffitt & Henry, 1989).

DECISION MAKING

In everyday cognition, strategic processing is used for making decisions. Complex decisions obviously involve more information, greater use of the strategic resources of the individual, and benefit from past experience and memory.

Often, however, past experience and memory can lead to incorrect decision making. Several logical fallacies or erroneous beliefs can result from the cognitive process of *framing* or "putting two-and-two together." On one hand, framing can lead to *illusory correlations* by biasing probability estimates. For example, what is the probability of a farmer in Wyoming buying a Toyota? What is the probability of a farmer in Wyoming buying a Toyota truck? Often, people give a higher probability to the second question, because they believe that since a farmer is the buyer, it is more likely that the purchase will be a truck than a car. However, the probability of buying the Toyota brand is not affected by whether it is a car or a truck. On the other hand, framing can lead to *the gambler's fable*, which implies that because a coin has been tossed and has come up heads six times, it will be more likely to come up tails than heads the next time. The odds are still 50–50, of course.

Does decision-making ability increase during adolescence? This complex question involves several of the other aspects of adolescent thinking discussed in this section such as hypothesis testing, planning ahead, and strategic processing. It also involves emotional aspects. As we discuss in the next section, decisions that deal with emotionally important issues tend not to bring out the most highly skilled cognitive abilities. Moreover, egocentrism, the focus of the next section, interferes with decision-making ability.

ADOLESCENT EGOCENTRISM

The failure to distinguish between one's own point of view and that of another person is the most general definition of Piaget's concept of **egocentrism**. In this sense, all persons are likely to be egocentric now and then; it is a part of the human condition, according to Flavell (1985):

> We experience our own points of view more or less directly, whereas we must always attain the other person's in more indirect manners. . . . Furthermore, we are usually unable to turn our own viewpoints off completely when trying to infer another's. Our own perspectives produce clear signals that are much louder to us than the other's, and they usually continue to ring in our ears while we try to decode the other's. It may take considerable skill and effort to represent another's point of view accurately through this kind of noise, and the possibility of egocentric distortion is ever present. [p. 125]

Thus, all thinking is potentially flawed by the assumption that our own point of view is the correct and accurate perspective. In adult life, Flavell (1985) noted, we are all at risk of being egocentric because there is always the danger that our inference about the other's perspective will be influenced by our own point of view. One may notice this when listening to others talk about their problems; there is a frequent tendency to interrupt and say, "I know just how you feel." Actually, it is unlikely that one knows *exactly* how another feels, but if one stifles the urge to interfere in that way and listens carefully, one may come closer to understanding the other's true feelings. In this instance, the thought, "I know just how you feel," would be an example of egocentrism, in the sense Piaget defined it. Note that Piaget's use of this term does not reflect any moralistic or evaluative judgments, as is often the case when one thinks of a person who is "self-centered" (Piaget & Inhelder, 1969).

> To take an example from adult life, every beginning instructor discovers sooner or later that his first lectures were incomprehensible because he was talking to himself, so to say, mindful of only his own point of view. He realizes only gradually and with difficulty that it is not easy to place oneself in the shoes of students who do not yet know what he knows about the subject matter of the course. [Piaget, 1962, p. 5]

William Looft (1972) described many of the forms that egocentrism may take from infancy through adolescence, adulthood, and old age. According to him, much of the progress involved in cognitive development represents overcoming the various forms of egocentrism that are characteristic of each stage. For example, the child (in the conservation of liquids task) who fails to recognize that the amount of liquid in a tall, thin glass is the same as the amount in a short, fat glass is responding egocentrically. The child fails to understand because the perception of that long column of liquid "looks like" a greater amount than in the short column, or the "fat" glass looks bigger than the "skinny" glass; thus, the way one dimension looks overwhelms the child's ability to consider both height and width simultaneously. The child cannot center attention on the perspective that differs from the one that seems obvious. When the child can "decenter" and shift from one perspective to the other, then the fact that height and width compensate for each other can be noted and the task solved.

During adolescence the ability to think about one's own thinking and to consider abstract possibilities frees the person from the egocentrism of childhood but produces new forms of egocentric thought. The egocentric thinking characteristic of adolescence has been described by Elkind (1967, 1978, 1980) in terms of two major themes: the imaginary audience and the personal fable. He also noted other manifestations, which he called pseudostupidity and apparent hypocrisy.

IMAGINARY AUDIENCE

The **imaginary audience** is the belief that other people are preoccupied with the adolescent's appearance and behavior. It is an "audience" because the adolescent feels he or she is the focus of attention. It is imaginary because usually others are not preoccupied with the adolescent (unless he or she makes a point of attracting attention). This form of egocentrism grows out of the adolescents' cognitive ability to think about thinking, to think about other's thinking, and the inability to distinguish between the focus of their own thoughts and the thoughts of others. If the adolescents are concerned with their own behavior, they egocentrically assume that others are equally concerned. According to Elkind (1967), this aspect of egocentrism partly accounts for the high degree of *self-consciousness* often characteristic of early adolescence. Likewise, the desire for privacy that is also typically expressed may reflect the wish to escape from the scrutiny of this "audience." Similarly, feelings of shame, self-criticism, and self-admiration may result from this imaginary audience.

Sometimes adolescents create an audience by loud or provocative behavior, but cannot understand adults' reactions to it.

A good deal of adolescent boorishness, loudness, and faddish dress is probably provoked, partially in any case, by a failure to differentiate between what the young person believes to be attractive and what others admire. It is for this reason that the young person frequently fails to understand why adults disapprove of the way he dresses and behaves. [Elkind, 1967, p. 1030]

Groups of adolescents are amusing in this regard. For, when they come together, each young person is an actor to himself or to herself and a spectator to everyone else. Sometimes groups of adolescents contrive to create an audience by loud and provocative behavior. Because they fail to differentiate between what is of interest to them and what is of interest to others, they cannot understand adult annoyance at their behavior. [Elkind, 1978, p. 130]

Similarly, Elkind (1978) suggested that vandalism committed by adolescents may involve this same egocentric principle. "The vandal is angry and wants to ensure that his or her audience will be angry too. In committing vandalism, the young person has the imagined audience in mind. . . ." (p. 130).

One humorous account of the difficulties of being an adolescent's mother suggested the extent to which this imagined audience behavior may be carried—and also the eventual demise of this form of egocentric thinking:

A 14-year-old of my acquaintance accompanied his mother and younger sister to the stationery store to buy supplies. When he got home, he realized he had bought the wrong paper.
"That's O.K.," his mother said. "I'll just take it back and exchange it."
"Oh, no, don't do that," responded the adolescent with horror. "They'll know I made a mistake, and they'll think I'm stupid."
"Son," said the mother, "somewhere, deep down, you know that's crazy."
"Yes," said the adolescent. And smiled. [Rinzler, 1979, p. C12]

According to Elkind (1967), the egocentrism of adolescence begins to decrease around age 15 or 16. The imaginary audience is gradually replaced by the person's own real audience in the sense that hypothetical reactions of the imaginary audience are tested against the actual reactions of the person's friends and other significant people. Thus, older adolescents gradually begin to separate their own perceptions from the perceptions of others. However, as anyone who has ever dropped a fork on the tile floor of a restaurant has noticed, even adults occasionally feel that everyone is paying attention to them although, in reality, they are not (Elkind, 1978). Thus, the imaginary audience may appear from time to time in adulthood as a reminder of the fact that we are all at risk for egocentric thinking.

Elkind and Bowen (1979) developed a measure of the importance of the imaginary audience, called the Imaginary Audience Scale (IAS), which consists of two aspects. The Transient Self (TS) items refer to potentially embarrassing situations that would happen only once. For example, "You have looked forward to the most exciting dress up party of the year. You arrive after an hour's drive from home. Just as the party is beginning, you notice a grease spot on your trousers or skirt. (There is no way to borrow clothes from anyone.) Would you stay or go home?" (p. 40). The Abiding Self (AS) items refer to potentially embarrassing situations that might occur more than once. For example, "If you were asked to get up in front of the class and talk a little bit about your hobby . . . [check one] I wouldn't be nervous at all. I would be a little nervous. I would be very nervous." (p. 41). Elkind and Bowen asked 697 4th-, 6th-, 8th-, and 12th-grade students to answer these and similar questions. Girls' scores were generally higher (more embarrassed or nervous) than boys' scores

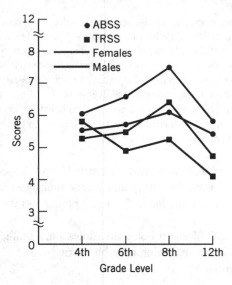

Figure 4.9 Grade-level differences in measures of egocentrism showing Transient Self scale (TRSS) and Abiding Self scale (ABSS) mean score for males and females. [*Source:* D. Elkind & R. Bowen. Imaginary Audience Behavior in Children and Adolescents. *Developmental Psychology, 15,* 38–44, Figure 1. © 1979 American Psychological Association. Reprinted with permission.]

(Figure 4.9). The 8th-grade girls and boys scored higher than any of the other students. This suggested that these 13–14-year-olds were more self-conscious and more nervous about revealing themselves to others than either older adolescents or younger children. Although this does not directly demonstrate that these 8th graders were preoccupied with an imaginary audience, the results are consistent with that interpretation.

Several empirical studies have investigated the imaginary audience phenomenon. In general, evidence has been found that it exists, but the explanation for it has been debated. For example, in a review of research on the topic Buis and Thompson (1989) questioned the link between IAS and adolescent egocentrism. Likewise, Lapsley found no evidence to support Elkind's idea that egocentrism is responsible for the IAS scores; instead, he suggested that the development of interpersonal understanding and perspective taking were better explanations than egocentrism (Lapsley, 1985; Lapsley & Murphy, 1985; Lapsley, Milstead, Quintana, Flannery, & Buss, 1986). Similarly, Cohn et al. (1988) concluded that the IAS appears to be associated with self-consciousness, not with egocentrism. Likewise, Jahnke and Blanchard-Fields (1993) found no support for a link between cognitive development and the imaginary audience.

Nonetheless, evidence of the imaginary audience has been found among many different groups of adolescents, including women first-year university students, perhaps associated with their entry into a new environment (Peterson & Roscoe, 1991), and Native American adolescents (Markstron & Mullis, 1986; Mullis & Markstron, 1986). Other studies have concluded that social experience and socialization are important in explaining IAS scores (Hauck, Martens, & Wetzel, 1986; Hudson & Gray, 1986; Pesce & Harding, 1986) and that education and counseling could encourage the decline of the imaginary audience phenomenon (Hauck, Martins, & Wetzel, 1986).

THE PERSONAL FABLE

A second manifestation of adolescent egocentrism, according to Elkind (1967), is a result of an overemphasis and overdifferentiation of one's feelings and a belief in one's uniqueness. He calls this the **personal fable**, which is the adolescents' belief in their immortal, special, and unique existence. In part, this results from the belief that they are at "center stage" performing before their imaginary audience. It also results from their inability to separate those characteristics that are unique to themselves from those that are common to all persons.

> One example is the daughter who said to her mother, "You just don't know how it feels to be in love;" or a son who says to his father, "You just don't understand how much I need that metal detector." The young person typically believes that his or her feelings or needs are unique, special and beyond the realm of understanding of others, particularly adults. . . .
>
> The reverse confusion is also familiar. This occurs when the young adolescent feels that his or her personal preoccupation and concern is shared by everyone. A young man may feel that his nose is too long, that everyone knows his nose is too long and that everyone, naturally, thinks he is as ugly as he thinks he is. Arguing with him about the fact that his nose is not too long and that he is in fact, good looking, has little impact. [Elkind, 1978, p. 131]

Other examples of this phenomenon may include adolescents who become pregnant, infected with AIDS, or addicted to drugs, because they believed that they were exempt from the risks of conception, infection, and addiction, thinking, "It happens to others, but not to me."

According to Elkind (1978), this personal fable is reduced as adolescents develop intimate friendships, learn there are many shared human characteristics, and realize that they are not as unique as they once thought and feared. This reduces the sense of loneliness that may accompany the personal fable. However, as with the imaginary audience, remnants of these feelings of being somewhat "special" and protected from harm remain during adulthood. It may be that they help one to cope with life in a world of accidents, disease, and personal losses by a belief that bad things happen to others, not to oneself.

As with studies on the imaginary audience, there is little empirical support for the link between cognitive development and the personal fable, but it may be linked with growth in interpersonal understanding (Buis & Thompson, 1989; Elkind, 1985; Hudson & Gray, 1986; Jahnke & Blanchard-Fields, 1993; Lapsley, 1985; Lapsley & Murphy, 1985; Lapsley, Jackson, Rice, & Shadid, 1988; Lapsley, FitzGerald, Rice, & Jackson, 1989).

PSEUDOSTUPIDITY AND APPARENT HYPOCRISY

Two other aspects of adolescent egocentrism were also noted by Elkind (1978). One he called *pseudostupidity*—the capacity to think about many different possibilities, to seek complex motives for behavior, and to overintellectualize trivial situations. "Consequently, young adolescents often appear stupid because they are, in fact, too bright" (p. 129). He gave an example of telling his son about some pizza sauce on the son's left cheek by pointing to his own left cheek; the son kept wiping his right cheek, thinking his father was not thinking of the son's perspective. The cartoon character Charlie Brown often suffers from pseudostupidity.

PEANUTS reprinted by permission of UFS, Inc.

The other aspect of egocentrism Elkind called *apparent hypocrisy*, meaning that young adolescents feel they do not have to abide by the same rules they feel so strongly others must follow. This results in part from the same process as the personal fable: one is unique and different from everyone else. However, it also reflects the young adolescents' new ability to think in terms of abstract principles while, at the same time, they have not yet mastered the ability to move from these principles back to specific situations. He gave as an example a group of young people who were marching to support a particular ecology campaign, but left a massive amount of litter along their path.

These topics have not been studied empirically, but have been found to be present in some adolescent novels (Matter, 1982).

EXAMPLE: ADOLESCENT SEXUALITY

Before concluding this discussion of adolescent thinking, let us briefly illustrate some of the points by examining the relationship of cognitive development and sexuality in adolescence. We will focus much more attention on the topic of sexuality later (Chapter 9).

It would be logical to expect that the capacity to think about abstract ideas and the unique adolescent forms of egocentrism would affect adolescents' development of sexual ideas and thoughts about sexual behavior and love. For example, according to Inhelder and Piaget (1958) even ideas about sexual attraction may be elaborated into romantic fantasies by abstract thinking: "What distinguishes an adolescent in love from a child in love is that the former generally complicates his feelings by constructing a romance or by referring to social or even literary ideals of all sorts" (p. 336).

Unfortunately, there has been very little research on the relationship between cognitive development and these topics during adolescence (Juhasz & Sonnenshein-Schneider, 1987; Pestrack & Martin, 1985). On the one hand, we might expect that the ability to think using formal operations would allow the adolescent to think about sexuality in abstract terms and to separate the various components of sexuality and gender roles in a manner similar to the "combination of liquids" problem described earlier. But on the other hand, adolescents may be unusually concerned about their sexuality and sexual behavior; this concern might affect their ability to think about these topics in objective and logical ways. Thus, they might not use formal operational thinking even if they can because the topic is too personally relevant (Blanchard-Fields, 1986; Covell & Abramovitch, 1988; Mohr, Sprinthall, & Gerler, 1987). Clearly, this area deserves to be studied further (Kramer & Melchior, 1990).

In a similar line of thought, Breese (1978) applied the characteristics of adolescent egocentrism to an analysis of adolescent sexuality. Although his analysis is not based on empirical data, he argued that adolescents fail to distinguish between the thoughts of others and their own thoughts. Thus, being primarily concerned with themselves, adolescents think others are as obsessed with their sexual behavior and sexuality as they are themselves. Moreover, the imaginary audience may be involved in the adolescent's self-consciousness about sexuality. Because it is created by the adolescent, this "audience" knows "what to look for in the way of cosmetic and behavioral sensitivities and sexual inadequacies" (Breese, 1978, p. 276). Thus, feelings of sexual inadequacy, guilt, shame, embarrassment, self-criticism, and bragging about "sexual conquests" each may reflect the adolescent's beliefs about what the imaginary audience expects.

The other aspect of adolescent egocentrism, the personal fable, may also affect sexuality: "Only [I] can suffer so from sexual deprivation, or experience such exquisite sexual rapture" (Breese, 1978, p. 276). Also, the personal fable may affect the use of contraception. Adolescents may not use contraceptives "partly because their personal fable convinces them that pregnancy will happen to others but never to them so they need not take precaution" (Elkind, 1974, p. 94). Cvetkovich (1975) also noted that adolescents may believe that they are sterile because they have had sexual intercourse many times without pregnancy resulting (the sterility fable) or that pregnancy will not result the first time, or the first few times (the gambler's fable). Alternatively, it may be that social experience and perspective taking are better explanations than egocentrism for adolescents' beliefs about pregnancy and sexually transmitted diseases. In either case, we would expect there to be a link between cognitive development and thinking about sexuality during adolescence.

According to Elkind, sexuality also plays a role in resolving these forms of egocentric thinking. That is, social interaction and personal relationships, such as falling in and out of love and the experience of intimacy, are among the processes that help the adolescent gradually develop the ability to differentiate the thoughts of others from those of oneself, while simultaneously integrating the feelings of others with one's own emotions.

In conclusion, the characteristics of adolescent egocentric thinking are based on Elkind's observations, and only the personal fable and the imaginary audience have been demonstrated through empirical research. However, as Elkind (1978, 1985) noted, these concepts may provide useful insights into aspects of adolescent behavior that otherwise might be perplexing. For example, they can provide cues for understanding a variety of behaviors during adolescence such as sexuality, vandalism, self-conscious concern with physical appearance, peculiar styles of dress or taste in music, shyness in speaking publicly, desire for privacy, and risk taking; these concepts may also stimulate additional research on these important topics. Of course, other factors may also be involved in these behaviors, especially in individual cases. Moreover, it appears that cognitive development may not be the best explanation for these phenomenon, and that the development of interpersonal understanding and the process of separation-individuation, discussed in Chapter 2, may be responsible for adolescent egocentrism (Jahnke & Blanchard-Fields, 1993).

We have now completed the description of the characteristics of adolescent thinking abilities. As noted earlier, cognitive development and egocentrism affect all aspects of thought. Thus, everything that adolescents think about may be thought about differently from the way it was conceptualized during childhood. This does not mean that adolescents *always* use these patterns of thinking, but once they are able to use this abstract form of thinking, it allows them to think about everything in new ways. Moreover, because thinking abstractly is new to the adolescent, it may be used just for the sake of using it. However, sometimes the old ways—concrete operational thinking—are adequate for the task, or are used for reasons such as lack of familiarity with the topic or because the topic is too personally relevant. In addition, some adolescent thinking may be different from adult thought because it reflects adolescent egocentrism.

Because so many aspects of the adolescent's life are changing as a result of physical growth, social development, and sexual maturation, this new ability to evaluate social and emotional beliefs is especially important. The psychological significance of the social and physical issues that confront adolescents adds to their inclination to examine them with these new intellectual powers.

Issues that have never or rarely been considered by the adolescent will take on enlarged significance and meaning. Topics of identity, society, existence, religion, justice, morality, friendship, and so on, are examined in detail and are contemplated with high emotion as well as increased cognitive capacity. [Keating, 1980, p. 215]

In the next chapter we focus on some of these social and psychological effects of adolescent cognitive abilities.

CHAPTER SUMMARY

1.   Cognition is the way we think about and know things. Cognitive processes include paying attention to particular stimuli, recalling previous experiences from memory, solving problems, and understanding the physical and social world, including oneself.

2.   Information processing is the cognitive activity that allows one to solve problems, make decisions, organize activities, and cope with everyday situations. Information flows from various inputs through the cognitive system, where it is attended to, transformed into a meaningful code, compared with other information stored in memory, and then output as a verbal response or a memory for later use.

3.   The information processing system may be thought of as consisting of two parts: *structural* aspects that are neurologically based, and *functional* aspects that parallel software and depend on external factors such as practice, familiarity, learned strategies, and computational aids.

4.   Functional aspects, especially cognitive functioning in areas of one's expertise and the growth of information in specific domains of knowledge, clearly increase during adolescence and thereby improve the ability to process relevant information on topics of expertise. Expertise refers to systematic knowledge in which some underlying organizing structure provides keys to perception, procedure, and response.

5.   Sensory inputs are attended to, perceived, and comprehended by the basic processing capacity. Those areas of lesser or greater knowledge are processed differently, with the latter being more likely to involve automatic responses. Self-regulat-

ing processes (metacognition) oversee this information processing and are able to think about thinking and thus to regulate it when necessary, seeking more information (knowledge acquisition), or countering automatic responses that are inappropriate (performance skills).

6.   Information processing abilities grow at different rates in various domains of knowledge based on the individual's talents, experience, and practice. There may be variations in performance between individuals of the same age in their knowledge acquisition, performance, and metacognition skills, and among each individual's domains of knowledge or expertise.

7.   Cognitive achievements that suggest adolescence is a crucial transition in the development of critical thinking are increased automaticity and functional capacity, greater knowledge in a variety of domains of content, wider range and better use of strategies for applying or gaining knowledge, and recognition of the relativity and uncertainty of knowledge.

8.   Piaget discovered that cognitive abilities develop as children grow older. He described an invariant sequence of different types of cognitive organization that defines this process of development.

9.   The term *operation* refers to those actions that a person performs mentally that form a coherent and reversible system. In the stage of concrete operations the child is able to perform a variety of operations on objects that are physically present and on thoughts about such objects. Experiments that demonstrate concrete operational thought include conservation of liquids, substance, and volume.

10.   The period of formal operations involves the mental ability to perform logical operations on the operations of the concrete period. It involves an ability to think about nonpresent objects, the future, possibilities, and hypotheses that are not concrete and present. Experiments that illustrate this period of cognitive development are the balance beam, pendulum, and the combination of liquids.

11.   Not all adolescents, or even adults, seem to reach the more advanced stages of formal operations. It may be that the sophistication of concrete operations, and of formal operations, has been underestimated. In general, there is a range of performance among adolescents when they solve cognitive problems.

12.   There are five major characteristics of adolescent thinking ability from Piaget's perspective: thinking about possibilities, thinking through hypotheses, planning ahead, thinking about thoughts,

and thinking beyond old limits. This does not mean that adolescents always use these patterns of thinking, but they gradually begin to apply them to more and different ideas and situations.

13.   Other characteristics of adolescent thinking ability from the information processing perspective involve greater experience, more efficient memory, and greater skill in selective attention. Strategic processing and decision-making abilities probably also increase overall, but depend on the particular skill involved.

14.   Egocentrism is the failure to distinguish between one's own point of view and that of another person. Empirical research on two major themes of adolescent egocentrism, the imaginary audience and the personal fable, have found interpersonal development to be more important than cognitive development for understanding this phenomenon.

KEY WORDS

accommodation	concrete operations	expertise	metacognition
assimilation	dialectical thinking	formal operations	operation
chunking	domain	imaginary audience	personal fable
cognition	information processing	long-term memory	short-term memory
cognitive processes	egocentrism	mapping	

REVIEW QUESTIONS

1.   What is cognition? List several examples of cognitive processes?

2.   Explain the statement: "The way in which we think about something—whether a physical object, event, or person—reflects the meaning it has for us."

INFORMATION PROCESSING MODEL OF COGNITIVE DEVELOPMENT

3.   Give some examples of how your mind has engaged in *information processing* during the last 5 minutes.

4.   What is the difference between structural and

functional aspects of information processing? How are functional aspects related to *expertise*?

5.   What domains of expertise do you possess?

6.   Cite some tasks that have become *automaticized* for you.

7.   Give some examples from recent television commercials or political ads that are designed to reduce critical thinking by presenting *pieces of knowledge*, or irrelevant information, so one might conclude incorrectly that "I can't tell which is correct."

8.   Describe the various components and their interaction shown in Figure 4.3 in your own words.

9.   What does it mean that "Adolescents may

be thinking based on different metacognitive principles than those of their parents?" Give an example.

PIAGET'S THEORY OF COGNITIVE DEVELOPMENT

10. What is meant by the term *concrete operations*? At what stage of cognitive development does it occur?

11. Explain the significance of the *conservation* tasks in Piaget's research. Can you duplicate these studies with children you know?

12. Describe the early adolescent's thinking abilities at the time concrete operations thinking has been achieved. Why is it called *absolute* reasoning?

13. What are the general characteristics of formal operational thought?

14. Describe the difference between the concrete and formal operational solutions to the balance beam, pendulum, and combinations of liquids problems.

15. Why do many adolescents (or even adults) not use formal operational thinking, according to Gray?

16. What is the evidence that emotional issues

hinder the thinking of adolescents? (Refer to Figure 4.6.)

17. Describe the major point shown in Figure 4.7 (regarding the association between emotional events and cognitive development) in your own words.

ADOLESCENT THINKING ABILITIES

18. List and summarize the five major characteristics of adolescent thinking abilities based on Piaget's theory.

19. List and summarize the five typical characteristics of adolescent thinking abilities from the information processing perspective.

ADOLESCENT EGOCENTRISM

20. What does the statement, "We are all at risk of being egocentric in our thinking" mean?

21. Give some examples of times you have experienced the *imaginary audience*.

22. How may the *personal fable* affect adolescents' risk of auto accidents, pregnancy, or contracting HIV/AIDS?

23. How does adolescent egocentrism affect adolescent ideas about love and sex?

Chapter 5

Social Cognition: Thinking About Social Topics

Cognitive development affects the way we think about other people, our friends, ourselves, and social, moral, and political values. This general topic is called **social cognition**.

> Social cognition is cognition about people and what they do and ought to do. It includes thinking and knowledge about the self and others as individuals, about social relations between people, about social customs, groups, and institutions. [Flavell, 1985, p.159]

In a sense, all thinking is social because we are embedded in a social context and we learn to think within that social context. There is a difference, however, in our thinking regarding physical objects and persons or social interactions. Moreover, we learn beliefs and attitudes in a social environment, and we apply them within a social context. Thus, the focus of this chapter is on the ways in which cognition and cognitive development affect the ways adolescents think about social topics.

In the first section we examine the insights provided by the information processing perspective about the ways in which individuals think and develop expertise in the social domain. In the next sections we discuss the effects of cognitive development during adolescence on three groups of socially relevant topics: conceptions of others, conceptions of oneself, and conceptions of social rules.

INFORMATION PROCESSING PERSPECTIVE

It may be recalled from Chapter 4 that we develop *expertise* within particular *domains* of knowledge. We consider social cognition as a particular set of domains in which one develops varying degrees of expertise through social learning (as discussed in Chapter 2). For example, one develops skills in understanding and interacting with persons of different ages; one's degree of expertise may differ based on the gender or the race/ethnicity of the person. In general, the model is one of increasing expertise based on a broader range of experience as one develops from childhood to adolescence.

The information processing approach to social cognition emphasizes three main questions: (1) What is stored in memory that affects thinking about social topics? (2) How does this stored information affect the processing of new information, judgments, choices, and social behaviors? (3) How is the stored information changed by new information, reflection, and reappraisal? (Sherman, Judd, & Park, 1989). This approach can be applied to any topic in social psychology such as stereotypes, changes in self-concept, and forming impressions of others. Each of these topics may be seen as a domain of knowledge in which one's skill changes with experience and other factors that affect one's ability to process information.

As noted in Chapter 4, the cognitive developmental theory and the information processing perspective may be seen as complementary. Greater recognition of the processes of information processing enhances our understanding of cognitive development; likewise, greater attention to development can enhance the significance of the information processing view.

INFORMATION STORED IN MEMORY

Social cognition, like all cognitive activities, is dependent on a vast storage of relevant information in memory. One type of information stored in memory is the judgments, inferences, and summaries regarding a particular social domain. Some of these memories are recorded moment by moment as the information is presented; others are learned from the teachings and experience of other people. A second type of stored information is the raw data from which the summary judgments are made. That is, one's memory consists both of *abstractions* and of specific *instances*. Thus, when one is asked to think about a "fat man" or a "ballet dancer" or a "Muslim," one might think of a generalized image (abstraction), or a specific person (instance). Moreover, one has *emotional responses* about the social object, which is one way that social cognition differs from cognition about nonsocial objects. When the social object involves oneself, there is also a *temporal dimension*: one has a past and a future in addition to one's present self (Sherman et al., 1989).

STORED INFORMATION AND THE PROCESSING OF NEW INFORMATION

In general, information that is consistent with stored information is more likely to be remembered than is inconsistent information. In this way, stereotypes about individuals and groups are often maintained because information that is consistent with the stereotype (i.e., stored information) is remembered, but information that may disconfirm the stereotype is likely to be ignored or discounted as an exception. Similarly, information that confirms one's self-perception is likely to be remembered, but information that is inconsistent with one's self-perception is likely to be ignored. Likewise, people tend to select social situations that provide information that is consistent with their stored information and to perceive situations that differ as if they were consistent with their expectations (Arkin & Baumgardiner, 1985; Swann, 1984). For example, an American traveling in Europe may expect restaurant menus and service to be similar to those at home and, in England, to have a difficult time getting used to looking out for traffic that travels on the left (instead of the right) side of the road.

These points are based on concepts discussed in Chapter 4. In particular, they are examples of *expertise* and *automaticity* as applied to the social domain. Fiske (1993) described three types of automatic processing that are important for understanding social cognition:

1. *Preconscious automaticity* refers to reactions that are facilitated without awareness of the stimuli or the process and without conscious intervention. An example might be gender, racial, or age-related assumptions about a person whose characteristics are not known, such as the spouse of one's professor.

2. *Postconscious automaticity* occurs when the stimulus is known, but the implications of the stimulus are ambiguous. For example, gender stereotypes or stereotypes about adolescents are triggered by a recognition of the salient characteristics of the person and may lead to automatic, but inaccurate, assumptions about the type of music or activities that the individual enjoys.

3. *Goal-dependent automaticity* is the process by which one's goal determines what is perceived. Consider the situation where you must select classmates for a softball game; then consider the classmates you would select to organize a dance. We generally infer traits to persons based on our goals, and rapid inference makes sense from a pragmatic point of view. To consider all of the relevant person and situation variables requires a great deal more cognitive capacity and effort. If one must make such decisions frequently, one's procedural efficiency may speed up, however.

HOW IS STORED INFORMATION CHANGED BY NEW INFORMATION?

When possible, new information is assimilated into existing structures of knowledge. However, when it is discrepant and compelling, *accommodation* of the existing structures of knowledge may be required. Attitude change, rejection of stereotypes, and reevaluation of oneself or others are examples of this type of accommodation of existing knowledge on the basis of new information. The likelihood of the new information having an impact depends on the nature of the information (e.g., several examples are more impressive than a single case), the nature of the individual (e.g., how open or rigid is the person's attitude), and the nature of the situation. For example, most people would assimilate new information if forced to confront it, but might not accommodate it into their existing knowledge unless they had a chance to reflect, model, or desire the change. Thus, a simple educational lecture might have limited value, but role-playing a situation might have more impact because it personalizes the information. Similarly, having a peer give the information is often more likely to have an effect than when a teacher gives the same information.

Consider, for example, an educational program to promote responsible behavior among adolescents to reduce the threat of infection with the sexually transmitted virus, HIV, associated with AIDS.

Early HIV prevention interventions were primarily information-based, using schools as the vehicle for disseminating information through teacher-administered didactic presentations. . . . The findings on this point are clear. Knowledge about HIV alone is not sufficient to motivate the adoption or maintenance of HIV-preventive behavior. . . . Trained peer educators are a more credible source of information and could serve also as positive role models who could dispel misconceptions that all adolescents engage in high-risk behaviors. . . . Peer-assisted behavioral interventions might lead more readily to the adoption of HIV-preventive social skills through small group interaction, training and through modeling. [DiClemente, 1993, pp. 160–161]

Thus, the information processing view of social cognition is one important approach to provide understanding of a variety of social skills and domains of social knowledge. It cannot be applied, however, without also considering and understanding motivation, group dynamics, learning theory, and individual differences (Sherman et al., 1989). Moreover, social variables such as socioeducational status and cultural background are also important to consider (Schneider, 1991).

As noted in Chapter 4, the information processing perspective does not emphasize age or developmental changes very much. Thus, although social cognition is a very active field (Fiske, 1993), it can currently shed little light on the ways in which adolescents process social information differently from children or adults. To examine these differences, we need to discuss social cognition from a cognitive developmental perspective.

DEVELOPMENTAL PERSPECTIVE

If cognitive development affects the way we interpret the physical world, then it also affects the way we interpret the social world of our daily lives. According to Inhelder and Piaget (1958), "the structural transformation [of formal operations] is like a center from which ra-

diate the various more visible modifications of
335). One interpretation of this idea, supporte
and Eisert (1981), is that formal operations fu
wide area of social and emotional functionin
eas of thinking, regardless of the content of
zational core assumes that emotional and in
For example, we can think of "a personally
cated cognitive levels . . . [or] a sensitive,
conserve volume" (Tomlinson-Keasey & Ei
unusual, however, because both emotional and
derlying organizational core. Thus, this model
emotional development with the general charac
based largely on questions involving physics, su
time, it allows for different levels of understanding ...
tude, and experience.

According to Flavell (1985, pp. 122–125), there are eight trends in the development of
social cognition that parallel nonsocial cognition from childhood to adolescence. These
trends incorporate Piaget's theory with the information processing perspective but emphasize the former because of the focus on developmental themes.

1. *Surface to depth.* Children tend to judge objects on the basis of their surface appearances. Similarly, they tend to pay attention to external characteristics of social interactions,
other people, and themselves. They emphasize physical appearance and behavior, but do not
pay attention to hidden aspects of social phenomena, or the causes that lie beneath the surface. However, adolescents (unlike children) make inferences about the causes and meaning
of behavior and appearances; they look beneath the obvious surface characteristics into the
deeper, covert processes of behavior.

2. *Spacial and temporal centrations.* Younger children pay attention to the present situation. Similarly, young children tend not see through social facades, but take the obvious
message of behavior as the only one. Thus, if a person appears to be very happy, the child
recognizes this, but may not note subtle signs that the happiness is forced and not genuine.
Older children consider what may have happened in the past to produce the behavior, or
what may happen in the future as a result of the behavior. Adolescents can focus on all manner of abstract influences on the behavior or appearance, and they can consider abstract possible consequences.

3. *Invariant formation.* As cognitive development proceeds, children begin to recognize
that many attributes of the person do not change. For example, personality, gender role,
identity, and many other characteristics do not change even though there may be variations
in moods or behavior from day to day. In adolescence, each of these characteristics becomes
understood in the abstract so that a wide range of behaviors can be evaluated and synthe-
sized in terms of these personal characteristics.

4. *Quantitative thinking.* Gradually, children come to think that rewards and punishments
should be determined by what the individual deserves; the criteria to decide this also become more sophisticated with age. Notions of "fair" and "unfair" are involved. Typically,
these involve a quantitative measure of precisely how much is fair. In adolescence, the

ermine what is deserved become more abstract, and the measurement of "fair-becomes less concrete.

inking about thinking (metacognition). It is during adolescence that individuals are cially likely to focus on thinking about their own thoughts, and the thoughts of others. nis thinking about psychological processes is known as *metacognition* and is especially characteristic of adolescence. It may involve heightened introspection, examination of one's own thoughts and feelings, questioning of one's values and beliefs, and concern about the thoughts of importance to other people in one's life.

6. *Abstract and hypothetical thinking*. Also during adolescence, as noted in the earlier points, individuals become able to think about abstract possibilities. This includes oneself, specific individuals, groups, and people in general. In addition, abstract ideas about morality, politics, and religion, as well as about oneself and one's future, all become not only possible, but also compelling social objects of one's thinking.

7. *Egocentrism*. We discussed the particular forms of egocentrism that affect adolescent thinking in Chapter 4. We also noted that egocentrism, in the sense of being distracted by one's own point of view, affects thinking about social phenomena just as it affects thinking about objective tasks in the sort of experiments Piaget developed.

8. *Understanding the sense of the game*. Adolescents and adults (unlike children) know that other people have different perspectives from themselves and that these different perspectives may affect their perception of reality. Often, they find pleasure in playing games that involve understanding—or attempting to guess—the perspective of the other person. Telling jokes, bluffing, and in other ways thinking about the ways other people think and see the world are typical activities of adolescents that reflect this aspect of cognitive development.

According to Flavell (1985), a number of different aspects of social cognition are affected by cognitive development from infancy through adolescence: perceptions, feelings, thoughts, intentions, personality, the self, and morality; he also noted artistic capacities, friendship, empathy, and humor. Other authors include identity, sexuality, political values, attitudes, religious beliefs, and love. Unfortunately, there is relatively little empirical research on the connection between some of these topics and cognitive development. Thus, we will include only those topics most relevant for adolescence and will limit our focus to topics where there has been at least enough research data to warrant discussion. These topics are perception of other persons, concepts of friendship, perception of oneself, one's sense of identity, political ideas, and thinking about moral issues.

CONCEPTIONS OF OTHERS

We begin with a discussion of the development of an adolescent's conceptions of other people. We focus on two aspects: perceptions of other persons, and the development of concepts of friendship.

PERSON PERCEPTION

A study by Livesley and Bromley (1973) of 320 English boys and girls between the ages of 7 and 15 focused on the description of themselves and other people they knew. It was found that younger children, about 6 or 7, focused on general characteristics such as appearance, family, location, and self-referential (egocentric) terms. "She is very nice because she gives my friends and me toffee. She lives by the main road. She has fair hair and she wears glasses. She is 47 years old." (Livesley & Bromley, 1973, p. 214).

In contrast, respondents in middle childhood were found to focus more on personality traits, including attitudes, interests, and abilities, although these were not integrated into an internally consistent impression and the child was probably not aware of the conflict. For example, one 10-year-old said: "She is quite a kind girl. . . . Her behaviour is quite good most of the time but sometimes she is quite naughty and silly most of the time." (Livesley & Bromley, 1973, p. 218).

During adolescence, respondents developed more organized portraits of the person they were describing; this included a broader range of ideas such as the other person's perceptions, contradictory personality traits, and different levels of personality. For example: "She is very reserved but once you get to know her she is exactly the opposite" (Livesley & Bromley, 1973, p. 222). Their study found that the use of *organizing* and *qualifying* statements (e.g., "once you get to know her") were used by over half of the respondents between 12 and 13 years of age, and that such statements increased during adolescence. They also noted that adolescents began to distinguish between observation and inference; interpretations were justified by supporting evidence.

> These subjects have become capable of dealing rationally with systems of psychological ideas; their thinking about other people has become flexible and capable of self-correction; their ideas about other people are functional in the sense that they are connected with the facts of observation and with the demands of personal adjustment. [p. 223]

Further development along these same lines was noted among groups of young adults. For example, one wrote: "She is curious about people but naive, and this leads her to ask too many questions so that people become irritated with her and withhold information, although she is not sensitive enough to notice it" (p. 225).

In summary, Livesley and Bromley (1973) noted six general developmental changes in the description of personality from childhood to young adulthood: greater number of categories; increased flexibility and precision in their use; greater coherence, complexity, organization, and selectivity of ideas; more qualifying and connecting terms; greater ability to interpret and analyze behavior; and more concern with presenting the material in a convincing manner (p. 227).

Other studies on this topic (Shantz, 1983) reported that the increase in qualifying and organizing statements has been found to occur not only between the ages of 12 and 14, but again between 14 and 16 years of age. In addition, this increase indicates an awareness that the adolescent is only one interpreter of the person's behavior and that other interpretations are possible. Shantz also noted that during adolescence people (and their behavior) tend to be described as a product of the interaction of personal characteristics and situational characteristics, which reflects the adolescent's awareness of the factors that interact to produce human behavior (p. 506). This appeared to be particularly true when the person being described is a peer who is liked by the individual giving the description.

There are two problems with these studies that should be noted, however. First, "free" descriptions of individuals, which is the method used in these studies, involve describing persons in one's own words. Thus, increased sophistication in verbal ability and vocabulary may be involved in the age differences in the descriptions. Other methods of studying person perception need to be used to validate these findings. Second, the link between cognitive ability and these characteristics has not been adequately explored. Livesley and Bromley (1973) noted that respondents in higher intelligence groups used more organizing terms than those in lower intelligence groups (p. 206). But does this reflect the level of cognitive development, or other factors? Nonetheless, these data are consistent with the notion that cognitive development affects the way adolescents understand other people.

The information processing approach also has focused research on person perception. It does not take a developmental view, but instead studies the process by which individuals draw upon stored information to make judgments about persons (Sherman et al., 1989). One factor that is important is the *accessibility* of the information to consciousness; for example, vivid memories, prejudices, and personal characteristics affect which memories are drawn upon to interpret one's perception of another person. A second factor is *representiveness*; that is, does the person represent some more general class or group. Of course, this can lead to bias and incorrect attribution of characteristics to an individual. Third, the *predictive utility* of the information is relevant because some information is more useful than others; for example, certain stereotypes are recognized to be false or are invalidated by other aspects of the individual. By stressing the importance of seeing the person accurately, the perceiver is more likely to use information that focuses on the uniqueness of the individual.

CONCEPT OF FRIENDSHIP

Friendship involves a relationship between individuals who like each other; friends are companions who help each other (Berndt & Perry, 1990). A developmental sequence of stages in the way children and adolescents think about friendship represents an important aspect of social cognition. Thus, we discuss this social cognitive aspect of friendship here. Then, because friendship is so important for understanding adolescence, we return to the broader topic in Chapter 8.

Several studies have identified three general changes in descriptions of friends and thinking about friendship from childhood to adolescence: (1) a shift from thinking about friendship in terms of playing together and giving each other goods to more abstract attitudes such as caring for one another, sharing feelings and thoughts, and providing comfort to one another; (2) a change from having the friend satisfy one's own desires to the idea of mutual sharing; and (3) a progression from a focus on concrete behavior, such as being nice, toward greater emphasis on enduring relations in spite of occasional conflicts (Shantz, 1983).

Similarly, Berndt and Perry (1990, pp. 272–274) noted that, although many aspects of

♦ **BOX 5.1   STAGES IN DEVELOPMENT OF IDEAS ABOUT FRIENDSHIP**

Stage 0   **Momentary Playmate**. Child does not distinguish between his/her perspective and friend's perspective; friends are valued for physical and material characteristics. "He is my friend." Why? "He has a giant Superman doll and a real swing set." (Approximate ages 3–7.)

Stage 1   **Assistance**. Child can take other's point of view, but does not recognize the importance of give-and-take reciprocity. "She is not my friend anymore." Why? "She wouldn't go with me when I wanted her to." (Approximate ages 4–9.)

Stage 2   **Fair-Weather Cooperation**. Reciprocal relations and other person's perspective are understood; both parties are seen as necessary for friendship to work. However, focus remains on serving self-interests. "We are friends; she likes me and I like her. We do things for each other." (Approximate ages 6–12.)

Stage 3   **Intimate and Mutual Sharing**. Collaborative relationship with others for mutual interests. Friends share secrets, feelings, and seek to help each other with personal problems. Limitation is that friendship is seen as exclusive and a possessive relationship. "He is my best friend. We can tell each other things we can't tell anyone else; we understand each other's feelings. We can help each other when we are needed." (Approximate ages 9–15.)

Stage 4   **Autonomous Interdependence**. Complex, overlapping system of relationships in which each person gives strong emotional support to the other, but also recognizes the importance of independent relationships for meeting the other's needs. "One thing about a good friendship is that it's a real commitment, a risk you have to take. You have to be able to support and trust and give, but you have to be able to let go, too." (Approximate ages 12 and older)

Source: Based on Selman and Selman, 1979, pp. 71–72; Selman, 1980, pp. 136–142.

friendship have been found in research studies to remain similar during childhood and adolescence, there are three distinctive features of adolescent friendships:

1. Early adolescents view their friendships as intimate and supportive relationships more often than do younger children. . . .

2. Early adolescents regard loyalty or faithfulness as more critical in friendships than do younger children. . . .

3. Under conditions in which competition and sharing are opposed to each other, early adolescents compete less and share more equally with friends than younger children do.

One series of studies by Robert Selman identified five stages in the development of ideas about friendship, based on his interviews with over 250 persons between the ages of 3 and 45 (Box 5.1). In the interviews he presented a dilemma involving friendship to the respondent and asked a series of relevant questions. An example of one such dilemma is: "Kathy has been asked by Jeannette, a new girl in town, to go to an ice-skating show with her the next afternoon. But Kathy has already made a date with her long-time best friend, Debby, to plan a puppet show. To complicate matters, it is clear that Debby does not like Jeannette" (Selman & Selman, 1979, p. 72). Interview questions focused on a number of issues about friendship such as trust, reciprocity, jealousy, and so on. The responses were analyzed in terms of the reasoning behind the individual's answer to reveal the structure of the person's thinking. Often it was necessary to ask for clarification. For example, two respondents said that it depends on how close the friends were. When asked what "how close" meant, the 15-year-old said, "Someone who shares lots of the same values as you," but the 5-year-old said, "If she moves down the street, real close, they can play a lot" (Selman & Selman, 1979, p. 72).

These studies have indicated that there is a progressive age-related development through these stages during childhood and adolescence. For example, in a 2-year follow-up study of 48 children 6 to 12 years old, there was a general progression upward through the stages for 40 of the children, and none reverted back to earlier stages (Cooney & Selman, 1978). In contrast, however, Pellegrini (1986) found a greater range of variability, with almost half of the fourth- to seventh-grade students in the study showing evidence of three different levels of ideas about friendships. Such children may be seen by their peers as disruptive and might benefit from training about friendship reasoning. Similarly, Selman also noted that the level of thinking about friendships did not always correspond with measures of formal operations, at least for some of the adolescents in his study who were referred to a child guidance clinic for problems in getting along with others (Selman, Jaquette, & Lavin, 1977). He attributed this, at least in part, to interpersonal problems that inhibited the development of social concepts.

Selman (1980) also studied individual self-awareness, conflict resolution in friendships, leadership in peer groups, and concepts of punishment in parent–child relations. In each area he described stages that parallel the stages of friendship and form a general model of social-cognitive development in interpersonal understanding. He suggested that these stages reflect several influences, including the periods of cognitive development identified by Piaget, with formal operations coinciding with stage 3 in his model (p. 181). Similarly, Keller and Wood (1989) found that level of cognitive development and social class influenced friendship reasoning over time in a longitudinal study of 9–15-year-olds.

A different method of studying friendship has found a similar progression of stages. Bigelow (1977) had teachers ask 480 students in Canada and another 480 students in Scotland between the ages of 6 and 14 to write essays about what they wanted their best friends to be like. These were analyzed in terms of categories of *friendship expectations*. Some characteristics did not change with age, such as the importance of liking each other. Only those categories that increased in importance with age in both samples were included in the analysis as developmental changes; that is, they were omitted by the younger students, but emerged as a major theme among older students. The analysis indicated there were three separate groups of expectations that became important at different ages. *Stage 1* focused on common activities and being physically near to each other; these expectations tended to focus on superficial aspects of friendships. *Stage 2* emphasized admiration and not violating rules of social behavior. *Stage 3* included empathy, understanding, and disclosures about oneself to one's friend.

Bigelow noted that the majority of students between age 13 and 14 were responding in stage 1 or 2; only 44% described friendship expectations categorized as stage 3. This finding would seem to contradict the idea that adolescents' level of cognitive development is associated with their conception of friendship. He suggested two possible explanations for this apparent discrepancy. One was that adolescents may comprehend more advanced ideas about friendship than they expressed in their written essays. Alternatively, practical social considerations may be more influential in friendships in early adolescence than the adolescents' cognitive skill. Of course, as we noted in Chapter 4, many adolescents do not perform standard tests of cognitive development at the formal operations level, so it is not particularly surprising that adolescents also frequently do not perform at the highest levels of friendship concepts.

One interesting application of these studies is that children and adolescents who have difficulty forming friendships may conceptualize the meaning of a friend at a different level (either higher or lower) than their peers. Thus, counseling that focuses on the development of concepts about friendship may be helpful. Likewise, pairs and groups of close friends may form, in part, because they share similar levels of friendship concepts (Cooney & Selman, 1978).

In conclusion, friendship is a significant aspect of adolescent development, and friendships are involved in the transition from childhood to adulthood in two ways:

> First, friendships themselves are transformed between childhood and early adolescence into more complex, psychologically richer, and more adultlike relationships. Second, friendships have an influence on the changes in self-perceptions, attitudes, and behavior that accompany the transition from childhood to adulthood. [Berndt & Perry, 1990, p. 281]

Thus, the link between the development of ideas about friendship and cognitive development is likely to be interactive. Greater awareness of the thoughts and feelings of one's friends may be influential in increasing one's own level of cognitive development, and vice versa. Similarly, as noted in Chapter 4, intimate sharing with friends may reduce egocentrism among adolescents (Elkind, 1978).

CONCEPTIONS OF ONESELF

In the next section we focus on the development of two aspects of the conceptions of oneself: self-perception and a sense of one's identity.

SELF-PERCEPTION

An important aspect of our lives in American society is the idea that we are unique individuals who possess a **self** that is relatively consistent across different situations, is essentially similar to the self we were at younger ages, and that can be seen by others in generally similar ways to the ways in which one sees oneself. Thus, just as our perceptions of others develop in complexity and abstractness, so also our conception of ourselves would be likely to develop from childhood to adolescence.

In general, the ideas one has about oneself appear to reflect the development of cognitive abilities (Harter, 1990a). On one hand, the content of self-descriptions evolves toward more abstract and differentiated conceptions of oneself as a person. On the other hand, adolescents become more aware of and concerned about their "real" or "false" selves and the inconsistency of oneself in different social situations (such as interacting with one's peers or one's parents).

Adolescents become aware of the inconsistency of a person's behavior in different situations and are concerned about which is the "real" and which is the "false" self.

Self-Descriptions

Livesley and Bromley's (1973) study on the ways children and adolescents in England perceived other people included essays written about themselves. Children around age 9 described themselves in more abstract and sophisticated ways than younger children, but they did not perceive the self as a unified concept. There was little organization or overall structure in these descriptions of the self. For example, one 9-year-old boy gave this description of himself:

> I have dark brown hair, brown eyes and a fair face. I am a quick worker but am often lazy. I am good but often cheeky and naughty. My character is sometimes funny and sometimes serious. My behaviour is sometimes silly and stupid and often good. . . . [Livesley & Bromley, 1973, p. 238]

Adolescents, in contrast, tended to give better organized, more structured, coherent, and consistent descriptions of themselves. They also focused more on beliefs, attitudes, and values. Livesley and Bromley suggested this may indicate the adolescents' attempts to understand themselves and to form a coherent sense of identity. One 14-year-old girl described herself in these words:

> I am a very temperamental person, sometimes, well *most* of the time, I am happy. Then now and again I just go moody for no reason at all. I enjoy being different from everybody else, and like to think of myself as being fairly modern. Up till I was about 11, I was a pretty regular churchgoer (R.C.), but since then I have been thinking about religion and sometimes I do not believe

in God. When I am nervous I talk a lot, and this gives some important new acquaintances a bad impression, when I am trying to make a good one. I worry a lot about getting married and having a family, because I am frightened that I will make a mess of it. [Livesley & Bromley, 1973, pp. 239–240]

As this example suggests, adolescents tended to show greater social awareness than younger children. They focused on the ways others see them, what others think of them, and the effects their behavior has on others. Many appeared to feel they were moody or irritable and were concerned about the effects of this on others. They were also concerned about feeling "different" from others—they wanted to fit in with the crowd, but did not want to lose their identity within the group (Livesley & Bromley, 1973, p. 240).

Damon and Hart (1988) described four developmental levels in the ways in which children and adolescents describe themselves that are similar to the pattern described above. *Level 1*: The self is made up of simple behaviors, moods, or likes and dislikes. *Level 2*: During middle childhood the self is described in comparison with others. *Level 3*: In early adolescence the self is seen in terms of characteristics or social skills that affect one's relations with others or one's social appeal. *Level 4*: In late adolescence, beliefs, one's philosophy and life plans, and inner thoughts are used to describe one's self.

Real Versus False Self

When dealing with "real" and "false" selves, the developmental task is to integrate a variety of different selves into a coherent conception of oneself as a multidimensional person who behaves in different but appropriate ways in different situations. Harter (1990a) described her research findings in terms of a three-stage sequence in the development of a coherent *self-theory*. In these studies, adolescents list characteristics of themselves in various social roles (e.g., with parents, friends, dates, at school, at work), and then identify those characteristics that are in conflict with each other (e.g., depressed versus cheerful; laid back versus anxious).

> The youngest adolescents, ages 11 to 13, detect a few opposing attributes in their self-portraits; however, they rarely report that such opposites cause them conflict. There is a dramatic peak in middle adolescence (ages 14 to 16) in that not only are far more opposites identified, but these opposites generate considerable internal conflict and distress. These adolescents are very troubled over the contradictions within their personality. . . .
>
> Such conflict diminishes considerably among older adolescents. Although these adolescents still identified opposing attributes, there was much less concern, distress, and conflict. Rather, they gave descriptions of how such opposites could harmoniously coexist within their personality. [p. 214]

The increased conflict experienced by the middle adolescents suggests that they can perceive the conflict, but cannot integrate it. They are especially concerned when they behave one way in a particular role, but behave differently in another role (e.g., with the mother versus with the father). The explanation Harter (1990a) suggested is that adolescents develop the ability to detect inconsistencies between social characteristics in midadolescence, but are not able to integrate them into an *abstract system*, where contradictions are seen as normal, until late adolescence.

During midadolescence, the awareness of a discrepancy between one's "true" and "false" self becomes an important concern and one is likely to agonize about which self-characteristics make up the "real me," according to Harter (1990a, pp. 216–217). In her studies, Harter found that adolescents are more likely to display behaviors they regard as false with class-mates or romantic partners, less likely to do so with parents, and least likely to do so with close friends. In interviews, adolescents indicated several motivations for these false self-behaviors:

> (a) significant others encourage or provoke the display of false self-behaviors; (b) one is driven to engage in these behaviors to impress or please others; (c) one is experimenting with the display of attributes and their social impact, particularly with classmates and romantic partners; and (d) one must protect or conceal one's real self out of fear that it would meet with disapproval or not be understood. [Harter, 1990a, p. 218]

Similar characteristics of adolescent thinking about the self were discussed in Chapter 4 as examples of egocentrism. For example, Elkind's (1967) concept of the *imaginary audience* reflects adolescents' focus on the ways others see them and their belief that others are as concerned with the adolescents' behavior and feelings as they are themselves. Likewise, the *personal fable* reflects the adolescents' feelings of being unique or different from others.

However, although adolescents may become better able to think about and describe a more complexly organized sense of self, the *content* of the self appears to remain generally stable during adolescence. Studies of the self-concept, which are based on the respondents' selection of prepared statements that are "like oneself," show few age difference during adolescence (Offer, Ostrov, & Howard, 1981, p. 117; Siegel, 1982, p. 540). These studies refer to the content of the feelings about the self, not about the complexity of the person's thoughts about the self. Thus, there may be more change in the way adolescents think about themselves than in the characteristics they attribute to themselves.

IDENTITY

Closely related to the perception of oneself is one's sense of identity. As we discussed in Chapter 2, according to Erikson (1968) the sense of identity involves a sense of continuity and consistency of the self over time. Thus, it would seem that the capacity for abstract thought, considering hypothetical possibilities that go beyond old limits, and thinking about the future would be very much involved in resolving this issue. For example, Berzonsky and Barclay (1981) argued that:

> Formal-reasoning strategies are necessary in order to experience identity achievement as de-scribed by Erikson [1968]. Specifically, one must be aware of a context of alternatives and pos-sibilities and then actively attempt to examine, consider and choose among them [p. 82].

Marcia (1980), who has defined four modes of dealing with the identity issues of late adolescence, suggested that formal operations is a necessary condition for identity achievement. It is not, in itself, sufficient for achieving identity; but he felt no respondents should be classified in the Identity Achievement mode who did not also show formal operational thinking (p. 180). Similarly, Berzonsky and Barclay (1981) suggested that those individuals who did not use formal operational thinking in resolving identity issues were adopting socially prescribed roles and values instead of working out their own unique identity.

They suggested the importance of using measures of identity achievement that adequately differentiate "formal-achievers" from "concrete-achievers" (p. 83). Similarly, Spencer (1988) argued that cognitive development is important for identity development among African-American adolescents who must distinguish between racial attitudes and personal identity.

However, studies that have focused on the connection between formal operations and identity have been not conclusive. In part this appears to reflect the difficulty of adequately measuring the achievement of formal operations. For example, one study obtained a positive correlation between formal operational thinking and identity (Wagner, 1976). But this relationship increased with age when one measure of formal operations was used and decreased with age when another measure was used; moreover, the two measures of formal operations were not correlated. Other studies have found no relationship between identity and cognitive development (Protinsky & Wilkerson, 1986; Wagner, 1987). However, Chandler, Boyes, and Ball (1990) found that *relativistic* thinking, available to adolescents with formal operational ability, was associated with more mature identity status.

Thus, there is much theoretical support for the link between the achievement of a sense of identity and formal operational thinking (Harter, 1990b). The empirical basis for concluding that this link actually exists is not as strong, however. Further research is needed to clarify this matter, especially with regard to such advanced forms of thinking as relativist thinking and other post-formal operations. We discuss the complex topic of identity development in detail in Chapter 10.

CONCEPTIONS OF SOCIAL RULES

We focus on two aspects of the development of conceptions of social rules: political ideas and moral development.

POLITICAL IDEAS

The effects of cognitive development during adolescence is not limited to the perception of others and oneself. The adolescents' growing ability to think abstractly also affects their ability to understand social and political ideas and to evaluate different systems of government. Research on this topic has focused on age differences in three aspects of political thinking: the quality of political thought, the decline in authoritarianism, and the concept of a perfect society.

Joseph Adelson (1971) studied political ideas among adolescents by asking the respondents to imagine that 1,000 people had migrated to a remote island to form a new society. They had to form a government, set up a legal system, and cope with all the problems of establishing some sort of order. The interview consisted of a number of detailed questions about possible situations that might arise. Using this technique, he and his colleagues interviewed over 400 adolescents between the ages of 11 and 18, reflecting all socioeconomic classes in three Western countries; about 50 of these respondents had been interviewed twice at 2- or 3-year intervals. He found that neither gender nor social class were as significant as age differences in political thought.

There is a profound shift in the character of political thought, one which seems to begin at the onset of adolescence—twelve to thirteen—and which is essentially completed by the time the child is fifteen or sixteen. The shift is evident in three ways: first, in a change in cognitive mode; secondly, in a sharp decline of authoritarian views of the political system; and finally, in the achievement of a capacity for ideology. National differences in political thought, though present, are by no means as strong as age effects. A twelve-year-old German youngster's ideas of politics are closer to those of a twelve-year-old American than to those of his fifteen-year-old brother. [Adelson, 1971, pp. 1014–1015]

The change in *cognitive mode* involved the capacity to use abstract ideas instead of being limited to concrete behavior. For example, older respondents said that the purpose of laws is "to ensure safety and enforce the government"; in contrast, younger respondents said laws exist "so people don't steal or kill." Similarly, older respondents talked about the more abstract concepts of "the community" or "society," whereas younger respondents tended to personalize their ideas of government by speaking of the President or the mayor. In addition, older respondents indicated some awareness of time as an important perspective. That is, they began to grasp the importance of the past in affecting present events, and they could imagine possible future consequences of present events and choices. Younger respondents were less likely to think about long-term consequences, focusing instead on the short-term. Other characteristics of adolescent thinking were also noted among these respondents. Older adolescents expressed a more complex understanding of the causes of behavior, whereas younger adolescents tended to think in more simplified terms of good people and bad people. Older respondents also were more likely to use hypothetical and deductive reasoning, including an analysis of the costs and benefits of various alternative possibilities.

The shift away from *authoritarian* views was evident in the adolescents' responses to questions about law-and-order issues. Generally, younger respondents felt that any measure was appropriate if it stamped out crime. For instance, the younger respondents said hiring police informers, hiding spies in the closets of homes, and having closed-circuit television monitors in public and private spaces would all be permissible to enforce a law against cigarette smoking. "To a large and various set of questions on crime and punishment, they consistently propose one form of solution: punish, and if that does not suffice, punish harder" (Adelson, 1971, p. 1023). In contrast, older adolescents' more critical and abstract views led to an understanding of individual rights, competing interests, long-term outcomes that outweigh short-term benefits, and a balance between goals and the means used to reach those goals. Using an index of authoritarianism, 85% of the youngest respondents were rated high, compared with only 17% of those in their senior year of high school. "The decline and fall of the authoritarian spirit is, along with the rapid growth in abstractness (to which it is related), the most dramatic developmental event in adolescent political thought" (Adelson, 1971, p. 1026).

A third change noted by Adelson and his colleagues was the beginning of an ability to form an *ideology* based on some general principles. He noted that the great majority of adolescents did not form idealized concepts of a perfect society (utopia), nor did they engage in extensive and thoughtful criticism of the present society, or even care very much about ideal forms of government. However, they did develop an understanding of principles that were the basis for a more or less organized set of political attitudes and that formed a basic political ideology. These principles involved individual and community rights that transcended more immediate and concrete solutions. The content of these ideologies typically reflected the influence of parental values as well as the growth of knowledge about politics from a variety of sources. Thus, the gradual development of an understanding of political principles might involve either conservative or liberal views on the balance between community and individual rights.

Another study, by William and Ellen Crain (1974), used a similar interview procedure. They asked 54 boys in Chicago, aged 8, 11, and 16, to establish a new government on an island "where everyone can live together as well as anyone ever could" and classified the responses into four types (Figure 5.1). A more recent study conducted with 6–15-year-old Italian children found four similar types of responses (Berti, 1988). In the Crains' study, *type 1* responses focused on concrete, personally relevant things and people; often they did not even mention government figures until questioned about them. They supported authority, but focused on a personally "close" society. For example, "Over here is a drug store and kids are riding their bikes to the drug store. . . . There would have to be some houses. . . . They would need a grocery store, make it kind of big" (p. 110). This type of response was typical of the 8-year-old boys.

Type 2 responses emphasized governmental institutions, often copying those in the United States, but did not provide any relationship between the institutions or attempt to limit their power by some system of competing authority. They tended to assume that the leader would only do "right" things. One boy said: "Here's the President, he makes the laws, and the Vice-President, he helps. Uh, the Senators, and the Governors are over here. . . ." (p. 110). This response type was most common among the 11-year-old boys.

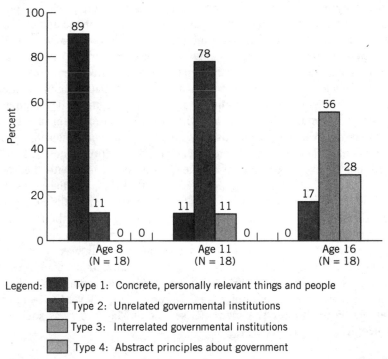

Figure 5.1 Distribution by type of response for 54 boys in three age groups asked to establish a new government on an island where everyone can live together as well as anyone ever could. Type 3 and 4 responses imply formal operational thinking ability. [*Source:* Crain & Crain, 1974, p. 109, Table 1. Data used with permission of the author.]

◆ *Profile*

LAWRENCE KOHLBERG

 The son of a wealthy businessman who had the benefit of college preparatory schools and special tutors, Larry Kohlberg joined the Merchant Marines and traveled around the world after high school. He served on a ship that was smuggling Jewish refugees from Europe into Palestine despite a British blockade, and here he faced the issue of justifying disobedience to the law and authority. This question became the central focus of his lifelong work in moral development.

He attended the University of Chicago and, by taking only final exams (which was then allowed to provide credit for the entire course), completed his bachelor's degree in 1 year. While pursuing his doctoral degree at the University of Chicago, he encountered Piaget's work on moral development. This model of moral thought that gave central place to the individual's cognitive development was the basis for Kohlberg's 1958 doctoral dissertation and remained his primary focus. His straightforward research methodology involved presenting moral dilemmas and noting what respondents said about them. Initially, he described six basic stages, which were refined and elaborated upon for the next 30 years. A 20-year follow-up longitudinal study of his dissertation subjects and the publication of a revised scoring system culminated this work in 1981.

He taught at the University of Chicago (following a brief appointment at Yale) until 1968, when he joined the faculty at Harvard University Graduate School of Education. He was a pioneer in the field of social cognition, arguing that cognitive development was the key to understanding gender role identity and virtually all other topics in social development in addition to moral development. He also described ways in which education can influence moral development without indoctrination of any particular set of values. His focus on the role of justice and of principled civil disobedience was consistent with the social and political movements for civil rights during the 1960s and 1970s. During the 1980s, he was heavily involved in moral education and, along with colleagues, started the *just community* approach in schools and prisons; he also commuted on a weekly basis to the Bronx, New York, where he had instituted moral development projects in two inner-city schools.

On January 17, 1987, he was reported missing; his body was eventually found in marshlands bordering Logan Airport in Boston. He had suffered since 1973 from a disease, contracted on a trip, that sapped his energy and made him continuously dizzy and nauseated; he suffered severe pain, disability, and depression for 13 years. He apparently ended his life at age 59 by drowning. A memorial service in May 1987 was attended by several hundred people.

[*Source:* Based on Rest, J., Power, C., & Brabeck, M. (1988). Lawrence Kohlberg (1927-1987). *American Psychologist, 43,* 399–400.]

Type 3 responses emphasized the ways in which the institutions were interrelated. The goal was to have a well-organized government that would make the society function. "The big word is agreement. In order to have a government and a people, you have to have harmony between them, and in order to have harmony, you have to have agreement. You can't have conflict because it won't work" (p. 115). This type of response was most common among the 16-year-olds.

Type 4 responses involved the consistent use of abstract principles such as: "My government would be based on the principle that the government is there to serve the people, rather than the other way around, so I would, of course, have all the officers elected . . ." (p. 111). Only five respondents provided this type of response, and they were all in the 16-year-old group.

The authors suggested that type 3 responses involve some characteristics of formal operational thinking such as structuring both hierarchical and horizontal relationships (e.g., checks and balances). However, type 4 responses more clearly demonstrate formal operational thought in the use of abstract principles (Crain & Crain, 1974, p. 118).

Obviously, political attitudes of adolescents involve many influences in addition to cognitive factors. Additional research is needed on the development of political thinking in adolescents, especially from an information processing perspective (Torney-Purta, 1989). However, the studies described here illustrate the relationship between political ideas and adolescent thinking abilities. Moreover, these studies reflect the importance of cognition for understanding one's relationship within the broader social structure of society. We follow this theme in the next section with a focus on moral development.

MORAL DEVELOPMENT

The final example we discuss of the effect of adolescent cognitive development on social ideas is thinking about moral issues. This topic, known as **moral development**, has received much more empirical research than other topics in this section on social cognition. As a result, there are many diverse and competing views of moral development that are too complex to be summarized here. Therefore, we focus on one approach to the study of moral thinking that has been directly influenced by the cognitive developmental theory of Piaget. This view, proposed by Lawrence Kohlberg (1958, 1981, 1984), has provided a major focus for research in the general area of moral development.

Kohlberg, attempting to avoid the conflicting views about what specific behavior is right or wrong, focused his attention on the structure of thought about moral issues, not on the content of moral values. Thus, he asked children, adolescents, and adults to respond to a variety of moral dilemmas by asking them specific questions that tapped their thinking about the problem. One of these hypothetical dilemmas involved a man named Heinz whose wife was dying of cancer and needed an expensive drug that the local druggist could provide at a very high cost; unfortunately, Heinz could not afford it. Heinz broke into the store and stole it. The respondents were asked whether Heinz should have done that, and also a number of other relevant questions. On the basis of a complex scoring system, their responses were evaluated according to the level of moral thinking that was involved. In the two decades after Kohlberg developed his scoring system, he modified various elements of each level of response. The latest scheme consisted of six stages, divided into three levels (although he has also suggested the possibility of a more advanced seventh stage; Kohlberg, 1981, 1984). These are summarized in Box 5.2.

◆ BOX 5.2 THE SIX STAGES OF MORAL JUDGMENT PROPOSED BY KOHLBERG

Level A. Preconventional Level

Stage 1. The Stage of Punishment and Obedience
Right is literal obedience to rules and authority, avoiding punishment, and not doing physical harm. The interests of others are not considered; they are not recognized as possibly differing from one's own. Actions are judged in terms of physical consequences.

Stage 2. The Stage of Individual Instrumental Purpose and Exchange
Right is serving one's own or other's needs and making fair deals in terms of the exchange of concrete things or services. Conflicting individual needs are recognized and are dealt with through giving each other equal treatment and earning each other's goodwill.

Level B. Conventional Level

Stage 3. The Stage of Mutual Interpersonal Expectations, Relationships, and Conformity
Right is playing a good (nice) role, being concerned about other people and their feelings, being loyal and trusting with partners, and following rules and expectations. The focus is on individual relationships, shared feelings, agreements, and expectations that are more important than individual interests. One places oneself in the other's shoes. There is no consideration of a generalized social system, however.

Stage 4. The Stage of Social System and Conscience Maintenance
Right is doing one's duty in society, upholding the social order, and maintaining the welfare of society or the group. The social system defines roles and rules. The person at this stage takes the viewpoint of the system and considers individual relations in terms of the social system.

Level B/C. Transitional Level

This level is postconventional, but not yet principled. Choice is personal and subjective; it is based on emotions, ideas of "duty" and "morally right" that are arbitrary and relative. The person at this transitional stage takes the viewpoint of one who is outside the system making decisions without commitment to society; one can pick and choose obligations, but there is no principle that governs the choices.

Level C. Postconventional and Principled Level

Moral decisions are generated from rights, values, or principles that are (or could be) agreeable to all individuals within a society that is fair and beneficial.

Stage 5. The Stage of Prior Rights and Social Contract or Utility
Right is upholding the basic rights, values, and legal contracts of a society, even when they conflict with the concrete rules and laws of the group. The person at this stage considers the moral point of view and the legal point of view, recognizes that they conflict, and finds it difficult to integrate them. The viewpoint is that of a rational individual who is aware of values and rights that may conflict with social attachments and contracts.

Stage 6. The Stage of Universal Ethical Principles
This stage assumes guidance by universal ethical principles that all humanity should follow. The basic moral premise is respect for persons as ends, not means. When laws violate universal ethical principles, one acts in accordance with principles such as justice, equality of human rights, and respect for the dignity of human beings as individuals.

Source: Based on Kohlberg, 1981, pp. 409–412.

These stages of moral development have been examined using both cross-sectional (by age) and longitudinal studies, some in a number of different cultures. For example, urban middle-class boys, aged 10, 13, and 16, in the United States, Taiwan, and Mexico were studied (Figure 5.2). The 10-year-old boys responded more often with stage 1 thinking than with stage 2, and more often with stage 2 than stage 3, and so on. In contrast, 16-year-old boys

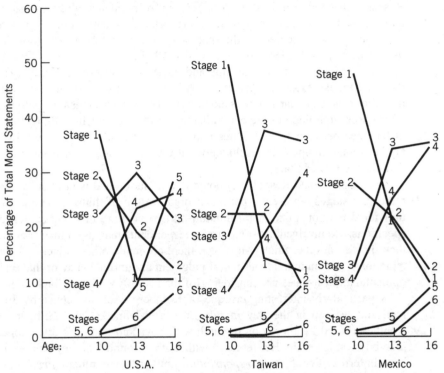

Figure 5.2 Moral development of middle-class urban boys in the United States, Taiwan, and Mexico. At age 10, the stages are used according to difficulty. At age 13, stage 3 is most used by all three groups. At age 16, U.S. boys have reversed the order of age-10 stages (with the exception of 6). In Taiwan and Mexico, conventional (3–4) stages prevail at age 16, with stage 5 also little used. [*Source:* Figure 1.1 from *Essays on Moral Development (Volume 1)* by Lawrence Kohlberg. Copyright © 1981 by Lawrence Kohlberg. Reprinted by permission of HarperCollins Publishers, Inc.]

reversed this order, except that few responded with stage 6 concepts. Kohlberg (1981) noted that stage 6 has been redefined since these data were analyzed and that stage 6 is now "a rare stage of adult development rather than something found and scored among young adolescents" (p. 5). In fact, his later data indicated that stage 6 responses occurred among less than 5% of adults (p. 192). Moreover, a longitudinal study of 50 working-class and middle-class boys between the ages of 10 and 16 first interviewed in 1955 and at 3-year intervals indicated that responses were typically at stages 2, 3, and 4 at age 16–17; there were no stage 5 modes of response until the boys were in their 20s. This longitudinal study is important also because it indicated that the boys did develop through the stages, without skipping any or reverting back to lower stages over the time of the study (pp. 255–256). Other longitudinal studies, as well as cross-sectional studies, also found general upward progression through the stages with increasing age (Carroll & Rest, 1982).

Theoretically, formal operational thinking is associated with stage 4 of moral development. The ability to think in terms of abstract ideas would be necessary to consider such abstract concepts as the social order or social system that defines roles and rules, for example.

Research that has examined the link between respondents' ability to use formal operations and moral development has generally supported this connection, although the results have depended, to some degree, on the specific measures of formal operational thought that were used (Carroll & Rest, 1982, p. 441; Zeidler, 1985).

There are a number of problems and questions concerning Kohlberg's scheme. Among these are the issues about whether stages 5 and 6 are as universal across different cultures as the other stages; perhaps there is an American or Western bias built into these stages (Crain, 1992). Research findings are contradictory on this point: Chiu (1990) found that there were differences between United States and Chinese school children in Taiwan; Hau and Lew (1989) found comparable results between Chinese students in Hong Kong and Kohlberg's data for the United States.

Also, Carroll and Rest (1982) noted that an individual is not "in" a particular stage, but rather the stages represent a particular organization of thinking about moral issues and an individual may organize moral thinking in two or more different stages, depending on the specific issues involved. At some times, respondents may use a much lower level of thinking than they do at other times. Moreover, there are many other influences—such as family interactions—on an individual's moral judgment and moral behavior that this cognitive-developmental analysis does not consider (Hoffman, 1980; Walker & Taylor, 1991).

A particularly interesting critique of Kohlberg's scheme concerns differences between men and women in the way moral issues are defined. Carol Gilligan (1982) noted that Kohlberg based his theory on research with boys and that girls often appear to score lower than boys on his scale. Her research with women found that they tend to define moral problems in terms of conflicting *responsibilities* rather than conflicting *rights* (as in the Kohlberg scale). That is, women tend to make moral judgments on the basis of a recognition of interconnected human relationships in which each person has a responsibility for others and cares for their welfare. This is shown in an **ethic of care** that she found to be more characteristic of women than of men. In addition, she suggested that women tend to make moral decisions based on pragmatic rather than abstract considerations, preferring to attach names and faces to the persons involved in the moral dilemma; are reluctant to speak out because they might hurt others whom they care for; and suspect that their voice would not be listened to even if they did speak. For all of these reasons their performance on the Kohlberg scale may appear to be "inferior" to that of men, but in reality it may be a different, but equally significant, moral voice. Empirical studies are only beginning to explore this perspective. One study with 233 participants between the ages of 5 to 63 years over a 2-year interval found support for Kohlberg's stage model (Walker, 1989). Responses were scored according to both Gilligan's and Kohlberg's models, and little relationship was found between the two scales. Also, very few gender differences were found in either measure, although there were clear developmental trends on both measures. Thus, gender differences may not be as significant a critique as Gilligan suggested. Nonetheless, she may have identified a different dimension of moral development that is important to consider.

In conclusion, the relationship between cognitive development and adolescents' thinking about social ideas is by no means fully understood. As noted in Chapter 4, formal operational thinking does not appear to be used by all adolescents, or even all adults. Whether this reflects an inability to measure this thinking process, sociocultural and educational factors, or the absence of a universal developmental progression to this stage is not known. If, in fact, a large proportion of adults do not reach formal operational thinking, then it can hardly

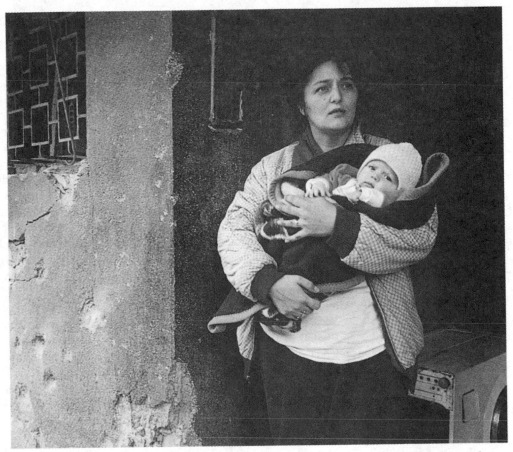

Women tend to make moral decisions based on pragmatic rather than abstract considerations and suspect that their voice would not be listened to even if they did speak.

be considered as a prerequisite for adolescent social development. Blasi and Hoeffel (1974) argued that concrete operational thinking is adequate for typical adolescent functioning and suggested that factors other than cognitive development are responsible for social development in adolescence.

> In fact, one of the main characteristics of adolescence, perhaps the central one, consists precisely in a new subjectivity, i.e., in moving away from the external world and in making the inner world the focus of one's experience. [p. 359]
>
> These developments appear to consist more in a change of perspective, in a shift of focus and in the formation of new attitudes than in the acquisition of entirely new cognitive skills, as the explanation in terms of formal operations would imply. [p. 360]

In their view, formal operations may enhance these self-reflective abilities, but they do not define or produce them. Thus, formal operational thinking may be required for solving various physical problems, but it is not required for dealing with complex social and psychological issues, according to Blasi and Hoeffel. This idea is consistent with the information processing perspective: individuals may differ based on their experience and expertise in various domains of social cognition, but the concept of formal operations does not shed much light on the important factors in information processing.

Similarly, Lapsley (1990) noted that "there are important developments in social cognition during adolescence, but they simply cannot be counted on to occur during early adolescence" (p. 197). Instead, although changes are taking place, their occurrence is gradual rather than sudden. Moreover, they are likely to vary quite a bit from one individual to another.

This point of view is consistent with the idea discussed earlier in this chapter that cognitive abilities form an organizational core of human functioning that affects all aspects of behavior mediated by cognition. Likewise, the development of thinking is not identical with emotional development; instead, the two aspects of adolescent development interact, as discussed in Chapter 4 (Haviland & Kramer, 1991). Thus, cognition helps adolescents understand their emotions, themselves, and their relationships. In turn, these relationships and emotional experiences enhance cognitive development by reducing egocentrism and providing opportunities for the growth of social cognition.

In the following chapters we focus attention on the noncognitive psychosocial influences such as the adolescent's social environment, schools, relations with parents, peers, sexual feelings, and issues of identity. The concepts in this chapter nonetheless provide a framework for understanding these diverse topics because, in an important sense, the way an adolescent thinks about these ideas gives them their meaning.

Following this chapter is our first interlude, an interview with Sarah, a 12-year-old girl. Throughout the interview her use of cognition and social cognition is apparent, especially as she discusses her self-perception and her friends.

CHAPTER SUMMARY

1. Social cognition is thinking about people and their social activities. It includes thinking about oneself and others, about interpersonal relationships, group relations, social institutions, beliefs, and attitudes.

2. The information processing view of social cognition focuses on a person's thinking about social topics as a domain of knowledge in which each individual has some degree of expertise, based on past experience and learning.

3. Memory is the basis for social cognition. It consists of abstract judgments, inferences, and summaries of social information as well as specific instances of social events and persons. Memories about social events often tend to involve emotional

responses and, if oneself is involved, they may include a temporal dimension.

4. Social cognition often involves automatic processing, which can lead to erroneous or stereotypic reactions. Preconscious automaticity occurs when the social stimulus is not known; postconscious automaticity occurs when the stimuli is ambiguous; goal-dependent automaticity occurs when the demands of the goal are the basis of the judgment.

5. New social information can change information stored in memory if the information is compelling, the individual is open to change, and the situation prompts acceptance of the information (such as by providing a peer model or encouraging role-playing to personalize the information).

6. Cognition may be seen as an organizational core in that cognitive development affects the way one thinks about all objects of thought, both physical and social, including thoughts about other people, one's friends, oneself, social ideas, and political values.

7. The development of social cognition from childhood to adolescence includes the following changes: greater focus on underlying characteristics of persons and situations, on future consequences of behavior, and on the continuity of some characteristics of persons. It also involves more abstract ideas of fairness, thinking about thinking, hypothetical ideas about oneself and others, adolescent egocentrism, and understanding other people's perspectives.

8. Adolescents, in comparison with younger children, tend to describe other people in more organized verbal portraits and to include a broader range of concepts. These concepts include contradictory personality traits, different levels of personality, and a greater understanding of the factors that interact to produce human behavior.

9. There is a developmental sequence of stages in the way children and adolescents think about friendship. Adolescents think about friendship in terms of abstract attitudes such as caring for one another, sharing feelings and thoughts, providing comfort to one another, mutual sharing, and emphasizing enduring relations in spite of occasional conflicts.

10. Adolescents tend to give better organized, more structured, coherent, and consistent descriptions of themselves than do younger children. They also focus more on beliefs, attitudes, and values and show greater social awareness. Adolescents focus on the ways others see them, what others think of them, and the effects their behavior has on others.

11. During middle adolescence, contradictory aspects of oneself are recognized but are often not integrated into an abstract conception of oneself in which it is normal to have contradictory characteristics. Many adolescents therefore are concerned by the distinction between real and false self-presentations to others.

12. The use of formal operational thinking is believed to be necessary for achieving a sense of identity, or a sense of continuity and consistency of the self over time. However, empirical data on this idea are inconclusive.

13. The adolescents' growing ability to think abstractly also affects their ability to understand social and political ideas and to evaluate different systems of government. This involves the use of more abstract ideas, a decline in authoritarian views, and the beginning of an ability to form an ideology based on some general principles.

14. Kohlberg's view of moral development focuses on the structure of thought about moral issues, not on the content of moral values. His model consists of six stages, with stage 4 associated with formal operations. Gilligan proposed an alternate model to the view that morality is based on competing rights, by focusing on an ethic of care.

KEY WORDS

ethic of care

moral development

organizational core

self

social cognition

REVIEW QUESTIONS

1. Give several examples of topics that would be considered to involve social cognition.

INFORMATION PROCESSING PERSPECTIVE

2. Recall the discussion of social learning in Chapter 2 and discuss how it applies to the development of expertise in social domains of cognition.

3. Assume you just met a rude, pushy young man. Describe the *abstract* judgments and inferences you might make, based on the information stored in your memory. Can you think of an *instance* of such a person? What is your *emotional* response?

4. Give an example of a stereotype that is likely to result from *postconscious* automatic thinking.

5. Why is goal-dependent automaticity a potential liability for an adolescent who is looking for a date to the school dance?

6. Describe why an HIV/AIDS educational program is likely to be more successful in changing the information stored in memory if it is conducted by peers and involves role-playing exercises.

DEVELOPMENTAL PERSPECTIVE

7. Imagine the *organizational core* of cognitive development as if it were the hub of an old-fashioned wheel with spokes and with the rim representing social cognition. Draw the diagram. Think of the spokes as representing the interaction of emotional and cognitive factors. Is the "wheel" round, or are some spokes "longer" than others?

8. Give an example of each of Flavell's eight trends in the development of social cognition from childhood to adolescence.

CONCEPTIONS OF OTHERS

9. Summarize the changes between childhood and adolescence in the use of organizing and qualifying statements with regard to perceptions of others.

10. Compare the models of change in friendship perceptions proposed by Shantz and by Berndt & Perry with the stage theories of Selman (Box 5.1) and with Bigelow's three-stage model of friendship expectations. How do these models overlap? In what ways do they differ?

CONCEPTIONS OF ONESELF

11. Give examples of each of the four levels in Damon and Hart's model of self-descriptions.

12. What is the cognitive explanation Harter provides for the dramatic peak in recognition of opposite characteristics in oneself that result in considerable internal conflict during middle adolescence?

13. Give some examples of false *self-behaviors*. How are they related to the imaginary audience discussed in Chapter 4?

14. Why is it thought that formal operational thinking is necessary for an adolescent to develop a sense of identity?

CONCEPTIONS OF SOCIAL RULES

15. Describe and give some examples of the change in cognitive mode in adolescents' development of political ideas, based on the Adelson study.

16. What other changes in political thinking were identified in the Adelson study?

17. In the moral dilemma proposed by Kohlberg, do you think Heinz should have stolen the drug? Why or why not? How do your responses compare with the stages shown in Box 5.2? Is it difficult to place your answer into a single stage?

18. Why is moral development thought to be related to cognitive development? To formal operations?

19. Summarize the data presented in Figure 5.2 (moral development levels of boys in three countries) in your own words.

20. Explain Gilligan's idea that some people base moral decisions on an *ethic of care* instead of a model of conflicting *rights*.

Interlude

◆

Sarah, Age 12

◆

"I don't want to die and know that my life didn't make a difference."

Sarah was an early adolescent white girl at the time of the interview with one of the coauthors (DK). She lives in an affluent suburban community with her parents and had recently returned from a trip to Paris with her mother. She is intellectually advantaged in terms of her school and family environment; she also is somewhat more physically mature than her age-mates and classmates. She has an extensive friendship network, mentioning 11 different people, including best friends (Sally and Jackie) and one good friend (Paul). Her relationships with her parents and younger sister are also friendly and apparently free of unusual conflict.

This interview provides an insight into early adolescence, where the developmental issues center on accepting how one looks and learning to use one's body and mind effectively, according to Havighurst (see Chapter 1). Also, we may see how the social context of Sarah's life affects her experience of adolescence (see Chapter 2). Moreover, this interlude illustrates many of the themes of cognitive development and social cognition discussed in Chapters 4 and 5. Sarah is skilled in many domains of information processing and shows the most advanced levels of concrete operational thinking. There are occasional glimpses of formal operational abstract thought, but as intelligent as Sarah is, the types of adolescent thinking discussed in Chapters 4 and 5 have yet to emerge fully. In particular, it is instructive to note her level of social cognition, such as the description of friends and her own self-perceptions.

How old are you now? Twelve. *What kind of school do you go to?* Public school, middle school, grades six through eight. *What grade are you in?* I'll be in the eighth in September. *How do you feel about school?* I like it. *What about the other students, do you like them?* Most of them, all but a couple. *What about your teachers, do you have favorite teachers, any you dislike?* I like all my teachers except for one. *Which one don't you like?* Mrs. J., she's my English teacher. *What about activities at school? Are there any you particularly like?* This year I did debate team and the school paper for my activities, and I do the Idea Program, which is like the gifted program at my school during my lunchtime, and I do the after-school sports, but at my school there are no serious sports, but one of my best friends is running for class president next year so maybe we'll get some serious sports then.

What are the subjects in school that you enjoy the most? Art, Math, the Idea Program, probably English, and French is okay I guess. *You said you're in the Idea Program for gifted students. Tell me about that.* Well, let's see, there are about five classes in Idea, and we have this during our lunch period instead of lunch and then study hall, so it's a 40-minute period, and I think there are like 40 kids in the program, and the Idea Program, uh, our school runs from kindergarten to ninth grade, and some of it is the best program in the state, and this year we did futuristic problem solving as our topic and we had teams, and we had to do problems, like we had terrorism, medical technology, students dropping out, and that was it. And also last year we did relativity and time.

How many students are in your school all together? Six hundred about, give or take a few. *Do you have plans about your future studies?* Um, well, what do you mean by that? *Are you going on, I assume, to high school?* Yes, I'm going to high school. *And then what?* Well, in high school I want to be in all the honors classes, because then you can get a higher than 4.0 average in this town, and so that's one of my goals. *What kind of an average?* Higher than 4.0 if you're in all honors classes. Obviously I want to go to college; I don't really know where I want to go, I'd like to go with one of my friends, Kathy, though. She wants to go to Stanford, but I think she should go to the best school she's accepted to. This year she took SATs, we took the SATs in the Idea Program, and she scored 1020.

Do you have a best friend? In a couple of different states I have; yes I'd say that um, I only have one best friend, she's in Utah, she moved this year, or if you want to stay in town I'd have to say Sally; she's a good friend. *Your best friend that moved to Utah—how long did you know her?* Well she lived on our street in third grade and that's how I met her, then we became better friends in fourth grade, and through fifth, sixth, and seventh we were best friends. *Was she kind of a special chum?* Yeah, I guess so. *But now she's moved away.* She moved January 29th; I had a going-away party for her here. *Do you still keep in touch with her?* Yes, I've written to her a lot of times. She came here a couple weeks ago, I think; her brother's graduation—it was June sometime. Her brother's up at Lake Placid for a special sports academy and he just graduated so she went up there and she stopped back here on her way back to Utah.

So, do you have any best friends now, just the one? Let's see, Sally, she's one of my best friends, and I guess one of my guy friends, Jackie, they're both really good friends. They're who I talk to the most and do the most things with. *So one of your best friends is a girl, and one is a boy?* Yes. *What do you like to do together?* Swim, I don't know, we do different things all the time. Like, let's see, the

last weekend I was here before I went to Paris, they were over here swimming on Saturday, and Friday and we were at Paul's house and we played basketball and listened to music; it just depends on what we want to do, go out for pizza.

Are you part of a kind of social group of some sort? At school there really are no tight groups, I wouldn't say so at school, but I'm with the church down the street, they have a youth group that I go to every Tuesday night, but there's nothing really with school. *Are you involved with friends in other activities than the youth group, anything else?* Yeah, Sally, Yves, and I are signing up for windsurfing lessons down at the beach. That's the sort of "come as you are" for the first lesson, then they do whatever you haven't done the next day. Let's see, I'm supposed to be working out for softball all this year and next year I'm going to try out for the all-star team in Bellport, because our school wasn't much for sports so you have to go outside the town for that, and also we belong to a tennis club and I do tennis up there, but it's sort of a family club, not necessarily your friends.

What do you think makes a good friend? Let's see, well, gotta be smart, because it's easier to carry on a conversation. And someone who's definitely nice, not a hypocrite. Most of my friends have pretty good senses of humor I guess. Someone I can talk to, and someone who actually does things and not just be sort of like, "I don't know what I want to do, I don't know what I want to be, I don't know what I want to do with my life"; someone who has some goals.

Are there some things you talk to your friends about that you don't talk to your parents about? Yeah. *What kind of things?* Um, to start with, music, because my parents listen to country music. And I guess what we're doing in school because I mean, my parents know about it, but if I want to talk about a certain teacher or something, I guess I'd talk to my friends about that, and um, if we're talking about our other friends I guess I'd turn to them rather than to my parents.

Are there some things you can talk to your parents about that you can't talk to your friends about? Yes. *Like what?* Well, my mom does a lot of politics in this town, and besides Sally, none of my other friends really know about that. So politics is a topic that we can talk about, because politics doesn't usually come up in conversations with my friends. The other things I can talk about with my parents I can talk about with my friends; basically it's the same between my friends and my parents.

Tell me a little about your family, do you have brothers and sisters? I have one sister, 20 months younger than me I think, yes, 20 months. *How do you get along with her?* Just fine, I get along better with her now than I used to, 'cause I guess since we're both older. And I guess I get along with her friends, one of her friends, Linda. My sister is Cindy; she's Jan; and I'm Marsha—like from the "Brady Bunch." That's like a joke we have. And when Linda is spending the weekend out at our house and so is my friend Kathy, we had like a Brady Bunch sleepover and we watched all the Brady Bunch reruns. *So you get along with her pretty well, she joins in your activities and you in hers?* A fair amount, but not like everything I do I do with my sister, but she knows my friends and they know her.

Some people feel that their relationship with their parents changes as they grow up, others say no; what about you? I guess so, because my parents, I guess they're more at my level now and I'm not the little tiny one that has to always look up to them, and I can tell them what I'm really thinking. I don't have to agree with everything they say, and I can actually carry on a conversation with them that's a conversation you wouldn't have with them as a little kid. *You feel you can actually talk to them now, that you're on an equal level. How long has that been the case?* I don't know, a couple of years, from maybe fifth grade.

Have the rules changed now that you've grown up a little? There aren't that many rules that I have to follow. We can swim in the [backyard] pool when there's someone at home rather than having to have someone outside [in case of emergency]. I don't have a babysitter anymore. I've never really had a bedtime but I go to bed basically the same time every night, and it gets a little later year by year, but there's never any actual rule about that.

What about going out at night? Um, I have to come back. *Any special time?* Well, I have to tell them what I'm doing, and they haven't actually said, "You have to be home by this time," 'cause they know I won't stay out forever. The latest I've ever been out was 11 o'clock, and that's not too late because if they know where we're going to be then that's fine.

Do you find that you have more things you wouldn't discuss with your mother now that you're getting older? Not really, I mean, I don't really see any difference. *What about your father?* No. *How is your relationship with your mother?* I don't hate her, and I love her—it's just normal. I can joke around and say "I'm just as smart as you are" or something, or say "I'm almost as tall as you now," but it's not—nothing bad. *And how about with your father?* Um, same thing. My dad likes to try and embarrass me but I get to choose whether or not I get embarrassed, because I'm not an easily embarrassed person. For instance, he does this thing where people try to teach their dogs to swim at our country house, all the rich people teach their dogs to swim, and he gets on top of the deck and he starts yelling, "Don't drown that dog, I'll take it! Please, please, don't drown that dog!" But see, he's done that twice and the second time I decided to embarrass him more and I said, "No dad, you can't have that dog. I get to have that dog!" So I mean, he's my friend. Sometimes we get a little bit impatient with each other, though, when we're trying to carry on a conversation and we keep interrupting each other. *You can talk to your mother about pretty much anything?* Yes, I mean, school, my grades, whatever, my friends. *And with your father?* Yes, I talk about whatever I want with him.

Do you have grandparents? Yes, on my mother's side both grandparents, and on my father's side neither. When I was not even 1 my grandmother on my father's side died, and I never knew my grandfather on that side. *Do you see your mother's parents a lot?* Um, they live out in Arizona, but we go out there say, once a year, twice last year because we had to go to a wedding out there. And they come out here, so I see them a fair amount considering how far away they are. I know people who have their grandparents living with them or across town and they see them every night or every weekend or something, so not as much as other people, but a fair amount considering we live halfway across the world. Well, not across the world, just across the country.

You just got back from Paris? Yes. *Were you there with your family?* I was with my mom, because my dad didn't want to go to Paris again because he doesn't like to travel in a big group. So my dad and my sister went down to Puerto Rico with another dad and his daughter. My mom and I went to Paris with one of my New York City friends from when I was a little-bitty baby. She's my age but she looks older, so I hang out with her. *Did you have a good time?* Yes.

Now I want to ask you about something a little different, about the physical changes that girls go through in adolescence. If it's too private, you don't have to answer. I don't mind. *Where did you learn about those physical changes?* My mom, school, friends I guess, well, not really friends. *Not your friends so much?* Well, I mean, I have a couple of friends who are older than me, but not really. *You learned from your mother.* Yes. *And have you had sex education in school?* Yes, since fifth grade. *Have any of the changes begun for you yet?* Yes. *How do you compare with other members of your class in terms of maturation?* Well, I'm 5'8" now I guess, maybe a little over. The people who I'm friends with are like, 6'2" and 5'11"; I'm friends with tall people. But compared to my class I'm actually very, very tall. Also, when I was in kindergarten they were holding most kids back, and I was never held back, so my friends are like 14 right now, and I'm still 12. So the people who are tallest in my grade are like up to my shoulder, and so actually I'm taller than most of them. *So you're a little ahead of other people your age.* Yes, my age and my grade.

What changes have you noticed? Have your breasts developed? Yes. *How's that been for you?* No different. I mean, it doesn't really make a difference to me, because I am considered more or less one of the guys. One of the last days of school we were playing "Mercy" in the back room and there

were only two people who could beat me, and I get respect for that. I am not treated like a girl, and nobody makes fun of me like other people would. Like one of my friends, she gets picked on because she is a girl and 'cause she like works hard. Some of the guys make her feel like "Oh, you are straight as an umbrella." *So they treat you like one of the guys?* Yes. *Were you surprised how you were treated?* No. Not at all. *Do you think it could be embarrassing?* I lost my bathing suit top a couple of times—no big deal, that's about it.

Have you had any crushes or sexual feelings for other people? Sure, I had a crush on a few guys. I have been asked out by a couple guys, but I never wanted to go out with them. We played spin-the-bottle at parties, but I truly find that boring. I like being friends with people, but in this town if you're going out, that usually leads to not being friends anymore, because they don't want to speak to each other any more or see each other any more, and people make it the biggest deal in the world. I mean there are people who might be going out with someone, but never see that person. It's just like a status. I don't really think that's a big deal because it just doesn't work. I mean my friend, Mark, his girlfriend just dumped him 2 weeks ago and he's not happy. She's a year older, and she's not happy, and so forth. It's just a big mess I don't think it's necessary. *So, you have not started dating?* Not what other people would consider dating; I mean, I've gone to movies with guys, in other places it might be considered a date. I went out with one guy for a while, but it's too complicated. *So basically you have been involved with guys; did it involve kissing?* Yes. *Have you had any other sexual experience?* Yes, I kissed a guy I was going out with, and I hug my friend Don, but no, it's no big deal. *Have you discovered masturbation?* No.

What are some of your favorite activities? What do you like to do? Basketball I like, eating I like, it's a good sport. I am involved in a club at school. Until this year I was doing community service with that and then right now they are going to build a gazebo for the park, because the old gazebo rotted. And I like hanging out. *Where do you like hanging out?* Well, since we are only in eighth grade, there is no [special place]. There's the town depot where the older kids go to. Actually it's the old train depot; high school kids go there to hang out, and there are some supervisors there. But we hang out at the beach, people's houses, a pizza place, sometimes downtown, but the downtown area scarcely exists, I have to say. In the downtown area one place we go to is up on the train tracks. We can go where the highway comes across and the train tracks come across. You go up there, and then there is another building, I swear the Mafia lives there, I swear the Mafia is in this empty building. Then, there's an entire underground parking lot where we take our bikes; half-way down you can dump your bike down there and go in there. And then there's Ed's, which is a music shop downtown. *Do you take your bikes to the town?* Yes, and we can go up there on the speed bumps, and you can bump. My friends all have mountain bikes; I have gotten pretty good at that. It's like going on sidewalks, you can jump. And we go on the golf course at night; we go on the golf cart trails; but you can go faster than golf carts. Old men chase you around trying to catch you, but they can't. It's the short cut from Eddie's house to Jackie's house.

Any shopping malls, where you go? We will go there, but we find it a joke. I have gone to so many malls before and that was fun; but I am not a mall rat who goes shopping and, you know, likes big stores that you can go in. There's this store called Candy Candy, and we know the guy who works there, it's Jackie's older brother who works there, and we go in there to talk to him, but we don't really hang out in the mall much, 'cause it's summer. In the winter we go there sometimes, but I see these people there that are really scary. One of the places is just like fancy, and another place has Chinese food. We don't want to eat Chinese food in the mall.

How often do you watch TV? I really don't watch much TV, 'cause I don't have much time to. But if I do watch any, I'll watch MTV. Whatever is on the videos, but they don't have anything I watch regularly. I watch very little TV for my age, maybe 2 hours a week at most. *Do you watch it alone?* Yeah, I guess so, or my dad comes in there. *Do you*

watch TV with your family? We have TVs but they are rarely turned on, and we don't watch TV as a thing.

What about video games? Do you play video games? We used to have a Nintendo I think, but it's probably in the basement. I mean that can be fun. Down the street we've got friends, and they play more than we do; and sometimes we go over there, and it's a joke to watch them play with no hand and eye coordination when it comes to those games.

Do you have a computer? My dad's business computer, family computer, and right now I have a computer in my room. It's a MAC PC; it was from dad's 50th birthday, the big five-0. He got a laptop computer with some extra screens and you can hook it up at home. But he put the MAC into my room. It's a pretty good computer. It's got an upgrade, so it has more memory now. *What do you use it for?* School, and I have two programs called "Sim" and "Sim-Life." On Sim-Life you create animals and you put them into habitats they give you in the simulator. They give you a planet and you have to change it. Sometimes the planet is burning when you get it, to start with, and you have to figure out how to stop that. It's a MAC system, and all my friends have that. My mom has a CD-ROM which has an encyclopedia on it. It's not exactly like a computer, but my dad just got a fax machine, and a couple of my friends do too. And we would fax each other a spelling list that we had forgotten or whatever. But I must admit I have hacked actually with other computers. See, in this town there's these two guys, "Postman" and the "Iridescent Mailman." I don't know who they are, but these two guys made a tape of all these kinds of things, and it's just like you get them and you read them and it's just hysterical.

Do any of your friends use drugs or alcohol? Nope, I mean none of my friends. There's one; she's not my friend actually. She's got a couple of friends who I would stay away from. Also the snobs in our school; they do drink, but they do that as like status. But none of my friends do. *So it's around but your friends don't do it?* Yes, Paul used to, but we stopped him, because we said we wouldn't be around him if he did, and when his two best friends stopped talking to him, he stopped. That was something he picked up from where he used to live. Supposedly everyone has a big problem with drugs and alcohol, but my friends don't do that 'cause I guess we are smart or something. And we can have fun without that.

You mentioned the church youth group that you are in. Yes. *Is religion important to you?* To be quite frank, not really. I mean I'm not christened and so I don't have a religion, but all my friends are in it, and I like going because I do learn something about religion. And I do think that is important, and it's good to know about God. But I am not actually superstitious that if I don't do this or that I am not going to Heaven. I mean I believe there is right and wrong, but I don't believe you have to dictate straight from the Bible. We read from the Bible and I learn a lot from that, 'cause I don't do a lot with Sunday school. *Do your parents go to church?* No, no they don't. We'll go on Christmas and Easter, and say when people we know in the choir have a solo or something, we'll go to watch that. Or if I stay over at a friend's house and we will go to church in the morning.

What do you do when you spend time alone? I put my stereo on. I guess it's really not alone when you are talking on the phone is it, 'cause you are talking with someone else? *Do you spend a lot of time on the phone?* A fair amount, more than I do watching TV, 'cause on school nights we mostly don't do things, 'cause we would rather do homework, but then I like to talk with people. Also, I tend to go out on the roof and watch the world go by. And I do my art when I'm alone, like sketching and portraits from photographs. I have never actually done a portrait like a person just sitting there. And time alone I read a lot. But I guess I should be reading harder books than I read, according to my parents.

What do you like to read? Stephen King, I picked that up from my uncle, and also Michael Crichton (I am not sure quite how you pronounce that); he wrote *Jurassic Park* and *Rising Sun*. I also like Madeline L'Engle; she wrote the, oh, what is it called? It's a whole series. I'll think of the first one in a second, but it is an entire series of books that have to do with relativity, and stuff. I can't remem-

ber the name of the first book. And she wrote a bunch of other books that have to do with this guy who is in them, and he does mindless things and it's sort of science fiction and she sort of uses them and then some of it is hard to explain, but they are more complicated than other stuff I've read.

Do you keep a diary? My mom made me keep one while I was in Paris. I wrote for 3 days. It had a ledger-type thing where I would write down important thoughts, and sometimes I write down important things or quotes I remember. But I don't exactly keep a diary of "today I did this, today I did that."

How would you describe yourself at the age of 12? Let's see, if I wanted to describe myself I would have to say that I am an optimist. I'm pretty smart. I guess I hang out with people who are more like most of my friends, older than me. Jackie came up with a name of how we should classify ourselves, because in our school everyone sort of has their names like the jocks, and the snobs, the cheerleader-type people. But we're "unique individual level extremist" or something; it was some bizarre name. Some other complicated name. *Unique individual level extremist?* Yeah. I think my friends are partly chosen because they listen to the same music. Also, the people I am friends with this year I really wasn't friends with last year. I really didn't know them that well. I've known Sally since first grade, and I have been friends with her most of the time. But Paul, he is one of my good friends, I didn't know him last year. I signed his yearbook, "I really don't know who you are, but have a great summer and everything." But this year we've been really close with a group of about 10 people that I didn't know before. And I like who I am friends with now. In the beginning of the year we were friends with a larger group of people, but then we cut down the group into a pretty small group of people and it sort of is a shame all the people that I am going to know from now until senior year will be the same 'cause we won't have anyone else in our high school so it's the same people. But it is better to keep to a small group we think.

How would you like things to work out for you? Well, I don't know. I would like to be President of the United States, but not for 24 years, can't do that [until age 36]. Let's see, I also would like to be a stand-up comedienne, but that doesn't have much of a future. And I'd like to be an artist, but that doesn't have much of a future, because people really don't make much money that way anymore. I would like to be in charge of things and I think people are messing up, and the candidates this year for President really made me sick. This is a role that I want: I want other people's kids to be at a public speech or watching TV or something, and I'll be up there and my friends will go, "That's our President, I went to school with her!" And then I mean, I would really like to stay in touch with the friends I went to school with now.

I really don't want to get married or have kids, because I don't want kids really. And I don't have time to babysit. I really like my little cousin, but I don't want kids. And I think the way most people's relationships or marriages are going, it's not really worth it to people 'cause everyone gets so messed up in divorce and everything.

I don't want to die and know that my life didn't make a difference. I want to be important, but when you think about how tiny and minuscule our little lives are compared to the entire universe, it's just so big when you think about that. And you think we don't matter and you're just one person and you have to be something as one person. I mean 'cause there are some people, let's say like Jesus or Ghandi or Helen Keller, one person who really made a difference, and I would like to be like that, but I am not. I can be, but I don't know about myself. I know some of my friends are actually going to be really important, but I don't know about myself. And you can tell by how they act, how they carry themselves, and what their goals are. And also there is sort of something about the way someone looks at you the first time you meet them, not as if they are judging you because I hate that, but as if they are wondering what they should expect from you. I think I want to be important or do something for people. It reminds me of that movie, you know the one with Jimmy Stewart, it's a Christmas movie and he was going to commit suicide. "*It's a Wonderful Life.*" Yeah. Until he thought his life didn't matter, then it did. I mean

so far my life doesn't really matter. *You hope someday it will?* Yes.

I wonder if there are other things that you think we should know about adolescence. We are writing this book about teenagers, what do you think we should know? OK. I think that the way you're approaching this I don't like that, like [wanting to interview] suburban kids, because to be quite frank I hate this town, and I'd love to get out of here. And the way you categorize people based on where they come from and who they are and what they want to do. Within the school there is a whole different category of people and you could find a whole bunch of different things out of that. If you heard a conversation like between two people there would be a lot of things you wouldn't understand, because a lot of kids have inside jokes and like sign words, and the way they talk and like if they are talking about a band or a sort of person, like one guy I know we call him "Turkey Lurkey" and so you would get really confused if you heard that, and we have inside jokes and stuff like that.

And I think maybe today people are a lot deeper than they should be. Like I know people who are like, "I know I am going to die tomorrow." I mean that is just too deep for people our age. And people should just totally lighten up. A lot of people don't know how. I read poetry and it's something to do to get my mind off things. And I guess with poetry it is something I only read it to a few people. I hope people trust one person or another and have some understanding of these people. Like Jackie, some people feel they have to tell someone; he always assumes that I will go and not say anything. He has told me a lot of stuff he hasn't told anyone else. And Sally is always whining and we're just always kidding around with her about this. For one thing I know that kids keep to themselves.

I think kids are smarter than people think they are and that they have an understanding of things better than other people do. I think that, say 2 years from now, things are going to be a lot different than they are now, because at this age people are a lot different than at my parent's age, because we think differently. And I think people set higher goals. I don't know anyone who said they wanted to be like something small. No one wants to be something small. Everyone has the highest goals in the world, and they always want to do something.

I think my generation is going to come up with the cure for cancer, 'cause my friend Abby, I think she had a pretty good idea about a way to get rid of tumors. She would have it under a controlled laser. You know how people get them inside their brain and they don't want to burn away tissue to get to it, so maybe a controlled laser she's talking about. And I think it has to do with genes 'cause, you know about P53? *No.* Well it's a certain gene, and they think it might have to do with cancer because usually a disorder in this gene is related with cancer cases. So I'm thinking that people should have physicals to check on that gene, because the way it starts out is when it destroys the gene is usually when the cancer started and if they can figure how long they have had cancer by how long the gene has been distorted, they can come up with a supplement for that gene. And genetic engineering is getting very involved right now, so maybe the cure for cancer will come out of that. Someone came up with sharp cartilage so tumors couldn't cling to it, but I don't think that is going to work. *Fascinating.* Maybe, maybe not.

What name would you like to use for this interview? Oh, I had a pet name once, now I can't remember it, but for one thing Clarissa or Lynn mean graceful and I am not graceful. Just something boring like Sarah. You know, they never ask what name you want, never. *So it's Sarah.* Sure make it's either Sarah or Meredith.

Chapter 6

❖

The Social Ecology of Adolescence

❖

Young people grow up in a social environment that differs from one generation to the next. Historical influences, such as economic affluence or depression, war or peace, epidemics and famines, technological changes, and a variety of population characteristics affect the experience of growing up and becoming an adult. Within any particular generation there are also significant differences among adolescents because of socioeconomic background, ethnic culture, and racial discrimination. Moreover, adolescents spend a great amount of time with their family, with friends, and in school. In addition, adolescents are important consumers of the mass media, including television, music, and film. Moreover, many adolescents are beginning to work, which further defines their niche in the structure of their society. Each of these influences interacts with the others. Together they produce the social ecology of adolescence.

Ecology may be defined as the interrelationship between the environment in which an organism lives and the organism itself. This chapter is concerned with the mutual accommodation of growing adolescents and the changing environment in which they live near the beginning of the 21st century. This analysis includes both immediate settings such as the school and larger social contexts such as one's community or nation.

We begin with a focus on population characteristics of the society because the relative number of adolescents compared with persons of other age groups directly affects the scarcity or abundance of resources for adolescents. Next we discuss junior high and high schools, both as social institutions and as social settings of considerable importance foradolescent lives. Then we examine adolescents and work, emphasizing the significance of work experiences as a social setting for adolescents. Next, we focus on popular music, music videos, video games, and television as important components of the social ecology of adolescence. We conclude the chapter with a discussion of the effects of growing up in an ethnic or racial culture different from the dominant society in the United States.

This chapter provides an introduction to the social world of adolescents. Obviously, the school, family, and peer group are important aspects of the adolescent's social ecology. For example, one study found that adolescents spend most of their time in four social settings: 29% of their waking hours are spent with friends; 27% is spent alone; 23% is spent with classmates; another 2% is spent with coworkers; and 19% is spent with the family (Csikszentmihalyi & Larson, 1984, p. 71; Larson & Richards, 1989). Although the influence of family and friends will be implicit in much of the discussion in this chapter, these relationships are such important topics that they will be discussed extensively in the next two chapters.

POPULATION DEMOGRAPHICS: LESS MEANS MORE

Following the Second World War, men and women returning from the war, a growing economic affluence, and general optimism about the future led to a great increase in childbirth, resulting in a *baby boom*. The increase in the birth rate began in 1945 and continued until around 1960, when it declined to a much lower rate (Figure 6.1). Because of medical advances, such as the discovery of sulfa and penicillin, fewer of these children died in childhood than in the past, so this increased birth rate resulted in a "bulge" in the population representing those who became adolescent between about 1957 and 1972. This generation will

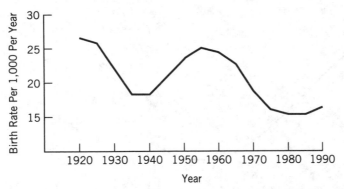

Figure 6.1 After reaching a low point in the 1930s, the birth rate climbed to a post-World War II peak in the 1945–1960 period, and has since declined noticeably. (The birth rate is the ratio of births in a given year to the average population; annual birth rates are here averaged over 5-year periods to bring out the longer term pattern.) [*Source:* Compiled by Easterlin, 1980, Figure 1.1, p. 8; U.S. Bureau of the Census (1992). *Statistical Abstract of the United States, 1992*, p. 64. Washington, DC: U.S. Government Printing Office.]

continue on into old age in far higher numbers than in previous generations, leading to a "senior boom" of retired persons in the 21st century. In contrast, the generation of adolescents born during the following period of relatively low birth rates (the so-called "baby bust" generation), who became adolescent after the mid-1970s, will have a much lower proportion of age-mates throughout their lives.

The relative number of age-mates in one's generation, and the proportion of one's generation to the rest of the population in the country, are important influences on a large number of characteristics in one's life. The effects may be divided into two types. First, the relative number of persons in each age group within society is known as the **age composition** of the population. Second, these population patterns may have **age-specific** effects on members of one particular age group. We will discuss both types of effects.

EFFECTS OF AGE COMPOSITION OF THE SOCIETY

The impact of the growth, and subsequent decline, in the birth rate after 1960 had a significant effect in our country. For example, the greater number of children during the 1950s and 1960s required building schools and hiring teachers; in the 1970s and 1980s, many of these schools were closed, and there was much less need for new teachers. Likewise, colleges experienced a dramatic increase in enrollment during the 1960s and 1970s, but enrollment leveled off around 1980, and the number of college-aged persons (age 18–24) will drop dramatically until around 1995 (Figure 6.2). Because most of those persons are currently alive (having been born before 1982), these population patterns are based on solid evidence. Immigration and movement from one school to another may affect enrollment in individual schools, however.

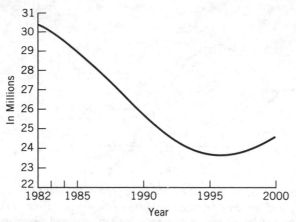

Figure 6.2 Projected population of persons in the United States aged 18–24 from 1982 to 2000. [*Source:* U. S. Census Bureau, *Current Population Reports*, Series P-25, No. 922, Table 2.]

AGE–SPECIFIC EFFECTS

Within the generation of young persons born during the baby boom, we also note effects of these population patterns. These age-specific effects are especially interesting for our developmental perspective, and they clearly illustrate the importance of analyzing the impact of social ecology on human development. Consider the difference between those adolescents who were born in the 1950s during the baby boom and those who were born in the 1970s when birth rates were much lower.

> For large generations, the typical story is one of crowding; for small generations, it is one of nurturance and special attention. At home, for large generations the pressures of sibling rivalry are high, and mom and dad are hard pressed to give time to each child's physical and emotional needs. At school, classrooms are overflowing, and inexperienced teachers, aided sometimes by volunteer assistants, are likely to be one's fate. Competition is everywhere severe—in class, in extracurricular activities, for part-time jobs. Because of the pressure of numbers, entry standards are likely to be raised. Experience will be required for jobs where previously on-the-job training was the norm (but where is one to get experience?); admission standards to the "best schools" are likely to be raised. [Easterlin, 1980, p. 30]

These conditions of high or low competition with one's age-mates follow throughout one's life, depending on whether one was born in a period of high birth rate or low birth rate. Periods of transition from high to low birth rates produce an intermediate degree of competition. Thus, one generation—such as those born during the low birth-rate period of the 1930s—would be favored with less competition with their age-mates compared with those born during the 1950s, who would face much greater competition. Those born during the 1970s would again have relatively less competition with their age-mates. All three generations are living within our society today, yet the social ecology of each generation is quite different. For example, the election of President Clinton and Vice President Gore reflected a change in political leadership from the pre-World War II birth cohort to the post-war (baby boom) generation.

Economist Richard Easterlin (1980) noted this pattern in birth rates and analyzed the age-specific effects of these changes on a variety of characteristics relevant to human development. According to his analysis, many of the aspects of adolescence and young adulthood that have received so much attention in recent years may be explained, at least in part, by the influence of birth rates on the baby boom generation. For example, young people born during a baby boom would be more likely than those born during a period of low birth rate to: (1) have more difficulty finding a good job and advancing up the career ladder; (2) delay marriage because of the scarcity of jobs and therefore produce more illegitimate children; (3) put off having children after marriage because of lower earning potential due to the effects of intense competition; (4) have greater marital stress and higher divorce rates; (5) have greater psychological stress, resulting in higher rates of suicide, crime, and feelings of alienation; and (6) for young women who choose motherhood, have a need to combine a job with care of children because of economic pressures (p. 4).

Whereas the picture Easterlin painted of economic competition, psychosocial stress, and political alienation for the baby boom generation is distressing, the opposite effects were predicted for the generation born in the 1970s. Thus, he saw a shift toward the patterns of the 1950s when this low birth-rate generation reaches adulthood in the 1990s. That is, there would be expected to be an improvement in earnings and employment opportunities; a shift to earlier marriages and increased birth rates; a slower increase in young women working in jobs and more opportunities for older women to work; lower rates of divorce and illegitimacy; lower suicide and crime rates; and less political alienation (p. 134).

Whereas the cyclical pattern he described would appear to be set to repeat with a high birth rate in the 1990s, it is possible that other social changes such as increased use of contraception, changed attitudes about women's roles, and greater understanding of the effects of a high birth rate may reduce the size and the effects of the baby boom of the 1990s. Therefore, it is possible that the "good news" he predicts for the decade of the 1990s might be continued for several decades into the future.

These provocative ideas provide an insight into the social and economic influences that may affect one generation of adolescents differently from the generation that preceded them, or the generation that follows them. It is a good example of the importance of social ecology for the understanding of human development. It also provides concrete evidence for the outer-physical dimension in the dialectical analysis of transitions discussed in Chapter 1.

Critics of this analysis point out that many other factors are involved in these complex social problems in addition to population patterns. Crime rates, for instance, reflect delinquent behavior in adolescence and drug abuse that have multiple causes not directly related to having been born during a baby boom (see Chapters 11 and 12). Moreover, although the various measures reported by Easterlin may increase or decrease at the same time, this does not mean that population patterns actually cause these changes either directly or indirectly. It may be that other factors—such as a decline in parental authority, or television, or liberalizing of gender role standards—are responsible for these changes and simply happen to occur at the same time as the maturing of the baby boom generation. It is unlikely that a single explanation is able to account for such a wide variety of social conditions. However, his argument has a logical basis—that population density produces stress that is manifested in these diverse ways—and it is well grounded in everyday observation of young adults competing for jobs, houses, and graduate schools, and delaying marriage and childbirth until economic prospects improve. As with most creative ideas, it is probably partly right and partly wrong. Nonetheless, Easterlin's analysis has called attention to these phenomena in different ways and has suggested interesting implications. For example, the current focus on high divorce and crime rates may give way, in the 1990s, to a concern with the political alienation and psychosocial distress of the middle-aged baby boom generation.

This discussion calls attention to the larger social context of adolescent lives (Bronfenbrenner, 1977). In the next section, we focus on one of the most important immediate settings in the social ecology of adolescence—the school. Obviously, the social conditions we discussed in this section have affected the schools to a great extent.

SECONDARY SCHOOLS

The junior high or high school is a social environment that has a significant daily influence on the lives of adolescents in the United States. It is a social center for meeting friends, making dates, and seeking peer-group support. It provides a testing ground for one's popularity, academic skill, and athletic ability. It is a miniature society where one can join clubs, run for office in student government, or remain uninvolved in anything outside the class-

The school is a social environment that has a daily influence on the lives of most adolescents in the United States.

room. One can find acceptance with the "socies" or the "jocks" or, if one is on the fringes, with the "slippies."

The school is also a social setting that has a variety of functions, including providing an education and skills for participation in a complex society; keeping young people occupied and out of the job market; preparing young people for college and work; enhancing social skills and ability to relate with others; and sorting young people into paths that determine much of their later pattern of life. Some of these functions are explicitly acknowledged, such as education and providing skills; these are known as **manifest functions** of the high school. Other functions are implicit in the way schools operate, but are not intentional goals; these are known as **latent functions**. An example of a latent function is the process of sorting adolescents into different paths such as "vocational" or "college-bound" tracks that implicitly limit or enhance the young person's chances of socioeconomic advancement.

In addition, the junior high and high school are an age-segregated society of persons who are nearly all between the ages of 13 and 19. Only a few people are of a different age—usually between 25 and 65; except for a few volunteers, these older people are paid to be there as teachers, administrators, or staff. Parents, young children, and other adults are ordinarily excluded except on special occasions.

There are other odd characteristics of this social setting, as well. Bells ring periodically. Public address announcements are made from time to time, occasionally in the middle of an interesting discussion. The day is divided into periods, and often something that happens in one period has no relationship to the next period. There are rules and regulations about all kinds of things, some enforced by adults and some by one's peers. Learning to cope with all of this is another important latent function of schools. One might question whether this odd social environment teaches coping skills that are relevant to adult life, or whether it simply teaches adolescents to respond passively to an environment over which they have little control.

For a variety of reasons, considerable attention is now being given to schools by educators, politicians, parents, and students. On the one hand, it is felt that secondary schools are not meeting their educational expectations and that a national effort needs to be undertaken to improve education. On the other hand, it is felt that the nation is blaming the schools for problems that are beyond their control but is unwilling to confront the social conditions that are causing the problems. Thus, any discussion of middle, junior high, and high schools in the United States today must consider the characteristics of these schools and their students, as well as the thoughtful recommendations that are being made.

Our focus in this section has three parts. First, we review the characteristics of secondary schools and their curriculum. Second, we discuss the effects of the transition from elementary school into a middle or junior high school. Third, we examine the social setting of the high school, including the informal and formal social structure of high schools and the effects of racial discrimination.

CHARACTERISTICS OF SECONDARY SCHOOLS IN THE UNITED STATES

Secondary schools are those housing the grades following primary school. They may include **junior high school** (grades 7–9) or a **middle school** that includes grades 6–8 or 7 and 8, both of which are followed by high school. Grades 9–12 are contained in about half of the country's public high schools. Others combine junior and senior high school grades (e.g., 7–12). Still others offer only grades 10–12, with the earlier grades placed in a junior high school or a middle school (Boyer, 1983; Entwisle, 1990).

There are approximately 18,000 public high schools in the United States with over 13 million students. Obviously, there is considerable difference among these schools. For example, 16% of all schools are in urban areas, 36% are in suburban areas, and 48% are in rural areas. In addition, there are about 6,000 private high schools with over 1 million students. About two-thirds of the students in private schools are in Catholic schools. The size of the school also varies greatly, with an average enrollment of 758 in public high schools and 215 in private high schools; of course, some public schools are much larger, and some private schools much smaller than these averages (Coleman, Hoffer, & Kilgore, 1982).

The vast majority of public high schools are **comprehensive high schools** in the sense that they offer both academic courses to prepare students for college and vocational courses designed to prepare students for work, as well as a general studies program for students whose goals are not clear. A few schools concentrate on specific programs such as the arts, business, or science; these are **magnet schools** that attract students from a wide area. Others consider themselves **alternative schools** and offer specialized programs for specific types of students.

Several dramatic changes have occurred in enrollment patterns of high schools in recent years. First, there was a large increase in student enrollment, and then there was a sharp decline (Figure 6.3). These trends reflect the general demographic patterns discussed in the first part of this chapter: the baby boom generation growing through adolescence in the 1960s and 1970s, followed by the generation that had a much lower birth rate. In addition, a greater proportion of high-school age adolescents graduated from high school in recent years than was true in the past (Figure 6.4). There also has been an increase in minority student enrollment in high schools, especially in urban areas.

The result of these trends is that high school students are more diverse in socioeconomic

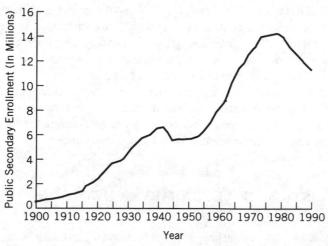

Figure 6.3 Enrollment in public high schools, grades 9–12, 1900–1990. [*Source:* National Center for Educational Statistics, *Digest of Educational Statistics 1992*, Table 39.]

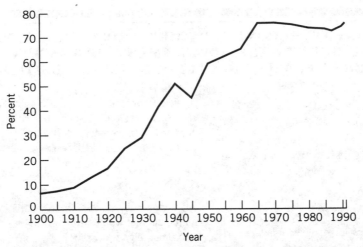

Figure 6.4 Public high school graduates as a percentage of the 17-year-old population; 1900–1992. [*Source:* National Center for Educational Statistics, *Digest of Educational Statistics 1992*, Table 95.]

and ethnic or racial background today than they were in the past when a smaller proportion of all adolescents attended high school and jobs were more readily available for persons without a high school education. Although these changes are clearly positive, they have forced schools to confront racism and other forms of discrimination and to provide an educational environment for a much more diverse student population than was the case in the past.

At the same time, a number of other social changes, such as the higher rate of divorce and adolescent pregnancy, have increased the strain on students and on schools. One national study on high schools noted:

> For many teenagers, the high school may be the only place to get support and ease the pain of personal trauma and deep hurt. It frequently becomes a crisis center—helping a pregnant girl, supporting a young student who has had a fight at home, or helping a teenager through the trauma of parental separation or divorce. [Boyer, 1983, pp. 37–38]

In addition, problems related to violence, students carrying weapons, and measures to promote safety have attracted considerable attention, especially in urban areas. Likewise, issues of sexual harassment, taunting, and unwanted physical contact have been reported to cause negative reactions such as not wanting to go to school, especially for girls (Barringer, 1993).

Moreover, many schools have faced serious financial problems that frequently result in too little money for teachers and guidance counselors, classroom equipment, and maintenance of the building. Although teachers' salaries have increased by 22% and money spent per pupil has nearly doubled between 1982 and 1993, schools in wealthy districts have benefited much more than urban schools (Celis, 1993).

A major study of high schools by the Carnegie Foundation for the Advancement of Teaching summarized 12 themes that schools must consider if they are to resolve the problems they face (Box 6.1). The important recommendations regarding preparation for work

♦ **BOX 6.1 SUMMARY OF RECOMMENDATIONS FROM THE CARNEGIE FOUNDATION FOR THE ADVANCEMENT OF TEACHING REGARDING PUBLIC HIGH SCHOOLS IN THE UNITED STATES**

I. Clarifying Goals

Every high school should establish clearly stated goals. School goals should focus on the mastery of language, on a core of common learning, on preparation for work and further education, and on community and civic service.

II. The Centrality of Language

The English proficiency of all students should be formally assessed before they go to high school. Intensive remediation should be provided in a pre-high school summer term and in the freshman year for students who are deficient in English.

All high school students should complete a basic English course with emphasis on writing.

The high school curriculum should also include a study of the spoken word.

III. The Curriculum Has a Core

The number of required courses in the core curriculum should be expanded.

In addition to strengthening the traditional courses in literature, history, mathematics, and science, emphasis should also be given to foreign language, the arts, civics, non-Western studies, technology, the meaning of work, and the importance of health.

IV. Transition: To Work and Learning

The school program should offer a single track for all students, one that includes a strong grounding in the basic tools of education and a study of the core curriculum.

The last 2 years of high school should be considered a "transition school" that includes advanced study in selected academic subjects, the exploration of a career option, or a combination of both.

Guidance services should be significantly expanded.

A new Student Achievement and Advisement Test should be developed to assess learning in the academic core and personal characteristics to help students make decisions more intelligently about their futures.

V. Service

All high school students should complete a service requirement that would involve them in volunteer work in the community or at school.

Students should have an opportunity to help organize, monitor, and assign credit for the service program.

VI. Teachers: Renewing the Profession

The working conditions of teachers must improve in terms of reduced teaching load, minimum preparation time, and freedom from routine monitoring of halls, lunchrooms, and recreation areas.

Good teachers should be given adequate recognition and rewards as well as a chance to advance within the profession.

Teachers should be supported in the maintenance of discipline based on a clearly stated code of conduct.

Teacher salaries should be increased substantially.

Outstanding students should be recruited into teaching.

Training of teachers must improve and continuing education strengthened.

Skilled professionals should be recruited to teach part-time.

VII. Instruction: A Time for Learning

Teachers should use a variety of teaching styles, and there should be an emphasis on the active participation of the student.

Classroom instruction should have high expectations, clear standards, and fair evaluations; students should be held accountable for their work.

Teachers should have a greater voice in selecting textbooks and should use more original source material in their classes.

VIII.   Technology: Extending the Teacher's Reach

Computers and other educational technology should be carefully evaluated and purchased only after considering their link with school objectives.

Computer companies should provide training for teachers and establish a fund to develop high-quality, school-related computer programs (software).

All students should learn *about* computers and the social importance of technology. In addition, students should learn with computers and learn from computers.

The use of other technologies, such as television, videocassettes, and film, should be greatly increased.

IX.   Flexibility: Patterns to Fit a Purpose

The class schedule should be more flexibly arranged to permit larger blocks of instructional time, especially in courses such as laboratory science, foreign language, and creative writing.

Small high schools should expand their education offerings by using off-campus sites, mobile classrooms, or part-time professionals to provide a richer education for all students.

Large high schools should organize themselves into smaller units to provide a more supportive social setting for all students.

Special arrangements should be developed for gifted and talented students, including residential academies that might be located on college campuses.

Remedial programs should be fully funded by the federal government because they have demonstrated their effectiveness.

High schools, working with a community college, should have an arrangement to permit dropouts to return to school part time or full time or engage in independent study to complete their high school education.

X.   The Principal as Leader

The role of the principal as the leader of the local school and its key educator must be reaffirmed and strengthened.

XI. Strengthening Connections

A comprehensive partnership should be formed between high schools and colleges to smooth the transition of students into higher education, to allow able students to accelerate their academic programs, and to strengthen the high schools.

Partnerships between high schools and businesses should be established to provide volunteer services, apprenticeship experience, enrichment programs, awards and grants to outstanding teachers and principals, and to help schools improve their facilities and equipment.

XII.   Excellence: The Public Commitment

Parents, other citizens, local school boards, state agencies and legislatures, and the federal government must work together to help bring excellence to our public schools.

Source: Adapted from Boyer, 1983, pp. 301–319. *Note:* Some material is summarized; see original source for specific recommendations and exact wording.

and the inclusion of a service component in the high school curriculum will be discussed later in this chapter.

One focus in this study was on the important role of the principal in the high school. It noted that schools with a high level of achievement and a feeling of community within the school had a principal who was an effective leader. Such a leader brought the diverse elements of the school together in a way that make them work (Boyer, 1983, p. 219).

Another focus was on the organization of the school to provide the benefits of a small school as well as the advantages of a large school. Considerable research has demonstrated that students in small schools benefit from greater opportunity to participate in activities (because there are fewer students competing for a place on the team, in the play or club, etc.), and from greater emotional support within the smaller community of students and teachers (Gump, 1980). Nonetheless, large schools provide a wider range of educational opportunities, advanced courses, and specialized programs that attract only a small proportion of the total student group. One way to provide the benefits of both types of schools is to divide schools of over 1,500 students into subunits of 500 students each. The subunits might each meet in the same physical building, but they could have separate programs, faculties, and extracurricular activities. Care must be taken, however, that students are not segregated by socioeconomic status, racial, or ethnic factors (Boyer, 1983, p. 235). Another way to achieve this goal is to develop mobile classrooms that could travel to smaller schools for a semester and provide specialized courses that would otherwise not be available.

TRANSITION FROM PRIMARY TO SECONDARY SCHOOLS

Making the transition from elementary school into the secondary school appears to cause some difficulty for many adolescents. You might recall your own experience and the differences between the ecology of the two schools. In many cases, the elementary school has a smaller total number of students and there are fewer people within one's own grade. Thus, there is less competition with regard to school performance or sports participation. Also, the atmosphere is often different, with a more impersonal and structured emphasis in the secondary school. In addition, one may have classes with different groups of students during the day and may see friends only once or twice during school. Finally, one's friends from elementary school may not have gone to the same secondary school, or may no longer be as friendly in this new and somewhat strange environment.

Several studies have focused on this period of transition from elementary to junior high school, and most have found it to be associated with a decline in school grades; this decline was predictive of dropping out of school later on (Simmons & Blyth, 1987). The decline in grades was found for African-American and white girls and boys when their grades in grade 7 were compared with their grades in grade 6 in a study of 12 schools in Milwaukee, Wisconsin (Simmons, Black, & Zhou, 1991). The decline was especially marked for African-American boys (Figure 6.5). Attitudes toward school also plummeted for African-American boys and girls; only white girls reported that they liked school better in grade 7 than they did in grade 6 (Figure 6.6). Other symptoms of problem behavior were high in African-American boys if their socioeconomic background was lower class or blue-collar, but not for those from white-collar and higher social classes. Aspirations to attend college decline for white boys and girls, perhaps as a result of greater competition, but do not decline for African-American boys and girls.

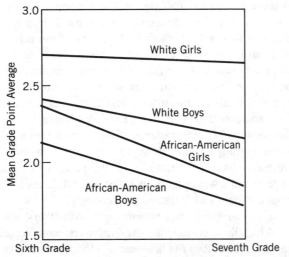

Figure 6.5 Grade-point average for African-American and white students in sixth and seventh grades, by gender. [*Source:* R.G. Simmons, A. Black, & Y. Zhou. African-American Versus White Children and the Transition Into Junior High School. *American Journal of Education*, *99*, 481–520, Figure 2. © 1991 University of Chicago. Reprinted with permission.]

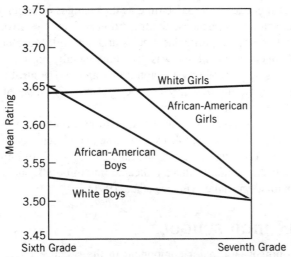

Figure 6.6 Liking school ratings for African-American and white students in sixth and seventh grades, by gender. [*Source:* R.G. Simmons, A. Black, & Y. Zhou. African-American Versus White Children and the Transition Into Junior High School. *American Journal of Education*, *99*, 481–520, Figure 10. © 1991 University of Chicago. Reprinted with permission.]

Studies that have examined students who stay in elementary school until eighth grade and then transfer to high school tend not to find such a marked drop in grades. However, careful analysis indicates that this lack of effect is the result of the private or rural school systems where this type of arrangement predominates. That is, students who live in rural areas or those who attend private school differ from those urban children who attend a junior high school. Thus, comparisons between different school systems have shown that "the presence or absence of a major school transition is less critical than the type of school the child is in during the early adolescent years (Eccles, Lord, & Midgley, 1991, p. 532).

Eccles and her colleagues (1991, 1993) identified four school environmental variables that help explain why many students have difficulty with the transition into junior high school. (1) There is greater emphasis on control and discipline, less personal relationship between teacher and student, and fewer opportunities for individual choice and self-management in junior high school compared with elementary school. (2) Junior high classes involve more situations where one can compare one's performance with others, which leads to a decline in motivation for all but the best students. (3) Classwork tends to require lower level cognitive skills than was the case during the last year of elementary school. (4) Junior high teachers use higher standards for judging students' performance, which leads to a decline in grades. For example, they compared the responses of the seventh-grade teachers with the same students' sixth-grade teachers:

> As predicted, the seventh-grade teachers believed students needed more discipline and control than did sixth-grade teachers; and the seventh-grade teachers rated the students as less trustworthy than did the sixth-grade teachers. Finally, the seventh-grade teachers felt significantly less efficacious than did sixth-grade teachers in their ability to influence the learning of all of their students. [Eccles et al., 1991, p. 535]

Thus, the difficult shift from elementary to secondary school seems not to reflect an inherent difficulty because it occurs at the same time as the changes of puberty, or because the change is necessarily upsetting, but because the transition is from a relatively positive environment into a less positive one. In particular, Eccles and her colleagues noted that the students were moving into an environment that was "developmentally regressive"; that is, "they were experiencing decreasing opportunity for autonomy and self-control as they got older rather than the increasing opportunities they felt they deserved because of their increasing maturity" (Eccles et al., 1991, p. 537).

Additional research is needed on this important transition for adolescents, but the present information suggests that educators need to examine the social ecology of the junior high school to reduce the negative aspects of this transition. The concept of a middle school was intended to do this very task, but studies have indicated that middle schools tend to be more like junior high schools than was hoped (Eccles et al., 1991).

ADOLESCENTS IN HIGH SCHOOLS

The high school environment is a major component in the social ecology of adolescence. Because adolescents spend a great amount of time in schools, and schools exert a great deal of influence on the daily life of adolescents, it is important that we now examine the intricate pattern of adolescents' adaptation to this social environment. There are several major patterns in this adaptation, each of which influences the others. First, many adolescents form themselves into groups, or **cliques**, which are separate social units that are based on similarity in age, sex, neighborhood, and interests (Cusick, 1973, p. 161). This social organization of students reflects the complex patterns of adult social life. It does not appear to reflect some sort of unified adolescent culture (McClelland, 1982, p. 490). Second, formal social organizations and the implicit sorting of students into one particular track of studies influences the patterns of social interaction. Third, racial discrimination affects the social environment of many schools. Let us discuss each of these aspects of the social ecology of high schools.

Social Groups Within the School

Think back for a moment to high school. Remember the physical building and the way it was organized. Remember the places where people used to gather, and the different groups that gathered in those places. Recall the organized activities: student council, special interest clubs, the band, sports, and the dances. Think of the people who were popular. Where did you fit in that pattern of social groups? What characteristics determined who was in each of the various groups? Was there a group that we might call a "leading crowd" at the school? How did people get into that group? Were there after-school hangouts that were especially popular with some students. Perhaps there were some activities, like "dragging Main Street," that were important signs of social status for some people.

Clearly, the social environment of high school involves a lot more than just classrooms, the athletic field, and the senior prom. As the Carnegie Commission report noted:

> Schools are places of strict boundaries, both physical and social. One student, sitting with us in the school cafeteria, explained the social geography of the room. "Of course there are cliques. There are cliques everywhere. Behind you are the jocks; over on the side of the room are the greasers, and in front of you are the preppies—white preppies, black preppies, Chinese preppies, preppies of all kinds. The preppies are the in group this year. Jocks, of course, are always in and greasers are always out." [Boyer, 1983, p. 206]

Studies of high school subcultures have identified a variety of groups (McClelland, 1982, p. 401). Among the groups identified were the following types: fun, academic, delinquent, conformist, bohemian, rebellious, and political militants.

Studies by participant-observers who observed the social groups as daily participants in the high school reported a diversity of unrelated groups. For example, Cusick (1973) described one school as follows:

> The groups there really were discrete social units, narrowly bounded not only by age, sex, and neighborhood, but chiefly by interests. . . . The data suggest that rather than a society or even a subculture, there is a fragmented series of interest groups revolving around specific items and past patterns of interaction. These groups may be the important social referent, not some mythical subculture or "adolescent society." [Cusick, 1973, p. 161]

A study of boys in one particular Midwestern high school (Todd, 1979) found that although there were a few highly visible cliques, most boys appeared to have some close friends but did not identify with any particular clique. The social organization seemed best described by two differing styles. One group Todd called the "citizens" and the other the "tribe." The "citizens" were highly involved in various school activities, agreed with the formal social structure of the school, and used this structure to satisfy their interests and find peer interaction. These students were not ordinarily highly involved in either athletics or other special interest groups such as drama or the newspaper. In contrast, members of the "tribe" were not interested in school activities and often had conflicts with school rules and authorities; however, they did find considerable informal social interaction within the school. They were a group distinct from the "greasers," who tended to be more disruptive, and also distinct from those students who were politically active or those involved with drugs (pp. 180–181). Todd suggested that the "citizens" may be well prepared for mixing intellectual and social activities as adults, whereas members of the "tribe" may be prepared for social interaction with peers on the job and in the community when they leave school. He implied that the "citizens" are likely to be college bound, whereas members of the "tribe" are heading for work or military service. In both groups there were some boys who were unsatisfied. "Few of the boys [in the tribe] were pleased with their futures or the high school experience, for that matter, although most were resigned to both" (p. 183). Some of the "citizens" were also isolated and low in self-esteem, especially those who were not doing well in their studies. "These boys have bought citizen values but do not measure up as well as they would like, and they seem to take it personally" (Todd, 1979, p. 183).

Although many of these studies of the informal social organization of high schools have focused on white, middle-class students (Gottlieb & Heinsohn, 1973), it appears that the schools reflect much of the variety to be found within adult society. As we note in the next section, formal school structures and racial discrimination also affect these informal social networks—much as they do in the adult world.

Formal Social Organization of the School

Schools have at least five functions: sorting, training, certifying educational accomplishments, providing custodial care, and socializing adolescents for adult roles (Kelly, 1979, p. 7). These functions often affect the social organization of the school. McClelland (1982) noted: "Schools as institutions, we would conclude, are relentlessly engaged in the process of sorting students, on the basis of their behavior and academic ability, into categories of good and bad, success and failure" (p. 408). On one hand, these formal sortings—such as tracking—may place students in similar classrooms and provide them with a chance to form groups. But on the other hand, there is no reason to assume that students will use these formal groupings to organize their own social structure. In fact, McClelland (1982) argued that the student social structure may attempt to reduce or negate "the definitions of inferiority that the school inevitably imposes on most students" (p. 408).

Another way schools attempt to influence the social interaction of students is through various extracurricular (or cocurricular) activities. Participation in these activities has been found to be related to improved race relations, higher levels of self esteem, educational aspirations, feelings of being in control of one's life, lower delinquency rates, and, for males, academic ability and grades (Holland & Andre, 1987). However, many high school students are not involved in extracurricular activities, and those that are involved generally are a selective sample, according to data cited by the Carnegie report.

Nationwide, 53 percent of all students do *not* participate in any nonvarsity sport or athletic activity; 85 percent do *not* belong to pep clubs or take part in cheerleading, debating, or drama;

more than 80 percent do *not* participate in either student government or the school newspaper; and over 78 percent are not members of chorus or dance, or band or orchestra activities. [Boyer, 1983, p. 207]

Involvement in these activities is more common for white, male, college-bound students, for students with higher grades, and for students from middle-income families (Boyer, 1983, p. 208). This self-selection of students who participate in extracurricular activities may explain the association of activity with self esteem and other characteristics noted above. In fact, as the previous discussion indicated, the students' own social structure may influence whether a particular student (i.e., a "citizen" or a member of the "tribe") is interested in these activities or not. Moreover, 70% of schools have policies intended to keep students who are failing academically from participating in extracurricular activities (Celis, 1993). We explore this issue from a different perspective in the next section.

Race and Social Structure in the School

Typically, persons who are similar in socioeconomic, ethnic, and racial background tend to group together, although shared interests can also bring diverse people together. So-called *magnet* schools that attract students with similar specialized interests or career goals may have social groups that are organized around those shared interests. However, racism and discrimination in the adult society of the surrounding community is usually reflected in the social organization of the school. Let us take a detailed look at this process in one school.

Nobuo Shimahara studied the social organization within an urban high school in an industrial area of the northeastern United States. The community where the school was located, which he called Everest, was mainly middle class. However, it contained:

> upper-middle-class families in its northern and western sections, middle- and working-class families in the center, and lower-class families on the southern fringe. It included multiethnic groups and a wide spectrum of political and religious persuasions. In this respect teachers at the school often described Everest as "typical" of the eastern part of the nation. [Shimahara, 1983, p. 111]

African-American families lived in three distinct neighborhoods (one was middle class, another was lower and working class, and a third was mixed). These residential patterns produced informal neighborhood groups of African-American adolescents. The high school had about 1,000 students; 69% were white, and 30% were African-American; Asian and Hispanic students made up 2%. The study focused on the entire junior class in 1981–1982; 50 students were interviewed in detail. Interviews were also conducted with teachers, administrators, and counselors; relevant school records were examined; and extensive observations of student behavior were made by three researchers over a period of two school years.

Segregation by race was generally evident in informal settings such as the halls, cafeteria, library, and free activities in gym class. In the cafeteria, African-Americans and whites sat at separate rows of tables. When passing in the halls, African-American students talked to each other more than to white students and vice versa. In the library, white and African-American students occupied tables in different areas of the room. When boys in gym class formed three voluntary teams, one basketball team was exclusively white; another was all African-American except for one boy; and the hockey group had all white students. In contrast, some formal settings with shared interests and goals were fully integrated, including the football team (27 African-Americans, 23 whites, 2 Asian-Americans) and the student council (18 whites and 9 African-Americans), but not the basketball team (18 African-Americans out of 20 players).

The students suggested four reasons for this pattern of segregation. First, it was comfortable and spontaneous; one African-American student commented: "Blacks and whites feel comfortable with their own kind of people, you know. As we sit and talk with our friends, we're separate, but there is no hard feeling against white kids" (p. 115).

Second, persons from the same group were felt to "know each other better." A third factor was pressure from others in the group to remain with one's own group. Students reported there was pressure in both African-American and white peer groups to avoid too much association with the other group. This took the form of "teasing" or "ridiculing," and some noted that no African-American student wanted to be "considered white." One African-American student commented: "As far as black students are concerned, they get not only peer pressure against being with whites, but they were brought up by their parents not to socialize with whites. The way they were brought up has a lot to do with their suspicion and distrust of them" (pp. 115–116). Fourth, students explained the segregated social interactions as reflecting the neighborhood divisions in the community: ". . . they grew up in different environments" (p. 116).

Not surprisingly, student friendship patterns generally reflected racial segregation. In a random sample of the entire junior class, 84% of the whites and 78% of the African-Americans indicated that their four best friends were of the same race as the respondent. In a closer analysis of 16 of the students, only 2 had close friends of the other race; both students were on the student council. It seemed clear that the social context was important for establishing friendships. Because these social contexts were generally segregated, friends were usually of the same race.

The school also grouped students into various levels of academic classes on the basis of grade-point average, test scores, teacher recommendations, and desires of the student and parents. The manifest function of this tracking (as noted earlier) is to promote learning and effective teaching for students of differing levels of ability. The latent function may be revealed by the fact that: "only three black students in the entire class of 357 students were placed above Section III in both English and math" (p. 121). This limited the opportunity for African-American students to interact in formal settings with white students in the top half of their class. Shimahara noted that this tracking reduced African-American students' access to "cultural capital," which he defined as "a total body of knowledge, skills, and symbols that serves to determine individual competence in social mobility and influences individual cognitive orientation toward life and society" (p. 122). This led to different patterns of socialization for the white students and for the African-American students, in general. Shimahara concluded:

> I suspect that racial separation in the school was considered natural by students and school personnel because it did not result from plot or plan; it was a consequence of actions woven into the fabric of everyday face-to-face interaction. Likewise, I suggest that no plan has been developed at Everest High School to place black students in lower sections and to limit their exposure to cultural capital because of their race. Instead, the typification of social interaction in day-to-day life in the school led to these consequences. What Everest did, however, was to perpetuate the structure that society interposed to separate blacks from whites and to relegate blacks to lower strata. [Shimahara, 1983, pp. 125–126]

Other studies of adolescents in a variety of schools have found similar patterns of social organization based on race (e.g., Noblit & Collins, 1980; Woods, 1979). It is important to note, however, that *separatism* differs from segregation that is forced by external authority; it does not necessarily imply discrimination or prejudice. Most minority groups (and adolescents themselves are, in a sense, also a minority group) experience a dialectical tension between separatism and assimilation (Hecht, Collier, & Ribeau, 1993, p. 64). However, discrimination can affect all minority adolescents, as the study by Konopka (1976) of young girls suggested:

They always put Indians down and that's not fair. When they put Indians down, that's when I don't like them. (16, *American Indian, urban*) [p. 117]

It was not so hard for me because I already knew how to speak English. But for people who do not speak English well, it is very hard. . . . I am making good grades and I hope to be able to finish high school. (15, *Chicana, urban*) [p. 118]

I didn't have no interest in school because nobody showed no interest in me. (16, *Oriental, urban*) [p. 123]

Although the implications of these findings for high school education, desegregation, and the reduction of racism in adult society are important, they are beyond the scope of our discussion here. However, we focus on other aspects of this issue in the final section of this chapter in the context of growing up in both a minority and the majority culture.

ADOLESCENTS WHO WORK FOR PAY

This chapter has focused on the social context of high school as one dominant setting for understanding the ecology of adolescence. Later chapters focus on two other major settings, the family and the peer group. A fourth context is becoming more important for understanding the social ecology of adolescence: work settings. A greater proportion of adolescents than at any time during the past 40 years are now working part-time, and there is no longer a difference between the numbers of male and female adolescents who work (U.S. Department of Labor, 1987). In one national study of high school seniors, only 7% said they had not worked for pay (Bachman, Johnston, & O'Malley, 1987). These high rates of adolescent employment are not found in other industrialized countries and thus are a unique aspect of adolescence in the United States (Steinberg & Dornbusch, 1991).

In addition, educators are recommending that various kinds of work experience be integrated into high school programs. For example, the Carnegie Commission report, described earlier (see Box 6.1), urged the development of a period of transition during the last 2 years of high school to prepare students for work or college. It also recommended a volunteer service component for all high school students. This service would be in the community or school and would not be paid. It would involve a minimum of 30 hours for each of the 4 years in high school.

They could tutor younger students; volunteer in the school cafeteria, office, audio-visual center; or maintain sports equipment and playing areas. They might also move beyond the school to libraries, parks, hospitals, museums, local government, nursing homes, day-care centers, synagogues, or churches. [Boyer, 1983, p. 210]

Part-time work is more frequent for adolescents in the United States than in many other countries.

Moreover, the report recommended that businesses form links with schools to provide apprenticeship experiences and part-time and summer jobs for high school students to assist them in planning their future (Boyer, 1983, p. 276). Some schools have such work programs, including volunteer work and work for pay. Their aim is to provide students with a greater understanding of working and, in some schools, to provide an opportunity for group discussion of the experience during school time (DeParle, 1992).

Clearly, work can provide a useful way to explore possible careers, to learn about one's skills and interests, and to gain greater self-confidence and a sense of providing a useful service. Supervised work in a setting related to school and a possible job can be an effective link between the often sterile classroom and one's future goals. But what effect does the typical part-time job, for instance in a fast-food restaurant, have on the adolescent?

One effect of working may be to reduce the amount of time available for homework or school-related activities. Another effect is to enhance the income of a student, which may teach the practical skills of managing money and can involve saving money for the expense of attending college. However, the money can also increase the purchasing power of the student and serve primarily to finance purchases of cars, clothing, records, and other products marketed specifically for adolescents. Likewise, work can expand the social experience and contacts of adolescents. At the same time, it may also reduce parental control over the adolescent. A respondent in one study of high school seniors commented:

> People here work, and they get their money to go have a good time. You've got your car, and in order to have your car you've got to work to pay for it. The reason you've got a car is so you can go around and have a good time. That's the whole process right there. [Green, 1990, p. 431]

Several cross-sectional studies have indicated that working may have positive effects on adolescents in terms of punctuality, dependability, and self-reliance (Steinberg, Greenberger, Garduque, Ruggiero, & Vaux, 1982). In one study, high school students who reported less conflict between their jobs and school were more motivated and less cynical about working; likewise, those with jobs that made use of their skills and abilities were less cynical about work (Stern, Stone, Hopkins, & McMillion, 1990).

However, these studies also suggested that spending more time at work is related to more absence from school, less enjoyment of school, and lower grades. Also, working was related to less time spent in family activities (but did not affect peer relations), and was associated with more negative attitudes about work. In addition, it is related to cigarette, alcohol, and drug use. Some of these effects of working were probably the result of repetitive jobs that provide little opportunity for learning and exposed the adolescents to environmental, interpersonal, and personal stress (Mortimer, Finch, Shanahan, & Ryu, 1992a, 1992b; Steinberg et al., 1982; Steinberg & Dornbusch, 1991).

One major study of 10th to 12th grade students in nine high schools in two states found clear evidence that part-time work can have negative effects on adolescents, especially if the time spent working exceeds 20 hours a week (Steinberg & Dornbusch, 1991). The sample consisted of about 4,000 adolescents; 8% were African-American, 14% were Asian-American, and 9% were Hispanic-American. The students completed questionnaires, and the results indicated that working was significantly related to grades in school, time spent on homework, and frequency of cutting classes. These results are shown in Figure 6.7. Time spent on homework and grade-point average showed a sharp drop for those who worked over 20 hours a week; the effect on grade-point average was not found for the African-American and Hispanic-American students, however. In addition, the study found that working was associated with drug and alcohol use, delinquency, lower self-esteem, and greater autonomy from their parents. The authors concluded:

> Compared with their classmates who do not work or who work only a few hours each week, students who work longer hours report diminished engagement in schooling, lowered school performance, increased psychological distress and somatic complaints, higher rates of drug and alcohol use, higher rates of delinquency, and greater autonomy from parental control. Workers do not have any advantages over nonworkers with respect to psychosocial development. In general, the deleterious correlates of employment increase as a direct function of the number of hours worked each week. [Steinberg & Dornbusch, 1991, pp. 309-310]

Another major study of random sample of 9th grade public school students in St. Paul, Minnesota (Mortimer et al., 1992b) found that 52% were working for pay. This study compared those who were working with those who were not working and found that part-time

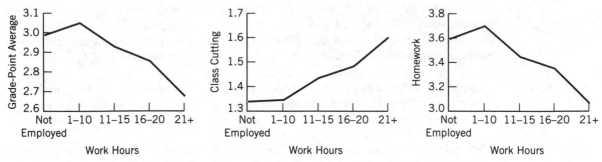

Figure 6.7 Relations between hours of work per week and grade point average, time spent on homework, and class cutting. [*Source:* L. Steinberg, & S.M. Dornbusch. Negative Correlates of Part-Time Employment During Adolescence: Replication and Elaboration. *Developmental Psychology*, *27*, 304–313, Figure 1. © 1991 American Psychological Association. Reprinted with permission.

work itself does not necessarily have deleterious effects. Instead, the amount of time spent working and the characteristics of the work have important effects. In fact, there was some indication that "low-intensity employment" may be beneficial. Also, boys who reported that the work gave them useful skills showed positive effects of working (the relationship was not as strong for girls). In contrast, stress at work (such as time pressure, being drained of energy, or exposure to excessive heat, cold, or noise) had negative effects for boys. For girls, negative effects were noted when the work interfered with schoolwork. Perhaps gender roles that emphasize the importance of schoolwork for girls and work skills for boys help to explain these findings.

It is important to note that these two studies focus on very different age groups of adolescents (10th to 12th grade vs. 9th grade). The 9th grade students often had informal neighborhood jobs such as babysitting, newspaper delivery, or yard work. The length of time students had worked had no relationship to problem behavior for girls but did have a negative effect for boys. However, the *intensity of formal work* (number of hours per month in commercial establishments or organizations) was significantly related to school problem behavior and alcohol use and smoking for girls (Mortimer et al., 1992a).

From these studies we cannot definitely conclude that work produces negative effects, because students who already had school problems or a propensity to use alcohol or cigarettes may have sought out work opportunities. Likewise, students who seek autonomy from parents might well choose to work so they can buy a car to spend time away from home. The St. Paul study by Mortimer and his colleagues is intended to be a longitudinal study, so the students will fill out questionnaires several times during their high school years. Perhaps this research will provide more definitive answers. At present, the best conclusion seems to be that the number of hours of work per week during the school year should be limited to reduce the risk of negative effects on adolescents (Steinberg & Dornbusch, 1991).

Because cross-sectional studies cannot provide clear answers about whether these findings actually reflect the effects of working or whether they reflect the characteristics of adolescents who choose to work, Steinberg and his colleagues (1982) studied a group of 10th and 11th grade students who had never worked before the study began. The respondents filled out questionnaires at the beginning of the study and again a year later. One-third of the 228 students who completed the second questionnaire were working at that time; 44% had not worked at all during the year. The types of jobs included food service, manual labor, retail sales, cleaning, clerical work, skilled labor, and child care. The sample was about 60% female, 80% white, 9% Hispanic, and 10% other. About one-quarter of the respondents had parents who were described as professional; one-third had parents described as white collar and management; and 43% had blue-collar parents. The statistical analysis allowed comparison of the change in each individual from the first questionnaire to the second, considering whether the person began working or not, the person's gender, and other background factors. The results indicated that working had different effects on girls than on boys. Generally, girls who were working showed more evidence of increased autonomy than boys did. It appeared that boys who worked were conforming to social expectations, rather than achieving autonomy from their parents; and, in fact, their relationship with the family improved. In contrast, girls who worked appeared to have been breaking away from the family and traditional social expectations; their closeness with their family declined sharply. Similarly, girls showed more gains in self-reliance if they worked than did boys. Likewise, Stern et al. (1990) found that girls showed greater motivation to perform work well and less cynicism about work than did boys.

In the longitudinal study by Steinberg et al. (1982), the more time the respondents worked, the greater their feelings of competence, pleasure, and persistence at work for both boys and girls. Working was also associated with less time spent on homework and a decline in school enjoyment; but, in contrast to other studies, it did not affect school performance, as measured by grade-point average. Likewise, although working reduced closeness with peers, it did not reduce the amount of time spent with peers. However, working led to more materialistic and cynical attitudes about work and greater acceptance of unethical work practices, although these variables differed by gender and the socioeconomic status of the students' parents. For example, boys became more materialistic (i.e., interested in the material benefits of working), but girls did not. Students from professional families became less cynical and less tolerant of unethical practices, whereas students from white-collar families became more so.

In summary, the effects of working on adolescents who are also students are not clear cut. In general, the evidence indicates that the effects are mixed, with longer hours of work having more negative effects; but working itself may have some positive benefits, depending on a variety of factors such as stress at work. The effect of part-time work on grades and homework is complex because many students spend little time on schoolwork outside of school and students who choose to work may differ from those who do not work in their interest and skill in academic achievement.

Finally, most respondents in these studies were working for additional income; few were working to help support their family or to gain work experience. However, the number of adolescents who work out of necessity is obviously greater among adolescents who drop out of school, as well as those who get married, live on their own, or provide income for their family. We discuss dropping out in Chapter 11. Choosing a vocation is discussed in Chapter 10.

MEDIA, TELEVISION, AND MUSIC

An important and often controversial aspect of the social ecology of adolescence is the popular media. Television and newspapers report adolescents rioting after watching a film depicting violence and aggression, concerned parents and civic leaders urging a ban on recordings of rock music with offensive or suicidal imagery, and general concern about the impact of video recordings, video games, and television itself. On the one hand, the media is a big business that seeks to sell products to willing buyers; naturally, sensation and controversy often lead to enhanced sales of the products of mass media. On the other hand, our nation is committed to freedom of speech, especially artistic and journalistic expression. Thus, for example, legislation to label compact disks (CDs) that contain offensive lyrics may lead to increased sales of those very disks. Parents, who may wish to limit the kind of videos or CDs their adolescents buy, may eventually defer to the adolescents, who will buy the CD or video with their own earnings and use them when the parents are not around, in the privacy of their own room, or with headphones.

Of course, popular music has long been important to adolescents, and the type of music adults prefer often has its roots in adolescence or young adulthood (Holbrook & Schindler, 1989). It may be that engaging adolescents in discussion about the music currently popular can elicit themes of development and lead to consideration of alternative perspectives and better communication with peers. Moreover, music popular during the parents' adolescence often dealt with similar themes in different ways so that it might provide a bridge between the generations (Mark, 1988). For example, the protest music of the 1960s and 1970s was in the folk idiom instead of rock, but was concerned with human rights, war, and the nuclear threat; similar themes are involved in some rock music today, but the latter tends to be less hopeful than the earlier folk music. It may be that social movements of the 1960s and 1970s extended the limits of tolerance so that contemporary songs about radical despair, world destruction, and suicide have resulted; other social factors associated with alienation may also be involved (Arnett, 1991a).

Several interesting studies have focused on rock music and its branch known as *heavy metal music*. Rosenbaum and Prinsky (1991) created a fictional case history of an adolescent whose parents were concerned about the music, clothing, and posters on the bedroom wall favored by their 15-year-old son. Ten out of 12 hospitals with adolescent care programs recommended that the boy be hospitalized, and most believed drug abuse was likely, although the case history specifically denied drug abuse or suicidal signs. The study concluded that there is a danger that adolescents may be stigmatized by their membership in a "punk" or "heavy metal" subculture in ways that could be harmful. Another study found that rock lyrics are often misunderstood, especially by younger listeners at concrete levels of cognitive development. Moreover, because lyrics are poetry, there often are multiple meanings so that adult critics of rock music and adolescent listeners may hear different themes (Greenfield et al., 1987). In fact, one reason given for watching music videos in a survey of adolescents was to find out what popular songs mean (Sun & Lull, 1986).

It should be noted that one clear effect of rock music is temporary hearing loss under some conditions (Danenberg, Loos-Cosgrove, & LoVerde, 1987). This study tested hearing of 20 junior and senior high-school students and 7 faculty or staff after a school dance. All but one student and one adult showed signs of noise-induced hearing loss just before leaving the dance. Six of the participants were tested again 3 days later. Although the hearing loss was assumed to be temporary and recovery was expected within 24 hours, only two of the students showed complete recovery after 3 days; the other 2 students and 2 adults showed only partial recovery. The authors suggested that holding rock concerts in high school cafeterias or gyms and other sites not acoustically suited for such high-volume sound may add to the problem. The risk is not limited to rock music, as classical musicians also have been found to show evidence of noise-induced hearing loss (Axelsson & Lindgren, 1981). For this reason, symphony orchestra musicians often wear ear protectors, especially if they sit in front of high-volume instruments.

James Lull (1992) noted that popular music has a particular influence on adolescents. Television, he felt, is part of family life, but popular music is part of peer-group life. Moreover, subcultures may be organized around music and provide a place for young people to meet at concerts and to share in the social experience and ideology of the group.

> Multiple sensory involvement with music gives it special meaning as an agent of communication. . . . [A]*ctive participation with a medium increases its potential as an agent of socialization* and there may be no more dramatic example of this than the actions of youth as they employ and enjoy popular music. The heavy beat, sexual lyrics, and aggressive tone of much popular music resonates with the emotional character of many adolescents, giving them abundant popular culture material with which to identify and a resource to exploit for personal and interpersonal objectives. Generally, young people use music to resist authority at all levels, assert their personalities, develop peer relationships and romantic entanglements, and learn about things that their parents and the schools aren't telling them. [Lull, 1992, p. 27]

Research on subcultures based on music and musical tastes among adolescents indicates that the social ecology of the school may play a major role in the choice of music subculture. For example, Roe (1987) concluded that those students who are successful in school tend to accept the school's culture; those who are failures adopt antischool subcultures. In a study of adolescents in Sweden, he found that higher school achievement was associated 2 years later with a preference for mainstream popular music, but lower school achievement was linked 2 years later with a preference for punk and rock music, as well as a greater orientation toward peers (Roe, 1983). This suggested that music preferences reflect relative success in school achievement and that the link is mediated by peer involvement.

> The more successful students, even when they come from the lowest social status background, show a greater liking for classical and mainstream music forms. The failing students move instead toward socially disapproved and oppositional music and at the same time orient themselves more fully to school peer groups. [Roe, 1987, p. 227]

Likewise, a study of "defiant" rock music enjoyment and use found that, although rebellious students did not enjoy such videos more than less rebellious peers, they enjoyed nondefiant rock music less and consumed it less than their peers (Bleich, Zillmann, & Weaver, 1991). Thus, it seemed that adolescents who preferred defiant music were, in fact, rejecting conventional rock, which is consistent with a rejection of other conventional (or school-related) culture. This view is in contrast to the idea that the defiant rock is in some way exerting an antisocial influence on otherwise conventional adolescents.

[T]he findings fail to support the notion that rebellious youths selectively engross themselves in defiant rock music. Surprisingly, such music proved to be highly appealing to nonrebellious youths. . . . On the other hand, rebellious youths have apparently great difficulty relating to romantic and other themes that dominate nondefiant music. [p. 363]

Similar findings were reported by Arnett (1991b). He found that adolescents who liked heavy metal music reported more "reckless" behavior such as driving while drunk, driving fast, having sex with someone known only casually, using drugs (for boys); having sex without contraception, shoplifting, or damaging property (for girls). Such adolescents also were higher on a measure of "sensation seeking" and were more self-assured about sexuality and dating. Thus, this music preference fit with several other characteristics that were consistent with the high level of sensation in the music itself.

It is interesting that the studies of adolescents who like heavy metal music tend to be based on samples that are disproportionately white and male. For example, 75% of the respondents to a sign posted in a store in suburban Atlanta recruiting participants in the study by Arnett (1991a) were white males. Therefore, he used a comparison group of boys from a nearby high school in his study. In general, Arnett (1991a) concluded that adolescent boys who liked heavy metal music were coping with a pervasive state of alienation shared by many in our contemporary culture. He felt that there were adaptive features to their use of heavy metal music, however, such as the ability of some to use it to purge themselves of anger. Other findings are summarized in Box 6.2.

Another study found that adolescents' use of music could increase their feelings of loneliness (Davis & Kraus, 1989). That is, the content of the music, such as sad or unhappy lyrics, might intensify rather than purge the lonely feelings. The study did not focus on heavy metal music, however, so the type of music might also be a relevant consideration. Based on data reported by Larson and Kleiber (1993), it is also probable that the adolescent listens to the music alone, for example in the bedroom, and engages in reflections and self-examination while listening. This situation could intensify any feeling the person had; thus a lonely person could find their feelings of loneliness increased.

The study by Larson and Kleiber (1993) also found that listening to music was more enjoyable than some other forms of media use such as watching television. Although television was the most frequently chosen media, its use diminished among adolescents between junior high school (12.9% of their time) to senior high school (7.2% of their time). Television also tends to become more of a solitary activity, with less time spent watching with the family as adolescents grow older. Music videos, VCRs, and video games were also relatively infrequently used—less than .5% of their time (Kubey & Larson, 1990; Lowery & De Fleur, 1983, p. 338). In general, the data indicated that adolescents shift from watching television with the family (especially on weekend mornings and evenings) to listening to music. Those that spend more time with television tend to be more family oriented. Those who spend more time with music tend to be more peer oriented (Larson, Kubey, & Colletti, 1989).

These data by Larson and his colleagues are based on a time-sampling methodology where a sample of adolescents are beeped by researchers using an electronic pager at 2-hour intervals seven times during the day and evening for 1 week. In response to the beep they were asked to complete a brief questionnaire about what they were doing, where they were, and the characteristics of their subjective feelings at the time. The adolescents were ran-

◆ BOX 6.2 SUMMARY OF FINDINGS FROM A QUESTIONNAIRE STUDY OF 52 WHITE ADOLESCENT MALES (AGE 14–20) WHO LIKED HEAVY METAL MUSIC

1. The most often cited reason for their preference was that they liked the musical talent and skill of the performers.

2. The bands they liked also attracted them because of the social consciousness in the songs.

3. Most (48%) paid most attention to the music, or to a combination of music and lyrics (41%); few put lyrics first (11%).

4. Most listened to heavy metal music when they were angry (43%); others listened to it whenever they had a chance (23%).

5. Although the songs they liked were bleak and despairing, many reported that it relieved their anger or made them feel better. That is, for 54% it seemed to purge them of their angry or negative feelings.

6. Nearly all had attended a heavy metal concert (88%), and most described it as a release of aggression, especially "moshing" or slamdancing (running into other dancers haphazardly) or stage diving (running on stage and jumping off into the crowd).

7. Many had a dream of being on stage, and over half tried to play a guitar or other rock instrument.

8. Parents usually disliked the music (57%), but few forbid it (according to the boys), although many restricted them from playing it loudly when the parents were present. Some parents encouraged their interest. Thus, rebellion or defiance against the parents did not seem to cause their enthusiasm for heavy metal music.

9. Over half said that most or all of their friends liked heavy metal music and it provided a strong bond among them by attending concerts, discussing music, listening together, and sharing recordings. Nearly all, however, had some friends who did not like it.

10. A substantial number (31%) reported strong hostility toward school and found the regimentation and structure of school hard to take.

11. They were generally less religious than the boys in the comparison group of boys who did not like heavy metal music.

Source: Arnett (1991a).

domly selected from fifth to ninth grade public school students in two suburban Chicago communities; one community was middle class, and the other was working class; both were almost entirely white. The communities had access to cable television, but only 35% had hookups; 85% of the households had VCRs. Data were collected during the school year because media use was quite different in the summer (Larson & Richards, 1989; Larson et al., 1989).

Other studies have found ethnic differences in media use. For example, Blosser (1988) reported that African-Americans and Hispanic-Americans from Chicago public school grades 2, 4, and 7 viewed more television than whites. The use of home video games, in contrast, was related to socioeconomic status.

In the suburban Chicago study by Kubey and Larson (1990), use of video games and VCRs was reported to be much more psychologically arousing than was traditional television. Video game use was also found to be much higher among boys than girls (80% compared with 20%) and among middle-class compared with working-class boys. Video arcade

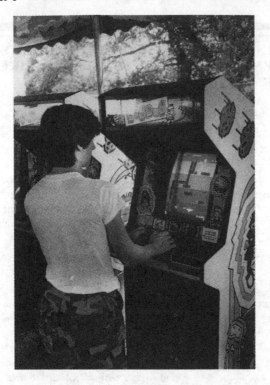

Video games often contain violent and antisocial values and seldom allow for cooperative rather than competitive play.

games were found to be even more arousing. Braun and Giroux (1989) observed adolescents in video arcades and analyzed the most popular video games. Most games allowed the players to compete sequentially, a few provided only solitary play, and none allowed for cooperative play. Many games were observed to contain violent and antisocial values.

Music videos are very popular in some communities. Sun and Lull (1986) reported on a sample of students in an ethnically diverse high school in San Jose, California, where 80% said they were viewers. For those who watched music videos, the average amount of time spent was over 2 hours of viewing per day. Most of the adolescents watched for information relevant to their social world, to appreciate the music, and for enjoyment or entertainment.

> They watch MTV to see particular groups, singers, and concerts, or have a generalized attraction to the musical content of MTV. . . .
>
> Respondents see the images as "visual aids" or "pictorial translations" of the *meaning* of the various songs they represent. Some students said that videos give "more meaning" to a song than they themselves would conjure up or that the videos promote "a whole new meaning" or a "different perspective" on the meaning. [Sun & Lull, 1986, pp. 120, 121]

Music videos were found to be similar to television viewing in terms of arousal; the only exception was when the teenagers were alone and, in some cases, reported dancing with the videos (Kubey & Larson, 1990).

The issue of parental control of media use has received some research attention. Lin and Atkin (1989) reported that parents were more likely to set limits on VCR use for male than for female adolescents in a sample of midwestern 7th and 10th grade students from middle-class suburban families. Also, adolescents with higher levels of academic performance reported more parental mediation of TV and VCR use. In this study, the average number of television sets in the household was three; 72% subscribed to cable TV, and 78% had a VCR at home. Parental control, either in general or over television use, also was found to reduce the impact of television on adolescents in a national survey of 10–14-year-olds. In contrast, adolescents who watched television with their parents or discussed television with them were more likely to be affected by the views expressed on television than those who did not (Rothschild & Morgan, 1987).

The role of the media in portraying violence has also received research attention. The link between television violence and behavior in children has been studied extensively, and it has been concluded that television violence has a causal effect on aggressive behavior (American Psychological Association, 1985; Lowery & De Fleur, 1983; Wood, Wong, & Chachere, 1991). Its effect on adolescents appears to be less important than the influence of other media, however. One study compared violence seen on TV, home video, and cinema among a sample of 801 German adolescents. Lukesch (1988) found a significant correlation between the amount of violent content of the media that the respondent watched or read and the amount of delinquent behavior. The relationship was much higher for VCR and cinema viewing of violence, despite the fact that such viewing was less frequent than viewing television or the other media. Moreover, the statistical analysis indicated a causal relationship from viewing video violence to delinquency. Among the delinquent behaviors measured were aggression against teachers, aggression against schoolmates or things, trouble during classes, reduced attention during classes, and mild delinquency such as riding a bus without a ticket.

In conclusion, it should be noted that the effects of television are mixed. On one hand, television may be found to be related to a variety of negative characteristics. For example, it may replace other activities, such as social interactions, athletic exercise, or studying. In a study of 401 middle-class boys attending high school (90% were white) Tucker (1987) found:

> Light television viewers were more physically fit, emotionally stable, sensitive, imaginative, outgoing, physically active, self-controlled, intelligent, moralistic, college bound, church oriented, and self-confident than their counterparts, especially heavy television viewers. Furthermore, light television viewers were less troubled, frustrated, and shrewd, and used drugs less frequently, particularly alcohol, than moderate and heavy television watchers, especially the latter. [p. 415]

However, these data do not indicate that television viewing caused the negative characteristics to appear; it is equally likely that persons with those behaviors were inclined to watch television, or vice versa. Moreover, Greeson (1991) concluded from his study of adolescents watching music videos that, although video images may affect the individual, individuals also analyze and evaluate media presentations, and some groups, such as older adolescents or females, interpret and respond differently to videos than others. Thus, the meaning of the video and its impact is determined by the interaction of the video and the individual.

Of course, television, video recordings, cable television, and other technological innovations also have great potential for educational, informational, social, and psychological development (Huston et al., 1992). Some studies also have found indications that the cognitive processes involved in watching videos, especially among adolescents, stimulate important and unique knowledge structures that deserve additional investigation (Blanchard-Fields, Coon, & Mathews, 1986). This aspect of the social ecology of adolescence is very likely to be the topic of considerable research in the future.

GROWING UP IN TWO CULTURES

One final example of the social ecology of adolescence is the fact that many adolescents grow up in two different cultures at the same time. This means that Hispanic adolescents in the United States experience the cultural expectations of the particular Hispanic culture in which their parents grew up as well as the cultural expectations of the dominant Anglo-European culture of the United States in which they are growing up. African-American adolescents, Asian-American adolescents, and other minorities in the United States likewise feel the effects of their unique cultural heritage as well as the influence of the dominant culture. Similar patterns exist in any country with minority groups (Wakil, Siddique, & Wakil, 1981).

Relatively little research has focused on these interesting aspects of adolescent development (Jones, 1989). However, the topic is particularly important in a pluralistic society such as ours, especially because the proportion of minority adolescents is increasing more rapidly

Adolescents have the potential to develop bi-cultural competence.

than the nonminority group. It is also important because much research has focused on white adolescents, or has assumed that all adolescents are essentially similar in cultural background. Moreover, minority adolescents have the potential to develop **bicultural competence** that allows them to draw upon a broad repertoire of skills and knowledge (Spencer & Dornbusch, 1990).

In this section we focus on some of the characteristic issues that confront adolescents who are growing up simultaneously in two cultures—their minority culture and the dominant culture. We stress the general themes that help us to understand the effects of this experience for all minority cultures, noting some of the ethnic differences that are especially important. This discussion is based on impressions and reports of individuals, as well as on some exploratory studies. More precise studies of these influences on adolescent development are necessary before we can state any firm conclusions.

In the following section many of the observations are based on a study of Chinese-American adolescents (Sung, 1979, 1985). There are two reasons for this: first, the issues are similar (but not identical) for other minority groups; second, Asian adolescents have received less attention in discussions of minority adolescents than the larger groups of African-Americans (Gibbs, 1990), Mexican-Americans (Ramirez, 1990), and Puerto Ricans (Inclán & Herron, 1990).

IMMIGRANT ADOLESCENTS

The special issues faced by immigrant adolescents are complex. *Language* is a major one. The language of school, the teachers, and other students may be different from the language spoken at home, or in one's home country. If we recall the concerns with being accepted by one's peers, the hypersensitivity because of the *imaginary audience*, and the fact that some adolescents can be very cruel to people who differ from themselves, we see that language can be a very special concern for adolescents who have immigrated from another country. Moreover, an adolescent may speak English better than his or her parents and therefore have to serve as a "translator" for the parents. This makes the parents dependent on the adolescent in an unusual way. In addition, feeling uncomfortable speaking in English may lead a person to be more shy, withdrawn, and self-conscious than he or she was before moving to this country. This is particularly stressful for adolescents who were popular and outgoing in their former peer group.

Cultural conflicts are another important issue for immigrant adolescents and their parents. The social expectations and values in the previous culture may be quite different from those in the new culture. For example, the Chinese culture teaches children not to fight; this is a very important value, and those who do fight have low social status (Sung, 1979, p. 92). In contrast, males in the United States are expected to stand up for themselves and to fight if necessary. Thus, Chinese adolescent males who do not fight are thought to be "sissies," and those who do fight are punished by their parents. Similarly, Chinese adolescents are taught to value education, and sexual interests are seen as distractions from learning. Dating is unfamiliar to most Chinese parents because their own marriage was essentially arranged for them. Open discussion or displays of sexuality are very embarrassing to Chinese girls, and Chinese boys are also expected to keep sexual feelings hidden until marriage. The contrast with sexual attitudes among adolescents in the United States is striking. Sung (1979) observed a dramatic example of this cultural conflict during her study in a Chinatown school:

A young Chinese girl had been forbidden by her parents to walk to school with a young Puerto Rican boy who was in the habit of accompanying her every day. To make sure that the parents were being obeyed, the grandmother would walk behind the girl to see that she did not walk with the boy. Grandma even hung around until her granddaughter went into class, and then she would peer through the window to make sure all was proper before she went home. Naturally, this was embarrassing for the girl, and it must have been noticed by the homeroom teacher. He exploded in anger at the little old lady and made some rather uncomplimentary remarks about this being the United States and that Chinese customs should have been left behind in China. . . . What he could have done was explain to the girl, or even to the entire class, the cultural values and traditions of her parents, so that she could understand how they thought and why they behaved in such a fashion. [pp. 93–94]

Immigrants from Hispanic countries also frequently report conflicts between the restrictive attitudes toward females and the more tolerant attitudes in the United States. Although adolescent boys are relatively free to express their "macho" impulses, girls are protectively guarded by their parents and brothers (Inclán & Herron, 1990). As in Chinese families, issues of dating, curfew, and kissing represent serious cultural conflicts for many families of Puerto Rican girls. Similar conflicts have also been reported among Indian and Pakistani families in Canada (Wakil, Siddique, & Wakil, 1981).

Another example of cultural differences is in styles of interpersonal relations, such as the expression of affection. Some African-American, Hispanic, and Mediterranean cultures are exuberant in emotional expression, in contrast to the reserved English and Scandinavian cultures, and in further contrast to the Chinese and Japanese cultures. Sung (1979) pointed out that in the very reserved Chinese culture, affection is never shown in public, even with one's spouse. Even a greeting between close friends does not involve a handshake, because it is traditional to clasp only one's own hands in greeting. Thus, Chinese adolescents may be perceived as cold and aloof. At the same time, they may wonder if their parents love them, or each other, because affection is never shown. Although these adolescents see expressions of affection in the popular media, and may want affection, they are unable to demonstrate it because of their earlier upbringing (Sung, 1979, p. 96). Thus, exuberant emotional expression may seem inappropriate, even if it is also envied, by adolescents from more reserved cultures. In turn, these Asian and Northern European adolescents may be seen as unemotional, uncaring, and detached. Because the dominant culture in the United States largely reflects Northern European values, many white people may therefore seem on the one hand to be too outgoing by Asian adolescents and, on the other hand, to be disinterested or cold by African-American, Hispanic, and Mediterranean adolescents.

Style of dress and attitude about spending money also differ between cultures in ways that are very important for adolescents. The Chinese traditionally value thrift and avoid purchasing on credit. Thus, clothing and home furnishings are expected to be extremely modest, reflecting the fact that most income is being saved. In contrast, the dominant culture in this country values the accumulation and display of material possessions. This may lead Chinese adolescents to envy the stylish clothing of their school mates, to feel their parents are "money-hungry," and to avoid inviting friends to visit their homes (Sung, 1979, pp. 97–98). Still other cultures value the public display of stylish living, while scrimping on the private furnishing of the home. These adolescents may also avoid inviting friends to their home, although they have a fashionable wardrobe for school and may regard less well-dressed adolescents as socially inferior.

As suggested by these examples, *relations with parents* may be a very important aspect of this cultural conflict. The parents reflect the "old" culture, while the adolescent is seeking to be accepted by the "new" culture. Thus, whether the issue is dating, sexuality, expression of affection, or attitude about money, adolescents who have immigrated are likely to experience more conflict than nonimmigrant adolescents. Moreover, if the adolescent speaks English and the parents do not, or is more skilled at the various bureaucratic tasks and computer forms so important to life in the United States, the adolescent is likely to be caught in the middle between the parents (and other family members) and the new culture. Not only is this a demand on the adolescent's time and daily responsibility, but also it makes the parents less powerful than they were in the old culture. Thus, the adolescent may not be as able to depend on the parents for support and guidance as would be the case in the "old" culture, or for adolescents in the dominant culture.

This loss of parental power also results from the direct effects of immigration. Typically, at least for Chinese immigrants, the social status of the father's job is much lower in the United States than it was before immigrating, largely because of the language barrier. For example, in Sung's (1979) study, only one out of ten fathers with a professional background found a similar position after immigration; half the former businessmen and five-sixths of the skilled laborers wound up with lower status jobs, usually in restaurant work; moreover, a high proportion appeared to be unemployed (pp. 149–150). Mothers also began working, usually for the first time, after immigrating. Their work was typically in factories making clothing where they were paid according to how many pieces they sewed. Because hard work and long hours increased their piece-work wages, these women could make a comparatively good income, which tended to reverse the traditional roles of husband and wife in the family. All of this increased the strain on the family already coping with the dramatic change in cultures. Although her piece-work job allowed her to take a few hours off to fix meals and oversee the children, she worked long hours. Often the father also worked long hours in a restaurant. As a result, the adolescents in Sung's study had relatively little contact with their parents. For example, even though 82% lived with both parents, 32% did not see their fathers on a daily basis, and 21% did not see their mothers daily (Table 6.1). Not surprisingly, the adolescents tended to feel lonely, ignored, and neglected. Nonetheless, they generally felt close to their parents, and over half of the boys and two-thirds of the girls felt closely supervised by their parents; however, 29% of the boys reported they were not supervised by anyone—a finding that may be related to the emergence of male teenage gangs in Chinatown (Sung, 1979, pp. 152–153).

One additional aspect of the experience of immigrant adolescents is the difference in *educational level* between the parents and the adolescent. In the Sung study, half of the fathers had a high school education (reflecting the traditional Chinese emphasis on education for males); mothers were more poorly educated. The adolescents, however, almost universally wanted to attend college. This goal was often one of the reasons the parents immigrated: to provide better opportunities for their children. Yet it also created another difference between the adolescents and their parents. Furthermore, it meant that the parents could not be role models for their children. Although this is not unusual for adolescents today, there are few role models in the Chinese community for the path these adolescents seek to follow; they are particularly lacking for females, two-thirds of whom wanted a career (Sung, 1979, p. 155).

Although these data obviously refer to families of one group of Chinese high school

Table 6.1 CONTACT WITH AND CLOSENESS TO PARENTS OF CHINESE HIGH SCHOOL STUDENTS

	Father (N = 270)		Mother (N = 270)	
	No.	(%)	No.	(%)
Live with parents				
Yes	222	82	232	86
No	27	10	21	8
No response	21	8	17	6
Hours see parents daily				
0	86	32	57	21
1–2	40	15	10	4
3–5	96	36	87	32
6–8+	48	18	116	43
Days see parents weekly				
0	58	21	45	17
1	40	15	10	4
2–5	31	11	19	7
6–7	141	52	196	73
Closeness to parents				
Distant	17	6	5	2
Not close	46	17	25	9
Somewhat close	78	29	78	29
Very close	106	39	147	54
No response	23	9	15	6

Source: Sung, 1979, Table 10-2, p. 152. Reprinted with permission.

students, it is reasonable to expect similar patterns among other immigrant families of adolescents in urban areas. Discrimination because of language, race, or other restrictions tends to limit first-generation immigrants to low-status jobs. Family stress because of the cultural discontinuity, mothers working for the first time and possibly earning more than the fathers, the disparity in education between adolescents and their parents, and the lack of role models in the culture for the adolescent's career goals probably are true for most immigrant families. Differences between the old and the new culture in many of the issues discussed in later chapters (such as relations with parents, peers, and sexuality) generally make the resolution of these adolescent concerns more difficult for immigrants. In addition, cultural conflicts are clearly related to the development of a sense of identity for those adolescents who are both American and something else. We discuss this issue in more general terms in the next section.

AMERICAN-BORN ADOLESCENTS

Many adolescents born in this country also experience conflicts between their culture and the dominant white, middle-class culture of the United States. There is great diversity of people in our heterogeneous society; this is especially evident in large urban areas, but is apparent in most sections of the country. These differences reflect ethnic and racial background, religious tradition, and lifestyle. In some instances, there is a largely self-sufficient neighborhood of people of the same group, or one may be an isolated family. Generally, there is a support network of one's family and other relatives, as well as some community groups that provide a cohesive link among members of the community. Informal social networks often provide assistance and links with other similar communities across the country or with the homeland. There may be shared language, heritage, and traditions that provide cohesion among the members. There may also be subgroups within the culture. The adolescent, therefore, grows up within this culture but also grows up within the dominant culture, which may differ considerably from the culture at home. This can result in cultural conflicts that are similar to the conflicts experienced by immigrants. However, many of these conflicts are also long-standing divisions within our society that are manifested in racial and ethnic discrimination. Thus, unlike some immigrants who may eventually assimilate into the dominant culture more or less, other adolescents are prevented from assimilation by discrimination.

African-American adolescents, for example, have learned that race is a characteristic that affects many aspects of life in the United States. They have been described as an "endangered species" in terms of education, unemployment, delinquency and crime, substance abuse, unwed-teenage pregnancy, violence, homicide, and suicide (Gibbs, 1989; Hammond & Yung, 1993). Even though their family may have lived in this country for generations, they are still seen as nonwhite, whereas a German family that immigrated two generations ago is fully accepted in the dominant white culture. As a result, the African-American culture has evolved a separate heritage within the dominant white culture. It exerts pressure on African-American adolescents as clearly as the "old" culture puts pressure on immigrant adolescents. Similarly, Asians and Hispanics experience discrimination by the dominant culture and may exert pressure on their adolescents to maintain their cultural identity (Gibbs & Huang, 1990). Thus, one theme of growing up in two cultures is the **dual identity** of being oneself in the larger culture and also being a member of one's ethnic, racial, or religious culture.

For example, LaFromboise and Low (1990) noted that Native American youth "often feel stranded between two cultures" that differ in language, religion, and cultural values. They also are aware of their parents' "often hopeless attitudes resulting from overwhelming impoverishment and discrimination" (p. 119).

Similarly, Inclán and Herron (1990) described the cultural clash between being American and being Puerto Rican, the generational clash in moral standards and cultural practices between parents and adolescents, the socioeconomic clash between wealthy mainstream communities and the disadvantaged "culture of poverty," and the developmental clash between the agrarian idea that one is a child until one becomes an adult and the urban-industrial idea of a stage of adolescence. They suggested:

> When working with Puerto Rican adolescents, therapists need to be aware of their own values and experiences and how these may influence their approach. Whereas for therapists the issue might present itself as *how* to succeed in the mainstream world, for their adolescent clients the issue may be a more basic one of "*Should* I aim for the mainstream world as a framework for success?" [p. 260]

The pressure on adolescents from minority groups to remain true to their cultural identity is important in our society, but it places a unique burden on these adolescents. Earlier, we

◆ *Profile*

VERA S. PASTER

Few psychologists are more experienced in the social ecology of adolescence than Vera Paster, whose professional life has focused on providing comprehensive mental health services to children and adolescents. Currently, she is a professor in the Department of Psychology at City College of City University of New York, where she is in charge of training a new generation of clinical psychologists to work with children and adolescents.

Born in the Bronx section of New York City, she initially intended to major in art at Hunter College in New York, but decided she could not make a living in that field. With a friend, she interviewed faculty in all of the departments of the college and decided that the one she knew nothing about was psychology. Thinking that it sounded interesting, she changed her major to it. As graduation neared, she learned that she would have to attend graduate school if she was to work in psychology. She applied to three different schools, was accepted in each, and decided to attend Clark University where she earned a Master's degree in 1949. Unable to get a job after graduation, she discovered that she needed first to do an internship. Sensing that her race would prevent her from being accepted (Dr. Paster is African-American), she got married; but after returning from her honeymoon in Mexico, she found that, in fact, she had been accepted. After completing the internship at Rockland State Hospital in New York, she found a job in a mental health agency and also went to school at night to earn a Ph.D. in psychology from New York University, which she earned in 1962.

discussed some of the ways this can influence the social organization within the school and the pressures it may place on adolescents. It is especially clear in schools, where success in academic courses can require, or be thought to require, "acting white." In turn, successful African-American students may be criticized by their peers for rejecting their black identity. Noblit and Collins (1980), in a study of a Southern high school where the college preparatory curriculum was dominated by whites, noted:

> The relatively proficient black students found success and their ethnic heritage to be in direct contradiction. They had to reject their culture for the purposes of schooling; the contingencies of success at CHS required it and they adapted. Nevertheless, the adaptation taught many lessons, not the least of which was to distrust whites. [p. 78]

Similarly, Steinberg, Dornbusch, and Brown (1992), in a study of 15,000 students in nine different high schools, found little peer support for academic achievement among African-

As she rose through the ranks in the agency, she was assigned to the Bronx, where she worked in the schools in her childhood neighborhood, eventually becoming a supervisor for the Bronx. In time, she became the first woman and the first African-American to be named Director of the New York City Bureau of Child Welfare. In the 1970s she organized an innovative community mental health center in Harlem. Returning to the Bureau of Child Welfare, she received a grant from the National Institute of Mental Health to provide training for the professional staff with the philosophy: "The life of that child has to be different as a result of our intervention."

Challenged by the prospect of developing the first program of mental health services for children and adolescents in the state of Massachusetts, she worked in Boston as Associate Commissioner for Mental Health for 4 years, where she established the first child abuse program that involved all of the relevant agencies working together. Learning of a faculty position at City College, she applied and returned to New York City in 1981.

Her work with adolescents has focused on primary prevention: providing alternative outlets for minority youth to build self-esteem in positive directions and to tap their wisdom in order to get them engaged on their own behalf. She has also been involved with a special program for very bright minority adolescents attending public schools and with an alternative high school that provides a wide range of health, recreation, and social services to adolescents in the inner city.

Dr. Paster was elected president for 1986–1987 of the American Orthopsychiatric Association, which established an award in her name to promote ethnic minority student development. She was named psychologist of the year in 1984 by the Association of Black Psychologists. She was also elected president of the Society for the Psychological Study of Ethnic Minority Issues, a division of the American Psychological Association.

Although her work in psychology leaves little time for other activities, she and her husband enjoy theater, music, and opera. They have four grandchildren.

American students. Even high-achieving African-American students reported very limited peer support, and many avoided contact with other African-American students. In contrast, Asian-American students reported extensive peer support and often formed study groups with other Asian-Americans. The study focused also on parental factors in achievement. They found that students who reported that their parents used an *authoritative* style that combines warmth, firmness, and a democratic pattern of decision making generally showed higher levels of achievement in school than those whose parents used an authoritarian style. However, in this study white adolescents typically experienced both the authoritative style of parenting and also peer support for high achievement. In contrast, Hispanic adolescents experienced neither peer support nor authoritative parenting because their parents tended to use the authoritarian style. Asian-American adolescents experienced strong peer support for achievement that offset the influence of their authoritarian parents, who seemed less involved in schooling than the other groups of parents. As noted above, African-American adolescents in the study did not experience peer support for academic achievement, which

High-achieving African-American students do not always have peer support and may avoid contact with peers who do not support their goals and ambitions.

undermined the positive effects of authoritative parenting and their parent's encouragement of academic achievement.

We conclude by noting that ethnic and racial minority adolescents face a number of unique issues as they cope with the transition of adolescence. For example, how does one deal with questions of interracial friendships and dating? Is it worthwhile to take the risks that may be involved, or should one not cross the "color line?" Can one strive for success and achievement in white society and yet be faithful to the "brothers and sisters" who are living in poverty because of racism and discrimination based on social class? Is it possible ever to achieve one's sense of identity so firmly that racist behavior by others will not bring back hatred about being seen as "second class?" What determines which whites can be trusted and which ones cannot? Can the anger about discrimination be transformed into something that is life-enhancing? These questions represent some of the issues that result from growing up in two cultures. They probably have no clear answers. Of course, they differ somewhat from one cultural group to another, reflect social and historical changes, and affect whites as well as minorities in our society.

There is a sense, as well, that these issues are relevant for adolescents who discover that they, as individuals, are members of a minority. For example, lesbian and gay male adolescents who discover their sexual orientation and seek to involve themselves in the emerging lesbian and gay community find similar conflicts between that culture and the dominant culture. As they seek to identify themselves with their gay "brothers and sisters," they may feel alienated from the larger culture. They may also find themselves alienated from their families. In that regard, they differ from other minority groups because they often cannot turn to their parents for support against the discrimination they experience. Unlike other minorities, whose parents teach their children to cope with rejection because of their minority status and provide role models for them, lesbian and gay male adolescents are sometimes rejected by their parents and may have few positive adult role models who are known to them. Nonetheless, they must cope with developing an affirmative identity as a member of a minority group (Uribe & Harbeck, 1991).

We have been able to give only a brief overview of the kinds of concerns and issues that are involved with experiencing adolescence simultaneously in two (or more) different cultures at the same time. Discrimination is a significant experience for many adolescents, and the pressures come from both cultures at once. These cultural differences provide much potential richness for adolescents in this country, but too often they are ignored, devalued, and used to limit growth instead of to enhance it. Nonetheless, they provide a very important component in the social ecology of adolescence.

The next two chapters expand our focus to other very important aspects of the adolescent's social environment. Chapter 7 discusses the family and relations with one's parents; Chapter 8 describes the peer group, friendships, and dating.

CHAPTER SUMMARY

1. Ecology may be defined as the interrelationship between the environment in which an organism lives and the organism itself. The school, family, and peer group are important aspects of the adolescent's social ecology. This chapter provides an introduction to the social world of adolescents.

2. Population characteristics of the society directly affect social ecology. The relative number of age-mates in one's generation, and the proportion of one's generation to the rest of the population in the country, are important influences on a large number of characteristics in one's life, according to Easterlin.

3. Population patterns produce conditions of high or low competition with one's age-mates throughout life, depending on whether one was born in a period of high birth rate or low birth rate, respectively. Lower opportunity for employment and advancement, delayed marriage, more illegitimate births,

and higher rates of divorce and suicide may be related to the stress produced by competition among those born during a period of high birth rate.

4. The high school is a social environment that is a social center, a testing ground for one's abilities, and a miniature society of its own. Its functions are to provide an education and skills; keep young people occupied and out of the job market; prepare young people for college and work; enhance social skills and ability to relate with others; and sort young people into paths that affect much of their later life.

5. There is considerable difference among the thousands of high schools in this country, and there is growing diversity among the millions of high school students. Various social changes and severe financial problems have added to the challenges faced by high schools. Serious criticisms have also been raised about their performance in educating young people.

6. The transition from elementary to secondary school often causes some difficulty for many adolescents. These problems appear to reflect characteristics of the junior high school and its social environment, which has been found to be more impersonal, more competitive, developmentally regressive, and have higher grading standards than elementary schools.

7. The Carnegie Commission report focused on a number of problems in public high schools that can be corrected. Their recommendations included providing a more coherent pattern of courses, strengthening English instruction, reorganizing the school day and the school environment, improving working conditions of teachers, reaffirming the important role of the principal, and providing adequate funding for education.

8. Studies of the social environment of the high school have identified a number of social groups. These may include a "leading crowd" and a variety of interrelated groups that reflect participation in athletics, special interests, involvement in school activities, interest in social activities, and various groups that are on the fringes of social acceptability.

9. Racism and discrimination in the surrounding community are usually reflected in the social organization of the school. In a typical high school in the northeast, segregation by race was generally evident in informal settings such as the halls, cafeteria, library, and in free activities in gym class. In addition, academic tracking led to different patterns of socialization for the white students and for the African-American students.

10. A greater proportion of adolescents are now working part-time than at any time during the past 40 years; they are also working more hours each week than previously. Working more than 15–20 hours a week during the school year appears to have negative effects on health and on the adolescent's homework and closeness with friends. Working under stressful conditions was also associated with increased cigarette and marijuana smoking.

11. An important and often controversial aspect of the social ecology of adolescence is the popular media: videos, television, and music. Studies on rock music have noted parallels in themes with folk music of previous generations of adolescents. Research on heavy metal music suggests that it may provide a release for anger, but may be associated with reckless behavior. Listening to music alone can increase loneliness, and loud music can affect hearing. Violence in television and films has been found to be associated with aggression and delinquency.

12. Many adolescents grow up in two different cultures at the same time. Immigrant adolescents face several special issues including language, cultural conflicts, relations with parents, and difference in educational level between the parents and the adolescent. Discrimination because of race may also be a factor.

13. One theme of growing up in two cultures is the dual identity of being oneself in the larger culture and also being a member of one's ethnic, racial, or religious culture. Ethnic and racial minority adolescents face a number of unique issues as they cope with the transition of adolescence. These include remaining true to one's culture while also developing an identity that allows one to function effectively in the dominant culture.

KEY WORDS

age composition	**cliques**	**ecology**	**manifest functions**
age-specific	**comprehensive high**	**junior high school**	**middle school**
alternative schools	**schools**	**latent functions**	**secondary schools**
bicultural competence	**dual identity**	**magnet schools**	

REVIEW QUESTIONS

1. Compare the term *ecology* with the idea of dialectical interaction (Chapter 1) and contextualism (Chapter 2). Are these different ways of making a similar point? Are there differences between these ideas?

POPULATION DEMOGRAPHICS: LESS MEANS MORE

2. What are some of the effects of the *boom* and *bust* cycle of birth rates in the United States after World War II?

3. Describe the distinction between age-specific effects and age-composition effects. Cite an example of each.

SECONDARY SCHOOLS

4. List three *latent functions* and three *manifest functions* of secondary schools in the United States.

5. What type of high school did you attend, according to the categories used in the text (e.g., comprehensive, grades 9–12, etc.)?

6. Did your high school comply with any of the recommendations from the Carnegie Foundation published in 1983 (Box 4.1)?

7. What aspects in the social ecology of junior high schools appear to cause students difficulty (e.g., decline in grades)?

8. One study described in the text focused on boys in a high school, some of whom were described as "citizens" and others as a "tribe." Based on your experience, is there a similar difference for girls?

9. What extracurricular or cocurricular activities did you engage in during high school? Why or why not? Did they have any effect on your self-esteem or educational aspirations?

10. The Shimahara study on racial separatism was reported in 1983. Have there been changes since that time with regard to race relations in the schools you are familiar with?

ADOLESCENTS WHO WORK FOR PAY

11. What are some of the psychological benefits associated with part-time work?

12. List some of the negative effects working can have on adolescents.

13. What do you conclude is the best advice to give adolescents about whether and how much to work?

MEDIA, TELEVISION, AND MUSIC

14. Explain the statement: Television viewing is part of family life, but popular music is part of peer-group life.

15. Describe the characteristics that differ between adolescents who only listen to defiant rock music as compared with youth who also enjoy non-defiant music.

16. What are some of the potential effects of adolescents' listening to music alone?

17. In what ways do music videos, video games, television, movies, and VCR viewing affect adolescents differently? Does the media cause the differences, or do different adolescents select different media, in your opinion?

GROWING UP IN TWO CULTURES

18. Give some examples of the concept of *bicultural competence.*

19. How are parent–adolescent relationships affected by growing up in two cultures for families who immigrate to the United States? Give several examples.

20. List several issues related to the concept of *dual identity* for adolescents growing up in two cultures.

21. How does the interaction of parental style and peer support lead to differences among African-American, Asian-American, and Hispanic-American high school students?

22. What are some parallels and some differences between lesbian and gay male adolescents and other groups of minority adolescents?

Chapter 7

♦

Growing Up Is a Family Affair

♦

In many respects growing up consists of learning to be physically and psychologically independent of one's parents. Infants start their progress toward independence with their first struggles to sit up and stand by themselves. Later, as preschoolers, they acquire such self-help skills as feeding and dressing themselves, and they begin to use language effectively to express their needs and influence their environment. During the elementary school years children expand their knowledge of the world and learn ways of managing their experience that make them increasingly self-reliant and less in need of supervision. Then, in adolescence, young people begin to seek psychological freedom from their parents—freedom to be their own person, to choose their own companions and pastimes, and to preserve the privacy of their thoughts, feelings, and belongings.

None of these steps along the way to independence proceeds in a vacuum. At every point the progress young people make toward self-sufficiency and how they feel about their own capacities is influenced by what their parents say and do. The psychological world of parents is, in turn, influenced by how their children are progressing toward maturity. Growing up is thus very much a family affair, shared by children and parents alike and by the family unit as a group. This is especially true in adolescence, because most parents of teenagers are at a transition point in their own lives, when having adolescent children signals to them that they are no longer young.

This chapter considers four key aspects of the family interaction processes that accompany and shape adolescent development: (1) the emergence of a new balance between autonomy and attachment in adolescents' relationships to their parents; (2) the impact of patterns of parental authority on adolescent attitudes and capacities for self-reliance; (3) the developmental influences of nontraditional family organization; and (4) the quality of relations between the generations, including the consequences of physical and sexual abuse.

AUTONOMY AND ATTACHMENT

In Chapters 3–5 we discussed the pubertal maturation and expanding cognitive capacities that begin to occur during the early adolescent years. These developmental changes leave young people with a different body and a different frame of mind. Now they have attained most of their adult height, have become more like grown-ups than like children in their physical appearance, and are nearing peak attainment of their basic mental abilities. They are capable of procreation, and they have accumulated considerable knowledge of the world around them.

As a consequence, adolescents begin to feel qualified to run their own lives and deserving of being treated as adults, and they enjoy exercising their capabilities and trying on adult roles for size. What adolescents want is **autonomy**, which is freedom to decide for themselves how to think, feel, and act. Few things cause more resentment and humiliation in young people than having their maturity belittled or their freedom limited.

We referred briefly in Chapter 3 to some observations by Gisela Konopka (1976), whose book, *Young Girls*, provides some first-hand accounts of how adolescents view family relationships and other aspects of their lives. Her research team interviewed over 800 12–18-year-old girls from various socioeconomic backgrounds living in different parts of the

Becoming grown up requires adolescents to learn how to handle new kinds of situations in which they may at first feel uncomfortable.

United States. Half of the group were minorities, including African-American, Hispanic-American, Inuit, Asian-American, and Native American adolescents. Here is how two of these girls expressed their concerns about adults not appreciating the adolescents' maturity:

> They don't understand the maturity we attain by the time we get to be sixteen or seventeen . . . they kind of still look upon us as a child and they treat you in that respect, when actually by the time you're that old, you're almost old enough to vote and get married and things like that. And you should be mature enough to accept more responsibility than they're willing to give you. (African-American, urban, age 17.) [p. 60].
>
> My mother and I are in complete conflict because she tried to baby me because I am her only child . . . I'm trying to grow up and she's not letting me. (White, urban, age 17.) [p. 66].

Although dating from the 1970s, these views of the girls Konopka interviewed are as relevant now as then—and probably have been and will be for a long time to come. There is good reason to believe that basic aspects of the way young people grow up and relate to their parents have a **universal** flavor. The content may change from one generation to the next, or from one society to another, but the developmental processes and types of interaction stay the same. Back in the days of ancient Greece, as described in the dialogues of Plato, Socrates asks a boy named Lysis whether his parents gratify all his wishes. In response, Lysis complains that, even though his parents seem to want him to be happy, his father will not let him drive the family chariot (cited by Hall, 1904, vol. 1, p. 514). Norman Kiell (1964), in a book called *The Universal Experience of Adolescence*, reports a wealth of such historical and cross-cultural evidence of the youthful quest for adult privileges.

Adults do in fact sometimes treat adolescents as being less capable or responsible than they are, for reasons we discuss in this chapter. By and large, however, adults foster adolescent striving for independence by encouraging and rewarding it. Thus young people become increasingly autonomous not only as a result of becoming physically and cognitively mature, but also because self-reliance is expected of them. In the home, most families provide a graduated series of expanded privileges and progressively less restrictive rules and regulations. For example, parents usually set curfews that they relax a bit each year, and they establish the age at which they will allow their adolescent children to date, use the family car, take out-of-town trips with their friends, and the like.

At school, the passage from elementary school to junior high is marked by having different teachers for each subject and changing classrooms several times a day rather than having one primary teacher and classroom; senior high school brings increased opportunities to choose which courses to take and increased responsibility for keeping up with homework assignments. In modern society, the primitive puberty rites mentioned in Chapter 1 have given way to numerous **mini-rites** by which we let young people know that they are considered ready for increasingly responsible self-determination. For example, most states set age 16 or 17 as the age at which adolescents can leave school, obtain a work permit, be licensed to drive, and be tried in adult court for breaking the law. As noted by the girl we quoted from Konopka's book, high school students are also aware that they are nearing an age when they can vote in elections and marry without their parents' consent.

The readiness of adolescents to become more autonomous and the encouragement they receive to do so result in increasing separation of children from their parents during the teenage years. However, the emergence of autonomy does not mean that adolescents become entirely "free" or "independent" of their parents. Although young people make rapid progress toward becoming their own person following puberty, their new-found freedom and independence are relative, not absolute; that is, they become freer and more independent than they were as children, but not completely so.

Psychological maturation in adolescence thus consists of growing increasingly self-reliant and taking increasing responsibility for regulating one's own behavior, but not becoming totally autonomous or independent. Adolescents and their parents continue to depend on each other in many ways, and the changes in parent–child relationships that occur during the teenage years involve a renegotiation of the **interdependence** between them—in terms of who will take how much responsibility for what—rather than any severance of the family ties that have previously bound them together. Accordingly, as we shall see, it is as important to recognize ways in which adolescents and their parents remain connected to each other as it is to identify how and why they begin to separate. It is also important to recognize how adolescent maturation evokes ambivalent feelings in family members and how these feelings are influenced by the midlife status of parents and the emerging sexuality of their teenage children.

BECOMING SEPARATE

Parent–child relationships change dramatically during puberty. Compared to younger children, adolescents who have begun to experience pubertal growth begin to spend less time with their parents and to feel less emotionally attached to them; they become more likely to criticize and disagree with their parents; and they become increasingly assertive and unwilling to submit without question to their parents' authority. These changes have been formulated by Laurence Steinberg (1989) as the **distancing hypothesis**, which states that pubertal maturation produces a growing distance between young people and their parents.

The distancing hypothesis has been confirmed in numerous research studies in which it has been demonstrated that puberty ushers in diminished attachment to parents, increased family conflict, and greater adolescent involvement in decision making (Collins, 1990; Paikoff & Brooks-Gunn, 1991; Papini, Roggman, & Anderson, 1991; Smetana, 1988). Two of these studies, which involved real-life observations of family members interacting with each other, are of particular interest. In one, 93 families with 5th- to 12th-grade children were asked to work on a family interaction task in which they had to resolve conflicts concerning how adolescent behavior should be regulated. The older the children were in these families, the less likely they were to concede to their parents' opinions without expressing their own point of view (Smetana, Yau, & Hanson, 1991).

In the other study the investigators stationed themselves in a shopping mall and an amusement park and unobtrusively observed 122 pairs of mothers and their children age 6–18. During the initial 30 seconds of this observation, note was taken of whether mother and child were interacting by touching, smiling, talking, or gazing at each other. Figure 7.1

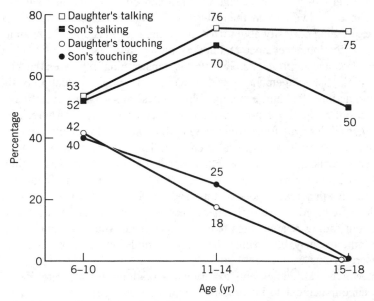

Figure 7.1 Frequency of touching and talking during a 30-second observation of mother–daughter and mother–son dyads. [*Source:* Based on data reported by Montemayor and Flannery (1989).]

shows the main result of the study: Early adolescence was a transitional period of increased physical distance in which the style of parent–child engagement shifted from touching to talking (Montemayor & Flannery, 1989).

Research on these changes in parent–child relationships during adolescence has consistently indicated that they are triggered by **pubertal status** and not by **chronological age**. What matters with respect to young people and their parents beginning to separate from each other is not how old a boy or girl is, but rather how physically mature he or she has become (Steinberg, 1987a, 1988). Steinberg's research involved both cross-sectional comparisons among 10–15-year-old boys and girls who were rated for their level of pubertal maturation on the basis of their physical appearance, and a longitudinal follow-up of these same youngsters 1 year later when they were age 11–16. Regardless of age, those boys and girls who were pubertal, compared to those who were still prepubertal, reported less feeling of cohesion with their mothers, less feeling of acceptance by their fathers, and a greater sense of emotional autonomy.

The strong relationship between pubertal maturation and emotional distancing in families of adolescents derives in part from the increased competencies of physically maturing children; for the most part, they are more capable of fending for themselves and are more interested in doing so than children who have not yet begun their growth spurt. In addition, those children who have begun to grow tall and look like adults are the ones most likely to receive the kinds of independence-fostering from adults that promotes autonomy. Parents, in particular—when they are influenced by their youngster's physical development to begin treating him or her less like a child—can exert a powerful impact on progress toward self-determination and self-reliance.

Stuart Hauser (1991), who observed and collected information from 133 14- and 15-year-old young people and their families over a 3-year period, concluded that the ways in which parents talk to their teenage children can either *enable* or *constrain* the teenagers' learning to be individuals in their own right. Talk that is enabling consists of explaining things, expressing curiosity about what the young person is doing, engaging in joint problem solving, expressing acceptance and understanding, and encouraging the expression of independent ideas and impressions. Talk that is constraining expresses detachment, lack of curiosity, subtle discouragement, or even direct mockery or devaluation of the young person's views and actions. Parental enabling helps adolescents separate from their families and develop the self-regulating autonomy that is expected of adults, whereas parental constraint discourages adolescents from even trying to think and do for themselves.

By and large, the developmental events that lead adolescents to separate psychologically from their parents, as well as most other aspects of family relationships in adolescence, proceed in just about the same way for girls and boys. According to Steinberg (1987b), who is one of the leading researchers in this area, differences between sons and daughters are found less frequently than differences between mothers and fathers when questions are asked about family relationships. On the other hand, there is some evidence that becoming autonomous may be a somewhat more complex process for girls than for boys, for two reasons.

First, whereas all adolescents experience a readiness to separate from their parents and receive encouragement to become more independent, girls in our society are more likely than boys to experience as well some subtle and sometimes not so subtle pressure to remain close to and embedded in their family. This kind of mixed message is rooted in old stereotypes that men go off to work while women stay at home. As we indicate later in this chapter when discussing dual-earner families, there is little support in fact for such a stereotyped belief. Nevertheless, what adolescent girls report about their life at home leaves little doubt that they are still encouraged more than boys to value closeness to the family (Bartle, Anderson, & Sabatelli, 1989; Stern, 1990). As a result, girls may have to work harder than boys to reconcile family separation and connectedness in their own minds, and they may need more time to become comfortable in asserting autonomy.

Second, whereas early physical maturation generally accelerates adult treatment of children as becoming grown up, thereby helping them acquire autonomy, other consequences of early puberty are more problematic for girls than for boys. To elaborate on our discussion in Chapter 3 of this gender difference, boys who mature early tend to be bigger and stronger than their peers, and their mature appearance and athletic prowess are socially beneficial; girls who mature early grow taller and heavier than their peers and are conspicuous for their breast development, which is not in keeping with present-day emphasis on being slim and exposes them to social situations for which they are psychologically unprepared. An early adolescent boy who shaves and has big muscles is admired by all. An early adolescent girl with a shapely figure is at risk for being giggled at by the boys in her class, whistled at by the older boys in her school, and regarded by adults, including her own parents, as needing special supervision to keep her out of trouble.

Not surprisingly, then, when Savin-Williams and Small (1986) asked a sample of 133 parents about their experiences with their adolescent children, the results indicated a clear relationship between the timing of their child's puberty and their experience of difficult and conflicted relationships with them. These parents reported experiencing more conflict with early maturing daughters than early maturing sons and more conflict with early maturing than late maturing daughters, but less conflict with early than late maturing sons. With respect to becoming comfortable with increased autonomy and new ways of relating to their parents, then, girls who mature early may face some special difficulties that delay their progress toward autonomy compared to boys.

REMAINING CONNECTED

Normal adolescent development involves learning to be psychologically independent from one's parents, as we have just discussed. It also involves turning increasingly toward relationships outside the home, as we discuss in Chapter 8, and seeking an identity in one's own right, which we take up in Chapter 10. These developments cannot be achieved if adolescents remain childishly attached to their parents; however, they are not served by becoming totally disconnected from one's family either.

There is good reason to believe that maturation should not be measured by how far adolescents have moved outside of relationships with their parents, nor should adolescent progress toward autonomy be regarded mainly as a matter of separation. Instead, the transition to mature self-reliance is best viewed as a process of **individuation**. Adolescents individuate by becoming capable of separating themselves from their parents and thinking for themselves, while at the same time continuing to participate as family members and collaborating with their parents in resolving issues in their lives. From this perspective, being an autonomous individual and being in an interdependent relationship with one's parents are not mutually exclusive; instead, autonomy and interdependence are two complementary features of normal family growth during adolescence. Research with families has consistently demonstrated that, at the same time as adolescents are actively engaged in trying to become distinct from their parents and to assert their own views, they are also trying to understand and accommodate to their parents' views (Grotevant & Cooper, 1986; Smollar & Youniss, 1989).

Adolescents who are individuating in normal fashion display their continuing attachment to their family by maintaining psychological closeness to their parents, even though they are spending less time in their physical presence, and by seeking their advice, support, and approval. How close they feel to their parents and how closely they listen to them tends to vary, however, depending on which parent is involved and what the topic is. Mothers and fathers, in turn, differ on the average in how involved they are with their adolescent children and in which aspects of their children's development capture their greatest interest.

Research findings indicate that adolescents of both genders and all ages feel closer to their mothers than to their fathers and choose their mothers over their fathers when they are seeking advice to solve a problem (Green & Grimsley, 1990; Paulson, Hill, & Holmbeck, 1991; Youniss & Ketterlinus, 1987). In one study of 296 13–17-year-olds by Noller and Callan (1990), both girls and boys reported having more frequent discussion with their mothers than their fathers about their interests, relationships, general problems, and sex roles and attitudes. Only with respect to sex problems were boys equally likely to talk with their fathers as their mothers, whereas girls were much more likely to talk to their mothers than fathers about such matters.

The reasons for this difference in closeness to mothers and fathers are not clear. Among the possibilities suggested by other findings in the Noller and Callan study are more frequent initiation of conversations with adolescent children by mothers than fathers and a greater receptivity on the part of mothers to their adolescents' opinions. It may also be that mothers are more likely than fathers to be at home when adolescents are there and are thus simply more available. However this may be, there is also evidence that mothers in turn generally experience more closeness than fathers to their adolescent children (Paulson et al., 1991).

As for what captures a parent's interest, there are in most families clear differences between the topics of most concern to mothers and fathers. Mothers are particularly interested in monitoring their children's emotional states, keeping informed about their interpersonal relationships, and making sure they fulfill their household obligations. Fathers, on the other hand, are more likely to be attentive to their adolescent's progress toward self-reliance than their social life and to pay special attention to how they are doing in school and what plans they are making for the future (Power & Shanks, 1989; Youniss & Smollar, 1985, Chapter 5).

The extent to which both mothers and fathers strike a balance between closely controlling their adolescents and granting them autonomy is not based solely on their personal preferences, however. Instead, most parents are influenced by how their children manage opportunities to exercise self-reliance. The more competence young people demonstrate in managing their own affairs, the more parents are inclined to grant them increased privileges; conversely, teenagers who seem childish and irresponsible tend to evoke parental insistence on their remaining dependent rather than free (Amato, 1989; Weissman, Cohen, Boxer, & Cohler, 1989). Hence, the ways in which parents influence their adolescent children to become separate while remaining connected is an interactive process involving both parental style and adolescent competence.

Adolescents benefit considerably when their parents are able to encourage them to rely on themselves while also making it clear that they can still turn to their parents for advice and a helping hand when they need it. In one study of 130 boys and girls in grades 7–9, Litovsky and Dusek (1985) found that those young people who perceived their parents as being warm and accepting and granting them autonomy felt better about themselves and were having more opportunity to learn social skills than those who were more likely to perceive their parents as controlling, cold, or rejecting. Other research has documented that parents who encourage their children to individuate while continuing to provide them with support enhance the self-esteem of their offspring and facilitate their becoming capable of taking on adult responsibilities (Berg-Cross, Kidd, & Carr, 1990; Collins, 1990; Grotevant & Cooper, 1986; Peterson & Leigh, 1990).

Adolescents also benefit considerably when they are able to maintain a sense of close attachment to their parents even while they are separating from them. When young people are asked to describe themselves and their family relationship, those who report feeling attached to their parents tend to be the ones who also report feeling psychologically comfortable with themselves and satisfied with their lives (Leung & Leung, 1992; Raja, McGee, & Stanton, 1992).

FEELING AMBIVALENT

Whenever they begin to separate from their parents and whatever the pace at which they become self-reliant, adolescents typically experience some ambivalence about the process and have some mixed feelings about giving up the protected status of their childhood. When teenagers begin to enjoy new privileges, they sometimes find themselves regretting the responsibilities that go along with them. Being "on their own" means that young people can no longer expect their parents to furnish their spending money, make difficult decisions for them, or shoulder the consequences of their mistakes in judgment.

Emancipation means further that adolescents must deal with unfamiliar situations in which they may feel awkward and inept, such as when they are expected to apply for jobs, make their own arrangements for music lessons or doctors' appointments, and act as an adult in dealing with sales clerks, auto mechanics, and waiters in restaurants. Adolescents usually have to fumble a bit until they develop confidence and skill in handling these situations, and they may suffer painful moments of uncertainty and embarrassment while they are learning to act grown up. At such times young people often yearn for the carefree days of childhood, when their parents took care of practical matters for them.

Because of such mixed feelings about becoming independent, most younger adolescents alternate from time to time between mature and childish behavior. One day they may take full responsibility for working out a difficult situation, and the next day they may turn helplessly to their parents for solutions to very simple problems. They may show surprisingly good judgment and sensitivity on some occasions, whereas at other times they act impulsively and with little consideration for others. These abrupt swings in apparent maturity do not reflect fluctuations in a young person's basic capacities for autonomy; they merely bear witness to the typical adolescent alternation between wishing to become an adult and longing to remain a child.

Like their children, most parents of adolescents have some mixed feelings about autonomy and attachment in their family. For the most part they enjoy seeing their children grow into and out of adolescence, but they experience regrets as well. Parents typically pride themselves on how their children look, what they know, and how much they can do, all of which reflect on their own qualities as people and as parents. They may take special satisfaction in seeing that their offspring have had a better start in life than they did and have better prospects for a rewarding adulthood. For many parents, moreover, the progress of their children toward adulthood brings a welcome realization that they are becoming free to do things that they felt unable to do while their children were young, such as taking a long trip or moving to a different environment.

At the same time, the increasing independence of adolescents and their increased exposure to various dangers and disappointments bring new concerns to the family. Most parents worry at least a little about how their youngsters will cope with social and academic frustrations; how they will handle sex, alcohol, tobacco, and drugs; whether they will drive safely; and whether their lives will be interrupted by some new war. Parents may consequently share with their adolescent sons and daughters some nostalgia for the earlier childhood years, when life was less complicated for them all.

Adolescence can also be a trying time for mothers and fathers who have relished their parental role and given child rearing top priority in their daily lives. To them the maturation of their children may signal the end of their most meaningful function in life. Even parents who have not been particularly child oriented often experience what is known as an **empty nest reaction**: They feel some sadness as their youngsters approach the age when they will move out on their own, leaving behind a home that is emptier, quieter, and less caught up with the excitement of a younger generation.

Undercontrol and Overcontrol

The mixed feelings that mothers and fathers of adolescents typically have about their parental roles can lead them to show widely different and occasionally inconsistent attitudes toward their youngsters' emerging autonomy. Some parents are especially eager to be free from child-rearing responsibilities and press their adolescents toward maturity at every opportunity. They have little tolerance for the normal tendency of early adolescents to act and want to be treated at times like children; during middle adolescence they try to hasten independence by requiring their sons and daughters to take full responsibility for their decisions and actions and by imposing few if any rules and regulations regarding their conduct—a stance that can be described as *undercontrol*; and in late adolescence they encourage their youngsters to move out of the house on their own as soon as it becomes feasible for them to do so. These are parents for whom the adolescent years of their children seem to plod on without end. "Will we ever be free to lead our own lives again?," they keep asking themselves.

The research that has identified intolerance for immaturity in some families has also identified types of families in which parents want very much to retain their child-rearing roles and feel uneasy about their adolescent youngsters growing up quickly (Constantine, 1987; Hauser, 1991; Reiss, Oliveri, & Curd, 1983). These parents enjoy and even foster childishness in their early adolescents, which means that they become upset with a junior high school daughter who wants to put on lipstick and a junior high school son who wants to go off with some older boys on an overnight camping trip. They promote dependency in their middle adolescents by regulating their behavior and making decisions for them as much as possible, which constitutes a pattern of *overcontrol* or *overprotection*. They encourage their older adolescents to continue living at home, even after they have finished high school and are attending college or working at a job.

For overprotective parents the adolescent years of their children go by too fast and threaten a family unity that is very important to them. Instead of looking forward to the time when their children will grow up and go their own way, these parents constantly wonder, "What can we do to keep this family together?" This kind of overprotection was seen by one of the girls in the Konopka (1976) study mentioned earlier in the following way, talking about her father: "He expects me to be his 'little girl' all my life and I think he is just not realizing that he can't have that; and that, I think, is what he expected out of me for a long time; he just wanted me not to do anything" (White, rural, age 16) (p. 69).

Both of these parental attitudes can have undesirable consequences. Adolescents who are undercontrolled may feel good about enjoying their parents' confidence and being free to run their own lives. However, they may also wonder whether their parents simply don't care enough about them to watch what they are doing and help them make important decisions. Adolescents who are overcontrolled know that their parents are determined to watch over them and guide their lives, which can be reassuring, but they may also resent being denied the freedoms that many of their peers have.

Most parents avoid the extremes of holding on to their child-rearing roles too long or letting go of them too quickly. Instead, they find some reasonably comfortable middle ground between exerting too much or too little control over their adolescent children. Nevertheless, because ambivalent attitudes toward one's children growing up are difficult to avoid entirely, even these parents treat their adolescent daughters and sons sometimes as incompetent children and sometimes as fully capable adults. Adolescents are in fact neither of these; as we are stressing throughout this book, they are in a developmental transition, no longer children but not yet adults. Hence what they need is a consistent, graduated experience in autonomy, with parents who respect their capacities but remain attached to them by standing ready to help them out when they get into situations they cannot handle. Two of Konopka's subjects describe their experience of this kind of parental support:

> I guess really they're [parents] the most important. Because they're always there and I can always go to them and they always say something that will make me feel better. And they support me in my activities and I don't know. They're just good all around. (White, urban, age 17).
>
> They're always there when I need them; they're always giving me what I need, always helping me out with problems, whatever. (Hispanic, urban, age 17.) [p. 71]

The Concept of Developmental Stake

The varying ways in which adolescents and their parents manage the process of becoming separate from and remaining connected to each other was nicely captured in the concept of **developmental stake** formulated some years ago by Vern Bengtson and J. A. Kuypers (1971). Developmental stake refers to the fact that both adolescent and parent generations have an important investment in teenage maturation.

Adolescents, said Bengtson and Kuypers, are invested in the *creation* of values and strategies. They are seeking to establish themselves as individuals in their own right, with their own personal life styles; they are trying to form their own attitudes toward major issues in life and toward institutions in society; and they are attempting to learn comfortable and effective ways of dealing with many new kinds of experiences. Parents, on the other hand, are invested mainly in the *validation* of values and strategies. They regard the adolescent generation as their social heirs and are eager for their children to adopt many of the same attitudes and ways of dealing with experience that they prefer. Parents are gratified when their children follow their example because this *validates* that their values and strategies were well chosen and are worth perpetuating.

As we elaborate when looking at adolescent values later in this chapter, most young people love and respect their parents and want to be like them, and some may even be determined to follow as closely in their parents' footsteps as they possibly can. One of the girls in Konopka's study expressed such total endorsement of her parents' values and strategies in these words:

> I guess if I could grow up and have the same attitudes like my parents, I would be happy. They teach me everything I know. I guess it is the way they brought me up, that I believe everything that they believe in as far as how to do things, how to get along, and that sort of thing. I think if I could be half of what my mother and father are, I'd be happy. (White, urban, age 15.) [p. 64]

As a group, however, Konopka's subjects reported a broad spectrum of feelings toward their parents, and even in generally harmonious families there is likely to be some conflict between the adolescent stake in creating new values and strategies and the parental stake in validating the old ones. To take some common examples, parents may want to see their children get an education comparable to theirs, but their adolescent children may not want to go to college even though their parents did, or they may be thinking about college when their parents did not go beyond high school. Parents may have their hearts set on their children going into their same trade or profession or joining them in some family business, but their adolescent children may not want to do the same work they do, and they may not be interested in whatever business their family may have.

Likewise with respect to family planning and social attitudes, adolescents who love their parents dearly may still come to feel differently from them. Parents may be looking forward eagerly to their children getting married soon and starting a family, even if they have to help them out financially; their adolescent children may be thinking about remaining single, deferring marriage until they can be financially independent, or marrying but not having children. Parents with middle-of-the-road political views may have adolescent children who become attracted to conservative or liberal causes that the parents find distasteful. Parents may be more interested in sports than in the arts, or vice versa, whereas their offspring develop an opposite preference.

Sometimes such differences between adolescents and their parents arise as reasonable and carefully thought out disagreements concerning such matters as the kind of career that best suits a young person's abilities. Adolescents may also come slowly and thoughtfully to the conclusion that they do not want to lead their parents' kind of life, as did one of Konopka's subjects:

> My mother is the type of person where she works and goes home. That's all she does. And like, that's what she wants me to do. I can't do that, cause I like to have my friends and I like to go out and have a good time and everything. I don't know, she doesn't understand it. (Asian-American, urban, age 16.) [p. 67]

The formulation of Bengtson and Kuypers helps to explain less reasonable situations in which young people decide to think and act differently from their parents mainly as a way of being their own person and pursuing the adolescent stake in creating new values and strategies. Parents in turn may become unhappy with adolescent attitudes and aspirations not because they can find logical fault with them, but because they threaten the parental stake in sustaining the generational continuity of values and strategies.

Aside from any conflicts that arise between them, adolescents and their parents can develop mixed feelings about their own generation's developmental stake. Sometimes adolescents may feel torn between modeling themselves after their parents and seeking to be part of a new generation of individuals in its own right. Just as mixed feelings about being independent can lead many young people to alternate between mature and childish behavior, ambivalence toward their stake in individuality can result in their changing their mind from time to time about how much they want to be like their parents and how much they want to be different from them.

For parents, wanting their children to choose to live as they have, as a validation of their own values and strategies, may conflict with wanting them to have a better life than theirs, perhaps one in which they find more happiness and avoid their parents' mistakes and misfortunes. This can lead to some paradoxical reactions among parents who are urging their children to lead different lives from theirs: They may feel gratified if their children ignore their advice and insist on being very much like them, and they may feel disappointed or even rejected if their children follow their advice by going into a different line of work from theirs or pursuing different kinds of interests. These kinds of interactions between the needs and attitudes of adolescents and their parents serve to demonstrate the theme of this chapter—that growing up is a family affair.

PARENTS AT MIDLIFE

Aside from whatever similarities and differences arise between parents and children, most parents are deeply affected by the successes and failures of their offspring and by the joys and sorrows that cross their lives. This aspect of the parental stake tends to be felt especially keenly by parents of adolescents. As young people mature physically and mentally and become increasingly self-reliant, their activities begin to touch directly on the hopes and aspirations their parents had when they were entering adulthood: to find someone to love, for example; to have a particular kind of family life; to reach some level of education or income and become successful in some business or profession; or perhaps to achieve fame or honor as an actor, an athlete, a dancer, a scientist, a musician, or a politician.

As parents observe their offspring becoming adults and choosing how to lead their lives, any ambivalence they feel about having adolescent children is often intensified by the fact that they have reached the middle years of their lives and have entered their own period of change. This event, which has become known as the **midlife transition** (Kimmel, 1990, pp. 124–140; Levinson, 1978), usually begins during the 40s, when many people begin to evaluate their lives and ponder their mortality.

Adults at midlife commonly recognize that they have lived more than half of their years and that, no matter how much success and happiness may lie ahead of them, they are starting to look at shrinking horizons. Their major commitments have been made, opportunities for new choices and new beginnings will be less frequent than before, and moments of happiness are unlikely to match the excitement of youthful triumphs and discoveries. With respect to their strength and energy, their physical appearance, and their sexual attractiveness, even adults who will retain their vitality and productivity for a long time to come recognize at midlife that they are on the downside rather than the upside of their years.

In addition to recognizing that they are growing older, parents of adolescents must also contend with the normal developmental process of **deidealization**. As sensitively described by numerous writers (e.g., E. H. Kaplan, 1991; Smollar & Youniss, 1989; Weissman et al., 1989), childhood tendencies to regard one's parents as all knowing and all powerful give way during puberty to more realistic perceptions of them as imperfect people, which we all are. From a child's perspective, parents know exactly what should be done and are in total control of what happens in the home. Even parents who behave badly or talk openly about personal inadequacies and failures are seen by their young children as people who should be respected and obeyed and whose difficulties are the fault of external circumstances beyond their control.

Psychological maturation during puberty gives young people increased capacity to recognize the personal virtues and shortcomings of their parents, and the emerging autonomy of adolescents encourages them to challenge parental judgments and decisions with which they previously would have complied without question—not because they no longer love and respect their parents, and not because they have suddenly become defiant and rebellious, but because it is natural and healthy for them to assert themselves as individuals who wish no longer to be treated as children.

The double-barreled stress that parents may be caused by having to surrender their position as idealized figures totally in charge of their child's life at the same time as they are contemplating their own future at midlife has been documented in some interesting research. Silverberg and Steinberg (1987, 1990) visited the homes of 129 families with firstborn children age 10–15 and asked questions about the adolescent's degree of emotional autonomy and the parents' level of self-esteem and self-satisfaction. Their findings confirmed that the concerns of mothers and fathers about their present and future life patterns are likely to become intensified when their same-gender child is forging his or her own independence.

Specifically, the more emotionally autonomous the sons in this study were from their father—as defined by having adopted less idealized images of them, having relinquished some of their childish dependencies on them, and having formed a more individuated sense of themselves as people in their own right—the more likely the fathers were to report being preoccupied with such midlife concerns as reevaluating themselves and reappraising their lives. Likewise, the more emotionally autonomous the daughters in this study were, the more likely their mothers were to report examining and reevaluating themselves. Importantly, however, for both mothers and fathers the amount of stress they experienced during their children's adolescence was lessened by their being able to remain comfortable with and committed to their own previous roles, especially in their work.

There is also evidence that the stress parents experience in contending with adolescent autonomy peaks during the early adolescent years, when pubertal changes are occurring at a rapid rate. Later on, when physical growth has tapered off and both adolescents and their parents have had some time to get used to the fact that yesterday's child is today's young adult, parental stress tends to decline. Such changes from preadolescence to early adolescence to middle adolescence are shown in Figure 7.2, which indicates the level of family re-

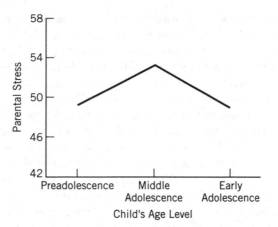

Figure 7.2 Level of experienced parental stress in relation to child's age level. [*Source:* From Small et al. (1988). Reprinted with permission of the Plenum Publishing Corporation.]

lated stress reported by parents of 139 10–17-year-old children studied by Small, Eastman, and Cornelius (1988).

Small et al. also found a clear difference between mothers and fathers in what it is that bothers them about their early adolescent child becoming separated. Fathers reported they were upset most not by their child wanting more autonomy, but by their not following paternal advice they way they used to. For mothers, on the other hand, stress experiences were related primarily to their children becoming more separate from them emotionally. These findings are consistent with the previously noted tendency for mothers to be more interested than fathers in helping their children manage their interpersonal lives, whereas fathers are more interested in promoting their children's progress toward autonomy.

In some families a difficult midlife transition may lead parents to reduce their involvement with their adolescent children. Adults may lose enthusiasm for life in their 40s and, grown old before their time, come to see the needs of their children as a burden they no longer wish to bear. Other adults in midlife may struggle to hold onto or recapture their youth by talking, dressing, and acting more like their adolescent children than their adult friends. They may even be drawn to love affairs with much younger men or women as a way of being reassured of their vitality and physical attractiveness.

When it occurs, such burn-out or pursuit of youthfulness can limit the extent to which parents' feelings of well-being are tied to events in their children's lives. Although this abdication of parenting may spare mothers and fathers some distress, their adolescent children typically suffer as a result. Research studies indicate a direct relationship between parents' ability to cope with midlife in an appropriate and mature way and the ability of their adolescent children to cope effectively with their experiences (Hauser, Borman, Jacobson, & Powers, 1991).

Aside from occasional situations in which parents in midlife become disinterested or detach themselves from their adolescent children, most take pleasure in observing their offspring progress toward adulthood and do well. They may especially enjoy seeing them do better than they ever did in various activities and have educational, career, social, and recreational opportunities that were denied them.

Even so, however, there is for most parents some pain mixed with this pleasure. Sometimes parents cannot avoid feeling envious as their adolescent children scale heights of achievement or find personal rewards that were never within the parents' grasp when they were young. Some parents may even feel relieved if their children pass up opportunities to do more than they did or become more than they are, as when a highly intelligent daughter or son of high school educated parents decides not to go to college.

Moreover, there is a negative side to having hopes and dreams for one's children, because they expose parents to disappointment should their offspring lack the ability or motivation to meet high expectations or take full advantage of opportunities. Because of such mixed feelings surrounding adolescent maturation, many parents are likely to alternate between enjoying and envying their children's opportunities and achievements. They consequently tend to vary in how encouraging and helpful they are. Feeling pleasure leads parents to promote and support as much as their youngsters are able to do; feeling envy leads them to make light of their aspirations and even stand in the way of their using their talents to the fullest.

Parents who fail to encourage their youngsters to realize their potential often generate resentment for their lack of support and sometimes even lifelong anger for having selfishly and senselessly stood between their children and the rewards of a full life. Parents who excessively pressure their youngsters to achieve can also foster resentment, because they, too, appear more concerned with their own needs than with the needs of their child. In both kinds of situations parents may breed rebellion against what they hold dear, and their adolescent youngsters may end up expressing their resentment by doing just the opposite of what the parents would like to see, for example, failing in school when the parents are demanding too much academic achievement, which we discuss in Chapter 11, or being determined to succeed academically when the parents are belittling their potential as a student.

Aside from how they view their adolescent children's accomplishments and opportunities, parents nearing middle age also have to come to grips with their youngster's increasing competencies. How do parents feel when they realize that their children are approaching or have even surpassed them in size and strength, in how well they can play tennis or the piano, in how much they know about chemistry or world affairs, and the like? Parents are usually proud of having offspring who are more talented and able than they are themselves, especially if they have actively encouraged or taught their youngsters various skills.

At times, however, being outdone or outshone by their teenage children is difficult for parents to accept, particularly if they are highly competitive people who are worried about becoming middle-aged. Then they may make light of their children's knowledge and abilities ("You're not as smart as you think you are"; "I can still beat you any time I want to"), primarily as a way of reassuring themselves that they are not yet growing old ("You've still got a long way to go before you catch up to me"; "I can still teach you a few things, Miss Smartypants").

Parents who show such negative reactions can put their adolescent children in a difficult situation, especially if they have been encouraging them all along to become knowledgeable and skillful people. Now these adolescents find that the more they know and can do, the more unhappy their parents become with them. Some young people who encounter this problem deal with it by keeping their talents hidden and their thoughts to themselves, at least when they are at home. Others may react by denying their own abilities in order to keep their parents happy. Then, as we elaborate in Chapter 11, they may pay the price of habitually doing less than they could have, not only in adolescence but in a lifelong pattern of underachievement.

DEALING WITH EMERGING SEXUALITY

As early adolescents go through their growth spurt and begin to develop adult sexual characteristics, capacities, and interests, their emerging sexuality temporarily complicates parent–child relationships. For pubertal adolescents, sexual arousal is now being experienced in new and exciting ways, and persons of the other gender are identified in part as sexual objects; that is, as people who can stimulate and satisfy sexual needs. Adults as well as agemates take on some identity as sexual objects, including their parents, and this is part of the complication. Regarding their parents as sexually active or attractive people, especially should any sexual arousal be experienced in their presence, is a distressing event that young people normally seek to avoid.

For parents of early adolescents, their pubescent children are taking on identity as sexual objects as well, and this is the other part of the complication. Parents are normally distressed to find themselves regarding their children as sexually attractive and potentially active, especially if sexual arousal occurs. As a consequence of these mutual needs to avoid sexuality in the family, there is typically a period of readjustment during early adolescence in which parents and children of different gender take some distance from each other and learn new ways of managing physical intimacy between themselves.

Steinberg (1981), whose research with families we have mentioned frequently in this chapter, has provided some interesting observational data that reflect changing family relationships associated with emerging sexuality. He visited the homes of 31 boys age 11–14 on three occasions 6 months apart. During each visit he rated the boys' physical status and observed how they interacted with their parents during a prescribed exercise that required the family to discuss certain questions and come to a group decision about them. He found significant changes in the tenor of these discussions over time in relation to the boys' physical status.

Specifically, as Steinberg's subjects matured physically and approached the peak of their growth spurt, there was increasing conflict between them and their mothers. Mothers and sons began to interrupt each other more frequently and to spend less time explaining their points of view to each other, and the sons became increasingly less likely to defer to their mother's opinion. Later in the pubertal cycle, after the period of maximum physical growth, these indices of mother–son conflict subsided. Fathers were also observed to interrupt their sons more often and to give fewer explanations of their views as the boys matured physically. However, in contrast to how frequently they took issue with their mothers, these boys usually deferred to their father's views and remained closely allied with him.

Early adolescent girls who begin to feel uncomfortable about the identity of their fathers as sexually active and attractive males are often inclined to react as boys do, by setting up some barriers between themselves and this parent of the other gender. Many girls at this age become highly critical of their fathers and sometimes seem to go out of their way to find fault with them and to be unpleasant, as if to discourage any physical or emotional closeness. For girls as well as boys, this type of strained, standoffish relationship with their parent of the other gender passes in time as they make progress toward individuation. By high school age most young people feel comfortable resuming some of the closeness they had with the parent earlier, as prepubertal children.

Like the 1981 Steinberg study, much of the research on emotional distancing that we discussed earlier confirms the likelihood that some other-gender parent–child discomfort will occur during early adolescence. With respect to boys, the increased conflict and tension and the decreased expression of warmth and involvement that normally rise and fall during early adolescence are much more characteristic of mother–son than father–son relationships (Anderson, Hetherington, & Clingempeel, 1989; Steinberg, 1987a). As for girls, relationships between fathers and daughters usually do not become as strained as relationships between mothers and sons. Nevertheless, fathers are not infrequently found to become increasingly flirtatious in their expressions of warmth toward daughters who are going through puberty, and pubescent daughters are more likely than sons to feel uncomfortable around their fathers and to avoid involvement with them (Hetherington, 1991; Hill, Holmbeck, Marlow, Green, & Lynch, 1986; Youniss & Smollar, 1985).

Discomfort related to the emerging sexuality of early adolescents also requires parents to orchestrate new ways of interacting physically with their adolescent children and new attitudes toward their behavior. New ways of interacting emerge in most families simply because of the young person's physical maturation. For fathers who have enjoyed having their daughters sit on their laps and for mothers who have enjoyed hugging their sons, the fact that the daughters now have breasts and rounded hips and the sons are tall, deep-voiced, and broad-shouldered often leads to second thoughts about such behavior. Where do you put your hands when you are holding your sexually developed child, and how much physical touching should continue when your children become adolescents? As for pubescent children, being hugged by the other-gender parent can bring a new kind of awareness of a mother's breasts or a father's strong arms and produce unwelcome sexual arousal. How, then, do you continue to respond to your parents' shows of affection without getting too close to them physically?

Most families struggle through some period of awkwardness with such questions until they complete a transition from parent–child to parent–adolescent kinds of physical interaction with which they are comfortable. Closely related to this problem is the question of how the family feels about nudity in the home. Attitudes toward nudity vary in different cultures, and what is considered proper in a particular family will depend on their cultural background. Nevertheless, most families have some code concerning what states of undress are proper for walking around the house and how much privacy people should have in their bedrooms or in the bathroom. Often this code has to be changed toward less nudity and more privacy when children pass into adolescence in order for family members to avoid feeling embarrassed or that they are behaving indecently.

As their children finish their early adolescent growth spurt and enter middle adolescence, parents also have to sort out some usually mixed attitudes toward their social and dating activities. As an important aspect of their alternating eagerness and reluctance to see their children grow up, parents often feel ambivalent about their youngster's sexuality. On the one hand, they want to see their adolescent children be socially popular and enjoy going out on dates. If they take vicarious pleasure in the sexual attractiveness of their sons or daughters, they may actively encourage dating and ask about the intimate details of their children's social lives.

On the other hand, parents sometimes worry that their adolescent children will misbehave or be taken advantage of sexually, and they may be particularly concerned about the risks of pregnancy and sexually transmitted disease, which we discuss in Chapter 9. Parents may at times also envy their children's sexual opportunities and attractiveness—especially if their own midlife transition includes concerns about no longer being sexually desirable. Then they may treat socializing as unimportant and discourage or prevent their children from becoming involved with girlfriends or boyfriends ("You've got plenty of time for that later on").

In this section we have discussed emerging sexuality primarily in terms of how the biological changes of puberty affect parent–child relationships during early adolescence. Emerging sexuality is influenced by social experience as well as biological change, however, and it has implications for peer as well as family relationships. Hence, we return to this topic in later discussions of dating (Chapter 8), sexuality (Chapter 9), and gender-role identity (Chapter 10).

PATTERNS OF PARENTAL AUTHORITY

Adolescents' progress toward becoming capable adults is substantially influenced by the manner in which their parents exert authority over them. By and large, parents who are able and willing to impose reasonable controls on their adolescent children while granting them gradually increasing autonomy help them gain self-confidence, self-control, self-reliance, and mature judgment. Parents who are overly controlling and restrictive are likely to undermine their child's capacity for autonomy, and parents who are unable or unwilling to maintain authority over their adolescent youngsters make it difficult for them to become responsible and self-reliant people.

Parents also foster their adolescent children's individuation and psychological maturity when they exercise authority in a loving manner. This is a matter not so much of *what* parents say and do, but *how* they say and do it. Parents who convey that they care deeply about their children's welfare are likely to have a powerful impact on them when they offer guidance or administer discipline. By contrast, parents who are perceived as hostile and rejecting seldom exert a positive influence on their children, even when they appear to be doing or saying "the right things."

These dimensions of *autonomy-control* and *love-hostility* in parental authority were formulated many years ago by Earl Schaefer (1959). Subsequent research confirmed that patterns of authority in families can be described largely in terms of how demanding and responsive parents are. Parental *demandingness* refers to establishing expectations and rules of conduct for children and monitoring their commitment to these expectations and their compliance with these rules—in short, what parents *ask* of their children. Parental *responsiveness* refers to being sensitive to children's needs, warmly supportive of their efforts, and broadly interested in what they are thinking, feeling, and doing—in short, what parents *give* to their children. Working with these dimensions, Diana Baumrind (1968, 1971) was able to demonstrate clear differences between three parental styles: **authoritative parenting**, which is high in both demandingness and responsiveness; **authoritarian parenting**, which is high in demandingness but low in responsiveness; and **permissive parenting**, which is low in demandingness but high in responsiveness.

The hallmarks of authoritative parenting are caring and warmth, appropriate demands and reasonable punishments, and firm control based on what is known as **inductive discipline**. Inductive discipline consists of explaining the purpose of rules governing the young person's behavior and being open to sound arguments for changing them. Parents who invoke inductive discipline say to their children, in effect, "Here are the reasons why it would be best for you to act this way; if you think you can convince me otherwise, I'm willing to listen."

Authoritarian parents, by contrast, show attention and concern but not much in the way of warmth and support, and they exercise firm control on the basis of **power assertion** rather than inductive discipline. Compared to authoritative parents, their demands are more likely to be inappropriate and their punishments unreasonable, and they set forth rules in an arbitrary fashion that is not open to discussion. Parents who are asserting power are saying, in effect, "I know what's best for you and you'll just do as I say, because I say so." Peterson and Leigh (1990) observed that inductive discipline is likely to be viewed by adolescents as "minimally sufficient" control, whereas power assertion is likely to be considered "functionally superfluous pressure."

With respect to permissive parenting, Baumrind's original category requires some amplification in light of subsequent research. There are, as she concluded, some parents who care about and are responsive to their children but choose to impose few demands or restrictions on them. Such parents typically believe that complete trust and full democracy in parent–adolescent relationships is beneficial, and they practice a type of permissiveness that can be called **indulgent parenting**. Other parents who exercise little control over their adolescent children do not really care very much about them and have disengaged themselves from child-rearing responsibilities. Permissive parents of this type practice what can appropriately be called **neglectful parenting** (Maccoby & Martin, 1983; Steinberg, 1990). The differences among these parental practices are summarized in Box 7.1.

How common are each of these four patterns of parental authority in families in the United States? To answer this question, a research team led by Laurence Steinberg collected information from approximately 4,100 14–18-year-old students enrolled in nine high schools in California and Wisconsin. This was a diverse sample of middle-class and working-class youngsters living in rural, suburban, and urban settings, and it included 9% African-American, 14% Asian-American, and 12% Hispanic-American students. These students completed questionnaires in which they described their parents in terms of their responsiveness (how accepting and involved they were) and their demandingness (how strict their supervision was). The frequency of the four parental styles, as reported by Lamborn, Mounts, Steinberg, and Dornbusch (1991) is shown in Figure 7.3.

As can be seen from Figure 7.3, the two most common patterns of parental authority as reported by this large group of adolescents are the authoritative and the neglectful, each accounting for about one-third of the total. Additional information collected by Lamborn et al. from these high school students demonstrated some sharp developmental differences between those from authoritative and those from neglectful homes. Those who were being reared authoritatively displayed significantly more self-reliance and social competence and a more positive attitude toward work than those who felt neglected; they were receiving significantly better grades and had a more positive attitude toward school; and they reported significantly fewer problems related to their behavior (e.g., school misconduct, drug use, delinquency) or sense of well-being (e.g., anxiety, tension, depression, somatic complaints).

As also can be seen from Figure 7.3, the remaining one-third of the adolescents in this study were about equally divided between the authoritarian and indulgent groups. On the various outcome measures, these two groups placed somewhere between the parentally advantaged authoritative and the parentally disadvantaged neglected groups in their level of self-reliance and social competence. Interestingly, however, youngsters from authoritarian and indulgent homes showed different patterns of strengths and weaknesses. Those students who described their parents as demanding but unresponsive (i.e., authoritarian) reported

♦ **BOX 7.1   DEMANDINGNESS AND RESPONSIVENESS IN FOUR PATTERNS OF PARENTAL AUTHORITY**

Parental Pattern	Demanding	Responsive
Authoritative	Yes	Yes
Authoritarian	Yes	No
Indulgent	No	Yes
Neglectful	No	No

Demanding: Establishing expectations and rules of conduct and monitoring commitment and compliance
Responsive: Being sensitive to needs, warmly supportive of efforts, and broadly interested in thoughts and feelings

fewer behavior problems and a more positive orientation toward school than those whose parents were responsive but undemanding (i.e., indulgent). On the other hand, those with indulgent parents reported greater social competence than those with authoritarian parents and showed more self-reliance.

In further work with these same data, the observed relationships between parental style and adolescent development were examined separately for adolescents from different ethnic and social class backgrounds. The percentage of authoritative families was found to be somewhat higher in middle-class than in working-class families and in white than in minority families. However, the adolescent outcome of parenting styles cuts across such family differences. Whatever their family background, adolescents benefit most from being reared in an authoritative way, by parents who are both warm and firm; compared to adolescents who are reared in nonauthoritative ways, they are more competent socially and in the classroom, more confident in their abilities, and less likely to feel bad or get into trouble (Steinberg, Mounts, Lamborn, & Dornbusch, 1991). As we elaborate in Chapter 8, authori-

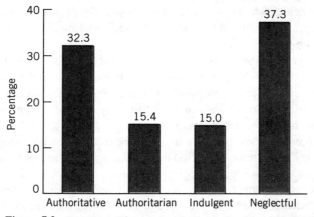

Figure 7.3   Patterns of parental authority in families of 4,081 high school students. [*Source:* Based on data reported by Lamborn et al. (1991).]

tative parenting is also associated with advantageous choices in the peer groups with which adolescents affiliate themselves (Durbin, Darling, Steinberg, & Brown, 1993).

The influence of parental style on adolescent development may be complicated in some families by differences between the two parents. What happens, for example, if one parent is inclined to be authoritative while the other parent leans toward permissiveness? Johnson, Shulman, and Collins (1991) examined this question in a study of 385 5th-, 8th-, and 11th-graders who were asked to describe their mothers and fathers as being either authoritative or permissive. Among the 5th-graders, only 9% described their mothers and fathers as differing in their parental style, whereas the other 91% perceived them as exercising authority in similar ways. Of the 8th-graders, 23% perceived a difference between their parents in this regard, and 31% of the 11th-graders saw one parent as authoritative and the other as permissive.

Hence, perceived inconsistency between parental styles appears to increase during the adolescent years, but remains relatively infrequent. When parental differences do occur, they are likely to be disadvantageous for young people. Among the Johnson et al. subjects, those who reported inconsistency between their parents showed lower self-esteem and poorer performance and adaptation in school than those whose parents were seen as similar in their exercise of authority, even when both were permissive. Findings reported by Wentzel and Feldman (1993) similarly indicate that adolescents whose parents have reared them in an inconsistent fashion show less self-control and less academic motivation than youngsters whose parents have held similar attitudes and expectations.

The research findings concerning parental patterns of authority, like those concerning autonomy and attachment, have clear implications for how parents can best serve the developmental needs of their adolescent children. Authoritative parents are already giving their children every advantage with respect to how they wield their authority and should strive only to sustain a united, consistent front in doing so. Neglectful parents are doing their children a disservice and should strive to become more engaged and invested in the responsibilities of parenthood.

As for the approximately one-third of authoritarian and indulgent parents, the ways in which they limit their children's psychological growth frequently derive from misperceptions of what is best for young people. For example, parents may think that by being permissive they can help their children learn to be on their own. Hence, they readily give in to their children's demands for more freedom and greater self-determination, which also helps to avoid unpleasant arguments.

More often than not, however, taking this easy way out achieves the opposite of what was intended. Adolescents press for privileges because they are no longer children, but they need to have limits set for them by people older and wiser than they because they are not yet adults. Just as adolescents do not want to become totally detached from their parents, they also do not want to be totally free to make decisions. They recognize that they need guidance and control, no matter how reluctant they may be to admit it. When guidance and control are lacking, they often worry about doing the wrong thing or losing control of themselves.

For this reason, young people who are prematurely left to their own devices tend to shy away from independence rather than embrace it. Sometimes they may brag to their peers about how self-reliant they are and how much they enjoy their freedom, and their peers may envy the liberty they appear to have. In truth, however, unguided adolescents are more likely to be apprehensive about acting on their own than self-confident. They have been freed from restraint only to become prisoners of their inexperience, uncertainty, and lack of familiarity with the ways of the world.

Furthermore, adolescent children of permissive parents often keep pressing for more and more privileges, not so much to get their own way as to force their parents to take a stand and set some limits. This kind of adolescent pressure—known as **testing the limits**—is sometimes applied for negative reasons alone, to see what one can get away with. Limit testing can also be employed for positive purposes, however, as an effort to provoke restrictions that will provide some guidance, bolster a young person's self-control, and demonstrate that parents care enough to make an effort.

Along with steering clear of permissiveness, parents also need to avoid exerting control in an authoritarian fashion. Parents who deny their adolescent children the opportunity to make their own decisions prevent them from practicing self-control and learning self-reliance. Being authoritarian is not a matter of how strict parents are, as is sometimes thought, but how willing they are to discuss rules, regulations, and punishments with their children. Typically, the main complaint that adolescents have about their parents' discipline is not having a chance to present their side of the story; it is not strictness, then, but an autocratic denial of participation in decision making that interferes with adolescents' learning to be independent.

In fact, children of strict parents usually benefit from having the parental guidance, the externally imposed limits, and the evidence of parental strength and effort that children of permissive parents lack. Adolescents may compare notes on how closely their parents control their behavior and tell each other that those with the least controlling parents are the most fortunate. However, so long as strict parents are not being authoritarian and are not preventing their children from participating in peer-group activities, they are usually not frustrating their independence strivings.

NONTRADITIONAL FAMILY ORGANIZATION

For many years the literature on adolescent psychology assumed that young people grow up in a "traditional" family headed by a mother who stays home and takes care of the children and a father who goes to work and earns the family's living. Contemporary trends in our society have made this kind of family organization much less common than in the past. In 1955 60% of families in the United States were organized around an intact marriage, a father as sole wage earner, a mother as full-time homemaker, and school-age children living at home; today, according to some reports, fewer than 10% of all households fit this traditional family image (Jackson & Sikora, 1992). Increasing numbers of children are spending their adolescence in **dual-earner families**, **one-parent households**, and **reconstituted families**, each of which can have special implications for the child's psychological development.

DUAL-EARNER FAMILIES

An increasing number of married women entering the labor force has made the dual-earner family commonplace in the United States. Employment among mothers of preschool children grew from 18% in 1960 to 57% in 1987, and it is estimated that by the mid-1990s 70%

♦ *Profile*

DIANA BAUMRIND

Diana Baumrind grew up in New York City and attended Hunter College, where she earned her bachelor's degree with a joint major in philosophy and psychology. Later, as a graduate student at the University of California at Berkeley, she pursued a joint doctoral program in social and clinical psychology. At this early point in her career, she was influenced mainly by a distinguished group of researchers at Berkeley who pioneered in developing the psychology of group dynamics, and she did her doctoral dissertation on group structure. One of the early models in group dynamics theory that she learned about from her mentor, Dr. Hubert Coffey, a student of Kurt Lewin, involved distinguishing between two kinds of group structure—*authoritarian* and *permissive*. With important implications for her future work with families, she became interested in whether there is a third kind of common group structure, one that is more democratic than an authoritarian group but less controlling than a permissive group.

Dr. Baumrind was not particularly interested in child development or family relationships, however, until she became involved in rearing her own three children. Then, wanting to be an effective parent, she set out to become as informed as she could about factors that promote good adjustment in young people. In addition to her own reading, she spent 3 months visiting prominent child development research laboratories around the country. The end result was a decision to devote her career to developmental research, and she brought to her work the models she had learned in studying group dynamics. Thus was born her seminal formulation of authoritarian and permissive patterns of parental discipline and a third, integrative category, known as *authoritative parenting*. Her concept of authoritative parenting, as elaborated in numerous articles and book chapters, has been widely demonstrated to distinguish between effective and ineffective parenting.

For over 30 years Dr. Baumrind pursued a productive career as a research psychologist at the Institute for Human Development at UC Berkeley. Recently retired officially, she continues to work as before on projects concerned with the antecedents of successful and unsuccessful adjustment. The recognition she has received for her work includes the G. Stanley Hall Award in developmental psychology from the American Psychological Association.

---

of the mothers of infants and young children will be employed, most of them full-time (Scarr, Phillips, & McCartney, 1989; U. S. Bureau of the Census, 1988). Among the major reasons for this growth in dual-earner families over the years have been (1) increased family financial need fueled by continuing cycles of inflation, when the dollar loses value, and recession, when well-paying jobs become harder to find and keep; (2) expanding opportunities for women in many types of occupations; and (3) changing social attitudes concerning the appropriateness of women and men sharing bread-winning and home-making roles. Barring unusual circumstances, there is every reason to believe that mothers who enter the work force when their children are young will remain in it during their children's adolescence.

Although many working mothers pursue careers they find gratifying and for which they have prepared themselves, most take the best available job they can find because they need or want the income for their family. Nevertheless, surveys indicate that most employed mothers would not leave their jobs to stay home with their children even if they had enough money, and the majority of full-time homemakers say they regret not having prepared themselves to pursue a career. Not only among professional career women (who are a small minority in the work force), but also among working-class mothers with jobs as waitresses, factory workers, and domestics, most are committed to their jobs, satisfied with their diverse roles, and interested in continuing to work (Scarr et al., 1989).

Dual-earner families thus appear to be well on the way to replacing one-earner families as the tradition in our society. With respect to the atmosphere young people experience at home when both parents work, dual-earner families benefit from the material advantages of having two incomes but also have to contend with some sources of strain. Parents who both work may have difficulty finding enough time and energy outside of their jobs to take care of their children, manage household affairs, and still enjoy some rest and relaxation. They may also find it more difficult than single-earner families to decide when and how many children to have, and they may have to choose whether to take advantage of a job opportunity for one spouse that would require the other spouse to give up his or her job.

Research reports indicate that several factors typically influence how well working couples handle such family strains (Anderson-Kulman & Paludi, 1986; Baruch & Barnett, 1987; Bernardo, Shehan, & Leslie, 1987). First, strain is minimized when husband and wife can agree on a routine of shared family responsibilities with which they both feel comfortable. Whether this routine involves a traditional division of labor or whether it is a less traditional routine in which the wife gets the car fixed and the husband does the cooking is not important; what matters is that both parents feel satisfied with their arrangement and avoid criticizing one another for letting their job interfere with what they are supposed to be doing around the house.

Second, the possibilities of strain in a dual-earner family are greatly reduced when husband and wife are mutually supportive of each other, and in particular of the wife's working. Husbands need to appreciate their wife's employment not only as a source of income but also as a valuable opportunity for her to be an independent person. Wives need to enjoy their work outside of the home and to feel comfortable in their role as a working person without becoming concerned that they are neglecting their children or shirking their homemaking responsibilities.

Third, and perhaps most important of all, the peace of mind of two working parents is directly related to the availability of affordable and dependable day care when their children are young and appropriate supervised after-school activities when they are older. Middle-class parents have some advantage over working-class parents in this regard. Relatively well-off dual-earner couples can more easily afford to hire housekeepers and babysitters, treat themselves to frequent vacations and entertainment, and pay for a second car, a microwave oven, someone to cut the grass, and other goods and services that make their life easier. Less affluent couples who work have little money for such things and cannot as easily juggle their work schedules, arrange for help in caring for their children and their home, and still find the time and means to relax. This is not to say that higher socioeconomic status families typically adjust well and lower status families poorly when both parents work, but only that working couples who are financially well-off have more resources for minimizing the strains of maintaining a dual-earner family.

For many years psychologists were concerned that, even in the best of financial circumstances, children, especially as infants and preschoolers, would be adversely affected by their mother's working. To the contrary, however, considerable research indicates that maternal employment is unlikely to have any negative consequences as long as parents are comfortable with the mother's working and maintain a positive atmosphere in the home. Whether or not mothers are employed does not by itself make any difference in the stability of infants' attachments to either of their parents; day care for infants and preschoolers has not been demonstrated to have any necessarily harmful effects on family relationships; and after-school arrangements of various kinds for older children whose parents are at work, provided that they involve interactions with other children in a safe environment, are unlikely to contribute to emotional or behavioral problems (Gamble & Zigler, 1986; Lamb & Sternberg, 1990; Lovko & Ullman, 1989; Volling & Belsky, 1992).

As for adolescents in particular, working and nonworking mothers have not been found to behave differently toward their teenage children in any systematic way, nor have any consistent relationships been identified between the employment status of women and the psychological adjustment of their adolescent youngsters (Gardner & LaBrecque, 1986; Lamb, 1982; Scarr, 1984). In fact, adolescents may benefit from their mothers being employed, if working helps their mothers feel more satisfied with themselves and their lives than they would otherwise. By providing a positive role model of competence and achievement, working mothers may also help their children avoid rigidly differentiated attitudes toward what men and women should do. With particular respect to girls, a research review by Lois Hoffman (1984) indicates that daughters of employed mothers are often reported to do better in school, feel more self-confident, and more frequently become career oriented than daughters of nonemployed mothers.

ONE-PARENT HOUSEHOLDS

Consider these facts about the American family:

1. The divorce rate in the United States rose sharply from the 1960s to the 1980s and now stands at 4.8 divorces per 1,000 people. Compared to the marriage rate of 9.7 per 1,000 people, this means that one divorce is being granted for every two marriage licenses being issued.

2. Three times as many children are experiencing the divorce of their parents as did 40 years ago, and twice as many (currently about 20%) are living in one-parent households.

3. It is estimated that almost half of the marriages begun in the 1980s will end in divorce and that as many as 50% of today's young people may live part of their lives in a one-parent household before their 18th birthday (Hernandez, 1988; Jackson & Sikora, 1992; National Center for Health Statistics, 1989; O'Leary & Smith, 1991).

This information has an important bearing on personality development because children of divorced parents are more likely to show adjustment difficulties than children from intact families. In elementary school they adapt less well socially, feel less positively toward themselves and their parents, and are more likely to misbehave than youngsters whose parents have remained together (Amato & Keith, 1991; Emery, 1988). As adolescents, they do less well in school and are more likely to drop out than classmates from intact families; they show less self-control and less mature approaches to problem solving; they feel less capable of managing stress and are less optimistic about their future prospects; and they are more likely to become depressed and withdrawn (Featherstone, Cundick, & Jensen, 1992; Hodges, 1991, Chapter 2; Irion, Coon, & Blanchard-Fields, 1988; Mulholland, Watt, Philpott, & Sarlin, 1991; Zimiles & Lee, 1991). Children from disrupted families appear in disproportionate numbers among patients in mental health settings, are more likely than other children to receive psychotherapy as adolescents, and have more difficulty making the transition from late adolescence to adult roles as parents and wage earners (Aro & Palosaari, 1992; Dickson, Heffron, & Parker, 1990; Raphael, Cubis, Dunne, & Lewin, 1990; Wallerstein & Corbin, 1991).

These findings have to be interpreted carefully, however. First of all, adjustment difficulties, especially those serious enough to require professional care, are by no means an inevitable consequence of divorce. Many young people withstand family breakup without suffering serious long-term consequences. It is only on the average that children of divorce are more likely than their peers to have psychological problems; divorce is a risk factor for such problems, but it does not always cause them (Barber & Eccles, 1992; Hetherington, 1989, 1991; King, 1992).

Second, parents who stay together but get along poorly are just as likely as parents who divorce to have children with behavior problems. The research in this area suggests that this is because parents who are in conflict, whether they separate or stay together, provide poorer models for their children, are less consistent in their discipline, and put more stress on their children than parents who have a comfortable marital relationship or an amicable divorce. Long-term adjustment difficulties are caused not by divorce itself, but by the family discord that breeds divorce (Forehand, Wierson, Thomas, Armistead, Kempton, & Neighbors, 1991; Johnston, Gonzalez, & Campbell, 1987; Long, Forehand, Fauber, & Brody, 1987; Smith & Jenkins, 1991).

Third, not having both parents living at home does not necessarily mean that a young person is receiving less parental attention than a youngster in an intact family. As most people know from their experience, and as the family studies we are citing confirm, divorced parents vary widely in how often they see their children and how much support they give them; likewise, parents living at home differ in how much they care about their children and help them grow up. Some children in intact families may have two disinterested parents who ignore them (the neglectful parents noted earlier), whereas children in one-parent households may have a devoted noncustodial parent as well as other relatives who see them often—which is why children of divorce are best described as being part of one-parent *households*, not one-parent *families*.

Further information on the developmental outcomes of living in a one-parent household has come from two sources: research on father-absent families and studies of how parents and their children are affected by the process and aftermath of divorce.

Effects of Father Absence

Although fathers are being granted custody much more frequently than in the past, fewer than 10% of divorce decrees give child custody to the father, and over 90% of children in single-parent households are living with their mother (Santrock & Warshak, 1986). Thus most children of divorced parents will be without a father in the home for at least some period of time. Whether growing up in a household without a father will be associated with developmental difficulties is associated with several factors.

First, the younger the children are when their father leaves the home, the greater their risk of being affected in some adverse way (Radin, 1981; Sales, Manber, & Rohman, 1992). This means that adolescents are less likely than younger children to suffer detrimental effects from their father's being absent, although some teenagers and adults as well are found to show persisting consequences of not having had a father from early in life, such as chronic or recurring feelings of loneliness.

Second, father absence resulting from divorce is more likely to have negative effects than the father's dying. As distressing as a father's death may be, it constitutes an unavoidable and understandable reason for his absence. When a father is gone because of divorce, especially if he has deserted the family, his absence may signify rejection and abandonment. Children who feel rejected and abandoned often ask themselves some painful questions ("Why didn't he love me enough to stay with me?") and come up with some self-critical answers ("I'm not a good person") that rarely cross the minds of children whose fathers have died.

Generally speaking, children who are deprived of fathers through death fare better emotionally than those who experience paternal loss through divorce or desertion (Adams, Milner, & Schrepf, 1984, Chapter 4). Compared to children of divorced fathers, those with deceased fathers express fewer negative attitudes toward their families and are less likely to develop behavior problems or become psychologically disturbed during their adolescence or as adults (Landerman, George, & Blazer, 1991; Tennant, 1988).

Growing up without a father is most likely to produce adverse affects as a result of interfering with normal gender role development. There is substantial evidence that being able to experience close and warm relationships with adults of both genders helps young people form a clear sense of their gender identity, feel comfortable with being male or female, and view the other gender in a positive light (Hodges, 1991, Chapter 8). Gender role development may be particularly problematic for boys in father-absent families. Fathers play a key role in transmitting values to their sons, setting a masculine example for them, and imposing controls on their behavior. Hence, in families that are suffering adverse effects of an absent father, boys are usually found to be having more problems than girls (Fry & Scher, 1984; Stern, Northman, & Van Slyck, 1984).

Although less so than boys, girls also benefit from having a father in the home. A study reported some years ago by Mavis Hetherington (1972) provides a revealing glimpse of the manner in which father absences of different kinds may affect heterosocial behavior in adolescent girls. Hetherington observed 13–17-year-old girls attending a community recreation center, some of whom were from intact families and some of who had lost their fathers through death or divorce. Of those without fathers, some had suffered the loss early in life (before age 5) and some later. None of the girls had any brothers, and none of the father-absent families had had any males living in the house since the death or divorce. Figure 7.4 shows comparisons among these groups of girls in how often they engaged in four kinds of social behaviors.

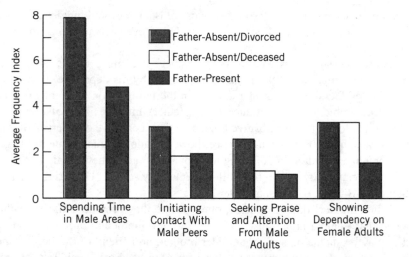

Figure 7.4 Social behavior of father-absent and father-present adolescent girls in a recreation center. [*Source:* Based on data reported by Hetherington (1972).]

As can be seen, the adolescent girls with divorced or deceased fathers behaved differently from girls with fathers and differently from each other. Compared to girls from intact families, those whose fathers had died tended to be shy, timid, and socially inhibited around males and to avoid them. Girls of divorced fathers, by contrast, were noticeably forward with males and inclined to seek their company and attention. Both groups of girls without fathers appeared to be more dependent on adult women than girls from the intact families. Each of these effects of father absence was found to be more prominent in girls who had experienced early rather than later separation.

As a third factor, the economic circumstances of a family can influence its response to father absence, for better or worse. Loss of the father often means a lowered family income, in which case material deprivation may increase the risk of developmental difficulties. As in the case of dual-earner families, on the other hand, one-parent households that are well off financially may have resources for minimizing possible detrimental effects of an absent father—not the least of which is reducing the strain, work demands, and energy drain experienced by the divorced or widowed mother.

However, although there is general agreement that affluence can ease the burden of father absence, research has thus far been inconclusive concerning whether detrimental effects of living in a single-parent household are solely the result of economic hardship. In the Ontario Child Health Study, interviews were conducted with over 3,000 6–16-year-old children from 1,869 households. Those children who were from single-parent households were having more developmental difficulties than those from two-parent households, but their families were also the ones experiencing the most economic and social hardship; when the comparisons were controlled for such hardship, no relationship was found between single-parent household status and either emotional problems or difficulties in school (Blum, Boyle, & Offord, 1988). On the other hand, in another carefully conducted large-scale study involving a national sample of 6,710 12–17-year-olds, an elevated incidence of deviant adolescent behavior in mother-only households was found even when family income was controlled (Dornbusch, et al., 1985).

Fourth, possible negative effects of a father's becoming absent can be minimized if other people are available to fill any gaps that are left by his departure. When father absence occurs in childhood, having a stepfather join the family soon after may reduce the risk of adjustment problems. The entrance of stepfathers into the lives of previously father-absent children is found to have positive effects on their cognitive and personality development, especially among boys; as we shall see, however, adolescents frequently have more difficulty than younger children in adjusting to stepparents, and a new stepfather may not be as helpful to a teenage boy as to a boy still in elementary school (Hetherington, 1991; Lamb, 1986; Santrock, Sitterle, & Warshak, 1988).

When mothers do not remarry, other people may provide sufficient fatherly support and attention to help a father-absent child avoid developmental problems. An uncle or grandfather may be such a person, or an older brother, or a friend of the family, and even the close involvement of a grandmother has been found to head off psychological problems in father-absent children. Last, but certainly not least, the ability of a child's mother to carry on as sole head of the family and provide a warm loving relationship can also minimize any adverse effects of growing up without a father in the home. Each of these situations involves what is called a "buffering" effect: strong support from other adults, especially the parent at home, can buffer young people against maladaptive reactions they might otherwise have to the loss of the parent who is gone (Breier, Kelsoe, Kirwin, Beller, Wolkowitz, & Pickar, 1988; Hodges, 1991, Chapter 2; Wierson, Forehand, Fauber, & McCombs, 1989).

Effects of Divorce on Parents

Divorce does not necessarily result in an unhealthy environment, and parents and children may survive a divorce psychologically unscathed or even better off than before with respect to their prospects for an enjoyable and productive life. However, no matter how many problems a divorce seems certain to solve, and no matter how clear and compelling the reasons for it appear to be, family breakup almost always leaves a stressful period of transition in its wake.

In the Virginia Longitudinal Study of Divorce and Remarriage, Hetherington and her colleagues conducted a 6-year study of 72 white middle-class boys and girls whose parents were divorced when they were preschoolers, along with their divorced parents and a like number of children and their parents from nondivorced families. During the first 2 postdivorce years the divorced families experienced more emotional distress than the nondivorced families, reported more health and behavior problems, and struggled with adjusting to new roles and other life changes associated with their altered family situation. By the time 2 years had passed, however, the majority of the parents and children in these divorced families were feeling considerably better and were adapting reasonably well to their circumstances (Hetherington, 1989; Hetherington, Cox, & Cox, 1982).

Other research has identified some of the reasons why divorce is so often a stressful experience. For one thing, couples may see their divorce as a major life failure, even when they are relieved at having escaped from a joyless or unpleasant marriage. They must explain to themselves and to their friends and relatives why they were not able to sustain a loving relationship that had once been strong enough to lead them to marry. When one spouse insists on the divorce while the other one still feels the original love or at least a commitment to the marriage, the rejected spouse often suffers the additional emotional strain of feeling unattractive and unwanted.

Another problem is that divorced parents must usually go through a period of relative social isolation. Being divorced can mean fewer opportunities to see former friends and less pleasure in being with them. Social invitations from married friends may even stop coming or be awkward to accept. Separation tends to be especially stressful for fathers initially, because they typically are the ones who move out of the family home and lose opportunities to see their children, and because they are less likely than their wives to have people with whom they can talk comfortably about their marital problems. These problems pass in time, as divorced people get over their hurts and rebuild their lives with new relationships and new routines. But for at least the first year, divorced people are found to be more socially isolated, to have fewer sources of emotional support, and to feel more anxious, depressed, angry, rejected, and incompetent than married persons (Hodges, 1991, Chapters 1 & 8; Jacobs, 1983; Weinraub & Wolf, 1983).

In such circumstances divorced parents are understandably likely to have difficulty meeting the needs of their children. Especially for the custodial parent, the task of filling both parental roles, providing emotional support, and taking care of financial and practical matters can be very demanding. This is all the more true when the absent parent had been the sole wage earner or had taken full responsibility for certain aspects of running the family that the custodial parent must now take on, no matter how unfamiliar or unwelcome they are—whether grocery shopping, doing the laundry, fixing a leaky faucet, balancing the checkbook, taking the children to the dentist, or finding and keeping a job. When these burdens are added to their social isolation and preoccupation with their shattered marriage, diminished parenting is frequently the result. Depleted in time and energy and preoccupied with their own needs, recently divorced parents tend to be less sensitive to their children's concerns, less affectionate, less communicative, and less consistent in their discipline than they were previously or are likely to be after a year or two has passed (King, 1992; Sales et al., 1992; Wallerstein & Corbin, 1991).

Effects of Divorce on Children

Children of divorce must live not only with unwelcome changes in the parenting they receive, but also with psychological reactions of their own to the breakup of their family. In the California Children of Divorce Project, Judith Wallerstein and Joan Kelly (1980) examined such reactions in 60 pairs of divorcing parents, their children, and their children's teachers, whom they interviewed at three points in time: just after the separation, about 1 year later, and 5 years later.

Wallerstein and Kelly found that almost all young people experience the divorce of their parents as a painful and traumatic event. With few exceptions, such as when a parent has been violently abusive or seriously disturbed, they oppose their parents' decision to divorce, no matter how much marital strife there has been in the home. Rather than being relieved by the divorce, even when it eliminates trying circumstances, they resent their parents' inability to keep the family together, they fear for the future, they yearn for the absent parent, and they often feel guilty for having in some way been the cause of what has happened.

On the basis of further follow-up information obtained from some of these children 10 and 15 years after their parents' divorce, Wallerstein expressed concern that many of them are still haunted by disturbing memories of family strife, still feel sad that their childhood or adolescence was burdened by a divorce, and harbor fears of being disappointed in their own love relationships (Wallerstein, 1987; Wallerstein & Corbin, 1991). Such findings do not mean that children of divorce are doomed to lifelong unhappiness and unfulfillment. To the contrary, King (1992) concludes from a review of the relevant research that, within 2 years following a divorce, 50 to 75% of children will be functioning adequately and feeling good provided that (1) their family is economically stable, (2) their custodial parent is adjusting reasonably well and is maintaining a good relationship with them, and (3) they are still in touch and on good terms with their other parent. At the same time, however, there is accumulating evidence that for many young people divorce is more than just an acute crisis in their lives; even when it does not cause serious psychological problems, family breakup may contribute to nagging concerns about self-worth and lingering discomfort in heterosocial relationships for many years to come (Allison & Furstenberg, 1989; Forehand et al., 1991; Kalter, 1987; Southworth & Schwarz, 1987).

Among preadolescent children, boys are more reactive to divorce than girls and are more likely to misbehave and become emotionally upset when their parents separate. By adolescence, however, the gender differences tend to disappear, and teenage girls are just as likely as boys to show adjustment difficulties should their parents divorce (Frost & Pakiz, 1990; Reid & Crisafulli, 1990; Smith & Jenkins, 1991).

This difference appears related to variations in general between girls and boys in their susceptibility to developmental problems. Prior to puberty, boys are more likely than girls to display many different kinds of psychological disturbance and to become more easily upset by stressful situations. As teenagers, by contrast, girls and boys are equally likely to become disturbed and upset. Among adolescents who have emotional or behavior problems, the boys are more likely than the girls to have had problems in childhood, whereas the girls are more likely to have first developed their problems in adolescence (Peterson, 1988; Weiner, 1992). Problematic response to divorce is most likely an example of this general trend, with gender differences appearing in childhood but not in adolescence.

As summarized by numerous writers, extensive research on children's response to divorce also reveals some clear age differences (Hetherington, 1991; Hodges, 1991, Chapter 2; King, 1992; Sales et al., 1992). Young children, because of their limited capacity to understand what is happening, are especially prone to unrealistic feelings of anger and guilt, and they often revert to whining, clinging, infantile behavior that they had previously outgrown. School-age children are better able than preschoolers to weather divorce without such developmental setbacks, because their greater cognitive maturity allows them to understand the divorce more realistically and to communicate their feelings about it. Nevertheless, they ordinarily suffer some depression and loss of self-esteem, and they feel bitter toward their parents for not being able to patch up their differences.

Adolescents are sufficiently mature to avoid most of the adverse effects of divorce on younger children. However, the kinds of developmental tasks they are working on make them vulnerable to some special kinds of problems in the wake of divorce. The research we have been citing identifies four such problems in particular:

1. The adolescent process of separating from parents and forming attachments outside the home is often disrupted by divorce. It is difficult to finish blending doses of closeness and independence into a mature relationship with a parent when that parent disappears from one's daily life. In addition, young people may become preoccupied with the events surrounding a divorce at the expense of keeping up with the academic, social, and recreational activities through which they are becoming autonomous individuals.

2. Adolescents' age frequently results in one or both of their divorcing parents treating them as adults at a time when their continuing maturation would be better served by distinct parent–child roles. Parents who turn to their teenage children for comfort and support following a divorce tend to give them more autonomy than they would otherwise, and to expect them in return to take on some of the responsibilities of the absent parent. Although adolescents in this circumstance may bask briefly in the glow of being treated as grown up, they soon begin to suffer from being depended on rather than having parents on whom they can depend. In this same vein, divorced parents who prematurely cast their teenage children as adults often find it difficult to exercise the kinds of authority and discipline over them that adolescents still need in order to continue learning self-control and self-reliance.

3. Adolescents whose parents have gone their separate ways often find it difficult to believe that marriage can provide enduring commitment in a loving relationship; or, if they do believe it, they worry that, created in their parents' image, they are doomed to fail in their efforts to make a happy and lasting marriage. These concerns in adolescent children of divorce can lead them to avoid marriage or, if they do marry, to avoid letting their marriage become an important part of their lives. Sometimes a self-fulfilling prophecy is the unfortunate result: Fear that marriage will be impermanent and disappointing leads to holding back from a full commitment to it, which in turn contributes to a marriage that is less stable and less rewarding than it otherwise could be.

4. Adolescents are more likely than younger children to be distressed by their divorced parents' involvement in new romantic relationships. As we noted earlier, teenagers often prefer to view their parents as nonsexual objects who no longer care much about or engage in physical sexuality. When divorced parents begin to date and develop new relationships, their adolescent children may experience discomfort they would not otherwise have. Moreover, a divorced parent's finding a new love interest may stir up some very mixed feelings in teenage children. They may feel happy in part, because the parent now has a fuller life again; yet they are also likely to feel envious and resentful, because they will have a less exclusive relationship with the parent, and they may even feel disappointed that the parent is not remaining faithful to the original marriage, no matter how disastrously it ended.

Issues of Custody and Visitation

The healing passage of time helps young people overcome the stress of divorce, as does having previously been reasonably well adjusted. Children who have been getting along well outgrow adverse reactions to their parents' divorcing more easily than those with prior psychological problems, and they are less likely to suffer any serious or persisting difficulties in dealing with the family breakup. Psychological well-being following divorce also depends on how much meaningful contact children are able to have with both of their parents and whether the divorced parents are able to maintain a friendly relationship. The more opportunity young people have to see both parents and share important aspects of their lives with each of them, the better off they will be and the less likely to suffer psychological damage from the divorce (Folberg, 1991; Healy, Malley, & Stewart, 1990; Maccoby, Depner, & Mnookin, 1988).

This last fact raises an interesting and sometimes controversial question concerning how custodial and visitation rights should be arranged following a divorce. One traditional view argues for a **joint custody** arrangement in which children live part of the time with their mothers and part of the time with their fathers (Roman & Haddad, 1978). This kind of arrangement gives young people ample opportunity to share their lives with each parent and continue working out developmental issues with both of them.

As a drawback, however, joint custody requires children of divorce to move back and forth between two homes. Especially when these homes are any distance apart, this arrangement can be very disruptive. Instead of having one home to call their own, these children of divorce must pack up and move regularly and keep readjusting to households with different schedules, different regulations and expectations, and maybe even a different set of new stepparents and stepsiblings. As another potential problem, joint custody calls for parents to coordinate complex arrangements in a responsible manner. Most authorities who favor joint custody in general believe that it can do children more harm than good if their divorced parents are unable to communicate and cooperate with each other or are still involved in seeking sole custody of their children (Buchanan, Maccoby, & Dornbusch, 1991; Gardner, 1991; Goldstein, 1991).

As a counterpoint to the potential disadvantages of joint custody, another traditional view argues for assigning custody to just one parent and arranging visitation rights for the other one (Goldstein, Freud, & Solnit, 1973). This allows young people the stability of growing up in just one home. Unfortunately, however, parents with visiting rights typically see their children much less often than parents who share joint custody of them (Arditti, 1992). Moreover, visiting parents often cannot avoid being outsiders in their children's lives. They may plan enjoyable activities together, but going shopping or to a ball game with your child is not the same as being involved on a daily basis with what he or she is thinking, feeling, and doing.

Research findings indicate that single custody with visitation works best when visits occur frequently on some routine basis (Loewen, 1988). Yet visits can do more harm than good when parents are not on friendly terms with each other. If divorced parents are psychologically at each other's throats, their children are likely to get caught up in their conflicts and become saddled with divided loyalties. In such circumstances more frequent access to both parents leads not to well-being, but instead to an increased frequency of emotional and behavioral problems (Buchanan et al., 1991; Johnston, Kline, & Tschann, 1991).

Thus, both joint custody and single custody with visitation have potential advantages and disadvantages, and there are specific circumstances in which it seems reasonable to expect that one will work better than the other. However, even though some authorities believe that joint custody at its best is more beneficial than single custody at its best (Luepnitz, 1991), available research does not yet provide a definitive answer one way or the other (Sales et al., 1992).

In light of the potential problems encountered by young people in the wake of their parent's divorcing, a final question to pose is whether parents who have their children's best interests at heart should stay together, no matter how troubled their marriage has become. This, too, is a controversial question for which there is no ready answer. The findings summarized in our discussion have led many child specialists to encourage parents to keep their home and family intact for the sake of their children, at almost any cost. Others argue that, despite the potentially adverse effects of divorce, children in calm, loving, single-parent households are better off than those living in families that are intact but ridden with strife and bitterness. A disinterested, rejecting, or hostile parent, from this point of view, is more detrimental to a young person's development than an absent parent. Conclusive evidence that will tell us which is better—an intact, unhappy home or a divorced family—is yet to come, and there may not be any single solution that is correct in all cases.

RECONSTITUTED FAMILIES: STEPPARENTS AND STEPCHILDREN

In everyday conversation references to stepparents and stepchildren often carry negative connotations. Fiction and biography are full of cruel stepmothers and abusive stepfathers. Everyone knows how mean Cinderella's stepmother was while favoring her natural-born daughters. And when Anna Freud referred in 1958 to adolescence as the "stepchild" in psychoanalytic theory, her meaning was clear: She was pointing out that adolescent development had been overlooked, ignored, considered of only minor importance, and relegated to second-class citizenship in much of the previous literature.

Negative associations to growing up in a stepfamily are important for us to put in proper perspective because most children of divorce subsequently become children in reconstituted families. Of adults who divorce, 80% of the men and 75% of the women remarry eventually, and 30% of all marriages are remarriages for at least one partner; 40% of families today can expect to become stepfamilies before their youngest child turns 18, and about 25% of children and adolescents will spend some time in a stepparent home (Glick, 1989; Hetherington, 1989; Hodges, 1991, Chapter 9). Like one-parent households, then, reconstituted families are a common feature of growing up in America.

Considerable attention has been paid to whether children living in stepfamilies are better or worse off than those who live with their biological parents. To be useful, studies of this question should take two considerations into account. First, most stepchildren have previously been children of divorce. If they are still recovering from the adverse effects of the divorce, and especially if their biological parents are in conflict, any problems they are having may have more to do with the divorce than with their being in a stepfamily. Second, even though young children, and especially boys in mother-custody homes, are likely to benefit from the advent of a stepfather, becoming a stepchild is a transitional event that can be expected to require some readjustments and almost always produce some temporary distress. Accordingly, the impact of stepfamily living can be measured adequately only after sufficient time has passed to heal the wounds of divorce and complete the transition into being a stepchild.

Research conducted with these considerations in mind indicates that living with a stepparent and stepsiblings does not have any uniform effects, for better or worse. On the average, children in stepfamilies do not differ from children living with both biological parents in their intellectual and cognitive achievement, social competence, self-esteem, or level of adjustment (Ganong & Coleman, 1984; Santrock et al., 1988). When emotional or behavioral problems do occur in stepchildren, moreover, they are associated not with the structure of the family but with family discord (Borrine, Handal, Brown, & Searight, 1991; Fine, Donnelly, & Voydanoff, 1991; Kurdek & Sinclair, 1988). As we have consistently seen, then, how family members get along with each other is much more important than who is living in the home when it comes to the psychological well-being of adolescents.

These findings concerning the influence of a stepfamily, when compared to findings concerning children of divorce, pose an interesting question. As mentioned on page 249, children of divorce on the average show more developmental difficulties than children from intact families; yet stepchildren, most of whom are children of divorce, do not differ on the average from children in intact families. This might suggest that transition into a stepfamily can over time have beneficial effects well beyond any that have yet been demonstrated. Further research is needed to explore this possibility.

Although we recognize that there is no universal handicap for adolescents in having their parents remarry, and there are perhaps some distinct benefits to remarriage in many circumstances, it is necessary to recognize as well that the transition into stepfamily living causes some strain. The increasing frequency of nontraditional family patterns has not changed the basic feelings of many people that the "ideal" family is a closely knit biological unit. Hence many stepfamilies, parents and children alike, strive to recreate the close and exclusive parent–child ties that typically exist in intact biological families. The fact is, however, that most stepchildren have biological parents living elsewhere, and children of divorce usually benefit from keeping in touch with their biological parents. Strain results when the stepchildren are encouraged and expected to be members of two households while also being encouraged and expected to limit their relationships to the stepfamily.

Becoming a stepchild is also likely to cause adolescents some specific strains in relation to their developmental concerns. The time when they are working to establish autonomy and become separate from parents is not an easy time for them to meet expectations of becoming attached to a new stepparent. Similarly, the time when they prefer not to regard their parents as being sexually active is not an easy time for sons of divorced custodial mothers or daughters of divorced custodial fathers to have a stepparent enter the parent's bed. For these reasons, adolescents are found to be more troubled than younger children by their divorced parent's taking a new spouse and less ready to love and submit to the authority of a new stepparent (Hetherington, 1991).

In thoughtful discussions of stepfamily life, John and Emily Visher (1982; 1988) identified several tasks and issues with which stepparents and stepchildren must deal in order to adjust smoothly to each other. These include working through any sadness they are still feeling over the breakup of the previous family; developing a set of traditions and shared experiences for the new family; resolving any conflicting loyalties of children to their biological parents and stepparents, and of stepparents to their current and former spouses and to their biological children and stepchildren; and deciding how decisions will be made among this reconstituted group and what values will guide these decisions. The more easily and constructively such matters can be resolved, the more likely it is that adolescents will prosper in a reconstituted family and suffer no disadvantage relative to their peers; conversely, problems in managing these tasks and issues increase the risk of adjustment difficulties in young people.

RELATIONS BETWEEN THE GENERATIONS

Most people recognize that adolescents think, feel, look, and act differently from adults in many ways. They are of a different generation; they differ in maturity and previous life experience; and they are dealing with different developmental tasks and responsibilities. Moreover, as we mentioned earlier, the developmental stake of adolescents in becoming autonomous leads them to seek characteristics of their own, different from those of their parents. Among other things, then, their distinctive tastes and attitudes, their use of language, their favored styles of dress and grooming, and their preferred pastimes clearly set most adolescents off from adults.

Are adolescents in rebellion against society? How people answer this question is likely to be influenced by the kinds of glimpses of adolescents that have recently made an impression on them.

To some observers of young people, such distinctive features of teenage behavior have signified that adolescents, especially in modern times, are in rebellion against their parents, alienated from family life, and in conflict with the adult world. As formulated in the notion of a **generation gap**, this view holds that the prevailing pattern of relationships between the generations consists of poor communication and adolescent rejection of adult values (Kenniston, 1965; Mead, 1978).

For the most part, however, vivid tastes and preferences among the young are merely the trappings of adolescence. Superficial appearances only, they say little about the basic and essential commitments that determine the quality of the relations between the generations: commitments to a sense of values, to standards of conduct and decency, to mutual love and respect, and to the welfare of the family. Abundant research on these topics indicates that most young people get along well with their parents and share their sense of values; most adolescents are not in rebellion against either their family or their society; and poor family relationships and alienation are associated with psychological disturbance, not normative adolescent development.

Accordingly, the prevailing pattern of relationships between the adolescent and adult generations is one of harmony. In some families, however, this harmony may be disrupted by psychological disturbance in young people or by physical or sexual abuse by parents.

HARMONY PREVAILS

In two landmark studies, Elizabeth Douvan and Joseph Adelson (1966) directed a research team that interviewed a nationally representative sample of over 3,000 teenage girls and boys, and Daniel Offer (1969) examined in detail the life experiences of a group of high school boys over a 3-year period. Both investigations found that the majority of adolescents respect their parents, want to be like them, and maintain harmonious relationships with them and with other adults as well. Most of the young people with whom these researchers spoke were satisfied with their homes and tended to view their fathers as reliable and their mothers as understanding and sympathetic. Although these adolescents and their parents often disagreed on various trivial issues such as curfews, clothing, and use of the family car, their disagreements seldom threatened the basic bonds of affection that existed between them.

Subsequent research, involving large and socioculturally diverse groups of subjects, has consistently yielded similar evidence of predominantly positive relationships between adolescents and their parents. As summarized by many reviewers, these studies confirm that relationships between the adolescent and adult generations consist typically of harmony rather than strife, affection rather than alienation, and commitment to rather than rejection of family life (Collins, 1990; Hill, 1987; Paikoff & Brooks-Gunn, 1991; Peterson, 1992; Powers, Hauser, & Kilner, 1989; Steinberg, 1990). Hence, there seems little doubt that the generation gap is largely a mythical concept, at least with respect to the overwhelming majority of young people.

Nevertheless, the mistaken notion that adolescent development typically disrupts parent–child relationships and sets the adult and adolescent generations against each other has a very long history, and its origins and its appeal need to be recognized. The fact that adolescent progress toward independence leads adolescents to assert some individuality, as people different from their parents, has resulted in almost every generation of adults becoming worried—unnecessarily—about what their youth are coming to (Elder, 1980). According to Lauer (1973), a 4,000-year-old tablet discovered during the excavating of the biblical city of Ur carries the following inscription: "Our generation is doomed if the unheard-of actions of our younger generation are allowed to continue" (p. 176). Shakespeare expressed a similar disaffection for the waywardness of young people:

> I would there were no age between ten and three-and-twenty, or that youth would sleep out the rest; for there is nothing in between but getting wenches with child, wronging the ancientry, stealing, fighting. [*The Winter's Tale*, Act III, scene iii]

When such disrespectful or antisocial behavior on the part of some adolescents makes a vivid impression, adults such as Shakespeare may be led to condemn the entire youthful generation. In a similar vein, adolescents in trouble make good stories for the media, and we are much more likely to hear and read about disruptive adolescent behavior than about the constructive actions of young people. Specific vivid impressions and stark portrayals on television and in movies and newspapers can shape a distorted image of the number of adolescents who are at odds with their parents and their society, unless we keep constantly in mind the firm evidence that family strife and generational conflict are atypical patterns.

More specifically, research findings indicate that serious and persistent problems in adolescent–parent relationships characterize just 20% of families; another 20% experience intermittent relationship problems; and the remaining 60% of adolescents and their parents get along for the most part in harmonious fashion (Montemayor, 1986). In no more than 10% of families does adolescence bring with it a dramatic deterioration in the quality of parent–child relationships; when family strife and generational conflict do become pronounced, they are likely to be associated with psychological disturbance rather than normal development (Prange, Greenbaum, Silver, Friedman, Kutach, & Duchnowski, 1992; Steinberg, 1990).

Markedly rebellious behavior is normal only in the early adolescent years, when teenagers are just beginning to separate themselves from their parents. By middle adolescence and beyond, when young people have reached a point of directing many of their interests and energies outside of the home, serious rebellion against closeness with the family constitutes deviant behavior (Eccles et al., 1993; Hill & Holmbeck, 1987). The implications of these research findings are clear: Families that are at odds with each other tend to have disturbed children in their midst, and disturbed young people are much more likely than their well-adjusted peers to come from families that have ceased to function comfortably as a unit.

The data shown in Figure 7.5 and Table 7.1 demonstrate further this association between family problems and adolescent disorder. Figure 7.5 depicts differences between normal and disturbed 14-year-olds in three indices of parent–child alienation; the disturbed adolescents can be seen to be much more likely to be having communication difficulty and altercations with their parents and to be withdrawn from interacting with them. Table 7.1 reports differences in attitudes toward their family expressed by 13–18-year-old normal, delinquent, and psychiatrically disturbed youngsters; in each case, the more positive or less negative attitude was held by the normal group. Other studies of family communication confirm that parents

Adolescents whose parents get along poorly are more likely to have adjustment difficulties than young people from harmonious homes.

and their adolescent children generally feel that they understand each other (Newman, 1989). When they do not, however, and when family members do not perceive each other as being understanding, there is a strong likelihood of adjustment difficulties in the family.

What can be said, then, about the quality of relations between the adolescent and adult generations? The answer is consistent with our noting in the first section of the chapter that adolescent progress toward mature self-reliance involves both separating from one's parents and remaining connected to them. Like adolescents and their parents, the adolescent and adult generations are distinct in many ways but normally maintain warm, respectful, and interdependent relationships. Nevertheless, as they separate from their parents, adolescents become increasingly engaged in the broader social world around them. This leads us to examine in the next chapter how social relationships expand and mature within the adolescent generation. Before doing so, however, we need to recognize that in some families harmony may be destroyed not by adolescent disturbance but by abuse perpetrated by parents on their children.

PHYSICAL AND SEXUAL ABUSE

Reports of child abuse number more than 2 million cases per year in the United States, and, like other kinds of deviant behavior that most families prefer to keep from public knowledge, these criminal acts probably occur more frequently than is reported (Ammerman & Hersen, 1992). As further evidence of the extent of this problem, surveys suggest that approximately 11 to 14% of young people are likely to be physically injured by a parent during their developmental years (Briere, 1992, Chapter 1; Haugaard, 1992).

When violence intrudes on what otherwise would be a harmonious relationship between children and their parents, it is the adolescent age group that is most likely to be victimized. Researchers have found that harsh punishment in general is most frequently visited on

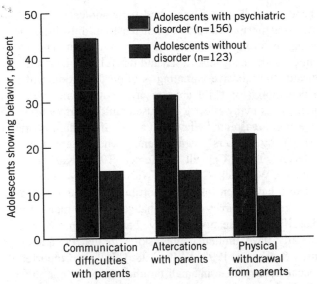

Figure 7.5 Parent–child alienation and psychiatric disorder at age 14. [*Source:* Based on data reported by Rutter, Graham, Chadwick, and Yule (1976).]

preschoolers and teenagers, who are the two developmental groups most inclined to oppose their parents' wishes. Perhaps because pubescence more often than early childhood coincides with a midlife transition that makes it difficult for parents to handle opposition from their children, adolescence is especially likely to be the time when physical abuse begins (Kaplan, 1991; Williamson, Borduin, & Howe, 1991).

Table 7.1 PERCENTAGE OF NORMAL AND DEVIANT ADOLESCENTS ENDORSING VARIOUS ATTITUDES TOWARD THEIR FAMILIES

Attitude	Psychiatrically Normal Adolescents	Delinquent Adolescents	Disturbed Adolescents
Very often I feel that my father is no good	17	25	24
Very often I feel that my mother is no good	11	18	18
I have been carrying a grudge against my parents for years	10	26	19
I try to stay away from home most of the time	28	49	46
I can count on my parents most of the time	76	66	67
My parents are usually patient with me	80	64	69
Most of the time my parents are satisfied with me	87	58	65
When I grow up and have a family, it will be in at least a few ways similar to my own	76	50	60

Source: Based on data reported by Offer, Ostrov, and Howard (1981) on the responses of several hundred 13–18-year-olds to the Offer Self-Image Questionnaire.

On the other hand, even though parents and their adolescent children can annoy each other, we have seen that normal developmental tensions only infrequently disrupt family harmony, and they hardly suffice to account for parental assault. The reasons why some parents abuse their children are many and varied and not fully understood. One consistent finding, however, indicates that abusive parenting is often the product of **generational transmission**: a large percentage of child abusers are people who were abused as children themselves, and perhaps as many as 30% of abused children grow up to be abusive parents. Accordingly, there is good reason to believe that abuse of children is often modeled after the example that was set by abusers' own parents, who taught them well but wrongly (Ammerman & Hersen, 1990; Cappell & Heiner, 1990; Kashani, Daniel, Dandoy, & Holcomb, 1992; Simons, Whitback, Conger, & Wu, 1991).

Several other factors have been found to contribute to violence in abusing families, but most of them involve general sources of strain that can lead to many different kinds of problems and are not specific determinants of abusive behavior. For example, parents who abuse their children generally have limited coping skills in general and poor parenting skills in particular (Hansen & Warner, 1992; Wolfe, 1985). It is also reported that physical abuse is more likely to occur in large than in small families, in poor than in well-off families, and in families in which parents are depressed, in poor health, or frequently intoxicated (Hansen, Conaway, & Christopher, 1990; Whipple & Webster-Stratton, 1991). Even though they appear regularly, however, such reports of family differences must be interpreted cautiously. Economically disadvantaged families with ill or alcoholic parents are especially likely to come under public scrutiny, and instances of child abuse under their roofs may be revealed more often than abusive behavior occurring behind the doors of affluent households.

The developmental consequences of growing up abused vary from one young person to the next, but they are rarely anything but negative. As would be expected, children who are abused often feel insecure in their relationships with their parents and subsequently uncomfortable, at least initially, in forming close attachments to anyone. The earlier the abuse begins, the more severe it is, and the longer it lasts, the more likely it is to generate not only developmental but lifelong problems in social adjustment. On the other hand, the more opportunity children have to develop normally before being subjected to abuse, and the more capable they have become of coping with stress, the better their prospects are for escaping psychological damage.

On the average, however, victims of physical abuse are at greater risk than other young people for arrested social, emotional, and cognitive development and for various kinds of psychological problems presently and in the future. We have already noted that abused children are more likely than their peers to become abusive parents. In addition, research findings indicate that victims of abuse, apparently because of their exposure to aggressive models in the home, are likely to show a high frequency of aggressive interactions with other young people while they are growing up and with other adults when they mature, both as perpetrators and victims of violence (Ammerman & Hersen, 1992; Conoway & Hansen, 1989; Eckenrode, Laird, & Doris, 1993; Hansen et al., 1990).

As evidence of the potency of parental modeling, the developmental risks incurred by physically abused young people are found in equal measure among children and adolescents who only observe violence in the home; even when not physically harmed themselves, they, too, are victims of abuse. It is estimated that spouse abuse, most commonly of a wife by her husband, occurs at least once in 20 to 30% of families, and interviews with children in violent families indicate that at least 40% and perhaps as many as 80% of these children have witnessed their father abusing their mother. Young people who witness family violence are more likely than their peers to become anxious or withdrawn, to display hostility, and to run away from home. They may also come to regard violence as an expectable or even appropriate way of resolving conflict. The daughters in such families often develop distrust of males and negative attitudes toward marriage; the sons often become abusive and violent themselves toward females (Geffner & Pagelow, 1990; Jaffe, Sudermann, & Reitzel, 1992; Kashani et al., 1992).

In some abusive families young people fall victim to sexual rather than physical abuse. No one can say with certainty whether sexual abuse of children is more prevalent in the 1990s than in past years; it is certain that sexual abuse is being reported much more frequently than ever before and that child specialists have become actively engaged in studying this problem and trying to identify its causes and effects.

Just how frequent is sexual abuse of young people? National surveys suggest that 20 to 30% of adult women and 10 to 15% of adult men in the United States were sexually abused as children or adolescents (Briere, 1992, Chapter 1; Finkelhor, Hotaling, Lewis, & Smith, 1990; Green, 1991). With respect to sexual abuse within the family, available data indicate that 6 to 10% of college students report having been sexually abused by a parental figure; that 10 to 20% of adult women in the United States may be survivors of incest; and that, at any one point in time, 1% of all children nationwide are involved in an incestuous relationship with a parent or parental figure (Haugaard, 1992; Haugaard & Reppucci, 1988; Lundberg-Love, 1990).

Both **sexual abuse** and **incestuous relationships** are broadly defined in contemporary usage. Sexual abuse includes inappropriate touching and fondling of young people by an older person as well as intercourse, and it also includes compelling or enticing children to observe sexuality or be observed sexually, as in watching a man masturbate or posing nude for pictures or movies. Incest refers to sexual involvement between members of the same immediate family, including stepparents as well as biological parents. These broad definitions allow for considerable variability in the form that inappropriate sexuality takes, and its causes and consequences are similarly likely to vary considerably. As one consistent finding, however, sexual abuse within families consists mostly of incestuous relationships between daughters and their fathers or stepfathers. Sexual abuse of boys, whether incestuous or not, is relatively infrequently reported, and much less is known about it than about sexual victimization of girls (Watkins & Bentovim, 1992).

Why fathers sexually abuse their daughters remains largely a mystery, despite a long history of efforts to account for such deviant behavior (Weinberg, 1955; Weiner, 1963). Research has shown that sexually abusive fathers are not seriously disturbed individuals, but rather tend to be insecure, socially inadequate men who experienced parental deprivation in their own youth and are immature in their sexual orientation. Somehow they manage to feel more comfortable getting sexual satisfaction from their children, over whom they can wield considerable control, than in tying to obtain it from adults who are more their equal. Sexual abuse within the family is generally not accompanied by physical abuse, but it is rarely an expression of affection. Instead, paternal figures who sexually abuse their daughters in middle childhood or adolescence tend not to have been closely attached to them or involved in caring for them as infants and preschoolers (Parker & Parker, 1986).

For a majority of young people, being sexually abused by a parental figure is a traumatic experience. Sexual abuse commonly leads to stress disorders that may persist for many years, even into adulthood, and be manifest in recurrent painful memories, episodes of depression, withdrawal from people and activities, and generalized anxiety and fearfulness (Graystone, de Luca, & Boyes, 1992; Kiser, Heston, Millsap, & Pruitt, 1991; McLeer, Deblinger, Henry, & Orvaschel, 1992). These harmful effects are more likely to result when abuse is perpetrated in the family than by a stranger, because it then constitutes a betrayal: someone who was trusted and depended on for kindness and concern has now selfishly exploited the victim in improper ways to meet his own needs. Like physical abuse, then, parental sexual abuse can undermine the capacity for trust and lead adolescents to become overly cautious individuals who shrink from close or intimate relationships (Brown & Finkelhor, 1986; Lundberg-Love, 1990).

Being sexually abused, even by a parental figure, does not inevitably produce psychopathology, however, and in all the studies of sexually abused children about one-third demonstrate few if any symptoms of disorder (Finkelhor, 1990; Kendall-Tackett, Williams, & Finkelhor, 1993). The less frequent the abusive events have been and the shorter the duration of an incestuous relationship, the better a young person's prospects are for overcoming the trauma they cause. Similarly, the less responsible they feel for having been molested and the less physically abusive the experience was, the less psychological damage young people are likely to incur as a result of being sexually abused. Finally, support from their mothers after sexual abuse by a paternal figure has been disclosed can also help girls to minimize the negative consequences of having been victimized; mothers who are accepting, sympathetic, and reassuring enhance their daughter's capacity to cope with what has happened to them, whereas those who are rejecting or blame their daughters for what has happened can make matters worse in their child's life (Briere, 1992, Chapter 1; Everson, Hunter, Runyon, Edelsohn, & Coulter, 1989; Haugaard & Reppucci, 1988, Chapter 4).

Even in the best postabuse circumstances, victims of sexual abuse in the family are likely to be struggling with confused attitudes toward sexuality for which they need psychological help. Having been forced or enticed into sexual interactions for which they were not emotionally prepared and often having received misleading messages about what constitutes appropriate sexual conduct, young people may develop either **hyposexual** or **hypersexual** reaction patterns (Green, 1991; Polit, White, & Morton, 1990; Tharinger, 1990). **Hyposexuality** involves fear and avoidance of sexuality and can lead adolescents to retreat from age-appropriate sexual encounters and become sexually unresponsive or inactive adults. **Hypersexuality** involves preoccupation with sexual thoughts and behaviors and can lead adolescents to act in markedly erotic and seductive ways, to be unusually sexually active or even promiscuous, and, as parents, to rear their own children in inappropriately sexualized ways.

CHAPTER SUMMARY

1. The hallmark of psychological maturation in adolescence is a young person becoming increasingly self-reliant and taking greater responsibility for his or her own behavior. As part of establishing their autonomy, adolescents begin to separate themselves from their parents by spending less time with them and taking a more active role in decisions that concern them.

2. Adolescent progress toward autonomy involves remaining connected to as well as becoming separate from parents. While learning to think for themselves, adolescents normally continue to participate as family members and collaborate with their parents in resolving issues in their lives. Thus, being an autonomous individual and being in an interdependent relationship with one's parents are two complementary features of normal family growth during adolescence.

3. Young people and their parents usually have some mixed feelings about adolescent autonomy and attachment. Adolescents enjoy having new privileges but often regret some of the responsibilities that go along with them. Parents take pride in seeing their children become self-reliant, but they may miss their previous parental role and worry about their adolescent youngster growing up too quickly.

4. Parents may respond with both pleasure and envy to the opportunities, achievements, and developing competencies of their adolescent children, especially in relation to their own midlife developmental transitions. At the same time as they may be reassessing their future prospects and shrinking horizons, parents must accommodate themselves to the fact that their offspring's childhood tendencies to regard one's parents as all-knowing and all-powerful give way during puberty to more realistic perceptions of them as the imperfect people that we all are.

5. The emerging sexuality of early adolescents temporarily complicates parent–child relationships in most families. Parents and adolescents often feel uncomfortable for a time about each other's being physically attractive and potentially sexually active. This discomfort may lead to some awkwardness and tension that diminishes in time as family members adjust to this aspect of adolescent maturation.

6. Parents who exercise control over their adolescent children in an authoritative manner that combines firm and explicit expectations with warmth and sensitivity to their needs help their children mature into self-confident and self-reliant adults. Parents who are authoritarian, demanding much but giving little support in return, deny their children opportunities to acquire social competence and gain

self-confidence. Parents who are permissively indulgent, showing love but providing little guidance and control, prevent their children from learning self-control. Parents who are permissively neglectful, offering neither direction nor warmth, place their children at risk for behavior problems.

7. Almost 70% of the mothers of young children hold full-or part-time jobs, and dual-earner families are well on the way to replacing one-earner families as the tradition in our society. Although working couples face some special strains, their mother's working has no necessary adverse effect on children or adolescents. Working and nonworking mothers do not behave differently toward their teenage children in any systematic way, and the adjustment status of adolescents is unrelated to the employment status of their mothers.

8. An estimated 50% of children born in the 1980s will spend part of their developmental years in a single-parent household, and, primarily as a result of divorce, about 20% are currently living with one parent. Divorce does not necessarily lead to developmental difficulties in young people; along with marital discord in intact families, however, it carries an increased risk for emotional upset and problem behavior.

9. Divorce almost always leaves a stressful period of transition in its wake. Parents have to adapt to disappointment, loneliness, social isolation, and, for many women, reduced financial resources; adolescents have to adapt to missing having both parents regularly available, resenting having to deal with the family breakup, and possibly becoming caught up in a continuing conflict between their parents. Adverse reactions to divorce are usually temporary, however, especially among young people who previously have been well adjusted and are able to keep in contact with both parents without having to struggle with divided loyalties.

10. Over three-quarters of adults who divorce later remarry, and most children of divorce subsequently become children in reconstituted families. Stepparents and stepchildren often have some difficulties in adjusting to each other. Contrary to much folklore, however, stepfamilies do not inevitably breed psychological problems, and young people in remarried families may get along better than children of divorce whose custodial parent does not remarry.

11. Contrary to the impressions of some observers that there is a gap between the generations, research findings demonstrate that most young people get along well with their parents and share their basic values and standards of conduct and decency. The typical pattern of relationships between the adolescent and adult generations involves harmony rather than strife, affection rather than alienation, and commitment to rather than rejection of family life. When family strife and generational conflict do occur, they are likely to be associated with psychological disturbance, not normal development.

12. Surveys suggest that as many as 14% of young people are physically injured by a parent during their developmental years. Abusive parents tend to be individuals with limited coping skills who were themselves abused as children. Victims of abuse are at risk for arrested personality development, for persistent feelings of insecurity in their relationships with other people, and for becoming aggressive adults and abusive parents. From 6 to 10% of college students also report having been sexually abused by a parental figure, and it is estimated that 10 to 20% of women in the United States are survivors of incest. Sexual abuse in the family is a traumatic experience that can cause persistent stress disorder, lingering concerns about whether people can be trusted, and confused and dysfunctional attitudes toward sexuality.

KEY WORDS

ambivalence	empty nest reaction	individuation	permissive parenting
authoritarian parenting	generation gap	indulgent parenting	power assertion
authoritative parenting	generational transmission	interdependence	pubertal status
autonomy		joint custody	reconstituted families
chronological age	hypersexuality	midlife transition	
deidealization	hyposexuality	mini-rites	sexual abuse
developmental stake	incestuous relationship	neglectful parenting	testing the limits
distancing hypothesis		one-parent households	
dual-earner families	inductive discipline		universal

REVIEW QUESTIONS

1. In what sense is growing up "a family affair?"

AUTONOMY AND ATTACHMENT

2. What developments lead adolescents to desire autonomy?

3. How do families and society in general encourage adolescents to become more autonomous?

4. Discuss the importance of interdependence between adolescents and their parents.

5. What kinds of evidence lend support to Steinberg's distancing hypothesis?

6. Why is becoming autonomous sometimes a more complex process for girls than for boys?

7. Discuss some common differences between mothers and fathers in how they communicate with their adolescent children.

8. How does adolescent maturation evoke ambivalent feelings in family members? Give some examples of how ambivalence may affect the actions of adolescents and their parents.

9. How does the Bengtson and Kuypers concept of "developmental stake" help to explain some types of conflicts and disagreements between adolescents and their parents?

10. Describe the impact that being in a midlife transition can have on how parents feel toward their adolescent children.

11. What implications does research on the distancing hypothesis have for the notion of reawakened oedipal conflicts in early adolescence?

PATTERNS OF PARENTAL AUTHORITY

12. List four typical patterns of parental authority and indicate the similarities and differences among them.

13. What are some of the apparent advantages for adolescents of being reared in an authoritative way?

14. Discuss the potential hazards of permissive parenting.

NONTRADITIONAL FAMILY ORGANIZATION

15. What kinds of factors can cause strain or help to minimize strain in dual-earner families?

16. Discuss the impact of maternal employment on adolescent development.

17. Why do studies comparing children of divorced parents with children from intact families have to be interpreted with special care?

18. List some factors that influence whether growing up without a father in the home has undesirable effects on child development.

19. In relation to the developmental tasks on which adolescents are working, what kinds of special problems are they vulnerable to if their parents divorce?

20. Discuss the advantages and disadvantages of joint and single custody for children of divorced parents.

RELATIONS BETWEEN THE GENERATIONS

21. Summarize the research findings on family relationships demonstrating that the generation gap is largely a mythical concept.

22. Why are adolescents at an age of special risk for being abused by their parents?

23. List some of the negative psychological consequences of being physically abused by one's parents.

24. What factors are likely to influence the psychological consequences of being sexually abused in adolescence?

Interlude

♦

Cesar, Age 16

♦

"The person I really look up to a lot is my father"

Growing up in New York City, Cesar, a 16-year-old Hispanic boy, had a choice among a variety of high schools; he chose one that specialized in technical education. He rides the subway (he calls it "the train") to school and almost everywhere else he goes. Riding through the urban landscape, he decided to become an architect. He learned about sex from cable TV, but has had no formal sex education; his lack of accurate information about contraception is striking because he has experienced sexual intercourse. His parents immigrated from Latin America, and he feels a very close relationship with his family; he is especially influenced by his father.

This interlude follows the chapter on family issues during adolescence. Consider the major topics in that chapter as you read this interlude: autonomy and attachment, patterns of parental authority, and relations between the generations. Also consider how Cesar's family is different from the nontraditional families described in the chapter. How did the various members of the family affect him and why do you think his father is so special? You may also think about the points raised in this interview that are relevant to the earlier chapters. Finally, in anticipation of the next chapter on dating, consider the following: How typical was his response to puberty? Is there evidence of formal operational thinking in the way he describes himself and others? What effect, if any, has growing up Hispanic in New York had on him? What is your reaction to his comments about high school? How did you feel about his first

sexual experience? Why is he not more popular with girls?

How old are you now? I'm 16. *What kind of school do you go to?* I go to New York Technical High School. They give you courses to choose. You get a choice of courses. I chose arts and science; it gives you a little bit of every course that other people choose. My friend, he chose the mechanical engineering course and I get a little bit of that and a little bit of architecture and machine shop also. *Why did you choose that school?* Because I liked the school. I knew a couple people that went there. And I like to draw, not really like an artist draws, a painting, but like architecture and architectural drawings; that's what I plan to major in in college. *So you plan to go to college?* Yeah. *And you want to major in . . .* Architecture. *How did you decide on that?* Well, at first I wanted to be a doctor and I was reading books on doctors and the body and everything. As I got older, 12 or 13, I would take the train to school and I would notice my surroundings, the buildings, you know; it really surprised me, to see the way everything was done and I wanted to know more about it. That's when I decided to study architecture. *Why did you decide not to be a doctor?* Well, because . . . I was interested for a while, and then I sort of changed; the environment changed my feelings toward being a doctor. *The environment changed that? How do you mean, the environment changed that?* What I really wanted to do was to design buildings, that's what really changed my mind. *Oh, seeing the environ-ment, traveling through it on trains . . . And walk-ing through it also.*

What are some of the things that stand out in your memory about the last few years? Anything particular about being an adolescent? You get to go to parties a lot; well I have, and I like that. My older brother, he's 18 now, and he drives, he's driving for 2 years, so we get to go to parties a lot. And he dri-ves, so that's quite convenient. *You enjoy parties?* Uh-huh. And going to movies also. And going to the [video game] arcades after the movies is fun too. *Do you do that alone, or with a group?* No, a group. I go with one cousin, and a couple of his friends and my brother also. *Guys, or guys and gals?* Guys and gals. I've had a girlfriend. We went out for a while, then things didn't work out. I don't know, she seemed kind of snobbish. I didn't get far with her. *What do you mean, snobbish?* Stuck-up; like she was pretty and all; she would act conceited. So I don't really like girls like that. She didn't seem that way at first. *How old were you when you started seeing her?* I was 14. I was a freshman. *How long did you date her?* About 2 months.

Do you remember when you first began to notice the physical changes of puberty happening to your body? Oh yeah. I started growing more in size, and my muscles started sticking out more. *About how old were you at that time?* I was 13½; my birthday is in July; it was like it was in June. One day I got re-ally sick, well, a little sick, and that's when I felt the change. *You really felt the change? You felt a little sick?* Somehow, yeah. *Were you one of the first guys in your class to start growing like that?* Oh no, there's this guy who was very tall; he's my age. We were in the same homeroom freshman year. But he was pretty tall; he was 5'9" and I was around 5'5". *How did you feel about those changes?* I didn't re-ally notice at first; I noticed changes in myself after-wards when I find out people start saying, "He's grown; he's grown a lot." And then I realized it; I feel surprised sometimes. *How about the physical maturation of the genitals? How did you feel about that? Pubic hair, penis getting bigger and all of that?* Uh, well . . . *It's kind of a sensitive ques-tion—the kind of thing people don't often talk about, but everybody experiences it.* Well, I was kind of surprised by it. I just noticed it. I was 13 and I still didn't have pubic hair and I was just waiting: when is it going to grow? When I was 14, going on 15 it started to grow. It took a while. *Did you go to the kind of school where guys sometimes shower to-gether and it was kind of obvious whether you had pubic hair or not?* No, we had locker rooms and we had separate things, so no one ever noticed. *So you could keep it pretty quiet?* Right. *Was it some-thing guys talked about?* In school, no one ever talks about it; not really. They just talked about girls—what they were going to do with this girl, and that girl's got a nice figure. *So you just kind of wondered when it would start and kept quiet about it?* Yeah.

Did you have any good friends at that time you could talk about sex with, or about development or feelings about it? My friend was not really that open. He just talked about girls, or really about sex; we talked about that a lot. And I didn't really feel like talking about it either. He told me once that he'd had sexual intercourse with a girl. And I was sur-prised because he didn't seem like that kind of a guy. It surprised me. *What do you mean, that kind of guy?* Well, like the guy who would after a couple of months knowing a girl instead of getting to know her a lot better, you know, dating her for like a year, I didn't think in 2 months he'd have sexual inter-course with her. *Seemed like he wasn't quite re-specting her enough?* Right.

Did you notice people reacting to you differently after you began to grow at puberty? Yeah, girls es-pecially. When I was younger I didn't look too great. I had my hair different, and they didn't even notice. I never noticed, well I did notice them, pretty girls, but they never looked at me. Now, when I got older, girls are starting to look my way. And that's how I'd meet girls; I know a lot of girls. So they started to notice me. *How about your own feel-ings? Did you start to notice girls more?* Yeah. There was this one girl; she's really a nice person. And she's pretty; she's very thin, but her face was pretty. And then, in just 2 years, she developed, rather quickly, and largely, you know. *So you no-ticed her and watched her development.* Right. I've known her since freshman year and I still know her, so I noticed the change.

Do you remember your best friend when you were around 12 or 13? Yeah. *Who was it, or did you have more than one?* I had one, really; no . . . two. One, his name was Larry; the other was George. And I still keep in touch with George; I don't know what happened to Larry.

What is your ethnic background? My parents are Ecuadoran. They come from Ecuador. *What about George and Larry; what was their ethnic background?* George, I'm not sure. Larry is Jewish. George, I think he's, I'm not sure, I never asked him.

How did you meet these guys? Well, George I met through my brother; he was in the same class as my brother was. *Oh, so he's older than you?* Right. Larry was in my homeroom in junior high school. So I met him there and I got to know him a lot better; we'd associate with each other a lot. *What kinds of things did you do together?* Well, we never really saw each other that much; Larry and I, we'd just go to school, like buddies; we'd just play football together, you know. We'd go swimming. We'd play with, not with each other, we'd be together a lot. *And then what happened?* That's when I started to meet George; you know, we became friends, then we became good friends; and we associated a lot together, we knew each other. *George was your brother's friend?* Well, my brother was never really good friends with him; but I became good friends with him, because I knew him. Just when I first met him I knew him. But it didn't bother Larry. He lived downtown, and he had this other friend downtown and they would go places together and it was, like, three's company. *What did you and George do together?* With George I went to the movies; with his girlfriend and a friend of his; and afterwards we went to the arcades and he went off somewhere with his girlfriend. And we stayed there for a while until he came back. Then we'd also go to, I think it was Macy's, a department store on 34th Street; and we just walked around to kill time; we went through the whole store. We were just looking at things, you know, having fun. We did a lot of things like that. We went to the park once to play some softball and

we were on opposite teams. We got into competition; I was trying to beat him and he was trying to beat me. And we did a lot of other things. *Why did you like him?* I found it easy to communicate with him, and go places. *Did his being older make a difference?* Uh-huh, yes. When I was 12 or 13 I wasn't able to go around too much, go all the way downtown and then come back by myself. I wasn't that privileged. When I got older, my mother began trusting me more and she let me go [alone]. *Are you still close to either of those guys?* Well, I haven't seen them for a while. *What happened?* Well, he wanted to go to Pratt, but I don't think he passed the test, so he went to another high school. *This was George?* Yes. After that I never even saw him again; we kept in touch, but after a while, just separated. I'd still call him a couple of times. *How long ago was it that you kind of split up?* The end of May [about 6 months ago].

Are you part of a social group of some sort in your school? Not really. I was on the soccer team. I wanted to join the tennis team, my freshman year, but I didn't have the time, nor did anyone tell me when the tryouts were. So I didn't really find out; I thought it was still being held, so . . . *Are there social groups at the school? People who kind of hang around together?* Yeah. We have teams; there are those guys who hang together—the football team especially, and the basketball team. And another—it's not really like a group, they're monitors; they're called the "SOS"; they have to go in to school early and have to stand in the hallways to make sure everyone goes in the right direction and take care of the elevator lines—those guys I think they hang out together the most because they go to the same homeroom. *It sounds like there's not a whole lot of social life at your school. People just sort of go in for classes and come home?* Oh no; there is in school, when you have friends, you go up to the lunchroom. The thing about them, other students, is that they like to cut a lot of classes and go to the lunchroom during lunch hours; they go to the lunchroom to see their friends, and they think it's hip, you know, cut class and go up to the lunchroom. I have fun when I change classes, everyone's talking during change of classes. But I don't cut class to go to the lunchroom. *Why not?* I don't find it really necessary to cut instead of going to class. I feel I need this education. I want to graduate with a New York Tech diploma and a high school diploma. At New York Tech, they give out a New York Tech diploma and a city diploma also.

How do you feel about school? I like it. The classes, a couple of them are boring. But I have some good ones too. And the people in my school are friendly, the guys I know. So I like it. *How do you feel about the teachers?* Oh, there's a couple of teachers I dislike. My English teacher, I don't like him. He gets too hostile; he gets too discouraged. Like if someone's talking in the back, he takes it out on the whole class and he starts screaming and yelling. And then he can't really hear or see—well, he can see and hear, but he screams at the wrong person. He starts yelling at someone for talking when he wasn't talking. *That bothers you.* Yeah, because he did it to me once; he started yelling at me and I wasn't talking. And I didn't like that. *What teachers do you like?* I like my architectural drawing teacher, my science teacher. *Why do you like them?* Because they don't get aggravated and they're not loud like my English teacher. And my Social Studies teacher is fun. I like funny teachers who tell jokes in class. My English teacher just wants to work and nothing else. I don't mind that, but he tries to crowd it on and get it over with and get tomorrow's work all done in one day; it's a little too much. *What about the other students? How do you like them?* Well, I like most of them; but some students I don't like. This one guy, he just gets on my nerves, I don't know why; just for no reason, he just starts to bother me. I just threatened him one day and he hasn't bothered me since. There's a couple of others that think they're hot, roaming around school, thinking they've got a lot of back-up from friends, when they really don't, when their back-up actually hates them also. *Sounds like a pretty complicated place.* Yeah, it is.

Any other activities beside soccer that you're involved in? Not really; I wanted to join the swim team, but then I decided not to because I didn't want to go swimming in this weather [winter]. You get out of the water and it's cold and I didn't want to get

sick. I play tennis during the winter, so I do that instead of swimming.

Does being Hispanic or from a Latin background have any effect on your social life at school? Not really, except some girls who like guys who are just from their place, like Puerto Rico. Some Puerto Rican girls just want Puerto Rican guys. And some girls that are pretty are Puerto Rican and just want Puerto Rican guys; that bothers me. *How do you feel about that for yourself?* Well, I feel that the girl is being unfair, because she's just looking for one background. I think that's unfair. *You don't feel the background is that important for girls you date?* Right. It doesn't matter where she's from if I like her.

Who are some of the adults, other than teachers, who have an influence on your life who you kind of look up to, or like? Let's see. There's this security guard I get along with, his name's Tony, but we call him Curly because he has curly hair. I almost got into a fight once with this guy, one on one. And Tony came up to me and grabbed me; he pulled me to the side and talked to me for a while. And he told me it wasn't necessary to fight; and he told me, "Cesar, who's the fool?" And I realized it was the guy that fights. So I look up to him because he was very reasonable and he knows what he's talking about.

Any other adults, people in the neighborhood, or the church? Well, the person I really look up to a lot is my father. He's very intelligent; he does a lot of things. Like, um, he's a cook at a restaurant; he also works around here with cars, he's also a mechanic. He works around here when some guys need help. What I like about him especially, I admire, is that he doesn't charge these guys; he does it for free because it's what he used to do when he was young. So I admire that generosity in not charging, because some jobs he does, like changing a transmission, it costs like $200 at a garage and he doesn't charge them anything. Sometimes they give him money; first he backs off, but if they end up giving it to him saying, "Here, here, take it," he'll take it afterwards, but he doesn't really want it. He just says, "It's ok." *What else do you like about him?* Well, he is a great pool player—plays pool, billiards, real good. And I watch him all the time when he plays. And I watch where he positions the pool stick and how he takes his shots. What I really like about him is that he's fair to all of us. He treats all of us evenly. And he's done a lot for me. I play tennis right now, and I've popped strings so many times it's unbelievable; I've popped like seven strings, one after another, and I have to go to this sporting goods store and he gives me the money for all of this. It's not because he gives me the money, but because he wants me to keep playing. *How do you get along with him?* I get along with him well. I talk to him. Any time I have a problem, I just tell him. I talk to my mother when my father's not there. But I really talk to my father. *You talk to him pretty well, pretty easily?* Yeah. *Has it always been that way, or was it different when you were younger?* Well, it was different when I was younger; I was kind of scared. He grew up and he taught us how to respect people and what to do when you're in another person's home. And if I was doing something wrong, he'd give me a certain look. And that's all. I'd just go and sit down, if I was fooling around; and that's why I was frightened. But then as I got older, I began to start talking to him; when I turned 12 or 13, I started opening myself up more. And I started asking him if I could go to the movies with my friends. At 13 he would tell me, "Not really, because you're still young, you're small"; I wasn't that big. At 14 he started letting me go. A lot of times, I'd ask permission; I always ask permission before I do things, so now if I know he's going to say, "No," I don't bother asking him. *You've learned what he'll say "Yes" to and what he'll say "No" to?* Right. Ever since I turned 13. *Do you also know how to get him to say "Yes" if you really want him to?* Yeah. I convince him; like, I give him the details of everything, and then he'll say, "Ok."

How about you and your mother. How do you get along with her? Oh, I talk to her a lot. But when it comes to problems, that's when I go to my father. My mother, she knows a lot, but since I'm a man, I don't think she can answer some male problems, so that's when I go to my father. And my mother, she tells me what to do, she tells me, "Put your sneakers away"; but I play around with her a lot, she's funny.

You enjoy that, the playful relationship and teasing each other? Yeah. *Has that relationship changed since you were a child?* No. *Still very much the same way?* Yes, uh-huh. *How do you get along with your brothers and sister? You've got two brothers and a sister.* I get along with my younger brother [age 12] the best; we do a lot of things together; we have fun; we play tennis together a lot. My sister [age 9] plays tennis also, but she's like butting in a lot. And she gets nosey. My older brother [age 18] is demandful: "You get out of here; get out of my room"; he tells us that; he gets on my nerves sometimes, but I don't bother, you know; I just keep quiet. Sometimes we have arguments over it. *Sure; it's natural enough. Are any other family members living with you?* No, but my brother, my oldest, he lives with my grandmother; I don't really get to see him often, but when I see him, we talk all right. We have conversations.

Where does your grandmother live? She lives uptown. *Do you see her very often?* She comes down almost every weekend; almost every weekend I get to see her. *How do you feel about her?* She's very nice. *Very nice?* Yeah. She didn't get mad one day. When we were small we broke this glass by accident. We were playing hide and seek, my brother and I; we were hiding behind the door and there was like this cabinet that had like a glass door and we crashed into it and it broke. And she just said, "It's all right. As long as you didn't get hurt." And so I like her. I liked her before. When we would go to visit she'd give us dinner, or give us cake or something. She always gives some good food for us. *Is she your only grandparent?* Yeah. She's my father's mother. My mother's mother died when she was young.

Is it sometimes a little difficult growing up in a family where your parents were born in another country; does that make a difference? Are they a little more traditional? Not really, I like being American. Because I go out, and some people think I'm Chinese; but I'm not. In Ecuador, most people have slanted eyes. I really don't notice that; I don't pay no attention if they start teasing me. *Do people sometimes tease you?* Oh yes. I was going to the store once and this fat guy started teasing me, and I paid him no mind; he started following me and asked if I was going home. I told him, "No." *You say you like being American, thinking of yourself as American.* Yeah. *And going out and acting American.* Yeah. *Do you sometimes get some conflict from your parents who may still think sort of like they were in the old country?* No. They really think it's important to be American. *They want that too.* Right. That's where you were born; that's the way you should be. *Do you speak Spanish?* Yes, I speak Spanish; I used to speak it very fluently, when I was around 10. Now I started speaking more English and then took up French. So, that's how my Spanish started getting a little awkward; but I can still speak it pretty well when I have to. *How do you feel about that?* Well, I feel kind of disappointed in myself for that, letting myself forget the words I used to know. In a way it helped me out in French, because French is associated with Spanish and English, so it helps.

Can we talk a little about sex? Sex, sure. *When did you discover masturbation?* Uh, 13. *How did you feel about it?* Well, I felt, like uh, how will I put this . . . [pause] I felt, like it was something very different, not normal. Like I was the only one doing it. Then I realized, I started talking to my friends. *You felt like you were the only one doing it?* Right. We played football, a lot of Saturdays (I've played football since I was 10), and I was outside and my friend, Luis, we got into a conversation, you know, masturbation, and he told us how many guys masturbate, because more than 85% of teenagers do it, masturbate. So that's when I learned it was normal. *How did you feel then?* I was glad about it. At first I didn't know what the word *masturbation* was. I learned it in junior high school. This girl asked me, "Do you masturbate?" I said, "What's that?" She said, "You don't know what masturbation is?" And I said, "No." And so she started to laugh. And she tells her friends, and they're over there laughing. These girls were in ninth grade and I was just in seventh. And they started giggling because I didn't know what it was. I didn't pay no attention. So I found out from my brother. Then I just laughed and felt embarrassed. *Why did you feel embarrassed?* Because I didn't know what the word meant, what it was.

How did you learn about sex? Well, on cable television; and also from my brother, he told me. My brother told me when I asked about masturbation, he started telling me about sex because he was taking a hygiene class, so he told me about it. And I learned the organs; because I wanted to be a doctor, I was reading books and I learned the reproductive system. *From cable TV, you mean, movies?* Yes, movies. We have Channel N and my brother would stay up late and he would sit there and I would walk in and watch. *Have you had sex education in school?* Well, not yet. We were supposed to have it in our senior year for hygiene; now they've changed it; all the sophomores have hygiene now.

When did you begin to notice sexual feelings toward other people? Fourteen years old; that's when I was [first enrolled] at New York Tech. I started noticing some of the girls in the trains. Most girls would wear these tight jeans, and pants, and shortcut shirts and for some reason it would excite me, yeah. I would feel like taking them home somewhere and just laying down. *Was there anyone in particular, or just kind of girls in general?* Mostly the good-looking girls, the ones who had the better figure, more developed.

Have you had any sex experiences with other people? Uh, yes, just once. *Would you tell me about it?* Let's see, well we started out, we were just kissing, then we went to her house; just after the kissing we came up to the house and kissed, and we just undressed and lay on the bed and had sexual intercourse. *Did either of you use a contraceptive?* Um, after she told me she had taken a pill. I didn't notice when she did; I guess she took a pill when she wanted to have sexual intercourse. *Did you have any thoughts about using contraception at the time?* No, I really didn't. In my sophomore year we had a speech class and our group decided (we split up into groups) and we decided to do a report on adolescence and we were talking about how girls and guys had sexual intercourse and how to protect yourself and that's when I learned that contraceptives were able to protect a girl from being pregnant, without harming her sex. Like the pill messes up the girl's hormones inside. And she could grow a moustache, or something. [His information on contraception is not accurate; see Chapter 9.]

How did you feel about having sex? Were you kind of nervous? Yeah, I was nervous at first, when we started undressing. But then afterwards, we were in the middle of it, I got calm, since I was reading books on the reproductive system, I made sure I didn't, you know, let loose, let go of my sperm, and that's when she had told me she took a pill, when I was backing out. *So you were going to pull out before you came because you were aware that she might get pregnant if you didn't?* Uh-huh. And as I got calm, and then she told me, she said, "It's all right." I just kept on and I came inside her. *How did you feel afterwards?* Well, I felt, like I did something, I'd experienced something that only adults do. And I knew that it wasn't only me, but I knew most humans have sexual intercourse. I wasn't alone. *You were not alone.* Right. I wasn't some special person. At first, I felt I'd done something special. But then I realized that everyone else does it. *So it wasn't especially good, I guess, or it wasn't anything especially bad, either?* Right. *You didn't feel guilty about it?* No.

Were you brought up in the church? Did that enter in at all because sometimes people do have guilt feelings about all this? Yeah, I was brought up going to church. This girl, you know, I got along with her well; and we decided, you know, why not, considering that night, what happened that day, you know, we went upstairs to her house and she took, I guess she took a pill, and afterward we had sexual intercourse. *She was more experienced, I guess?* Yes.

How would you describe yourself now, at the age of 16? Well, um, [pause] I'm someone with a lot of heart. Since the age of 15 I've started thinking about what's going on in the world and with everyone else, like some people who tease other people. I feel that people who are being teased aren't the fools, it's the people that are teasing them. I feel sorry sometimes for other people, some guys who are dumb and get teased. And like street bums, I feel sorry for them, because when you grow up you never know if you will have an education and opportunity like I do. I really feel something for them. I feel that if I was

able to burn a hundred dollars, if I was that rich, I'd give them a hundred dollars you know, to buy food or something.

So you're a guy with a lot of heart, and concerned about where the world's going and what's happening. What else? I like to have fun. I like to go to parties, like I said before. And I enjoy meeting girls a lot. *Do the parties involve drinking or smoking grass?* Well, I don't like smoking, so I don't smoke cigarettes or anything. Drinking alcohol, I drink lightly, I don't drink too much. I don't overdrink, get drunk, come home falling down. Also because my brother's there, and he doesn't like drinking, so I'm under pressure. He's good also, because he doesn't let me go too far. *It's nice having him around for that.* Right, so I don't go home falling down the steps or anything. I just drink to a certain extent; I don't exceed my boundaries.

What else about you—a guy with heart, somebody who likes parties . . . ? I'm active. I'm up for a lot of sports. I'm kind of lazy. I put down my book bag on top of my bed, and I think, "I'll take it off later"—everything is "later." And my mother doesn't want that, she wants me to do it now. And I want to do it afterwards, after I've done what I want to do. She wants me to do it now.

Do you think you know who you are? Do you think you have a sense of identity? In school I have an image, you know. I have to be nice, because that's how I am; everyone knows me as being nice. I do them favors. I don't ask them for favors. This girl, she asked me to do her homework because she had to go to the dean's office; so I did it for her. She just came and said, "Thank you." I just accepted it. So, I take that from my father. *Being nice and doing things.* Right, a nice person. *So it's an image at school you sort of have to live up to?* Right. And at home, I'm lazy. When I'm not home I'm doing other things. 'Cause at home I got used to this.

How would you like life to work out for you? I'd like everything to go a lot better. Well, everything is ok right now, but I'd like to have a little bit more money in order to buy myself another [tennis] racquet. And get a car. It's a lot to ask for. *It'd be important to have a car?* We have three, but one is in bad condition, one my father uses, and the other one my brother uses. So, also I'd have to get a license; I have a permit. *Is it pretty important to have a car in the city?* Yeah. Because you have to travel around. I go to play tennis on Friday afternoons from 4 to 6, so I could take the trains, but I come home to go with my friends; and my mother, she's been driving for about a year, but she's not too confident if the car stalls. *So you'd like to have a little more money to get some of the things that are important, a racquet, a car of your own. How else would you like things to work out?* I'd like girls to look at me, so many girls look at the guys we call "hard rock," tough guys with a lot of back-up that dress real tough and I'm not like that, so I don't attract girls. See, you have these things called "goose downs," you know, jackets, at my school that's like a fad now, everyone is wearing goose downs now. And some girls like those guys that wear them. I wish they could change, for my benefit, and for their benefit. *I think they will; it may take a few years before they realize how important it is to find someone who is serious, sincere, nice, instead of just somebody with a fancy coat.* And someone with gold chains. And dancing; I can dance, but some guys can dance better than I can and they attract the girls. I'd do that also; but some guys who are better than I am, the girls ask them to dance. I'm almost beat. We have this thing called break dancing, so we sometimes have those contests in school. And they play music and you dance on the floor, you know, you do certain spins; and I know how to do it and I'm almost even with those guys. But, you know, the girls, they always think you can do better, little by little. So I practice. If I'm better than they are, all the eyes will turn. And I've been putting down those guys who wear those goose down coats and that dress real good with gold chains on. I don't wear gold chains because I ride the trains, and I don't think—well, it's not too dangerous but you can never be too sure. So I don't wear them. *But you kind of like to put down those guys that are so popular with the gold chains and the goose down coats and get the girls.* Right.

I'd like to, you know, be able to put them down, kick 'em to the side. *Kick 'em to the side and the girls would be interested in you?* Not really for my dancing, I'd like to get—I've only gone out with like three girls and I know a lot more—but what I want in a girl is not to be looking for a dancer, but to be looking for a guy who's more kind, sensitive, generous and a guy that will respect her. And that's the kind of guy I am. And most guys in my school aren't like that. And most girls, they just go for those guys. I don't understand. Later on they'll realize "that was the guy for me, but I was blind."

Chapter 8

◆

Friends, Peers, and Dates: The Social World of Adolescents

◆

Adolescence is a time of rapidly expanding social horizons. As young people move from childhood into their teenage years, their increasing independence from their family is accompanied by a shift from home-centered to peer-group and community-wide activities. More time is spent with friends instead of parents and siblings, and recreation in the immediate neighborhood is replaced by participating in extracurricular activities at school, "cruising" popular gathering places, and going to concerts, parties, ball games, and other kinds of events in various parts of town. In this chapter we examine four aspects of adolescents' relationships with each other that define their social world: forming friendships, belonging to the peer group, dating and other "strategic interactions," and being lonely and shy.

FORMING FRIENDSHIPS

Friendships are special relationships between two people who care for each other and share important parts of their lives. Friendships need to be distinguished from friendly relations, and friends from acquaintances. Most people have numerous acquaintances and spend time with groups of people who are friendly with each other. However, an individual friendship involves just a two-person bond of common interests and reciprocal affection.

Compared to acquaintances, friends are fonder of each other, more extensively involved with each other, and more concerned about each other's welfare. More so than acquaintances, friends can be counted on to stick up for you when defense is needed and to put themselves out for you when help would come in handy, even if they have to make some sacrifice in the process. As the old saying goes, "A friend in need is a friend indeed." Simply put, then, friends are people who like each other a lot, help each other a lot, and spend a lot of time together.

In her book called *Young Girls*, which we have discussed in previous chapters, Konopka (1976) provides some first-hand accounts of how her culturally and socioeconomically diverse sample of 12–18-year-old girls viewed friendship and other aspects of their lives. Here is what three of them had to say about the nature of friends and how they differ from acquaintances:

> [A friend is] someone who . . . when you really need them, they will come. Someone who sticks close and is truthful and y'know, I won't really have to worry about them goin' out and tellin' your business or somethin' like that. (Black, urban, age 15.) [p. 85]
>
> I like people who are willing to listen . . . My friend and I, we talk to each other about our problems and we help each other . . . with our ideals and things. (White, rural, age 17.) [p. 85]
>
> Well, I only have about three tight friends, because I don't trust that many people with my feelings . . . the rest of them [friends] I consider acquaintances. (Black, suburban, age 15.) [p. 86]

In studies that involved talking with more than 1,000 12–19-year-olds about their relationships with parents and peers, Youniss and Smollar (1985, Chapter 6) found ample evidence of how important friendships are in the lives and social development of young people. It is with their close friends that teenagers typically engage in enjoyable activities that take place away from home and without their parents being involved, Youniss and Smollar noted,

Table 8.1 ADOLESCENT ATTITUDES ABOUT HAVING CLOSE FRIENDS

Statements About Friendships	Percentage Responding "True"
I have at least one close friend who means a lot to me	94%
My close friend values my friendship	92%
Once I become friends with someone, we stay friends a long time	92%
My close friend understands me better than my parents do	70%
I feel right now in my life that I learn more from my close friends than I do from my parents	70%
I'm more myself with my close friends than with my parents	68%
My friendships don't last very long	9%
I never had a real close friend	7%
Friends aren't really that important to me	5%

Source: Based on data reported by Youniss and Smollar (1985, Chapter 6) on 180 12–19-year-old students.

and it is with their close friends that they talk with people other than their parents about such topics as school, friendship, dating, sex, and their present and future plans.

As most people know from their own experience, it is not just having friends that counts, nor is the number of a young person's friends all that critical to them; what matters is having at least a few good friends. Table 8.1 shows what one group of Youniss and Smollar's subjects had to say about having close friends; their comments leave little doubt about the significance of such relationships in the lives of young people.

Willard Hartup (1989a), who was one of the first researchers to study peer interactions, drew a useful distinction between relationships with parents and relationships with friends. Children's relationships to their parents are *vertical* attachments to individuals who know more and have more social power than they do, he noted, and from these relationships young people gain protection and security and learn basic social skills. Relationships with friends, on the other hand, are *horizontal* attachments between individuals who are relatively similar in knowledge and power. It is in these horizontal relationships that young people elaborate their social skills, begin to learn about the complexities of competition and cooperation among equals, and first achieve intimacy in social relations. Hartup stressed that both kinds of relationships, vertical and horizontal, are necessary for adaptive development to occur.

Needing and wanting to have friends is thus a basic aspect of the human condition because sharing bonds of friendship is a pleasurable and rewarding experience that enriches peoples' lives, enhances their capacities to manage interpersonal relationships, and helps them feel good about themselves. There is much truth in the words of a song made famous by the entertainer, Barbara Streisand: "People who need people are the luckiest people in the world." By contrast, individuals who are disinterested in or incapable of forming friendships are often suffering from personality disorders that limit their sense of personal fulfillment, no matter what else they are able to accomplish. For this reason, having friends is generally regarded as an important social achievement, as an index of interpersonal skill, and as a sign of good adjustment among young people and adults alike.

With respect to adjustment, research confirms that young people who are psychologically disturbed have fewer and less stable friendships than their peers (Hartup & Sancilio, 1986); conversely, adolescents who have the benefit of supportive peer relationships have higher self-esteem, get along better in school, and less often become emotionally upset than those who lack such friendships (Berndt, 1992; Furman & Gavin, 1989). More than any other single symptom, in fact, poor peer relationships differentiate young people with emotional problems from those who are developing normally (Bierman, 1989).

Moreover, longitudinal studies have demonstrated a significant relationship between how well children and adolescents get along with their peers and how well adjusted they are later in life. For example, Ladd (1990) found among 125 kindergarten children that those who made new friends during the first 2 months of the school year made more gains in school performance during the rest of the year than those who did not make new friends; kindergartners who experienced rejection by their peers early in the school year, on the other hand, performed less well during the rest of the year than those who were not rejected, and they also were more likely to dislike school and to have poor attendance records.

In similar research with older children, Morrison and Masten (1991) examined the sociability of 207 third- to sixth-graders and again 7 years later when they were age 14–19. Those who were relatively socially isolated as elementary school students were more likely to show poor social skills and various kinds of psychological disturbance as adolescents. As a third example, Hightower (1990) reported a long-term study in which harmonious peer relationships among 141 subjects at age 13 were found to predict sound mental health at age 50. Abundant additional research leaves little doubt that positive peer relationships foster adaptive social and emotional development, whereas young people who get along poorly with their peers are at risk for subsequent psychological difficulties (Bierman, 1987; Kupersmidt, Coie, & Dodge, 1990; Parker & Asher, 1987).

Although young children form friendships, their emotional immaturity and self-centeredness typically restrict the degree of reciprocal understanding and support they are capable of providing each other. Children's friendships thus tend to be relatively shallow and fleeting until about age 9 or 10. Then young people start entering into deeper, more stable, and more other-directed relationships than they have had before, often in the form of what are known as "chumships." From this point on through adolescence, friendships continue to deepen and to complement relationships with parents.

THE EMERGENCE OF CHUMSHIPS

As we noted in discussing the contributions of Harry Stack Sullivan in Chapter 2, **chumships** are close relationships that many young people form during preadolescence with just one other person, usually of the same age, gender, and race. Preadolescent chums become inseparable friends who spend most of their waking hours together and share exclusively with each other their innermost hopes and fears. Seventeen typical features of this special kind of relationship are listed in Box 8.1. In developing this list for research purposes some years ago, Mannarino (1976) suggested that preadolescents who endorse ten or more of these items in describing how they get along with their best friend are probably involved in a chumship.

Sullivan (1953, Chapter 16) originally described several ways in which he felt that chumships differ from earlier childhood friendships. For many years his views were supported mainly by the impressions of other observers, in the absence of much systematic re-

◆ BOX 8.1 A CHUMSHIP CHECKLIST

1. Play games in which you both take turns being the leader.
2. Walk to school together.
3. Help out when one of you gets behind in his/her work.
4. Talk about girls/boys.
5. Share each other's games, etc.
6. Tell each other things you wouldn't tell anyone else.
7. Stick up for each other if another boy/girl is picking on one of you.
8. Sit together on the school bus.
9. Try to be on the same side when choosing teams for basketball, softball, volleyball, etc.
10. Do "fun" things together, such as going to the movies.
11. Tell each other if one of you has done something wrong.
12. Phone each other about school assignments.
13. Talk about what you want to be when you grow up.
14. Sleep over at each other's house.
15. Talk about your parents.
16. Find it hard to disagree with him/her on important things.
17. Go on a vacation or short trip with him/her and his/her family.

search. More recently, however, accumulating data have documented three developmental changes that he described, one involving cognitive-social maturation, a second having to do with similarities and differences, and a third relating to stability and change.

Cognitive-Social Maturation

Sullivan said that the time when young people find a chum coincides with the time when they start becoming truly sensitive to the needs and feelings of other people. Prior to this change, children are very self-centered in their relationships with their playmates and with their parents and siblings, as well. As preadolescents they begin to display other-directed concerns about what they can do to contribute to the happiness and well-being of other people, especially a chum.

We touched on this change from self-centered to other-directed relationships in Chapter 5, when we described how cognitive maturation makes it possible for children to understand each other better and take a more reciprocal approach to friendship relationships as they grow older. To study this relationship between chumships and maturing social cognition, McGuire and Weisz (1982) examined two central aspects of other-centeredness: **perspective taking**, which was measured by how well subjects could recognize the feelings of others and understand why they felt that way; and **altruism**, which they measured by observing such caring behavior as expressing support for a peer being picked on, offering to call the parents of a classmate who became ill, sharing one's lunch, and giving help to a classmate who had an accident.

McGuire and Weisz conducted their study with 230 fifth- and sixth-graders in a rural public school. Of these children, 109 showed a reciprocal best-friend choice with a classmate that was stable over a 3-week period and involved many shared activities. Those children who were actively engaged in such a chumship tended to be older than those who had no regular best friend, which is what Sullivan's developmental formation would predict. In further support of Sullivan's notions, children who had chums showed significantly higher levels of altruism and perspective taking than those who were chum-less.

This and subsequent research has confirmed that having close friendships is associated with being able and willing to understand and genuinely care about other people. Developmentally, children approaching junior high school age place increasing importance on sharing and loyalty in friendship relationships (Berndt, 1989; Clark & Bittle, 1992; Hartup, 1989b; Inderbitzen-Pisaruk & Foster, 1990). But what comes first? Sullivan felt that close interpersonal relationships are important learning experiences that foster emotional sensitivity to others, and many leading theorists have concurred that peer relations make a unique contribution to children's development of social skills (Bukowski & Hoza, 1989). Cognitive-developmental theorists in the Piagetian tradition (see Chapter 5) tend instead to regard the maturation of perspective-taking skills as a necessary foundation that precedes building mutual friendships.

Although we cannot resolve this theoretical difference, we can be sure that social skills and social interactions grow together. Slight increments in perspective-taking ability are likely to promote slight increments in friendship mutuality, which are in turn likely to promote a further increment in perspective-taking ability, and so forth. In understanding this and other aspects of personality development, recognizing which processes grow together and how they influence each other's growth may well be more important than identifying which one occurs first.

Similarities and Differences

Sullivan suggested that preadolescent chums are more likely to differ from each other in their background and interests than childhood playmates. Playmates are selected for comfort and support, he said, as companions who will think and act the same way as oneself. They will want to do the same things, and they will be predictable and easy to understand. Although chums must also be supportive and comforting, he continued, they are chosen in part because they are interesting and intriguing in some way: They have a different kind of family background from one's own, for example, or they have lived in different places, or they have some different talents or hobbies, or they have a different sort of temperament or style of relating to people. Although such differences tend to be far outnumbered by the many common characteristics that link chums, they flavor the relationship with a spicy taste of attitudes and circumstances different from one's own.

Studies of friendship choice have focused mainly on the kinds of similarities and common perspectives that attract people to each other. This work has confirmed our previous observation that childhood and adolescent friends tend to be similar in age, gender, and race (Clark, 1989; DuBois & Hirsch, 1990; Epstein, 1989; Tolson & Urberg, 1993). Young people who become friends are likely to feel the same way about school, to have the same heroes and favorite celebrities, and to want to spend their time in similar ways. One of Konopka's (1976) subjects stated, "All of my friends are a lot like me. You know, none of them are carbon copies, but enough like me so they can understand me and I can understand them" (white, suburban, age 17) (p. 86).

Nevertheless, Sullivan is not alone in suggesting that friends may be chosen partly on the basis of complementary rather than similar traits and interests. Such "unusual" friends ex-

◆ *Profile*

THOMAS BERNDT

Thomas Berndt entered college thinking about majoring in either physics or psychology. His enthusiasm for a course he took on learning theory and motivation helped him choose psychology as his career of choice. He subsequently entered the graduate program in developmental psychology at the University of Minnesota, from which he received his Ph.D. in 1975. As a graduate student, Dr. Berndt focused mainly on cognitive development and the work of Piaget. He became especially interested in the indirect implications of Piaget's concepts for the ways in which young people form friendships, and he decided that he would concentrate his own scholarly work on direct studies of how youthful friendships form and develop.

After completing his graduate studies, Dr. Berndt joined the faculty at Yale University and later moved on to positions at the University of Oklahoma and Purdue University. Since 1982 he has been Professor of Psychological Sciences at Purdue, and over the last 15 years he has become a leading scholar in the area of peer relationships among children and adolescents. His research has contributed important information concerning peer-group influence in young people, the nature of youthful friendships, and the significance of friendships in providing emotional support and promoting good adjustment.

Even when he is not teaching or writing about developmental psychology, Dr. Berndt involves himself with young people. Much of his spare time is devoted to family activities centered around his four sons, presently aged 5 to 18, especially sports and church activities. He has coached Little League baseball and soccer and also found time to teach Sunday school. His future research plans involve further study of how young people reconcile conflicts between their friendship needs and their individual needs: How do you choose, for example, between doing what your friend wants to do, which promotes your relationship with the friend, and doing something different that you want to do, which promotes being your own person?

pose people to ways of approaching life that differ from what they have previously learned or been taught, which can be a broadening and even exhilarating experience. Thomas Berndt (1982), whose research we cite frequently in this chapter, has said that these are "friends whom [adolescents] can idealize or friends who engage in behaviors that fascinate them but that they are afraid to perform themselves" (p. 1453). Other researchers as well have noted that similarities between friends can minimize disagreements and promote reciprocity but may also become boring and predictable; differences between friends, on the other hand, can lead to more conflict and compromise than people desire, but they can also bring excitement and enrichment to their lives (Epstein, 1989).

Most people appreciate that friendship relationships almost always involve some blend of similarity and complementarity. An example of this feature of friendship occurred in the life of Sigmund Freud. As an adolescent entering high school, Freud developed a close relationship with a boy who, like him, had a sharp, inquiring mind. This boy had a more relaxed attitude toward life than Freud, however, and ended up being expelled from school. Their relationship is described by Freud in some recollections of his adolescence written when he was age 71:

> I know that I made the acquaintance of Heinrich Braun during the first year at the gymnasium when we got our first "report card" and that we were soon inseparable friends. All the hours of the day which were left after school I spent with him, mostly at his home. . . . We . . . got along marvelously. I hardly remember any quarrels between us or times during which we were "mad" at each other. . . . He awakened a multitude of revolutionary trends in me and we reinforced each other in the overestimate of our . . . superior knowledge. . . . I admired him: his self-confident poise, his independent judgment; I compared him secretly with a young lion. . . . A scholar he was not, but I did not mind that, though I myself soon became *Primus* (first in the class) and remained it; in the vague feeling of those years I understood that he possessed something which was more valuable than all success in school and which I have since learned to call "personality." . . . Our relationship experienced its first interruption—I think it was during the Septima, the next to last grade—when he left school, unfortunately not voluntarily. [Quoted in Grotjahn, 1956].

Stability and Change

Sullivan believed that preadolescent chumships are more stable and enduring than peer relationships among younger children. Membership in elementary school groups tends to change rapidly, as new members are accepted and old members move on to some other group they find more to their liking. By contrast, Sullivan said, chumships are likely to last for several months, and some young people may have just one or two chums during the preadolescent period between middle childhood and the teenage years. Once more, research findings have born out Sullivan's impression. Children in the fourth grade, who at a typical age of 9 have reached the age when chumships begin to emerge, are found to have more stable friendships than children in the earlier elementary grades.

The main research evidence in this regard has emerged from some well-conceived studies by Berndt and his colleagues (Berndt & Hoyle, 1985; Berndt, Hawkins, & Hoyle, 1986). In one set of studies, children in the first, fourth, and eighth grades were asked in the fall to identify their close friends and then asked to do so again in the spring. The stability of the identified friendships from fall to spring was greater among the fourth-graders than the first-graders, but friendship stability did not increase between the fourth and eighth grades. At the same time, both the first-graders and the fourth-graders made more new friends during the year than they lost, whereas the eighth-graders lost more new friends than they gained. Consistent with the formation of chumships, these findings confirm (1) that friendships become more stable during the early elementary years, (2) that children by the age of 9 or 10 are already forming close friendship relationships that last several months, and (3) that between the fourth and eighth grades friendship choices become more selective and focused on closer relationships with a smaller number of peers.

In another set of studies, fourth- and eighth-graders were paired with a close friend in the fall and their friendship relationship was assessed in two ways: They were asked a series of questions about their friendship, and they were asked to work together on a task on which achieving a good performance would earn them a reward, but on which they had to choose between sharing or competing for use of a limited set of materials with which to complete the task. These same procedures were repeated in the spring of the school year. At both the fourth- and eighth-grade level friendship stability was high, with two-thirds of the children, both boys and girls, remaining close friends in the spring with their same partner from the fall. Whether friendships were likely to endure or dissolve during the school year was predictable from how these children talked about them in the fall. Generally speaking, the less they said about intimacy, mutuality, and similarity when responding to questions about their relationship with their close friend, the less stable the friendship was likely to be.

With respect to working on the task, the Berndt et al. studies identified some interesting changes between childhood (fourth grade) and early adolescence (eighth grade) in friendship attitudes toward competition and sharing. Fourth-graders working in pairs displayed less sharing with a close friend than with an acquaintance who was not a close friend. By contrast, the eighth-graders displayed more sharing with close friends than with acquaintances while working on the task. This finding is consistent with Sullivan's suggestion that mutual responsiveness between friends increases as childhood gives way to adolescence. Whereas children in collaborative problem-solving situations are likely to compete with a friend in order to enhance their success, adolescent friends are likely to place less emphasis on doing better or worse than on sharing equally in the effort, whatever the outcome.

The emergence of chumships as a more involved, exclusive, and stable pattern of friendship than children have experienced earlier marks the beginning of a series of major changes in social relationships that carry into and through the adolescent years. This preadolescent event has been important for us to consider not only for its continuity with developmental events of adolescence, but also because it sets the stage for how well or poorly some of these events will proceed. The time that chums spend together and the frank opinions they share, especially about each other, give chums valuable opportunities to learn more about the world and about themselves through the trusted eyes of their friend. The sharing that chums do also helps them become more comfortable in expressing feelings and concerns that would otherwise remain private and known only to themselves. The way chums listen to and care for each other expands their appreciation for what someone else really thinks and for how this may differ from outward appearances. By pointing out each other's mistaken impressions and seeking ways to translate their differences into common outlooks, chums increase each other's skills in recognizing and resolving interpersonal misunderstandings.

For this reason the experience of chumships helps prepare young people for increasingly intimate relationships later on. Children who enter adolescence without ever having had a chum may well be handicapped in this regard. Having had little practice in the kinds of behavior that sustain close and enduring relationships, they may suffer more anxieties and setbacks than other adolescents in the process of making and keeping friends. Young people who lack social skills honed by prior practice are at risk in particular for being disliked or rejected by their peers and for experiencing loneliness, as we shall see in later sections of the chapter.

HOW FRIENDSHIPS DEEPEN

As young people pass puberty and enter early adolescence, the close friendships they have begun to form in preadolescence become an even more important part of their lives, mainly for two reasons. First, because of the many new and potentially upsetting experiences in their lives, such as the pubertal changes in their bodies and the academic and social demands of junior high school, early adolescents are more likely than elementary school children to have things on their mind that they need to talk about—intimate, personal things that cannot be discussed with just anybody, but only with close and trusted friends who have some first-hand familiarity with the same concerns.

Second, at the same time as the need to discuss intimate concerns increases, the suitability of parents for listening and responding to such concerns decreases. Sometimes parents are too removed from their own adolescence to understand what their pubescent son or daughter is worried about; sometimes adolescents assume without asking that their parents will be insensitive or unsympathetic to their questions; and sometimes adolescent determination to be self-reliant deters teenagers from seeking advice that parents would in fact be able and willing to provide. Hence, even in loving and tightly knit families, adolescents typically feel an increased need for close friends in whom to confide.

As we noted in Chapter 7, adolescents' needs for friends does not signal the demise of involved and supportive relationships with their parents. To the contrary, adolescents talk with their parents about as often as younger children do. Evidence in this regard comes from an interesting study of adolescents' conversations reported by Raffaelli and Duckett (1989). These researchers used an experimental method in which subjects carry an electronic pager and are beeped several times a day, at which time they write down what they are doing. Over a 1-week period, Rafaelli and Duckett collected almost 15,000 reports of how a group of 401 fifth- to ninth-grade students were spending their waking hours.

The results, shown in Figure 8.1, indicate that both girls and boys in the ninth grade spend as much time talking with their parents as fifth- and sixth-graders. What changes over these years is the amount of time young people spend talking with friends, which is significantly greater for girls and boys in junior high school (grades seven and eight) than elementary school (grades five and six), and for girls is significantly greater in high school (grade nine) than in junior high. As can also be seen from Figure 8.1, girls in general spend more time talking than boys, and this gender difference widens from elementary school to high school.

The new experiences and needs of teenagers explain *why* friendships deepen during adolescence. As for *how* they deepen, we mentioned in Chapter 5 some sequential stages in the way children and adolescents think about friendships; among adolescents in particular, these stages are characterized by trends toward increasing **intimacy** and increasing **mutuality**.

Intimacy

People who have a psychologically intimate relationship with someone else share their innermost thoughts and feelings with that person and know him or her well. Intimate friends keep few secrets from each other. Certain that whatever they say will be kept in confidence and not used to embarrass them, they disclose themselves openly, confessing even their shortcomings, blunders, and self-doubts. Intimate friends know how the other person will probably react in various situations; they know the other's likes and dislikes; and they know

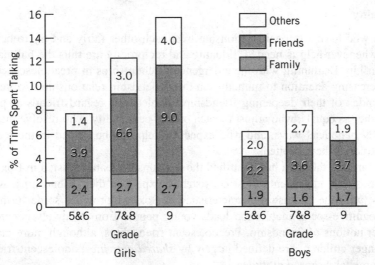

Figure 8.1 Age differences in whom young adolescents talk to. [*Source:* From Raffaelli and Duckett (1989). Reprinted with permission of Plenum Publishing Corporation.]

what he or she wants and fears. The two best clues to how intimate a relationship two people have are thus how much they reveal about themselves to each other, and how much they actually know about each other's personal and private characteristics.

We have already noted (Chapter 5) that children growing up are increasingly likely to describe friendship in terms of intimate sharing of feelings and thoughts and intimate personal knowledge of someone else. In a direct assessment of such developmental changes, Diaz and Berndt (1982) asked pairs of fourth-grade and eighth-grade best friends to provide information about each other's personality (e.g., what the friend worries about, what the friend gets mad about); about each other's preferences (e.g., favorite sport, favorite subject at school); and about each other's objective characteristics (e.g., the friend's birthdate and telephone number). As judged against actual information these children gave about themselves, the fourth-graders knew as much about their friend's objective characteristics as the eighth-graders did. With respect to thoughts, feelings, and preferences, however, the eighth-graders were significantly more knowledgeable than the fourth-graders about their best friends.

Research on friendship relationships also indicates that girls are more likely to be intimate with their close friends than boys. In addition to spending more time talking with friends than boys do (Figure 8.1), girls also place more value on conversation. Among the 12–19-year-olds interviewed in the Youniss and Smollar (1985) studies, the girls were more likely than the boys to report that they enjoyed "just talking" with their close friends, whereas the boys were more likely than the girls to say that they preferred to "do things" with their friends, such as play sports, rather than just engage in conversation. When these young people did talk with their close friends, moreover, the girls were more likely than the boys to discuss intimate personal matters, whereas the boys were more likely than the girls to keep personal problems and concerns out of their conversations.

Mutuality

People who have a mutual relationship treat each other fairly and try to be helpful to each other whenever help is needed. Equality and reciprocity are thus the hallmarks of a mutual relationship. Beginning with the emergence of chumships in preadolescence, young people pay increasing attention to mutuality in their friendship relationships. More so than before, as an index of their deepening friendships, adolescents regard friends as people who treat each other as equals, who adjust to each other's personality, who resolve their differences in mutually beneficial ways, and who expect to help and be helped in the relationship rather than exploit or be exploited.

Research in this area has identified the relationship features listed in Box 8.2 as the characteristics that adolescents most consistently expect in their friendships. A comparison of this list with the chumship characteristics in Box 8.1 provides some further indication of how cognitive-social maturation leads young people from relatively concrete to relatively abstract notions of friendship. Preadolescent friendships, although more mature than those of younger children, are defined largely by *shared activities*; adolescent friendships are defined largely by *shared attitudes*.

The increasing intimacy and mutuality that deepen youthful friendships were captured by Fischer (1981) in a study of 177 high school students (mostly age 16–17) and 180 college students (mostly age 19–20). These students were unmarried, predominantly white, and from middle-class backgrounds, with two-thirds of them at both age levels being female. They were asked to describe their relationship with the person closest to them, exclusive of family members, and their answers were coded for an emphasis on being *friendly* (a focus on shared activities), *intimate* (a focus on affection, attachment, and being able to communicate clearly), *integrated* (both friendly and intimate), or *uninvolved* (neither particularly friendly nor intimate). Among both males and females, the college students were significantly more likely than the high school students to report an intimate or integrated relationship with the person closest to them, as opposed to one that was uninvolved or focused mainly on shared activities (see Table 8.2).

Despite deepening friendship, adolescents eventually become reluctant to depend heavily on peer-group attachments, just as earlier they had become reluctant to depend exclusively on their parents. As they grow increasingly self-reliant, late adolescents become less interested in maintaining an extensive network of friends. They still welcome intimate and mutual relationships, but with fewer and more selectively chosen friends than before, and neither constant companionship nor constant reassurance from peers continues to be as important as it was.

In one study of this developmental change, Clark-Lempers, Lempers, and Ho (1991) asked 330 early adolescents (age 11–13), 481 middle adolescents (age 14–16), and 299 late adolescents (age 17–19) from several different schools in rural Midwestern towns to rate their relationship with their best same-gender friend on several characteristics. The early and middle adolescents reported more admiration, companionship, reliability, and satisfaction in their close friendships than did the late adolescents. Berndt and Perry (1990) similarly reported evidence that involvement with a broad circle of friends exerts more influence on the attitudes and behavior of fifth- and eighth-graders than of eleventh-graders. Taken together, such findings confirm that same-gender friendships are more important to young people in early and middle adolescence than in late adolescence, by which time adolescents have not

♦ **BOX 8.2 WHAT ADOLESCENTS EXPECT FROM THEIR FRIENDSHIPS**

1. Shared activities and interests
2. Loyalty and commitment
3. Cooperation and other prosocial responses
4. Help and support
5. Genuineness

6. Intimacy
7. Trust
8. Absence of conflicts

Source: Adapted from Inderbitzen-Pisaruk and Foster (1990).

only become highly self-reliant but are also likely to be investing themselves in other-gender relationships that reduce the intensity of their ties to same-gender friends.

In further work with a sample of 576 students in grades 6–12, Lempers and Clark-Lempers (1993) found that, at all grade levels, the girls tended to rate their friendships as involving more admiration, companionship, reliability, and satisfaction than did the boys, and the girls also attributed more affection, helpfulness, intimacy, and nurturance to their relationships with their close friends. Similarly with respect to gender differences, when Raja, McGee, and Stanton (1992) asked 456 female and 479 male 15-year-olds about their degree of attachment to their peers, the girls were significantly more likely than the boys to report communicating with, trusting, and feeling close to their friends.

Like the evidence of more intimate conversations among adolescent females than males, these findings are consistent with the widespread belief that girls are more interpersonally oriented than boys and attach more importance to close friendships; boys, on the other hand, are generally felt to be more interested in what they can accomplish than in whom they can befriend. We explore this belief further in Chapter 10 when we consider gender differences in how young people form their sense of personal identity.

Table 8.2 **TYPE OF RELATIONSHIP WITH PERSON CLOSEST TO THEM (EXCLUSIVE OF FAMILY MEMBERS) AMONG HIGH SCHOOL AND COLLEGE STUDENTS**

Types of Relationship[a]	*Males*		*Females*	
	High School (%)	College (%)	High School (%)	College (%)
Uninvolved (neither friendly nor intimate)	39	28	31	17
Friendly	24	23	26	11
Intimate	15	23	15	30
Integrated (friendly and intimate)	22	26	28	42
	100	100	100	100

[a] The difference between high school and college students in type of relationship is significant at the .01 level of confidence.

Source: Based on data reported by Fischer (1981) on 177 high school students (average age 16.9) and 180 college students (average age 19.1).

Stability and Change

Because adolescents form increasingly intimate and mutual relationships as they mature beyond childhood, it may seem reasonable to expect their friendships to become progressively more stable and enduring. On the other hand, dramatic biological and emotional changes are also occurring during adolescence. If young people are changing rapidly in how they look, what they like to do, and how they feel toward their parents and peers, isn't it reasonable to expect them to make a lot of changes in who their friends are?

As it turns out, neither of these reasonable expectations is the case: Friendships become neither more nor less stable during adolescence. Instead, as we have already seen, the stability of friendship choice does not change very much from preadolescence through the early and middle and adolescent years. Most of the close friendships that are made during these years last for several months at least, and their average stability remains about the same from late elementary school to late high school. As one way of reconciling these findings with reasons to expect either increasing stability or increasing change, Berndt (1982) suggested that biological and emotional developments in adolescence promote less stable friendships, cognitive maturation promotes more stable friendships, and the two cancel each other out.

However this may be, observers of young people have become less interested in whether their friendships endure than in why they change. Generally speaking, friends drift apart when they no longer meet each other's needs, and friendships lose their appeal when people cease to share the common interests and outlook that originally brought them together. Events that point people in new directions and toward new ways of thinking about their lives often lead them to seek new friends. Adolescents experience many such events, and they also vary considerably in the pace of their physical growth, cognitive development, and social maturation.

What often happens, then, especially during early and middle adolescence, is that previously good friends who are maturing at a different rate lose interest in each other. Should one of them suddenly grow much bigger and physically mature than the other, or become much more capable of thinking about abstract possibilities, or become much more self-reliant or attracted to the other gender, the friends may quickly run out of things to say to each other and do together. During this period of development, young people gravitate toward peers who resemble them in these aspects of maturation, and friendship patterns shift as some adolescents spurt ahead and others lag behind in their physical, cognitive, and social maturation.

Independently of maturational differences that may weaken bonds of friendship, close relationships can also be disrupted by conflict. Good friends can usually settle arguments more easily and resolve differences more peaceably than casual acquaintances or people who dislike each other, and disagreements among friends, once thrashed out, may at times strengthen their relationship by helping them understand each other better. On the other hand, close friendship involves certain expectations (see Box 8.2) that include absence of conflict.

What kinds of events are likely to cause conflicts that disrupt adolescent friendships? Youniss and Smollar (1985, Chapter 7) asked this question of their subjects. Both females and males most often mentioned *untrustworthy acts*, such as failing to keep a secret, breaking promises, lying, getting you in trouble, or going out with your other-gender friend. For girls the second most commonly mentioned source of conflict with friends was *lack of suffi-*

cient attention, such as ignoring you, not calling you, not coming to your party, spending time with other people, and leaving you out of plans. For boys the second-ranking unwelcome event was *disrespectful acts*, such as being rude, calling you names, putting you down, making fun of you, being bossy, or hitting or fighting with you. The third most frequently mentioned friendship issue was disrespectful acts among the girls and lack of sufficient attention among the boys. Fourth for both females and males as a source of conflict was *unacceptable behaviors*, such as being moody, conceited or stubborn, having a bad temper, bragging or acting stupid, quitting school, or drinking too much.

PEER VERSUS PARENTAL INTERACTIONS

The emerging self-reliance and social maturity of adolescents bring about some changes in how they interact with their parents. As they become involved in deepening friendships and expanding peer-group activities, young people have less time for their parents and less need for their attention. Increasingly, they turn to their own generation for close relationships and eventually for romantic attachments. The importance of friends to young people does not signify that their basic beliefs have become incompatible with those of their parents, however, or that parents are losing their influence to the teenage peer group. To be sure, the old notion of a generation gap led to widespread opinion that adolescents routinely reject their parents' values and advice in favor of peer-group standards. We took pains to discredit this generation-gap notion in Chapter 7, on the basis of considerable evidence, and there are also abundant indications that parents continue to influence their children throughout adolescence and are perceived as very important sources of affection, help, and support from age 11 to age 19 (Clark-Lempers et al., 1991; Lempers & Clark-Lempers, 1992).

At the same time, the source of the greatest influence on adolescent behavior varies with the type of issue being considered. Research findings indicate that young people are more likely to listen to their parents than to their peers when it comes to morality, educational and occupational plans, managing money, and handling interpersonal relationships other than those with their peers. They are more likely to listen to their peers in matters of choosing friends, handling peer relationships, and spending leisure time (Hunter, 1985; Sebald, 1989; Smetana, 1993; Wilks, 1986). Figure 8.2 gives some further examples of the frequency with which adolescents talk about various topics with their parents and friends.

These findings indicate that parents do become replaced to some extent as the deepening friendships and increasing peer-group involvements of their adolescent children result in parents' sharing some spheres of influence that were previously theirs alone. Yet these shifts do not diminish the continuing importance of parent–child interactions around certain kinds of issues, nor does becoming less dependent on one's parents result in becoming more susceptible to the influence of peers. Rather, as adolescents mature, both parental and peer influences become replaced by increasingly independent thinking. By late adolescence, neither parents nor peers hold much sway over youthful opinion. Young people continue to listen to what parents and peers have to say, but, as emerging adults in their own right, they prefer to chart their own course and rely on their own judgment.

Steinberg and Silverberg (1986) studied these developmental changes by questioning 865 10–16-year-old students from diverse socioeconomic backgrounds about their involvement and autonomy in peer and parental relationships. Compared to fifth- and sixth-graders, eighth-graders expressed less dependence on their parents and more dependence on their

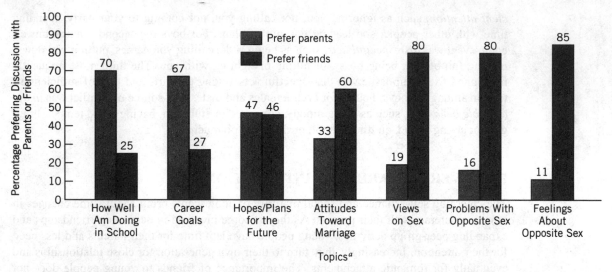

Figure 8.2   Percentage of adolescents preferring to discuss topics with parents or friends. [*Source:* Based on data reported by Youniss and Smollar (1985, Chapter 9).]

peers. By grades eight and nine, however, peer orientation had begun to diminish, parent orientation stayed about the same, and expressions of independence from both peer and parental influence had begun to increase.

In another study confirming changes over time in sources of peer influence, Furman and Buhrmester (1992) asked male and female fourth-graders, seventh-graders, tenth-graders, and college students to indicate which relationships were providing them with the most support. Among 107 students in the fourth grade, mothers and fathers were reported to be the most frequent providers of support. Same-gender friends were perceived as providing just as much support as parents among 134 students in the seventh grade and as providing more support than parents among 116 students in the tenth grade. Among 221 college students, romantic partners were reported as the most frequent providers of support.

In yet another study, Montemayor (1982) obtained some first-hand information from adolescents by arranging for them to be interviewed over the telephone on three randomly selected evenings at approximately 1-week intervals. The subjects, who were 64 tenth-grade students (30 males and 34 females) from predominantly middle-class families, were asked on each occasion to relate everything they had done the preceding day, for how long, and with whom.

The reports of Montemayor's subjects indicated that they were spending equal amounts of time with their parents and peers, but in different kinds of activities. Time with parents centered mainly around *task* activities involving some necessity or obligation—doing homework or household chores, eating, going shopping or to church services, and the like. Time with peers centered around *leisure* activities—playing sports, making small talk, or seeking some other entertainment.

What these data indicate is that peer and parental involvements do not compete with each other, as the generation gap notion would suggest, but are instead complementary. Adolescents are not torn between the expectations and demands of their parents and peers, but instead can be viewed as enjoying two beneficial but contrasting social worlds: One world consists of task-oriented interactions with parents that help adolescents learn to take responsibility and apply their energies constructively; the other world involves leisure-oriented interactions with peers that help adolescents improve their interpersonal sensitivity and role-taking skills.

In light of such findings, Youniss and Smollar (1985, Chapter 9; 1989) cautioned theorists to avoid describing parental and peer influences as if they compete for the hearts and minds of teenagers and pull them in different directions. They caution particularly against mistaken expectations that peer-group attachments will undermine the influence of parents, turn young people away from family values, and breed misconduct. To the contrary, as we have seen, the ways in which parents and peers influence adolescents are more likely to be complementary than adversarial, and both kinds of influence serve important and positive developmental purposes.

Research findings suggest, in fact, that the strength of adolescents' attachments to their parents and peers, far from being negatively correlated, are positively related to each other. Positive relationships with one's parents nurture intimate relationships with one's peers, and the more that adolescents view their parents as sources of support and as people to trust and confide in, the more they view their peers in the same way (Blain, Thompson, & Whiffen, 1993; Gold & Yanof, 1985; Raja et al., 1992). The broader influence of the peer group, beyond the impact of individual friendships, is the topic to which we turn next.

BELONGING TO THE PEER GROUP

Along with forming deepening friendships, adolescents become interested in belonging to some group of their age-mates who share common interests and attitudes. The appeal of peer-group belongingness stems from the transitional developmental status that children enter at puberty and their wish to separate themselves from their parents.

As we discussed in Chapters 1 and 7, early adolescents perceive clearly that they are no longer children. The size and shape of their bodies tell them they are almost grown up, and their emerging capacities to think in complex ways tell them they have much more in common with adults than with children. Yet they are still a long way from having adult status and privileges, especially before they become old enough to hold a regular job, get a driver's license, or finish school. No longer content with being children, not yet accepted as adults, and eager to avoid depending too much on their parents, adolescents from age 11 or 12 to 16 or 17 often feel a gap in their lives that is only partially filled by having a few good friends.

To close this gap, young people typically establish groups or cultures of their own that exist primarily to give them a sense of belongingness. Involvement in such groups provides opportunities for adolescents to share responsibility for their own affairs, to experiment together with ways of handling new situations, and to learn from each other's mistakes. The peer group also formulates codes of conduct in areas where young people are reluctant to rely on their parents' advice, such as how to manage peer relationships. Finally, adolescent cultures typically prescribe tastes in language, dress, hair styles, music, and leisure-time activities that differ from adult tastes. These group guidelines provide young people with some welcome relief from having to make decisions on their own, and they expand their sense of belonging to a clearly identifiable group that is not being run by adults.

As elaborated in this section, the importance of being accepted into a peer group leads most early adolescents to become concerned about conformity to group standards and popularity among their peers. During the high school years certain changes in group structure tend to moderate these concerns, and a broad peer-group orientation is gradually replaced by more selective friendships and by heterosocial interests.

CONFORMITY

Conformity consists of doing what other people around you are doing, or what you think they want or expect you to do, in order to make a favorable impression. Adolescents are more likely than people at other ages to become concerned for a time with conforming closely to the values and practices of their peer group.

In a classic experiment some years ago, Costanzo and Shaw (1966) were able to chart the waxing and waning of peer-group conformity during the adolescent years. These researchers asked 12 male and 12 female subjects at each of four age levels to judge which of a series of lines was the same length as a standard stimulus line. Although this ordinarily would have been an easy task, the situation was "rigged" by having each subject respond last after three

As one reflection of their need to feel part of an identifiable group, early adolescents show a high degree of conformity to some unique tastes and values.

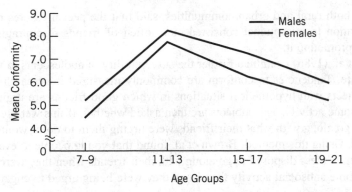

Figure 8.3 Conformity to peer influence as a function of age. [*Source:* From Costanzo and Shaw (1966). Reprinted with permission of the Society for Research in Child Development.]

of his or her classmates (who were working with the experimenter and had been instructed in how to respond) sometimes gave the right answer and at other times gave the wrong answer. The 24 target subjects at each age were assigned a conformity score based on how often they agreed with the incorrect peer judgments and had thus apparently been influenced by them.

As shown in Figure 8.3, susceptibility to peer influence was greater among 11–13-year-olds than among 7–9-year-old, 15–17-year-old, and 19–21-year-old subjects. Both males and females showed the same developmental pattern, but there was some tendency for the females to be more conforming than the males at each age level.

Subsequent research over the years has confirmed that conformity wanes among high school students after having reached a peak during the junior high school years. In how they think, feel, and act, middle and late adolescents tend to become more individualistic than they were as younger children and more likely to be influenced by what is pleasing to them and to other people in general than by the preferences of their immediate peer group (Brown, 1989; Gavin & Furman, 1989; Youniss & Smollar, 1989).

In real life, of course, adolescents rarely have to worry about judging the length of lines. Instead, according to reports from junior and senior high school students, they encounter five main types of pressures in their relationships with other teenagers: (1) pressures for peer involvement, such as spending free time with friends and attending parties and other social events; (2) pressures for participation in academic and extracurricular activities in school; (3) pressures for engagement with their families; (4) pressures for conformity to peer norms in dress, grooming, musical tastes, and the like; and (5) pressures related to misconduct, such as drug and alcohol use, sexual laxity, and delinquent activities (Brown, Clasen, & Eicher, 1986; Clasen & Brown, 1985).

In the opinion of several hundred adolescents questioned by Clasen and Brown (1985), by far the strongest among these five types of peer pressure are expectations of group involvement. Less keenly felt are pressures for school participation, family engagement, and peer conformity; pressures related to misconduct are the least intense of the five types. This finding documents further the fact that the influence young people exert on each other is not necessarily antifamily and promisbehavior. Moreover, many of the Clasen and Brown subjects, from both rural and urban communities, said that the peer pressures they did experience in relation to misconduct consisted more often of friends discouraging misbehavior rather than promoting it.

Brown et al. (1986) examined further the susceptibility of adolescents to various kinds of peer pressure. Tendencies to conform are commonly measured in research studies by presenting subjects with hypothetical situations in which good friends are urging them to participate in some activity. The subjects are then asked whether, if this were really happening, they would go along with what their friends were urging them to do or would do something else instead. Using this method, Brown et al. found that young people at every age from 12 to 18 were much less disposed to go along with their friends when they were being urged to engage in some antisocial activity than when they were being urged to engage in some neutral activity.

In general, these studies of conformity behavior bear out the expectation that early and middle adolescents are more likely to be influenced by attitudes of their peer group than either preadolescent or late adolescent youngsters. This age trend is not uniform across different types of peer pressure, however. By late adolescence pressures to socialize with group members and conform to group norms typically weaken, whereas peer urging to participate in school activities and avoid or engage in misconduct is likely to increase during the high school years (Clasen & Brown, 1985).

Most adolescents handle peer pressures to think, feel, and act in various ways without becoming unduly upset by them. Influencing and being influenced by friends is a natural and often helpful aspect of peer-group belongingness because groups allow young people to share in sometimes taking leadership and sometimes receiving guidance. Nevertheless, about one-fourth of teenagers report being troubled by peer pressure (Dubow, Lovko, & Kausch, 1990). Like the experience of peer pressure and the tendency to be influenced by it, being troubled by peer pressure increases in frequency during junior high school, peaks in the ninth grade, and then steadily declines (see Figure 8.4). In this same vein, early and middle adolescents are typically found to place more value on being a member of a well-established group than do preadolescents or late adolescents, and they perceive their classmates as showing more group conformity than do preadolescents or late adolescents (Gavin & Furman, 1989).

The gender differences as well as the age differences in conformity noted by Costanzo and Shaw have been consistently demonstrated by other researchers. Girls are somewhat more concerned about peer-group belongingness than boys, somewhat more inclined to conform to group expectations, and somewhat more likely to report being troubled by peer pressure (Dubow et al., 1990). When presented with hypothetical situations that measure disposition to conform, girls worry more than boys about the consequences of agreeing or declining to go along with the urgings of friends (Pearl, Bryan, & Herzog, 1990). When asked to describe how they feel about peer-group interactions, girls are more likely than boys to report having positive group interactions and being bothered by negative interactions when they occur (Gavin & Furman, 1989). This greater involvement of girls than boys in peer-group relationships is consistent with the greater friendship intimacy and attachment among girls that we noted earlier.

Before concluding this discussion of conformity, we need to call attention to the particular role of friends as a source of peer-group influence. Young people are less likely to be influenced by what large groups of adolescents like or do than by the attitudes and actions of

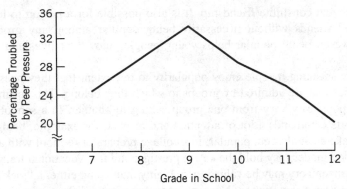

Figure 8.4 Percentage of boys and girls who feel troubled by peer pressure. [*Source:* Based on data reported by Dubow et al. (1990) on 1,384 junior and senior high school students.]

their close friends (Urberg, 1992). However, an interesting question to consider is whether close friends are similar to each other because they influence each other a great deal, or because it was similarities between them that led to their becoming close friends in the first place.

In discussing these alternatives, Tolson and Urberg (1993) concluded that similarities between friends can result from either friendship selection or friendship influence, or from a combination of both. Berndt and Savin-Williams (1992) went a step further to suggest that peer influences in friendship similarity may be overestimated, particularly with respect to how frequently young people are said to get into trouble "because of bad companions." Instead, apparent peer influence in such cases may be secondary to preexisting resemblances between friends, and choosing trouble-making friends may be a result rather than a cause of having a trouble-making disposition.

However this may be, anecdotal reports indicate that being able to fit in comfortably with their peers has been an adolescent concern for a long time and in many places. The great German writer Goethe tells the following story of going away to college some 200 years ago:

> My wardrobe, which I took with me to the university, was . . . very complete and fine looking. . . . I thought myself sufficiently well-dressed, but it did not last long before my lady friends . . . convinced me that I looked as if I had been dropped down from another world . . . I took courage and ventured at once to exchange my whole wardrobe for a new-fashioned one, suited to the place. [Quoted by Kiell, 1964, p. 340]

POPULARITY

Popularity refers to how well liked people are in the groups to which they belong. Being popular means being regarded by others as someone whose company, friendship, and esteem they would like to have. Popularity differs from friendship, which we discussed earlier, because a person can be liked and admired by other people without having any reciprocal peer relationships that constitute friendship. It is also possible for a person to have one or even several good friends without necessarily being popular among any group. Like having friends, however, being popular helps young people enjoy their lives and feel good about themselves.

Generally speaking, people enjoy popularity to the extent that they possess attributes or characteristics that are admired by groups to which they belong. This means that the determinants of popularity vary from one group setting to another. In a school where achievement in sports commands a lot of attention and respect, for example, being a good athlete will help make an adolescent popular; in a college preparatory school with a limited athletic program, good grades may hold the key to prestige; and in a vocational training school, skill in repairing machinery may be valued more highly than being either a "jock" or a "brain."

Because of such variation, adolescents may experience different levels of popularity in different groups to which they belong. Compared to a medium degree of popularity in his or her school, a devoutly religious youngster may be held in very high esteem in a church-related group, and an artistically talented girl or boy may be extremely popular in a summer camp program for dance, music, or painting. Nevertheless, some characteristics are found to be associated with popularity among young people of all ages, regardless of setting or social climate.

With few exceptions, the popular adolescents in a group tend to be warm, friendly, kindly, cooperative young people who care about their peers and are sensitive to their needs. They participate actively in what the group does and often take initiative in suggesting group activities and trying to include group members in them. They tend to be in confor-

Adolescents who are popular among their peers tend to have good social skills and to be concerned about helping other people feel good.

mity with prevailing group standards of dress, language, and conduct, often because they are trend-setters whose example is being followed by others. When conflicts arise, they deal with them directly and take a calm approach to resolving them (Bryant, 1992; Coie, Dodge, & Kupersmidt, 1990; Inderbitzen-Pisaruk & Foster, 1990).

By contrast, unpopular adolescents tend to be described by their peers and also by their teachers as being angry, aggressive, and argumentative young people or as being submissive, inhibited, and excessively dependent. In either case, they are seen as selfish, uncooperative individuals who seldom participate in group activities. Disliked adolescents also tend to be noncompliant and disruptive individuals who ignore group preferences, break rules, and deal with disagreements by refusing to face them squarely or by retaliating in an angry way (Berndt & Das, 1987; Juvonen, 1991; Parkhurst & Asher, 1992; Rubin, LeMare, & Lollis, 1990).

Becoming angry does not always stir dislike, however, and not all young people who are described as being aggressive are unpopular. Being assertive, becoming angry in situations that warrant anger, expressing anger directly, and, above all, defending yourself when attacked or provoked are characteristics that may be admired by an adolescent's group and enhance his or her popularity. Bossiness, temper tantrums, indirect retaliation (tattling on someone or stealing or vandalizing his or her property), and unprovoked verbal or physical attacks on others (especially bullying of weaker or less capable youngsters), on the other hand, are very likely to correlate with peer rejection (Coie, Belding, & Underwood, 1988; Lancelotta & Vaughn, 1989).

There are also some gender differences in the importance of aggressiveness in determining popularity. Although neither girls nor boys tend to like peers who are aggressive in the nasty or sneaky ways we have just described, girls place less weight on aggressiveness than on positive social characteristics such as being friendly and cooperative when they are asked to rate the popularity of their peers (Coie et al., 1990).

Young people who lack popularity usually fall into two distinct groups, some who are *rejected* by their peers and others who are *neglected* by them. Being rejected involves being disliked, whereas being neglected means not having many friends and not many enemies either, but not necessarily being disliked. Neglected adolescents may be accepted in their peer group, even admired for some of their attributes; however, because their relationships with members of their peer group tend to be distant and their involvement in peer-group activities minimal, they rarely become popular. Although neglected young people may be at risk for the problems of loneliness we will discuss later in this chapter, they are less likely than rejected adolescents to develop various kinds of emotional and behavior problems (Asher, 1990; Kupersmidt & Coie, 1990).

Table 8.3 shows how popular, rejected, and neglected young people can be differentiated on the basis of whether they are high or low in aggressiveness and social skills. As Table 8.3 also indicates, research on peer relations identifies a fourth type of young person who can be called *controversial* (Newcomb, Bukowski, & Pattee, 1993). Controversial adolescents are aggressive but also socially skillful. Instead of being consistently popular or unpopular, they tend to generate mixed feelings toward themselves. Depending on how hard they are trying to temper their aggressiveness with affability, they may be strongly liked or strongly disliked by different people at the same time and by the same people at different times.

To appreciate more fully the individual circumstances that can affect an adolescent's popularity, we need to consider two other issues. First, a young person's social skills, which play

Table 8.3 AGGRESSIVENESS AND SOCIAL SKILLS IN
FOUR PATTERNS OF PEER RELATEDNESS

	Popular	*Neglected*	*Rejected*	*Controversial*
Aggressiveness	Low	Low	High	High
Social Skills	High	Low	Low	High

Source: Based on research by Newcomb et al. (1993).

an important role in popularity, have a circular relationship with being popular. Second, there are some substantial continuities and discontinuities in popularity from childhood through adolescence.

The Circularity of Social Skills and Popularity

As children mature into adolescents, the degree to which they seek and enjoy each other's company becomes increasingly based on psychological considerations—how pleasant and relaxed they are, how capable they are of recognizing other's thoughts and feelings, how willing they are to be helpful, and how adept they are at managing social relationships, for example. In more specific terms, popular young people are found to be relatively skillful in initiating friendships, inserting themselves into a group conversation, resolving arguments, offering constructive criticisms, and judging the impression they are making. Unpopular youngsters are frequently lacking in these social skills (Adams, 1983; Kennedy, 1990; Miller, 1990; Putallaz & Wasserman, 1990).

But how do such skills originate? To some extent they come from cognitive maturation, as children grow capable of formal operational thought and perspective taking. Young people who lag behind their peers in developing basic skills for processing social information, such as being able to interpret subtle social cues accurately, often have difficulty functioning competently and feeling comfortable in social situations. The awkwardness and uneasiness of cognitively immature and socially clumsy adolescents can, in turn, lead to their being disliked and rejected (Dodge & Feldman, 1990).

As in sharpening any kind of skill, however, learning to handle social interactions smoothly and comfortably also comes with practice. Young people who are disliked by their peers and are excluded from peer-group interactions miss out on trial-and-error learning experiences that help build social skills. Even though a good friend may provide some of this kind of experience, effective socializing in the broader peer group is learned largely from group interactions.

This means that social skill deficits can *result* from as well as *lead to* being unpopular. When a socially anxious or inept young person is not well accepted, his or her social skill development may fall even farther behind those of the peer group, which can lead to his or her becoming even less well liked, and so on, and a **circular relationship** develops. However, this circularity can also operate in a positive direction. Improved social skills can increase a youngster's popularity, which gives him or her more opportunities for the kinds of peer-group interactions that sharpen social skills, which will make the person even more popular. With this in mind, specific training in social skills is sometimes recommended as an effective way of helping unpopular children improve their social adaptation (Furman & Gavin, 1989; Ladd & Asher, 1985).

The extent to which adolescents are friendly, relaxed, considerate, and energetic in interpersonal situations can also depend on as well as contribute to how popular they are. It is much easier to be pleasantly sociable when one feels accepted and well liked than when one senses imminent rejection. Likewise, being kind, thoughtful, self-confident, and enthusiastically involved in group activities leads to being accepted and popular, which in turn leads to feeling even more sure of oneself and enthused about participating in the group. On the other hand, selfish, demanding, anxious, withdrawn youngsters who feel disliked by their peers often become tense, embittered, self-centered, and disinterested in group activities, which leads to their being even more disliked.

For better or worse, people rarely stand by passively while such circular events shape their social status. Instead, they often act on the basis of certain **self-fulfilling prophecies**: that is, they cause things to happen by expecting them to happen. Young people who anticipate being well received in group situations tend to approach them with a degree of quiet confidence that contributes to such an outcome. By contrast, adolescents who doubt their self-worth and fear being rejected often act in ways that make their fears come true. Such young people are likely to invite rejection and ridicule by avoiding peer-group activities, by being timid and ill at ease in social situations, or by seeking attention and acceptance through bluster, bravado, and various kinds of outlandish behavior.

Continuity and Discontinuity

The popularity of young people among their peers shows a strong tendency to carry over from childhood into adolescence, for two reasons. First, the same factors are associated with popularity in the elementary grades as in junior and senior high school. As with adolescents, elementary school children who are well liked by their peers tend to be friendly, sociable, outgoing youngsters who participate in many group activities, comply with prevailing group standards, and treat others with kindness, acceptance, and sensitivity to their needs; unpopular children tend to be shy and withdrawn, to avoid group activities, and to put other people off with displays of indifference, insensitivity, and hostility (Cillessen, Van IJzendourn, Van Lieshout, & Hartup, 1992; Coie et al., 1990). Of particular importance, the types of aggressive and disruptive behavior that lead to young people being disliked by their peers tend to become stable and predictable early in the elementary school years.

In one study of kindergarten and first-grade children, for example, those with patterns of aggressive and disruptive behavior tended to show the same behavior problems 2 years later, as second- and third-graders, and to be disliked by their classmates on both occasions (Taylor, 1989). In a similar study involving children who rated each other as kindergartners and again when they were in the third grade, popularity was highly correlated from one time to the next, and being rejected was especially likely to be a stable classification (Howes, 1990).

Second, the experiences that shape social behavior and popularity begin having their effects when children enter elementary school. By the time they reach adolescence, their social status has already been forged by several years of interacting with classmates. Like the stability of factors associated with popularity, this cumulative experience promotes continuity from childhood to adolescence in how young people are regarded by their peers. In a demonstration of this continuity, Bukowski and Newcomb (1984) asked 175 boys and 159 girls to identify whom they liked and disliked among their classmates when they were fifth-graders attending several elementary schools and again after they had entered a consolidated middle school. The social reputation of these students as indicated by their peers was largely unchanged from their preadolescent to early adolescent years.

Third, social reputations that become established by early adolescence often resist change, even if a young person's behavior changes. Established reputations tend to create a bias that leads groups to judge their members not by how they are behaving now, but by how they have behaved in the past. The expectations that people have typically exert a powerful influence on what they think about each other's behavior and what they remember about each other's attributes. A girl who is expected on the basis of her reputation to be helpful may be perceived as being helpful even when she is acting selfishly; a boy who has been re-garded as timid may still be considered timid, at least for a while, after newly found self-confidence has helped him become fairly assertive.

Research on peer-group interactions confirms that young people respond more positively to popular than to unpopular classmates even when they are behaving in exactly the same way, and they overlook personality quirks or errors of judgment in popular classmates that they would consider laughable or unacceptable in unpopular classmates (Hymel, Wagner, & Butler, 1990). For young people to gain or lose popularity, then, changes in what their peers expect of them, as well as actual changes in what they are like or how they act, need to occur.

Yet popularity is not permanently fixed by the events of childhood. The passage through puberty into the adolescent years may often be marked by discontinuities in peer accep-tance. A girl who was a skinny "ugly duckling" may blossom into an attractive young woman who is popular with boys and admired by girls. A boy who was small and thin may emerge from his adolescent growth spurt as tall and muscular, thus bolstering his self-image and gaining new respect from others. Youngsters who mature rapidly in their capacity for formal cognitive operations may take on added appeal as group members, whereas previ-ously popular children who lag behind their teenage peers in cognitive maturation may no longer be as sought after as companions.

Additionally, the widening world of adolescence gives young people opportunities to uncover new and admirable talents. A boy who was too small to accomplish much in the football and basketball games of elementary school may become the star of his high school wrestling team in the flyweight class. A girl with vocal or dramatic talent that was untapped in elementary school may become a soloist or lead actress in the concerts and plays performed in high school. By taking advantage of such opportunities to shine, adolescents may be able to enhance both their sense of worthiness and their peer-group pop-ularity.

In reviewing research on the leisure-time activities of high school juniors and seniors, Larson and Kleiber (1993) singled out sports, artistic, and organizational activities in partic-ular as contributing to good psychological adjustment and positive emotional development. They attributed these beneficial effects to the pleasure and enjoyment that such activities can bring and to the useful skills that young people can learn from participating in them. They could well have added that doing well in such activities also helps young people feel good about themselves and look good to others—which enhances their popularity.

CHANGES IN GROUP STRUCTURE

We noted earlier that the importance of multiple friendships and peer-group belongingness diminishes during the high school years, to be replaced by deeper, more selective friendships and increasing heterosocial interests. These changes in adolescent social structure were described a number of years ago by Dexter Dunphy (1963), whose analysis in Figure 8.5 still fits typical teenage behavior. Boys and girls are shown as standing apart from each other at the beginning of adolescence, just as they did in elementary school (stage 1). Soon they begin to interact as boy–girl groups (stage 2), after which they enter a transition period when some boys and girls pair off as couples (stage 3). Then, adolescents get together largely in boy–girl pairs (stage 4), and by late adolescence this pattern gives way to couples whose closest relationship is with each other and who have only loose associations with other couples (stage 5).

To elaborate on this progression, it is helpful first to distinguish between **cliques** and **crowds** as these terms are used in contemporary research. Cliques refer to small groups of perhaps 5–10 young people who spend time together, develop close relationships among

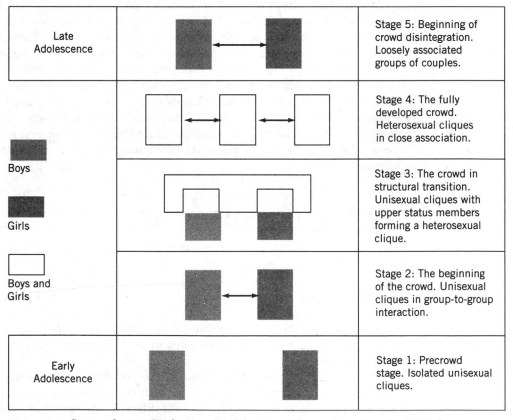

Figure 8.5 Stages of group development in adolescence. [*Source:* From Dunphy (1963).]

themselves, understand and appreciate each other more than anyone outside the clique, and regard the clique as their primary base of interaction with other groups of adolescents. Crowds are larger groups of young people who may or may not hang around together but are identified as sharing some particular set of attitudes or interests. Members of cliques are affiliated with each other, whereas members of crowds are affiliated with the reputation they have (Brown, 1989).

Earlier we mentioned two crowds that most groups of adolescents identify in their midst, jocks and brains. Such crowd labels typically indicate clearly the attitudes and interests attributed to crowd members, or say something about the crowd's social status. Other common crowd labels among junior and senior high school students are populars, preppies, druggies, bikers, loners, nobodies, unsociables, and nerds (Brown, 1990; Durbin et al., 1993). Young people usually do not choose the crowd to which they belong, in the way they choose friends, but are instead selected into a particular crowd and regarded as belonging to it on the basis of how they look and what they like to do. Interestingly, however, adolescents do not always recognize which crowd they are associated with by their peers. Research cited by Brown (1989) indicates that about 75% of jocks and druggies are likely to be aware that they are classified this way; among students whose peers regard them as loners, nobodies, or unpopulars, by contrast, fewer than 15% pick these categories when asked what they think their reputation is.

With further respect to the heterosocial developments sketched by Dunphy's stages, boys and girls who before adolescence had little to do with each other begin during adolescence to arrange parties in which they gingerly test the new sensations and feelings that are associated with emerging sexuality. They drink soft drinks, listen to music, dance, chase one another, wrestle, and perhaps do some experimental kissing in the corner, but strictly in the context of a group activity without any consistent pairing off. Later on they begin dating, and their socializing comes to involve couples who come as a pair, instead of just as groups of boys and girls. Over time, casual and occasional dating tends to become more frequent dating and then turns into "going steady" or at least narrowing the field to a few serious interests, which sets the stage for later, usually postadolescent decisions about engagement and marriage.

DATING AND OTHER STRATEGIC INTERACTIONS

Dating may need no explanation before we begin discussing it, but what are **strategic interactions**? The term was introduced by sociologist Erving Goffman (1969) to describe ways in which people behave toward each other when they are trying to convey, conceal, or obtain information through indirect means. He gives an example of card players using various comments and gestures to suggest that the hand they are holding is better or worse than it actually is. David Elkind (1980) subsequently applied this concept to adolescent social relationships, primarily in relation to his notion of the "imaginary audience," which we mentioned in Chapter 5.

Remember that the imaginary audience consists of people whose opinions are important to you and who are assumed to be observing and forming impressions of how you act, even if they are not actually present (Elkind, 1985; Elkind & Bowen, 1979). A broad imaginary audience of peers takes on special importance during adolescence, and early adolescents in particular are more likely than children or adults to draw their self-esteem from real or imagined audience reactions. Cognitive maturation provides the capacity for early adolescents to become more sensitive than they were before to what others are thinking, and needs for peer-group belongingness make them more concerned with making a good impression than they will be later, when conformity and popularity become less important (see Figures 8.3 and 8.4).

These developments make adolescents highly self-conscious with respect to "looking good" in front of their peers and showing themselves to every possible advantage. As one result, Elkind (1980) suggested, adolescents engage with each other in many interactions that are *strategic*: Instead of expressing directly what they think and feel or even enjoying what they are doing, they seek mainly to give a good impression of their attractiveness and social competence, for the benefit of whoever may be watching.

It may not immediately be clear how dating qualifies as one of these strategic interactions. Among late adolescents and adults dating is usually considered a pleasurable opportunity for companionship or a prelude to romance, not an occasion for "playing games" in the manner of one card player trying to bluff or finesse another. On the other hand, most people can recall times even from their late adolescence or adulthood when having a particular date was more a matter of making an impression than enjoying an interpersonal relationship.

Even more so for junior and senior high school students, the matter of who dates whom and when involves considerable playing to the audience. The idea of having a date and of other people knowing about it is often more exciting than the date itself. Moreover, when young people are still socially inexperienced, many of the ways in which dating couples interact are based more on strategies for avoiding ineptness than on direct discussions of what both of them would prefer doing.

WHEN DATING BEGINS

Young people typically begin to date sometime during early or middle adolescence. The actual average age when dating begins varies widely among groups of adolescents from different backgrounds. Very few youngsters have their first date before entering junior high school, and most have begun to date by the time they finish high school. Within this broad age range, adolescents usually begin to date around the time when doing so is approved and encouraged in their particular neighborhood, school, socioeconomic, and ethnic group.

This observation runs contrary to a common belief that young people become interested in dating when they reach puberty and develop secondary sex characteristics. The facts are clear, however, that dating behavior is determined primarily by cultural norms, not biological development, and that differences in physical maturation have little effect on the age at which adolescents begin to date (Gargiulo, Attie, Brooks-Gunn, & Warren, 1987; Sorensen, 1973; Westney, Jenkins, Butts, & Williams, 1984).

One of the informative studies in this regard was conducted by Dornbusch and his colleagues (Dornbusch et al., 1981) with data from the United States National Health Examination Survey, which involved a large representative national sample of adolescents. As one part of this survey, 6,710 12–17-year-olds were examined by a physician and rated on Tanner's 5-point scale of physical development that we described in Chapter 3 (see Figures 3.11–3.13). Among other questions, each of these young people was asked, "Have you ever had a date?"

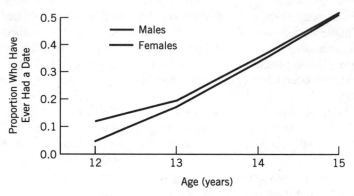

Figure 8.6 Proportion of boys and girls at Tanner stage 3.0 of sexual development who have ever had a date, by age in years. [*Source:* From Dornbusch et al. (1981). Reprinted with permission of the Society for Research in Child Development.]

Figure 8.6 shows the proportion of adolescents at four different age levels but all at the same intermediate stage of physical development (Tanner's 3.0) who reported having had a date. For boys and girls alike, beginning to date became substantially more prevalent from age 12 to 15, regardless of the fact that the 10-year-olds in this sample were as mature physically as the 15-year-olds. With respect to adolescents of the same age who differ in physical maturation, Figure 8.7 indicates no significant differences in the proportion of 12-year-olds who were dating, regardless of their Tanner level of development. The Dornbusch et al. data thus provide substantial evidence that the onset of dating in adolescents is determined not by biological maturation, but by social standards of typical and appropriate behavior at various ages in a young person's environment.

When dating does begin, it usually consists of one strategic interaction after another—not romance, not pleasurable companionship, not even an activity enjoyed for its own sake,

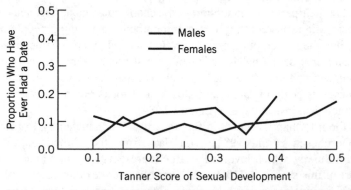

Figure 8.7 Proportion of 12-year-old boys and girls who have ever had a date, by Tanner's score of sexual development. [*Source:* From Dornbusch et al. (1981). Reprinted with permission of the Society for Research in Child Development.]

but an effort by adolescents to do what they think is expected without letting their inexperience and uncertainty make them look foolish. Consider, for example, the strategies and concerns that commonly accompany two aspects of dating among early and sometimes middle adolescents as well: getting dates and kissing goodnight.

The traditional pattern in which boys ask for dates and girls accept or refuse them is still the prevailing practice in our society, and both the question and the answer can involve some difficult decisions. A boy wondering whether to ask a particular girl for a date may find himself weighing the benefits of getting the date against the risk of being turned down. The more attractive and popular the girl is, the more pleased he will be if she accepts the date, but the more likely he is to have the deflating experience of being turned down. If she is not particularly attractive or popular, his chances of getting a date will be better, but her accepting will not be as gratifying to him.

And how should he ask for the date? To minimize any possible blow to his self-esteem—which is always on the line in these early boy–girl encounters—he could begin with, "Are you doing anything this weekend?" If the girl is busy, he thinks, she will tell him, and he will be spared from having to ask for a date that will not be accepted. But what if she says she is not busy and then declines an invitation to go out with him? Then the blow is much worse than it would have been if he had just asked her outright and been able to tell himself that the only reason she said "No" was that she already had other plans.

And what is a girl to say when a boy asks, "Are you busy this weekend?" Saying "No" can be distasteful, because it says in effect, "I have no plans, I'm dull and uninteresting, I never do anything, I have no friends to be with, and no one else has asked me out." If she feels compelled to say "Yes," in order to look good, then she loses the chance for a date. Saying "No" is not a good alternative, because she has no way of knowing whether the boy will then ask for a date or whether his plans for the date will have any appeal. It would be much easier if the boy were to come right out and say, "Would you like to go to the movies with me Friday?," but this is the kind of direct, nonstrategic approach that novice daters have difficulty managing because it provides them with no hedge against losing face.

In whatever way invitations are presented to them, girls may find it hard to decide which ones to accept. When a girl is asked out by a boy she doesn't like, she must decide whether to accept just in order to have some kind of date, especially if it is for a special event, or to decline and hope that she will hear from someone she likes better, which means taking the risk of winding up with no date at all. When a girl wants to go out with a particular boy, moreover, she has to steer some middle course between being too coy and reserved (in which case he may not notice her) and being too obvious about her feelings (in which case she may get an unwanted reputation as a flirt or "boy chaser").

For both boys and girls at the beginning of their dating experience, pleasure and disappointment in getting dates revolve around the peer audience. It's not the one-to-one time spent with a date that counts, it's having the date and having others know you have the date, and the more popular a person your date is, the more your self-esteem prospers. This is what is reflected in stages 3 and 4 in Dunphy's description (Figure 8.5) when a couple on a date interact more with their group of couples than with each other.

Kissing goodnight, even though it usually occurs in private, brings up a similar host of questions about what other people expect and how to preserve one's self-esteem. The boy, who is usually expected to initiate the kiss, has to worry about whether he will be rebuffed or, worse yet, be laughed at for a clumsy effort. He can decide not to try, but then he risks

Adolescents beginning to date usually have some anxieties about how to manage a goodnight kiss.

being seen as a coward (and remember, the imaginary audience is watching) or having the girl think he doesn't like her when he does. The girl has to decide when and with whom to permit a kiss—not too soon or with just anybody, or she loses a boy's respect and risks becoming known as a "hot number," and not too little or late, or she can lose a boy's interest and become known as a "cold fish."

There are no easy solutions to this problem. What usually happens is that beginning daters use a number of strategic interactions in words and gestures to convey their level of interest in kissing or being kissed to spare each other as much embarrassment as possible. For example, a girl who runs up her front steps is telling her date one thing about whether he should try to kiss her goodnight, and one who inches slowly up the steps standing close to him and holding his arm is telling him something else. Many other interactions during the process of arranging for, being on, and ending a date involve similar kinds of strategic maneuvering rather than direct communication as both parties make their best effort to preserve an appearance of social competence.

AS DATING MATURES

From an adult perspective, youthful concerns of the type we have been describing may seem silly and inconsequential. For adolescents, however, successful dating can be a crucial ingredient of self-esteem and peer-group belongingness. Adolescents who date regularly, compared to those who do not, are found to feel better about themselves and be perceived by their peers as having higher self-esteem (Samet & Kelly, 1987). Conversely, young people who do not date or who do so awkwardly often feel inferior to their more socially competent peers. Moreover, the increasing popularity of heterosocial activities among their peer group may cause nondating adolescents to become socially excluded.

Most adolescents feel at least a little inadequate and uneasy when they begin to date, and being afraid of "doing something wrong" on the first date is a common experience. With maturity and practice, young people develop social skills that increase their comfort and decrease their need for strategic interactions in dating relationships, and then dating gradually takes on romantic qualities of interpersonal interaction.

As one reflection of their heterosocial maturation, high school students tend increasingly to date people they want to *be with* instead of people they want to *be seen with*, and going out with someone who is popular becomes less important than dating someone whose company is really enjoyed. In one study of this developmental change, Roscoe, Diana, and Brooks (1987) asked sixth-graders, eleventh-graders, and college students about their reasons for dating and for selecting particular people to date. Egocentric reasons (that is, feeling good about myself and having a good time) were more commonly given by the early and middle adolescents, whereas the late adolescents were more likely to talk about reciprocal sharing of intimacy and companionship.

In this regard, the pleasure that adolescents derive from dating a certain person, and the likelihood of their wanting to date the same person again, depend in large part on whether they are dating for the same reason. The main reasons why adolescents date are generally agreed to be for recreation (having a good time), learning (improving skills in managing dating interactions), status (making a favorable impression by how often and with whom one has a date), companionship (sharing pleasurable activities with someone of the other gender), intimacy (establishing a special, close relationship with a person of the other gender), sexual experimentation, and courtship (looking for someone to have as a steady date or to marry) (Paul & White, 1990). If a boy and girl are dating for different reasons—for example, if one is seeking status and the other companionship, or one is looking for intimacy and the other for recreation—at least one of them will probably not enjoy a date together very much and choose not to repeat it. On the other hand, couples who meet each other's needs in a dating relationship are likely to enjoy going out together and to consider doing so steadily.

CALLING, CUTTING, AND CLIQUING

Elkind (1980) has described three other kinds of strategic interaction that often occur when young people are playing to the imaginary audience. *Calling* refers to being on the telephone, which is where many adolescents seem to their parents to be much of the time. Families with teenage children often face the challenge of keeping them off the telephone so that other calls can be made or received. A contemporary phenomenon among affluent families is having a separate telephone for an adolescent to use, or even a separate number; the marketing of home telephone equipment that allows for overriding of a busy signal has undoubtedly been buoyed by the needs of parents to maintain contact with the outside world via the telephone despite having a teenager in the home.

Adults typically use the telephone to give or receive information. Among adolescents, Elkind points out, being on the telephone can instead become an index of popularity and a source of self-esteem. Once on the phone, other strategies come into play. One of these is to stay on the phone a long, long time. Parents often assume that these long-winded discussions are solely devoted to projects or gossip. But they also have another reason, to give other potential callers the *busy signal*, or, with call waiting, to be able to say "I'm on the other line" or "I'm talking to so-and-so." A phone in use signifies a popular person, and the busy signal is a sign of popularity. Sometimes, of course, the adolescent may cut a conversation short because he or she is "expecting some other calls," which gives the caller the message that he or she is no one special and that others are waiting to call the popular person.

Cutting has to do with recognizing or ignoring other young people in public. Being recognized in front of an audience can boost a person's self-esteem, especially if it's warm and enthusiastic recognition from someone who is popular and admired. Being ignored often has the opposite effect of deflating one's self-esteem. You come up to someone you think you know well and think likes you, and the other person walks right by without noticing you, or returns an enthusiastic greeting with a luke warm acknowledgement, or maybe even goes out of his or her way to avoid you altogether. Then you feel humiliated in front of everyone who is or is imagined to be watching.

Because of their concerns about maintaining self-esteem and an appearance of adequacy, adolescents are acutely sensitive to the impact of cutting and being cut. Whether or not a peer should be recognized and with what degree of enthusiasm often becomes a strategic interaction that is carefully planned and executed to dispense rewards or administer punishment. As observers as well as actors in these interactions, adolescents take careful note of who is cutting whom and use this information to judge the social status of their peers as well as themselves.

Strategic considerations can also influence the companions adolescents seek, not for friendship but for purposes of *cliquing*. Cliques are small, tightly knit social groups, as we noted earlier, and they are used by their members to enhance their self-esteem and impress the broader audience with the company they keep. Being a member of some clique conveys that you have some special qualifications for acceptance into a highly selective group; not being included in any clique, on the other hand, can tell the audience that there is nothing special about you.

The strategies of cliquing sometimes lead to apparently unusual associations. A clique of attractive girls may welcome an unattractive girl into their group, for example, because comparisons with her call attention to how good looking they are. Although this may seem a selfish way of exploiting the unattractive girl, she may welcome the association. Being an accepted member of a clique of popular, attractive girls bolsters her self-esteem and shows the audience that she is an appealing person. Sometimes adolescents may even seek to associate with a peer because his or her family is well known or prominent in the community. In such strategic interactions the characteristics of the peer make little difference; what counts for the person seeking the association is having others take notice and be impressed by it.

BEING LONELY AND SHY

For young people who have difficulty forming close friendships and establishing peer-group belongingness, the adolescent years may bear bitter fruits of loneliness. **Loneliness** is a distressing, unpleasant experience in which your social relationships fall short of meeting your needs for companionship. The larger the gap that exists between how much friendship and intimacy a person would like to have and how much is currently available in his or her life, the more lonely that person is likely to feel.

Most people experience painful moments of loneliness from time to time, when changing

Adolescents who have difficulty becoming a participant in peer-group activities may experience a deep sense of loneliness and alienation.

relationships or unusual circumstances temporarily deprive them of their accustomed level of companionship. Such passing moments of situational loneliness seldom affect how people feel about themselves; usually they can easily be attributed to external events over which the person has no control. However, loneliness that persists or keeps recurring often fosters feelings of alienation and social inadequacy, especially among adolescents.

Alienation from peers is experienced as an acutely painful sense of being isolated from much of what life has to offer. There is no one to talk to, no one to share with, no one even for company in walking to school, sitting down to lunch in the cafeteria, or going to some special event. It's not that no one cares; most lonely adolescents have parents who care about them very much. It's that the peers don't seem to care, and they are the ones whose attitudes mean so much to how teenagers feel about themselves, particularly during early and middle adolescence. Alienated young people become passive spectators whose world is passing them by; alone and unnoticed, they watch in envy while their classmates carry on the activities of adolescence without them.

With respect to their sense of adequacy, junior and senior high school students and college students as well who say they are lonely also tend to report feeling inferior to other people, unable to assert themselves socially, incapable of making and keeping friends, and incompetent in academic and athletic as well as social situations (Berndt & Perry, 1990; Goswick & Jones, 1982; Inderbitzen-Pisaruk, Clark, & Solano, 1992). Sometimes they express anger toward other people, as if to blame them for their loneliness. More often they blame themselves for their predicament and feel anxious and depressed about it.

Holden Caulfield, the unhappy teenager in J. D. Salinger's *The Catcher in the Rye* (1945), also knew how depressing it can be to be lonely: "I felt so lonesome, all of a sudden, I almost wished I was dead." As for the anxiety that loneliness can cause, this is what one of the girls in Konopka's (1976, p. 92) research had to say: "Being alone just scares me. I don't know. Sometimes when I do feel lonely, I don't know how to handle it, because I am definitely not a loner . . . it just scares me" (white, urban, age 17).

LONELINESS AS A SUBJECTIVE EXPERIENCE

Young people who report feeling lonely are consistently found to have fewer social activities than their less lonely peers, to have fewer friends, and to experience less intimacy and mutuality in the friendships they do have (Asher & Wheeler, 1985; Kelly & Hanson, 1987; Rotenberg & Whitney, 1992). Nevertheless, what it means to be lonely cannot be measured by any objective assessment of social participation or of the quantity and quality of a person's friendships. As we have already implied, loneliness is a *subjective* experience, and basic theories about loneliness stress that whether the actual extent of a person's social life is satisfying or not depends on his or her felt needs for companionship and intimacy (Peplau & Perlman, 1982).

Just about anyone would feel lonesome in Robinson Crusoe's shoes, with no human company at all. Crusoe felt much better after Friday came along, and there are people who similarly, by virtue of their particular temperament or circumstances, have only modest needs for social interactions and interpersonal intimacy. Such people may be satisfied with occasional companionship, infrequent socializing, and only a modest degree of shared intimacy with their closest friends. Then there is the "social lion," who seems to have an insatiable need to be surrounded by friends or at least companions. This type of individual can feel lonely despite a crowded social calendar that most other people would find overwhelming. And finally, there is the "clinging vine," who has unusually strong needs to share innermost thoughts and feelings with close friends and feels unfulfilled or abandoned unless friends are constantly providing opportunities for such intimacy.

With respect to differences between quests for companionship or intimacy, Robert Weiss (1973) made a useful distinction some years ago between *social loneliness* and *emotional loneliness*. Social loneliness stems from subjective feelings that one lacks a sufficient number of friends or an adequate network of social relationships. Emotional loneliness derives from subjective feelings that one is lacking in close, intimate relationships with other people. As subsequently elaborated by other researchers, social loneliness is largely a matter of perceived shortcomings in the *quantity* of one's relationships, whereas emotional loneliness is a matter of perceived shortcomings in their *quality* (Asher, Parkhurst, Hymel, & Williams, 1990; Russell, Cutrona, Rose, & Yurko, 1984). Although these two types of loneliness have many features in common, the distinction between them is helpful in determining what kinds of steps should be taken in an attempt to overcome feelings of being lonely (Adams, Openshaw, Bennion, Mills, & Noble, 1988).

Of further importance to note, being lonely is not necessarily a function of being alone. A person who is unsatisfied with the relationships he or she has with others can feel lonely in the midst of a crowd. One male college freshman put it this way:

I do not feel my interests and ideals are the same as other peoples'. I get especially lonely when I realize that I am an isolated person, alone even in a group. It's depressing because I might always feel this way. [Cutrona, 1982, p. 299]

Whether being alone makes people lonely depends on when it happens and what they are doing at the time. This interaction was documented by Larson, Csikszentmihalyi, and Graef (1982) in an informative study of how adolescents and adults spend their time. These researchers asked 75 high school students, boys and girls from diverse socioeconomic backgrounds in grades 9–12 in a large suburban school, to carry an electronic pager with them for 1 week. Throughout the week, at random times within every 2-hour interval during the day and evening hours, they were beeped on the pager.

The subjects' task when they were beeped was to complete a short questionnaire indicating where they were, what they were doing and with whom, and their current state of mind. Similar data were collected from 107 working adults, men and women aged 19–65 in both blue-collar and white-collar jobs. The approximately 9,000 self-reports Larson et al. collected in this way indicated how these adolescents and adults divided their time among various activities at home, at work, in school, and in public, and whether these activities were more likely to take place alone or in the company of others.

As shown in Table 8.4, these adolescents were spending about one-fourth of their time alone, mostly while at home studying, reading, or doing household chores. By contrast, they were rarely alone while at school or in public. This difference suggests that being alone during some personal or work-related activity at home is much less likely to make a person feel lonely than being alone during leisure activities in public—which neither young people nor adults very often attempt to enjoy by themselves. In describing their state of mind, these subjects reported being able to concentrate better when they were by themselves, which fits with their using solitary time for work-related activities, but they also felt less happy, cheerful, and sociable than when they had company.

Among the adolescent subjects, such negative moods were especially pronounced when they were alone on a Friday or Saturday night. The particular unhappiness of being alone at times when other people are having fun together has been noted, among other places, in such laments as "being all dressed up with no place to go." Both the research data and common experience tell us that being alone is most likely to cause loneliness at times or in activities that are typically shared by groups of people, whereas in some circumstances being alone may be just what a person needs and wants.

ADOLESCENT SUSCEPTIBILITY TO LONELINESS

Because adolescents are seeking new kinds of peer-group relationships at the same time as they are loosening childhood ties to their parents, they become particularly susceptible to experiencing loneliness. In the early and middle adolescent years, young people are faced with separating from one set of relationships before another set is firmly established. Some junior high school students opt to remain childish rather than take on this challenge. They cling to previous ways of thinking and acting and use a close relationship with their parents to justify disinterest in becoming involved or popular with their age-mates. This is a costly choice because it undermines a young person's self-esteem and invites ridicule from peers, teachers, and most parents (except those who are still struggling with the need to have their offspring remain childishly attached to them).

Table 8.4 WHAT PEOPLE REPORTED DOING WHEN ALONE AND WITH OTHERS[a]

	Percentage of All Self-Reports			
	Adolescents (n = 2,734)		*Adults (n = 4,791)*	
Activity	*Alone*	*With Others*	*Alone*	*With Others*
Home				
Housework, other practical	6.7*	5.6	5.4*	8.6
Self-care	2.1*	0.5	2.2*	1.2
Studying (adolescents)	3.5*	1.4	—	—
Eating	0.6	3.1*	0.7	2.4*
Socializing (includes by phone)	2.6	5.4	—	3.8*
Watching television	2.0*	3.9	2.2	5.1
Personal reading	2.0*	1.4	1.5	1.4
Doing hobbies or art	0.7	0.5	0.3*	0.2
Idling, listening to music	1.8	2.5	2.4	3.3
Total at home	20.0	24.3	14.7	26.0
Work and school				
Working at work	1.6	2.2	5.9	20.9*
In class (adolescents)	0.0	15.6*	—	—
Other at work or school	1.2	13.5*	3.6	11.5*
Total at work or school	2.8	31.3*	9.5	32.3*
Public				
In transit	1.3	3.3	2.9	3.6
Other practical activities	1.2	6.2*	0.8	1.1
Leisure	0.6	9.0*	1.2	7.9*
Total in public	3.1	18.6*	4.9	12.6*
Total	25.9	74.1	29.1	70.9

[a] The table shows the percentage of times people reported themselves to be doing each of the activities when alone and with others. The percentages are based on the entire pool of self-reports for each sample. The asterisks indicate whether an activity occurred at a higher rate alone or with others for a significant ($p < .05$) number of people.

Source: Based on data reported by Larson et al. (1982).

As a preferred course of action, most adolescents brave the pain of relinquishing childhood ties and endure some loneliness while they are replacing these attachments with new relationships and more exciting activities. This normally occurring interlude of distress between the formation of new attachments prompted Anna Freud (1958) to describe adolescence as a period of "mourning." Just as people feel lonely and diminished while they are mourning the loss of a loved one who has died or gone away, adolescents may pass a temporary time of sadness over the loss of their childhood.

This kind of developmental loneliness is especially troublesome for adolescents who have been isolated from their peers during elementary school or find it difficult to give up childhood attachments. The mild sense of alienation that weighs on most adolescents from time to time can also be intensified by environmental obstacles to peer-group belongingness. For example, young people who live in remote areas without easy access to the places where their peers congregate may not have a chance to be accepted into a group, whatever their intrinsic capacities for becoming popular. Similarly, adolescents confronted with exclusive cliques into which they don't quite fit may suffer more feelings of alienation than they would in a school or community with a more open society.

Moves to a different school or community during early adolescence may also contribute to this kind of problem. Feelings of loneliness, sadness, irritability, and anger are commonly found among young people who are uprooted and taken away from friends on whom they have come to depend for companionship and support. Persistent negative effects of moving are not inevitable, and no systematic link has been found between the number of times people have moved while growing up and their subsequent susceptibility to loneliness (Rubin, 1982). Nevertheless, it takes an unusually outgoing and self-confident youngster to handle moves without some disruption of his or her social relationships and peer popularity. For most, having to start from scratch in making new friends and breaking into already established peer groups takes time and is not an easy task.

Escaping loneliness after moving is typically more difficult during early adolescence than it is in the childhood years, when group formation is more casual and neighborhood based,or in later adolescence, when group membership and activities have become less important than individual pursuits and relationships. On the other hand, there is as yet no clear evidence that susceptibility to loneliness varies with age among adolescents. In relation to the typical characteristics of their friendships, adolescents at all ages need at least some opportunity to disclose and unburden themselves to peers with whom they share intimacy, and any event that disrupts this opportunity can lead to episodes of loneliness.

School transitions can pose a particular hazard for adolescents because of their heightened vulnerability to loneliness. Early adolescents may have to face going to a junior high school different from the one that most of their sixth-grade friends will attend, and graduating from junior to senior high school may likewise occasion a new setting with little carryover of old friends and a corresponding period of feeling lonely. Likewise in late adolescence, going away to college may also give new birth to the specter of loneliness. Young people who leave their high school and their home town to attend college leave their social credentials behind and have to make a new start in establishing friendship and dating relationships. A female college freshman interviewed by Cutrona (1982) gave this description of her first 7 months on campus:

> Coming to a large university such as this was a big change for me. After being voted in junior high and senior high school "Best Personality" and "Most Popular," I had to start over. Walking a long distance, seeing nothing but strangers was rather difficult at first, but I find myself getting used to it.

In a research study that Cutrona conducted (p. 291), 98 female and 64 male college students in a large public university were assessed for loneliness at three points in time: 2 weeks, 7 weeks, and 7 months after arriving on campus to begin their freshman year. At 2 weeks, three-quarters of these new freshmen reported having experienced at least occasional loneliness since coming on campus, and over 40% reported their loneliness had been moderately to severely distressing. At 7 weeks, the frequency and extent of reported loneliness among these students had decreased significantly, and a further significant decrease was found at 7 months, when only one-fourth of them said they had experienced loneliness in the previous 2 weeks.

These data indicate the susceptibility of young people to loneliness but also how quickly most are able to adapt to new situations. Some other interesting research has examined the characteristics of young people that predict their susceptibility to becoming lonely and, as well, their ability to disperse clouds of loneliness when they threaten to close in (Inderbitzen-Pisaruk et al., 1990). First, and not surprisingly, those adolescents who resist and overcome loneliness most effectively are those who have good social skills. Conversely, loneliness is most likely to strike and persist in young people who are relatively insensitive to the needs and feelings of others, who have trouble initiating and sustaining conversations, and who feel awkward or uncomfortable in group situations.

Second, just as feelings of being inferior and incompetent are often found among people who report loneliness, having low self-esteem and limited self-confidence increases the vulnerability of adolescents to becoming and remaining lonely. Feeling good about yourself to begin with, on the other hand, helps you keep going psychologically when circumstances deprive you for a time of good companions and close friends, whereas people who have doubts about themselves to begin with are at risk for suffering distressing pangs of loneliness when companions and friends are not available. What did I do wrong to end up all alone, they wonder, and will I ever be able to do the right thing to make friends?

Third, young people who are prone to loneliness and those who are not differ in how they think about social problems in their lives, especially with respect to where they place the blame when they find themselves without companions and friends. Adolescents who are particularly susceptible to feeling lonely tend to attribute their lack of companions and friends to causes that are *internal* and *stable*. Internal causes constitute one's own fault, something about the way you are or the things you do that is responsible for your being in a socially unfulfilling situation. Stable causes consist of circumstances that are unlikely to change. By contrast to this self-blaming and pessimistic pattern of attribution, adolescents who avoid loneliness or overcome it when it occurs attribute their situation to *external* and *unstable* causes, that is, to events that are not one's fault and are not likely to be permanent.

COPING WITH SHYNESS

Persistently lonely people tend to be awkward and unassertive in making social overtures, highly self-conscious, and exquisitely sensitive to the slightest hint of dislike or rejection. A common word for this pattern of social ineptness, especially when it is combined with feelings of inadequacy and sensitivity to rejection, is **shyness**. Shyness is defined by a pattern of social anxiety and interpersonal inhibition arising in situations that raise the prospect of being evaluated by others. In such situations, shy people are motivated more by the need to protect themselves than by the desire to express themselves (Arkin, Lake, & Baumgardner, 1986; Leary, 1986).

People have recognized what it means to be shy for almost as long as they have been interacting with others, but little formal research on this very common aspect of personal relationships has yet been done. The most extensive work on this topic remains a large-scale project done by Philip Zimbardo in the 1970s in which thousands of people of all ages and from diverse backgrounds were surveyed about shyness. Zimbardo and Radl (1981) described shyness as

a mental attitude that predisposes people to be extremely concerned about the social evaluation of them by others. As such, it creates a keen sensitivity to cues of being rejected. There is a readiness to avoid people and situations that hold any potential for criticism of the shy person's appearance or conduct. It involves keeping a very low profile by holding back from initiating actions that may call attention to one's self. [p. 9]

About 80% of the people interviewed in Zimbardo's surveys said they were either shy now or had been at one time. This confirms what most people know from their own experience: almost everyone has moments of feeling shy or even thinking of himself or herself as a shy person—a child being overwhelmed by overly demonstrative adults, for example, or an early adolescent learning to approach the other gender. Being shy now was reported by about 40% of Zimbardo's sample, but the comments of these subjects identified many shades of shyness. Some people who consider themselves shy are only slightly hesitant or uncertain in their interpersonal relationships. Some are merely timid or easily embarrassed. For others, however, being shy can mount to an intense, chronic fear of people that makes any kind of social encounter unpleasant, if not unbearable.

People who carry such a painful burden of shyness into social situations are constantly afraid of saying or doing the wrong thing or not knowing what to say or do. They fear that whatever they reveal about themselves—their feelings, aspirations, past experiences, even where they live or what their parents do for a living—will give others something to criticize or laugh at. They fear being ignored or rejected, especially by people they want to like them. This degree of shyness often takes people down the path of loneliness, particularly if they yearn for the kinds of close personal relationships that their shyness makes it difficult for them to form and sustain. In an illustrative study of 159 college students by Jones and Carpenter (1986), those who scored high on a measure of shyness reported more loneliness and less satisfaction with their personal relationships than those who were not shy, especially with respect to having intimate relationships. The shy students in this sample were also likely to have small social networks and, compared to the nonshy students, the people to whom they felt closely related contained a larger proportion of family members as opposed to friends.

Like loneliness, shyness is a painful psychological experience to which adolescents become particularly vulnerable, especially during the early teenage years. Facing larger numbers of new people than before and being expected to act grown up, yet still lacking the social skills that further maturation and cumulative experience will help them acquire later on, junior high school students are more likely to feel shy and behave shyly than elementary school or high school students (Cheek, Carpentieri, Smith, Rierdan, & Koff, 1986; Hauck et al., 1986; Kelly & Hansen, 1987).

Another factor that may contribute to a temporary increase in shyness during early adolescence is the heightened influence at this time of the imaginary audience phenomenon that we have discussed. Young people who are highly sensitive to what the imaginary audience thinks may be especially inclined to avoid situations in which their actions are likely to be judged by others. As a result, shy young people who worry a lot about the imaginary audience may deprive themselves of the very kinds of social interactions that could help them enjoy friendships more and feel less uncomfortable and self-conscious. As evidence of this likely influence of the imaginary audience, Ishiyama (1984) found among 96 male and female tenth-graders that self-reports of being shy correlated with regarding shyness as an unacceptable and shameful experience and believing that it is noticeable by others.

Some researchers suggest that inborn differences in temperament, such as how easily a person adapts to novelty and change, may influence a young person's susceptibility to shyness from early in life (Kagan & Reznick, 1986; Kagan, Snidman, & Arcus, 1992). However, the work of Zimbardo and his colleagues demonstrated that shyness originates to a large extent in a variety of childhood experiences and how they are perceived. These include failure and rejection in social situations; doing poorly in school; being compared unfavorably with peers and siblings; losing parents or other supportive, confidence-building people; having parents or other models set a shy example themselves; and being deprived of opportunities for social interaction. Such experiences foster low self-esteem, vulnerability to feeling ashamed and embarrassed, and a tendency to label oneself as socially inadequate, and this is a combination of attitudes from which persistent shyness often emerges.

When children who are disposed to shyness or are already shy become adolescents, their fears interfere with their forming friendships, establishing peer belongingness, and becoming involved in dating relationships. Other disadvantages result as well, among both high school and college students. Those who remain shy tend to worry excessively about whether they are behaving in a socially effective way, and they sometimes react inappropriately out of fear of being evaluated negatively. In protecting themselves from anxiety by avoiding situations in which failure is possible, they deny themselves opportunities for competitive successes that could bolster their self-confidence and ease their shyness.

Even when they are talented, then, the concerns of shy young people about gaining acceptance and approval tend to make them followers rather than leaders, and they are relatively easily swayed by the views of others. They hesitate to share their opinions, they have trouble standing up for their rights, and they are often reluctant to express themselves in the classroom or other public situations. Ironically, the social aloofness of shy youngsters who feel less worthy than their peers and long for their approval may be misperceived as indicating snobbishness and disinterest in being friendly (Arkin et al., 1986; Zimbardo, 1986).

In addition to becoming more prevalent in adolescence, shyness also becomes a more stable and persistent characteristic than it is among children. Even though there are some shy adolescents and adults in whom social anxiety and inhibition were apparent even before they entered elementary school, longitudinal studies of shyness indicate only a modest correlation (.35) between grades three and four and little predictability from the third grade to grades five through seven in how much shyness children are likely to show. However, shyness in the fifth grade is significantly related to being shy over the next four years, and between grades eight and nine the correlation is substantial (.85) (Asendorpf, 1986). Consistent with this finding, young people who have established a pattern of shyness by the end of childhood are more likely than their peers to be socially reserved through adulthood and into their middle years as well (Caspi, Elder, & Bem, 1988).

Although persistent shyness can become a lifelong trait, shy children are not necessarily trapped forever in the clutches of timidity. Zimbardo reported that 40% of the late adolescents in his survey felt that social experiences in college had helped them become less shy than they were in high school. These young people described numerous ways in which interactions on campus had reduced their shyness by making them more open and outgoing, more relaxed in the company of other people, better able to put their best foot forward, and more appreciative of what other people have to offer.

Based on what they learned from their research about the nature and modifiability of shyness, Zimbardo and Radl (1981, Chapter 9) wrote a "Student's Shyness Handbook" in which they offered hints on how young people can help themselves overcome this problem. These include making a firm decision to become less shy and risk making social overtures; taking careful stock of what kinds of situations are most likely to make you feel shy; undertaking a personal improvement program designed to bolster your self-confidence and enhance your attractiveness to others; learning to enjoy your own company so that being alone does not necessarily make you feel lonely or inadequate; and practicing the kinds of social skills used in interacting with friends and dates. Aside from such self-help efforts, a variety of training methods have proved effective in assisting shy young people to become more socially active and comfortable (Alden & Cappe, 1986; Christoff, 1985; Glass & Shea, 1986).

CHAPTER SUMMARY

1. Friendships are special relationships between two people who care for each other and share important parts of their lives. Whereas children's friendships tend to be relatively shallow and fleeting, adolescents show increasingly deepening friendship relationships.

2. The maturation of *perspective taking* and *altruistic attitudes* in late childhood and preadolescence is associated with most young people entering into *chumships*. Chumships are close and exclusive relationships between two preadolescents who become inseparable friends and spend most of their waking hours together. In early adolescence chumships give way to a broader range of friendships that, over time, become increasingly *intimate* (including a high degree of self-disclosure and shared personal information) and *mutual* (involving a high degree of equality and reciprocity).

3. With deepening friendships, adolescents become more attached to their peers than before and more influenced by them. However, despite being more likely to listen to their peers than their parents about such matters as choosing friends and spending leisure time, they remain more likely to listen to their parents in matters of morality and educational and vocational planning. By the end of adolescence, both parental and peer influence have usually diminished in favor of increasingly independent thinking.

4. Conformity to peer-group standards increases from childhood to early adolescence but then declines during middle and late adolescence. The type and amount of peer pressure young people experience also vary with age, but at all grade levels pressures to participate in peer-group and school activities are more keenly felt than pressures to misbehave.

5. The determinants of popularity may vary among teenage groups, but being well liked is most commonly associated with having good social skills and being an active participant in group activities. Although peer-group standing often carries over into adolescence from patterns established in childhood, the nature and pace of developmental events during adolescence can produce marked changes in relative popularity.

6. Adolescents are highly conscious of the *imaginary audience*, which consists of people who are assumed to be observing and forming impressions of one's behavior even if they are not actually present. Many features of how young people interact with each other are *strategic*, in that their primary purpose is "looking good" to whoever may be watching.

7. Young people begin to date sometime during early or middle adolescence. The actual age when dating begins varies widely among groups of adolescents from different backgrounds and is determined primarily by sociocultural expectations, not physical maturation. With maturity and experience, adolescents gradually develop social skills that decrease their initial uneasiness and need for strategic interactions in dating relationships and pave the way for pleasure and romance.

8. Social relationships that fall short of meeting a person's needs for companionship lead to feelings of *loneliness*, which are most acutely felt when a person is alone at times or in activities that are typically shared by groups of people. Because of their need for peer-group relationships, adolescents are partic-

otible to feeling lonely, especially when emselves in unfamiliar surroundings. ..ver, most young people are capable of adapting quickly to new situations, and persistent loneliness rarely occurs.

9.   Poor social skills, combined with feelings of inadequacy and sensitivity to rejection, constitute *shyness*. Shyness is fostered by childhood experiences that lead to low self-esteem and vulnerability to feeling ashamed and embarrassed. In some individuals, shyness may become a lifelong trait. However, it is observed more commonly among adolescents than among either children or adults, and many young people have experiences as late adolescents and young adults that help them become less shy than they were in junior or senior high school.

KEY WORDS

altruism	conformity	loneliness	self-fulfilling prophecy
chumships	crowds	mutuality	shyness
circular relationship	friendships	perspective taking	strategic interactions
cliques	intimacy	popularity	

REVIEW QUESTIONS

FORMING FRIENDSHIPS

1.   How do "friends" differ from "acquaintances?"
2.   What do longitudinal studies show about the importance of childhood and adolescent friendships?
3.   List some typical features of chumship relationships.
4.   Discuss the issue of whether perspective-taking skills or close interpersonal relationships come first in social development.
5.   How does a blend of similarity and complementarity contribute to close and rewarding friendships?
6.   In what ways do chumships help prepare young people for increasingly intimate relationships later on?
7.   Why do adolescents have a greater need than children for close friendships with peers?
8.   What does the research on adolescent attitudes toward friendship suggest about gender differences in interpersonal orientation?
9.   Describe the kinds of circumstances that cause some friendships to endure and others to dissolve. What are the kinds of events that are most likely to disrupt adolescent friendships?
10.   In what ways do adolescents typically spend different kinds of times with their parents and with their peers?

BELONGING TO THE PEER GROUP

11.   Discuss differences in conformity behavior that are associated with the age and gender of young people.
12.   What characteristics usually contribute to young people being popular or unpopular with their peers?
13.   What does it mean to say that social skills and popularity are "circular" phenomena?
14.   List three reasons why popularity among adolescents is likely to carry over from popularity in childhood.

DATING AND OTHER STRATEGIC INTERACTIONS

15.   Give some examples of how "strategic interactions" influence the way girls and boys act toward each other when they begin to date.

16. How are chronological age, physical maturation, and sociocultural expectations related to the age at which adolescents start dating?

BEING LONELY AND SHY

17. What is the significance of saying that loneliness is a subjective experience?

18. Discuss the kinds of circumstances and events that make adolescents particularly susceptible to feeling lonely.

19. Identify some personal characteristics that can help adolescents avoid or overcome feelings of loneliness.

20. What kinds of childhood experiences are likely to contribute to shyness in adolescence?

Interlude

◆

Linda, Age 15

◆

"A good friend is somebody who cares for you; and you care for them"

Linda, an African-American 15-year-old girl living in New York City, was attending a Protestant, private all-girls high school where she received an award for general excellence last year. People and interpersonal relations are obviously very important to her, and she describes friendships, the way other people treat each other, and the way she feels about relationships in detail. At one point she comments: "Everything is worse because of people. But then again, if you didn't have people, you'd be lonely." She also shares her thoughts about teenage pregnancy, abortion, death, and suicide. She was interviewed by Alexandra Woods, a doctoral student in psychology at City College of C.U.N.Y.

This interview follows Chapter 8, on the social world of adolescence. Consider the major topics of that chapter as you read this interview: forming friendships, belonging to the peer group, dating, and being lonely or shy. This interview conveys a lot of feelings about being an adolescent. What memories does it bring back for you? Other questions to consider while reading this case are the following: What do you think about her feelings about getting angry, and her feelings about growing up? From Chapters 4 and 5, what is the evidence of formal operational thinking in her discussions of friendship, abortion, and suicide? Are there examples of Elkind's concepts of the imaginary audience and the personal fable in her discussions of friends and interpersonal relations? From Chapter 6, what is your reaction to her thoughts about schoolwork and about choosing a career? What difference does her social background have on her life? From Chapter 7, in what ways does she differ from Cesar in her relationship with her parents and the way she discusses them?

Did you start thinking that you were different or that you were changing when you became a teenager? No, not really. Well, all I could say is that people were saying I was more mature, getting more mature. And also I guess I had a lot more responsibility, because before your parents would say that you have to go and do your homework, you have to sit there and do it for an hour; now you have to divide your time. You have to know what your values are and do what you thought was right. So when I entered high school—which is really where I felt, wow, I'm a teenager, it really wasn't any different; it's just that you have to divide your time up. In my high school we get a lot of work. *What high school are you at?* St. Hilda's High School in the Bronx. And I mean, it's a lot of work. You have to know how to divide your time well, or you'll never get finished. In high school they don't push you to do the work. If you do it you do it; if you don't do it, then you can do anything else you want. When I got into high school I found out more about a lot of other people—because there are girls there (it's an all girls high school) who didn't want to do their work; there are girls there who never do their work. There are girls who study just to pass because the school is so tough. So I found out a lot about other people; that's basically it. Plus we have the responsibility when we go home to do your chores. And, you know, you have to make time for your friends also. *Sounds like for you some of the changes had to do with having to take a lot more responsibility yourself, and make some decisions yourself, and you talked about also learning about other people more. Was that part of it too?* Yeah, that really was because the more I learned about people, or I started to look at other kinds, that kind of made me laugh because I used to do that. You know, I'd feel, "Oh, you've been bad!" And I was surprised because it made me think about what I was doing more. And I'd think about what I was going to do before I'd say it or do it, something like that.

Where do you come in the family? Are you the oldest? Oh no, I'm the youngest. I've got an older sister—she's in college—she'll be 20 this year. And my mother and father. *Did your sister sort of tell you about what it was going to be like to be a teenager?* (laughs) No. Me and my sister don't get along that well. I think maybe she started to talk to me a lot more. To me she's like a teenager because she acts nowhere near 20; I don't know, maybe you do act that way when you're 20. It just seems like when she entered college she just changed, changed for the worse to me. She didn't tell me anything about it. It wasn't really a change to her. We don't hardly speak. Our personalities just don't go together. I think that maybe if I didn't live with her and I met her I might have liked her more, you know. But I really get to the point where I'm going to go crazy. *You say you and she are very different.* Oh well, it's just, you know how sometimes people do little things to bring the worst out of you. Well, that's what she does. We share a room also. She may clean up the room and throw something on my side, or something like that. And then she'll do other things—if she goes into the kitchen and doesn't wash up her dish—things like that will get me a little irritated because it makes more work for me. That's all I need! As I tell you, my schoolwork, it keeps me up; it takes me from about the time I get home until about 11 or 12 o'clock because I have to get tennis in because that's one of my favorite sports, so I make time for that. And usually I'll do extra work over the weekend so I can make time for tennis. It all works out. *So your time is really divided pretty much now between school and a lot of homework and a little bit of tennis too.* Uh huh. Tennis I love. *Do you play well?* Oh yeah, I hope to.

Also another thing I think is that it's an all girls school. I'd always gone to a public school. In my grammar school, everybody always tried so hard, you know. There were some people who really did try, but for some reason they just couldn't do it; but most of the people at my grammar school would try really hard. In high school I expected all the girls to be working hard and everything, but a lot of them are just concerned about boys. And the fact that I grew up on a block with a lot of boys—we've all become good friends on my block—but there's hardly any girls, maybe two girls, and I don't get along with them; they're pretty snobby. You know, boy-crazy girls, that's what they are; and all they talk about is boys—you can't carry on a conversation with girls who talk about boys a lot. *Sounds like you have a lot of friends who are boys, but you're not that into being boy crazy or hanging around girls who are boy crazy right now.* Right. I have maybe a few female friends; I think Carol and Millie are about the best friends, best girl friends that I have. I've also got cousins, but some of them live on Long Island. I may call them every 3 months or something. But Carol and Millie, we talk all the time. *Have you been friends a long time with Carol and Millie?* Well, Carol, I knew about her last year, but I really got to know her this summer. And Millie, I've known for about 2 years. I really got to know Millie the year before last; that's when we became good friends.

When you look back at the kind of friends you used to have as a little girl and the friendships that you have now, are they different? Well, to tell you the truth, most of the friends I have now, I've had for a long time. *Have they changed, those friendships, or are they sort of the same?* Well, they're sort of the same, you could say. Because basically I grew up with two other kids and they moved a couple of years ago. We've always kept in touch, you know. Those were the only two I really grew up with, besides my cousins. And most of the friends I had then I have now. Except for, let's see, when I was 10, I think I met a girl and her name was

H———, and also there was another friend named R———; and R———, I don't know, she just drifted away. R———, she's a nice person, but she's a gossip, because she knows everything about everybody else. She has a lot of older sisters and brothers and has a lot of influence on everybody. She's the fighting type. The reason why I drifted away from her is because of my sister. My sister can say some things about me that can get people to go away from me. But most of the things that she says are not that harmful. R——— was just one of the ones who was affected. And H———, well me and H——— still talk; but we're not the good friends we used to be because something happened around the block with a boy. She started this whole big argument with these boys. All these boys from the block up the hill would come down and meet the girls on my block and I felt bad. And my uncle stopped the fight and everything. It was hard for me to forgive her; but you have to forgive everybody.

You talked about some people you liked and some people you don't like so much anymore. What makes a good friend? Well, a good friend is somebody who cares for you; and you care for them. Somebody who trusts you, and likewise. And when they're down, you know, you try to bring their spirits up so that when they're happy, you're happy that they're happy. When they're successful, you're happy for them. And when they fail, you help them get over it. Someone who forgives you. Someone who, you know, really hooks into you. I guess they talk to you; they answer you; they're kind. I think many of my friends have wonderful personalities.

I also feel that, you know, just a few years ago, maybe a year or 2 ago, I met some people and they would say, "Oh I have very few friends; I have associates." I started to think about that because it was hard, you know, this was something totally new to me; I had never heard of it. *What did they mean?* They meant that there are people who are your friends, which are very few. And everybody says you have very few friends in this world. And they have people you just talk to, you know. I consider maybe an associate would be a person who you say hello and goodbye to. But there are other people who, you know, you really talk to; those are your friends. To me, now that they've said that, I look at all my relationships with other people and I've found out it is kind of true. Because I think that Carol and Millie are really my good friends. Other girls in my school I just say hello and goodbye to. And maybe there's two who stick out in all the rest. They're good friends. The rest are just hello and goodbye. Then the male friends I have—I consider all the boys on my block to be friends because they really watch out for me and everythingt. They care about me and call me and come over. And there are other boys I'd just say hello and goodbye to; you could call them associates. But "associates" is such a degrading word. If somebody calls me an associate, I feel as though they're saying you're less than a friend. You're like nobody, to me. So I'd rather say that they are friends. Because, I mean, you do talk to them and, you know, if they didn't care they wouldn't talk to you. *Sounds like you've been doing a lot of thinking about this.* Well, in a way I do.

How do you like school? To tell you the truth, I like school; school is OK. But the amount of work they give me, that makes me hate school. Last year I got an award for general excellence and this year I don't like high school because they give a lot of work. You look at the other schools and they give a diploma and they don't work as hard. So why should I? But then you have to look at what you're getting, in reality. You're getting an education which will last forever. While meanwhile they might not be learning anything and still get the diploma. And that would mean a harder life than you. So I don't look at it that way. In school I don't have that many friends, but I do talk to people. *You have sort of mixed feelings it sounds like about how much work it is.* Yeah, I think it's really the high school [I want, but] I don't know; it's still on my mind. I'm going back and forth [in my mind]. But I'm going to stay in this school because it's a very good school academically. But you know, people come in with stories. We get more tests than any school I've ever heard because we have a test every single day. I mean it's not like short little quizzes; there are tests on chapters which are 30 or 40 pages long, maybe 70. And you know, you have to really look at it. And to me it's an achievement;

it's a goal to get this diploma, because this is a challenge. *It sounds like it. What are the subjects that you enjoy most?* Well, my subjects which I enjoy most are—well, I might not enjoy studying for them because it takes a long time—but I enjoy chemistry, geometry; I like math, I love math—it's like a puzzle, you know, to figure it out. Spanish is ok; it's not one of my best subjects, but I do well in it, though. I really like Latin better than Spanish. Social studies, I do well in it. To me social studies is like a story and if you have all the facts, you put it together and make up a story; and religion, to me, for some reason I don't like religion. I mean I have faith and everything, but I don't understand why they test us on our faith. And sometimes the teachers mix me up. *Anything in particular that you find mixes you up?* Well, sometimes, you know, the fact that they're testing us on our faith really aggravates me. *What do you mean, testing you on your faith?* I mean they teach us things, you know, and it's things that we really already know. And I think all you learn in high school in religion is you love God and God is this, and you know it's not something you don't already know. And I really don't understand why they test us; I guess because it's a course, so you should be tested on it. But sometimes you put things down which are your own feelings and they mark it wrong. And that, in a way, brings your whole average down, so you pay for it.

When you think about the future, do you have any thoughts about what you'd like to be doing? Well, I'd like to go to college and then go to med school and become an anesthesiologist. *How come you chose that?* Oh, well, I wanted to become a doctor; but I think about doctors—my uncle's a doctor—and he really has a heavy schedule. And in a way I want to settle down, marry and have kids; but with a heavy schedule like he has—I mean, I look at him, and I say that could never be me. He leaves the house at 7 o'clock in the morning and gets home at 8:30 at night. I think an anesthesiologist, you have times, but they're not as strenuous as a doctor—where you have to go here, and here, and here. I really would like to become a doctor, but I mean if I could become an anesthesiologist, it's great—awesome. *How did you choose that? How did you*

choose anesthesiology? Oh, somebody told me about anesthesiologists and I had this thing for, you know, how you watch the monitors and everything else, and you put the IVs in, you know. Ok, my other uncle, he became an anesthesiologist; he said that it's not really different from being a doctor; it's like you're assisting a doctor, but you're really the one who's in control in the operating room because you're telling them exactly what's happening, and it's like being a doctor, to tell you the truth; it's just a different field. I guess you have to know just as much about everything that happens in the operating room like the doctor does. And I also like graphs and things like that. To me the human body is something else! You know, it's fascinating.

Any other careers that you've thought about? Oh, computer science, maybe chemistry—it's difficult, but I'm doing well in it. And lab technician. You know where I get that from? Quincy [on television]; I love that show. I just sit there and watch it. Computer science I don't think I'd be interested in because you're tapping buttons and it's boring to me. I don't know, I really haven't made up my mind yet. Probably will as a freshman in college, because there you'll know what you have to take and you'll go from there. *Where do you want to go to college?* Well, I want to go to Columbia, or a college in the city, or a college out of state. I don't want to go to a college in upstate New York. To me the towns there are so depressing and so deserted I don't think I could go back up there.

I was wondering about your family. You know, often teenagers feel their relationships change with their parents when they become teenagers; and other teenagers say no. Well, I don't really think so. Before, your mother was your mother; she told you what to do and you did it. If you didn't, then you got in trouble. Your mother would play with you and your father would play with you, things like that. But it's just, you know, they do the same thing— they talk to me, they play around sometimes. I have a good relationship with them. The only thing that I notice is that they get angry at stuff—they're the type of people who will take it out on you. So I'll just put in a little word there. *Like what?* Like, "Mommie, if you don't have anything nice to say, don't say anything at all." Because sometimes she comes home in a bad mood, or my dad, and they'll be angry. And I'll say, "If you're mad, I'll leave you alone." And that's it. You know, I say it in a very kind way. It seems as though everybody just gets to the point where they just do it. *Does it work when you say that?* Well, yes. Or I'll say, "Why are you being so mean today?" You know, it kind of brings them to their senses. It kinda tells them, you know, "Hey, why am I doing this; it is my job; it has nothing to do with her; why get mad?" *In some ways it sounds as if things sort of have changed. The way you started was to say that your mom is your mom and what she says goes; and now you're beginning to notice things about her more than you probably would have when you were 9 or 10.* Yeah, I do. I guess from looking at other people, the way they are.

Have their rules changed now that you've grown up a little? Yep. Well, I have a curfew—9 o'clock; in the summer it's 10. *What do you think about those hours?* Oh, it's good for a girl. What's a girl going to do all day long? That's basically it. The thing is, my parents—my dad works at night and my mom works in the day; and when summer comes, my mom works from 8 'til about 8 and my dad works at night. So I go to camp and stay there from about 8 to 5, so when I come home really there's nobody there. And when I used to come home from school there was always somebody there. But you know, things change. You know they're doing it for a good cause. You eventually see them when they get home. *But you don't see them as much as when you were younger?* Yeah, but I see them, you know. It's so neat! A lot of people say there's a generation gap and in a way there is because your parents, you know, sometimes they do things or they say things that they really don't understand. They forget how they felt when they were younger, when they were my age. I don't consider my parents old at all—or old-fashioned. Sometimes they do things or say things that they forgot they used to say when they were younger. *Can you give an example?* Uh, this is hard. Well, when you went out somewhere and you came in a little late and you say (like you're 5 minutes late and your

mother's yelling at you), "Don't you remember when you used to be late?" And they'll get angry after that. Sometimes me and my mother—I rarely have arguments with my father—sometimes me and my mother will have an argument and she'll really get angry. She doesn't understand because you feel . . . Oh, we'll play it a little bit different. You have an argument with your mother and like you just don't talk to her. Then when they start talking, you really don't feel like it; but then you finally get over it and say, "What am I doing? This is my mother." Sometimes I feel like my mom or my dad is acting like a kid because they don't talk to me. So, in a way, I realize that. I rarely have arguments with them, but on some occasions I do. I mean, I get over it real quick because there's always something I have to go and ask them, or something like that. And they always talk to me; and if they're still mad at me, I don't care, I'll still go and ask it. To me, we rarely have arguments, very rarely. That's just about it.

Do you find you have more things you wouldn't discuss with your mother now that you're getting older? Or are you just as open as you always were? I'm just as open as I always was. You know, things that happen outside, you know, my sister doesn't really want me to tell, and I'll tell my mom anyway and she'll get mad. *Something that might happen to your sister, you mean?* Something that just happened about 5 minutes ago—"Don't tell anybody." I mean, I might not tell her if they say, "Really, don't tell her." But I mean if it's something that happens out on the street and you know, and it's nothing major to me, as far as I'm concerned, but um, a lot of times, see my sister doesn't trust me because we had a little—we went up to this lady's house where my sister was babysitting just to see the New Year's fireworks. So, you know, there was nothing to it; it was just me, her, and this other girl and we went up there. Then when this lady came back—I'm sure she wouldn't mind, or we wouldn't have gone up there—but when the lady came back, this girl who lives across the hall from me said, "We had a nice party up at your house." And it really wasn't a party; and so my sister kind of blamed me for saying it, and I didn't even say it. So she tries to blame it on me, but I don't pay any attention to her. I get to the point where I say, "Hush up" (laughs). If the other person wasn't my sister, I would never talk like that. I get to the point where I say to myself, "I'm never going to talk to her again." It's not really anger; I never really get angry at anybody—I get irritated. Anger has its place when you're going crazy. *It sounds like some times you do get sort of mad at her.* I get mad, angry, uh at the upmost. *You don't like being angry?* No; I don't even like getting mad. How come? Because I like to be happy all the time. You know, I don't like to get angry because if somebody says the wrong thing to me I feel as though I might snap back at them. And I don't want to do that.

I want to ask you about something a little different which is just in terms of growing up physically, you know, and going through the changes that girls do in adolescence, where did you learn about that? Well (laughs), in a way that's a hard question. Where did I learn about that? Well, when we were younger me and my sister used to jump around and play. My grandmother and mother (laughs) came in; I guess we learned from that. And I learned from my mother. And then sometimes when you go outside and you hear about these people—they say some of the most disgusting things—and I guess you learn kinda from that. You learn from every place, you know. "Say, you're growing so big!" (laughs). *Who says that?* You know, your aunts and your uncles. And, "You're growing so tall!" "Growing to a woman." OK, all right, enough of that! In a way I don't want to grow up (laughs). *How come? It's a feeling that a lot of people have.* I was thinking recently—when you grow up, you know, you start becoming more conscious of yourself, your hair, and your face, and your weight; oh gosh. That's me. I'm overweight and I have to lose about 20 pounds. And it hurts. When I was a kid I didn't care about those things. I wouldn't even have to look in a mirror at myself, because my mother would do my hair. But now every morning I have to look at myself for a half an hour. *So you are more self-conscious in some ways because you have to take care of yourself; you have to look at yourself in the mirror.* It's really because of peers I guess—

because if you go out and you don't look right, there's somebody who is going to say something. And in a way I don't like examining myself in a mirror really close. There's always a girl or a couple of girls who give you looks. It really makes you want to go and hide. *They sort of look mean?* Yeah; I told my dad about it. He said, "They're just jealous!" I said, "Of what?" And he said, "Don't worry about it." So I've gotten to a point where I don't care; but I do notice it.

When you hear things on the street like you were saying, you hear things about sex or about developing, whatever, and they are really gross to you, would you feel comfortable in talking to your mother about it and telling her what you heard? Or is that stuff you really need to keep to yourself? To me it really doesn't last in my mind. I just know that I heard it, and it's nothing to go home and tell your mother about. If I heard anything about those things, you know, it's just a part of life; you hear it all the time—you hear it in jokes; you hear it on TV. To me it's just something that's there; it doesn't have to be; I'll forget about it. There are a lot of boys these days, and girls, and to me it's kind of surprising because they have sex, you know, a lot, and they're all in their teen years. They may even be 10. And it's surprising me you know, like "ha, ha, ha" they say. I don't know. It just seems that girls who haven't done anything, they're looked down on because they don't have experience. And if you don't have experience in this and that, it leads to other things. *What do you do about that?* To me it's . . . it doesn't bother me. When they start talking about inexperience—your first boyfriend starts saying all this stuff about inexperience, you know—I'll tell you no boy is ever going to push me, you know. There's a time when you have to say "No," you know. And I feel as though too many teenagers don't know how to say no. And I guess it's because of what's being exposed on TV and all this. It does make me feel out of place, because it's like you can tell. And you know that you're surrounded by all these people that are so experienced. If you go to a party or something, I don't know, I'll talk to them and everything but, it's just like this is not your crowd. I guess it's not hard; you don't even have to think about it. Me, I hardly ever think about it, unless somebody will say a joke about it. It doesn't bother me that much. *It sounds as if you have some pretty strong values and sometimes it makes you a little uncomfortable because you feel different from other people, but basically you just sort of go home.* Well, I have some friends and they go down South every year and they'll come back saying, "Oh the girls down South are the best." And I think, "That's really degrading to yourself, you know." They say they can get the prettiest girls down South; you know, that doesn't really make you feel good at all. It really kind of makes you feel bad. But you have to do what you have to.

Do you have thoughts about when you'd like to get married? Would you wait until after you finished college? Yes, uh huh. I guess between 22 and 28 (laughs). I don't know; I'm not giving a limit on this because you know if anybody who I really loved had asked me to marry him and he loved me, I guess I'd get married at 22. But not before because you're not really financially secure in college because you're just getting by yourself; so you have to be economically secure, you know, in order to get married.

You've just told me a lot of things; you're very articulate, which is a real pleasure. I'm wondering if there are other things that you think we should know. Here's this man writing a book about teenagers, and what do you think? I think, well, have you ever heard anybody say that people down South are friendlier than people up in New York? *I don't know. Sometimes I heard that they say that New York people aren't so friendly, but what are you thinking about?* Well, in a way I feel it's true because somebody told me about down South and they said that they really don't say anything bad about you down there. But here, if you're walking along a street, a person will make a snap at you for no reason. You know, it's anybody. That's what I find so bad about the subways because watching people do that to you, I mean, the main words around here— "dog" and this and that—it's terrible; and it can really degrade a person. And I feel that a lot of people, a lot of teenagers, are inconsiderate of each other because they just say all their friends are dogs; and it's really not good because they don't know—

and, I mean, they could say it to the person's face. But they don't care. And that's something that really strikes me as unusual because those are some pretty harsh words to be saying to a person. I mean, people shouldn't even be able to say that; they shouldn't even say anything like that. You know, they're not kind, you know. And I think it's everywhere; it's not just New York. And some people I think aren't ever affected; but those that are, you know, it really affects them. And they don't know how much damage they've done because I found out that if I got angry—I hate that word—if I got irritated, whatever it is, I'll say something. It won't click in my mind then what I said; but then after a while, "Oh gosh, I said this to this person; he'll really feel bad about it." And I don't think teenagers are too considerate of each other. *I'm wondering if maybe part of why you don't like to get angry is because you know that it hurts when people say mean things to you?* Yeah. 'Cause I tried to break up a fight between two boys and I was called something I don't like to repeat; so I didn't take it. And other experiences, you know. I've seen people get yelled at if another person was angry. You can see it on the person by the expression on their face; so that's just what I really think, yeah.

Teenage life really isn't that hard. It's not really that different from being a kid. When you were a kid you used to say things to other people that would hurt them. You did have some responsibilities—you had to carry your book bag home; you had to do your homework, you know, being a kid. I think it's all the same; it all levels out. You get into a role. Your mind begins to reason better. I guess when you reach adulthood, you might look back to your teenage years and say, "Oh how stupid I was to do that, or to think that," because you realize things about yourself and about others.

To me you can't really know about a person until you start talking to them. You can't really like or dislike them. You can just know a person to say hello and goodbye, but you can't really like them or dislike them because you really don't know who they are. You have to speak to a person before you can judge them. I think that also teenagers are harsh in their judgments. *Why do you think teenagers are harsh?* Because a lot of the things they say, you know. They'll say, "Oh, that's the prettiest girl"; and they'll see a male model and they'll say, "Oh, that's the handsomest boy." And people will be standing right there and that will hurt them maybe. There are other instances where they'll just go along, on the streets they call it "staffing"; and they'll be staffing on other people. *That means saying a mean thing?* Yeah. They'll be staffing on people and saying things about their mother and this and that and they'll say things about how they look. It's really hard to feel about it because you have to learn, because you'll have that all of your life. I mean people are harsh on other people because of their judgments, because they don't really look at what they have. And like we were just studying this book in school; it's called "Art." The main theme of the play is that you never really are a hundred percent perfect; and it's the truth. And also, we don't recognize what we have until we've lost it, some people; you know, like teenagers don't. Some have friends and they'll get into arguments over little things and never talk to them again. There are other people who will hold grudges against other people because they said this; and it's really a harsh thing, you know. It's hard to deal with. And I think that if you get into an argument over, you know, oh she's trying to become my friend, or she's trying to take one of my friends—they're friends, they're not leaving you. So, they won't ever talk to the other person (laughs). So you say I'm never going to have all these problems, but then you get to a point where you do have some of them. Or you say, "I'm never going to go through all those phases" and you see everybody else going through them.

A lot of people say public schools are bad, this and that; private schools are fun. No matter where you go, they always say something against the school. If you go to a private school, you're a snob; if you go to a Catholic school, you're stuck up. If you go to a public school, you're dumb. It's not true. Everybody is stereotyped. To me there's nothing wrong with going to any school. I feel you should go to a school where you're going to get an education. Wherever you go, if you listen in class, you will eventually get educated in some way or another. If people choose to do other things, if a person chooses to get pregnant, something like that, or they choose to make that move, I guess that's their choice. Teenagers all over have different choices. Sometimes they get mixed up. Sometimes they can't find the right move. I don't know. I've never been put in a situation like that. I know some people who have gotten pregnant. But they were older, you know, they were like 19 or 20. That was their decision.

I'll tell you, I don't know about abortion. My feelings are mixed on abortion. Because if you can have the child and support the child, then go ahead. If you can try to give the best to the child that you're going to have, you might as well have it. But there comes a point in your life where you're not able to, you know, raise the child correctly because you're too young yourself. So I really don't know about abortion. (laughs) I'll never think about it, you know. After you get in your 20s, then I feel that abortion is totally out. As for people who get pregnant, and they say that the baby's going to, you know, have water on the brain or something like that, that's kind of hard for me to think about too because if the child is going to grow up being unhappy because, as you know, children will feel the slightest defect—the first thing they'll notice is that defect—and they're asked about it, and that can make a child very sad. If it's not going to make the child happy and it's not going to make you happy because you're going to be struggling, then I guess you should; I'm not sure. I'm confused on that myself.

But my cousin, she was 6 years old when she recently died and that kind of struck me hard because nobody in my family had really died, you know, close to me. And she died because she had a disease. So it was kind of hard for me to think about death. Then I thought about teenagers committing suicide. All of these other people committing suicide. And I was thinking, well, why did she have to? People don't know how precious life is. No matter how hard things get, there's always a good time in our life. That's why I could never imagine myself committing suicide, because there's always something to enjoy in life. *What do you think about those teenagers that are in the papers, you know, there was a guy who seemed to be very successful and then committed suicide?* Well, in a way you just think they just had a lot of problems and they really didn't look at anything good in their life. They didn't look back on the good times that they had and about the future and what it held. When my cousin died, I was thinking about why couldn't she have taken one of their lives and they just have died, because I was really upset. I just didn't understand why a little girl should go through so much pain. You know, you think about things like that—a little girl dying in your family as a storybook tale; you never think it is going to come true. But when it does, you can really feel what those people in the stories felt. As for the people who do commit suicide, I guess it's because of their problems and because of pressures put on them by society. Society does put a lot of pressure on people. Everything is worse because of people. But then again, if you didn't have people, you'd be lonely.

I guess you can win. You can win by having friends. If you are happy with your friends, you'll survive. But if people don't have any—because where they go they don't have any friends, this and that—that might be a reason for committing suicide. Other people may think they're too fat, that's why they commit suicide. Other people may think that their life is going down the drain. They have to look at what they have. I guess if they really, really look at what they have—it might be a puppy or a bird, or something—if they look at what they have, they'll see, you know, a little light in things. People make life what it is. They have to make life what they want it to be.

Chapter 9

◆

Sex, Sexuality, and Romance

———— ◆ ————

Human sexuality involves the mind as well as the body. It reflects biological maturation, cognitive development, social learning, the peer group, and the family. It is neither an automatic physical reaction, nor the simple result of experience. Sexuality is unique for each individual. It is important to persons of all ages. It does not emerge for the first time at puberty; nor does it end when grandchildren are born.

This chapter explores the unfolding sexuality of adolescence. It focuses on the process of defining the meaning of one's own sexuality and integrating sexuality into relationships with other people. These are not simple processes, especially in a society that conveys many contradictory messages about sex. Often adolescents do not have someone they can talk with about their sexual feelings and questions about sex. Sometimes adults, and even other adolescents, become anxious or upset when sex is discussed openly. However, these important human feelings need to be explored and the questions answered frankly and honestly.

Much of what is known about human sexuality is the result of relatively recent research. Nonetheless, many myths and misconceptions about female and male sexuality continue to exist. Therefore, the goal of this chapter is to report the most relevant aspects of this research for the understanding of adolescent sexuality. We begin with a discussion of the development of sexuality, emphasizing prenatal influences, childhood experiences, and adolescent sexuality. The next section deals with questions and concerns adolescents often have about sexuality, especially masturbation, and issues in heterosexual relationships. The next topic is sexual orientation and homosexuality. Then we consider the interaction of sexual lust, romance, and intimate love. The final section focuses on some of the implications of sexual interaction during adolescence: contraceptive use, pregnancy, and sexually transmitted diseases including infection with HIV and the development of AIDS.

DEVELOPMENT OF HUMAN SEXUALITY

The origins of human sexuality begin before birth. In Chapter 3 we noted that the difference between males and females at birth results from the prenatal effects of a few strategically timed biochemicals, including androgens and MIS. If these substances are present, a male is produced; if they are not present, a female is produced. Several variations, some of which result in mixed or ambiguous sexual organs, or mismatches between the sexual organs and hormonal or chromosomal sex, were also discussed. In the next sections, we focus on psychosocial influences on the development of sexuality, but recognize the potentially important effects of prenatal and other physiological influences. We begin with a discussion of the general topic of gender identity and gender roles. Next, we note that each individual's sexuality is the unique result of the interaction of several factors including physiological influences, psychosocial experiences, learning, and the cognitive integration the person forms of his or her sexual and erotic fantasies, thoughts, and feelings. We conclude this section with a discussion of adolescents' attitudes about sexuality.

GENDER IS MORE THAN APPEARANCE

Most infants are born with genitals that can be readily identified as male or female. From the moment that the gender of the infant is revealed, complex social processes begin teaching the meaning of femaleness and maleness in the individual's particular society, social class, and family. Thus children learn that they are boys or girls and what behaviors are expected of them as boys or girls. It may begin simply with blue or pink blankets, but before long it involves a lengthy list of things that boys or girls should and should not do. Although some families may try to minimize the differences between their female and male children, school teachers, grandparents, other adults, books, the mass media, and other children also teach the children what boys and girls should and should not do. As a result, clothing, styles of grooming, types of games, and even the expression of emotions (boys do not cry; girls do not fight) differ between the sexes. This process is known as **gender-role socialization**; it involves teaching the behaviors that make up the gender roles associated with being a male or female.

Gender roles are not the same in every society. Margaret Mead (1949), in her classic study, *Male and Female*, described the variety of gender roles in different cultures.

> In every known society, mankind has elaborated the biological division of labour into forms often very remotely related to the original biological differences that provided the original cues. Upon the contrast in bodily form and function, men have built analogies between sun and moon, night and day, goodness and evil, strength and tenderness, steadfastness and fickleness, endurance and vulnerability. Sometimes one quality has been assigned to one sex, sometimes to the other. Now it is boys who are thought of as infinitely vulnerable and in need of special cherishing care, now it is girls. In some societies it is girls for whom parents must collect a dowry or make husband-catching magic, in others the parental worry is over the difficulty of marrying off the boys. Some peoples think of women as too weak to work out of doors, others regard women as the appropriate bearers of heavy burdens, "because their heads are stronger than men's." The periodicities of female reproductive functions have appealed to some peoples as making women the natural sources of magical or religious power, to others as directly antithetical to those powers; some religions, including our European traditional religions, have assigned women an inferior role in the religious hierarchy, others have built their whole symbolic relationship with the supernatural world upon male imitations of the natural functions of women. In some cultures women are regarded as sieves through whom the best-guarded secrets will sift; in others it is the men who are the gossips. Whether we deal with small matters or with large, with the frivolities of ornament and cosmetics or the sanctities of man's place in the universe, we find this great variety of ways, often flatly contradictory one to the other, in which the roles of the two sexes have been patterned. [pp. 7–8]

All children learn the gender roles of their society and attempt to relate these roles to their own behavior and their own identity. One part of this process involves identifying with and imitating other persons of one's own gender—such as the mother, sisters, aunts, and female teachers by girls (and parallel male figures for boys). A second part of this process involves being told how to behave and what to do and what not to do because one is a boy or a girl, by parents, playmates, and others. This requires learning about the gender role of the other gender, so that one knows what behavior should be avoided and how one's behavior should complement the behavior of the other gender. A third part involves the child's attempts to learn, internalize, and make sense of this information. Thus, the child's *cognition* plays an important role in this process of learning gender roles (Kohlberg, 1966).

Gender roles are deeply involved in sexual feelings and behavior. For example, in a study of 304 never-married midwestern undergraduate students, males were more likely to have their first sexual intercourse experience in a relatively casual relationship, but females were more likely to experience intercourse for the first time in a close relationship (i.e., steady partner, lover, or fiance); females were also more likely to have sexual intercourse again with

Gender roles are not the same in every society.

the first partner than were males (Darling, Davidson, & Passarello, 1992). Similarly, Pleck, Sonenstein, and Ku (1993), in a study based on a national survey of adolescent males, noted that males who hold traditional gender-role attitudes differ from those who do not.

> Males with traditional attitudes have more sexual partners, use condoms less, and have less favorable attitudes toward condoms. They disagree that males have a responsibility to prevent pregnancy, and are more likely to believe that making a partner pregnant validates their own masculinity. The greater frequency of sexual partners, the lower usage of condoms, and the contraceptive beliefs associated with traditional attitudes toward masculinity increase adolescent males' risks of unintended pregnancy, AIDS, and other sexually transmitted diseases. [Pleck, Sonenstein, & Ku, 1993, p. 26]

Examples of traditional attitudes can be found in statements such as: "it is essential for a guy to get respect from others"; "I admire a guy who is totally sure of himself"; "it bothers me when a guy acts like a girl"; "men are always ready for sex."

The link between gender roles and sexual behaviors and attitudes varies across dif-ferent cultures. What is normal in one culture is atypical or even abnormal in another. For example:

> A strong double standard exists concerning the sexual activities of Hispanic boys and girls. From a very early age, Hispanic girls are taught that female ignorance about sex is equated with purity and innocence. Sexual maturation, sexual intercourse, and the risks of pregnancy are infrequently discussed between Hispanic mothers and their daughters; in contrast, Hispanic boys may be encouraged by male family members to experiment with heterosexual relations soon after they reach puberty. . . .
>
> Gender inequality in sexual relationships is exacerbated by the frequent age differences between Hispanic partners. It is not uncommon for female adolescents as young as 13 or 14 to go out with men who are 5, 10, or even 15 years older than they. When such dramatic age differences exist, it is unrealistic to expect the young woman to "just say no" or to imagine that educational sessions promoting strategies for delaying sexual activity can succeed. [Fennelly, 1993, pp. 347–348]

To take another example, Hatano (1993) reported that Japanese adolescents follow a developmental pattern lasting 4 years on the average from sexual curiosity to dating; 2 more years pass before the first kiss; first intercourse follows 1 year later at age 20 or 21 (Table 9.1). Similarly, Asian-American adolescents are less sexually active than non-Asian peers. In a study by Chan (1993), Asian-American girls avoided and minimized expressions of sexuality in physical appearance, preferred to associate with boys when in a group, and limited physical contact to holding hands or kissing. Boys felt an expectation that they would not experience sex unless they were married or "very seriously involved." Violation of these family expectations would bring punishment, and the shame and disappointment of the family members would be internalized. First- and second-generation immigrants would particularly feel a burden of meeting their parents' expectations because of the parent's sacrifice in immigrating to this country. As noted in Chapter 6, adolescents who are growing up in two cultures often face strong conflicting demands from their parent's culture and from the culture of their peers.

A contrasting cultural attitude was shown in a study of 200 middle-class, African-American adolescent men, 11–19 years old, living in an inner city (Jemmott & Jemmott, 1990). The average age at first sexual intercourse was 11.1 years, and virtually all of the

Table 9.1 AGE OF FIRST EXPERIENCES OF SELECTED EVENTS BY MEDIAN
PERSON IN A STUDY OF SEXUAL ACTIVITIES OF JAPANESE YOUTH

Age (years)	Male	Female
< 11		Menstruation
12		Desire to approach opposite sex
13	Ejaculation	Sexual curiosity
	Desire to approach opposite sex	
	Sexual curiosity	
14	Masturbation	
	Desire to touch opposite sex	
	Sexual arousal	
15	Desire to kiss	
16		Dating
17	Dating	Desire to kiss
18	Touching opposite sex	
19	Kissing	Sexual arousal
		Kissing
20	Petting	Desire to touch opposite sex
	Intercourse	
21		Touching opposite sex
		Petting
		Intercourse

Source: Y. Hatano. (1993). Sexual activities of Japanese youth. *Journal of Sex Education and Therapy, 19.* Table 1, p. 135. © 1988 The Japanese Association for Sex Education. Reprinted with permission.

adolescents reported that they had engaged in intercourse; 94% reported having intercourse within the last year before the study. Nonetheless, 50% reported that they felt "young people should not have sex before getting married."

Herdt (1990) identified three patterns of sexual development that may be recognized in different societies. (1) In *linear development*, there is a continuous unfolding of sexual behavior from early childhood through adolescence to adulthood where, for example, heterosexual contact is permitted for children and expected for adults. (2) In *sequential development*, there is a dramatic change between behavior that is allowed children and adults; for example, children may be regarded as sexless, but at some point in adolescence or adulthood they are expected to become sexually active. (3) In *emergent development*, changing values within a society preclude predicting the outcome of a child's emerging sexuality and allow a range of possibilities for an adult's sexual expression; this pattern is found in rapidly changing societies such as the United States since the 1960s and some developing countries around the world.

SEXUALITY DOES NOT BEGIN IN ADOLESCENCE

As a result of earlier cultural beliefs in the United States, based on a sequential model of sexual development, there are still many myths about sexuality during childhood. For example, a widely accepted but incorrect idea is that sexuality emerges at adolescence and is wholly absent during childhood. This belief may be responsible for some of the peculiar ideas that are associated with adolescence, such as the notion that puberty marks the end of innocence and the beginning of strong sexual urges that need to be controlled. In fact, research has found that children have a wide range of sexual feelings, thoughts, and experiences (Calderone, 1983). Boys experience erection of the penis and girls experience lubrication of the vagina. It is not unusual for a boy or girl to discover the pleasure of stimulating the genitals using hands, bedding, clothing, stuffed toys, stairway banisters, table legs, and so on. Of course, before puberty, the boy's penis does not ejaculate (just as girls do not ovulate or menstruate). However, both boys and girls can experience the sensation of orgasm. Social taboos about studying children's sexual behavior have prevented researchers from analyzing this phenomenon carefully.

Children are also very curious about the similarities and differences between their bodies and those of others, both boys and girls. Some invent games such as "doctor" or "nurse" as a sort of script to examine one another's bodies. Others simply look, touch, and experiment in as many ways as they can imagine. Usually the exploration involves neighbors, friends, or relatives of about the same age. Children learn very early that sex is a big secret in our culture. Like other secrets, it can be shared with people about one's own age, but not with adults (Money, 1980, p. 45).

These consensual peer experiences are very different from sexual experiences that are coerced by adults, often family members who are older. Such experiences are usually traumatic, involving rape or other unwilling sexual contact, and can be quite harmful to the developing sexuality of the child or young adolescent. Kilpatrick (1992) contrasted the effects of consensual sexual contact with abuse in a study of 501 women. She found that 83% of the women with sexual experiences as children (including kissing and hugging) and 85% of the women with sexual experiences as adolescents reported that the experience was not abusive (p. 97). The majority of respondents reported positive reactions to experiences in which they voluntarily participated (p. 111). However, experiences that were forced or abusive did have significant negative effects on several measures of adult functioning (p. 114).

Adults sometimes become upset when they discover children exploring their bodies, either in masturbation or mutual sex play; this reaction can teach the children that sex makes others anxious, and they may learn to associate anxiety, fear, or anger with sex. Adults also may become upset when their children discover adults having sex. Peculiar things can happen at these moments. The child can become ashamed or feel guilty. Anxiety may momentarily paralyze the child (and the adult). The child might think that the parents are fighting. The adults may feel ashamed or guilty (perhaps remembering their own parents' reactions). This point about being caught and made anxious is important to stress because it can be one of the influences that helps to set the sexual stimuli and sexual fears that are exciting or inhibiting later in life.

It is impossible, however, to predict which childhood experiences will or will not be carried on into later sexuality, or how important they will be. For example, one's preferences for a specific skin, hair, or eye color, male facial hair, shape of female breasts, or male buttocks each may reflect experiences or persons from one's childhood. Likewise, a child who is sexually stimulated by receiving a spanking, seeing someone urinate, being tied up in a game, or while wrestling may find these activities sexually exciting in adulthood. Similar situations might be fascinating precisely because they are forbidden, secret, and taboo. Even if the behavior does not recur, it may be left in memory and resurface in sexual fantasy.

Thus, the gradual discovery of one's own sexual "turn-ons" during adolescence or adulthood frequently reflect childhood experiences (Money, 1980, pp. 37, 152).

All of these sexual experiences of childhood must be interpreted through the framework of the child's level of cognitive development. Thus, young children may think that a penis can grow just as breasts can grow, or that a penis can be lost just as teeth are lost (Money, 1980, p. 46). It is not uncommon for children to think that one can become pregnant by kissing, or have other illogical ideas about sexuality, even if they have been told basic sexual information. Therefore, sex education, and the child's understanding of sexual experiences, should be seen in terms of the cognitive level on which the child is thinking (see Chapter 4).

Thus, throughout childhood, children learn about sex and sexuality in a variety of ways. This learning usually takes place in the absence of adequate factual information, and with considerable emphasis on secrecy. If the sexual feelings or behaviors become known to adults, the adult response is often anxiety, denial, or invalidation, and so the young person may also become anxious, perhaps even upset or frightened. The message can be that the feeling or behavior should be ignored or avoided and it will go away. In addition, the response may be that the child, or the feeling, is wrong, unimportant, immature, or all of the above. In short, the adult's response may be confusing and difficult for the child to interpret. These feelings can become internalized by the child and are associated with sexuality. The result is that sexuality may be interpreted by the child as confusing, dirty, upsetting, unimportant, and best kept secret. Potentially serious misunderstandings about one's own and others' sexuality can be produced in this way.

Children also fall in love, sometimes with each other, occasionally with older persons and adults, and often with television, movie or music stars, and other celebrities. As in all aspects of childhood sexuality, these experiences have not been studied systematically. In fact, adults tend to minimize their importance by calling them "puppy-love," "crushes," "infatuations," and "hero worship." However, Money (1980) pointed out that these experiences can be very important, not only for the young persons at the time, but also for their later development. These intense emotional relationships may become eroticized (whether or not they involve explicit sexuality) and involve strong romantic feelings as well as expressions of affection. In some cases, so-called puppy love continues on through adolescence into a satisfying adult marriage. In other cases, so-called hero worship provides an environment for learning from the teacher, mentor, or friend, who may or may not be older than the other person involved.

In summary, multiple prenatal and childhood influences on adolescent sexuality are activated by the hormonal changes of puberty. The result is that "the profile of one's erotic turn-on imagery is as personally idiosyncratic as one's signature, one's face, or finger prints" (Money, 1980, p. 37).

ADOLESCENT SEXUALITY

Sexual feelings increase in intensity after puberty, reflecting the greater amount of sex hormones circulating in the body for both females and males (Udry, Billy, Morris, Groff, & Raj, 1985; Udry, Talbert, & Morris, 1986). Masturbation, sexual dreams and fantasies, daydreams, and tentative explorations of sexual behavior with others are typical. Romantic fantasies, feelings of falling in love, writing poetry, feeling uncomfortable or attracted by love scenes in movies, and wanting to be near sexually attractive persons are usual. Sometimes romantic stories or movies bring particular feelings of excitement that are essentially sexual. Sometimes photographs of near-naked models, whether in sexually oriented magazines or in television commercials, can be stimulating. Any of these activities may be private and secret; they may involve a close friend, or a group in a public setting such as a rock music concert. They can involve feelings of guilt, embarrassment, and shame; they can also include feelings of excitement, fascination, curiosity, and pleasure. If the activity involves others, it can bring feelings of support and mutual acceptance. Thus, adolescent sexual behavior clearly reflects both biological and social components as well as their interaction (Smith, 1989; Miller & Fox, 1987).

Drawing on their unique childhood experiences of sexuality, adolescents gradually begin to discover their own particular sexual interests. They also learn the sexual "scripts" that are shown to them by their immediate social environment (Gagnon, 1973). These include previous experiences in similar situations, fantasies and expectations, and stories from friends and in the popular media. The task of integrating one's own sexual feelings, moral values, and these sexual scripts into a reasonably coherent set of personal sexual beliefs and behavior is the primary struggle of adolescent sexuality. This task becomes more complicated because sexuality is linked with a wide range of nonsexual behavior and beliefs in our society (Marsiglio, 1988). Thus, the idea that "real men" are strong, do not show emotion, and are aggressive can be mixed up with male sexuality (Pleck et al., 1993). Similarly, the idea that "real women" are passive, emotional, and attractive can be mixed up with female sexuality. All kinds of peculiar ideas about male and female relations can result from these gender-role stereotypes.

> On the one hand, we are disposed by both our biological heritage and our past cultural heritage to be attracted to the same gender role stereotyped traits and characteristics that our ancestors found attractive in members of the opposite sex. On the other hand, to the extent that we embrace contemporary ideals of gender equality, we are likely to react negatively to the asymmetrical power relations and miscommunications that result when men view the world through the lens of power and status and women view the world through the lens of closeness and solidarity. When the issue is one of physical and sexual attraction, we are ruled by instincts that have their roots deep in the past. However, when the issue is one of trying to establish a nonexploitive, equal-partner relationship, we find these old instincts troublesome and aspire to be ruled by our ideals instead. [Ickes, 1993, pp. 82–83]

Obviously, the interaction of gender-role stereotypes, sexual scripts in our changing society, and the individual's own sexual interests produces a thicket of difficult issues for today's adolescent. Often the stereotypes conflict with the scripts: men should be both aggressive and affectionate, strong and tender; women should be both passive and assertive, emotional and strong. Frequently the stereotypes and scripts conflict with the individual's own sexual feelings. Moreover, one's own sexual feelings may conflict with one's emotional needs for a sense of security, acceptance, and understanding.

First dates, a night at the prom, moonlit walks, parking on the way home all involve settings where these conflicting stereotypes, scripts, and feelings are keenly experienced. This is especially true for adolescents whose sexual feelings are not easily integrated with social scripts and stereotypes. An adolescent who is very uncomfortable about sexual feelings may find these situations to be quite painful. An adolescent who feels sexual attraction to someone of the same gender would find these heterosexual scripts to be very alienating. One who is considered unattractive, or not stereotypically masculine or feminine, may feel ostracized from these socially prescribed rituals. Yet, there is considerable social pressure to fit into these scripts or risk being thought to be abnormal.

Adolescent sexuality emerges as a result of these adolescent experiences, which are built upon childhood experiences, and also reflect the influences of prenatal hormones and other varied factors. The pattern of adolescent sexuality is unique; no two persons have exactly the same sexual feelings and interests. Thus, there is no way of guessing the unique sexuality of another person, particularly because it is influenced by so many factors and is often complicated by stereotypes about gender roles and sexual scripts.

ADOLESCENTS' ATTITUDES ABOUT SEXUALITY

Sexual attitudes reflect the social context in which adolescents live. They vary between geographic regions of the United States, as well as between urban and nonurban areas.

> For instance whites who attend church tend to have more conservative sexual attitudes than whites who do not attend church; however, a similar association between sexual conservatism and religiosity does not hold for blacks. . . . Regional differences within the United States, as another example, confuse sex and racial differences in attitudes. In general men have more permissive attitudes than women and blacks tend to have more permissive attitudes than whites; however, . . . white men in New York were more permissive than black men in Virginia. . . . Another complication involves the fact that many factors which traditionally showed a strong relationship with sexual attitudes appear to be becoming less pronounced in recent years. . . . Men are not much more permissive than women today, and better-educated people now tend to have the same attitudes as people without advanced educations. [Dreyer, 1982, p. 567]

A national survey of adolescent attitudes about sexuality was conducted by telephone in 1987 when the respondents were 17–23 years old. The sample was selected to be representative of the United States population; they had been contacted in person in 1976, and a subsample was contacted in 1981 (Moore & Stief, 1991). In this third interview the respondents reported the following:

1. Two out of three females aged 18 had experienced sexual intercourse, as had one of four aged 17. By age 17, a majority of males had experienced sexual intercourse.

2. Eighty-seven percent felt that sex was wrong for those aged 14–15, and 52% felt that sex was wrong for those aged 16–17 (p. 365).

3. One out of ten white females, one out of four African-American females, one out of three white males, and one out of two African-American males felt their friends encouraged them to have sex.

4. Six out of ten females felt their mothers discouraged them about sex; about one-third of males felt their mothers discouraged them about sex (p. 367).

5. Eighty-five percent of the white females and 30% of the African-American females stated that they "want to wait until I'm married"; 53% of white males and 26% of African-American males felt that way (p. 368).

6. "Practical, nonmoral reasons also motivate youths, particularly whites, to postpone sex. Concern about pregnancy and catching a disease are important reasons for avoiding sex,

as are more opportunistic factors, such as not having found the right person or not having found an opportunity" (p. 368).

7. Respondents were very negative about pregnancy and abortion during adolescence (pp. 370–371).

Most of the adolescents in the study said they planned to marry during their 20s, but over half endorsed the idea of living together before marriage. Because many had experienced growing up in a divorced family, they had very negative attitudes about divorce and wished to avoid entering a marriage that might end; likewise, they had a strong preference for two-parent families and believed that emotional problems develop when parents divorce.

> In sum, data on the attitudes and values of contemporary youth do not support those who predict the demise of the family. In fact, they suggest considerable concern among young adults about the issues that older adults define as problems, such as adolescent pregnancy and divorce. As policymakers wrestle with developing approaches to the social problems associated with early sexual activity, pregnancy, abortion, and family disruption, they might do well to consider the attitudes and values of those who are the objects of their efforts. [Moore & Stief, 1991, p. 385]

Brooks-Gunn and Furstenberg (1990) pointed out the mixed messages about sexuality in our culture. Popular media emphasize sexual images, frequently unmarried characters who focus on issues of sexuality. There are few references to birth control on television, however. Sexuality is shown as dangerous, especially for girls, who are often portrayed as victims of sexual encounters who have limited power in sexual negotiations. Males and females are viewed as antagonists, with danger and desire coexisting as girls seek to maintain male relationships (pp. 66–67). In real life, however, adolescents (especially girls) are not encouraged to talk about sexual desire. Boys also do not usually discuss the physical changes of puberty or their first ejaculation. Girls seldom talk about masturbation, although about one-third are estimated to have done it by midadolescence (pp. 62–63). Thus, adolescents are likely to have a variety of questions and concerns about sexuality they dare not ask about.

QUESTIONS AND CONCERNS ABOUT SEXUALITY

Sex education is more prevalent in schools than it was in the past, especially as a result of the need for sexual information to reduce the risk of becoming infected with **human immunodeficiency virus** (HIV) associated with **acquired immune deficiency syndrome** (AIDS), which is a serious disease of the immune system that is transmitted from an infected person through specific bodily fluids (blood, breast milk, or semen; we discuss this disease in more detail in the last section of this chapter).

However, many adolescents continue to learn much of their information about sexuality from friends. In a study of 288 adolescents from five public schools including urban and rural communities and different ethnic groups, 44% indicated they received "a lot" of information from friends, compared with 36% from school and 26% from parents. Relatively little information was obtained from the church or from personal doctors and nurses (Davis & Harris, 1982). In a more recent study, Moran and Corely (1991) found that friends were a

Sex education is more prevalent in schools today than it was in the past.

source of information for over half of the respondents, but sex education was also important for over half of the Anglo and Hispanic males age 15–17. Learning about sexuality in a sex education class was related to reported condom use among those males who were sexually active (71% of those who used condoms vs. 21% of those who did not learned about sexuality in sex education classes).

Lack of sexual education is widespread in some groups, however. For example, one study found that urban and minority male adolescents were less well informed than suburban and white males about HIV/AIDS transmission and their risk of being infected (Bell, Feraios, & Bryan, 1990). Likewise, a study of 212 adolescents involved with the juvenile justice system found that, because of a lack of information, they were at high risk for sexually transmitted diseases, HIV/AIDS, and unintended pregnancy (Melchert & Burnett, 1990). Similarly, a study of middle-class, inner-city, African-American adolescent men found that their average score on a sexual knowledge test was only 62% correct, and several significant gaps of information existed:

For instance, 17% believed that a girl could not get pregnant the first time she has sex, 65.5% did not know that if a man removes his penis from the woman's vagina before he ejaculates, the woman can still become pregnant; 36.5% did not know more protection is achieved when contraceptive foam or jelly is used with a condom; 16% did not know that condoms can reduce risk of STDS [sexually-transmitted diseases]. [Jemmott & Jemmott, 1990, p. 355]

White and DeBlassie (1992) pointed out that teenagers may not be "developmentally ready for the responsibility that is required to be effective contraception users" (p. 188) and that sex can be a "quick fix" for interpersonal needs that have little to do with sexuality, such as loneliness, low self-esteem, affection, the need to vent anger, or an escape from boredom. They recommended that sex education focus on helping teenagers understand the reasons for sexual behavior to help them delay or avoid sexual activity. A variety of sex education programs that focus on abstinence have been developed. One study in Utah schools found a modest effect toward greater acceptance of abstinence for older students, but the junior high non-virgins showed more permissive attitudes after the course (Olsen, Weed, Daly, & Jensen, 1992).

Parental influences on adolescent sexuality are thought to be strong, but the process by which parents influence sexual behavior are not known. For a variety of reasons, many parents are uncomfortable talking about sexuality with their children. Thus, their influence may be indirect, involving social-cognitive abilities, decision-making skills, and feelings of self-efficacy (Brooks-Gunn & Furstenberg, 1989).

Likewise, other adults, including teachers and religious leaders, are sometimes unable to discuss sexuality frankly with children and adolescents. Even doctors and other health professionals may not be comfortable discussing sexuality with adolescents, and adolescents may not be comfortable talking about it with them. Many adolescent boys, for example, are uncomfortable undressing for a physical examination. Thus, feelings of embarrassment about sexuality can make it difficult for adolescents to find accurate information and to ask personal questions.

Although we cannot discuss sexuality in as much detail as a course in human sexuality, we can briefly discuss a few of the questions adolescents sometimes have about their own sexuality. For more detailed information, the local family planning clinic, Planned Parenthood office, or the Sex Information and Education Council of the United States (SIECUS) are good general sources.

Some of the most frequent questions involve the adolescents' understanding of their bodies. According to Sarrel and Sarrel (1981), many women have misunderstandings or lack information about their vagina. These include:

1. Normally a clear or cloudy white secretion is produced by glands in the cervix. Often when menstruation is explained, this normal secretion is not explained, leading adolescent girls to think it may be a sign of venereal disease, cancer, or pregnancy.

2. Over half of the 200 Yale women they questioned did not realize that the hymen is close to the skin surface. Many were also surprised to learn that the hymen still exists after intercourse, and were surprised at the normal size of the opening in the hymen.

3. Adolescent women may think of the vagina as something that hurts or is vulnerable. This idea may result from difficulties with tampons, pelvic examinations, recurrent inflammation of the vagina (vaginitis), or concerns about vaginal cancer. Some may experience uncomfortable contractions of the vagina (vaginismus) during intercourse or have other unpleasant experiences that make them think that sexual intercourse with men is for the man's pleasure only.

Similarly, men also have misunderstandings about their genitals. This may include the physical anatomy or their sexual response:

1. A pigmented line on the underside of the penis and in the middle of the pouch of skin (scrotum) enclosing the testicles, the epididymis that feels like a soft lump on each testicle, and the fact that one testicle usually hangs lower than the other are all normal.

2. Some adolescent males may worry about the large or small size of their penis, being circumcised, or about curvature of their erection. These variations are part of human diversity and ordinarily do not affect sexual satisfaction, although some sexual positions may be more satisfying than others for oneself or one's partner because of the shape or size of the erect penis.

3. Erection of the penis or ejaculation in nonsexual situations such as when in class or riding a school bus, when angry or frightened, or when wrestling or watching a fire may result from arousal of the **sympathetic nervous system**, which is activated to deal with emergency situations (and is primarily responsible for ejaculation), or from arousal of the **parasympathetic nervous system**, which functions when one is relaxed (and is responsible for erection and initial sexual arousal).

These topics are examples of the importance of open and sensitive discussion of sexual concerns by adolescents with informed adults. However, as Sarrel and Sarrel (1981) concluded:

> We feel that most adults have not recognized the nature of young people's emotional and sexual relationships. They tend to judge them in outmoded terms and do not offer the kind of help and support young people need. What adolescents need is much better information about their bodies, the bodies of the other sex, the psychology of human relationships, a chance to explore and question their own attitudes and beliefs, and above all some help in learning how to communicate intimately, i.e., how to talk about feelings, sex, contraception, fidelity, and trust to name just a few important topics. [p. 98]

MASTURBATION

As noted earlier in this chapter, many children discover methods of **masturbation**, which is self-stimulation of the genitals. They usually also learn that this behavior makes parents anxious, and learn to feel guilty about doing it; or they may learn that it is a private activity that is normal if it is done in an appropriate place and time. A national sample designed to be representative of the population of the United States found that 19% of men and women began masturbating by age 10; another 53% of the men and 25% of the women began between the ages of 11–13; by age 21, only 7% of men and 23% of women had not masturbated (Janus & Janus, 1993). In a study of African-American adolescent males, Jemmott and Jemmott (1990) found that relatively few (14%) reported that they had ever masturbated; perhaps this reflects a cultural difference, or the availability of sexual intercourse for this sample. In contrast, Sarrel and Sarrel (1981) reported that about 75–80% of Yale undergraduate men and women said that they masturbate. However, some of these women and men felt very uncomfortable about doing it, and 20% reported they do not masturbate.

Clearly, reported incidence of masturbation and other sexual activities varies in different groups of adolescents. In general, we have chosen not to focus on who does what sexual activity how often (see any current human sexuality textbook for a review of relevant studies). These data about groups of people do not provide much information about what is natural or normal for a specific individual and may cause someone to feel abnormal because they are atypical.

Finding ways to stimulate oneself sexually is a useful way to become acquainted with one's genitals and with the kinds of stimulation that are exciting. It is helpful to get to know one's sexual responses, and to accept those responses and one's genitals as a healthy part of oneself. This may involve examining one's body and sexual organs with a mirror and comparing one's unique physical characteristics with idealized diagrams and photographs. Genitals and breasts are as different from one person to another as is one's face. For example, both breasts are usually not perfectly symmetrical or the same size; their shape may change depending on the menstrual cycle or the season of the year. The shape of the nipples in both men and women vary from one individual to another; they also change at different levels of sexual excitement. Similarly, each man's penis may curve back toward the body, to the right or left, or stick straight out when it is erect. A woman's labia minor are usually not symmetrical, and their size varies from one woman to another. Testicles also vary in size from one man to another; in addition, they may hang very low, or be held tight against the body depending on the level of sexual excitement and body temperature.

Women may be unaware of the structure and feeling of their internal sexual organs unless they explore them.

> When someone first said to me two years ago, "You can feel the end of your own cervix with your finger," I was interested but flustered. I had hardly ever put my finger in my vagina at all, and felt squeamish about touching myself there, in that place "reserved" for lovers and doctors. It took me two months to get up my nerve to try it, and then one afternoon, pretty nervously, I squatted down in the bathroom and put my finger in deep, back into my vagina. There it was(!), feeling slippery and rounded, with an indentation at the center through which, I realized, my menstrual flow came. It was both very exciting and beautifully ordinary at the same time. [Boston Women's Health Book Collective, 1979, p. 26]

Men can also be unfamiliar with their genitals. For example, some men who are circumcised may confuse the foreskin (which is removed in circumcision) and the glans (the tip of the penis). If they do not know they were circumcised, and do not remember it happening, they may think that their penis is naturally uncircumcised. Thus, when they see an actual uncircumcised penis, where the glans is covered with a foreskin, they could think that this penis had the glans removed and that this is what is meant by circumcision. Being glad the tip of their penis was not removed, because it is so pleasurable, they would think they were lucky not to have been circumcised, when, in fact, they *have* been circumcised. There is debate over the importance and psychological effect of voluntary male circumcision (Lindeke, Iverson, & Fisch, 1986; Christensen-Szalansky, Boyce, Harrell, & Gardner, 1987; Williamson & Williamson, 1988). If the foreskin can be pulled back so the glans can be washed, there is no evidence that circumcision reduces the spread of disease. Also, some research indicates that the trauma of circumcision, usually performed without anesthetic, may have lasting psychological effects (Chamberlain, 1989; Richards, Bernal, & Brackbill, 1976).

Self-examination is important, not only for discovering one's sexual anatomy and gaining comfort with it, but also for noticing unusual changes from what is normal for oneself. This is important for both men and women because signs of testicular and breast cancer as well as of sexually transmitted diseases can be detected by self-examination. The counsel of a good physician on what to look for, and how to diagnose any abnormalities, should be a routine part of adolescent health care.

SEXUAL RELATIONSHIPS

Many adolescent concerns about sexuality focus on relationships with persons of the other gender. Note that we said *other gender*, not opposite sex. The idea that men and women are opposite implies many of the misconceptions that make heterosexual relationships more difficult than necessary. For example, it is often difficult to express one's secret feelings about

Self-examination is important to detect signs of breast cancer and other diseases.

sexuality to someone else, but if that other person is also "opposite" in sexuality, then it is almost futile to try; however, if that person is simply different in some ways, but has many of the same feelings and reactions, then communication may be easier.

One of the major misconceptions about heterosexuality is that the man is the expert who knows (or should know) everything about sexuality, that he should be strong, courageous, and take the initiative. In reality, one survey found that men strongly prefer women who take the initiative (Tavris, 1978). Masters and Johnson (1979) found a tendency for men to assume the role of expert; the result was that women felt they could not tell their partner what forms of stimulation they preferred at any particular moment, and men felt they could not ask. Pleck et al. (1993), reporting on the national survey of adolescent males (age 15–19) conducted in 1988 noted:

> With numerous background and personal characteristics controlled, traditional attitudes toward masculinity are associated with having more sexual partners in the last year, a less intimate relationship with the current sexual partner, and greater belief that relationships between women and men are adversarial. [p. 24]

Some adolescents believe women are responsible for contraception, but think only in terms of female contraceptives. Women are able to buy condoms, although they may feel embarrassed doing so. Nonetheless, if her partner did not prepare himself by having some available, a young woman can carry a condom with her. Even if she is using another form of birth control, unless she knows that her partner has not been infected with HIV/AIDS (or any other sexually transmitted disease), she would be wise to insist on this protection against infection, or to abstain from genital contact. A variety of studies on condom use has found that "communication/negotiation skills, the self-efficacy to request condom use, and the perception of HIV-preventive social norms are key factors associated with consistent use" (DiClemente, 1992b, pp. 48–49).

A common myth is that withdrawing the penis before ejaculation can prevent pregnancy. In fact, sperm may be present in the discharge from the penis before it is inserted in the vagina, so pregnancy can result whether there is an ejaculation or not. Likewise, infection with sexually transmitted diseases such as HIV/AIDS can result without ejaculation, so a condom is necessary even if the partner pulls out. Similarly, the contraceptive pill can be very effective in preventing pregnancy, but it does not protect against HIV/AIDS or other sexually transmitted diseases.

Another misconception is that men who are sexually stimulated will suffer physical damage or severe pain in the testicles if they are not able to have intercourse. Sometimes women feel it is their duty to help the man gain sexual release to prevent this physical "damage." Some men may believe this, too. Although discomfort or pain may sometimes occur in the genitals of both men and women during prolonged periods of intense sexual stimulation, it can be relieved quickly by masturbation (Masters & Johnson, 1979, p. 142).

It is often assumed that vaginal intercourse is the goal of heterosexual relations. This is not a valid assumption unless producing a child is seen as the only aim of heterosexuality. There are other pleasurable ways to achieve sexual satisfaction and emotional intimacy without vaginal intercourse. These include any combination of one-way or mutual masturbation, rubbing, cuddling, and caressing each other's body and the bodies together.

Oral stimulation of the genitals and especially anal intercourse may expose the partners to the virus associated with HIV/AIDS, so use of a condom is important.

Sexual fantasies are normal. One may enhance sexual activity by allowing the mind to imagine stimulating scenes or feelings that may or may not relate to the partner or the activity of the moment. These fantasies do not indicate that the sexual activity, or the partner, is unsatisfying. They simply serve to heighten the excitement and are not necessary for an intense sexual experience.

Sexual guidebooks can be helpful. But it is important to consider sexual guidebooks as if they were cookbooks: one need not make all the recipes, or like all the ideas that are suggested.

SEXUAL ORIENTATION

Adolescents are often confused and fearful about **homosexuality**, which is sexual attraction to persons of the same gender. Men whose sexual orientation is homosexual are known as **gay men**; women are known as **lesbians** if their sexual orientation is toward women. It should be noted that lesbians and gay men are not to be confused with *transvestites*, who dress in clothing of the other gender, or with *transsexuals*, who wish to become the other gender; transvestites and transsexuals may be heterosexual, bisexual, or homosexual in sexual orientation.

There is great pressure in our society to be 100% *heterosexual* and to avoid any sexual fantasies or feelings about persons of one's own gender. This pressure to avoid homosexuality may pose a conflict that can take the form of fearing same-gender sexual feelings in oneself or feeling hostile or uncomfortable toward persons who find sexual satisfaction in same-gender relationships. Sometimes these attitudes can result in violence against gay men and lesbians, which is a serious social problem (Garnets, Herek, & Levy, 1990).

A sizable proportion of men and women report having had some sexual contact involving orgasm with someone of their own gender. In the Janus and Janus (1993) study of a representative national sample, 22% of the men and 17% of the women reported they had had same-gender sexual experiences. Of these, 9% of the men and 5% of the women reported that they had frequent or ongoing same-gender sexual experiences. About half of these respondents indicated that their sexual identification was **bisexual**; that is, they were sexually interested in both men and women (Table 9.2).

Earlier in this century, psychologists believed that homosexuality was an emotional disorder caused by hormonal imbalance, physical abnormality, or an unusual pattern of parent–child relationships. For example, mothers were often felt to be responsible for homosexuality in their sons because they had overly close relations with them, and the fathers were too distant or cold for the son to use as a sexual role model. During the 1950s, research began to call these beliefs into question. One important finding, for example, was that gay men could not be distinguished from heterosexual men on the basis of standard psychological tests in use at the time (Hooker, 1957). Several years of accumulated research further questioned the idea that homosexuality was a mental illness. This research, combined with active advocacy by gay men and lesbians—many of them mental health professionals—led the American Psychiatric Association to remove the label of mental illness from homosexuality in 1974 (Bayer, 1981). The American Psychological Association in 1975 adopted a res-

Table 9.2 PROPORTION OF A REPRESENTATIVE NATIONAL SAMPLE OF ADULTS IN THE UNITED STATES WHO REPORTED THEY HAVE HAD HOMOSEXUAL EXPERIENCES, FREQUENCY OF THOSE EXPERIENCES, AND SELF-IDENTIFIED SEXUAL ORIENTATION

	Men	Women
Have you had homosexual experiences?	$n = 1,335$	$n = 1,384$
Yes	22%	17%
No	78%	83%
If you have had homosexual experiences, how often have you had them?	$n = 294$	$n = 235$
Once	5%	6%
Occasionally	56%	67%
Frequently	13%	6%
Ongoing	26%	21%
What do you consider to be your sexual identification?	$n = 1,333$	$n = 1,411$
Heterosexual	91%	95%
Homosexual	4%	2%
Bisexual	5%	3%

Source: S. S. Janus, & C. L. Janus. (1993). The Janus report on sexual behavior. New York: Wiley. Tables 3.14, 3.15, 3.16, pp. 69–70. Reprinted with permission.

olution in support of that decision and also urged "all mental health professionals to take the lead in removing the stigma of mental illness that has long been associated with homosexual orientations" (Conger, 1975).

One major study by the noted researchers Masters and Johnson (1979) examined whether lesbians and gay men differed from heterosexual persons of the same gender; the study concluded:

> No real difference exists between homosexual men and women and heterosexual men and women in their physiologic capacity to respond to similar sexual stimuli. In other words, there is no basis in physical fact for the oft-repeated dictum, "My way is better than your way." It is reasonable to speculate that, when absorbed, this finding should lead to significant modification in current cultural concepts. [p. 226]

Considerable research attention has been given to the origins of sexual orientation. One major study by the Alfred C. Kinsey Institute for Sex Research interviewed 979 lesbian and gay adults and 477 heterosexual adults who were similar to the lesbians and gay men in age, education, and religion (Bell, Weinberg, & Hammersmith, 1981). This study found that respondents' relationships with parents, especially the parent of the other gender, had "no significant impact on whether they turned out to be homosexual or heterosexual" (p. 189). This finding contradicted earlier assumptions about the effect of parents on their child's sexual orientation. Other traditional theories of the development of sexual orientation likewise were not supported by the data in this study. For example, there was no support for the idea that homosexuality results from having unusual relations with persons of the other gender, from being labeled as homosexual by others, or from being seduced by an older person (pp. 184–185). In contrast, they reached the following conclusion:

Our findings suggest that homosexuality is as deeply ingrained as heterosexuality, so that the differences in behaviors or social experiences of prehomosexual boys and girls and their pre-heterosexual counterparts reflect or express, rather than cause, their eventual homosexual preference. In short, theories that tie homosexuality to an isolated social experience cannot be expected to account well for such a basic part of one's being as sexual preference appears to be. [pp. 190–191]

These findings suggest that *sexual feelings* during childhood and adolescence are much more significant than had been previously recognized. They also suggest that an individual's sexual or erotic orientation in adulthood is influenced more by mental thoughts and emotions than by sexual experiences.

Additional conclusions from this study further strengthen the idea that sexual orientation—whether heterosexual or homosexual—is often determined by some combination of factors that operate early in life:

1. By the time boys and girls reach adolescence, their sexual preference is likely to be already determined, even though they may not yet have become sexually very active. . . .

2. Among our respondents homosexuality was indicated or reinforced by sexual feelings that typically occurred three years or so before their first "advanced" homosexual activity, and it was these feelings, more than homosexual activities, that appear to have been crucial in the development of adult homosexuality. . . .

3. The homosexual men and women in our study were not particularly lacking in heterosexual experiences during their childhood and adolescent years. They are distinguished from their heterosexual counterparts, however, in finding such experiences ungratifying. [pp. 186–188]

The findings of this study are consistent with what would be expected if sexual orientation was affected by genetic or physiological influences that operate early in life. Support for this idea has been provided in recent studies based on the postmortem comparison of the brains of gay and heterosexual men. This type of study became feasible as a result of the unusually high rate of death among self-identified gay men due to HIV/AIDS. Characteristics of the brains of gay men have been compared with men who were thought to be heterosexual, some of whom also died of HIV/AIDS. For example, LeVay (1991) found that an area of the brain associated with male sexual behavior was smaller in men who had been gay than in men presumed to have been heterosexual. Other studies have reported similar findings of differences in specific areas of the brain (Allen & Gorsky, 1992; Swaab & Hofman, 1990). Another line of support for this type of theory is that some evidence has been found of genetic linkage for sexual orientation in gay men and lesbians (Bailey & Pillard, 1991; Bailey & Benishay, 1993; Bailey, Pillard, Neale, & Agyei, 1993; Hamer, Hu, Magnuson, Hu, & Pattatucci, 1993; Pillard & Weinrich, 1986; Weinrich, 1987). The problem with this point of view is that even if differences in neuroanatomy are found, or if there are more homosexuals in families of gay men and lesbians, the explanation of sexual orientation is still elusive (Pillard, 1990). Recent research has suggested that there is a "gay gene" that may be a relevant influence for some gay men (Hamer et al., 1993). Thus, it is plausible that prenatal hormonal factors influence neuroanatomy at a critical period such that sexual orientation is affected (Money, 1987).

It seems implausible, however, that a single cause of sexual orientation would exist for all lesbians and gay men. Also, past studies on areas of the brain or genetics have focused almost entirely on men, and research has only begun to examine lesbian orientation in women. At this point, the most likely conclusion is that a combination of influences—both prenatal and postnatal—interact with childhood, adolescent, and adult experiences to influence sexual orientation. Moreover, the "data suggest that there may be different origins of sexual orientation for different individuals" (Garnets & Kimmel, 1991, p. 150).

The origins of bisexuality are also not known, although it appears that the developmental path for bisexuals may differ from that of both homosexuals and heterosexuals. Bisexuals are not simply unacknowledged lesbians or gay men, but this sexual orientation has received little research attention (Blumstein & Schwartz, 1977; Garnets & Kimmel, 1993; Masters & Johnson, 1979).

In summary, adolescents discover that their sexual feelings are directed toward persons of the other gender, or toward persons of the same gender, or both. For some, this may reflect childhood or prenatal influences that also were manifested earlier by sexual feelings. Others may choose a sexual orientation for a variety of reasons through a process similar to the choice of a sexual partner or other major aspects of one's life (Hart, 1981). It is likely that there may be different paths for different individuals in their development of sexual or erotic orientation. There might also be differences in the influences that are important for women and for men. Therefore, for many people, sexual orientation is as unchangeable as race or gender; for others it may be a matter of personal choice similar to one's religion or marital status. This argument may be used in support of antidiscrimination legislation that includes race, gender (or sex), religion, and marital status also including sexual orientation. Some people believe, however, that homosexuality is morally wrong or unnatural and oppose including lesbians, gay men, and bisexuals in antidiscrimination legislation. Others feel that this legislation should not be extended to any other groups.

Those adolescents who discover their sexual orientation is toward persons of the same gender often face considerable social stigma placed on same-gender sexual feelings, behavior, and relationships in our society. Thus, lesbian and gay adolescents learn to hide their sexuality, or face the stigma outright. Usually they cannot go to their parents for support, as members of racial minority groups do. Often they must cope with religious beliefs and cultural traditions that devalue their worth as individuals and invalidate their feelings and intimate relationships (Boxer, Cohler, Herdt, & Irvin, 1993).

Recently, these attitudes have begun to moderate somewhat, and lesbian and gay persons have found support and political power among one another. However, the individual adolescent must still deal with heterosexual bias in many social, school, and community activities. Mainstream television is also mainly silent about lesbian and gay youth, usually treating it only as a problem (Kielwasser & Wolf, 1992). Thus, often, gay and lesbian adolescents must deal with the issue alone and hide their sexual feelings from friends, teachers, and parents or risk antigay/lesbian violence (Gibson, 1989; Hunter, 1990; Hunter & Schaecher, 1987).

Malyon (1981) pointed out three styles of coping that lesbian and gay male adolescents use to deal with their sexual feelings. Some *repress* them out of their conscious awareness by using psychological defense mechanisms, only to find the feelings emerging again later in life, sometimes with distressing consequences. Others consciously *suppress* or hide the feelings. The psychological unrest that results, however, can delay the search for a sense of identity. Some persons seek to suppress the same-gender sexual feelings by heterosexual dating or marriage. A third response is *disclosure* of their sexual orientation. This may result in hostile reactions from one's peers and a painful confrontation with one's parents. In some cases, the adolescent is rejected by family and friends, or is subjected to harassment and forced to seek professional counseling. Because homosexuality is no easier to change than heterosexuality, attempts to enforce the adolescent's rejection of same-gender sexual feelings are very likely to be futile (Halderman, 1991).

Uribe and Harbeck (1991) described a counseling and educational project for gay, lesbian, and bisexual youth. They cited examples of how adolescents cope with being lesbian or gay:

> *Hack, age 17, Chinese.* The only way I have been able to deal with being gay is to throw myself into school activities. I am "Mr. Popular," and I hate every minute of it. Only one person at school, a lesbian, knows about me. My parents found out but they refuse to believe it. I don't like the social pressures on me. I have to go to school functions that for me are a total sham. . . .
>
> *Eleanor, age 18, Caucasian.* My parents don't know about me, and for now I don't see that it would do any good to tell them. I have never dated a guy. I've dealt with being a lesbian by throwing myself into my work. My parents think I'm going to be a doctor, so they leave me alone. I'm very wary of close friendships because they will find out about me, and I'm not ready for that. I guess I'm just not very sociable. [p. 15]

The social stigma and parental rejection may also lead the adolescent to run away from home to establish a self-sufficient life in an urban area where the social support of other gay persons can be found; unfortunately, prostitution for survival and other serious problems may result from such action. Sometimes the distress reaches the point that the lesbian or gay male adolescent is at a high risk of suicide (Remafedi, Farrow, & Deisher, 1991). We discuss runaways and suicide in Chapter 12.

Services now exist for gay and lesbian adolescents in many urban areas to provide safe opportunities for dating and socializing with peers of both genders parallel to those that are routinely provided for heterosexual adolescents (Martin, 1982; Rofes, 1989; Slater, 1988; Uribe & Harbeck, 1991).

When discussing homosexuality with adolescents, frequently there are questions about the nature of gay lifestyles, sexual behavior, and the risk of HIV/AIDS infection. Several resources focus on providing useful information and guidance to counselors, therapists, and physicians (Cranston, 1991; Gonsiorek, 1988; Murphy, 1991; Paroski, 1987; Peplau & Cochran, 1990; Savin-Williams, 1990; Slater, 1988; Sobocinski, 1990).

A final point is that adolescents sometimes wonder whether they might be lesbian or gay because they have had a few sexual experiences with others of their own gender, or because they have little interest or success in sexual relations with persons of the other gender. In such situations, it is useful to help the adolescent discuss his or her fantasies and to become comfortable as a unique sexual individual. Often the fear of homosexuality may be more harmful than the actual situation, which can reflect delayed sexual maturation, dislike of particular kinds of heterosexual acts, greater satisfaction from masturbation than from heterosexual relations, not having experienced sexual intimacy, or various forms of sexual inadequacy, none of which necessarily indicate homosexuality (Sarrel & Sarrel, 1981).

LOVE, LUST, AND ROMANCE

In earlier chapters we discussed Harry Stack Sullivan's interpersonal theory and his important concept of the chum, or close friend (see Chapters 2 and 8). In his theory, this relationship can represent the person's first experience with emotional intimacy, collaboration, and love. This chum relationship provides a number of significant new interpersonal experiences for the preadolescent who has such a chum. Although Sullivan (1953) described only male chumships, female preadolescents also experience similar relationships (McGuire & Weisz, 1982; Ursano, Wetzler, Slusarcick, & Gemelli, 1987).

A **chumship** is a collaborative relationship in which each person feels accepted and affirmed by another individual who is valued and trusted (see also the definition in Chapter 8). This sense of acceptance allows the chums to share many of their deepest feelings, questions, and uncertainties with one another. A chum ideally can reaffirm one's acceptability as a valued person who is unique; a chum can also offer his or her own experience and feelings, which are usually similar in important ways to one's own. This can greatly reduce the fear that one is different or that there is something "wrong" with oneself. Often, budding feelings about sexuality, masturbation, interest in sexually explicit magazines, romantic crushes, curiosity about the normality of one's body, and one's speed of physical maturation can be shared and discussed with one's chum in a way that reduces anxiety and fears of being abnormal or different.

> In fact, as a psychiatrist, I would hope that preadolescent relationships were intense enough for each of the two chums literally to get to know practically everything about the other one that could possibly be exposed in an intimate relationship, because that remedies a good deal of the often illusory, usually morbid, feeling of being different, which is such a striking part of rationalizations of insecurity in later life. [Sullivan, 1953, p. 256]

Of course, not every preadolescent experiences such a chumship, and the long-term results of lacking such a friend need not be negative. Some adolescents and adults who seek psychotherapy, however, are continuing to deal with issues of feeling unacceptable or different or alienated—problems that might have been resolved earlier by having a preadolescent chumship.

According to Sullivan, the major task of early adolescence is the integration of sexuality into the person's pattern of interpersonal relationships and feelings of worth as a person. This involves integrating the **lust dynamism** into the kind of collaborative, intimate relationship one had earlier with a chum. Recall from Chapter 2 that Sullivan's concept of *dynamism* refers to a pattern of recurring tension or a particular bodily zone of interaction with others. Lust refers to the tensions felt in association with the needs that have their culmination in sexual orgasm, and it involves the genitals as a zone of interaction with others. Because chumships are usually not explicitly sexual, and usually involve chums of one's own gender, this emerging lust dynamism is a major change. If the sexual feelings are directed at persons of the other gender, then the task is to develop relationships similar to chumships with a person of the other gender. If the sexual feelings are directed at persons of one's own gender, then the task is to avoid rejection and being stigmatized as gay or lesbian by hiding one's sexuality or choosing one's chums with great care.

◆ *Profile*

HARRY STACK SULLIVAN

Interpersonal relationships were the central theme in the theories and life of Harry Stack Sullivan, one of the most original psychological thinkers born in the United States. The grandson of Irish immigrants—his mother's family name was Stack, his father's was Sullivan—he was born in 1892 in a rural county in New York state. He understood the effects of prejudice, as his family was Roman Catholic in a mostly Protestant community during a time of strong anti-Catholic feelings, and he was the only Irish Catholic boy in his school. An only child (two previous babies died in their first year of life), he also knew social isolation and loneliness during childhood. The family farm where he grew up was remote, and social contact was primarily with relatives who occasionally visited; it was reported that his only friends were farm animals and pets. His emphasis on the importance of personal relationships in psychological development clearly relects this period of his life.

One of Sullivan's major contributions to psychology was his description of the preadolescent relationship described as a *chum*. This experience, which he thought could have a very positive effect on development, probably reflected the long friendship Harry began when he was 8½ with an older boy who was also somewhat of an outcast from his peer group. Another important concept was the emergence of the *lust dynamism* during adolescence. This may have also reflected his personal experience as a young man away from home for the first time at Cornell University in 1909. He apparently got into some sort of trouble, was suspended from college, and disappeared for 2 years. The details are not clear, but his biographer suggests that Harry experienced a delayed and unusually stormy emergence of sexual feelings and that this resulted in a schizophrenic episode. Later, as a psychiatrist, he was highly

An important task of adolescence is to resolve various conflicts among the needs for security, intimacy, and lust. For example, Sullivan noted that some children learn that their genitals are "not-me" in the sense of not being an acceptable and good part of their body. In that case, lustful feelings, which can be extremely powerful, collide with an equally powerful need for security, self-esteem, and feelings of personal worth. The result can be that the individual is unable to learn how to do anything about the lustful desires, and thus feels extremely lonely, restless, and abnormal.

A parallel conflict may arise between lustful feelings and the need for intimacy. That is, one would think of persons one has sexual feelings toward as different from those one has

respected for his insight into schizophrenia and his sensitivity to the importance of the social environment in its treatment.

In 1911 Sullivan experienced urban life and ethnic diversity when he entered a program from which he earned his medical degree in a combined college and medical school in Chicago in which a substantial proportion of the students were from Europe, Asia, and Africa. He also had serious financial problems and may have had a second schizophrenic experience before serving in the Army Medical Corps during World War I.

His professional career as a psychiatrist began in earnest in 1921 when he joined the staff at the Sheppard Enoch Pratt Hospital in Maryland. In 8 years, his work on the importance of emotional disturbances made him "a legend in both the clinical world and the world of the social sciences" (Perry, 1982, p. 190).

By this time he had met a man who was officially regarded as his foster son, James I. Sullivan, with whom he lived for over 20 years until his death. James managed Sullivan's household and his correspondence and writings, and he cared for him during extended periods of illness near the end of his life. In 1930 they moved to New York City, where Sullivan established a private practice of psychoanalysis. During this time he was part of a circle of influential thinkers from several different fields in the social sciences. He was instrumental in establishing a prominent school of psychiatry in Washington, D.C., and in New York City, and an interdisciplinary journal, called *Psychiatry*. Returning to Maryland in 1939, he began a series of lectures at Chestnut Lodge, a psychiatric hospital in suburban Washington. These lectures were recorded and became the basis for three books published after his death.

When the atomic bomb was dropped on Hiroshima, Sullivan, despite serious heart disease, decided that he had to take an active role in preventing war and reducing international tension. During the last years of his life he was deeply involved in these issues, and he died while in Europe working for this cause in 1949. He is buried in Arlington National Cemetery.

[*Source:* Based on Perry, H. S. *Psychiatrist of America: The Life of Harry Stack Sullivan*. Cambridge, MA: Harvard University Press, 1982.]

friendly feelings toward. The classical example of this conflict is the "prostitute versus good girl" dichotomy many men adopted earlier in this century. More contemporary versions of it may still be found among persons who have sex with people they do not really like, or who have sex while drunk and cannot remember the experience; these experiences often cause guilt for adolescents (Darling et al., 1992).

According to Sullivan, deciding what sexual activities one prefers and integrating these into the rest of one's life is the basic task of early adolescence. Its achievement marks the beginning of late adolescence. Usually this task involves a process of sexual unfolding and a series of transitional relationships, which we discuss in the next section.

TRANSITIONAL RELATIONSHIPS

The process of developing satisfying patterns of sexual intimacy is a gradual evolution that Sarrel and Sarrel (1981) have termed "sexual unfolding." There are many interacting components to this process, including one's past (childhood and preadolescent) experiences, sex education and factual knowledge, social norms and expectations, personal fears and anxieties about sex, and opportunities for interaction with potential sexual partners. It involves feelings about separating from one's parents, evaluation of oneself in relation to one's peers, moral values, and feelings of personal competence. Sexual relationships can be very confusing and frightening; they can also be very important opportunities for growth and occasions for learning about oneself in relation to others.

The variations in this process are enormous, and there is no one right way to develop sexual relationships. A useful approach was suggested by Goethals and Klos (1976, pp. 366–367) by their term "**transitional relationships**." These are relationships that are necessary experiences to aid the young person's development from one point to another in this evolution of intimate sexual relationships. A transitional relationship ordinarily ends when it has provided its contribution to the partners' development; if it continues past that point, it may begin to inhibit further growth. Many adolescents experience several of these transitional relationships between when sexual feelings emerge and when a mutually supportive loving relationship develops. Frequently, these transitional relationships provide information about oneself and therefore focus more on one's own feelings or the effect of oneself on others than on the other person. In part this reflects the egocentrism of early adolescence. But it may also reflect the importance of the questions about one's identity. Erikson (1968) argued that one cannot become truly *intimate* with another person until one has a fairly firm sense of one's own *identity*. These transitional relationships, especially during early adolescence, may serve to firm up one's sense of identity as a sexual person. Only later does the focus shift toward understanding the unique identity of the other person, thereby providing an opportunity for the emergence of true intimacy.

ROMANTIC LOVE

Most people fall in love for the first time during adolescence. As Money and Ehrhardt (1972) speculated, this may be triggered by a biological clock we do not still understand. Clearly, adolescent love is different from a child's love for his or her parents, from the day-to-day love of a long-term marriage, and from the love of a parent or grandparent for a child or grandchild. Very often the romantic love of adolescence is a kind of "being in love with love" combined with the developmental necessity to discover one's own identity from within a close relationship that involves sexual attraction.

Psychological research on love has only recently begun to emerge. One model that stimulated much interest was proposed by Sternberg (1986b, 1988a). His approach focused on three components of love: *intimacy, passion,* and *commitment.* Seven different types of love may be seen to emerge from combinations of these three components (Figure 9.1). For example, **romantic love** combines intimacy and passion. Sternberg commented:

> In essence, it is liking with an added element of physical or other attraction. In this view, then, romantic lovers are drawn to one another both physically and emotionally. Commitment is not a necessary part of romantic love, however. The lovers may realize that permanence is unlikely,

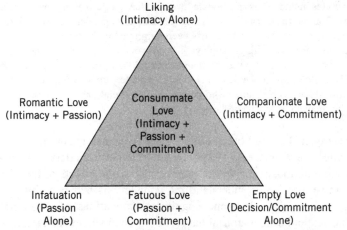

Figure 9.1 Kinds of loving as different combinations of the three components of love proposed by Sternberg: intimacy, passion, and commitment. [*Source:* R.J. Sternberg. Triangulating Love. In R.J. Sternberg & M.L. Barnes (Eds.), *The Psychology of Love.* © 1988 Yale University Press. Figure 6.2, p. 122. Reprinted with permission.]

impossible, or simply an issue to be dealt with at some future time. A summer love affair, for example, may be highly romantic, but without any real chance of lasting beyond the summer. [Sternberg, 1988a, p. 126]

Hatfield (1988) focused on the passionate aspect of love and noted that strong emotions can stimulate feelings that may be interpreted as sexual attraction under some circumstances. She cited the classic study of young men who participated in an experiment that involved experiencing a degree of fear while crossing a 450-foot-long suspension bridge "that tilts, sways, and wobbles over a 230-foot drop to rocks and shallow rapids below" (p. 203) in the presence of a "good-looking college woman." A greater number of men phoned the woman (a confederate of the experimenter) after the study if they experienced the suspension bridge as compared with another group who experienced crossing a solid bridge over the same river (Dutton & Aron, 1974). Additional evidence about reactions to high levels of emotional arousal suggests that "adrenalin makes the heart grow fonder" (Hatfield, 1988, p. 204). Thus, in a sense, motion precedes emotion—the physical reaction of the body to stimulation may produce the sensations we label as love, if we are in a potentially romantic situation. This situation may be especially important when one is making love: if one does it successfully, inducing a high level of emotion, then one is likely to interpret those feelings as love.

Hendrick and Hendrick (1992) noted the distinction between saying, "I love you," which can be "a promissory note that the relationship will endure" (p. 20) and "falling in love," which involves a variety of emotional reactions, both positive and negative. Their research has led to the idea that love is an attitude or set of beliefs that one has about another person. Thus, there may be several different kinds of love, reflecting differences in beliefs about love or individual differences about styles of love. Lee (1973, 1988) proposed six styles of love, and Hendrick and Hendrick (1992) measured them based on a scale of love attitudes (Table 9.3). They summarized their research findings in these words:

These love styles include Eros (passionate love), Ludus (game-playing love), Storge (friendship-based love), Pragma (practical love), Mania (obsessive, dependent love), and Agape (altruistic love). A scale based on the love styles has been employed with some interesting results. For instance, men appear to be more game-playing, with women sometimes more friendship-oriented, practical, and obsessive. It also may be that gender role is as or more important than actual gender where love styles are concerned. . . . The love styles are also implicated in the stability of dating relationships, with couples who continued their relationships more passionate and less game-playing than couples who broke up. [p. 86]

So far, researchers have not been satisfied with their understanding of love, especially romantic or erotic love. Berscheid (1988) pointed out that to understand "eros" we must understand human emotional experiences in general and the effects of the context of the relationship; we must also better understand the connections between physiological reactions, attitudes, and beliefs about love and cognitive explanations of emotional reactions. She noted also that sex and sexual arousal have seldom been studied as factors in love. She suggested that erotic love is, in fact, "about 90 percent sexual desire as not yet sated" (p. 373).

One of the most interesting discussions of romantic love is the analysis by de Rougemont (1956) of the **romantic myth** in Western culture. He argued that the quest for a perfect love is a culturally transmitted ideal that can be traced back to an idea that was considered a heresy by the early Christian church. One example of this mythical romantic ideal is the Tristan and Isolde legend, in which ideal love is one that is prevented from being consummated except in the eternity of death. This romantic myth is also portrayed in the story of Romeo and Juliet as well as in countless contemporary stories and movies. The essential ingredients are two passionate lovers who are drawn together but, for some unalterable reason, are unable to grow old together in mutual love. Thus de Rougemont argued, the image of love that is prevalent in our society leads us to seek passionate attachments that, in their fulfillment, sow the seeds of their own destruction. He suggested instead that "to *be in love* is not necessarily *to love*. To be in love is a state; to love, an act" (de Rougemont, 1956, p. 310). For example, from a Christian point of view, it is not correct to view love as a senti-

Table 9.3 SAMPLE ITEMS DESCRIBING SIX TYPES OF LOVING FROM THE LOVE ATTITUDES SCALE

EROS
1. My lover and I were attracted to each other immediately after we first met.
LUDUS
2. I try to keep my lover a little uncertain about my commitment to him/her.
STORGE
3. It is hard for me to say exactly when our friendship turned into love.
PRAGMA
4. I considered what my lover was going to become in life before I committed myself to him/her.
MANIA
5. When things aren't right with my lover and me, my stomach gets upset.
AGAPE
6. I try to always help my lover through difficult times.

Source: S. S. Hendrick, & C. Hendrick. (1992). *Romantic love.* Newbury Park, CA: Sage Publications. Table 4.12, p. 69. Reprinted with permission.

ment instead of as an act that is the result of a decision. The injunction "Love your neighbor as oneself" is a command to actively aid one's neighbor, according to de Rougemont.

Romantic love is especially important in adolescence, partly because it is so widely promoted by our culture, and partly because it fits adolescent egocentrism so well. That is, the adolescent is inclined to focus on personal feelings and to generalize these to a universal principle; thus, for an adolescent, feelings of love reflect ultimate love, and the abstract principle of loving another as oneself becomes reduced to the sentiment of romance. As noted in Chapter 4, the personal fable inclines an adolescent to think that no one has ever experienced the intensity of love that he or she is feeling.

In contrast, Maslow (1955) defined two types of love. One type is generous, therapeutic, and mystical. It is nonpossessive, does not diminish from being gratified, and is not tainted with anxiety or hostility. He called this **B-love** because it is love for the other person as a *being*: "B-love, in a profound but testable sense, creates the partner. It gives him a self-image, it gives him self-acceptance, a feeling of love-worthiness and respect-worthiness, all of which permit him to grow" (Maslow, 1955, p. 28). The second type he called **D-love** because it involves loving the other to make up for a *deficiency* within oneself. It is selfish love, a need for love.

Thus, Maslow's concept of B-love is an active love of one's most intimate of neighbors— one's lover. It is based not only on sentimental (romantic) love, as historical and contemporary Western mythology would suggest, but also on a decision to love. This decision must always have an arbitrary element that involves undertaking to bear the consequences of that decision whether the consequences turn out to be happy or unhappy.

This discussion is not intended to deny the significance of romantic love, which can be a wonderful and powerful experience. Both men and women, adolescents and adults, find the zest of this feeling to be an important source of satisfaction. However, it can occur most readily in situations that block its ultimate fulfillment. It thrives when the lovers are separated and the feeling blossoms in fantasies of what one feels about the image of the absent lover. It leads to high expectations about what the love relationship should involve, thereby often leading to disappointment when the actual relationship requires the chores of daily living, which are not always very romantic. It can also involve intense jealousy, which Sullivan (1953) noted is very unwelcome and extremely unpleasant (p. 279).

SEXUAL ISSUES

Transitional relationships generally begin with socially prescribed expectations about dating behavior. We discussed adolescent dating in detail in Chapter 8. In this chapter we focus on sexual issues that are involved in these experiences. One of the best discussions of this topic may be found in the writings by Lorna and Philip Sarrel (1979). We draw on their description of these issues in this section.

Issues about private space, exposing one's body or sexual areas to another person, and feelings about trusting another to accept one's body become central as dating progresses from casual contact to more explicit sexual interaction.

> The convention of the goodnight kiss contains some implicit permission for a prescribed amount of closeness and touching. But he might decide to go a bit further and touch her breast. How will she react if he does? Will he or she put a tongue in the other's mouth? Through nego-

tiating hundreds of such situations, in which conventions help to lessen the anxiety, young adolescents learn how to let another person get close, enter their private space, and touch in sexual ways. [Sarrel & Sarrel, 1979, p. 48]

Through this process, one learns about oneself, other's reactions to one's body, and those activities that feel good as well as those activities that bring anxiety or discomfort. It is important to note that one learns from positive experiences about one's likes, and from negative experiences about one's dislikes. Sometimes it is difficult to separate one's preferences from the context of the experiences, however. For example, discomfort in a situation with little privacy or space, or a partner who is rough or demanding, may be hard to separate in one's feelings from the activities that one found to be pleasant or unpleasant. Thus, a great deal of learning and cognitive evaluation of that learning is involved in this process of sexual unfolding.

Because sexuality is usually unknown and unexplored, initial experiences can be frightening and can undermine one's feelings of competence and control. In addition, fantasies about sexual orgasm as a loss of control or wild animal-like passion can cause fears about experiencing sexual arousal. Males may fear ejaculating in their pants; females may fear losing control of the situation and "being taken advantage of." Thus, it is not unusual for a person to hold back emotional feelings, or even to avoid orgasm, in an attempt to avoid losing control in early sexual experiences. Nor is it unusual for a person to feel disappointed about the experience of orgasm when it does not produce an intense feeling of abandon or ecstasy. Moreover, for men the anxiety of early sexual encounters, or abstaining from masturbation because of intended sexual relations, can cause premature orgasm, which can be very unsettling.

Most couples implicitly decide how far they want to go in their sexual experiences. Of course, some simply let sexual relations happen; but even then, this is often an implicit decision even if the partners do not take responsibility for the choice. Based on their experience as counselors in a university, Sarrel and Sarrel (1979) noted:

> Among the student couples who have their first intercourse experience during the college years, there is a great range in the length of time they "date" before having intercourse. We, and others, have noted a trend toward students sleeping together for weeks or perhaps months before deciding to have intercourse. The decision-making process itself can be very important, reflecting the individual personalities and the ability of a particular twosome to negotiate, to talk about feelings and to face their sexual behavior. . . .
>
> Once a couple begins to have intercourse on any regular basis, their relationship changes. Petting to mutual orgasm is certainly an important experience between two people, but placing the penis in the vagina, although it may be "only a matter of another inch or two" is realistically and symbolically on another plane. Issues of pregnancy and contraception enter the picture. Feelings about loss of virginity, if this is the first time, may be very complex. And the sex itself changes, now that intercourse is included. It may change for the better, in the sense of increased erotic pleasure and feelings of closeness or it may change for the worse because of pain, sexual dysfunction, possible decreased responsiveness for the female who was accustomed to responding to oral or manual stimulation, or a generalized pressure to "perform." [pp. 58–59]

Compounding these sexual issues are the social issues of peer pressure. In some settings, a person who has not had sexual intercourse may feel an implicit stigma about being a virgin. This can be true for both men and women. It is not uncommon for a socially popular or sexually attractive adolescent to be a virgin, even if everyone assumes he or she is sexually experienced. Similarly, it is not unusual for a heterosexually inexperienced person to feel that they may be abnormal, or perhaps homosexual. Also, such a person may identify any number of inaccurate reasons for this lack of experience: one's breasts may be too small, one's penis may be too small, one's sexual desires may be too strong or too weak, and so on. Such feelings can make an adolescent miserable and, if the person is already shy, increase the shyness (Sarrel & Sarrel, 1979).

Attention has also focused on ways in which adolescents are coerced into having sexual relationships in which they do not voluntarily consent (Craig, 1990; Feltey, Ainslie, & Geib, 1991; Levy, 1993). Sexual abuse was discussed in the context of family relations in Chapter 7. Here it is important to note the importance of **date rape** in which a couple who voluntarily agree to date find that one partner exerts control and power over the other to force compliance with some sexual experience that is not voluntary. A typical pattern is to use alcohol intoxication to weaken resistance, or to park in a remote location so that the partner must comply or be abandoned; sometimes a form of blackmail is used to force compliance by threatening to ruin the partner's reputation. A number of suggestions have been developed to reduce the risk of date rape (Box 9.1). In general, the point is to accept that "No" means "No!"

SEXUALITY AND ITS IMPLICATIONS

Most adolescents have sexual relations. About 60% of males and 53% of females age 15–19 reported they have experienced heterosexual intercourse at least once, according to nationwide studies of representative samples (Forrest & Singh, 1990; Sonenstein, Pleck, & Ku, 1991). The reported incidence of sexual intercourse has increased during the 1980s: for women, the proportion who are sexually active rose to 53% from 47% (Table 9.4); for men, the pattern was complex, with younger (under age 15) African-American males reporting lower rates in 1988 compared with 1979, but rates were higher for all groups after age 16 (Figure 9.2). Likewise, the birth rate in the United States is very high among teenagers (12.5% of all births in 1988), and it is more than twice that of Canada, England, and France, and six times that of the Netherlands. Moreover, about 2.5 million teenagers in the United States are infected with sexually transmitted diseases each year (Coates, 1992). The risk of HIV infection is associated with sexual intercourse, and therefore sexually active adolescents are at the forefront of the battle against AIDS (DiClemente, 1992a).

Because political pressure has blocked comprehensive nationwide studies of adolescent sexual behavior in recent years, we do not have good data on what proportion of adolescents engage in various sexual behaviors, or whether their sexual behavior is placing them at risk for HIV/AIDS (National Commission on AIDS, 1993). There is some evidence that adolescent males are responding to the HIV/AIDS epidemic by using condoms (Pleck, Sonenstein, & Ku, 1991). Also, the proportion of women (age 15–19) in nationwide studies who reported they used any form of contraception jumped from 48% in 1982 to 65% in 1988, mostly as a result of increased condom use (Forrest & Singh, 1990).

Some studies have reported decreased sexual behavior of young people compared with a decade earlier, which may be attributed to awareness of sexually transmitted diseases such as herpes and HIV/AIDS. For example, Murstein, Chalpin, Heard, and Vyse (1989) found

♦ BOX 9.1   DATE AND ACQUAINTANCE RAPE

Definition[1]

Date/acquaintance rape is forced, unwanted intercourse with a person you know. It is an act of humiliation, violence, and power. It can be with someone you know casually, with someone you have dated a few times, or even with someone you are having a relationship with.

I learned that a guy shouldn't want to have sex with a girl who doesn't want to. It isn't normal. If she's crying or begging him to stop or afraid of him, and he makes her do it anyway, that's sick. That is rape. I want to tell girls not to think that's normal.

— **Albert, 17**[2]

Keeping a Rape-Free Environment[1]

Men

- Know your sexual desires and limits. Communicate them clearly. Be aware of social pressures. It's ok not to "score."
- Being turned down when you ask for sex is not a rejection of you personally. Women who say "No" to sex are not rejecting the person; they are expressing their desire not to participate in a single act. Your desires may be beyond your control, but your actions are within your control.
- Accept the woman's decision. "No" means "No!" Don't read other meanings into the answer. Don't continue after "No!" Remember that it might be just as difficult for her to say "No" as it is for you to hear it.

- Don't assume that just because a woman dresses in a "sexy" manner and flirts that she wants to have sexual intercourse.
- Don't assume that previous permission for sexual contact applies to the current situation.
- Avoid the use of drugs and excessive use of alcohol. Alcohol and drugs interfere with clear thinking and effective communication.

Women

- Know your sexual desires and limits. Believe in your right to set those limits. If you are not sure, STOP and talk about it.
- Communicate your limits clearly. If someone starts to offend you, tell them firmly and early. Polite approaches may be misunderstood or ignored. Say "No" when you mean "No."
- Be assertive. Often men interpret passivity as permission. Be direct and firm with someone who is sexually pressuring you.
- Be aware that your nonverbal actions send a message. If you dress in a "sexy" manner and flirt, some men may assume you want to have sex. This does not make your dress or behavior wrong, but it is important to be aware of the possibility of misunderstanding.
- Pay attention to what is happening around you. Watch the nonverbal clues.
- Trust your intuitions. If you feel you are being pressured into unwanted sex, you probably are. Leave.
- Avoid the use of drugs and the use of alcohol. Alcohol and drugs may interfere with clear thinking and effective communication.

more sexual behavior reported among college students in New England in 1979 than in either 1974 or 1986; 1986 reports were similar to the 1974 levels.

Sonenstein et al. (1991) called attention to the vagueness of the term "sexually active." They analyzed the number of sexual partners and frequency of heterosexual intercourse based on data from the National Survey of Adolescent Males (1,880 never-married males aged 15–19 in the United States who lived in a household, i.e., were not homeless, runaways, or in institutions or the military). They found that adolescent men, especially African-Americans, reported fewer partners and less frequent intercourse within the 4

Options Available to Protect Yourself [3]

- Decide how much personal information you are comfortable giving out to people without jeopardizing your safety (phone number, address, whether you live alone, etc.).
- Be aware that if you accept a ride home with someone you don't know well or are led into an isolated setting (his car or apartment, your apartment), the opportunity exists for him to attack you.
- When you go out or leave a party with a man, let someone else know of your plans (the name of your date, when you will be coming home, etc.).
- If you and your date return to your apartment or room, call a friend or neighbor . . . "I told you I would let you know when I got home. Steve and I will be in my room."

What to Do If You Have Been Raped [3]

- Get to a safe place.
- Call a friend, family member, or the police for transportation to a hospital.
- Call a rape crisis hotline for support and information.
- Go to a hospital for treatment of external and/or internal injuries, tests for pregnancy and sexually transmitted diseases, evidence collection, and support services.

Remember . . .

- Don't shower, bathe, douche, change clothes, or straighten up the area. You will destroy evidence you may need.

- Reporting to the police is your choice.
- Consider seeing a counselor with special expertise in working with rape survivors.

What To Do If You Are Being Abused [2]

- If you are repeatedly coerced or forced to do sexual acts you do not want to do or you are afraid to say "No," you are being sexually abused.
- Take it seriously; it usually gets worse unless something is done to stop it.
- Tell your abuser the abuse must stop.
- Say it clearly if you don't want sex.
- Plan for your safety to avoid further abuse.
- Tell your parents or a trusted adult.
- Call the police or other authorities.
- Call a rape or domestic violence hotline.
- Find a counselor or a support group to help you deal with the relationship.
- Talk to friends.
- Do things for yourself that make you feel stronger.
- Take a self-defense class.

[1]*Source:* Los Angeles Commission on Assaults Against Women, Date/Acquaintance Rape Prevention Project.
[2]*Source:* Barrie Levy, *In Love and in Danger: A Teen's Guide to Breaking Free of Abusive Relationships.* Seattle: Seal Press, 1993, p. 90.
[3]*Source:* Women's Resource Center, University of California, Los Angeles, 1987.

weeks before the study in 1988 as compared with a similar study in 1979 (p. 166). They also noted that the sexual life of the average adolescent male was not as extensive as might be expected:

1. The mean number of partners for sexually experienced men in the last 12 months was 1.9; there was little difference by age group.
2. Mean frequency of intercourse was 2.7 times in the last 4 weeks; this leads to an estimate of 23 intercourse experiences within the last year, for the average sexually active man in the study.

Table 9.4 PERCENTAGE OF WOMEN AGE 15–19 WHO HAD EVER HAD INTERCOURSE AND WHO HAD EXPERIENCED INTERCOURSE IN THE PREVIOUS 3 MONTHS

	1982	*1986*
All women (age 15–19)	$n = 9,521$	$n = 9,179$
Had intercourse in last 3 months	40.0	42.5
Ever had intercourse	47.1	53.2
Non-Hispanic white	44.5	52.4
Non-Hispanic black	59.0	60.8
Hispanic	50.6	48.5
Never married (not cohabitating)		
Had intercourse in last 3 months	34.3	38.5
Ever had intercourse	42.1	49.5

Source: J. D. Forrest, & S. Singh. (1990). The sexual and reproductive behavior of American women, 1982–1988. *Family Planning Perspectives*, 22, Tables 3 and 4, p. 208. Reprinted with permission.

3. Sexually experienced respondents spent about 6 months of the last year with no sexual partner, on the average; only 20% had a sexual partner throughout the last year.
4. Sixty-nine percent reported having no more than one sexual partner during the past 12 months (p. 163).
5. Racial/ethnic differences were significant, but when the length of time the respondent had been sexually active was considered, many of these differences disappeared (p. 162).

Sonenstein et al. concluded: "A typical picture of an adolescent male's year would be separate relationships with two partners, lasting a few months each, interspersed with several months without any sexual partner" (p. 166).

Likewise, in another study among adolescent women, although 58% of those who were sexually experienced reported having more than one partner, only 8% who had sex within 3 months of the study had more than one sexual partner during that time (Forrest & Singh, 1990, p. 709).

Thus, it is important for us to put adolescent sexual behavior in its context:

> Sexual preoccupation and sexual experience may not have as large a place in the lives of teenagers as people commonly believe. Adolescents face myriad challenges, sexuality being only one of them. And, also in contrast to prevailing opinion, many teenagers do not have sex very often. [Brooks-Gunn & Furstenberg, 1990, p. 76]

As noted above, there are considerable differences among various groups of adolescents about sexual attitudes and behavior. Because these differences overlap, generalizations do not necessarily apply to any single individual.

Our discussion in the next section of this chapter focuses on the implications of sexual

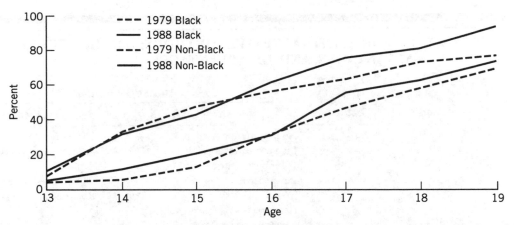

Figure 9.2 Cumulative proportion of never-married metropolitan-area males who had experienced intercourse before each age, by race, in 1979 and 1988. [*Source:* F.L. Sonenstein, J.H. Pleck, & L.C. Ku. Levels of Sexual Activity Among Adolescent Males in the United States. *Family Planning Perspectives, 23*(4), Figure 1, p. 166. © 1991 Alan Guttmacher Institute. Reprinted with permission.]

behavior during adolescence: use of contraception, pregnancy, and sexually transmitted diseases, including HIV/AIDS.

CONTRACEPTION

With the invention of the rubber condom in 1876, and its increased popularity when latex rubber condoms became available in the 1920s, the possibility of preventing pregnancy became a reality (Money, 1980, p. 144). Much of the credit for the contemporary birth control movement belongs to Margaret Sanger (1883-1966), who fought against considerable male opposition for the right of women to gain control over their risk of pregnancy. "After several arrests, some time in jail, and much harassment, her first clinic opened in New York City in October of 1916. Half a century later, Planned Parenthood clinics have become a vital resource in a world urgently needing population control" (Francoeur, 1982, p. 23). Sanger was instrumental in stimulating the development of modern birth control technology, including the contraceptive pill. Today there are many forms of birth control; however, some methods are much less effective than others (Box 9.2). Recently, a contraceptive known as Norplant, implanted in the upper arm, has become available and is thought to be effective for 5 years, but it is relatively expensive for an individual to obtain. Another recently approved contraceptive known as Depo-Provera is 99% effective for 3 months; it is injected by a physician or nurse, and the cost is expected to be similar to birth control pills (*New York Times*, 1992). A condom designed for women to use inside the vagina has also recently been approved (Leary, 1993).

For a variety of reasons, many sexually active adolescents do not use effective contraception. In a study of 1032 randomly selected Philadelphia teenage girls, Loewenstein and Furstenberg (1991) found that fewer than half under age 17 reported that they used birth control during their first intercourse (Table 9.5). Age at first intercourse, and whether

♦ **BOX 9.2   MAJOR CONTRACEPTIVE METHODS: THEIR EFFECTIVENESS, ADVANTAGES, AND DISADVANTAGES**

Method	Effectiveness	Most Effective Methods	
		Advantages	*Disadvantages*
Condom	90%	No prescription needed Man can be responsible for birth control Inexpensive No side effects Helps prevent spread of venereal disease and AIDS	Use may intrude on lovemaking Some men report decreased pleasure; others report prolonged pleasure Requires planning
Condom and foam used together	95–99%	Mutual responsibility of partners	Requires communication skills
Oral (pill)	90–96%	Gives most protection Regulates menstrual cycle Does not intrude on lovemaking	May cause side effects Requires medical supervision Long-term effects still being researched
Contraceptive implant (Norplant)	99%	Capsule implanted in arm every 6 months	Side effects possible Requires medical insertion Removal may be difficult Expensive initial cost
Contraceptive injection (Depo-Provera)	99%	Injection once every 3 months Highly effective	Weight gain and other possible side effects including increased risk of breast cancer
IUD	95%	Nothing to do just before intercourse String easily checked Inexpensive Plastic IUDs one-time insertion only	Insertion may cause temporary discomfort May increase menstrual cramps and flow Uterus may reject it Requires medical supervision May aggravate pelvic infection
Diaphragm with jelly/cream	83%	No side effects Jelly acts as lubricant No medical supervision after insertion Can be used as part of sexual foreplay	Requires planning May interrupt lovemaking for insertion
Contraceptive foam	75–80%	No prescription needed	Use may intrude on lovemaking
Contraceptive sponge and suppositories		Inexpensive No side effects Provides lubrication Highly effective if condom is also used	Can be messy Must be used every time Can provide too much lubrication

| Method | Effectiveness | Most Effective Methods | |
		Advantages	Disadvantages
Periodic (rhythm)	80%	No hormonal or mechanical device No cost No side effects	Requires careful monitoring of basal temperature, vaginal mucus, and menstrual cycles Instruction must be given by professional or experienced user May require many days of abstinence each cycle
Sterilization	Nearly 100%	Permanently unable to conceive or impregnate Nothing to think about Onetime only cost for surgery Available to either man or woman	Cannot change mind about fertility later

Less Effective Methods	
Withdrawal	Man withdraws penis from vagina just before ejaculation. This method is cost free, is always available, and has no side effects. However, man may forget, may mistime, or may impregnate with lubricating fluid before ejaculating.
Breast feeding for 12 months	A woman usually does not ovulate while nursing, but she may be fertile before menstrual periods resume. Actual effectiveness is 60%.

Ineffective Methods (Myths)	
Douching	Sperm travel faster into the uterus and tubes than a woman can travel to her douche. Also, the force of the douche spray may help propel the sperm into the uterus.
Holding back	A woman's orgasm or climax has nothing to do with getting pregnant.
Virginity	If sperm are deposited near the vaginal opening they may get inside even if the woman has never had intercourse.
Positions	Any position where there is penis–vagina contact can result in pregnancy whether sitting, standing, or lying down.

Source: Adapted from Chilman, 1983, Table 14.2, pp. 264–267. *NY Times*, 1992, A1, A14.

Table 9.5 INTERCOURSE EXPERIENCE AND USE OF BIRTH CONTROL
IN A REPRESENTATIVE SAMPLE OF ADOLESCENT WOMEN
IN PHILADELPHIA (*N* = 1032)

	Had Intercourse (%)	Intercourse in Last 4 Weeks (%)	Used Birth Control at First Intercourse (%)	Used Birth Control at Last Intercourse (%)
Age (yr)				
14	12	4	25	52
15	29	10	44	61
16	42	18	44	63
17	53	28	39	71
18	72	39	50	72
Age at first intercourse (yr)				
<14			21	57
14			36	61
15			42	73
16			50	72
17			65	69
18			64	80
Race				
White	34	17	54	71
Black	55	24	37	67
Hispanic/other	32	20	40	46
Education				
In school	40	18	44	68
Out of school	77	41	45	66

Source: G. Loewenstein, & F. Furstenberg. (1991). Is teenage sexual behavior rational? *Journal of Applied Social Psychology, 21,* Table 3, p. 968. Reprinted with permission.

HIV/AIDS was discussed with the partner, were found to be strongly related to use of birth control at last intercourse, as was whether or not contraceptive protection was felt to detract from the enjoyment of sex (p. 973). The authors concluded that simple knowledge about birth control and attitudes about pregnancy and motherhood are not likely to have an important effect on contraceptive use (p. 983). However, they noted:

> Our data suggest that the simplest, but perhaps potentially most effective strategy would be to increase access to contraception—to reduce its cost, the embarrassment associated with it, and to help teenagers find a method that they are comfortable with and that interferes minimally with sexual spontaneity and pleasure. [Loewenstein & Furstenberg, 1991, p. 984]

To understand the use of condoms and other forms of birth control, we must consider the individual adolescent and his or her beliefs about sexuality, pregnancy, contraception, and HIV/AIDS (Byrne, Kelley, & Fisher, 1993; Chilman, 1983). First, in order to have contraceptives available, one must acknowledge the possibility of engaging in sexual relations. This involves an admission that one is a sexual person who may engage in sexual behavior.

It also requires a recognition that sexuality is not a spontaneous act, but a probable outcome of a heterosocial interaction. Thus, there is a conscious decision involved in obtaining contraceptives that requires both *acknowledgment* that one is going to have intercourse and *planning* for intercourse.

Second, contraceptives are not automatically available. One must seek them out in a store (and face the public acknowledgment of the druggist or check-out clerk), or seek medical assistance to obtain more effective methods. Therefore, the adolescent must not only recognize the need for contraceptives, but *take specific action* to have them available when they are needed.

Third, if one is not involved in regular sexual activity, continuation of contraceptive pills reminds a woman on a daily basis not only of her sexuality, but also that she does not currently have a partner. Using the pill without having a regular partner can bring fears of becoming promiscuous. Moreover, a woman also needs to have condoms available to protect against HIV/AIDS.

Fourth, many women have concerns about the side-effects of contraceptives, such as excessive bleeding from the pill or IUD, weight gain, or other effects from the pill.

Fifth, some women fear they may be infertile, sometimes because of statements made by their physician such as "You might have trouble getting pregnant."

Sixth, there are a number of perceived benefits to becoming pregnant: it proves one is a woman; it provides a child (to love and who will love her); it proves one is fertile; it may increase a man's commitment; it would please a lover; it can attract attention; and it can be an episode of risk-taking or thrill.

Finally, it may be thought that the risk of becoming pregnant is not very great, and one can obtain an abortion if necessary (Chilman, 1983, p. 116–117).

In addition, as noted in Chapter 4, the adolescent's level of cognitive development may inhibit planning for the possibility of intercourse (a formal-operations task during a period when this level of development may only be emerging). Similarly, adolescent egocentrism can also interfere with contraception because the imaginary audience is watching and the personal fable implies that bad things will not happen to oneself (Dembo & Lundell, 1979; Johnson & Green, 1993). For example, in a study of 300 adolescents age 14–19, those reporting that they were sexually active and used contraceptives had higher scores on a measure of formal operations and lower scores on a measure of the imaginary audience than those who were sexually active but did not use contraceptives (Holmbeck, Crossman, Wandrei, & Gasiewski, 1994).

Sarrel and Sarrel (1979) noted that some couples have worked out a system of sharing responsibility, for example by alternating using a diaphragm for several months followed by several months of using a condom. Today, this would require that both partners have tested negative for the virus associated with HIV/AIDS.

Use of condoms is not only a form of contraception, but also a means of preventing infection with HIV/AIDS and other diseases. In general, effective communication skills, self-confidence sufficient to request condom use, and the belief that use of a condom to prevent HIV/AIDS is socially acceptable have been found to be associated with consistent use of condoms by adolescents (DiClemente, 1992, pp. 48–49). Pleck et al. (1991) found that one-third of sexually active adolescent males (age 15–19) in the National Survey of Adolescent Males reported that they used condoms all the time; one-third used condoms sometimes. The authors found that condom use reflected a cost–benefit analysis by the adolescent: condom use was related to his degree of concern about HIV/AIDS and to his belief in a man's responsibility to prevent pregnancy (p. 742). Consistency of condom use was reported to be higher among African-American than among other groups of adolescent men (p. 743). The authors concluded:

> These findings imply that consistency of condom use by adolescent males could be improved by continued educational efforts emphasizing the benefits of condoms in preventing AIDS and pregnancy and by encouraging women to insist that men use condoms. The findings suggest that education directed toward a male's personal risks regarding pregnancy may not work as well as emphasizing responsibility in contraception and general social norms that support condom use. Negative concerns about reduction of sexual pleasure could be mitigated by development of more sensitive condoms or educational efforts promoting the potential erotic aspects of condom use. [Pleck et al., p. 744]

It is interesting to note that the reduced sensitivity men report when using a condom can be interpreted either as a disadvantage or as an advantage. In a survey for the magazine *Consumer Reports* (1989), about half of the men felt that condoms reduced pleasure, but the other half of the men found this reduced sensitivity to be an advantage because it allowed the man to prolong the sex act and have better control, which may benefit adolescent males who feel they ejaculate too quickly.

ADOLESCENT PREGNANCY

There has been a marked decline in adolescent childbearing, but not in adolescent pregnancy, from its peak in 1957. Because adolescent sexual intercourse has increased greatly during this period, these data indicate the greater use of contraception and abortion by teenagers. Studies of these phenomena have focused primarily on females, tending to ignore the role and feelings of the male partners; this is true, in general, for contraception, abortion, and parenthood.

Zabin and Hayward (1993) reviewed the data on adolescent sexual behavior and childbearing and concluded:

> There are two quite different problems of adolescent sexual activity and pregnancy in the United States today. One involves sexual initiation in the midteens and accidental pregnancy that generally terminates in abortion. The other involves sexual onset in the early pubertal or postpubertal years and accidental conception during the teen years, also often resulting in unintended abortion but very frequently in childbearing. Whereas the first problem knows no geographic, social, or economic boundaries, the second has become a familiar pattern in our most disadvantaged communities. [p. 115]

Although adolescent parenting is costly for society and may have some negative effects on the parents, especially on unwed mothers and underemployed fathers, the effects do not seem to be as negative or long-lasting as media reports would lead one to believe. Frequently, support from other family members helps to relieve the burden. Moreover, when balanced against the characteristics of the mothers before they became pregnant, the effects of childbearing alone are not as significant, in general, as the complex social and situational deficits imposed by the poverty, sexism, and racism experienced by many of these young mothers. "In general, and on the average, early childbearing would seem chiefly to add to the vulnerabilities of an already troubled population of young people" (Chilman, 1983, p. 143).

Children born of mothers under the age of 18 tend to have low birth weights, a higher incidence of mental retardation and learning disabilities, and greater physical complications than the children of mothers over age 18. Moreover, infant mortality rates are much higher for babies born to mothers under the age of 15 (Dreyer, 1982, p. 590). However, it is difficult to assess the relative effects of mother's age and other factors that may be related to adolescent motherhood, such as low income, racial/ethnic discrimination, and other situational deficits (Fennelly, 1993).

A remarkable study by Furstenberg, Brooks-Gunn, and Morgan (1987) began in 1966 with a sample of over 300 teenage women and their children who were interviewed periodically until 1984 when the children were 18 years old. Five years after giving birth, the detrimental effects of premature parenthood were clear in terms of educational, occupational, and marital decisions that lowered the women's relative economic position. However, there was notable variation among the group of young mothers. At the conclusion of the study, many of the mothers had found routes out of poverty by returning to school, finding stable employment, becoming married, and obtaining voluntary sterilization to prevent further childbirths. Those who became economically independent, compared with those dependent on welfare, had children who were doing better in school and reported less deviant behavior. However, about one-quarter of the respondents had remained primarily dependent on welfare. The authors noted that social programs that focus on teenage mothers need also to include males.

> Ameliorative programs focusing on education, job training, and stable job opportunities for disadvantaged males may be as important as similar programs for teenage mothers that we advocate. Put more forcefully, the problem of teenage parenthood cannot be solved by simply directing services exclusively to females. Indeed, our failure to address the marginal position of males in disadvantaged communities may contribute to the perpetuation of teenage parenting. [p. 153]

Finally, the surprising diversity of the mothers later in life had clear implications for their children: the children's chance of success is affected not only by the circumstances of their birth, but also by the success of their mothers (p. 129).

Zabin and Hayward (1993) recommended several intervention strategies: (1) educational services, to increase the level of knowledge; (2) family planning services; (3) improving the self-concept, aspirations, and skills of adolescents at risk for teenage parenthood; (4) pregnancy detection and counseling to provide choice early in the pregnancy and to identify adolescents who are at high risk for conception; (5) high-quality obstetrical care; (6) sexually transmitted disease diagnosis and treatment; (7) services for young men. They stressed the importance of confidentiality, services close to where the adolescent spends her or his time, and free and flexible care (pp. 90–113). Fennelly (1993), focusing on Hispanic youth, stressed the importance of culturally sensitive programs that involve the parents.

Miller and Paikoff (1992) reviewed a variety of adolescent pregnancy programs and concluded that successful programs must be carefully planned and intensive. They found no simple solution exists, but that a combination of approaches can be effective:

Providing knowledge (JUST SAY KNOW) and encouragement for teenagers to wait (JUST SAY NO or NOT YET), and encouraging or dispensing contraceptives (JUST SAY NOT WITHOUT USING SOMETHING) are fundamental approaches. Postponing sexual intercourse and contraceptive approaches are not mutually exclusive . . . (Zabin, 1992). Furthermore, these strategies can be made more effective by increasing motivation and skills to avoid pregnancy and by helping teens understand that they could have much to gain by avoiding pregnancy until they are older (I HAVE OTHER THINGS TO DO). [p. 282]

SEXUALLY TRANSMITTED DISEASES

Sexual relations usually involve considerable intimate contact with another person. Thus, a variety of diseases may be passed from an infected person, who may or may not have symptoms of the disease, to his or her sexual partner. These diseases are known as **sexually transmitted diseases (STDs)**. These diseases are not caused by sexual behavior. The diseases are caused by bacteria, viruses, and other organisms that one may be exposed to during sexual contact. One may have all the sex one desires in a mutually exclusive (monogamous) relationship without increasing the risk of disease. However, if one has more than one sexual partner, or if one's exclusive partner has other partners, each of whom may also have different sexual partners, then the risk of disease increases greatly.

Therefore, persons with more than one sexual partner should be examined by a physician or clinic to avoid passing any disease. It is possible that the individual will have to ask specifically for an STD checkup of all the bodily organs used in sexual contact so that they will be examined. Depending on the number of partners and the type of sexual activity, check-ups should be done at least once every 3–12 months; if one is active with many partners, then once a month checkups are advised, and one should become well-informed about the serious health risks that may result from the current epidemic of STDs.

Not surprisingly, some persons with STDs avoid checkups. Unfortunately, many of the symptoms of the diseases go away by themselves, but the disease does not. One can transmit the disease without having symptoms. The disease may recur or cause severe long-term consequences. Some of the more common STDs are listed in Box 9.3; HIV/AIDS is discussed in the next section.

Lesbian women appear to be relatively free of STDs (Robertson & Schachter, 1981). However, sexually active gay men are especially at risk for two other diseases in addition to those listed for men in Box 9.3: hepatitis and enteric diseases. Hepatitis, a viral or bacterial infection of the liver that can cause permanent damage to the liver, may be fatal and may be related to the later development of liver cancer; a vaccine is now available and is usually recommended for gay men, hospital workers, and persons who have contact with blood. Enteric diseases are a group of bowel infections caused by parasites or bacteria.

Francoeur (1982) suggested a number of commonsense basic health principles for reducing the risk of STDs:

One night stands, casual pickups and sexual intimacy with persons you hardly know pose a much greater risk than long-term relations with someone you know fairly well. The more sexual partners you have, the greater the risk of STD.

Proper and consistent use of a condom and washing after sexual activity can reduce the risk when one is not monogamous or sexually exclusive.

For a woman on the pill, a condom provides additional protection against the increased tendency to vaginal infections that comes with the effect of the hormonal pill on the vaginal environment.

Vaginal contraceptives, foams and creams, may provide some protection for both men and women.

Watch for sores, rashes, or discharge around the vulva or penis, or elsewhere on the body, especially the mouth. Avoid kissing or oral sex with cold sores.

Wash sexual organs with soap and warm water before and after contact. Urinate soon after intercourse. [p. 321]

As with all aspects of sexual behavior, responsibility for healthful sexual activity rests with the individual. For many reasons, including adolescent egocentrism ("it can't happen to me"), young people are likely to take risks in their sexual lives. Also, as will be discussed in Chapter 12, they may avoid physical examinations and fail to follow the prescribed treatment for a disease. Therefore, education for effective health promotion and sensitive, supportive medical care needs to be provided for adolescents, especially those who are sexually active.

ACQUIRED IMMUNE DEFICIENCY SYNDROME (AIDS)

Adolescents today are coming of age in the era of HIV/AIDS (Brooks-Gunn & Furstenberg, 1990). Although the number of reported cases of adolescents with HIV/AIDS is relatively small (about 1% of all cases), it has increased steadily. Of course, because of the lengthy incubation period, many young adults who develop the disease may have been infected when they were adolescents. Statistically, adolescents with HIV/AIDS are more likely to be female than is the case for adults; the method of transmission is more likely to be heterosexual sex than is true for adults; and over half of adolescents with HIV/AIDS are members of minority groups (pp. 60–61).

Most adolescents know the ways in which persons become infected by the virus associated with AIDS, the human immunodeficiency virus (HIV): semen or blood from an infected person, which can enter the body during sexual intercourse or by sharing IV needles; at birth or from breast milk if the mother is infected; and by transfusion of blood from an infected person.

However, a majority of sexually active adolescents who have participated in research studies have reported that they engage in unprotected sexual intercourse that puts them at risk of infection with HIV. In addition, adolescents who are incarcerated are less likely to be informed about HIV/AIDS and also are more likely to be engaging in risky behavior than adolescents in school. Moreover, information about the transmission of HIV/AIDS has generally not reached non-English-speaking immigrant groups (Hingson & Strunin, 1992).

Educators should discuss adolescent beliefs about AIDS and should emphasize the growing susceptibility of adolescent females to infection. They should reinforce the fact that while some drugs, such as AZT, can prolong the lives of HIV-positive persons, no cure exists and that sexual abstinence and not using injection drugs are the most effective forms of avoiding infection. For those adolescents who do not refrain from sexual activity, educators should emphasize that condom use is critical. Further, educators should demonstrate how to use condoms correctly and should indicate where condoms can be obtained. Perhaps even more important, adolescents need to receive instruction on how to negotiate safety with a potential sexual partner. Role-playing exercises might be particularly helpful in teaching these communication and negotiation skills. [Hingson & Strunin, 1992, p. 29]

◆ BOX 9.3   COMMON SEXUALLY TRANSMITTED DISEASES

Candida albicans vaginitis (*moniliasis, vaginal thrush, yeast, candidiasis*; fungal infection). The organism is frequently present in the mouth, vagina, and rectum without symptoms; it can be present under the foreskin of an uncircumcised male. It can be carried from the rectum to the vagina by menstrual pads or by wiping after bowel movements. It may follow oral sex, coitus, or antibiotic medication. It occurs more commonly when a woman is taking contraceptive pills, and during pregnancy. Symptoms include thick, white, cream-cheeselike vaginal discharge; yeast-like odor; irritation; and itching.

Gonorrhea (bacterial infection). It is transmitted through sexual contact (vaginal, oral–genital, anal) with someone who has it. Symptoms appear within 2 weeks of contact; 80% of women and up to 20% of men have *no symptoms*. In women, symptoms are greenish or yellow-green vaginal discharge and irritation of vulva. In men, symptoms are painful urination and discharge from the urethra. In both sexes, it may infect the throat through oral–genital contact, or the anus through anal intercourse. Serious long-term effects may occur if it is not treated.

Hemophilis vaginalis (*vaginitis*; bacterial infection). This organism is frequently present in females with no symptoms; in males it may be a cause of non-specific urethritis (NSU); see below. Symptoms include a profuse creamy white or gray vaginal discharge and foul odor.

Herpes genitalis (*herpes simplex II, genital herpes*; viral infection). This is transmitted through direct contact with blisters or open sores through petting, sexual intercourse, and anal or oral sex. Avoid oral sex or kissing if partner has a cold sore on or in the mouth (*herpes* I causes cold sores and may be active in sexual infection). Symptoms include tender, painful blisters on sexual organs and surrounding areas; painful urination or bowel movements; blisters in vagina or on cervix (not painful); tender and enlarged lymph glands; and possible fever. Symptoms erupt for an infectious period and then go away while the disease is dormant; the blisters reappear from time to time. They may be reactivated by stress, hormone changes, sunbathing, food allergies, cold, or fatigue. Use condom or abstain from sexual contact in the affected area when symptoms arise and until all external signs of the infection are gone in both partners. The risk of cervical cancer is increased in women with herpes and a Pap smear every 6–12 months is recommended; herpes may be linked with cancer in males. There are serious dangers to an unborn child.

Nongonococcal urethritis (*NGU, NSU*). The signs and symptoms resemble a mild gonorrhea infection. One common cause is *Chlamydia*, a bacteria-like organism. Depending on the cause, it may or may not have serious effects on the infected person and unborn child.

Pubic lice (*crabs*; parasitic). Lice are ransmitted by skin-to-skin contact, and also from bedding, clothing, toilet seats, and chairs. Symptoms include itching, pinhead-sized dark spots on underwear (may be eggs

As noted above, condoms are more likely to be used if peers support condom use and if the individual perceives that the benefits of condom use outweigh the costs (DiClemente, 1992b; Pleck et al., 1991). For example, does embarrassment or lack of stimulation "cost" more than the "benefit" of responsibility and safety? Use of drugs or alcohol is also related to risk of HIV infection, because responsible decisions are more likely to be made when one is sober.

In addition to education about HIV/AIDS transmission and prevention, skill training in negotiating responsible sexual behavior, changes in adolescent attitudes about condom use, and effective outreach to adolescents who are homeless, incarcerated, and non-English speaking, public health efforts must also focus on helping adolescents obtain HIV testing.

or bloodspots), and possible rash. Over-the-counter medications may kill the active lice, but not all eggs, so a reinfestation is possible. Kwell (requires a prescription in many states) is more effective. Boil underwear and dry-clean or launder in hot water all possibly infected clothing and bedding.

Syphilis (bacterial infection). This is transmitted through sexual contact (vaginal, oral–genital, anal) with an infected person. Fluid from syphilitic sore or rash infects skin. Symptoms appear within 3 months of contact. A painless sore (*chancre*) appears where the bacteria entered the body but disappears in 1–5 weeks; the disease then produces other symptoms, which again disappear; then it attacks internal organs. Serious long–term effects are possible if not treated; serious effects are also possible on a fetus infected in the womb. A blood test is available.

Trichomonas vaginalis (*Trich, TV*; parasitic). This is transmitted by a parasite found in some men and women with no symptoms; it is passed back and forth during intercourse, with the male rarely showing symptoms. It may be transmitted during lesbian lovemaking through vaginal contact. It is also transmitted by moist towels, bathing suits, underwear, washcloths, and toilet seats. Female symptoms are yellowgreen or gray, thin, foamy vaginal discharge; foul odor; and vaginal irritation. It often flares up around the time of menstruation. It is more common among women taking contraceptive pills. If un-treated, it may be linked with cervical cancer in women and urethral blockage in men.

Venereal warts (*genital warts*; viral infection). These are transmitted by direct contact with warts through vaginal, anal, or oral sex. Painless warts appear 1–3 months after contact. They are detected by examining genital areas regularly with fingers (especially in and around vaginal and rectal openings) and looking for new bumps in the skin. Visually, they appear soft, pink or red, in single or multiple clusters in most areas of the body; in dry areas, they are small, hard, and yellow-gray. They are highly contagious and can spread into the vagina and rectum. They may be transmitted to the child at delivery.

Medical advice should be sought for all of these diseases. Partners who may have been the source of the disease, or who may have picked it up from you, should be contacted as soon as the disease is diagnosed. Note that a person may carry one of these diseases without having symptoms, but can transmit it to a partner. It is important to follow the treatment procedures carefully and to ask the physician any questions you may have. If your physician is uncomfortable, or makes you feel uncomfortable, find another doctor. A toll-free hotline, operated by the Centers for Disease Control, is available to answer questions about sexually transmitted diseases: 1-800-227-8922

Source: Adapted from Francoeur, 1982, pp. 322–331.

This blood test may be performed anonymously, and it can provide an important opportunity for early education, intervention, and treatment, if necessary (English, 1992). The test determines whether the body has produced *antibodies* to the HIV virus; if there are antibodies (a positive result), the individual has been infected with HIV and is at risk for eventually developing AIDS. A positive result also is an indication that the person can transmit the virus to others by sexual contact (but not by ordinary household contact), and that medical treatment may be beneficial. A negative result indicates that no antibodies have been formed, but it is possible that one has been infected recently; therefore, a second test several months later is needed to confirm the negative result. Of course, if an adolescent has not engaged in sex or

All adolescents are potentially at risk for HIV/AIDS every time they have sexual relations or use IV drugs.

used IV drugs (or had a blood transfusion or was born to or nursed by an infected woman), there is no reason to expect an HIV infection. If one is negative, then there is an important motivation to remain uninfected; moreover, two uninfected sexual partners who do not use IV drugs or have sex with anyone else can have sex without fear of HIV infection.

Obviously, education about the risk of infection by the use of IV drugs that are used with needles contaminated with another person's blood and treatment for IV drug abuse are also important components of HIV/AIDS prevention programs.

Finally, it should be noted that the fear of HIV/AIDS can be an important public health problem in itself. That is, the irrational fear of catching HIV/AIDS from mosquitos, public toilets, or from donating blood can lead people to behave in irresponsible ways (Kirby, 1992). Similarly, the fear of persons with HIV/AIDS can lead to unrealistic anxiety and inappropriate behavior. Because the virus is transmitted only in specific ways, one can touch, hug, and share a meal with a person with HIV/AIDS just as with any other person. For example, one study found that adolescents who know someone with HIV/AIDS had significantly lower anxiety about interacting with persons with HIV/AIDS than those who did not (Zimet et al., 1991).

This chapter has focused on one of the major themes of the developmental transition during adolescence. We have discussed the emergence of sexuality from its prenatal and childhood origins into fully adult sexual behavior. The development involves a process of transition from early adolescent sexual feelings to mature sexual interaction where one is responsive to the needs of one's partner and takes responsibility for the consequences of that behavior.

The next chapter focuses on another major theme of adolescence: the development of a sense of identity. As we will see, an individual's sexual identity is an important aspect of that process.

CHAPTER SUMMARY

1. Human sexuality reflects the influences of hormones, cognitive development, social learning, one's culture, the peer group, and the family. An individual's sexuality is as unique as his or her fingerprint.

2. From the moment that the gender of the infant is revealed, complex social processes begin teaching the meaning of femaleness and maleness in the individual's particular society, social class, and family.

3. Gender roles are not the same in every society. They affect attitudes about sexual behavior and may influence perceptions of responsibility for preventing pregnancy.

4. Throughout childhood, children learn about sex and sexuality in a variety of ways. The gradual discovery of one's own sexual turn-ons during adolescence or adulthood frequently reflects childhood experiences including puppy love, crushes, infatuations, and hero worship.

5. Sex education is more prevalent in schools than it was in the past. Yet, many adolescents continue to learn much of their information about sexuality from friends. Adolescents who do not receive accurate information may carry misconceptions or fears about their bodies and sexuality into adulthood.

6. As adolescents seek to understand their sexuality, they often explore and examine their own bodies through masturbation. They usually experiment with heterosexuality, and many of their concerns focus on relations with persons of the other gender.

7. Adolescents usually discover that their sexual feelings are directed toward persons of the other gender (heterosexual), or toward persons of the same gender (homosexual), or both (bisexual). Adolescents who come out as lesbian or gay may have to cope with hostile reactions from persons whose support they need most, such as their parents.

8. According to Sullivan, the major task of early adolescence is the integration of sexuality into the person's pattern of interpersonal relationships and feelings of worth as a person. This task involves deciding what sexual activities one prefers and integrating these into the rest of one's life. Conflicts between the needs for security, intimacy, and lust are typical during this process.

9. Dating, as a socially defined pattern of social–sexual interaction, provides an important opportunity for developing the skills, feelings of competence, and experience necessary for intimate relationships. Many adolescents experience several transitional relationships between the point when sexual feelings emerge and when a mutually supportive loving relationship develops.

10.   Very often the romantic love of adolescence is a kind of "being in love with love." It may be an attempt to discover one's own identity in a close relationship that involves sexual attraction. In contrast, Maslow defined B-love as an active love that is generous, therapeutic, mystical, and nonpossessive; it is based on an active decision to love and to bear the consequences of that decision.

11.   Concerns about private space, exposing one's body to another person, and feelings about trusting another to accept one's body become central as dating progresses from casual contact to more explicit sexual interaction. Another theme of initial sexual exploration is the process of separating from one's parents and becoming responsible for one's own behavior.

12.   Over half of all young people engage in heterosexual intercourse before the age of 19. There are considerable differences among adolescents in sexual behavior, but the typical sexually experienced adolescent is not very sexually active.

13.   For a variety of reasons, many sexually active adolescents do not use effective contraception. As a result there has been an increase in teenage pregnancy, abortions, and illegitimate births.

14.   Adolescent parents, especially single mothers, tend to be burdened with social, economic, psychological, and family problems that existed before they became parents. The complex social and situational deficits imposed by poverty, sexism, and racism appear to be even more significant than the effects of childbearing alone.

15.   Sexually transmitted diseases are not caused by sexual behavior; they are caused by bacteria, viruses, and other organisms that one is more likely to be exposed to if one has more than one sexual partner. Education for effective health promotion and sensitive, supportive medical care needs to be provided for adolescents, especially those who are sexually active.

16.   Acquired immune deficiency syndrome has placed the present generation of adolescents in jeopardy. Because no cure or vaccine exists, education to inform adolescents about AIDS and to enhance the adolescent's self-confidence to refrain from IV drug use and sexual contact or to follow safe sexual guidelines is the only effective prevention.

KEY WORDS

acquired immune deficiency syndrome (AIDS)	D-love	human immuno-deficiency virus (HIV)	romantic love
bisexual	gay men	lesbians	romantic myth
B-love	gender-role socialization	lust dynamism	sexually transmitted diseases (STDs)
date rape	homosexuality	masturbation	transitional relationship

REVIEW QUESTIONS

DEVELOPMENT OF HUMAN SEXUALITY

1.   Explain the statement: "The origins of human sexuality begin before birth."

2.   Give three examples of gender-role socialization.

3.   What is the effect of traditional gender role attitudes of adolescent males, according to the study by Pleck et al. (1993)?

4.   What is (are) the most striking contrast(s) between the sexual behavior of Japanese, Hispanic, and African-American adolescents, as reported in the text?

5. Describe some of the ways children learn about sexuality.

6. What effect did Kilpatrick (1992) find in her study of women who had consensual sexual experiences as children and adults?

7. Explain the statement: "One's sexuality is as personally idiosyncratic as one's face, signature, or fingerprints."

8. How do adolescents learn sexual *scripts* such as how to behave on a date?

9. Do the attitudes expressed in the nationwide study of adolescents differ from yours? Are they different from attitudes of adults you know?

QUESTIONS AND CONCERNS ABOUT SEXUALITY

10. Why do some adolescents lack information about sexuality?

11. What was the difference in condom use between adolescent males who learned about sex from friends and those who learned about it through sex education?

12. Are there sound reasons to encourage adolescents to explore and to examine their own body and sexual organs? What are they?

13. How would you explain the finding in the Jemmott and Jemmott (1990) study where 94% of the men said they had sexual intercourse within the last year, but only 14% said they had ever masturbated?

14. What implications does the term "opposite sex" convey regarding sexual relations? Do you prefer the term "other gender" or "opposite sex?" Why?

15. How does the traditional male gender role affect sexual behavior and intimacy according to Masters and Johnson (1979) and Pleck et al. (1993)?

16. What is the role of fantasy in sexual activity?

SEXUAL ORIENTATION

17. Gay men are sometimes confused with transvestites; what is the actual difference between them?

18. What is known about the cause of heterosexuality, bisexuality, and homosexuality? Is it biology or choice?

19. Describe some of the difficulties a lesbian adolescent might experience because of social attitudes about homosexuality. Are they different than for a gay male adolescent? Why?

LOVE, LUST, AND ROMANCE

20. How do transitional relationships differ from chumships? What is the function of each type of relationship for the adolescent's development?

21. In Sternberg's model of three components of love, what type does intimacy and passion (without commitment) produce?

22. What does Hatfield's conclusion that "adrenalin makes the heart grow fonder" imply about making love?

23. Describe the characteristics of the romantic myth in Western culture (e.g., Romeo and Juliet).

24. Contrast B-love with D-love. Where would B-love fit on Sternberg's model (Figure 9.1)?

25. What would you teach adolescent boys about date rape? What would you want adolescent girls to know?

SEXUALITY AND ITS IMPLICATIONS

26. Describe the major characteristics of what is known about adolescent heterosexual behavior.

27. What are some of the reasons adolescents do not use contraception and how can their use be encouraged?

28. Summarize the main findings of the Furstenberg et al. longitudinal study of teenage women and their children.

29. List several sexually transmitted diseases that can be prevented by the use of a condom (in addition to HIV/AIDS).

30. What are the major goals of HIV/AIDS prevention and education programs? How do these compare with the goals of pregnancy prevention programs?

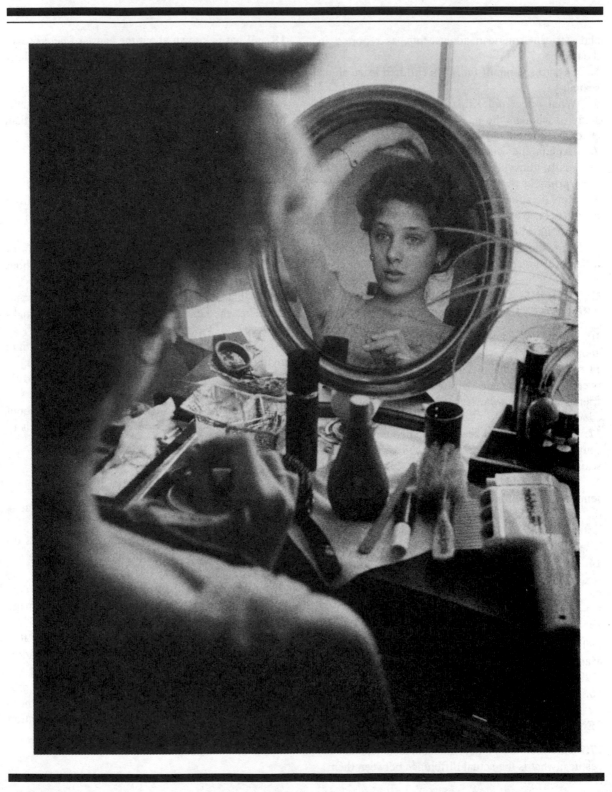

Chapter 10

◆

Forming a Sense of Identity

◆

In a great American play, Arthur Miller's *The Death of a Salesman*, Biff at age 34 confesses to his mother, "I just can't take hold, Mom, I can't take hold of some kind of life."

In a less famous but also psychologically sensitive piece of fiction, a novel by Romain Gary called *The Ski Bum*, Lenny is a young man who chooses detachment from family, country, love, and work. To a young woman he wants to take to bed but not into his heart, he recommends the following philosophy: "Trudi, when two people begin to stick together for good they end up by having jobs, kids, homes, cars, problems, and that's no love no longer, that's living. We don't want that" (p. 21).

These expressions of being unable or unwilling to make commitments reflect failure to complete the final phase of adolescent personality development: the formation of a **sense of identity**. Achieving a clear sense of one's identity is usually the last step in the several-year transition from childhood to adulthood. Although identity formation is thus primarily an adolescent process, it begins in infancy with life experiences that influence the concepts people form of themselves.

During the first 2 years of life children gradually develop a sense of being separate from other people. From ages 2 to 5 they begin to feel psychologically as well as physically discrete from other people, become aware of the anatomical differences between girls and boys, and take on some gender-typed preferences and behavior patterns (e.g., girls play with dolls and boys play with trucks). In middle childhood self-perceptions are sharpened by peer-group comparisons that identify how one's abilities, attitudes, and interests are similar to or different from those of others. At this time also, specific attitudes toward what boys and girls should do mature into broader concepts of gender-differentiated roles that shape a young person's subsequent masculinity and femininity (Damon & Hart, 1988; Harter, 1990a; Huston & Alvarez, 1990; Ruble, 1984).

These phases in the development of a self-system lead during adolescence to **identity formation**, which builds on what young people have learned about themselves as individuals having certain distinctive characteristics. A sense of identity consists of being reasonably sure of what kind of person you are, what you believe in, and what you want to do with your life. Forming an identity involves achieving an integrated view of your aptitudes and capacities, your values and preferences, and your ways of reacting to and being perceived by others. Once achieved, this integrated view generates a feeling of certainty and purpose in moving from the past to the future and lends continuity to how people think, feel, and act from one time and one situation to another. James Marcia (1980), a leading researcher on identity formation, has provided this further elaboration of what it means:

> [Identity is] a self-structure—an internal, self-constructed, dynamic organization of drives, abilities, beliefs, and individual history. The better developed this structure is, the more aware individuals appear to be of their own uniqueness and similarity to others and of their own strengths and weaknesses in making their way in the world. The less developed this structure is, the more confused individuals seem about their own distinctiveness from others and the more they have to rely on external sources to evaluate themselves. [p. 159]

The first section of this chapter elaborates the nature of identity formation and its place within the adolescent transition from childhood to adulthood. Three subsequent sections address (1) steps along the way in the process of identity formation, which include, in addition to *identity achievement,* the way-stations of *identity diffusion*, *identity foreclosure*, and *identity moratorium*; (2) individual differences in identity formation in relation to family, gender, ethnic, socioeconomic, and vocational-choice influences; and (3) the relationship between identity formation (which is a normative feature of development) and adolescent turmoil (which is not).

THE NATURE OF IDENTITY FORMATION

The role of identity formation in adolescent development was first delineated by Erik Erikson (1959, 1963, 1968), whose work we introduced in Chapter 2. As noted there, Erikson's developmental scheme divides the life cycle into eight stages, each of which poses a particular psychosocial challenge or "dialectical struggle" for the individual. He sees the primary developmental challenge of adolescence as preparing to meet adulthood with a cohesive and comfortable set of self-perceptions and aspirations:

> The wholeness to be achieved at this stage I have called a sense of inner identity. . . . Individually speaking, identity includes, but is more than, the sum of all the successive identifications of those earlier years when the child wanted to be, and often was forced to become, like the people he depended on. [Erikson, 1968, p. 87]

Sometimes people have difficulty learning enough about themselves and their surroundings to forge an identity that fits realistically with their personal characteristics and harmoniously with their environment. Then they experience what Erikson called **identity confusion**. This kind of confusion involves feeling very uncertain about oneself and one's possibilities in life, and it often interferes with taking full advantage of one's talents and opportunities.

DIMENSIONS OF IDENTITY FORMATION

Erikson's notions concerning identity formation as the central theme of adolescent development have been extended by numerous personality theorists and examined in an extensive research literature. This subsequent work has clarified the following seven dimensions of what it means to achieve a sense of identity:

1. People achieve identity to the extent that they are able to invest themselves in a relatively stable set of commitments. The less willing or able they are to make such commitments—as in the cases of Biff and Lenny mentioned at the beginning of the chapter—the more likely they are to lack a sense of identity.

2. The kinds of relatively stable commitments necessary to achieve a sense of identity involve deciding on (1) a set of values and beliefs to guide one's actions, which defines an **ideological stance**; (2) a set of educational and career goals to direct one's efforts in work, which constitutes an **occupational stance**; and (3) a gender orientation that influences one's forms of acquaintanceship and intimacy with males and females and establishes an **interpersonal stance**.

3. Identity formation is influenced jointly by *intrapersonal* factors, which comprise an individual's inborn capacities and acquired personality characteristics; by *interpersonal* factors, which include identifications with other people whose example is followed and respect

♦ *Profile*

ERIK H. ERIKSON

Erik Erikson would certainly acknowledge that his interest in the concept of identity reflects his own personal history. He was born in Germany of Danish parents in 1902, but his parents separated a few months before he was born. When he was 3 years old, his mother married a local pediatrician, and Erikson took his stepfather's name, Homburger, as his middle name. Erikson's mother and stepfather were Jewish, but he himself looked like a typical tall, blond, blue-eyed Dane; he was even called "the goy" (non-Jew) by Jewish boys. As a result, he was rejected by both Jewish and non-Jewish peers.

After graduating from high school, he spent several years traveling as an itinerant artist; according to his theory, this would be called a period of "moratorium." At the age of 25, an old school friend, Peter Blos, invited him to come to Vienna, where Erikson taught in an experimental school and was trained as a Montessori teacher. He also studied psychoanalysis with Anna Freud, one of the founders of the school where he taught, and was analyzed by her as a part of his training in analysis. While in Vienna, at age 27, he and a Canadian-born dance student, Joan Moivat Serson, were married and began a family.

The rise of Hitler forced the family to leave Europe in 1933. He settled in Boston, where he was welcomed as New England's only child analyst and met some of the influential social scientists of the day, including the anthropologists Ruth Benedict and Margaret Mead. Because of their influence, he went to the Pine Ridge Reservation in South Dakota to live with and to learn about the Sioux tribe of Native Americans; later he also studied the Yurok tribe in northern California. He moved on to San Francisco where he resumed his practice as an analyst and also participated in a study of normal children who were observed and inter-

for other people whose advice is heeded; and by *cultural* factors, which consist of the broad societal values to which a person is exposed while growing up in a particular country, community, and subcultural group.

4. Identity formation involves a several-year process of trying roles and ideologies on for size. Adolescents consider various job and career possibilities, they date and make friends with different kinds of people, and they weigh the merits of alternative social, political, economic, and religious attitudes. Because successful identity formation requires an active effort to examine types of work, friends, potential mates, and philosophies of life carefully before choosing among them, young people typically vacillate for a time in what they like to do and with whom.

viewed over a period of many years. Clearly he was exploring areas that Freud had not described—children growing up in different cultures and the lives of normal children.

During the Second World War, Erikson treated servicemen in a veterans' hospital. Many of the men appeared to be troubled because they could not reconcile their role as soldiers and killers with their previous role as civilians. He noted again, as he had in his studies of Native Americans, that conflicts involving *identity* could produce emotional distress that was as severe as the problems resulting from sexual conflicts that Freud had described earlier. Thus, although Erikson remained loyal to Freudian theory, he expanded it to include identity conflicts and other sociocultural influences. He described his ideas about these conflicts during eight stages of life in his classic book, *Childhood and Society*, first published in 1950. That same year he left the University of California because he refused to sign a loyalty oath that had become required of all faculty members during that period of anticommunist fervor; he resigned in protest when some of his colleagues were fired.

Erikson continued elaborating his ideas and teaching at the Austen Riggs Center in Stockbridge, Massachusetts, a center for treatment of emotional problems, and at Harvard University, where he was hired as a member of the faculty in 1960 even though he had never earned a formal college degree.

In 1985 he published the first of two other highly influential books, *Young Man Luther*, which was about the life of Martin Luther, the theologian who was important in the Protestant reformation. *Ghandi's Truth*, published in 1969, was about the man who led the struggle to remove the British from India by the use of nonviolent techniques and won Erikson both a Pulitzer Prize and a National Book Award. These books illustrated his genius for using psychological insights to understand people from different cultures and historical periods. After a brief illness, Erikson died in May of 1994 at the age of 91.

Sources: Based on Coles, R., *Erik H. Erikson: The growth of his work*, Boston: Little, Brown, 1970; Crain, W. C. *Theories of development*, Englewood Cliffs, NJ: Prentice Hall, 1980; Elkind, D., & Weiner, I. B. *Development of the child*. New York: Wiley, 1978.

5.   The better developed their sense of identity has become, the more fully people appreciate how they are similar to and different from others, and the more clearly they recognize their assets and limitations. The less well developed their identity, on the other hand, the less well people comprehend their own distinctiveness, and the more they need to rely on external opinions to evaluate themselves.

6.   People who have a clear sense of their personal identity generally feel good about themselves, work constructively toward well-defined goals, seek out and feel comfortable in close relationships with others, and remain relatively free of anxiety, depression, and other symptoms of emotional distress. Identity confusion, on the other hand, is often associated with low self-esteem, difficulties in setting and working effectively toward realistic goals, susceptibility to becoming emotionally upset, and strained interpersonal relationships.

7. Although achieving identity lends continuity and stability to people's lives, the process of identity formation never really ends. Adolescence comes to a close with the establishment of fairly firm commitments to ideological, occupational, and interpersonal stances. However, most adults revise their identities from time to time as they encounter new experiences and different roles, as, for example, when they decide to make a career change or when they first become a spouse, parent, boss, grandparent, widow, or retiree (Adams, Gullotta, & Montemayor, 1992; Josselson, 1989; Marcia, 1980; Waterman, 1982).

THE TIMING OF IDENTITY FORMATION

Although achieving a sense of identity becomes the primary developmental task of adolescence, young people do not begin immediately on becoming pubescent to wrestle with questions of who they are, what they believe in, and what they want to do with their lives. Other concerns come first, as we have discussed previously: adapting to rapid and dramatic changes in their bodies and cognitive capacities (Chapters 3–5); learning how to separate themselves from their parents and become self-reliant (Chapter 7); forming new patterns of relationships with their peers of both genders and becoming comfortable in their sociocultural environment (Chapters 6 and 8); and finding ways of enjoying romance and sexuality (Chapter 9). Not until adolescents have formulated some answers to how they feel about

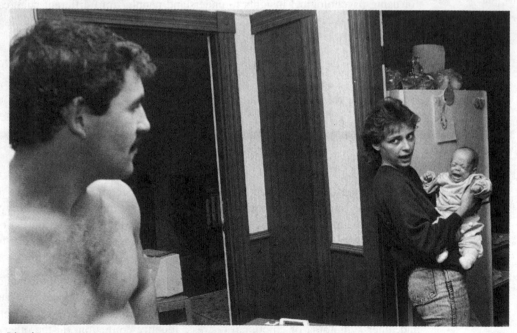

Identity achievement and the end of adolescence often occur earlier for young people who enter the working world and start a family after graduating high school than among those who go on to college.

College life gives young people opportunities to defer taking on adult roles and responsibilities.

these aspects of their lives are they ready to think about how all of these answers might fit together into an integrated sense of identity.

In addition to requiring a synthesis of diverse attitudes that have already been formed, identity achievement may require being able to think about oneself in a conceptually abstract way. Hence, the maturation of capacities for formal operational thinking may well have to precede being able to come to grips with identity issues. As reasonable as this sounds, we noted in Chapter 5 that there is, so far, no conclusive evidence that formal operations are necessary for identity achievement to occur. However, three areas of research do suggest that at least some aspects of cognitive maturity are closely associated with identity formation.

First, in studying specific kinds of Piagetian tasks used to measure formal operational thinking, Wagner (1987) found significant positive correlations between the identity level of 10–18-year-old subjects and their "combinatorial operations," that is, their ability to synthesize ideas in some meaningful fashion. Second, Chandler and his colleagues demonstrated that mature identity formation requires "relativistic doubt"; relativistic doubt emerges in adolescence when the absolute certainty that characterizes childhood thinking gives way to recognizing that things may not be as they appear and that events may have more than one plausible explanation (Boyes & Chandler, 1992; Chandler et al., 1990). As we mentioned in Chapter 4, relativistic doubt is available to adolescents with formal operational capacities, but not to those who still think exclusively in concrete operational terms. Third, Rothenberg (1990) concluded from an extensive research project on creative thinking that the development of creative capacity occurs primarily during the adolescent years and helps to establish a coherent sense of identity in young people.

Generally speaking, research studies also confirm that most of the work on identity formation takes place in late adolescence. Prior to the high school years, very few young people show much interest in contemplating lifelong commitments in any serious way. Then, from age 15 to 18, adolescents begin to pay increasing attention to exploring possibilities, sorting out their commitments, and seeking an identity. However, especially among young people who attend college, the greatest gains in identity formation occur between 18 and 21. Even among high school seniors who have already made seemingly stable commitments, the new and broadening experiences of college life often lead to some rethinking and further identity development (Adams, 1992; Grotevant, 1992; Patterson, Sochting, & Marcia, 1992).

Particularly with respect to occupational stance, the processes of exploration and commitment may extend well beyond the adolescent years. Moreover, young women who are interested both in careers outside the home and in traditional homemaking roles may marry and bear children early in their adult lives and defer until some later time a resolution of their higher educational and vocational objectives. This unique aspect of female identity formation is given special attention in our discussion of gender differences and vocational choice.

IDENTITY STATUSES: STEPS ALONG THE WAY IN IDENTITY FORMATION

The manner in which young people progress in their identity formation can be elaborated in terms of some discrete steps along the way, which are known as **identity statuses**. Adolescence typically begins in a status that Erikson called **identity diffusion**. Diffusion is a state of affairs in which the person has not made any firm commitments to an ideological, occupational, or interpersonal stance and is not currently considering any such commitments. Any tentative commitments that do occur tend to be short lived and quickly replaced by other equally tentative commitments.

After they grow to know themselves physically, cognitively, interpersonally, socially, and sexually, adolescents begin to reflect on the kinds of long-term commitments they might like to make. Erikson labeled this state of affairs an **identity moratorium**: Alternative choices are considered, different roles are experimented with, and final decisions are deferred during a period of active uncertainty.

Sometimes adolescents find that the uncertainty of contemplating alternatives while deferring decisions about the future causes more anxiety than they wish to endure. Then they may choose to remain in or revert to a state of identity diffusion, in which they put aside thinking about choices and commitments, or they may opt for what Erikson termed **identity foreclosure**. In the foreclosure status the person latches onto a convenient set of beliefs and life goals that comes along early, usually through being suggested or modeled by someone else, without ever going through a process of weighing other alternatives.

Adolescents who are able to shake themselves loose from identity diffusion and to avoid identity foreclosure slowly work their way through a period of identity moratorium until they settle on the relatively stable commitments that constitute **identity achievement**. Compared to people whose identity is foreclosed, and who have taken on commitments belonging to others, those who achieve identity are more likely to experience a sense of ownership in relation to the choices they have made. Our understanding of this developmental progression has been advanced by the availability of reliable instruments for measuring these four identity statuses and by research on the personality characteristics that are associated with each of them.

MEASURING IDENTITY STATUS

Empirical research on identity formation began with the development of the Identity Status Interview by Marcia in 1966. In this method of measuring identity status, subjects are asked a series of questions designed to reveal the extent to which they are considering or have made commitments to an occupational goal and to political and religious beliefs and attitudes. Responses are then coded by judges for their resemblance to the four identity statuses: *Achievement* is scored for evidence of firm commitments following a period of active uncertainty; *moratorium* for current uncertainty and an active weighing of alternatives; *foreclosure* for indications of firm commitments without any prior period of actively exploring alternatives; and *diffusion* for the apparent absence of commitments or of any effort to form them. Based on the averages of the judges' ratings, subjects are classified as belonging to one of the four identity status categories (Marcia, 1980). Some illustrative questions and answers from the Identity Status Interview are listed in Box 10.1.

Although Marcia's interview method helped to clarify the nature of identity formation and was an important impetus to research on the topic, it has some serious limitations. First, the Identity Status Interview evaluates commitment only in the two areas of ideology and occupation and does not ask about interpersonal attitudes. As we noted earlier, an individual's interpersonal stance is of equal importance with his or her ideological and occupational stances as an aspect of identity formation.

Second, assigning people to only one overall identity status can mask meaningful differences among their ideological, occupational, and interpersonal stances. One young person may have settled carefully on a career (achievement), be struggling with questions of ideology (moratorium), and not yet have begun to think seriously about interpersonal commitments (diffusion); another may have foreclosed on an interpersonal commitment (e.g., early

◆ **BOX 10.1 EXAMPLES OF THE IDENTITY STATUS INTERVIEW**

Question	*Typical Answers*
How willing do you think you would be to give up going into [a possible occupation mentioned by the interviewee] if something better came along?	Well, I might, but I doubt it. I can't see what "something better" would be for me. [Achievement]
	I guess if I knew for sure I could answer that better. It would have to be something in the general area—something related. [Moratorium]
	Not very willing. It's what I've always wanted to do. The folks are happy with it and so am I. [Foreclosure]
	Oh sure. If something better comes along, I'd change just like that. [Diffusion]
Have you ever had any doubts about your religious beliefs?	Yeah, I even started wondering whether or not there was a god. I've pretty much resolved that now though. The way it seems to me is . . . [Achievement]
	Yes, I guess I'm going through that now. I just don't see how there can be a god and yet so much evil in the world . . . [Moratorium]
	No, not really, our family is pretty much in agreement on these things. [Foreclosure]
	Oh, I don't know. I guess so. Everyone goes through some sort of stage like that. But it really doesn't bother me much. I figure one's about as good as the other. [Diffusion]

Source: From Marcia (1966).

engagement or marriage), be in a moratorium with respect to career choice (exploring but undecided), and be diffuse about ideology (e.g., not caring much one way or the other about political beliefs), and so on.

Third, even though judgments based on interviews can be reliable, they require careful training of judges and involve the individual administration of the interview to each subject. As an alternative, self-report questionnaires, although lacking some of the richness of interview methods, are usually easier to score reliably and administer to large numbers of subjects.

For these reasons, a variety of self-report scales and inventories have been constructed to extend Marcia's method to broader coverage of identity domains and to facilitate large-scale data collection. The currently most widely used such measure is the Extended Objective Measure of Ego Identity Status (EOM-EIS) developed by Grotevant and Adams (1984). The EOM-EIS is a questionnaire that asks subjects to rate 64 statements about exploration and commitment for the degree to which they are self-descriptive. Half of these items pertain to ideological identity formation and comprise eight statements about occupation, politics, religion, and philosophical life style; the other half of the items concern interpersonal identity and comprise eight statements each relating to friendship, dating, sex roles, and recreation.

Whereas the EOM-EIS treats the occupational domain as an aspect of ideology, we have spoken previously of ideology, interpersonal orientation, and educational and occupational goals as three equally important aspects of identity formation. In terms of the processes of exploration and commitment that it involves, we believe that choosing a career does indeed stand apart in developmental significance from choosing political, religious, and philosophical beliefs. Accordingly, even though the EOM-EIS research that we are going to examine next has not singled out occupational identity status, we discuss vocational choice as a topic in its own right later in the chapter.

SEQUENTIAL CHANGE IN IDENTITY FORMATION

First with the Identity Status Interview and later with the EOM-EIS, researchers have been able to examine how identity status changes over time. Following a model proposed by Waterman (1982), identity formation during adolescence can be described as proceeding in either a *progressive* fashion, a *regressive* fashion, or a *stagnant* fashion, and most young people will display some variation of one of these three patterns.

Adolescents typically begin the process of identity formation in a state of diffusion, as we noted earlier, not yet very much interested or engaged in sorting out their personal identity. In the progressive pattern described by Waterman, maturation from adolescence to adulthood typically involves progressing from an initial diffusion to a moratorium and then to identity achievement that remains in place. As a common alternative progressive path toward maturity, a person who has settled on certain commitments may subsequently find them less comfortable or less rewarding than they previously seemed to be. Then identity achievement may give way to some rethinking (moving back to a moratorium) that leads to a new and more satisfying sense of identity (progressing once more from moratorium to achievement).

Another way in which people often progress toward identity formation involves opting for foreclosure at some early point but later on entering a moratorium and moving toward identity achievement. This sequence typically occurs when foreclosed young people encounter life experiences that challenge their hastily formed commitments and convince them to think about them more carefully—such as finding out in college that one does not have much aptitude for or interest in some long-held career goal.

Goethals and Klos (1976) gave a good example of this last sequence in a report of personal interviews with college students, one of whom described giving up an earlier occupational foreclosure to consider other possibilities:

> I'm a psychology major. I originally wanted to go to grad school for a Ph.D. in clinical psychology. That's one option. Or work for a while. Or (my latest idea) go to law school. And in the next year before I finally have to decide, I'm sure I'll come up with two or three (at least) more options. [p. 195]

Unlike progressive shifts in identity formation, regressive shifts involve three ways of moving away from rather than toward identity achievement. A person with a foreclosed identity may give it up not in order to think some more about it (moratorium), but instead because of losing interest in prior commitments and not caring about replacing them. Then the person will be reverting from foreclosure to a state of identity diffusion. In a similarly regressive way, people in a moratorium may give up on the effort to find worthwhile commitments and sink back into diffusion, and people who have achieved identity may lose their sense of purpose—perhaps in response to unfortunate life experiences—and become identity diffused, without feeling any urge to seek new commitments. Most of us can think of people we know or know about who have shown these various patterns of progressive and regressive identity formation.

As for stagnant identity formation, two variations may occur. In some cases, young people remain indefinitely in the diffusion status without ever making a serious effort to work out identity issues. In other instances, teenagers foreclose their identities permanently and, without any further thought, carry into adulthood a set of goals and values to which they became committed in early or middle adolescence. Generally speaking, the persistence of identity diffusion and identity foreclosure reflects psychological immaturity. Although there are some gender differences in the implications of foreclosure that we will consider in the next section, most people with stagnant identity formation have been unwilling or unable to give serious attention to the developmental task of asking "Who am I?" and "What do I believe in?" Identity achievement, on the other hand, constitutes the mature resolution of such questions, and a moratorium signifies a constructive growth process in which answers to such questions are being sought.

Patterns of movement between identity statuses have been studied cross-sectionally for the most part, by comparing groups of young people at different ages. Cross-sectional differences in identity status, as measured by the EOM-EIS, are shown for the ideological and interpersonal domains in Figures 10.1 and 10.2. These findings, based on a large sample of girls and boys in grades 7–12, confirmed that early adolescents fall largely into the diffusion and foreclosure categories. With advancing age, the percentage of diffused and foreclosed young people decreases, while the percentage who are identity achieved increases sharply. Even so, only about one-third of the 12th-graders in this study demonstrated identity achievement, which is consistent with the expectation that the most dramatic changes in identity status occur in the late adolescent years from age 18 to 21.

Similar large-scale studies of the percentage of late adolescents showing each of the four identity statuses are not yet available. However, actual scores of 268 18–22-year-old male and female college students on the EOM-EIS are reported by Benson, Harris, and Rogers (1992). As shown in Table 10.1, these students scored highest by far on identity achievement and second highest on moratorium, with diffusion and foreclosure ranking third and fourth.

Also at the college level, Prager (1986) used an interview method to assess identity status in 86 female undergraduates. With respect to their occupational commitment, political and religious beliefs, and sexual values, these young women showed significant association between their identity achievement and their age and amount of college experience. The older they were and the more years they had been in college, the more likely they were to be have achieved identity. Taken together, hese findings from seventh-graders through college students demonstrate typical adolescent progression toward identity achievement and help to

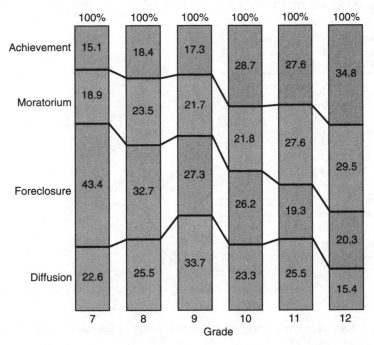

Figure 10.1 Ideological identity status among 7th- to 12th-graders. [*Source:* Based on EOM-EIS responses of 1,691 male and female adolescents studied by Christopherson, Jones, and Sales (1988).]

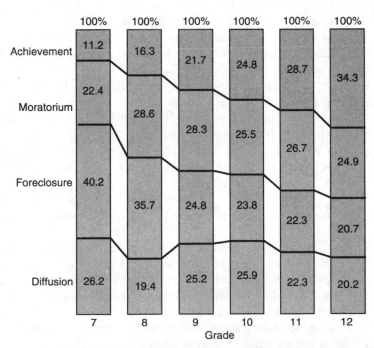

Figure 10.2 Interpersonal identity status among 7th- to 12th-graders. [*Source:* Based on EOM-EIS responses of 1,691 male and female adolescents studied by Christopherson et al. (1988).]

Table 10.1   IDENTITY STATUS SCORES
AMONG 18–22-YEAR-OLD
COLLEGE STUDENTS

Identity Status	Mean Score	
	Males (n = 127)	Females (n = 141)
Achievement	64.1	67.7*
Moratorium	49.6	49.5
Foreclosure	38.2	36.8
Diffusion	42.3	39.9*

*Significantly different from males at .05 level of confidence.

Source: Based on data reported by Benson, Harris, and Rogers (1992).

confirm that the achievement of a sense of personal identity is the most mature outcome of the identity formation process.

IDENTITY STATES AND IDENTITY TRAITS

How people think, feel, and act is influenced jointly by their states and traits. A person's **states** consist of how he or she is reacting to a current set of circumstances. For example, someone sitting down to take an exam or getting up to make a speech may feel anxious. This anxiety will be a transient reaction to the situation, and the state of anxiety it represents will pass when the exam is over or the speech is finished.

Although most people become anxious when they have to perform in some way, some keep fairly calm during their performance whereas others become too nervous to perform at all. Such individual differences in how people react to similar situations are determined by their **traits**, which are persistent tendencies to respond to experience in certain characteristic ways. Whenever the question is asked, "What kind of person is he (or she)?" the usual answer is a list of trait descriptions. A person being called on to perform might be someone who would be described as characteristically "nervous," "tense," and "high strung," or as "relaxed," "self-confident," and "unflappable." Differences in these traits would influence how calm or upset the person is likely to be in an anxiety-provoking situation.

This distinction is important because identity status exerts both state and trait influences on how people feel, think, and act. When identity has been achieved or has become stagnated in diffusion or foreclosure, it influences behavior as a persistent tendency to behave in certain ways. When identity is in flux, its influence is transient and changeable. This means that personality characteristics associated with each of the four identity statuses may be either habitual dispositions or temporary states, depending on whether the person's identity status is relatively fixed or in the process of progressing or regressing.

Achievement Status

Research findings confirm that young people in the identity achievement and moratorium statuses are more mature in virtually every facet of their personality development than those in the foreclosure and diffusion statuses. Identity achievers in particular are likely to be self-directed and self-confident people who are fairly free from anxiety, view themselves in positive terms, and feel good about what they can and will do with their lives. They tend to be the kinds of people who, although sure of themselves and their roles, remain open to new ideas. They confront problems directly but make decisions only after searching out and evaluating relevant information and considering carefully the consequences of their decision (Berzonsky, 1992; Berzonsky, Rice, & Neimeyer, 1990; Marcia, 1980; Papini, Micka, & Barnett, 1989; Shain & Farber, 1989).

Identity achievement and moratorium adolescents are also more likely than foreclosed or diffused adolescents to feel relaxed and comfortable in social situations. They are typically interested in and concerned about other people, as opposed to being preoccupied with their own needs and problems; they tend to be helpful and cooperative individuals who facilitate positive interpersonal interactions; and they are relatively agreeable to sharing their thoughts and feelings with others (Adams, Ryan, Hoffman, Dobson, & Nielson, 1984; Slugoski, Marcia, & Koopman, 1984). As would be expected, then, adolescents in an achievement or moratorium status more easily become engaged in intimate relationships with other people than do those in foreclosure or diffusion.

This interpersonal aspect of identity formation does not mean that identity-advanced girls and boys necessarily develop heterosocial interests sooner than their less mature peers. To the contrary, some important early research by Josselson, Greenberger, and McConochie (1977a, 1977b) suggested that adolescents who are progressing well toward identity achievement tend to take their time about getting involved in dating and sexuality. They anticipate being able to handle and enjoy heterosocial activities when they get around to them, and they rarely feel any urgent need to thrust themselves into socializing.

By contrast, adolescents who are less advanced in identity formation often lack confidence in their social skills. They may consequently feel a need to prove themselves socially and tie down commitments that spare them from having to worry about where their next date or next kiss is coming from. For this reason, adolescents who precede most of their peers in dating, going steady, and getting engaged may be showing identity foreclosure in their interpersonal stance, not mature progress toward identity achievement and true interpersonal intimacy.

Moratorium Status

Because they are engaged in positive progress toward identity achievement, adolescents in a moratorium status share with identity achievers a relatively high degree of self-directedness, self-reflection, and self-esteem. However, as might be expected from their being in a situation of indecision, in which they are actively exploring alternatives but have yet to make firm commitments, moratoriums are more likely than adolescents in any other identity status to feel uncertain about things and to lack fixed opinions. They tend to be especially ambivalent when it comes to choosing between going along with what others are thinking and setting their own agenda. When parents, peers, and teachers are asked to describe an adolescent who is in a moratorium, they are likely to do so in one of two ways. If they are feeling generally positive toward the person, they tend to see him or her as a flexible, sensitive, interesting, stimulating individual; if at the moment they are displeased with this same moratorium adolescent for some reason, they tend to see him or her as being nervous, indecisive, unpredictable, and irritating (Marcia, 1980).

Foreclosure Status

Adolescents in the foreclosure status have opted for premature commitments as a way of avoiding the challenge and uncertainty of making informed, self-determined choices. Not surprisingly, then, foreclosed adolescents show a higher degree of conformity, conventionality, rigidity, and dependence on authority than young people in other identity statuses. Compared to more mature youngsters in the achievement and moratorium statuses, they are less reflective, less independent, less self-confident, and less inclined to think for themselves. Because reflection and delay make them uncomfortable, adolescents in foreclosure are also likely to be more impulsive than their peers. On the other hand, for as long as they succeed in sustaining their commitments, while keeping their eyes closed to alternative possibilities, foreclosure adolescents are often the least anxious of the four identity status groups (Berzonsky, 1989; Bourne, 1978; Cella, DeWolfe, & Fitzgibbons, 1987; Papini et al., 1989).

The rigid conformity and unquestioning certainty that accompany identity foreclosure often make a favorable impression on other people, mainly adults, who are likely to praise foreclosed adolescents for their reliability, steadfastness, and sense of purpose. These qualities rarely help foreclosed adolescents enjoy good peer relationships, however. Typically they have a hard time relaxing in social situations and dealing with unplanned events or unexpected circumstances. They tend to be emotionally reserved rather than spontaneous and to limit themselves to carefully orchestrated friendship and dating relationships, and they often make premature personal commitments as a way of skirting exploration and avoiding uncertainty.

In a confirmation of such premature commitment, Lutes (1981) found that 18–21-year-old college students who were married were more likely to be identity foreclosed than identity achieved; a comparison group of unmarried college students were evenly divided among achieved, moratorium, and foreclosed conditions, with only a few instances of diffusion. Identity foreclosed college students have also been found by Slugoski et al. (1984) to gear their interpersonal stance to protecting their beliefs against being challenged or having to be evaluated. The foreclosed subjects in their study tended to relate to others in either an antagonistic manner (thereby resisting external influence) or in an acquiescent manner (thereby embracing external influence). Being either antagonistic or acquiescent allowed these students to establish and maintain certain attitudes and beliefs without putting themselves in interpersonal situations where they would have to defend or reconsider them.

There is also reason to believe that adolescents who are inclined to identity foreclosure differ from other young people in how closely they are attached to their families. Some theorists have proposed specifically that the patterns of family separation and individuation we discussed in Chapter 7 exert considerable influence on the identity status that young people are likely to show (Grotevant & Cooper, 1986; Josselson, 1989). With particular respect to identity foreclosure, adolescents in this identity status typically do remain strongly attached to their parents. Reluctance to separate emotionally from their parents contributes substantially to the preferences of foreclosed adolescents to avoid challenge, to commit themselves early on to what is familiar, and to value security over experimentation. We will have more to say about family influences in identity formation later in the chapter.

Diffusion Status

Like foreclosed adolescents, young people in the relatively immature identity diffusion status show less self-esteem, less self-directedness, and less self-control than those in the achievement or moratorium status. Sometimes the detached and disinterested approach to life that characterizes diffused adolescents is appealing, however, and they may be described by others as carefree, charming, and free spirited. Yet identity diffusion is the least adaptive of the four statuses, and young people who persist in this status are at high risk for developing psychological disturbances (Akhtar, 1984; Marcia, 1980).

Although adolescents with identity diffusion may not display much anxiety, they are often apathetic and socially distant. They tend to be shallow and self-focused individuals who are easily influenced by peer pressure but rarely impress their peers as people to depend on or confide in. Unlike achievement and moratorium adolescents who seek out new information, and unlike foreclosed adolescents who cling to old information, diffused adolescents generally avoid information of any kind. In similar fashion, they cope with problems by deferring action, and they deal with decisions by putting off making them. Whereas foreclosed young people are more likely than their peers to show persistent attachment to their families, adolescents with identity diffusion tend to be notably separate and disconnected from their families (Adams, Abraham, & Markstrom, 1987; Berzonsky, 1992; Josselson, 1989; Slugoski et al., 1984).

Now that we have reviewed the personality characteristics associated with each of the four identity statuses, we can see in Box 10.2 a concise summary of some of the major differences among them. The information in Box 10.2 was provided by ten active researchers on identity formation who were asked by Mallory (1989) to sort 100 statements about personality traits according to how well they describe people in an achievement, moratorium, foreclosure, or diffusion status. The Box lists characteristics that were regarded by these experts as most or least typical of each status for both males and females.

As a final item of interest, the interviews reported by Goethals and Klos (1976) included some comments from a college senior who had not made any applications either for a job or for further education. His words provide the following personal perspective on what it means to be persistently identity diffused:

> However, in my own case, I can't really say that, until recently, I have ever been overly preoccupied with the whole issue of making decisions. They aren't terribly enjoyable for me, and I make them only when it is absolutely necessary, which usually means that the consequences of not doing so would constitute a threat to the peaceful state of suspended animation in which I much prefer to remain. Whether they are trivial, routine choices, like deciding what flavor ice cream to order, or more important ones, such as choosing a college or a career, my tendency is almost always to avoid committing myself as long as I possibly can and eventually make the decision primarily on the basis of my immediate inclination. I suppose that's not an ideal way of going about things . . . It enables me to avoid a long and careful consideration of the course that the rest of my life should take. My problem is that, when I do reflect seriously upon my future, feelings of emptiness and despair often arise. [pp. 178-179]

♦ **BOX 10.2   CHARACTERISTICS TYPICALLY ASSOCIATED WITH IDENTITY STATUSES**

Most Typical	*Least Typical*
Identity Achievement	
Values own independence	Self-defeating
Clear, consistent personality	Brittle ego-defense system
Ethically consistent behavior	Reluctant to act
Warm, compassionate	Withdraws from frustration
Productive	Lacks personal meaning
Moratorium	
Values own independence	Emotionally bland
Philosophically concerned	Represses conflicts
Basically anxious	Satisfied with self
Rebellious, nonconforming	Calm, relaxed in manner
Introspective	Submissive
Foreclosure	
Sex-appropriate behavior	Rebellious, nonconforming
Satisfied with self	Unpredictable
Conventional	Unconventional thought
Moralistic	Lacks personal meaning
Conservative values	Introspective
Identity Diffusion	
Unpredictable	Clear, consistent personality
Avoids close relationships	High aspirations for self
Brittle ego-defense system	Warm, compassionate
Reluctant to act	Productive
Lacks personal meaning	Dependable, responsible

Source: From Mallory (1989).

A good question to consider at this point is what kinds of adult lives people are likely to have if they end their adolescence in an achieved, moratorium, foreclosed, or diffused identity status. Very little longitudinal research has been done to answer this question. However, some suggestive findings have emerged from a study by Josselson (1987, 1989), who interviewed 34 young women first when they were college seniors and again 12 years later, when they were in their mid-30s. As might be expected, those women who were foreclosed as college seniors showed the least change and remained basically the same psychologically as they were at age 21—purveyors of their heritage, carrying on family traditions, and remaining committed to activities and interests they had chosen as late adolescents but in reality had pretty much decided on as children or early adolescents.

The identity diffused college seniors in Josselson's sample were also basically unchanged in their mid-30s. They had gone in many different life directions, but, in Josselson's words, they ad typically functioned as "leaves blown by the wind," sitting back and letting events structure their lives rather than initiating constructive action to establish any such structure. The identity achieved women had fared best, altering their commitments somewhat over the years to enrich their lives but basically continuing in a purposeful way to implement the self-chosen identity of their adolescence. The moratorium group was the least predictable and most heterogeneous group over the 12 years of the study. Some had benefitted from favorable circumstances and strong support from friends and loved ones and gone on to form a solid sense of personal identity; others remained as uncertain as before, still searching and experimenting but not yet decided on how best to direct their lives.

INDIVIDUAL DIFFERENCES IN IDENTITY FORMATION

Beyond the patterns of identity formation that characterize adolescent development in general, there are developmental differences among young people that influence how they progress through this phase of growing up. To begin with, adolescents who have fared well as children in mastering developmental tasks are relatively likely to progress smoothly toward identity achievement; conversely, the more adjustment difficulties a young person has had before puberty, the more likely he or she is to travel a bumpy trail on the way to identity achievement, with periods of regression as well as progress and perhaps with stagnation in an immature identity status. In addition to this continuing impact of previous adjustment, individual differences in identity formation are shaped by family relationship patterns, gender influences, ethnic and minority group membership, and issues of vocational choice.

FAMILY RELATIONSHIP PATTERNS

As we discussed in Chapter 7, most families strike a balance between attachment and separation in rearing their adolescent children. They allow and encourage increasing self-reliance and self-determination while also requiring and expecting continuing commitment and belonging to the family. Such a balance in the individuation process fosters positive progress toward identity achievement. The increasing autonomy that adolescents are granted frees them to consider alternative commitments and beliefs and to make up their own minds about the kind of person they are and what they want to do with their lives. At the same time, continued connectedness to a supportive family gives adolescents a secure base from which to explore possibilities without worrying about getting lost at sea.

Instead of striking a separation-individuation balance that facilitates identity formation, parents may sometimes stress connectedness at the expense of autonomy for family members. Adolescents in this type of family are encouraged to adopt their parents' ideologies as their own and to follow a life path that their parents have set out for them. Consequently, they are more likely than their peers to foreclose their identity and to have difficulty maturing beyond foreclosure in their identity formation. A different but equally problematic result is likely should parents emphasize self-reliance at the expense of family support. Adolescents who are left too much to their own devices in finding their way in the world lack the secure base of operations that family attachment can provide. Fearful and uneasy about exploring uncharted territory without an adequate fall-back position, they may choose not to do so at all—and thereby remain mired in identity diffusion.

To elaborate this critical impact of parental style on identity formation, let us review how decisions are made in the three types of families we discussed in Chapter 7: *authoritarian* families, in which parents discourage their adolescent children from expressing opinions regarding their own behavior and rarely permit them to participate in decisions about what they should do; *authoritative families*, in which adolescents are encouraged to be a part of discussions concerning their behavior, although final decisions are usually made or approved by their parents; and *permissive* families, in which parents make relatively few decisions for their adolescents and turn over to them much of the responsibility for governing their lives. As might be expected, studies of the relationship between identity status and these family styles indicates that steady progress toward mature identity formation is closely associated with parental controls that promote independence within the context of supportive parental authority (Allison & Sabatelli, 1988; Benson et al., 1992; Cooper & Grotevant, 1987; Markstrom-Adams, 1992).

Specifically, *authoritative parents* are well positioned to help an adolescent son or daughter progress toward identity achievement. Their supportive, accepting, and responsible but not domineering stance fosters security in considering alternatives. Their children become accustomed to questioning the way things are and to taking independent action, while at the same time knowing that they can rely on their parents for help and advice when they need it. Being on their own but also having their parents right behind them gives valuable self-assurance in taking on the uncertainty of a moratorium and working to turn it into identity achievement.

Authoritarian parents, because they tell their children what to think and do, often promote identity foreclosure rather than movement through moratorium to identity achievement. Their offspring simply put on the clothes that are laid out for them, accepting their parents' choices and preferences as their own. The possibility remains that they will reconsider this foreclosure later on, in response to broadening experiences that lead them to question their parents' views. More commonly, a strong relationship will persist between having been reared in an authoritarian home and being identity foreclosed.

In some cases adolescents may rebel against the dictates of authoritarian parents and insist on finding their own way in life. Young people who enter a moratorium for this reason, in rebellion against authoritarian parents rather than with the support of authoritative parents, face an especially difficult challenge in achieving identity. Not having been encouraged to make their own decisions, they have little experience in thinking for themselves and little confidence in being able to do so wisely. Instead of being able to turn a moratorium into identity achievement, authoritarian-reared adolescents often give up any active rebellion sooner or later; then they either return to an endorsement of their parents' way of life or regress to a state of diffusion in which they stop thinking about their future.

Permissive parents, while giving their youngsters free rein to make their own decisions, seldom guide them in choosing well or facing up to their mistakes. As a result, permissively reared adolescents tend to shy away from considering alternatives. Like authoritarian-reared adolescents, they may be inclined to foreclose on their parents' preferences. This is not always easy to accomplish, however, because permissive parents are not very forthcoming about what their preferences are, especially when it comes to setting standards of conduct for their children and recommending life goals for them. As a result, permissively reared adolescents can be left uncertain about what to do as well as hesitant to test out possibilities, which makes them more likely than their peers to remain identity diffused.

As the opposite side of this coin, young people in different identity statuses are likely to differ in how they view their family. Those in a foreclosure report the closest relationship with their parents. Compared to peers in other statuses, they are most likely to express positive attitudes toward their mothers and fathers and to regard their family as child centered. They see their parents as possessive and intrusive, but also as supportive and encouraging, and they are willing and eager to involve them in their decision making.

Identity diffused adolescents are the least involved with their parents. They describe their mothers and fathers as indifferent, inactive, and detached, or as rejecting, overcontrolling, and unfair. Compared to adolescents in the other identity statuses, those in diffusion are most likely to perceive their families as lacking in effective coping skills, emotional cohesion, and channels of communication.

Adolescents in the moratorium and achievement statuses fall in between these two extremes. They are neither detached from their parents nor entirely at peace with them. More than the family oriented foreclosed adolescents and the family alienated diffused adolescents, adolescents in moratorium are relatively critical of their parents' views and relatively at odds with them about how they should lead their lives. As a moratorium resolves into identity achievement, these tensions gradually diminish and are replaced by mutual respect, although not necessarily agreement, concerning the young person's occupational, ideological, and interpersonal commitments (Adams & Jones, 1983; Campbell, Adams, & Dobson, 1984; Papini et al., 1989; Quintana & Lapsley, 1990).

Taken together, these findings support the expectation that identity exploration and subsequent commitments will be found in greatest supply in families that are characterized by openness and emotional connectedness. This research on family relationship patterns must be interpreted cautiously, however, because it demonstrates *associations* and not necessarily *cause-and-effect relationships*. Could it be, for example, that the parents of an identity diffused adolescent became uninvolved as a result of their daughter or son showing little interest in doing anything or becoming something? Similarly, have authoritarian parents caused their youngster to become excessively dependent on them, or have they responded to an overly dependent child by providing guidance that was constantly being sought? Additional longitudinal research is needed to determine the sequence in which parental styles and adolescent identity status influence each other over time.

GENDER INFLUENCES

In Figures 10.1 and 10.2, we examined age-related changes in the percentage of junior and senior high school students showing each of the four identity statuses in the ideological and interpersonal domains. Figure 10.3 indicates the percentage of males and females among these same 1,691 students who demonstrated each identity status.

As Figure 10.3 indicates, girls tend to mature somewhat more rapidly than boys in their identity achievement. In the ideological domain, 56.7% of the girls compared to 41.6% of the boys were either identity achieved or in moratorium and working actively toward achievement status; in the interpersonal domain, 57.7% of the girls compared to 42.9% of the boys were identity achieved or in moratorium. There are also some gender differences between the ideological and interpersonal domains. Note that in the ideological domain, the

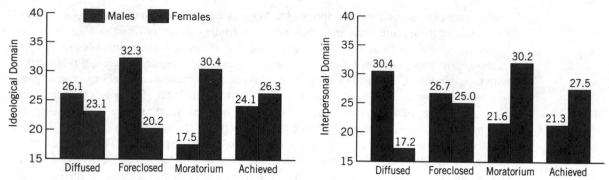

Figure 10.3 Identity status distribution among male and female 7th- to 12th-graders. [*Source:* Based on EOM-EIS responses of 1,691 male and female adolescents studied by Christopherson et al., (1988).]

boys were similar to the girls in frequency of diffusion and showed lack of maturity primarily through being more frequently foreclosed (32.3% of the boys versus 20.2% of the girls); in the interpersonal domain the boys resembled the girls in foreclosure and showed immaturity primarily through being more frequently diffused (30.4% of the boys versus 17.2% of the girls).

These findings suggest that concerns about beliefs and occupational goals and concerns about interpersonal relatedness play somewhat different roles in the identity formation of adolescent males and females. As we shall see next, research findings do in fact confirm gender-identity differences in interpersonal and intrapersonal orientations, gender-role orientation, and adjustment.

Interpersonal and Intrapersonal Orientations

There is good evidence to indicate that females are generally inclined to focus on *interpersonal* aspects of their identity formation, such as their attachments and connections, and males on *intrapersonal* matters, such as their individuation and achievements. What this means is that late adolescent females are more likely than males to learn about themselves from the kinds of people with whom they have good relationships; among late adolescent males, identity is more likely to be formed on the basis of *what* they are doing rather than *with whom*. Commitments to ideology and vocation are more central to the identity concerns of boys than of girls, whereas girls are more likely to be concerned than boys about commitments relating to friendship, dating, love, sex, and marriage (Cosse, 1992; Dyk & Adams, 1990; Josephs, Markus, & Tafarodi, 1992; Patterson et al., 1992; Paul & White, 1990).

In a similar vein, observations of same-sex late adolescent friends reveal that female pairs tend to talk more often and in greater detail about interpersonal relationships and to value friendship for its *intimacy*; male pairs tend to talk more often and in greater detail about activity-oriented topics and to value friendship for its *instrumentality*, that is, for its usefulness in helping to achieve some purpose or goal (Reis, Senchak, & Solomon, 1985; Richards & Larson, 1989). Studies of both junior and senior high school students indicate that, in general, girls are more involved than boys in the personal lives of their friends and more concerned about their welfare (Gore, Aseltine, & Colten, 1993; Skoe & Gooden, 1993).

In an interesting demonstration of such gender differences, over 1,500 college students were asked to write brief stories about a series of pictures that portrayed two people in some kind of interaction. The female students attributed significantly more warmth, closeness, and communication to the interactions between the characters in their imaginative stories than did the male students; the male students did not appear to be avoiding or denying intimacy but were simply less likely than the females to think of it or consider it important in writing their stories (McAdams, Lester, Brand, McNamara, & Lensky, 1988). Hence it seems reasonable to conclude that gender differences in intimacy are matters of preference rather than capacity. There is no basis for doubting that males can desire and experience intimacy just as deeply as females, or that females are every bit as capable of being instrumental as males. What distinguishes the genders with respect to their identity formation are the priorities generally assigned to intimacy by adolescent girls and to instrumentality by adolescent boys.

As we noted at the beginning of this chapter, identity formation in general and gender-role identity in particular have their origins in developmental experiences going back to early childhood. What is noteworthy about adolescence with respect to the development of interpersonal and intrapersonal orientations is **gender intensification**. Gender intensification refers to the fact that the distinctions young people draw between what constitutes femininity and what constitutes masculinity increase with age and begin to crystallize following puberty. Whatever beliefs children have about gender-determined characteristics of people *intensify* during their adolescent years, which is part of the reason why boys and girls become so increasingly different from each other as teenagers. With specific respect to the greater preference for sociability among girls and for instrumentality among boys, this difference in orientation is present earlier in life but becomes especially pronounced during adolescence (Biernat, 1991; Huston & Alvarez, 1990; Richards & Larson, 1989).

The prevailing interpersonal orientation among young women and the intrapersonal orientation among young men does not rule out individual differences within as well as between the sexes. In any group of adolescents some minority of the boys will be more concerned about becoming proficient in interpersonal relationships than about developing their individual talents, and some minority of the girls will be paying more attention to honing their skills than to how they are getting along with others. This raises an interesting question: Are the boys who differ from the usual pattern in this way showing evidence of some feminine identification, and are the girls who differ from the usual pattern displaying masculinity?

There is no simple answer to this question because it cannot be separated from society's views concerning what constitutes appropriate gender-role behavior. As an important case in point, the last generation has seen dramatic changes in how career goals are viewed for men and women. The frequency with which girls as well as boys are encouraged to develop and use their talents has increased greatly, and the number of women who aspire to enter challenging careers—including many that had earlier been almost entirely the province of men—has grown enormously. Correspondingly, men are much more likely than in the past to share child care and homemaking responsibilities with their wives, to support their wives' career activities outside the home, and even to subordinate their own career goals to those of

More frequently than in the past, women are forming their occupational identities around challenging and distinguished careers—as exemplified by Janet Reno, Attorney General of the United States.

a wife with more talent or better prospects. These societal changes may make it seem less masculine, or not masculine at all, for a young woman to be preoccupied with career aspirations, and less feminine for a young man to be interpersonally oriented.

Masculinity, Femininity, and Androgyny

In concert with society's accepting views toward a broadening range of individual differences in gender-role orientation, accumulating evidence suggests that people are likely to benefit from being able to adopt some of the interests and attitudes traditionally associated with the other sex. It may well be that an identity based not on femininity or masculinity alone, but on **androgyny**, facilitates becoming a competent, flexible, and well-adjusted person. These notions about androgyny were first formulated by Sandra Bem (1974, 1975), who explained the concept in the following way:

> It is now the "androgynous" person, capable of incorporating both masculinity and femininity into his or her personality, who is emerging as a more appropriate sex role ideal for contemporary society. Theoretically, such a person would have no need to limit his or her behaviors to those traditionally defined as "sex appropriate" but would have the psychological freedom to engage in whatever behavior seemed most effective at the moment, irrespective of its stereotype as masculine or feminine. [Bem & Lenney, 1976, p. 48]

Bem developed a gender-type questionnaire, the Bem Sex-Role Inventory (BSRI), that can be used to classify people as primarily masculine, feminine, androgynous, or undifferentiated in their gender-role orientation. The BSRI, like the EOM-EIS measure of identity status we mentioned earlier, has become widely used and has fostered considerable research on the implications of gender-role differences for identity formation. Studies of large numbers of late adolescent college students indicate that androgynous young people, whose attitudes and interests involve some integration of traditionally feminine and masculine personality characteristics, do form a comfortable and rewarding sense of identity more easily and more rapidly than those who are rigidly or stereotypically feminine or masculine. Late adolescent girls who are firmly feminine and boys who are firmly masculine in turn progress more smoothly in their identity formation than those whose gender type is undifferentiated (Dyk & Adams, 1990; della Silva & Dusek, 1984; Tzuriel, 1984).

The apparent fact that androgynous adolescents have some advantage over their gender-typed and gender-undifferentiated peers in resolving their identities raises the question of whether androgyny is generally conducive to good adjustment. Among junior and senior high school students, androgynous young people tend to be popular among their peers and to report fewer feelings of loneliness than their masculine, feminine, and gender-undifferentiated peers. However, masculine boys are also widely accepted as friends and companions, and feminine girls a little less so, and it is only the adolescents with cross-gender characteristics—masculine girls and feminine boys—who are likely to be rejected (Huston & Alvarez, 1990).

Other research strongly suggests that both boys and girls generally benefit from integrating aspects of the other gender's orientation and that androgynous individuals feel better about themselves and adapt better to their experiences than young people who are rigidly gender typed (Harter, 1990b; Ruble, 1984; Schiedel & Marcia, 1985). On the other hand, in all of these studies there have been some young people with strong masculine or feminine orientations who have shown better adjustment than some androgynous individuals, and it would be a mistake to regard androgyny as an ideal toward which all people should strive. Rather, in light of present knowledge, it is probably more accurate to conclude that a wide range of individual differences in femininity, masculinity, and androgyny can be associated with positive personality development; poor adjustment becomes likely only when a person is having difficulty differentiating any clear sense of his or her gender-role orientation or is developing a cross-gender orientation.

Moreover, even though our society is defining appropriate gender-role behavior less narrowly than before, prevailing attitudes still regard men as being responsible chiefly for working and supporting their families and women as being responsible chiefly for taking care of the home. When asked what they would like to be when they grow up, most young boys and girls still express preferences for traditional gender-typed occupations, such as boys becoming doctors and girls becoming nurses (Huston, 1985). At the junior and senior high school levels as well, career interests remain largely gender typed, although differences between boys and girls have become less pronounced and less simplistic than they were at an earlier age (Barber & Eccles, 1992).

Three studies are informative to note in this regard. In the first of these studies, Gorrell and Shaw (1988) asked 292 5th-, 8th-, and 11th-grade students in a small town, semirural setting three questions about several jobs traditionally regarded as men's or women's jobs: "Who can do these jobs?," "Would you like to do these jobs?," and "Could you learn to do these jobs?" These young people showed few gender differences in the kinds of jobs they would like to have or believed that they could do; however, when it came to what kinds of jobs they thought they could learn to do, they clung to traditional gender-typed beliefs.

In the second study, Schulenberg, Goldstein, and Vondracek (1991) administered a career interest inventory to 699 students in grades 7–12 in a rural community. They found substantial differences consistent with gender-role stereotypes; the boys, for example, scored higher on science and technology-related interests and the girls scored higher on art and service-related interests. However, there was also a fair amount of individual variation in the career interests of these adolescents and clear evidence that their preferences were being influenced not only by their gender but also by their educational aspirations, their certainty about pursuing a particular career, and their family background.

The third study included an examination by Sandberg, Erhardt, Ince, and Meyer-Bahlburg (1991) of the "ideal" career designated by 78 male and 67 female 13–18-year-old city-dwelling students from middle- to upper-class homes. Together, these boys and girls nominated 68 distinctly different careers as their ideal. Of these 68 careers, only 16 were chosen by both the males and the females; the remaining 52 were nominated by one gender only. Table 10.2 lists the 12 occupations most commonly mentioned as ideal by each gender; only medical doctor, lawyer, and veterinarian appear on both lists.

Table 10.2 CAREERS MOST FREQUENTLY NOMINATED AS IDEAL BY ADOLESCENTS AGED 13–18

Males (n = 78)	*Females (n = 67)*
1. Architect	1. Teacher
2. Medical doctor	2. Secretary
3. Athlete	3. Medical doctor
4. Electrical engineer	4. Biologist
5. Lawyer	5. Fashion designer
6. Musician	6. Lawyer
7. Store owner	7. Musician
8. Carpenter	8. Psychologist
9. Electrician	9. Reporter
10. Manager/administrator	10. Social worker
11. Mechanic	11. Person who works with animals
12. Veterinarian	12. Veterinarian

Source: Based on data reported by Sandberg et al. (1991).

Identity Status and Adjustment

Much of what we have said in this chapter indicates that the moratorium and achievement statuses in identity formation reflect positive personality development and should be encouraged, whereas the foreclosure and diffusion statuses handicap a person's adaptation and should be avoided or outgrown. Some of the early research with the Identity Status Interview suggested that there were gender differences in this regard, in particular that college women who were identity foreclosed might behave more similarly to identity achieved women than those in a moratorium. These findings led to the conclusion that the foreclosure status is more adaptive for women than for men, presumably because of traditional expectations that young men should think carefully about their future prospects and possibilities, whereas young women should find their identity in the role of wife and mother without considering other alternatives (Marcia, 1980).

In light of changing societal attitudes, this formulation is probably outdated. Despite persisting gender-role traditions, young women these days, especially among college students, are as likely as young men to be sorting through their commitments and beliefs and to be doing so with the support and encouragement of their parents, peers, and teachers. Moreover, because the Identity Status Interview does not address interpersonal issues, it is possible that the early identity research yielded some misleading results concerning gender differences. Not surprisingly, then, more recent studies using newer methods confirm that women as well as men who are in an identity moratorium resemble identity achievers more than identity foreclosures (Patterson et al., 1992). In other words, identity achievement and identity moratorium are likely to be associated with better adjustment than foreclosure and diffusion among both males and females.

On a more individual basis, however, there may well be instances in which identity foreclosure is more adaptive for some women than it is for most men. This is especially likely for girls growing up in a very traditional environment in which there is strong family and social support for foreclosure and little encouragement or tolerance of exploration. In such circumstances young women may be tempted to accept the comfort and solidity of doing what is expected of them with respect to career and family goals, rather than take on the uncertainty of a moratorium process that will alienate them from their loved ones. Given a choice of this kind, settling into a low stress, interpersonally connected, and perhaps still productive foreclosure may prove more adaptive than striking out alone to wrestle with a disconcerting moratorium.

As a further aspect of gender differences in the implications of identity foreclosure, young women are more likely than young men to opt for foreclosure on a temporary basis. As we noted earlier, foreclosure once adopted in late adolescence tends to stay that way unless the individual encounters some broadening life experiences that prompt some reevaluation of values and goals. However, a person wanting to pursue a career and have a family, but unable to do both at the same time, may decide first to marry and have children and then at some later time think through career possibilities. This involves choosing foreclosure for the present but fully intending to move on to moratorium in the future. This type of situation, which occurs almost exclusively in the lives of young women rather than men, produces a foreclosure that may be a temporarily adaptive resolution of personal identity.

A study by Grotevant and Thorbecke (1982) provides one additional perspective on gender-related aspects of occupational identity. They found that gender differences in a group of high school juniors were less likely to involve identity status itself than the meanings that are attached to a particular status. The boys and girls in their study were making similar kinds of progress toward achieving occupational identity. Among the boys, however, thinking about future careers involved primarily an instrumental focus on what challenges they wanted to take on and what they thought they could accomplish, and there was little concern about possible negative attitudes other people might have toward their objectives or their efforts to achieve them. By contrast to these boys' self-centered focus on mastery, the girls in the sample were thinking about occupational commitments primarily in terms of being diligent, avoiding competition, and having other people approve of their goals. These findings fit closely with the indications in general that young men are relatively intrapersonally oriented in their identity formation and young women are interpersonally oriented.

ETHNIC AND MINORITY GROUP MEMBERSHIP

There is no evidence that identity formation proceeds any differently among adolescents from various ethnic backgrounds. By and large, wherever they live and whatever their cultural heritage, young people making the transition from childhood to adulthood pass through a period of consolidating their personal identity in which they begin as diffused, enter a moratorium, and end up as identity achieved. Some may become foreclosed along the way, temporarily or permanently, and others may have varying degrees of success in bringing moratorium to a satisfying resolution. To be sure, broad cultural differences may produce different patterns of outcome than typically are found in the United States; a rigidly authoritarian culture, for example, just like an authoritarian family, may foster a high frequency of early identity foreclosure. Nevertheless, the basic process of identity formation and the status of a young person's identity as diffused, foreclosed, in a moratorium, or achieved appear to be universal.

Research in the United States with African-American, Asian-American, and Hispanic adolescents has confirmed that they go through the same type of identity formation process and demonstrate the same identity statuses as white adolescents (Grove, 1990; Taylor, 1989). However, for those young people whose ethnic background makes them a minority group in our society, and probably for ethnic minorities in other parts of the world as well, identity formation may become complicated. With respect to establishing one's sense of identity, then, we need to extend our discussion in Chapter 6 of what it means to grow up in two cultures.

Two factors in particular have been observed to complicate the identity formation of minority group adolescents. First, in deciding what kind of person they want to be, minority young people often experience conflicts between the values and preferences modeled by their ethnic group and those endorsed by the majority culture. Second, prejudice and discrimination may limit the opportunities for minority youngsters to explore alternative commitments and life directions within the context of the broader society (Markstrom-Adams, 1992; Phinney & Rosenthal, 1992). According to Baly (1989), for example, African-American youth on the average have just as high occupational aspirations as their white peers, but have substantially lower expectations of realizing their aspirations. Low expectations concerning what one can hope to achieve, whether warranted or not, can dampen the urge to pursue possibilities and thereby curtail the identity formation process.

The research on this important subject is sparse and not yet very conclusive (Phinney, 1990). Nevertheless, there is adequate evidence to indicate that minority group adolescents, while dealing at times with different kinds of questions, do not necessarily have more difficulty than other adolescents in achieving a sense of identity, and that minority youth often progress smoothly in their identity formation if they have been reared in ways that promote both a strong sense of ethnic pride and a tolerant appreciation of cultural diversity.

In one study of the relationship between ethnicity and identity, Phinney and Alipuria (1990) obtained self-report information from 196 male and female college students from Asian-American, African-American, and Mexican-American backgrounds. As might be expected, these minority young people were paying significantly more attention to issues of ethnicity than were a comparison group of white students. The more they were thinking about these issues, and especially if they felt they had resolved them, the more likely these minority students were to report feeling good about themselves. The students in this study who scored high on a measure of ethnic identity were also more likely than low scorers to report that their parents had taken pains to prepare them to cope with living in a culturally diverse society (Phinney & Rosenthal, 1992). Other researchers have concluded similarly that racial pride is an important ingredient of positive identity formation and that minority group young people benefit from experiences that promote a positive sense of identification with their ethnic group (Spencer & Markstrom-Adams, 1990; Ward, 1990).

The benefits of ethnic group identity for minority adolescents raises some interesting questions with respect to the impact of ethnic assimilation. Having equal opportunity is without doubt advantageous for minority youth seeking to utilize their talents and fulfill their potential. Identity exploration and accomplishments aside, however, being just like everyone else is not conducive to maintaining racial pride or a strong sense of ethnic identity. Ward (1990), for example, argued that black student organizations help African-American adolescents come to terms with ethnic differences and appreciate the unique qualities of being black; on the other hand, she argued, educational institutions that place a priority on integrating minority students into school and campus groups may pay too little attention to racial differences and encourage minority students to reject their ethnic identity. Ward suggested that some racial barriers can play a constructive role in personality development while young people are defining their self-concept, and she cautioned against an extent of social integration that drives a wedge between minority young people and their racial ties and cultural background.

Yet, separation among cultural groups also has some drawbacks, whether it occurs in response to discrimination or as a positive effort to preserve ethnic identity. Rotheram-Borus (1990), comparing African-American, Hispanic, Asian, and white high school students, found that those who reported a strong ethnic identification were more likely than those with less ethnic identification to report ethnic pride and a preference for racial separatism over assimilation. However, those who preferred separatism also described more ethnic group conflict in their lives and less interest in using the English language. Phinney and Rosenthal (1992) contended further that efforts to preserve ethnic identity may not always foster personal growth. Whereas racial pride combined with cultural openness contributes to identity achievement, they pointed out, minority adolescents may sometimes focus on their ethnicity as an oppositional identity, that is, as a way of defining oneself in contrast to the dominant culture. An oppositional identity, based on rejection of the broader society and negative rea-

As illustrated by the life of Malcolm X, a strong identification with one's ethnic or racial group can be a source of pride and self-esteem for many young people, but it can also bring them into conflict with the majority culture.

sons for being what you are (i.e., not being like them), can stunt an individual's psychological growth along with contributing to racial group tensions.

VOCATIONAL CHOICE

Achieving a sense of identity involves considering alternative educational and career goals and making a commitment to some that seem advisable. Vocational choice is thus an integral aspect of identity formation. The relationship between identity formation and choosing a vocation revolves primarily around when adolescents begin working full time and how they decide what kind of work they want to do.

Most adolescents work at part-time jobs during high school, and most young people who go on to college continue to work while in school or during the summer. Those who do not attend college typically begin working full time after leaving high school, but the jobs they take usually do not constitute a career choice. In a detailed analysis of the work experience of late adolescents, Hamilton (1990) pointed out that most adolescents who become full-time workers immediately following high school tend to continue in the same kind of undemanding and unrewarding jobs they had previously held on a part-time basis, mainly in retail sales, food service, clerical work, and unskilled manual labor. Evidence cited by Hamilton indicates in fact that only 14% of the jobs held by 16–21-year-olds require a high school diploma. Neither the occupants of these jobs nor their employers expect that they will be long-term employees, Hamilton added. Instead, these positions are filled temporarily while noncollege young people continue to think about finding a career that appeals to them.

This means that adolescents who finish their formal education with high school usually set out in a career direction a few years later, at about the same time as their college-going peers are completing a course of study that has prepared them to go on to graduate or professional school or to enter the job market in a serious way. For both groups of young people, choosing a vocation is a complex social psychological process, and occupational psychology is a broad field of study in its own right. Moreover, career choice is just one phase of a lifelong process that also includes career preparation, career development, career satisfaction, possible career change, and career decline and retirement (Lambert & Mounce, 1987; Morrison & Adams, 1991; Spokane, 1991).

We will concern ourselves here just with the fact that how people go about choosing a vocation typically reflects how they are going about forming their identity. This close relationship is apparent when we consider the four events widely regarded by occupational psychologists as governing the process of vocational choice (Blustein, Devenis, & Kidney, 1989; Neimeyer & Heesacker, 1992; Young, 1983):

1. Becoming knowledgeable about one's talents and interests.
2. Becoming familiar with the world of work, especially in relation to how certain kinds of jobs match one's talents and interests.
3. Becoming capable of making difficult decisions and ready to settle on a career choice.
4. Responding to a variety of family, school, peer-group, and sociocultural circumstances that make some types of work more attractive and available than others.

In the comparable language of identity formation, these events involve acquiring self-knowledge, trying on possible future roles for size, becoming able to make enduring commitments, and being influenced by a variety of individual experiences that lead some people in one direction and others in a different direction. With respect to deciding on an occupation, then, research findings indicate that young people who are relatively mature in their identity formation tend to make occupational decisions in a rational, systematic manner marked by exploration and self-reliance. Foreclosed adolescents, by contrast, tend in an unsystematic manner and with minimal exploration to pursue decision-making strategies that depend heavily on the views of others. The more diffused they are in their identity, the more likely adolescents are to avoid exploration altogether and to make vocational decisions—if they make them at all—on an intuitive basis, that is, choosing to do what feels right or seems convenient, without giving the matter much thought (Blustein et al., 1989; Blustein & Phillips, 1990; Neimeyer & Heesacker, 1992).

Adolescents who progress in normative fashion from identity diffusion through a moratorium to identity achievement eventually choose a career direction that fits their interests and aptitudes. So long as they have sufficient opportunity to learn about different kinds of work, they gradually narrow the list of reasonable career possibilities open to them and finally decide on one that seems to suit them well. Any problems that arise in reaching this decision can usually be solved by their learning more about themselves or about the world of work. Vocational guidance counselors can sometimes be helpful in providing such information, including both descriptions of the nature of certain kinds of jobs and suggestions based on the use of specialized aptitude and interest tests (Lowman, 1991). Armed with enough information of this kind, young people are ordinarily able to resolve uncertainties about vocational choice without undue difficulty.

On the other hand, as we have already suggested, young people who are not progressing smoothly toward identity formation may develop problems in choosing a vocation that cannot be solved by information alone. Studies of career development from the junior high school through the college level have identified distinct types of indecision, some based on a lack of relevant information, but others related to a general pattern of disinterest or difficulty in making any kinds of decisions (Lucas & Epperson, 1991; Slaney, 1988; Vondracek, Hostetler, Schulenberg, & Shimizu, 1990). Among young people who are generally indecisive, some are too identity diffused to form any specific interest pattern ("I can't think of any kind of job that appeals to me very much"). Others may be stuck in a moratorium because of strong competing interests that they are unable to put in rank order ("There are still three or four different things I could see myself doing, and I just don't know which one I'd like best, so I'm going to keep my options open until I'm able to make up my mind").

Among adolescents who are apparently being decisive but are in fact identity foreclosed, one further possible obstacle to rewarding career choice involves being unrealistic. Young people who respond more to what others want and expect of them are at risk for various kinds of vocational maladjustment: choosing a career they will not enjoy, for example, or one that is too demanding for them to qualify for or succeed in, or one that does not fully utilize their abilities and is therefore unfulfilling. When such unrealistic choices occur, they often reflect maladaptive family and gender-role influences on identity formation. In the next chapter we look in more detail at how such influences can contribute to problems of underachievement in school.

IDENTITY FORMATION AND ADOLESCENT TURMOIL

In closing this chapter, we need to answer an important question: To what extent does the normal process of identity formation, with its uncertainties and experimentation with alternatives, lead to maladaptive turmoil during the adolescent years? There is an influential view that the challenges of forming an identity and coping with other developmental tasks of adolescence can be expected to cause young people to behave in peculiar and erratic ways, even to the extent that emotional upset and apparent psychological disturbance become typical features of adolescent development. In looking briefly at this commonly held view, we will see that it is largely a mythical notion. The evidence points overwhelmingly instead to psychological well being among most young people, prevailing stability in identity formation, and considerable continuity in personality development through the adolescent years and into adulthood.

NORMATIVE ADOLESCENT TURMOIL: A MYTH THAT WON'T GO AWAY

The views of Anna Freud, whose important contributions we introduced in Chapter 2, carry great weight in the field of child study. With respect to **adolescent turmoil**, Freud maintained that adolescence disrupts the continuity of personality development and produces stormy, unpredictable behavior: "Adolescence constitutes by definition an interruption of peaceful growth which resembles in appearance a variety of other emotional upsets and structural upheavals. . . . To be normal during the adolescent period is by itself abnormal" (Freud, 1958, pp. 257 and 267).

Freud went on to say that because "peaceful growth" is interrupted, adolescents normally display maladaptive thoughts, feelings, and actions that might suggest psychopathology if they occurred in adults. Erikson (1956) incorporated this benign view of apparent psychopathology into his theory of identity formation: "What under prejudiced scrutiny may appear to be the onset of a neurosis is often but an aggravated crisis which might prove to be self-liquidating and, in fact contributive to the process of identity formation" (p. 72). This impression has been echoed repeatedly over the years, primarily by psychoanalytic writers, in the following kinds of statements:

> Although puberty may take many courses, we think primarily of stormy and unpredictable behavior. [Eissler, 1958, p. 224]
>
> During the ongoing struggle for identity, many more or less severe symptoms may arise. . . . It is generally agreed that adolescence comes to an end after a painful struggle, of greater or less duration. [Deutsch, 1967, pp. 34 & 37]
>
> Frequently these young people give us a distorted picture, puzzling to the clinician. . . . At times, one can hardly differentiate between psychopathology and normal growth crises. [Ekstein, 1968, p. 347]
>
> If there is anything that can be considered typical of the adolescent period, it is this quality of identity diffusion. [Giovacchini, 1978, p. 326]
>
> In working with adolescents it is a most difficult task to tease out in the clinical picture what is a normal disturbance due to the developmental upheaval of the age and what constitutes a truly psychopathological condition. [Blos, 1983, p. 106]
>
> It seems safe to assert that all adolescents are probably shaken by emotional storms and troublesome floods of impulse. . . . In any event, the predictable state of affairs for any given youngster is a condition of episodic turmoil. [Noshpitz, 1991, pp. 128 & 129]

The notion of normative adolescent turmoil suffers from the same shortcoming as the concepts of adolescent rebellion and the generation gap that we mentioned in Chapter 7. It emerged not from a representative sampling of young people, which is the only way to determine what is typical, but instead from encounters with adolescents being treated for emotional or behavioral problems. Clinicians listening to their teenage patients talk about their lives assumed that what they were hearing was painting an accurate picture of what most adolescents are like. By contrast, when researchers have looked at identity formation and other features of personality development in nonpatient adolescents, such as groups of students responding voluntarily to questions at home or in their classrooms, turmoil has been as unlikely as alienation to emerge as a normative aspect of adolescence.

More specifically, a large number of studies have been reported in which 12–21-year-old nonpatient young people from a broad range of backgrounds have been carefully evaluated with respect to the nature and extent of their psychological problems. These studies have consistently found that about 20% of adolescents are likely to be maladjusted, as defined by having psychological problems that interfere substantially with their adjustment at home, in school, or in social situations. Interestingly, a 20% prevalence of significant psychological disorder is almost exactly what is found among the adult population, which strongly suggests that adolescents are no more likely than adults to appear disturbed unless they are in fact disturbed (Offer, Howard, Schonert, & Ostrov, 1991; Offer & Schonert-Reichl, 1992; Powers et al., 1989; Weiner, 1992, Chapter 1).

As for the remaining 80% of adolescents who are not disturbed, many may experience occasional mild episodes of anxiety or depression as they grapple with uncertainties and suffer through disappointments; rarely, however, do they lose more than momentarily their capacity to function effectively. Aside from not experiencing substantial turmoil or significant psychological disturbance, this large majority of young people demonstrate to researchers that they enjoy their lives, are happy with themselves most of the time, take pleasure in work well done, feel comfortable with their sexuality, are hopeful about the future, and anticipate being successful in what they try to do (Offer, Ostrov, Howard, & Atkinson, 1992). Finally in this regard, ample evidence indicates that knowledgeable observers will have little difficulty distinguishing between normative developmental concerns and serious disturbances of adjustment; symptoms of disorder indicate disorder in adolescents, just as they do in adults (Elmen & Offer, 1992; Strober, 1986).

Despite the convincing nature of such research findings, the myth of normative adolescent turmoil should not be too quickly dismissed. Even in the face of evidence to the contrary, a surprisingly large number of mental health professionals and pediatricians still view adolescence as a tumultuous phase of development in which the absence of serious problems signifies that something is amiss (Offer & Boxer, 1991; Swedo & Offer, 1989). Familiar and long-held opinions do not easily yield to the weight of new facts; as Peterson (1988) aptly put it, "Most people believe they know what adolescence is like and are unreceptive to findings that challenge their beliefs" (p. 584).

Like the companion myths of adolescent rebellion and a generation gap, the turmoil notion has found its way into the fabric of common parlance as well as clinical practice. Parents are advised, "Don't worry, she'll grow out of it"; self-appointed authorities tell us to make allowances when adolescents get out of line because "most teenagers get a little mixed up trying to find themselves"; in Leonard Bernstein's musical *West Side Story*, the members of a teenage gang urge Officer Krupke to go easy on them because "we're not delinquent, we're misunderstood."

These kinds of advice, whether offered in earnest or in jest, and whether appearing in popular media or in the professional literature, share a regrettable feature: They minimize the significance of outlandish or disturbed behavior and downplay the need for resolving the adjustment difficulties that such behavior usually indicates, as we discuss in Chapters 11–13. So long as this myth refuses to go away, people interested in adolescent development need to keep constantly in mind how inaccurate and misleading it is.

STABILITY AND ADAPTATION IN IDENTITY FORMATION

The refutation of the generation gap notion in Chapter 7 drew on findings from an extensive national survey by Douvan and Adelson (1966) and an intensive longitudinal study by Offer (1969). The results of both investigations were also unequivocal with respect to normative adolescent turmoil. The 3,000 adolescents in the Douvan and Adelson survey showed little evidence of normative turbulence or instability, and it was only the adolescent at the extremes "who responded to the instinctual and psychosocial upheaval of puberty by disorder" (p. 351).

Offer followed his original group of high school students through 4 years of college and found that very few of them gave any indications of personality disarray between ages 14 and 22 (Offer & Offer, 1975). Research over the years has indicated that the most common pattern of personality development during the teenage years is what Offer (1991) called **continuous growth**, which consists of smooth and adaptive progress through adolescence into young adulthood. The second most common pattern he called **surgent growth**, which involved adaptive but irregular progress toward maturity: The young person sometimes stands still developmentally and sometimes concentrates considerable energy on mastering developmental tasks. The remaining adolescents, about one-fifth of teenagers, display **tumultuous growth**, which comprises the kinds of inner unrest and overt behavior problems that the notion of normative adolescent turmoil incorrectly ascribes to most adolescents.

Hence, as we have already noted, numerous studies of representative samples of nonpatient adolescents have documented that turmoil is the exception rather than the rule and that an interruption of peaceful growth is definitely not necessary for normal adolescent development to occur. These findings are consistent with longitudinal evidence of considerable continuity in the personality characteristics and adaptive capacities that people show from early childhood into and through their adolescent years. Although children change in many ways as they grow up, through maturation and in response to experiences from which they learn, they are likely to retain many of their relative positions among their peers from one age to another; thus, for example, those who are more aggressive, more dependent, more outgoing, more self-satisfied, or better adjusted at one time will be so at another time (Alsaker & Olweus, 1992; Cairns, Cairns, Neckerman, Ferguson, & Gariepy, 1989; Lerner, Hertzog, Hooker, & Hassibi, 1988; Rutter, 1989; Verhulst & van der Ende, 1992).

Accordingly, adolescent development is mostly a slow, steady process in which maturation occurs gradually and without tumult. With particular respect to identity formation, there may normally be some unevenness in the process, as we noted earlier (e.g., identity achievement in occupation combined with moratorium in interpersonal relatedness), and there may also be some alternating periods of progression, regression, and stagnation. By and large, however, the way in which adolescents view themselves changes only gradually over time and is marked more by consistency than by disruption or instability. The more change adolescents do perceive in themselves, the more likely they are to have adjustment difficulties rather than to be developing normally.

Much of the research concerning the nature and stability of how adolescents view themselves has employed a self-report instrument developed by Offer and called the Offer Self-Image Questionnaire (OSIQ). OSIQ data collected from many thousands of teenagers have played an important part in demonstrating that adolescents are not normally in the throes of turmoil and that those who are markedly upset, especially in relation to forming their identity, are not functioning normally (Offer et al., 1981, Chapters 8 & 9). The 11 scales of the OSIQ and what they measure are shown in Box 10.3.

One of the informative studies using the OSIQ is the Toronto Longitudinal Study (Golombek & Marton, 1992), in which 59 boys and girls were interviewed when they were in the fifth grade and on three subsequent occasions, when they were age 13, 16, and 18 years old (corresponding roughly to early, middle, and late adolescence). These young people completed the OSIQ on each occasion, and Table 10.3 shows how the OSIQ scales correlated from one time to the next. Although the magnitude of these correlations is modest, almost all of them indicate a significant degree of continuity in these self-image characteristics across the teenage years that goes far beyond chance expectation.

♦ **BOX 10.3 THE SCALES OF THE OFFER SELF-IMAGE QUESTIONNAIRE (OSIQ)**

1. *Impulse control.* A measure of the extent to which the person can manage stress without losing control.

2. *Emotional tone.* A measure of the degree of affective well being.

3. *Body and self-image.* A measure of how well the adolescent has adjusted to his or her body.

4. *Social relationships.* A measure of interpersonal attitudes and friendship patterns.

5. *Morals.* A measure of how well conscience is developed.

6. *Vocational/educational goals.* A measure of how well the adolescent is performing as a student and in planning for his or her vocational future.

7. *Sexual attitudes.* A measure of feelings, attitudes, and behavior toward the other sex.

8. *Family relationships.* A measure of the quality of the adolescent's relationship with his or her parents.

9. *Mastery of the external world.* A measure of adaptation to the immediate environment.

10. *Psychopathology.* A measure of the presence of psychological disturbance.

11. *Superior adjustment.* A measure of coping skills.

Source: Based on Offer et al., (1981).

Table 10.3 STABILITY COEFFICIENTS FOR OSIQ SCALES FROM EARLY TO MIDDLE TO LATE ADOLESCENCE

	Correlations		
OSIQ Scale	*Early to Middle Adolescence*	*Middle to Late Adolescence*	*Early to Late Adolescence*
Impulse control	.71	.69	.55
Emotional tone	.65	.56	.52
Body and self-image	.55	.64	.46
Social relationships	.57	.54	.49
Morals	.37	.43	.26
Sexual attitudes	.53	.50	.28
Family relationships	.45	.67	.49
Mastery of the external world	.61	.53	.25
Vocational/educational goals	.32	.41	.21*
Psychopathology	.53	.69	.44
Superior adjustment	.60	.53	.57

*Except for this correlation, all of the other correlations indicate relationships that are statistically significant well beyond a .05 level of confidence, which shows they are not a chance occurrence.

Source: Based on data reported by Golombek and Marton (1992) from a longitudinal study of 59 adolescents.

CONTINUITY IN PERSONALITY DEVELOPMENT FROM ADOLESCENCE TO ADULTHOOD

As a final contradiction to notions of adolescent turmoil, longitudinal studies have demonstrated considerable continuity in personality development not only from childhood through adolescence, but also from adolescence into adulthood. People do change as they get older. They learn more, fill new roles, and seek new means of coping with changing circumstances in their lives. By and large, however, people remain basically the same in how they think, handle interpersonal relationships, and are perceived by others. For better or worse, adults tend to display many of the same general personality characteristics and the same relative level of adjustment that they did as adolescents.

The most extensive longitudinal studies of personality development were started by the Institute of Human Development of the University of California at Berkeley in 1928 (Bronson, 1972; Eichorn, 1973). As part of this project, interview, test, and rating scale data were collected at regular intervals for two groups of people: one group followed from age 12 to age 50 (the Oakland Growth Study) and another group followed from age 12 to age 40 (the Guidance Study). Table 10.4 lists 34 traits that were assessed in this research, grouped in the following categories: ways of approaching and processing information, forms of interpersonal reactions, responses to socialization influences, and manner of self-presentation. The many substantial correlations ratios in the table (those larger than .50) indicate considerable stability over the time period studied. The findings thus strongly suggest that these traits are established by early adolescence and are not greatly affected by the process of adolescent development or by subsequent adult experience.

Several other ambitious research projects have provided impressive evidence in the same vein. Bachman, O'Malley, and Johnston (1979) examined change and stability in a representative national sample of 1,628 boys followed from entry into 10th grade to age 23. The picture that emerged from their data was one of stability, not change: "Contrary to what might have been expected by those who view adolescence as a period of great turbulence and stress, we have found a good deal of consistency along dimensions of attitudes, aspirations, and self-concept" (p. 220). In a subsequent follow-up of high school seniors into adulthood, Rodgers and Bachman (1988) similarly reported prevalent stability with little change in these subjects' feelings of happiness and life satisfaction as they moved through this life transition.

Vaillant (1978) conducted a 35-year study of 268 male college sophomores, 94 of whom were still available for interviews at age 54. The adequacy of the high school adjustment of these men, as rated from the information they gave as college students, was significantly related to the adequacy of their adult psychological adjustment. Good social adjustment in adolescence was clearly predictive of good social adjustment at midlife for these men, and poor adjustment at midlife was typically preceded by poor adjustment in adolescence.

Jessor, Donovan, and Costa (1991) collected longitudinal self-report information from two groups of subjects: one group of 384 girls and boys studied when they were in junior high school (grades 7–9) and again when they were age 25 to age 27, and another group of 184 college freshmen followed up when they were age 30. The correlations these subjects showed on several psychosocial measures are shown in Table 10.5. These correlations are not of the same magnitude as those in Table 10.5, perhaps because they are based on

Table 10.4 **TRAIT CONSISTENCIES FROM ADOLESCENCE IN THE OAKLAND GROWTH STUDY (OGS; AGES 12–50) AND THE GUIDANCE STUDY (GS; AGES 12–40)***

Items	Females		Males	
	OGS	*GS*	*OGS*	*GS*
Ways of approaching and processing information				
Esthetically reactive	.85	.60	.76	.80
Verbally fluent	.66	.69	.79	.81
Wide interests	.72	.69	.79	.84
Prides self on objectivity	.65	.51	.79	.60
Introspective	.57	.70	(.49)	.66
Thinks unconventionally	.66	.71	(.27)	.65
Ruminative	.54	.66	(.18)	.51
Has concern about body	(.38)	.54	.51	.51
Forms of interpersonal reactions				
Arouses liking	.60	.68	.71	.63
Assertive	.69	.76	(.47)	.68
Socially poised	.76	.72	.67	(.49)
Values independence	.69	.63	.50	.52
Aloof	.74	.59	.60	.58
Distrustful	.57	(.49)	.55	.56
Responses to socialization influences				
Fastidious	.69	.70	.71	.63
Sex-typed behavior	.59	.67	.52	.77
Rebellious	.70	.75	.61	.73
Overcontrolled	.64	.72	.61	.79
Undercontrolled	.70	.66	.72	.73
Pushes limits	.67	.69	.77	.64
Feels victimized	(.47)	.52	.74	.65
Manner of self-presentation				
Interesting	.74	.77	.62	.65
Cheerful	.69	.70	.62	.67
Satisfied with self	.57	.70	.57	.67
Satisfied with appearance	.67	.55	(.48)	.56
Talkative	.72	.63	.65	.68
Intellectual level	.80	.78	.87	.86
Rapid tempo	.64	.72	(.44)	.62
Physically attractive	.73	.69	.60	.67
Basic hostility	.62	.66	.63	.56
Self-dramatizing	.69	.71	.71	.69
Self-defeating	.61	.57	.75	.61
Fearful	.73	.57	.61	.58
Reluctant to act	.63	.55	(.40)	.67

*Correlation ratios ≥ .50 indicate significant consistency. Correlations less than .50 are shown in parentheses.

Source: Based on data reported by Haan and Day (1974).

Table 10.5 STABILITY COEFFICIENTS FOR PSYCHOSOCIAL MEASURES FROM JUNIOR HIGH SCHOOL AND COLLEGE AGE TO ADULTHOOD

	Males		Females	
Psychosocial Variables	*From Junior High (n = 162)*	*From College (n = 84)*	*From Junior High (n = 222)*	*From College (n = 100)*
Value on achievement	.05*	.33	.05*	.13*
Value on independence	.35	.33	.25	.33
Expectation for achievement	.36	.27	.16	.18*
Expectation for independence	.33	.23	.18	.28
Social criticism	.34	.59	.36	.50
Alienation	.37	.42	.30	.41
Self-esteem	.42	.57	.31	.28
Attitudinal intolerance of defiance	.35	.53	.27	.37
Religiosity	.56	.64	.45	.73
General deviant behavior	.33	.14	.28	.38
Church attendance	.43	.43	.34	.39

*Except for these correlations, all of the others in the table identify a relationship beyond chance expectancy at or well beyond the .05 level of confidence.

Source: Based on data reported by Jesser et al. (1991).

self-report questionnaires rather than the more broadly based ratings of subjects by the investigators that were used in the Berkeley studies. Nevertheless, they provide one further demonstration of beyond-chance stability and consistency in individual differences in various personality characteristics across time.

Numerous other studies have confirmed that personality development is usually not disrupted by adolescence, but rather proceeds in a continuous fashion through adolescence into adulthood (Brody, 1988; Caspi, Elder, & Bem, 1987; Mussen, 1987; Stevens & Truss, 1985; Tubman, Lerner, Lerner, & von Eye, 1992). Moreover, the overall consistency of psychological and behavioral functioning from adolescence to adulthood has been demonstrated to apply to abnormal as well as normal development. Adolescents who show signs and symptoms of psychological disorder rarely outgrow them. Those who *appear* disturbed are likely to *be* disturbed and *remain* disturbed unless they receive adequate treatment. Furthermore, the severity of psychopathology in adolescents who receive treatment is consistently found to predict their level of adjustment as adults (Weiner, 1992, Chapter 1).

CHAPTER SUMMARY

1. Forming a sense of identity consists of becoming reasonably sure of what kind of person you are, what you believe in, and what you want to do with your life.

2. Achieving identity involves making relatively stable commitments to a set of values and beliefs (*ideological stance*); to a set of educational and career goals (*occupational stance*); and to a gender orientation that influences patterns of relationships with males and females (*interpersonal stance*). This takes place over a several-year period of experimentation with alternative roles and attitudes, especially during late adolescence.

3. Identity formation begins with a state of *diffusion* in which young people have not yet made or begun to think seriously about commitments. Sometimes adolescents opt next for *foreclosure*, which consists of commitment to a convenient set of beliefs and life goals without much exploration of alternative possibilities. More often, however, diffusion is followed by a *moratorium*, which is a period of active uncertainty and weighing of alternatives, and then by the gradual resolution of a moratorium into *achievement* of identity. In some instances identity formation becomes stagnant in the diffusion, foreclosure, or moratorium statuses, and not uncommonly some *progressive* and *regressive* shifts occur among them.

4. Parents who rear their children in an authoritative fashion are likely to help them progress through an identity moratorium toward identity achievement. Adolescents with authoritarian or permissive parents, on the other hand, are more likely than authoritatively reared children to become mired in identity diffusion or to opt for identity foreclosure.

5. Girls are likely to mature somewhat more rapidly than boys in their progress toward identity achievement. Late adolescent females are generally inclined to focus on *interpersonal* aspects of their identity formation, whereas males tend to focus in *intrapersonal* matters and to form their identity more on the basis of *what* they are doing than *with whom*.

6. Societal expectations with respect to gender-appropriate behavior have become considerably more flexible than in the past. Accordingly, both a clearly defined sense of masculinity or femininity and a mixture of traditional masculine and feminine orientations (*androgyny*) are associated with better adjustment than an undifferentiated gender identity. For both boys and girls, identity achievement and moratorium are more adaptive among late adolescents than identity diffusion and foreclosure, although temporary foreclosure may sometimes be quite adaptive for young women who want to be homemakers and also to have a career.

7. Identity formation proceeds in similar ways among adolescents from different ethnic backgrounds. However, minority group youngsters may face some special challenges in making choices between their ethnic identity and the values of the majority culture.

8. Vocational choice is an integral aspect of identity formation. In choosing a career, as in achieving identity in general, the most optimal decisions usually consist of commitments made following a period of exploration and on the basis of ample relevant information.

9. Contrary to widespread belief that adolescence usually constitutes a state of turmoil and an interruption of peaceful growth, disruptive crises occur only infrequently during the process of identity formation; when they do occur, they reflect psychological disturbance, not normal development.

10. Personality development proceeds in a continuous fashion through adolescence and into adulthood. For better or worse, adults tend to display many of the same general personality characteristics and the same relative level of adjustment they did as adolescents.

KEY WORDS

adolescent turmoil	identity confusion	identity status	states
androgyny	identity diffusion	ideological stance	surgent growth
continuous growth	identity foreclosure	interpersonal stance	traits
gender intensification	identity formation	occupational stance	tumultuous growth
identity achievement	identity moratorium	sense of identity	

REVIEW QUESTIONS

THE NATURE OF IDENTITY FORMATION

1. Discuss the relationship between being able to make relatively stable commitments and achieving a sense of identity.

2. In relation to their influence on identity formation, distinguish among intrapersonal factors, interpersonal factors, and cultural factors.

3. How are people who have a well-developed sense of identity likely to differ from people with identity confusion?

4. What kinds of research findings suggest relationships between cognitive maturity and identity formation?

IDENTITY STATUSES: STEPS ALONG THE WAY IN IDENTITY FORMATION

5. Describe the basic differences between the four identity statuses delineated by Erikson.

6. What kinds of methods have Marcia and other researchers used to assess identity status?

7. How do progressive, regressive, and stagnant patterns of identity formation differ from each other?

8. In what ways are the identity achievement and moratorium statuses generally indicative of greater maturity and better adjustment than the identity foreclosure and diffusion statuses?

INDIVIDUAL DIFFERENCES IN IDENTITY FORMATION

9. Discuss the likely impact of authoritative, authoritarian, and permissive parenting on adolescent identity formation.

10. How are adolescents in different identity statuses likely to differ in how they feel toward their parents?

11. In what ways do gender-identity differences appear related to differences in interpersonal and intrapersonal orientation among adolescent boys and girls?

12. Of what significance is the distinction between androgyny and gender-role uncertainty?

13. What does it mean to say that societal attitudes toward appropriate gender-role behaviors have a bearing on whether identity foreclosure is adaptive for young women?

14. How can minority group membership complicate the process of identity formation?

15. Discuss the impact that identity status can have on the process of choosing a vocation.

IDENTITY FORMATION AND ADOLESCENT TURMOIL

16. Summarize the evidence indicating that the notion of normative adolescent turmoil is a myth.

17. Of what importance is Offer's distinction between continuous, surgent, and tumultuous personality development during adolescence?

18. What do longitudinal studies show about the continuity of personality development from adolescence to adulthood?

Interlude

---◆---

Carol, Age 17

---◆---

"We laughed the whole time and that was really a great night."

This subject is a 17-year-old white girl named Carol. She was interviewed by Andrea Mowatt, a doctoral student in psychology at the University of South Florida. The interview was conducted in May 1993, shortly after Carol had graduated from high school. Carol lives in St. Petersburg, a city of about 500,000 people in the southeast. Carol attended a small private school where she was an outstanding student and very active in extracurricular activities. She has been accepted and will be attending college in the fall. She is from an intact family, with two parents at home and two sisters. Her father owns a small business that has been successful, and the family would be described as upper middle class.

This interlude provides an opportunity to review the concepts of identity formation, identity statuses (both the stages and traits), individual differences in identity formation, and the continuity in personality development during adolescence discussed in Chapter 10. In reading this interview, consider Carol's progress in developing an identity and also relevant themes from earlier chapters such as the relationship with her parents, friends, dating, and attitudes about sexuality.

Would you tell me about your adolescence? What things particularly stand out in your memory? Okay—I think that it was a real learning experience. In high school I think I learned a lot about other people, and I learned there were people that I liked and there were people that I didn't like and I made my own group of friends. I learned that I really don't like fakeness and fake people who just try

to be your friend whenever they need you. I don't like that—and I learned about myself. I learned, you know, that I was interested in the environment and what type of person I was, and I knew who I wanted to be with and wasn't worried about if I was the most popular person or whatever; I just wanted to be myself.

How do you feel about what kind of person you are? I'm happy with myself because I see all the people in school, like those fake people. You can just tell that they're not really happy; they just seem to be happy. I just know that later in life, they are happy now, but I just have a feeling they will look back and regret—I just don't think I will be doing that.

And how would you describe yourself? Um . . . weird. *Why weird?* I don't know, I'm just different, like sometimes I wear fun clothes, and just different things. I like being different but I don't like trying to be too different—like everybody else—I just like being myself, and that's one of the main things about me.

What kinds of things stand out in school for you during adolescence? I don't know, I have a job up in Massachusetts. I could go there every summer—so that's a really big part of my life 'cause I have friends up there. I really like working. It's fun because I get to be with a lot of people and I just love the beach and everything, so my summers are a really big part.

Do you remember when you first noticed the physical changes of puberty happening to your body? Yeah. I was about in eighth grade. *What did you notice first—what happened?* Um, my hair. It went from being totally straight to wavy and it got real dark; it used to be blonde, really. *Okay, any other physical changes?* Just in high school I used to be kind of heavy. In high school I started running, in ninth grade, and I lost so much weight. I mean not like a ton, I wasn't like noticeably like fat or anything, but you can just tell was it like baby fat and I lost it.

Would you say you were first in your age group to begin maturing? One of the first, but not like in the very beginning. *Okay, how did you feel about those changes in your body?* You know at first there are little things, you notice them and they're a little embarrassing, but I think later you get used to it. *Did you notice other people treating you differently because of these changes?* No. *Boys or parents or anybody?* No. *It didn't really seem to make a difference?* No.

Let's talk about your parents. How would you describe your relationship with your mother and father during your childhood? I think that I had a really good relationship with them. I've always been able to communicate, talk to them, and they were always there for me. *That's great. Is your relationship with your mother about the same or different than it was in your childhood?* I think that it's pretty much about the same, but I think that I just talk to her more now, but just a little more as a friend, but it's always been the same. *What kinds of things do you talk about?* I talk about my friends and about boyfriends and stuff and just what I do; she's interested in my life. *And she's pretty receptive to that?* Yeah. *Okay. How about your relationship with your father, did it stay about the same or change during adolescence?* I think that my relationship with my father changed. *In what way?* I think I can talk to him more now than when I was a child just because, when I was younger, I think he was more of like my father, you know, and that I looked up to him but I was kind of afraid of him in a way, not afraid of him as in like getting hurt or anything. He was just my father, you know, I guess I didn't really talk to him as much when I was younger, but now that I'm older, I think I have a lot more to share with him.

Were there other family members, brothers or sisters, grandparents, living with you during adolescence? Yes, in my later years, while in high school, probably tenth grade till graduation there was my two older sisters. One's 24 and one's 27. *So they came back to live with you?* Yes. *How did you get along with each of them?* I got along with them very well. They were really friends; I talked to them about everything. *And were you closer with one than another?* Yeah, a little bit, just with Sylvia a little closer because she was the younger one and I think we have a lot more in common.

What are a couple of your most vivid memories of your family during adolescence? My sister got married when I was a junior in high school and that was just a real big time for my family. Actually, the whole year, from the year before she got married, because we did a lot together and she got to come down a lot. I miss her because she lives in Michigan. I don't get to see her that much. So, you know, it was a good time that whole year because we would just plan everything. We redid our house, so we really made a lot of big changes.

Do you remember your best friends when you were around 12 or 13 years old? Yeah, I've had the same best friend. *Have you?* Yeah. *Who was it? Or, who were they?* Okay, well my friends D———, M———, and S———, but I've been best friends with D——— since first grade, best friends with M——— since 6th grade, and with S——— since 4th grade. *How did you meet them?* In grade school. *What were the kinds of things you did together?* Well, D——— and I did everything together. She used to come over to my house every day after school because her mom worked, so we'd just be together like till like 6:00 every night, and we went to birthday parties and stuff like that—what you do as little kids. And then S——— came, she was like my very best friend. S———, I remember I met her in fourth grade. She came from New Jersey; I met her in third grade, actually, and then we became friends and, when we were older, we used to go shopping and stuff and sit under the pier and we used to walk. We used to do a lot of fun things because she lives by a park, and we used to like play games in the park and stuff like that. And with M—

——, I used to spend the night at her house and we always had a blast. *Did the four of you do things together?* In grade school, yes, and then my friend S—— went to a different high school and D—— and M—— and I went to the same high school, and everybody's always called us the triplets throughout high school 'cause we did everything together. And so we, you know, we're all best friends. I always invite S—— out because she's my best friend, and then, they get along with her, but I don't think they do stuff with her on her own, like when I invite her and we all go together; yeah they get along great, but just that they never call her or anything like that. In fact, in school, M—— and D—— and I do a lot together 'cause we all went to the same high school, so we used to do lipsynch contests and stuff and that was a real big part 'cause that was really fun. We used to win all the time and everybody hated it. So that was really fun, we did a lot together and, we went to dances and stuff together, like homecoming and prom, and it was always real exciting, you know. We would get together and come over and get pictures and stuff.

How do you feel about going away to college now, are they going to the same school? Well my best friend S—— is going to the same school, in fact. And D—— and M—— are going to the same school together too. They're rooming and they're going to the state university. But, I'm really glad that I'm getting away from them, I think, just 'cause I want to move on and I know I'm gonna meet a lot more people, and I'm not even really upset about it, you know. I mean I know I'm gonna miss 'em, but I know I'm going to keep in touch.

Okay, now that you're moving on to college, I would like to have you look back for just a minute over your high school years and ask you how did you feel about high school? About the other students? The teachers? The activities? Well, I think we had a lot of opportunity at my school. Since it is such a small school you can be involved in a lot of clubs and everything and a lot of sports. Like when during freshman and sophomore year I did four sports. I did soccer, cheerleading, track, and cross-country. *Busy girl.* Yeah, and then I got bad knees in sophomore year and actually I didn't do track. After sophomore year my knees were like shot, so I couldn't do anything else. I cheered in 11th grade, but just for football season. We have a lot of clubs during school, we have an activity period every week, and that's fun because you can choose three clubs and go to one each week. And I think it's a lot of fun because you meet a lot of people who aren't in your grade, who you don't have classes with, and I think that's good. And the other students at my school and the teachers, um, I like all the teachers. I never really had a problem with any of the teachers. I know that a lot of students do. I think one of the big problems is that like they don't have a lot of respect and none of the students really respect the teachers, I don't think. *What makes you say that?* Sometimes in class, I just can't believe like the way people act and stuff. They just act up so much, they just talk right through class, they don't pay attention, or they talk back to teachers a lot. You know, people have hit teachers and everything, and they get kicked out. I just think that, I don't know, they've gone to a small school all their life and they never really learned what they had to do. I don't think you can ever get away with what we do in my school in a public school. But, you know, it kind of bothers me sometimes—I don't think people really have respect and I don't think people realize, since it is such a small school and we get very special attention, that they're gonna have to go out into the real world and they're not gonna be able to get away with things, and I think that's gonna be a problem. Even in just academics I think a lot of my friends always say, "Oh can we extend a deadline?" and stuff like that, and a lot of teachers do that, and I don't think that's really good either because, I mean, it's great when you don't have to write your paper that night, but I think it's not gonna help a lot of kids. I think they're gonna go to college and expect the same and they're not gonna be able to do that.

What would you say were your favorite courses or the things that you were most interested in in terms of academics? I think I really started to like English. I hated English as a kid, but I liked it 'cause it was more literature and more analysis and stuff, and I really learned a lot about English. So

I really liked that class. And I love science, except for physics—I hated physics this year—but I loved chemistry, that was my favorite class last year. *So you have a science background, is that what you're planning on going into for school?* Yeah, what I want to major in. I find it very interesting.

Who were some of the adults who had an influence on your life? Well, my parents, definitely. I know that they have been a big influence in my life, and, I don't know, I think they're the main influences as adults. I guess some of my parent's friends, too; they're close friends. We spend a lot of time with them and, you know, I have fake "aunts" and "uncles" and stuff like that. A lot of them just 'cause they talk to me. I think they help me decide what I want to do with myself.

When did you begin dating? I guess it really wasn't until last year, junior year. That's when I had my first boyfriend. *Would you tell me about one or two of your most memorable dates during adolescence.* I don't know; well, one of my most memorable dates wasn't even with a boyfriend, it was just with a friend. We went to the homecoming dance together. He was a senior and I was a sophomore and he was the funniest guy you'd meet. And we went with his other friend, his best friend, who was a senior, and a friend of mine who's a sophomore also, it's a girl. So, we went together and we all went out to dinner, and it was the funniest thing, we laughed the *whole* time because it was a fancy restaurant and he just kept like making noises or hitting his plate or something, but not on purpose, because he was trying to be all mature, and I just know that was funny because we laughed the whole time, and that was a really great night—it was one of the best nights.

Can you think of any memorable dates you had with your boyfriend? I don't know; I remember the first date I went out with my boyfriend that I have now, with him and then my best friend and her boyfriend, 'cause my boyfriend is best friends with her boyfriend. That's how we met. So I remember going, it was just funny, 'cause he was actually still dating his old girlfriend at the same time. But, it was fun, because we really got to know each other well; you know, we had never really talked that much before. I think that the most memorable are

when I had a lot of fun and laughed a lot. *And where did you go on that first date?* We went to Ruby Tuesdays, and it was fun because their other best friend—'cause there are three guys, three best friends—and the other one that wasn't with us, he works there, so we kept talking with him and we were just joking around about like cockroaches in the salad bar and 'cause the friend that worked there told them that he had seen that and we got salad so they didn't tell us until after we got our salad, and we were all laughing about that. Then we went to Blockbuster Video and rented *Singles* and we watched that at his house. It was just fun.

Would you be willing to talk about your sex life during adolescence? Sure. There's not really anything to talk about. *How did you learn about sex?* I had this one friend that was older, she was like 3 years older than me. You know, I really don't talk about it. I rarely think about sex because I don't really plan on doing anything any time soon. It was never really a major part of my conversation, but if she was talking about it or whatever, I think I learned a lot of it from that. Of course, you learn it in school, but I mean that's just what you learn in the books. *Did your sisters or your parents ever sit you down and talk to you about it?* Not really. I don't think they have ever really been worried about it. I mean because they know me so well, they don't think that I'm gonna go do anything crazy. *When did you begin to notice sexual feelings towards other people?* I don't know, I guess maybe when I had my first boyfriend, just 'cause that's when you first started really kissing people and stuff like that. So I guess that would be the time; it was my junior year, the beginning of it. *Okay, and would you describe a couple of your sexual experiences with other people other than actually having sex, were there other people that you were attracted to or had feelings toward?* Yeah, like my boyfriend right now, I think we are really close and when we're kissing or whatever I just think we're really open about what we are doing or what we're talking about. It's not that he doesn't ever do anything that I don't want him to do, like if he starts like putting his hand somewhere I just move it. I think that's really good, you know, we're very open about it and I like that. *So you've never had inter-*

course? No. *You're not planning on it?* No. *If you did, would you use birth control?* See I don't think so, I just know I'm just like so afraid that would screw up your body and it's not always 100% sure. I don't really know—I haven't really like thought about what I would do to prevent pregnancy or anything. *How about condoms?* Oh, yeah. We would definitely use that just because, you know, so much disease and everything.

How would you describe yourself now at age 17, after high school graduation, going to this school? Oh, I think I'm really ready to move on with my life, get to college; I'm really excited about it. I think I'm excited about meeting a lot of new people, 'cause I've had great friends in high school, but I just know that I'm gonna meet a lot more people that maybe have a lot more in common with me because it will be a much larger school and you can kind of choose your friends, even though in high school you do too, but then I went to a small school and there were only seven people in my class, so I think I'm just gonna be able to meet a lot more people and just think that will be fun.

Do you think you know who you are? Do you have a strong sense of identity? Yeah I feel that I do, now. I think that in ninth and tenth grade I was a little unsure. But I really think I know who I am right now, I just know that I'm an honest person and I have very strong beliefs and I'm not afraid to stand up for them. Like if someone says something to me I disagree with, I'll tell them. I really like that about myself. I think that's a good quality to have in anybody. I think that people need to stand up for what they believe in. And I think that I'm a leader; you know, this year I was in the student council, I was vice president of student council. Even though it may not seem like a lot of leadership, it is really important, and I'm also not afraid of telling people what to do. I don't like to seem very bossy, but I just don't let people like walk all over me, but I think that was a really important part of what I learned about life this year as being vice president. I learned that to be a leader you need to be able to tell people what to do, you need to take control. I think my honesty and my values; I just have very strong values.

What are some of your values? Well, my family is really important to me. I wouldn't want to do anything against my family. Yeah my family's very important to me, like when my whole family gets together in town when my sister comes down and we all do things together, that's most important, more important than my friends. I do stuff with my family first, and I think my religion is very important to me. I don't think I could get through a lot of times without praying to God. I find that it's very important; I go to church and everything. I just go there and I listen, then I go home. It doesn't really have an effect on me, but I think just my faith. Then also, I don't drink and stuff. It doesn't bother me that people do because I know that everybody does and I don't care. That's the only thing that bothers me 'cause everybody thinks I care just 'cause I don't drink. I couldn't care less what other people do, just as long as they're careful. But, I think that's been a really strong part of me, helped build my personality that I don't and that I won't. Like if people try to push me around or whatever, I just don't do it just 'cause I know what I want to do. 'Cause I want to be healthy, and that's really important, plus I don't like the taste of it, but, being healthy is also pretty important and I don't want to harm myself.

How do you want to life to work out for you in the future? Well, I am going to Duke next year, so I think I'll go there and I'm not gonna declare a major right away, but I'm interested in geology because I want to work with the environment. I wanted to major in a science and that one has a lot to do with earth science, and maybe even learn about anthropology or archeology or something like that. Then I'm pretty sure, if I major in geology, I'll go to graduate school, probably at the state university. I'm thinking of maybe chemical oceanography to get a master's degree. I don't know what I want to go for yet, depending on how long it will take, but I want to work with environmental regulation. Work for a company, maybe even EPA, that's my goal. But, I don't know, that's tough, but I want to do something like that. And then after I have my career set I want to get married. I don't want to get married right away. Hopefully I'll have a serious boyfriend at the time, but then after I get married I'll probably still work and not have kids right away. Then after I have kids I think that I want to stay home with the kids just 'cause I think that's important, but I don't know, maybe just for their earlier years. Then I want to open a store, that's what my parents do, and I just think it's really neat just 'cause I've been with it all my life, so I want to own my own store, but, like an environmental store with all environmentally safe products and things like that; but that's my long-range goal.

If you could sum up your adolescence in just a paragraph and describe how you feel about it as you look back over the years, what would you have to say? Well, I think that I was very lucky. I think I had a very easy adolescence, 'cause you know I went to a private school; that was, I think, a major part, 'cause it was small and I felt very sheltered. Some people might think that's bad. I don't really see why that's bad because if you're not experiencing all the violence or other things in society, like all the bad things, people are thinking, "Oh you're so shel-tered," but I really don't see what's wrong with that. I was glad I was sheltered. The same adolescent things happened, like people drink, you know, I mean just the same things like that. They go through the same things. There's a period where everyone starts smoking and everybody starts just doing all that kind of stuff. So you go through all that the same, you just don't see all the violence or the fighting and things like that, and I like that, but it's not that I don't know it exists, so I'm prepared to face it. My teachers, I had some good ones, so I think they helped me out a lot in deciding what I want to do, what I was interested in. Also, like I said before, my family really were a lot of help. It was very easy for me because my family was always there and I could always communicate with them. So, I think that was very important. *It sounds like it was a pretty good experience.* Yeah it was. It was a very good experience, and I have really good friends and I found a boy who I want to be with and found myself and I really think it was a very good experi-ence. *Thank you very much, Carol.*

Chapter 11

◆

Problems in School and the Community

◆

Some of the physical, cognitive, personal, and social achievements discussed in Chapters 3–10 come easily, whereas others demand determined effort to master developmental tasks. Most adolescents eventually mature into reasonably self-reliant and well-adjusted adults, but many run into some behavior problems along the way. This chapter concerns the two behavior problems that most commonly interfere with normal adolescent development and identify special needs for help in growing up: problems in school involving learning and attendance, and problems in the community involving delinquent behavior. In the next chapter we consider three other behavior problems that constitute potential pitfalls for adolescents—use and abuse of drugs, running away, and suicidal behavior—and we also look at challenges young people may face in confronting chronic illness, physical disability, and death and dying.

Adolescent behavior problems have two important features in common. First, they vary widely in severity from occasional difficulties that deviate only slightly from typical patterns of behavior to persistent or recurring episodes of serious maladjustment. In school, for example, a learning problem can range from working somewhat below capacity in one subject to failing completely in every subject; an attendance problem can range from fleeting anxiety about some aspect of being in the classroom to total refusal to attend school at all.

Second, each of these problems has many different possible causes. Considerable effort has been expended at times to pinpoint some single reason why young people become delinquent, or abuse drugs, or harm themselves. Such efforts are misguided, however, and their conclusions are misleading. These problems are complex behaviors that do not result from any one aspect of what people are like or what they have experienced. The most that can be said about a delinquent, for example, is that he or she has broken the law. Aside from having behaved illegally, delinquents are not any particular kind of people who have any particular kind of condition or are responding to any particular kind of situation. Instead, like the other adjustment difficulties we discuss in these next two chapters, delinquency is a multiply determined pattern of behavior fostered by several different types of personality characteristics, psychological conditions, and situational events.

PROBLEMS OF SCHOOL LEARNING AND ATTENDANCE

Being in school and achieving at the level of their ability help young people feel good about themselves, and being an adequate student promotes cognitive development, social maturity, and positive planning for the future. Many adolescents who do poorly or drop out of high school develop low self-esteem, remain psychologically immature, and fail to realize their intellectual and occupational potential.

Longitudinal studies confirm clearly that how adolescents do in high school predicts how they will do in college or at work. In one such predictive study, McCall, Evahn, and Kratzer (1992) compared the academic performance of 6,720 high school juniors and seniors with their educational and occupational status 13 years later, when they were 28–31 years old. The early adult accomplishments of these young people were more clearly related to the grades they had earned in high school than to how intelligent they were. Bright students who had received lower grades than would have been expected on the basis of their mental abilities showed just about the same level of accomplishment later on as classmates who were less academically talented but had managed to earn the same grades.

The subsequent careers of students in the McCall et al. study who performed below their capacity in high school tended to show the following specific characteristics: (1) their first full-time job was not commensurate in status or income with their mental ability, but was comparable to the first jobs of other students who had earned grades similar to theirs; (2) they completed fewer years of postsecondary education and were less likely to graduate from college than students of similar mental ability who had performed at their capacity during high school and thereby received better grades than they did; and (3) even 13 years after high school, they were holding lower status jobs and earning less money than students of equal ability who had out-performed them in high school, whereas in both respects—status and income—their jobs were comparable to those of less able students who had matched them in high school achievement.

These findings demonstrate how long-lasting the effects of learning problems can be. McCall et al. (1992) reported that a small percentage of young people who fail to utilize their abilities in high school may blossom later on and achieve educational and occupational goals consistent with their abilities. For most, however, the achievement level laid down in high school predicts the level of later accomplishments, whatever the person's level of ability.

The consequences of failure to realize learning potential are especially unfortunate among adolescents who drop out of school. The dropout rate of young people who leave high school before graduating in the United States presently stands at about 15%. Follow-up studies have indicated that these high school dropouts in their mid-20s are much more likely than high school graduates to end up in the ranks of the unskilled and unemployed, to be working, if at all, in low-status and low-paying jobs, and to be uninvolved in the affairs of their society (Bachman et al., 1979; Reyes & Jason, 1993; Wetzel, 1987).

With respect to psychological development, being in school keeps adolescents involved in learning experiences that build cognitive skills and in school-centered peer relationships that sharpen social skills. Young people who drop out or are unable to attend high school typically lose out on opportunities to broaden their knowledge and improve their basic abilities to read, write, and do arithmetic. Additionally, without the stimulation of assignments that encourage abstract thinking, they may fall behind in attaining the capacity for formal operational thought. Missing out on participation in school social events and extracurricular activities such as sports, music, dramatics, and hobby clubs can also result in adolescents' feeling alienated from the mainstream of teenage life and failing to develop their special talents to the fullest.

As for teenagers who remain in school but do poorly, their self-esteem suffers from a daily regimen of competition and evaluation in which they constantly come up short. Even for those who consider school unimportant, the constant experience of being identified as less competent than their peers can be painful and demoralizing. A vicious circle can get started in this regard: Doing poorly can result in criticism and embarrassment; the young person tries to ease his or her distress by paying less attention to schoolwork; this reduced attention leads to even poorer work; and poorer work results in even more criticism and embarrassment.

Adolescent learning problems can in many cases be traced to handicaps that have been present since early childhood. The most important of these are subnormal intelligence and two types of developmental disorder in children with adequate intelligence: specific learning disabilities, especially **dyslexia**, an inability to read at grade level; and **attention deficit hy-**

peractivity disorder (ADHD), a developmental disorder characterized by an age-inappropriate extent of inattentiveness, impulsiveness, emotionality, and hyperactivity. Although teachers and mental health professionals who work with adolescents need to be familiar with how these conditions can affect behavior and performance in junior and senior high school and on into adulthood, developmental disorders are problems more of child than of adolescent development (Barkley, Anastopoulos, Guevremont, & Fletcher, 1991, 1992; Hinshaw, 1992; Weiner, 1992, Chapter 7; White, 1992).

Poor school performance that begins in adolescence usually occurs in students who have no apparent learning handicaps but have nevertheless been receiving lower grades than they are intellectually capable of earning. This kind of gap between ability and performance constitutes **academic underachievement**. Because ability and performance have been measured in many different ways in studies of academic underachievement, it is difficult to specify the probable frequency of this problem among any particular group of adolescents. We do know from the findings of McCall et al. (1992) and others that academic underachievement occurs two to three times more frequently in high school boys than girls. We also know that academic underachievement tends to arise in the presence of certain family, school, gender-role, and personality influences.

FAMILY INFLUENCES IN UNDERACHIEVEMENT

Young people usually identify closely with their parents' feelings about school and education. Parents who value the educational process and respect the efforts of their childrens' teachers foster positive attitudes toward school, whereas parents who belittle teachers or doubt the usefulness of formal education promote negative attitudes. Similarly, when parents say that education is important but show little personal interest in reading, learning, or intellectual discussions, they can influence their children to downplay the significance of school in their lives.

Research comparing achieving and underachieving high school students of comparable intelligence indicates that achievers are typically more highly motivated to perform well academically and attach more importance to working hard and learning something in school (Carr, Borkowski, & Maxwell, 1991; Wentzel, 1989; Wentzel & Feldman, 1993). Research confirms further that the parents of achievers are generally more interested in how their children are doing in school and more encouraging with respect to their performance in the classroom; these parents more actively promote intellectual interests in their children and foster a positive attitude toward teachers and the school; and they are more likely than the parents of underachievers to value educational attainment and to express clear expectations of attainment by their children (McCall et al., 1992; Steinberg, Lamborn, Dornbusch, & Darling, 1992; Wood, Chapin, & Hannah, 1988).

Studies have also demonstrated that parental involvement in teenagers' lives influences their scholastic performance, for better or worse. When parents keep track of where their children are and what they are doing, children spend more time on homework; when parents discuss decisions and plans for the future with their adolescents, pay attention to their grades, and show interest in their assignments, their adolescents receive better grades (Dornbusch, Ritter, Mont-Reynaud, & Chien, 1990; Eckenrode et al., 1993; Fehrmann, Keith, & Reimers, 1987; Steinberg, Elman, & Mounts, 1989).

At times such differences in parental support for educational accomplishment have been attributed to family income level. Because middle- and upper-income parents tend to be well educated, it was said, they are likely to regard schooling as important in preparing for later life. Hence, they could be expected to speak well of the benefits of becoming educated and to discuss with their children the significance of what they were learning in school. Low-income parents, it was said, tend to be minimally educated, to regard school as an alien and unsympathetic institution, and to attach little importance to their children's doing well academically. Hence, they could be expected to pay relatively little attention to their children's school activities, show relatively little interest in what they were studying, and offer relatively little praise for their classroom achievements.

Given contemporary cultural diversity and expanded access to educational opportunities, such generalizations regarding disadvantaged families are no longer valid. In the first place, disadvantaged high school students can be as different from each other as they are from students from affluent families. In one study of Hispanic tenth-graders attending an inner-city high school, for example, Reyes and Jason (1993) were able to distinguish between groups of academically successful and unsuccessful students. The successful students had passed all of their courses as ninth graders and had been absent less than 10% of the time; the unsuccessful students had failed three or more courses in the ninth grade and had an absenteeism rate above 20%. Yet most of the students in both groups were from low-income, one-parent households in which parent education averaged below the fifth-grade level, and the two groups did not differ in these respects.

How these two groups of disadvantaged adolescents did differ involved their attitudes toward being in school. The successful students expressed satisfaction with their school and their activities in it, whereas the unsuccessful students tended to be highly critical of the school and to complain in particular about how they were being treated by their teachers and principal.

Second, families within any subcultural group can also think differently and influence their children in different ways. In studies of low-income African-American students, for example, comparisons of those who were doing well in school with those who were doing poorly have demonstrated clear differences: The parents of the achieving students were found to be more interested in their children's education, more knowledgeable about the school system, more supportive of academic achievement, and more likely to provide an intellectually stimulating environment, such as by having books in the home and setting aside adequate space for studying (Clark, 1983; Scheinfeld, 1983).

Manaster, Chan, and Safady (1992) studied 151 Mexican-American migrant high school students who were considered at high risk for school learning problems by virtue of their sociocultural background but who in many instances were in fact doing well academically. These successful students, compared to their underachieving peers, were found to be more fully acculturated, to have a clearer sense of their personal identity, and to have higher occupational aspirations and expectations. The unsuccessful group were more likely to come from families that were larger, poorer, more rural, and composed of more family members who had been born in Mexico.

Third, in addition to being diverse in their attitudes toward education, Hispanic and African-American adolescents and their parents do not differ from white Americans on the average in the values they place on achievement. In Chapter 7 we discussed a large-scale research project in which Steinberg and his colleagues collected various kinds of information from several thousand students who were attending nine different high schools and came from a broad range of ethnic and socioeconomic backgrounds. The African-American and Hispanic 14–18-year-olds in this large sample were just as likely as other students to value education, and their parents were just as likely as other parents to harbor aspirations for their children's success in school. The Hispanic and African-American students did tend to do less homework and receive lower grades than other students; however, this appeared to be related to their parents' difficulties in becoming supportively involved in their children's school learning and to lack of peer-group support for their academic achievement, not to antieducational values (Steinberg, Dornbusch, & Brown, 1992).

These findings suggest that parents influence the academic attitudes and achievements of their children through the environment they create at home, not by their socioeconomic status or by their minority group membership. Compelling evidence to this effect appears in Figure 11.1, which summarizes the results of 101 different studies of the relationships among academic achievement, socioeconomic background factors, and atmosphere in the home (as measured by parents' attitudes toward education, parents' aspirations for their children, family participation in cultural and intellectual activities, and availability of reading materials). Figure 11.1 indicates that measures of home atmosphere correlate more strongly with academic achievement than any single or even combined group of socioeco-

A home environment that provides intellectual stimulation can foster motivation to do well in school.

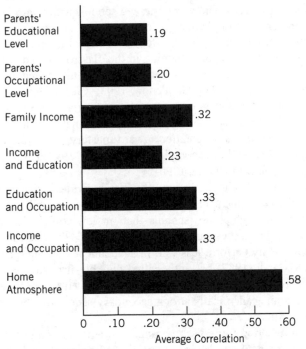

Figure 11.1 Average correlations among academic achievement and family background factors. [*Source:* Based on an analysis of 101 studies by White, 1982]

nomic indicators. This leaves little doubt that many lower income parents succeed admirably in creating a home environment that fosters learning (reading to their children, helping them do their homework, taking them to cultural events, encouraging them to go to college), whereas many economically advantaged parents may not.

SCHOOL INFLUENCES IN UNDERACHIEVEMENT

Able adolescents whose experiences at home have motivated them to achieve in school may nevertheless be prevented from doing well in the classroom by educational circumstances that limit their opportunities to study and learn. A widely publicized circumstance of this kind is the failure of elementary schools to prepare young people adequately for secondary school and college work. This problem is most acute in inner-city and depressed rural areas, where educational resources are frequently in short supply. Students who attend under-equipped and understaffed schools where they sit in crowded classrooms listening to bored or inept teachers may not acquire the basic academic skills and study habits they will need later on. Children who begin secondary school without having learned to multiply, read fluently, or take examinations, for example, and adolescents who enter college without ever having had to write a composition or conduct a laboratory experiment are ill prepared to meet the educational demands that await them.

Research studies have documented that the climate created by elementary and secondary schools and the teaching methods they prefer make considerable difference in how students behave and how much they learn. The more oriented schools are toward learning, the better behaved their students are and the better grades they earn; likewise, academic motivation and accomplishment increase when schools stress educational objectives, show respect and support for students, foster a sense of belonging in the classroom, and get students personally involved with their teachers and with school activities (DuBois, Felner, Brand, Adan, & Evans, 1992; Good & Weinstein, 1986; Goodenow, 1993; Kasen, Johnson, & Cohen, 1990). As for teaching strategies, there is good evidence that learning is facilitated by adapting course materials to student characteristics, presenting these materials in small steps, modeling correct examples, stressing an orientation toward mastery, encouraging class participation, and rewarding effort as well as accomplishment (Ames, 1992; Brophy, 1986; Gamoran & Nystrand, 1991; Pokay & Blumenfeld, 1990).

Aspects of the climate in a school that can influence individual achievement also include the overall intellectual level of the student body. Students of equal ability tend to form lower academic self-concepts in high-ability schools than in low-ability schools. Because students' conceptions of how well they can expect to do influence the grades they actually earn, equally able students usually perform less well in academically strong than in academically weak schools, which Marsh (1987) has aptly called the "big-fish–little-pond effect." In the absence of ample support and encouragement, then, adolescents may underachieve simply as a result of attending an academically strong secondary school in which they form a self-image of being a poor student.

Underachievement resulting from discouraging experiences in school is especially likely to occur among work-oriented and socioculturally disadvantaged adolescents who are not college bound. Teachers frequently expect less from their low-income than from their middle-class students and underestimate the abilities of their disadvantaged students (Entwisle, 1990; McCall et al., 1992). These disadvantaged young people come, in turn, to expect less of themselves than of their more advantaged peers, which leads them to put less effort into their studies; this reduced effort suggests disinterest in school and leads to low grades, which "justify" giving these students less attention.

Similarly with respect to students' future goals, schools frequently devote more of their resources to college-bound students than to those without such aspirations; often schools set more demanding requirements for their potential collegians than for their other students and pay more attention to whether they are performing adequately (Rosenbaum, 1991). This can leave students in a noncollege track feeling rejected and unimportant academically, which in turn can lead them to study less, learn less, and underachieve.

The impact that such expectations can have on how students actually perform in school is frequently referred to as the **Pygmalion effect**. Pygmalion was a sculptor who, according to legend, breathed life into a statue he was carving and made her into exactly the kind of woman he wanted her to be. The use of this term to describe influences in the classroom was coined by Rosenthal and Jacobsen (1968), who did some of the early research on this subject.

The educational impact of a school's climate tends to vary with its size as well as its philosophy. Schools that are large and impersonal may fail to involve their students adequately. Overcrowded inner-city schools serving disadvantaged youngsters are particularly prone to this problem, but it is not theirs alone. Large suburban junior and senior high schools furnished with abundant resources and attended by affluent students often provide their strongest programs at the top and bottom of the intellectual range. There are ample opportunities for gifted students to take accelerated courses, and there are excellent special educational services for slow learners. In between, however, many students of average ability may get lost in the shuffle.

Outside of the classroom, as well, a large school's athletic teams, performing groups, and even its clubs and service societies are often available to only a small percentage of the student body who are especially talented and determined. Research studies confirm that students in smaller schools enjoy more opportunities for participation and experience more emotional support in their community of students and teachers than students in larger schools (Entwisle, 1990). Students who lack such participation and support may lag in developing the kinds of involvement that make the school experience an important part of their lives and motivate them to do well in the classroom.

There is considerable evidence that being involved in multiple school activities and feeling a sense of commitment to their school contributes to adolescents receiving better grades; moreover, even when extracurricular activities do not affect a student's grades, they have been found to reduce the likelihood that a student will drop out of school (Marsh, 1992; Melnick, Sabo, & Vanfossen, 1992; Wentzel, 1992).

An interesting study relating school participation to academic performance was conducted by Gifford and Dean (1990), who compared 771 ninth-grade students who were attending a junior high school (grades 7–9) with 825 ninth-graders who were attending a senior high school (grades 9–12). The ninth-graders in junior high school settings were significantly more involved in extracurricular activities than those who were in a senior high school setting, and they were also earning significantly better grades.

GENDER ROLE INFLUENCES IN UNDERACHIEVEMENT

In Chapter 10 we discussed how gender-role concerns about success can influence a young person's occupational identity formation. Stereotyped attitudes about what constitutes appropriate behavior for males and females can also affect how hard adolescents work in school. Boys in a school or peer-group environment in which academic effort and attainment are viewed as feminine may hesitate to do their best in their studies to avoid being considered anything other than a regular guy. Girls surrounded by people who think that scholastic excellence and career mindedness are masculine characteristics may hesitate to give any indication that they value their studies over their social life, in order to avoid having their femininity called into question. As clear evidence of how gender-role concerns can stifle academic enthusiasm, most people can recall instances in which they or a classmate tried to conceal how well they had done on a test or in a course to avoid being seen as a brainy girl or a bookish boy.

In today's society such anxieties are being moderated by the desire of many people, both male and female, to get away from rigid gender-role definitions. A conviction that all talented people should realize their potential has largely replaced the socially acceptable "gentleman's C" of earlier years and the restriction of career-minded girls to teaching, nursing, and social work. Particularly among college students over the last generation, there has been a substantial increase in goal directedness among males and a marked reduction among females in conflict between intellectual and interpersonal needs. Wasting opportunities to become informed and to prepare for a future career is now less commonly regarded as normal adolescent behavior, and students of both genders are less inclined than before to devalue intelligence, competence, and ambition among their female friends (Deaux, 1985; Jacklin, 1989; Tittle, 1986).

Despite such signs of progress, however, stereotypes die hard. We noted in Chapter 10 that prevailing attitudes still hold men as being responsible chiefly for working and supporting their families and women as being responsible chiefly for taking care of the home. As reflections of these attitudes even in contemporary times, junior and senior high school teachers have been found to interact more frequently with the boys than the girls in their classes (Entwisle, 1990; Tittle, 1986); fathers have been found to be more concerned with the achievements of their sons than of their daughters (Bronstein, 1988); and high school boys were more likely than girls to be interested in learning about new kinds of technology (Taylor, Boss, Bedard, & Thibault, 1990).

Moreover, there remain clear gender differences in how young people view their own capacities and achievement potential. In one study of 279 junior high school students, Stipek and Gralinski (1991) administered a questionnaire measuring achievement-related beliefs before and after a mathematics exam. The girls reported a lower opinion of their abilities than the boys and had less expectation of doing well on the exam. After taking the exam and getting their scores, the girls were less likely than the boys to attribute success to high ability and failure to bad luck, and they were more likely than the boys to attribute failure to low ability. The girls in this study also took less pride in success than the boys and were less likely to believe that effort could bring them continued success. Can there be any doubt that such negative attitudes will put a damper on academic enthusiasm and contribute to students' achieving below their capacity?

In another study having similar implications, Poole and Evans (1989) asked 1,061 15–18-year-old students about their perceived level of skill in dealing with educational and work situations. The girls in their sample gave themselves lower competence ratings than the boys and saw themselves as being less personally effective; the boys rated themselves as possessing more ability than the girls, being in better health, and enjoying more success. To the extent that feeling able, competent, and successful contributes to realizing one's potential in the classroom, these findings identify the continuing possibility, even today, that some girls may underachieve as a result of gender-related doubts about their abilities and their prospects for doing well academically, regardless of how hard they work.

One further indication of contemporary gender differences in academic achievement orientation, at least during adolescence, comes from a study in which Gustafson, Sattin, and Magnusson (1992) followed the educational careers of 450 women from the eighth grade until age 26. At age 26, 70% of these young women were either married and rearing children without having had any postsecondary education, or they had pursued a college education and had no children. Only 15% of the sample had combined further education beyond high school with child rearing; the remaining 15% had neither gone to college or become a mother.

PERSONALITY INFLUENCES IN UNDERACHIEVEMENT

Academic underachievement in adolescence often reflects a personality pattern that involves considerable anger that young people feel toward their parents but are not able to express directly, concerns about rivalry that lead to fears of failure or fears of success, and a passive-aggressive style of dealing with stressful situations. No element of this pattern is unique to adolescents who have school learning problems. In combination, however, they frequently contribute to a reluctance or refusal to achieve, especially in families that value education, and young people with these characteristics can often be predicted to show a form of school learning difficulty called **passive-aggressive underachievement** (Marcus, 1991; McCall et al., 1992; Weiner, 1992, Chapter 7).

Anger Toward Parents

Passive-aggressive underachievers tend to resent their parents for being too authoritarian and expecting or demanding too much from them. These parents typically put pressure on their children for higher grades than the children could earn even if they did their best. Often the parents also insist on academic goals or career directions that are important to them but do not appeal to their son or daughter (such as getting into a prestigious college or becoming a lawyer or physician).

Passive-aggressive underachievers cannot easily express their resentment directly, and they seldom complain openly about their parents' demands and expectations. Instead, they vent their anger indirectly, through poor school performance. Doing poorly is an effective means of retaliation, especially when low grades frustrate parents' aspirations and make them visibly upset. "How can you do this to us?" such parents will ask their underachieving adolescent. They should be asking, "How can you do this to yourself?," because underachievement often ends up as a self-defeating maneuver that prevents young people from realizing educational and career goals of their own.

Concerns About Rivalry

Passive-aggressive underachievers typically suffer from **fears of failure** or **fears of success** that inhibit their academic efforts. Those who are afraid of failing have little confidence in themselves and doubt their ability to match the accomplishments of their parents and siblings. When trying to do something, they become discouraged at the slightest hint of criticism or an unsuccessful outcome. The more their family expresses disappointment in them ("Why can't you get the marks your brother does?"), the less they try to achieve.

To salvage some self-respect, adolescents who fear failure often set unrealistically high goals for themselves and then work only halfheartedly in pursuit of them. This can be an effective way of denying one's limitations and minimizing the shame of any failure. Ambitious goals provide a ready-made excuse for not reaching them, and lackadaisical effort helps preserve the fiction that "I could have done better if I had wanted to, but I really didn't feel like working hard." Operating in this way, fear-of-failure adolescents can be observed to move through life very carefully. They rarely risk making a mistake; they put out minimal effort to avoid seeming incapable should they fail; they deny having tried hard even when they have; and they pride themselves on what they accomplish without much work ("I got a C without even reading the assignment").

By contrast, adolescents who are afraid of succeeding believe in their talents but worry that doing well will cause other people, especially those with less ability, to envy or resent them. To avoid being disliked for their abilities and accomplishments, success-fearing young people often make light of them. They set limited goals that are easily within their grasp ("I'll be happy to get a C average, that's all I'm working for"), they put in just enough effort to reach these goals, and they deny any further aspirations ("I couldn't hope to do any better"). Unlike fear-of-failure adolescents, who blame their difficulties on any source but themselves, success-fearing adolescents usually attribute their failures to personal short-comings and their accomplishments to external factors that bring them no credit, such as luck.

Passive-Aggressive Style

Passive-aggressive behavior consists of purposeful inactivity by which people express anger and resentment that they cannot bring themselves to show openly. In approaching their schoolwork, passive-aggressive underachievers carefully avoid doing what it takes to earn good grades. They study less than their achieving peers, they postpone finishing assignments, and they put much less energy into their studies than they seem able to muster for extracurricular activities.

Passive-aggressive underachievers also take steps to make sure that their grades stay down rather than go up. They may read widely and keep themselves informed about many things, but they manage not to learn very much about matters that are likely to come up in class discussions or on examinations. They keep silent in class, even when they have something to contribute; they "forget" to write down assignments or "accidentally" study the wrong material; they "misunderstand" the directions on a test or "overlook" the last page of

Some students keep their grades down by finding time to do almost anything except their school work.

questions. By using these and similar kinds of "mistakes" and inactivity, passive-aggressive underachievers undermine their chances of performing at the level of their intellectual abilities.

TRUANCY AND SCHOOL PHOBIA

Adolescents who are not old enough to quit school sometimes refuse to attend, and some young people who could legally drop out remain enrolled but still show two patterns of school refusal: *truancy* and *school phobia*. Youngsters who are persistently truant or school phobic suffer many of the same consequences as dropouts. Removed from day-to-day interactions with classmates, they miss out on opportunities to improve their social skills and to develop a sense of belonging; absent from school, they experience academic failures that diminish their self-esteem and hamper their preparation for rewarding adult work.

Truancy consists of skipping school to spend time in what the adolescent considers to be more enjoyable ways. Truant adolescents usually dislike school and are doing poorly in their studies. While out of class they look for fun away from home, typically in the company of other truants and without their parents' approval. **School phobia** is a reluctance or refusal to go to school because of intense anxiety experienced in the school setting. As summarized in Box 11.1, youngsters who become school phobic differ in several respects from those who become truant, especially in having positive attitudes toward school learning (Berg, 1991; Sommer, 1985; Weiner, 1992, Chapter 6).

Despite their positive attitudes toward learning in school, school-phobic youngsters express a dread of going to school and often develop physical complaints that lead their parents to keep them at home, such as a headache, a stomachache, nausea, or a sore throat. Although they may exaggerate such complaints, school-phobic youngsters frequently suffer real physical distress at the prospect of being in the classroom, including pain, diarrhea, vomiting, and even fever. In some instances, either in addition to or instead of physical complaints, school-phobic students list various criticisms of the school situation as their reason for not wanting to attend: The teachers are unfair; the work is boring; the bus ride is too long; the other students are unfriendly; and so forth.

◆ BOX 11.1   DIFFERENCES BETWEEN TRUANT AND SCHOOL-PHOBIC STUDENTS

School-Phobic Students	*Truant Students*
1. Like school	1. Dislike school
2. Are doing average or above-average work in school	2. Are doing poorly in school
3. Are concerned about falling behind in their studies	3. Have little interest in their studies
4. Express eagerness to be able to return to school	4. Express wish that they didn't have to attend school
5. Have their parents' consent to be out of school	5. Are out of school without their parents' approval
6. Spend their time out of school at home	6. Spend their time out of school away from home

Whether expressed as physical complaints or criticisms of the school, school-phobic apprehensions cannot be ignored. If these youngsters are forced to go to school, they often become so ill or upset that they have to be sent home. Yet numerous reports indicate that neither their physical ills nor their criticisms tell the whole story (Berg, 1991; Last, 1992; Weiner, 1992, Chapter 6). Their bodily symptoms, although physically real, come and go quickly depending on whether they are being pressured to attend school. Weekends usually bring dramatic symptom relief, for example, followed on Sunday night or Monday morning by a sudden relapse. Criticisms of the school turn out to be rationalizations rather than the real reason for their not wanting to go. Modifying the situation, such as by driving them to school instead of having them take the bus, or even transferring them to a different school, improves matters temporarily but is soon followed by new criticisms to justify staying at home.

The underlying anxieties of school-phobic students often go unrecognized by parents, teachers, and family doctors who concentrate on reducing their real physical distress or resolving their seemingly reasonable complaints about school. In one important study from the past, for example, Tyrer and Tyrer (1974) found that more than two-thirds of a group of adults with a clear history of childhood school-phobic episodes had never been referred for psychological help. For this reason, the frequency of school phobia is difficult to determine. The best estimates are that this condition occurs in 0.5 to 1.0% of the school population each year, and that it is present in 3 to 8% of young people who are seen by mental health professionals (Hersov, 1990; Last & Strauss, 1990).

School phobia most often appears between the ages of 5 to 7 and 11 to 14 (Blyth & Simmons, 1983; Hersov, 1990). These two peak periods correspond to major transitions in a young person's life: the early years of elementary school and entrance into junior or senior high school. School phobia beginning in childhood differs in several important respects from school phobia beginning in early adolescence, however, and these differences define what are commonly referred to as *acute* and *chronic* forms of the problem.

Acute school phobia appears suddenly in children who have not previously shown adjustment difficulties. This form of the problem is especially likely to occur in younger students who are anxious about being separated from their parents or are responding to conflicts in the family through defiance and efforts to assert control over their parents (Atkinson, Quarrington, & Cyr, 1985; Bernstein, Svingen, & Garfinkel, 1990). Although episodes of acute school phobia may recur, they usually respond to treatment in just a few days or weeks (Blagg & Yule, 1984; Durlak, 1992).

Chronic school phobia develops gradually in students who already have a history of adjustment problems, sometimes including acute school phobia, and it becomes a lingering inability to attend school that can extend over months or even years. This form of school phobia occurs mainly among adolescents rather than younger children, and in teenagers it can be difficult to treat and a threat to normal development. Chronically school-phobic young people tend to withdraw not just from the classroom but from their friends and other previously enjoyed activities as well, and their condition often becomes complicated by generalized symptoms of anxiety and depression (Bernstein, 1991).

The more time that chronic school phobics spend at home instead of in the classroom, the more opportunities they lose for academic learning and cognitive and social maturation. Chronic school-phobia thus is a more serious condition and requires more extensive treatment than acute school phobia. With adequate intervention, however, the majority of young people with this condition are also able to return to school. This is the case even among chronic school-phobic youngsters whose adjustment difficulties are sufficiently serious to require treatment in a psychiatric hospital. Berg and Jackson (1985) found in a follow-up study of 168 such adolescents that half were able to overcome their problems and remain free from serious adjustment difficulties as young adults in their 20s. The recovery rate was even more favorable for those who first received treatment before age 14.

In contrast to younger children, adolescents who become school phobic are usually responding to unpleasant experiences in school rather than concerns about separation (Last, 1992; Weiner, 1992, Chapter 6). These experiences are seldom mentioned by adolescents as their reason for not wanting to go to school, usually because they are too painful for them to talk or even think about. Particularly common among early adolescents who become school phobic are embarrassments related to concerns about their bodies. For example, an athletically inept boy who is humiliated in his gym class may develop headaches or stomach upsets that, significantly, appear only on the days when he has gym. A physically advanced 11-year-old girl who is self-conscious about her breast development may become so upset about her classmates staring at her—whether or not they really are—that she begins to find excuses for staying home. In senior high school, when adolescents are dealing with concerns about dating and interpersonal relationships, school phobia may be precipitated by social rejections that make a young person feel unbearably uncomfortable or unattractive in the company of his or her peers.

TREATMENT

As is the case for all adjustment difficulties, problems of school learning and attendance are treated with a wide variety of methods and approaches. The choice of treatment depends mainly on the specific nature and source of the problem and how severe it has become. Even so, there is rarely just one way of helping an adolescent overcome a particular problem, and in most specific situations at least a few equally effective treatment alternatives can be identified.

Ironically, the problems of school learning and attendance that are the easiest to understand are the ones that are the most difficult to modify. These involve adolescents who are doing poorly in school because they see little to be gained from trying to do well or who are staying away from school because they dislike being there. Such attitudes develop over many years in response to negative family, neighborhood, and school influences, and by adolescence they have often become part of the individual's basic value system. Hence to be successful, any treatment must promote a value system in which academic success is seen as rewarding and useful for the future, while at the same time helping underachieving students improve their basic academic skills and their confidence in these skills.

Although this kind of treatment is typically simpler to describe than to implement, considerable success has been achieved in improving the school performance of unmotivated and unprepared students through direct efforts to modify negative influences on them and build up their academic abilities. These include special instructional programs for training academic skills; counseling with students to improve their self-concept as students, build their confidence in their abilities, increase their pleasure in being successful, and expand their appreciation of the advantages of becoming as well educated as they can; and working with parents to encourage them to support the educational efforts of their children, such as by discussing homework assignments with their child and praising good work (Barth, 1986, Chapter 8; Fehrmann et al., 1987; McCall et al., 1992; Weiner, 1992, Chapter 7).

When underlying anxieties are involved in school problems, as they are in passive-aggressive underachievement and school phobia, psychotherapy can help young people identify the nature of their concerns and resolve them in ways that are more adaptive than working at less than capacity or staying home. Especially when these problems have only recently begun and contrast sharply with generally good adjustment in other respects, prospects for rapid improvement in response to appropriate intervention are usually fairly good. However, the longer the problem has persisted before help is sought and the more it has affected a young person's life outside of school as well, the longer and more difficult the treatment is likely to be.

Adequate treatment for passive-aggressive underachievers and school-phobic youngsters often extends beyond individual discussions with a therapist. Because attitudes toward parents and the parents' own behavior are so frequently involved in these problems, work with the parents of underachieving and school-phobic students is often an essential feature of such therapy. In addition, numerous behavioral techniques have proved helpful in reducing the anxieties of school-phobic youngsters and hastening their return to the classroom. These techniques include training exercises in how to deal with anxiety-provoking situations in school; a program of gradual reintroduction to school, such as initially attending just one class at a time; and a formal attendance contract in which students participate in negotiating what will be expected of them (Bernstein & Borchardt, 1991; Last, 1992; Taylor & Adelman, 1990).

BREAKING THE LAW: DELINQUENT BEHAVIOR

We stated in the introduction to this chapter that delinquency consists of behavior that violates the law. Although this statement is accurate as far as it goes, it does not address the complexity of defining and measuring delinquency. Delinquent behavior can occur infrequently or repeatedly; it can range from minor misdemeanors to major felonies; and it can involve **status offenses**, which are acts that are illegal only by virtue of the person's age. Truancy and running away are crimes in 15-year-olds, for example, but not in 18-year-olds. To complicate matters further, only some of the adolescents who break the law are caught; of those who are caught, only some are arrested; of those who are arrested, only some are brought to trial; and of those who are tried, only some are adjudicated as delinquent.

These circumstances make it difficult to say how much delinquency there is, who should be called a delinquent, and which young people should be studied to learn more about the nature and origins of delinquent behavior. Any general statement about teenage delinquency that overlooks these complexities should not be taken seriously. In particular, global references to "juvenile delinquents" that are made as if these youngsters constitute some uniform group warrant skepticism rather than belief. *Delinquency* can be uniformly defined according to the acts it consists of, regardless of who does them or why; *delinquents*, on the other hand, are, from a psychological point of view, a very heterogeneous group of young people.

Some young people who commit delinquent acts can best be described as *socialized* delinquents because they are psychologically well-adjusted members of a delinquent subculture. Other adolescents who break the law are manifesting a *characterological* disorder marked by chronically irresponsible, aggressive, and inconsiderate behavior. In a third common pattern, delinquent behavior emerges as a *neurotic* symptom of underlying needs and concerns that a young person has been unable to resolve in other ways (Quay, 1987; Weiner, 1992, Chapter 8).

FREQUENCY OF DELINQUENT BEHAVIOR

Although the extent of juvenile delinquency is not known for sure, statistical reports from the U.S. Department of Justice indicate that approximately 4% of 10–17-year-olds in this country appear in juvenile court each year for offenses other than traffic violations. Compared to their numbers, adolescents are disproportionately likely to enter the criminal justice system. In 1986, for example, young people age 13–17 constituted 9.0% of the population but accounted for 19.9% of arrests (Flanagan & Jamieson, 1988). On the other hand, as shown in Figure 11.2, juveniles under age 18 accounted for a smaller percentage of arrests in 1986 and 1990 than they did in 1977 and 1981. The reasons for this substantial decline in the proportion of juveniles among persons arrested have not yet been determined; it can be said, however, that the decline exceeds any expectation based solely on a declining proportion of young people in the general population.

National statistics also identify gender differences among arrested adolescents: males outnumber females by a ratio of 3.4 to 1 (Flanagan & Maguire, 1992). This gender difference may be influenced by the apparent fact that police officers are more inclined to arrest teenage boys than girls who have committed the same offense. There is also evidence that lower socioeconomic status young people living in poor neighborhoods are more likely to be arrested than middle-class adolescents from advantaged neighborhoods (Binder, 1988; Gold, 1987). Hence the official data on young people who come before a judge may say more about who gets arrested for crimes than about who commits them.

As a further item of interest, the 3.4 to 1 ratio of arrested boys to girls in 1990 represents a gradual decline since 1979 from what was then a 3.9 to 1 ratio. Does this mean that more females than before are getting into a traditionally male activity (lawbreaking)? Or does it mean that law enforcement officials are less likely than before to make allowances for delinquent behavior when the offender is a girl? No one knows the answer for sure, but, perhaps

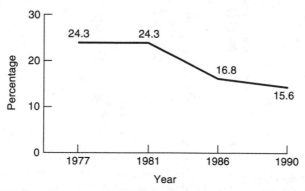

Figure 11.2 Percentage of total arrests involving juveniles (under age 18) (excluding traffic offenses). [*Source:* Based on data reported by Flanagan and Maguire, 1992]

in parallel with changing gender-role influences on achievement-related behavior, we are seeing how societal trends toward less rigid definitions of gender-appropriate behavior can lead to a changing male–female distribution of juvenile court cases.

With further respect to societal trends, the publicity that surrounds serious juvenile crime sometimes contributes to exaggerated impressions of how badly adolescents behave and how many young criminals there are. A closer look at the official statistics on the nature and frequency of juvenile lawbreaking is informative in this regard. In 1990 62.6% of the total arrests of juveniles were for various kinds of misdemeanors rather than more serious crimes against people or property (e.g., assault, rape, robbery, arson). Three status offenses—curfew violations, running away, and liquor-law violations—accounted for 18.6% of juvenile arrests, while vandalism, disorderly conduct, drunkenness, and minor violations of drug laws accounted for another 16.2% (Flanagan & Maguire, 1992).

Figure 11.3 shows further that an increase in arrests for serious crimes during the 1980s was more of an adult than a juvenile problem. Between 1981 and 1990 the total number of arrests among juveniles increased at only a fraction (one-seventh) of the rate of increase among adults, and juvenile arrests for serious crime actually decreased while the adult rate was increasing by almost one-third. Although violent crimes increased among juveniles, they did so at only three-fifths the rate of increase among adults.

To put delinquent behavior in further perspective, surveys indicate that fewer than 10% of young people who break the law are chronic, repetitive offenders and that this small fraction of youthful lawbreakers accounts for approximately half of the offenses committed by adolescents (Elliott, Huizinga, & Menard, 1987; Farrington, 1989). Longitudinal studies also indicate that the vast majority of adolescents who break the law, especially those who commit status and trivial offenses, begin and end their delinquency with their adolescence. Very few youthful lawbreakers are found to be persistently antisocial people who start be-

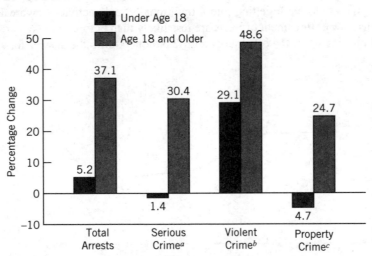

Figure 11.3 Arrests among juveniles and adults showing percent of change from 1981 to 1990. [a]Violent crimes and property crimes. [b]Murder, forcible rape, robbery, and aggravated assault. [c]Burglary, larceny–theft, motor vehicle theft, and arson. [*Source:* Based on data reported by Flanagan and Maguire, 1992]

having badly as preadolescent children and continue doing so as adults, and occasional minor offenses by adolescents do not necessarily predict any future misconduct or psychological maladjustment (Farrington, 1983; Loeber, 1990).

When marked misconduct does begin in childhood, on the other hand, a continuing pattern of problem behavior may follow in its wake. Research findings indicate that prepubertal antisocial behavior substantially increases the likelihood of a young person becoming seriously and repetitively delinquent by late adolescence; in turn, adolescents who are seriously and repetitively delinquent are more likely than young people in general to show criminal behavior as adults and also to have adjustment problems in their work and interpersonal relationships (Patterson, Capaldi, & Bank, 1991; Robins & Price, 1991; Stattin & Magnusson, 1989; Tolan, 1987).

In gauging the frequency of delinquent behavior, the official delinquency statistics tell only part of the story. They do not account for so-called **hidden delinquency** that goes undetected. In response to questions from survey researchers, about 80% of adolescents in the United States typically report having committed one or more delinquent acts for which they could have been arrested but were not (Johnson & Fennell, 1992; Tolan & Loeber, 1993). Consistent with the official statistics, most of these self-reported offenses are minor crimes, and most of the perpetrators are infrequent offenders. Undetected delinquents commit the same kinds of offenses as official delinquents, for the most part, and they do so for the same reasons; hence, most of what has been learned from studies of identified delinquents is generally considered applicable to undetected delinquents as well (Weiner, 1992, Chapter 8).

MISCONDUCT AS GROUP BEHAVIOR: SOCIALIZED DELINQUENCY

Socialized delinquency involves illegal behavior associated with membership in a subculture that endorses *antisocial* standards of conduct. The members of such deviant subcultures collaborate in committing crimes that reflect their customary way of life and that from their perspective constitute entirely appropriate behavior. This pattern of delinquency is also referred to as "gang," "subculturally deviant," or "group type" delinquency, and it is characterized by social rather than solitary acts. Socialized delinquents rarely commit crimes by themselves, and they have not been found to differ behaviorally from nondelinquents in any major ways aside from their lawbreaking. According to Quay (1987), however, they account for an estimated one-third of young people who are being held in correctional facilities.

Subcultures that foster group delinquency value successful lawbreakers and reject peers who decline to participate in antisocial activities. In this kind of environment, delinquent adolescents find acceptance and belongingness, whereas nondelinquents feel outcast and unworthy. Far from being alienated or socially inadequate, then, socialized delinquents typically form good interpersonal relationships within their delinquent subculture. They are satisfied, secure, loyal, and respected members of a supportive social group, and psychological studies indicate that they are no more likely than adolescents in general to demonstrate adjustment difficulties (Arbuthnot, Gordon, & Jurkovic, 1987; Quay, Routh, & Shapiro, 1987).

Consistent with their being psychologically well adjusted members of their group, socialized delinquents have usually enjoyed good family relationships during their early life. As infants and preschoolers, they have had attentive parents and siblings who helped them develop adequate capacities for judgment, self-control, and interpersonal relatedness. Later,

Membership in a delinquent gang can give adolescents feelings of belongingness that are difficult for them to give up.

however, in elementary school and as adolescents, they have usually lacked parental supervision and been influenced less by their family than by antisocial models in their neighborhood. Socialized delinquency thus tends to be associated with growing up unsupervised in a loving but loosely organized home that is located in a deteriorated, high-delinquency neighborhood (Dishion, Patterson, Stoolmiller, & Skinner, 1991; Elliott, Huizinga, & Ageton, 1985; Farnworth, 1984; Lyon, Henggeler, & Hall, 1992).

These risk factors for socialized delinquency are typically observed to exert their influence interactively. Parents in conflict-ridden homes who get along poorly with each other and with their children tend to lack interest in monitoring their delinquent youngsters' whereabouts and requiring them to comply with family rules and regulations. Adolescents who lack firm and dedicated parental supervision tend to be relatively susceptible to peer influence toward misconduct. Antisocial peer models are relatively numerous in disadvantaged or deteriorated neighborhoods, and such neighborhoods, because of their usual dense population and clutter of buildings, complicate the parental task of keeping track of where their children are and what they are doing (Farrington, 1986; Snyder & Patterson, 1987; Steinberg, 1986, 1987).

Yet socialized delinquency is by no means a unique product of economic disadvantage or inner-city neighborhoods. Economic hardship has not been shown to bear any relationship to delinquency independently of inconsistent parental discipline (Lempers, Clark-Lempers, & Simons, 1989). Delinquent adolescent groups are found at all socioeconomic levels, and the actions of delinquent gangs are as disturbing and unacceptable to poor adults as to affluent adults. Moreover, even though delinquent groups are found more often in lower income neighborhoods, delinquency is very much a middle-class phenomenon also, including the formation of trouble-making gangs (Lowney, 1984; Richards, Berk, & Foster, 1979). Neither lack of community cohesion nor inadequate parental supervision is limited to poor neighborhoods. Wealthy suburbs, with their sometimes transient population of families on the move and parents preoccupied with their own goals and interests, can also fail to provide young people with an adequate sense of direction and belonging.

MISCONDUCT AS PERSONALITY DISORDER: CHARACTEROLOGICAL DELINQUENCY

Characterological delinquency consists of illegal behavior that reflects an essentially *asocial* personality orientation. Unlike socialized delinquents, characterological delinquents are usually loners who have no group membership or loyalties. They commit their crimes either by themselves or in temporary alliance with other delinquents whom they seldom regard as friends. In further contrast to socialized delinquents, they do not show two faces to the world, one a face of trust and loyalty for members of their subculture and the other a face of disaffection and disdain for people outside their group. Instead, characterological delinquents trust no one and are loyal only to themselves, even though they may pretend trust and loyalty when it serves their purpose to do so.

The misconduct of characterological delinquents represents not so much an intent to break the law as a consequence of disregard for the rights and feelings of others and an inability or unwillingness to control their behavior. They do as they please, without hesitation and with little concern for how their behavior affects others; they take what they want aggressively and without regard for how others may suffer in the process. Characterological delinquency is also known as undersocialized or solitary-type delinquency, and the interpersonal orientation and behavior patterns of characterological delinquents constitute in budding form a condition known as *psychopathic* or *antisocial personality disorder*.

Psychopathic or **antisocial personality disorder** is the most common personality disorder that emerges during adolescence, and it usually comes to light in connection with characterological delinquency. The two basic elements of psychopathic personality are an underdeveloped conscience and an inability to identify with other people. Because they lack conscience, psychopaths feel little guilt about trampling on the rights and well-being of other people. Because they lack identifications, they are essentially loveless individuals whose emotional relationships are fleeting and shallow. They do not hate other people in the way that socialized delinquents may hate "outsiders"; instead, they simply do not care enough about other people to have strong feelings toward them one way or another. As far as they are concerned, other people exist to be used and manipulated, not to be taken care of or depended on. Psychopaths are self-centered individuals who blame other people or circumstances for whatever difficulties they cause or encounter, and they feel fully justified in doing just as they please (Harpur, Hare, & Hakstian, 1989; Meloy, 1988).

These features of their personality make psychopathic young people highly likely to engage in characterological delinquent behavior. Usually they refrain from antisocial acts only when they are concerned about being caught and punished, and rarely because of any internal standards of decency and propriety. Contrary to common belief, however, there is no direct relationship between psychopathy and criminality. Lawbreaking may occur for subcultural and neurotic reasons as well as because of characterological defects, and not all psychopaths become criminals.

◆ *Profile*

HERBERT QUAY

As a young man just out of high school, Herbert Quay joined the army and served in the headquarters of General Douglas McArthur's army of occupation in Japan following World War II. There he became interested in a career in industrial relations, and after his discharge he enrolled as a business major at Florida State University. At Florida State he divided his time between his studies and playing on the tennis team, and he also began to shift his interests from industrial relations to psychology. When he graduated, he had a tentative offer to stay on as a graduate assistant in the Athletic Department and coach tennis. When this possibility did not materialize, he decided to stay on anyway and get a master's degree in psychology.

Completing his master's in 1952, Dr. Quay took a position as a clinical psychologist at the Florida School for Boys, a state correctional center that immersed him in the problems of delinquent behavior. He stayed at the Florida School for only 1 year before moving on to Milledgeville State Hospital in Georgia for 2 years and then on to the University of Illinois to pursue his doctorate, but his experiences in Florida had much to do with his career-long commitment to unraveling the origins of conduct problems in young people. In the first 16 years after he received his Ph.D. he served terms on the faculty at Illinois and at Vanderbilt, Northwestern, and Temple Universities. In 1974 he went to the University of Miami as Professor and Director of the Program in Applied Social Sciences, and from 1984 until his retirement in 1992 he served there as chairman of the Department of Psychology.

As a scholar, Dr. Quay is widely known for his extensive research and writing on delinquent behavior, but he is also the author of numerous books, chapters, and articles concerned with many different types of abnormal psychological development in young people. He could also be just as easily recognized for his distinguished professional contributions as for as his research. In addition to helping build an outstanding program in child clinical psychology in his department at Miami, he founded the *Journal of Abnormal Child Psychology* and for over 20 years served as its editor. He also served a term as president of the section on clinical child psychology of the clinical division of the American Psychological Association and in 1991 received the section's Distinguished Contribution Award.

Dr. Quay continues to play tennis in his retirement, but he is also actively engaged in further exploration of the ways in which the dispositions of young people to seeking various kinds of rewards may relate to their likelihood of misbehaving.

Most people have known some individuals in their lives who show psychopathic features, who are selfish and self-centered individuals who heartlessly exploit people and circumstances to their own ends but stop short of overt criminal acts. Nevertheless, because of their generally aggressive, asocial attitudes and their lack of concern for the welfare of others, psychopaths are found to be more likely than most other kinds of people to behave in ways that violate the law. Quay (1987) reported that psychopathic youth constitute about one-fourth of the adolescents institutionalized for delinquent behavior.

Although the origins of psychopathic personality are not fully understood, people with this disorder have usually experienced parental rejection and neglect, beginning early in life. Love and affection seldom came their way during their preschool years, and consistent discipline and well-intended supervision were likewise conspicuously absent during their middle childhood and adolescence. Reared in this way, young people grow up with little capacity to feel warmth and compassion toward others and have little expectation of being loved or nurtured by them. Instead, they tend to see the world as a hostile and uncaring place in which quarter is neither asked nor given, consideration is neither tendered nor received, and survival and success depend on looking out for yourself (Deutsch & Erickson, 1989; Feehan, McGee, Stanton, & Silva, 1991; Simons, Robertson, & Downs, 1989; Snyder & Patterson, 1987).

As might be expected, then, the most reliable known predictor of this personality disorder is growing up in a home in which there is considerable conflict, little family cohesion, and one or both parents are themselves asocial. Psychopathic parents are prime candidates to ignore or abuse their children and fail to teach them the meaning of self-sacrifice and respect for others. Perhaps for this reason, research findings demonstrate that having a criminal parent is a major risk factor for juvenile delinquency (Haddad, Barocas, & Hollenbeck, 1991; Rutter et al., 1990; Veneziano & Veneziano, 1992).

Knowing that criminal tendencies run in families raises the interesting question of whether this phenomenon derives from the way parents rear their children, or from genetic dispositions they transmit to their children, or from some combination of genetic and experiential factors. The available data so far suggests that criminal tendencies are jointly determined by constitutional and environmental factors, but no specific genetic determinants of psychopathic personality disorder have yet been identified (Plomin, 1989; Weiner, 1992, Chapter 8).

MISCONDUCT AS COMMUNICATION: NEUROTIC DELINQUENCY

In **neurotic delinquency** young people commit illegal acts neither as well-integrated members of a delinquent subculture nor as a reflection of personality disorder, but instead as an individual effort to communicate some specific unmet psychological needs. Like many other neurotic behaviors, neurotic delinquency is thus symptomatic of underlying concerns that it serves indirectly to express.

Whereas socialized and characterological delinquency often involve recurrent antisocial conduct that becomes a way of life, neurotic delinquency typically consists of occasional, situationally determined episodes of lawbreaking. These episodes usually begin soon after the emergence or intensification of some personal problem that is generating feelings of tension, remorse, or discouragement, and they tend to stop soon after this problem has been resolved in some way. Accordingly, this pattern of misconduct is sometimes referred to as "acute," "accidental," "situationally provoked," or "anxious-withdrawn-dysphoric" delinquency. Although adolescents who misbehave for these reasons do not fit usual stereotypes of being a juvenile delinquent, anxious-withdrawn-dysphoric youth account for one-fourth of institutionalized delinquents (Quay, 1987).

Two types of needs are particularly likely to contribute to neurotic delinquency. First, needs for recognition and respect sometimes lead a young person who feels unnoticed and unappreciated to misbehave in some dramatic fashion. Acts of daring and bravado may occur for this reason, such as climbing the school flagpole or attempting to shoplift in front of a store clerk. This purpose is also served by behaviors that embarrass or disrupt the "establishment," such as calling in a bomb threat that results in the school or a movie theater being emptied and searched. Because their misconduct can communicate to others only if they learn about it, neurotic delinquents manage almost without exception to get themselves caught. No matter what penalties follow, they enjoy their temporary notoriety. The use of public antisocial behavior to gain recognition and peer status, especially in young persons suffering from low self-esteem, has been widely noted in clinical and research studies (Blatt, Hart, Quinlan, Leadbetter, & Auerbach, 1993; Weiner, 1992, Chapter 8).

Second, young people who are experiencing distressing problems that they are afraid or embarrassed to tell anyone about, or whose expressions of concern are falling on deaf or disinterested ears, may resort to visible acts of delinquency as a way of communicating a need for help. Their delinquent behavior then forces others to recognize the existence of a problem and do something about it. For example, inattentive parents who are called before a school principal or a juvenile court judge to discuss their child's misbehavior can no longer deny or overlook that he or she is in distress.

The problem most commonly associated with the use of delinquent acts to communicate needs for help is an underlying depression. Uncharacteristic aggressive behavior and the sudden onset of stealing are often observed in young people who have recently begun to feel lonely, isolated, discouraged, and helpless. This kind of delinquency is particularly common following the loss of some important person in an adolescent's life, such as loss of a parent through death or divorce (Chiles, Miller, & Cox, 1980).

The previous life pattern of neurotic delinquents usually contrasts sharply with their present pattern of misconduct. Instead of the childhood history of impulsive, aggressive, and inconsiderate behavior that typically accompanies characterological delinquency, neurotic delinquents tend to have been well behaved in the past. Often others who know them well are genuinely surprised that they of all people have suddenly lost respect for law and order.

Similarly, unlike the family circumstances surrounding characterological delinquency, neurotic delinquents typically have stable, caring, and law-abiding parents. This is not to say that family problems play no role in neurotic delinquency. To the contrary, neurotic delinquents are often using misbehavior as a hostile act against parents who are failing to recognize their needs, and the parents of these adolescents are in turn usually angry at them for how they are behaving. When delinquent patterns reflect neurotic rather than characterological difficulties, however, any current falling out between parents and their children exists along with more basic feelings of love and affection and a sincere wish to draw closer together.

TREATMENT

For delinquent behavior as in instances of academic underachievement, the best approach to treating the problem depends on what is causing it. Neurotic delinquency, like passive-aggressive underachievement, reflects underlying concerns that can usually be identified in a relatively short course of psychotherapy. When previously unrecognized or unmet needs that have fostered delinquent behavior get communicated and responded to in therapy, the motivation to misbehave ebbs rapidly. In fact, it is not unusual for neurotic delinquents to stop getting into trouble as soon as arrangements have been made for them to begin psychotherapy, even before the work of the treatment has begun, apparently because their use of delinquency to communicate a need for help has achieved its purpose.

Especially when depression related to some loss or disappointment has led to the delinquent behavior, having a regular relationship with an understanding and interested therapist often stems the misconduct, regardless of what is discussed in the treatment sessions. On the other hand, most groups of delinquents will include some whose basic problems are emotional, not behavioral (Armistead, Wierson, Forehand, & Frame, 1992), and treatment programs that fail to recognize and deal with underlying depression in a delinquent adolescent may have little impact.

In a study of 91 adolescents with behavior problems who were treated with a management-oriented approach aimed at reducing their problem behavior, those who were depressed at the beginning of the treatment showed much less improvement than those who initially gave little indication of being depressed (Exner & Weiner, 1982, pp. 140–142). What the depressed misbehaving adolescents in this study apparently needed and did not receive was intervention aimed at resolving their depressive concerns. In a contrasting study, disruptive students who were given opportunities to talk about previous loss experiences in a school-based counseling program showed a reduction in angry outbursts and improved school performance as well (Fleisher, Berkovitz, Briones, Lovetro, & Morhar, 1987).

Socialized delinquents are rarely interested in or responsive to traditional forms of psychotherapy. They are, after all, relatively comfortable and well-integrated members of their peer group, and they tend to see any problems they have as residing in society, rather than in their own psychological makeup. However, despite the long odds against getting socialized delinquents to reject the antisocial values they share with their peer group, two approaches have shown some promise.

One of these approaches employs neighborhood- and home-based programs intended to encourage subcultural delinquents to pursue ways of having fun and making money that will not get them into trouble with the law. These programs promote the Police Athletic League, provide job training and vocational counseling, instruct parents in reinforcing socially acceptable behavior, and try to show delinquents how their current behavior is wasting their talents and energies and could be replaced by nondelinquent means of getting ahead in school and work situations (Clark, 1992; Gottschalk, Davidson, Gensheimer, & Mayer, 1987; Henggeler, Melton, & Smith, 1992; Miller & Prinz, 1990; Nelson, 1990).

The other approach concentrates on training delinquent adolescents in specific academic, social, and employment skills. This approach emerged from indications that juvenile offenders, especially those who become repetitive lawbreakers, tend to lack basic learning, living, and working skills that could help them achieve success and feel comfortable outside of their delinquent subculture. The results of such training efforts indicate that carefully designed programs aimed at increasing these skills can reduce the frequency of repetitive delinquency, especially when they are combined with parent management training that improves parent–child interactions (Cunliffe, 1992; Jensen & Howard, 1990; Serna, Schumaker, Hazel, & Sheldon, 1986; Shore & Massimo, 1979).

Some of these psychotherapeutic and educational efforts are also used with characterological delinquents, but rarely with much success. The relationship of characterological delinquency to psychopathic personality disorder makes it extremely difficult to treat. Delinquents with this kind of psychological disorder rarely trust or identify with other people, nor do they reflect critically on their attitudes and behavior, nor do they feel any need to change. Hence they provide few opportunities for effective psychotherapy to occur, and their basically asocial, self-centered orientation to the world is seldom touched by social-action or skill-training approaches to reducing delinquency. What few prospects there are for altering the behavior patterns of characterological delinquents are mostly limited to intensive long-term treatment in a residential setting (Condry, 1987; Marohn, 1993; Meeks & Cahill, 1988; Stone, 1993).

There is also reason to anticipate that some developmental aspects of socialized and characterological delinquency will influence their outcome in different ways. Socialized delinquents, being by and large well-adjusted group members, may, in the process of becoming adults, affiliate with new companions whose values differ from the antisocial standards of their adolescent friends. Even delinquent gangs who remain close as adults may become wiser as well as older, and they may decide for themselves that there are better ways to spend their time than fooling around and risking arrest.

This kind of self-determined decision to stop breaking the law is sometimes referred to as the "natural cessation" of delinquency. In one study of natural cessation, Mulvey and LaRosa (1986) found in a group of untreated but reformed late adolescent delinquents that their behavior change had in fact been preceded in each case by their arriving at a changed perspective on their current behavior and future prospects and resolving to change the former in order to improve the latter.

Such positive developmental changes seldom occur among characterological delinquents. They may become more clever and wiser to the ways of the world, but otherwise maturity brings to young people with characterological disorder only a further crystallization of their maladaptive attitudes. Hence characterological delinquents typically persist in inconsiderate, irresponsible, and antisocial behavior, and as adults they are significantly more likely than socialized delinquents to be convicted and imprisoned for criminal behavior.

CHAPTER SUMMARY

1. Attending school and achieving at the level of their ability helps adolescents feel good about themselves and continue to mature. Young people who do poorly or drop out of school often develop low self-esteem, remain psychologically immature, and fail to realize their intellectual and occupational potential.

2. *Academic underachievement* is a gap between ability and performance that arises in relation to a variety of influences: a *family* environment that discourages intellectual pursuits; a *school* setting that limits opportunities to study and incentives for learning; *gender-role* attitudes that inhibit educational ambition; and *personality* problems involving anger toward parents and concerns about rivalry that foster *passive-aggressive underachievement*.

3. *School phobia* is a reluctance or refusal to at-

tend school because of intense anxiety experienced in the school setting. Although it is an easily treatable condition among younger children, it can become chronic and persistent in adolescents and seriously interfere with their academic learning and their cognitive and social maturation.

4. Approximately 4% of 10–17-year-olds appear in juvenile court each year, and an unknown larger percentage commit delinquent acts for which they are not arrested. Although *delinquent behavior* can be uniformly defined according to acts that break the law, *delinquents* are a psychologically heterogeneous group.

5. Some juvenile lawbreaking is *socialized delinquency* that is associated with good psychological adjustment within a subculture that endorses *antisocial* standards of conduct. Some is *characterologi-*

cal delinquency that reflects an essentially asocial orientation associated with a *psychopathic personality disorder*. And some is *neurotic delinquency*, in which the misconduct is symptomatic of underlying concerns that it serves indirectly to express.

6. The best approach to treating delinquent behavior depends on what is causing it. Neurotic delinquency usually responds quickly and well to psychotherapy. Sociological delinquency calls for family and community programs of intervention and various kinds of skill training. Characterological delinquency rarely responds to these treatment approaches and can be modified, if at all, only by intensive long-term treatment, usually in a residential setting.

KEY WORDS

academic under-achievement

acute school phobia

antisocial personality

attention deficit hyperactivity disorder (ADHD)

characterological delinquency

chronic school phobia

dyslexia

fears of failure

fears of success

hidden delinquency

neurotic delinquency

passive aggressive behavior

passive-aggressive underachievement

psychopathic personality

Pygmalion effect

school phobia

socialized delinquency

status offenses

truancy

REVIEW QUESTIONS

1. What does it mean to say that delinquency and other behavior problems have complex causes?

PROBLEMS OF SCHOOL LEARNING AND ATTENDANCE

2. What are some likely negative consequences of doing poorly in high school or dropping out?

3. How can parents help their adolescent children earn better grades and avoid underachievement?

4. Discuss the relationships between family background factors and the academic performance of adolescents.

5. Describe some aspects of the "climate" in a school that can affect how well students do in their studies.

6. What kinds of research findings indicate that long-standing gender-role stereotypes can still discourage females from achieving at the level of their capacity?

7. List the three defining characteristics of passive-aggressive underachievement.

8. How can concerns about rivalry contribute to underachievement?

9. What are the major differences between truancy and school phobia as reasons for not attending school?

BREAKING THE LAW: DELINQUENT BEHAVIOR

10. What factors make one adolescent more likely than another to be arrested for committing the same offense?

11. Summarize the research findings concerning the continuity of misconduct from childhood to adolescence to adulthood.

12. In what sense are socialized delinquents often psychologically well adjusted?

13. Describe the typical attitudes and behavior patterns that characterize psychopathic personality disorder.

14. What kinds of information about previous behavior patterns and family relationships help to distinguish neurotic delinquency from characterological delinquency?

15. Discuss the types of intervention that appear to work best in reducing socialized, characterological, and neurotic delinquency.

Interlude

❖

Brad, Age 18

❖

"I think I've found me now because, you know, I'm finding acceptance all over the place"

Brad, a white 18-year-old, had just graduated from high school in a small town when he was interviewed. He discusses his brief experience with drinking and marijuana, meeting and falling in love with a local minister's daughter, his relations with his parents, and early sexual experiences, and he describes the social ecology of his high school. He seems to have made considerable progress in his development of a sense of identity in the last year or two, and many of his experiences illustrate themes we described in earlier chapters. His discussion of drugs also sets the stage for the next chapter on pitfalls and challenges during adolescence.

Questions to consider while reading this case include the following: In what ways is Brad a fairly typical adolescent boy, and in what ways is he unusual? What is your reaction to his relations with his parents? Why did he have so few close friends, as he seemed to be fairly popular and to date quite a bit? How did the definitions of social status in his high school affect him? Why did his teachers have such an important influence on him? Were his sex education and early sexual experiences unusual? Has his developing sense of identity followed the process described by Marcia in Chapter 10? What is unique about being an adolescent in a small town? With regard to the last chapter, how would you evaluate his "delinquent" behavior? What type does it express?

How old are you now? I'm 18; I'll be 19 in September. *Would you tell me a little bit about your* *adolescence? What things particularly stand out in your memory of it?* Well, I went a little wild when I was a sophomore. I was a good student right up through until I hit my sophomore year and then I got into the drinking and smoking and the rough group. Then I decided that wasn't for me when I was a junior and I've been "straight" from then on, but I've always been, I don't know, open, pretty well accepted, had quite a few friends. Like to have a good time. But I went to church, I always went to church. And when I was a junior I started listening to what went on in church rather than just going. *Anything else that stands out in your mind?* It seems like my last year of high school was a big step, from junior to senior for me was a big step, it was a big change in attitude. A few people notice; they think I'm more mature or something. I don't know, it just seemed to happen. I guess I've worked harder, and I've settled down to make something.

Sounds like the sophomore year was kind of a bad time for you, or difficult? It was trying to be accepted more than anything else. I worked with a bunch of rowdy people who smoked dope and drank and played rock and roll; I played the guitar and had a band. So I decided I'd follow their footsteps and be accepted in the wide range, you know. But when I had those friends and I had friends ranging from 22 to my age, 16 then, probably, and to be 16 and to have friends that were 22 was kind of a thing for most people. *So you played the guitar and had a band?* Well I had a band then, but I don't have one now.

You mentioned the church as being pretty important to you. Yeah, it is now. And I've always gone. I've started listening to it, it seems. *What do you mean?* Well, I started paying attention. I felt there was something there for me. I picked up a girlfriend who happens to be the minister's daughter, when they moved here, you know. So I went to church and then it just started to make sense to me, what they were saying; it never did before; I never really cared before. *Anything in particular?* Well, I don't know, I always felt, it seems weird, but since I was a little kid, I've always felt I was going to be a minister. I don't know why. I'm going to go to college; I may go to college for that afterwards. It's not a calling, but there's a feeling there ever since I was, I don't know how high, in Sunday school looking up at the minister. I always wanted to be one. In the church, my church, you can find just as much acceptance as anything else I've ever wanted, without abusing myself. *You feel accepted by the people there?* Oh yeah.

Do you remember when you first noticed the physical changes of puberty happening to your body? How old were you then? I really don't have any idea. Seems like my grade grew up quicker, you know; we had parties when we were in fifth grade. We had kissing parties and no one knew how to kiss and dancing parties, you know, and everyone thought that was a big thing. Older people had them, so we had them. *That was back in fifth grade?* Yeah, in fifth grade. Dating games in fourth grade, even. Someone was going with her for a week and dropped her and went with someone else for a week. Sixth, seventh grade I guess, I really couldn't pinpoint it. *That's about when you began to notice the changes?* Yeah. Seventh grade, come to think of it. *Any particular memories of those changes?* Well, I noticed there were especially attractive girls, you know, the way you looked at girls changed. They were something we wanted to get ahold of. In seventh grade, I remember one girl; it was weird but, I guess that's probably when it hit most, when it started. *What about with your own body? Did you notice changes there?* Of course I noticed. I just figured they were normal, I suppose. Playing sports the way I did, you're always in the locker room, you know. It was subconscious—you see other guys who are in high school, but you just figured you'd get there someday. *Were you about the first in your age group to mature or were there others that were more mature than you were?* I think there were others more mature than I was. Yeah, I was about average; there were a few who were done and a few who were even further back, who always wore their underwear in the showers, or something. I was just about average, I'd say. *Anything that you particularly were bothered by during that period with the physical changes?* Well, let me think. I always wanted it to hurry up and change, you know, you don't like to be not like the older boys. I remember I had a hard time adjusting at first to taking showers with other guys because I was always by myself; but I got over that as soon as you find out that's what they do. I do remember going to the doctor during that period. Before going to the doctor, mother was always there. Now mother's not there; you're alone with the doctor. I felt a little weird taking my pants down for him. He acted as if it was nothing, and I thought, "What're you doing!" *What about changes in your voice, was that a big thing for you?* (Laughs) I had the regular squeaks and I got made fun of, of course. *Who made fun of you?* Oh, you know, friends; we'd make fun of each other 'cause all my friends were in the same age group; we had a great time. *How did you feel about all of these changes you were going through in your body?* Well, I just figured they were normal. My parents never told me what to expect or anything, so I just took 'em in stride.

Let's talk a little bit about you and your parents. How would you describe your relationship with your mother and father during childhood? Well I was the firstborn, so I was spoiled. I don't know why, but I was sort of rebellious, I was mouthy. *What do you mean mouthy?* Oh, I used to sass back, you know, want my own way, and just persisted anyway, stubborn. But I've always been mouthy, sassy; well, not now, but then I was. As far as I can remember I always had been; always had fits and stamped and had temper tantrums and the works. *Did they punish you pretty bad for that?* Oh, I got hit quite a bit. Not actually quite a bit; I imagine I deserved it, but I did get hit. *Just a slap?* A pound on the butt, hit in the head every once in a while, nothing serious; I mean they didn't kill me, they just let me know that I wasn't doing what I should be doing. *Were you sort of close to your mother or father?* No. Never have been. Not now either, not now. We get along fine and proper; I tell them if it's really bad, but I keep to myself. They keep to themselves. *How do you feel about that?* Well, it could be better, but at least I know they care, they know I care. Sort of a silent agreement. *Something that's not talked about much.* Yeah, but it's there. *You know that they're there if you need them?* Oh yeah, definitely. If I have any trouble and it's bad, they'll be there.

Is your relationship with your mother about the same now as it was then, or has it changed in the last few years? It's changed. With my father it's stayed pretty steady. But with my mother it's changed because I talk more to her now. I come home from work and flop down in a chair and we talk about what happened at work. She's mouthy like I am, or sassy or smart, or whatever, so we kid around a lot. We get along better. *But it's still kind of the same with your father?* Yeah, it's the same. Ma, I don't come home and cry on her shoulder or anything; but, you know, if anything really bad, she's there; we talk a lot more. My father, I can talk to anytime I want, but he doesn't offer, doesn't loosen up very often. It's just that he's constantly there; if we need each other, he'd be there. *But you don't really talk much?* No, not to my dad. *You don't do much together, you and your dad?* No, he's busy; I'm busy. We go fishing every once . . . , we go hunting, we always hunt together. But when I played sports, we'd probably be out playing sports together, we'd fish together. Now I've got other interests; he's got other interests. He coaches Little League, he's a Little League manager, and I'm glad. It gets him in with the other kids; I mean I'm not resentful of that or anything. I think he did a pretty good job. I don't feel neglected.

When you were a sophomore, you mentioned kind of getting in with a different crowd and getting into some things you weren't very happy about. How did your parents deal with all of that? Well my parents always told me not to hang around with these guys, not to drink. But I figured I was big enough to take care of myself, and I told them so. And when I started smoking dope, they didn't know, hardly nobody knew. But they had an idea. So they'd accuse me of it when I hadn't even been. *How did they get an idea?* I don't have any idea. My mother has a second sense, or something; she knows everything I do; she's always known everything I've done. I don't really know. She just figured that the people I hung around with smoked so I must be. I'd imagine that's how. But she never said anything to me; my father did. But I hadn't even been, the time they accused me. *Were there any fights or disagreements about that or over that whole period?* Well there was a difference. My father drinks beer every once in a while, so if I had an occasional beer, he wouldn't care. My mother hates it when he drinks beer. So my father wouldn't say anything if he found out I drank beer; my mother probably would. But my father would go off his rocker if he thought I was smoking dope. And my mother would probably say something, or give me a lecture: "I never thought you'd do this" or, you know, the typical guilt trip. But she wouldn't get upset like he would. She never said anything to me. He did. Just once. *Just once about smoking dope?* Yeah, I quit it, anyways, shortly after. It wasn't worth the hassle; it wasn't worth the price. *Why did you start smoking dope?* Well, that was a summer project of the people I was working with. I refused to smoke it; I'd drink a little bit, but I wouldn't smoke. They said that by the end of the summer they'd have me smoking it. I said no. Every day all summer they'd bug me to smoke and every day I'd say no until finally they wore me down and I said, "Well, if it means that much, I will." So I started and people thought that was cool and a few people thought that was really cool to smoke dope with them. Tried it with a couple people to see what it does; I was young and foolish and didn't know what was going on. A new experience. *How did you react to it?* Well, it took me five or six times to get the effect. Then I bought some, just to be cool, you know, to have it. And I tried it a few times, a few different times and then I had, I don't know if you can have a bad trip on dope, but I didn't have a very nice one. I just said, "That's enough of this bullshit."

I just quit. Nobody bothered me too much about it anyway. I didn't care if they did; I wasn't going to do it; I didn't like it.

You mentioned also that you did quite a bit of drinking during that period, did you get in trouble with that at all? Tremendous; I thought I should have been an alcoholic because I drank every day all summer. At least a beer a day, even on Sunday. I got drunk quite a few times a week. I don't have a drinking problem; didn't have a drinking problem. But I did drink a lot. I never got in trouble for it; they never caught me. I could walk by my parents drunk and they wouldn't even know. I got caught drunk once, but that was only because I was very drunk. That was one of the first times I ever drank; I was a sophomore. I didn't drink a bit until then; a beer was a big thing. Then I went out one night with friends and drank whiskey and I'd never drunk whiskey before and drank and drank and drank and didn't feel it or nothing and said, "This is pretty stupid." And I stood up and, you know the story, that was it. I was too drunk to do anything but pass out. And I only had a few hours before I had to go home. Walked into the house and I couldn't lock the door. I figured my parents were in bed and I turned around and they were both standing right there and it was sort of a give-away. *What happened?* I said "good night" and stumbled up the stairs and went to bed. Woke up in the morning hung over. My father asked me if I wanted a beer. He figured that would drive home the point. I don't know if you've ever been hung over, but the last thing you want is something else to drink in the morning. My mother just came in and said, "How come you went to bed early last night?" I said, "I didn't feel too good." She said, "Well, I'm not impressed." And that was it. My father just asked me where I got it, and said "You shouldn't do that." And my mother just said, "I'm not impressed." *How did you feel about their reaction?* I thought it was pretty neat. It was sort of like you see on TV when the kid gets drunk and the parents didn't get upset. I thought that was the kind of reaction I'd like to hear from them. You know, that it's a part of growing up and that they can accept it. Everybody tries it, not everybody, but a good part of the people. I was

happy with their reaction, but when it came down to telling people what my parents said, I thought it was pretty funny that they didn't do anything about it. So I figured I could go out and do it again. That was the only problem with what they did. So I did go out and do it again. But I really wouldn't want to get in their shoes either; I wouldn't know how to handle that kind of situation. They did the right thing, I think. They couldn't have punished me because at that point in life I would have just gone out and done it again to spite them. I think they knew that, so they just let me know that they didn't particularly care for it—maybe that my own head would steer me clear, given time, but not when they wanted it. *I guess it was several months then, that you were . . .* Yeah, it was all summer, all summer from June to September, I drank like a fish. *Why did you stop?* I got a girlfriend; it seemed like really a big change at that point. I'd had girlfriends all summer here and there, a few at a time, and you know, two or three a week, great fun; but I picked this one up and she was a little bit different because I fell in love with her, or whatever. She didn't care for drinking. She wouldn't have said anything if I did drink, but I just, something told me it was time to turn around and do something right for a change. Because I knew it wasn't right drinking all the time and partying. I mean, you could see some of the people I was with, burned out crispy—they couldn't even function. And I didn't care to be like that. So I guess common sense sort of took hold then. *As you look back on it now, why do you think you went through that that summer?* Just to be cool, I think. Just to do what everyone else was doing. To be accepted.

Do you remember your best friends when you were around 12 or 13 years old? Best friends? I really had no best friends. I haven't had a best friend for . . . I do have a best friend now. My best friends would have probably been my cousin—he was all right—and my next door neighbor was probably my best friend then. He was a year older and further up in school than I was. Yeah, at that point that's who they were. We chummed around since day one, I think. Lived on the same street. *What kind of things did you do together?* Oh we did everything. Built tree houses, went fishing, went running, went bike riding, built carts, raced carts; did everything kids do; painted everything we could find. As we got older we picked up BB guns and then guns, you know. All the typical things boys do. Hunting together then. Played sports together. *Did you feel pretty close to them?* Well in a way; they were pretty good friends, but we had a falling out every once in a while. I was not ever really close to anyone at that age anyway, besides myself. *You didn't confide in them very much?* No, I've never confided in anybody that I know of. *Did they confide in you?* No, I don't think so, not really. I can't remember any personal problems they were going through, or any changes they wanted to talk about or anything; I don't know if they were and didn't tell me or what. *I guess you kind of kept to yourself, kept your feelings to yourself.* Yep, always.

I was stuck in between being almost a jock, as people would say now, and being just your "average Joe." I had trouble because people would expect me to play sports just to hang around with the jocks and leave other people alone. They do. But I always had friends in all classes; I had smart friends, I had people who were in drama, and guys who were in chorus—which some of those athletes would think were faggots just because they sing. I felt I was a little bit more open minded than them. I used to have trouble though because I wasn't like that. I wouldn't stick to one group; I had friends all over the place, people I liked.

I guess there are a lot of different cliques in high school? Yeah, unreal. Always was, though, even from fifth grade up: who was going to be where they were going to be [in terms of social status]; who was going to be popular and who was going to be down on the bottom. They really come to light in high school, though. *What were some of the cliques in high school? You mentioned the jocks.* There were the jocks, and the dummies. Uh, at Marshall jocks and nonjocks are the big ones. After that they divide the people who are smart and don't play any sports, guys, are almost considered faggots. Because a lot of the Marshall athletes are not in the higher grades, are not right up there, you know. *They aren't real good students?* Right, and they re-

sent people who are. So they make fun of them. Marshall is a very sports-oriented school. Kids are growing up, they just get that driven into their heads, "If you don't play sports you aren't anything."

You say you've got a close friend now? Well, yeah, Jeff, he goes to Sunday school with me. We've been friends for a long time. We've been close friends because it seemed like he went through his change just about the same time I went through mine. He tried everything almost, like I did, and we came back to church at the same time; we seemed to fall together. So we went through about the same thing and we could talk to each other about what we were going through. And we just became closer and closer until we're probably best friends now. He's one that will tell me stuff and I'll tell him stuff. You know, I don't hesitate at all to talk to him. *He's sort of the first real close friend you've had?* Probably. Real close, yeah, he's the first one.

Who are some of the adults that had an influence on your life? Adults, um, I have positive and negative influences; you probably want them both, right? Adults at the end of our street, a good, nice bunch of people, they've always been there, but they drink a lot. They always let their kids drink, and their kids are always cool; so you go over there and you're cool. So we'd go over there; they were really nice to me, I don't say they were a negative influence, but they were really lenient as far as drinking goes. They had trouble letting me drink because my mother wouldn't let me go to the end of the street and they didn't want to get into trouble. But still the fact that they permitted drinking by minors in their house, or let them use their [vacation] camp for parties, was enough to make me maybe resent, uh wonder, why my parents weren't the same. Why my parents wouldn't let me have the same freedom.

A positive influence. Well, my girlfriend's father is a minister. He's younger, about 40 I think, but he's the first one who took any interest really in youth groups and the kids in the church. So he was really good help. I guess that's why I listen to him, you know. He's a friend from the start. He's been a real good influence on me. *What denomination of church is that?* Baptist.

What about in high school? Any teachers, or anybody there have an influence on you? Any teachers? Let me think. I had a couple super, super teachers. My English teacher my junior year was one of the best teachers that ever has lived, I think. She was tough; oh, wasn't she tough. "You do it my way and you do it right." So I respected her, almost feared her, but not quite—there's a fine line there. She liked me; I liked her. And she was tough and I knew it, so I worked up to her standards. She was the first teacher there to make me really work. She was really a super teacher. I had another one who started out my freshman year—I had him when I was a freshman, junior, and senior. I had him for physical science, chemistry, and physics. He started out my freshman year with the same attitude that he's always kept. He'd come into the class and he'd intimidate you. He says, "You're here; if you don't study, you flunk; I don't care. If you do study, you pass. That's good. I want you to pass; but if you flunk, that's your own problem." So you know from the start he wants what's good for you, but he's not going to make you do anything; you have to do it yourself. So one teacher makes you go; and the other one lets you do it yourself. But both of them in their own way are super, super teachers. The one who didn't care you wanted to work for; and the one who did care you had to work for, but you wanted to, I don't know why. They were good teachers.

And my last English teacher was a good teacher. As you get older though you talk more to them, you're more one-on-one; it's not a teacher–pupil scared-to-death situation. As a freshman you're intimidated by everything anyway, but as you get older—my senior year—every teacher I had was like talking to a person for a change. And it was really great. My senior year was probably the best for me. I talked to my history teacher and I talked to the principal, he was a super principal, and I talked to all of my teachers and they talked to me like we were people. It was a long time in coming, but it was worth it. "You know what you've got to do when you get out of high school and I'm going to help you do it."

So I had really good teachers and a really good senior year. A lot of friends at school—a lot of faculty friends, I mean. *Faculty more than students?* Uh, well it depends on how you look at it. I have a lot of friends all over, because I was on both sides here. I played stage band, I'd sing in the chorus, but I played basketball and I played sports, and I played intramurals. You know, so I had friends all over the place. I had a lot of friends and I like to think I'm well liked, that I like just about everyone. So I had a lot, a lot of student friends. But the faculty was just as much of a friend as the students at Marshall in that last year. It's too bad, it seems like there's one group of us and we were always in the top class, you know. But it didn't matter to us. I don't know if you would say we were more mature, because I don't like to say that I'm more mature than anybody, but we didn't care what you did. We were all friends, whether you played basketball, or whether you sang, or whether you danced ballet, it didn't matter. And that top group was the one that was the friendliest with all the teachers in high school. So I had a lot of friends; the faculty was a friend to me just as much as the students were.

I guess you've partly answered this already, but when did you begin dating? (Laughs) Eighth grade and I remember that because I was scared to death to ask a girl to the eighth grade graduation dance. She'd mostly already said yes, because you know how you do: "Will you ask someone to telephone me?" Word always gets around before you get around to asking. I was still scared to death to ask her. That was in the eighth grade. And from then on it was a steady stream—whoever showed up. But I dated from the end of my eighth grade year through to my junior year. *What did you mean, "whoever showed up"?* Oh it wasn't hard to find girls, I don't know why. I wouldn't say I'm exceptionally good looking. But I always went roller skating, always there were some girls hanging around I could stop and talk to. I went with a local girl for a while; went with a best friend for a while. There's always girls once you get your [driver's] license; it opens up new horizons, you can go to the next town. You've got a little bit more mobility and you've got a little bit more area to cover, so a few more girls.

Would you tell me about one or two of your more memorable dates—either good or bad? Well, I had one girlfriend at home that I asked to the eighth grade graduation dance and I went with her for quite a while. Then I went out to Wisconsin on the youth group trip and met a girl from Tennessee and I went out with her or that girl from Marshall; the girl from Tennessee was my second girl; I felt rotten all the way back, so I'd never do that again. I remember that; it was a bad dating experience, a bad move—dating somebody while you're dating somebody else. So from then on I decided that if I think I like somebody else, I'll just get rid of the one I was going with. So I do that instead. I don't know if it's much better for the girl or not. I didn't much care, actually.

Any especially good dates? Uh, especially good dates? Not really. My girlfriend that I have now I've had for a year or so. When I first went out with her I thought that was pretty nice, but every time you go out with a girl for the first time you think that's pretty nice anyway. So I don't remember any really special dates. With my girlfriend now we have special times, when we go out for a real date, go riding around, talk. But I don't remember any memorable dates. *What kind of things do you do with her?* With my girlfriend? Well, we don't have sex; so we just, I don't know, we play games and we occupy ourselves the best we can because now there are definitely desires whether you're a minister's daughter or a minister's son-in-law, or whatever you are. That's kind of life, I guess. So we talk, we play games, we drive around and visit people. We visit my grandparents. We visit her grandparents. We just try to be good, try to be decent, I mean to each other. *I guess you're pretty serious about her?* Yeah, I guess so. Yeah. *You mentioned "the minister's son-in-law"; have you had some thoughts in that direction?* Oh yeah, that'll be someday; after I get out of school, I hope. *After you get out of college, you mean?* Yeah.

Would you be willing to talk about sex a bit? Yeah, sure. Well, I can't talk too much, I don't know too much. I've had a few weird experiences, but, what do you want to know? *When did you discover masturbation?* Uh, I don't know when, I don't know what grade I was in. I didn't know what it was, I

know that. That was different. *What was your reaction, what was it like?* Well the first time I didn't know what was happening. *You were really surprised when you ejaculated and something came out?* Yeah. I didn't have any idea about what was going on and what it was. Except maybe from the Boy Scout manual about wet dreams, stuff like that. About that time though you start having your sex education films, then you find out what's going on. But the first time I was ignorant; I didn't know what was going on. *What happened? What did you feel? What did you do?* Actually I can't remember. I remember it was at night and it was in bed, but I don't . . . [pause] I don't really remember. All I know is that when I came, you know, what is this? Smell it, feel it, wipe it off. *I guess it was sometime after that then that you found out in sex education what it was all about?* Yeah. I didn't know. I mean, I had an idea; but I didn't know what was going on or why this would happen anyhow.

How did you learn about sex? Was it sex education, or friends, or what? Oh, I'd imagine it was mostly, well I can't say mostly, you have your sex education films—so you'd learn the basics. Friends have fathers who read *Playboy* or something else, you know, and you always think that's a big thing to sneak in while they're working, lift up the bed and pull out the magazine and read it even if you didn't know what was going on, you'd learn. We learned by word of mouth, books. I never read books, facts, or how-to, or anything like that, but dirty magazines. Pick up the language and then try to figure out what it means. *Your parents didn't tell you anything?* No, they didn't tell me a thing. Probably scared to. *What do you mean?* (Laughs) Probably didn't want me to run around and find . . . I don't know. I don't know why my parents didn't tell me. Maybe they were too embarrassed. I know when it comes time for me someday [to tell my kids] I may be, not ashamed or anything, but it's kind of a tough thing to talk about, or a tough thing to handle, right off the bat, you know: "Son, I want to talk about sex." Because actually, kids now-a-days know more than kids when I was that age; and I imagine that when my father was the age that I knew, he probably didn't. Because I learned when I was in fifth grade. I went to a party, one of these parties. And the girl I was with took me upstairs to her bedroom and I didn't know what was goin' on at all. Thank God, somebody else came up and kicked us out. I remember that I guess she knew what to do; I didn't know what to do. Given time she probably would have taught me, I guess. *This was fifth grade?* Yes! That's scary; my little sister is already going into eighth. Better keep my eye out for her (laughs).

Would you describe a couple of your sexual experiences with other people? Oh, I can't say I've had sex, really, but I've had the opportunities that I never took advantage of because I just didn't feel like I should. So I wasn't, uh, really bent on sex, premarital sex, at all; I just didn't feel I should bother with someone I didn't love. I had a girl that I was making out with pull my pants down. I think that was my sophomore, going into junior year. And I wouldn't go with her. *You wouldn't go with her?* I wouldn't have sex with her. *You mean intercourse?* Right. *That's what she wanted?* Yeah. It's not what I wanted. I just let her, actually. But I just didn't think that was right. *So what happened?* I just didn't do anything. I wasn't hardly excited anyway. We were making out and she pulled my pants down; then I was really turned off! I just said "No thanks." *Was she about the same age you were?* Just about. And another girl I could have had intercourse with, I took her to a place and I was planning on it, but it just didn't feel right. I was inexperienced and didn't really know what to do. And she certainly didn't. And so I just said, forget it, it's not worth it; I'll find someone later. It was a big thing in that year. The guys were always saying, "You gotta get it, you gotta get it." I thought to get it would be nice, but I don't have to kill myself to get it. I guess to them it was like drinking and smoking dope and having sex; with me it was always a little bit different. *That was your sophomore year?* Yeah, sophomore year. So I've had chances to, but I can't say I really ever have; played around some. *What do you mean, "played around"?* Oh, petting, I guess you'd call it. I've had girls with their clothes off, everything, all except for actual intercourse. *What kept it from going to intercourse, was that your decision?* Yeah. Seemed like if I wanted it right now, I could proba-

bly go to my girlfriend. I just don't feel that I want to right now. I think more in terms of responsibility and if something happens I'm not fit to take care of it. I mean, I'd like to, but I still have a long time to live and I plan on doing it right. *What about birth control? The couple times you got close to intercourse, did you have birth control?* I had a rubber. But didn't need to use it. Didn't do anything.

You mentioned a couple of "weird" experiences; did we cover those? We covered them, I didn't go into details. One was the girl pulling my pants down—weird for me. Usually it's the guy, but this was the girl, and I was completely [turned off], no way. I had a couple of girls who just didn't know where anything was, you know. Almost my age and I was amazed at how little they knew.

How would you describe yourself now, at age 18, almost 19? Average. Have the same problems I think as a lot of people do. I think I have a little bit more self-control than some people. I try to have self-control; I don't like being out of control. That's one of the reasons I don't like to drink. Um, I've got my head on almost straight. I still do some things that I don't like to do, even if it's just swearing, or even just having a desire to drink, or grab another girl, or, you know, things like that. I look at them now as temptations for me because I shouldn't be doing that. I think I'm pretty mature for my age. I think I've got a long way to go, but I'm started right anyway. I work pretty hard; work hard at my jobs. Try to do the best I can.

Do you think you know who you are? Have kind of a sense of identity? For a change I do. I think that's one of the reasons why my senior year things settled. I'm in touch with myself, you know. It's kinda weird to say that, but you know I floated around between being sassy and being wild and being rotten and being me and I think I've found me now because, you know, I'm finding acceptance all over the place. My girlfriend, my work, especially my work. I really like working. I work hard now at everything I do. I don't have to, to tell the truth. I could get good grades without studying. For the last year or so I enjoyed studying and getting something out of it. You know, you work on a physics problem for 8 hours and it's driving you foolish, but when you solve it there's almost no better feeling in the world because you've done it yourself. You've worked hard and you've passed yourself. Lately, my job and my attitude, everything has just changed and just picked up. It's all going full steam ahead. I like it. So I think I'm happy. I'm happy now.

How do you want life to work out for you? Well, I want to go through school, get a 4.0 (laughs), just want to go to school and study hard and get my money's worth; since I'm paying I'm going to study. I'm going to work hard and get a real good education. I should be fit when I come out, I'm not sure really, but I'm thinking of a double major. I may go to seminary after that. But I may even be fit to teach English, or write—journalist or writer—I like to write. I figure I'll get married, have a couple of kids, and be your average guy on the block with his house and his car. That'd be a little more than average for me, I guess. I'd like to be a pastor or minister of a church. I like reading the Bible; I like studying it; I like talking to people and I like helping people. Especially I enjoy helping people. If people have a problem I'd just as soon talk to them as, you know, I like being nice (laughs). I haven't been nice for so long, and it really is a selfish world if you want to go along with it, at times, look out for number one:

"You're breaking your mother's heart because you're smoking dope; that's her problem as long as you're having fun." I like being nice; I don't care if I scratch somebody's back and they don't scratch mine anymore. It doesn't matter; I'd just as soon do anything for anybody. If they don't want to do it for me, then I guess that's their own problem. But I did it for them, so they don't have any gripe. You know, I'm happy.

Postscript——Brad was still residing in the small town where he graduated from high school at the time the 2nd edition of this book was being prepared 10 years after the original interview. It was easy to reach him by telephone and to learn the general outline of his life after high school.

He became a minister after studying for four years in a Christian liberal arts college in New England where he majored in biblical studies and American history. Not formally ordained, he has served two local Baptist churches and works as a supervisor of a residential program for troubled children and adolescents. He is married and has three children (but he did not marry the minister's daughter discussed in the interlude). He said that becoming a minister had been his ambition, "and that's what I am."

Chapter 12

Pitfalls and Challenges

In Chapter 11 we looked at the two behavior problems that most commonly interfere with normal adolescent development, problems involving school learning and attendance and problems involving delinquent behavior. In the present chapter we turn our attention to some other developmental pitfalls and challenges that may undermine the well-being of young people and call for special help to overcome.

With respect to developmental pitfalls, we will focus on using and abusing drugs, running away, and attempting and completing suicide. All three of these topics receive considerable attention in the newspapers and other media, and rightly so, because falling victim to them can threaten not only the psychological adjustment of young people, but also their health and even their lives. As we will note, the coverage these pitfalls receive sometimes conveys that they are more widespread than they in fact are; nevertheless, they occur with sufficient frequency that knowing something about them is an important aspect of being knowledgeable about adolescent development.

With respect to other developmental challenges, the chapter considers problems that adolescents may have to face in adjusting to chronic illness and physical disability and in coping with death and dying. In contrast to the public attention paid to drug abuse, running away, and suicidal behavior, the topics of illness, disability, and death and dying tend to be overlooked or ignored—perhaps because of the psychological pain of facing them squarely. They, too, are part of everyday life for many young people, however, and familiarity with the psychology of illness, disability, and death is accordingly part of being familiar with the psychology of adolescence.

USING AND ABUSING DRUGS

Few topics in adolescent psychology have been studied with more concern and less clarity than problems related to taking drugs. Articles in the professional literature and stories in the popular media regularly call attention to the mental and physical ill effects of drug abuse and to the social evils that attend drug addiction and illegal drug trafficking. Unfortunately, however, these articles and stories frequently overlook individual diversity and changing patterns in drug use.

For example, occasional use of mild drugs is not uncommon among young people but usually has little bearing on how well they are adjusted or what will become of them in the future. Heavy use of drugs, on the other hand, is an infrequent event that has grave psychological implications and constitutes **drug abuse**. Statements about youthful drug taking that fail to distinguish between *use* and *abuse*, but instead refer broadly to some "percentage of adolescents" who "use drugs," lack precision and rarely merit consideration. To be of value, statements on this subject must take account of some complex relationships that exist among (1) the frequency with which certain kinds of drugs are used; (2) several stages and categories of drug use; and (3) various personal, social, and family factors associated with using drugs.

FREQUENCY OF ADOLESCENT DRUG USE

Table 12.1 indicates the percentage of 12–17-year-olds in a representative nationwide sample who reported ever having used various drugs or having used them within the last month. These data reveal some of the complexities in describing adolescent drug use. In the first

Table 12.1 INCIDENCE AND PREVALENCE OF DRUG USE REPORTED
BY 12–17-YEAR-OLDS IN 1990

Drug	Percent Reporting Any Use Ever (Incidence)	Percent Reporting Use Within Past Month (Prevalence)
Alcohol	48.2	24.5
Marijuana	14.8	5.2
Stimulants	4.5	1.0
Sedatives	3.3	0.9
Hallucinogens	3.3	0.9
Cocaine	2.6	0.6
Heroin	0.7	—[a]

[a] Less than 0.5%.

Source: Based on data reported by National Institute on Drug Abuse (1991), *National Household Survey on Drug Abuse: Population Estimates 1990.*

place, the frequency of reported use varies widely for individual drugs. Alcohol is by far the most widely used drug among young people, and it is the only one that approaches use by a majority of 12–17-year-olds. With the exception of alcohol, in fact, the prevailing pattern among adolescents is *nonuse* of drugs, from almost 85% who have never tried marijuana to over 99% who have never used heroin.

Second, the percentage of young people who have ever used a drug (which is the *incidence* of drug use) differs substantially from the percentage who are currently using it (which is the *prevalence* of its use). Table 12.1 indicates that the percentage of 12–17-year-olds who ever use drugs far exceeds the percentage who become even occasional users. The prevalence for use within the past month ranges from 50.8% of those who have ever used alcohol down to less than one-fourth of those who have ever used cocaine or stimulants. Because the "ever used" statistic is frequently given in reports on drug use, especially when the problem is being dramatized, it is important to keep in mind that this figure says nothing about the prevalence of current use.

Third, the frequency of drug use among adolescents increases as they grow older. As shown in Figure 12.1 for alcohol, marijuana, and cocaine, senior high school students are more likely to report current use than the combined group of 12–17-year-olds, and high school seniors are more likely to report recent drug experience than high school freshman. It should be noted further that these data on high school students come from adolescents currently enrolled in high school. Hence, they represent the approximately 85% of teenagers nationwide who stay in high school, but not those who drop out. To the extent that high school dropouts as a group are more likely to be involved with drugs than adolescents who remain in school, these findings may underestimate drug use prevalence for young people of high school senior age.

Fourth, in addition to considering differences related to type of drug, pattern of use, and age of user, discussions of adolescent drug taking need to recognize trends over time. Drug use increased sharply in the United States during the 1960s and 1970s, but in the 1980s it began to level off and decline. As shown in Table 12.2, current use of all drugs by adolescents and young adults as well has been decreasing slowly but steadily. As a further index of

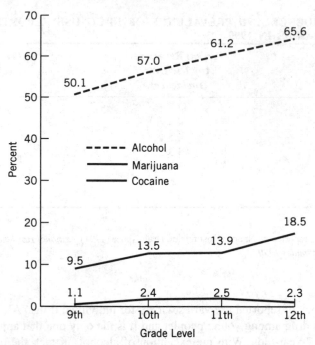

Figure 12.1 High school students reporting use of alcohol, marijuana, or cocaine within past month. [*Source*: Based on data reported by Flanagan and Maguire, 1992].

Table 12.2 PERCENT OF ADOLESCENTS AND YOUNG ADULTS REPORTING DRUG USE WITHIN PAST MONTH

	1974	1976	1979	1982	1985	1988	1990
Age 12–17							
Alcohol	34.0	32.4	37.2	30.2	31.0	25.2	24.5
Marijuana	12.0	12.3	16.7	11.5	12.0	6.4	5.2
Stimulants	1.0	1.2	1.2	2.6	1.6	1.2	1.0
Sedatives	1.0	—[a]	1.1	1.3	1.0	0.6	0.9
Hallucinogens	1.3	0.9	2.2	1.4	1.2	0.8	0.9
Cocaine	1.0	1.0	1.4	1.6	1.5	1.1	0.6
Heroin	—	—	—	—	—	—	—
Age 18–25							
Alcohol	69.3	69.0	75.9	70.9	71.4	65.3	63.3
Marijuana	21.8	25.2	25.0	15.5	12.7	34.4	27.4
Stimulants	3.7	4.7	3.5	4.7	3.7	2.4	1.2
Sedatives	1.6	2.3	2.8	2.6	1.6	0.9	0.7
Hallucinogens	2.5	1.1	4.4	1.7	1.9	1.9	0.8
Cocaine	3.1	2.0	9.3	6.8	7.6	4.5	2.2
Heroin	—	—	—	—	—	—	—

[a] Less than 0.5%.

Source: Based on data reported by National Institute on Drug Abuse (1991), *National Household Survey on Drug Abuse: Population Estimates 1990.*

Making personal decisions about how to deal with drugs and alcohol has become an important part of growing up.

these changes over time, survey data indicate that the prevalence of daily alcohol consumption among high school seniors declined by almost 40% between 1979 and 1988, from 6.9% to 4.2% who reported using alcohol every day. Similarly, daily use of marijuana was reported by 1 in 9 (10.7%) high school seniors in 1978, but by 1 in 37 (2.7%) in 1988 (Johnston, O'Malley, & Bachman, 1989).

These survey findings indicate that the use of intoxicating substances other than alcohol is not widespread among adolescents in the United States, and furthermore that regular current use of drugs including alcohol is infrequent. These findings run contrary to what many people believe and to widely publicized concerns about curbing youthful drug abuse. This discrepancy between fact and impression, like the mythology of adolescent turmoil discussed in Chapter 10, appears to derive from inappropriate generalizations from un-representative samples, particularly disadvantaged and patient populations of young people.

Substance abuse problems are especially prevalent in deteriorated neighborhoods with high crime rates, and problematic drug use usually runs high among adolescents seen in mental health settings (Greenbaum, Prange, Friedman, & Silver, 1991; Weiner, 1992, Chapter 10). However, neither disadvantaged nor patient populations are representative of young people in general, and assuming that they are contributes to misleading impressions about adolescent drug use nationwide. On the other hand, the generally low prevalence of adolescent substance use does not negate the severity of drug abuse as a social and mental health problem. To the contrary, the fact that heavy drug use is normatively infrequent signifies that, when it does occur, it cannot be written off as "just one of these things a lot of adolescents do these days." Substance use is not an everyday phenomenon among young people, and its occurrence calls for careful professional evaluation of a possible drug-abusing pattern that constitutes psychological disorder and requires treatment.

STAGES AND CATEGORIES OF DRUG USE

Some years ago Denise Kandel (1975) identified a sequence of four stages in youthful drug use: (1) drinking beer and wine; (2) drinking hard liquor; (3) smoking marijuana (which is often referred to as a **soft drug** to indicate that its effects are relatively mild in comparison with other drugs); and (4) using such other substances as stimulants, sedatives, hallucinogens, cocaine, and heroin (which are usually called **hard drugs** to indicate that their effects are relatively powerful compared to marijuana). Her findings and those of other investigators indicate that, with few exceptions, only young people who have used drugs at one stage become users at the next stage. Thus almost all adolescents who drink hard liquor have previously drunk beer or wine; almost all who smoke marijuana have previously drunk hard liquor; and almost all who become involved with hard drugs have had prior experience with marijuana. Previous nonusers of drugs rarely try marijuana without having progressed through the stage of alcohol use, and drinkers rarely experiment with other illegal drugs without having first tried marijuana (Mills & Noyes, 1984; Van Kammen, Loeber, & Stouthamer-Loeber, 1991; Yamaguchi & Kandel, 1984).

The fact that hard drug use evolves from soft drug use—which is known as the **stepping-stone hypothesis**—does not mean that one drug necessarily leads to another. Adolescents who drink are not always on the way to using marijuana, and those who use marijuana are not destined to become hard drug users. On the other hand, the stepping-stone hypotheses does predict that the likelihood of using a substance at a particular stage will be higher among young people who have used a substance at a previous stage than among those who have not. In the original work by Kandel and Faust (1975), for example, a 6-month follow-up study of high school students found that 27% of those who smoked or drank subsequently tried marijuana, whereas only 2% of those who neither smoked nor drank did so. Similarly, 26% of the marijuana users in their sample had gone on to try stimulants, hallucinogens, or heroin, but only 1% of those who had never used marijuana did so.

Patterns of drug use can also be usefully categorized as *experimental*, *social*, *medicinal*, or *addictive* (Weiner, 1992, Chapter 10). Young people who manifest **experimental drug use** try mild drugs once or perhaps a few times out of curiosity or to have a new experience and then stop using them. For young people who never go beyond this experimental use, drug involvement cannot be said to constitute any kind of personal or psychological problem.

In the case of **social drug use**, young people take drugs as a way of participating in a group activity with their peers. Although adolescents may sometimes get together primarily to share a drug experience, social drug use is largely limited to parties, dances, and other special occasions. Like experimental drug use, then, social use tends to involve only occasional and infrequent drug involvement. Among drug-using adolescents in a study of 2,635 junior and senior high school students by Novacek, Raskin, and Hogan (1991), those who gave group belongingness as their main reason for using drugs reported using drugs significantly less frequently than those who said that they used drugs mainly as a way of feeling better or being able to cope with everyday problems, which brings us to medicinal drug use.

Medicinal drug use is the taking of a drug to relieve anxiety or tension or to enjoy a drug experience for its own sake. Because of the purpose it serves, medicinal drug use is much more likely than social drug use to become a regular or customary way of dealing with or escaping from life problems. In the Novacek et al. study, those students who reported regular use of alcohol and drugs said they did so primarily to relieve nervousness or depression, to escape problems, to relax, or to enjoy their effect, and rarely for purposes of belonging. Medicinal drug use is thus an individual experience for the most part; although two or more people may take drugs together for medicinal purposes, they are likely in doing so to focus more on their own experiences than on any interpersonal interaction.

Addictive drug use, which is also an individual experience, consists of habituation to one or more drugs. Any drug can become habit forming if a person comes to depend on its effects to feel good physically or mentally. The defining characteristic of addictive drug users is that they suffer real physical or psychological distress (**withdrawal symptoms**) when they are deprived of drugs. As a result, addictive drug users are the most likely of these four types to use drugs regularly and frequently.

The differences between these four categories of drug use help to distinguish between drug *use* and drug *abuse*. From a psychological point of view, using a drug is not in itself an abuse; people can take small amounts of mild drugs (alcohol and marijuana) occasionally without doing themselves any harm, as far as is known (Marlatt, Baer, Donovan, & Kivlahan, 1988; Newcomb & Bentler, 1989). Legal and moral issues aside, then, it is the frequent use of drugs and the taking of hard drugs that are most likely to *abuse* a person's physical and psychosocial functioning. Experimental and social drug use seldom results in such abuse, whereas medicinal drug use may have this result, and addiction to a drug always constitutes drug abuse.

The previously noted differences between lifetime incidence and 30-day prevalence of drug use among adolescents suggest that youthful drug *abuse* is relatively infrequent. The vast majority of adolescents who have tried drugs appear to be experimental or social users, inasmuch as only a small minority of them show the pattern of current, regular drug taking that characterizes medicinal or addictive use.

This distinction has important implications for whether psychological disorder is present. Numerous investigators have found substantial evidence of emotional disturbance in drug abusers, whereas experimental and social types of drug users are generally about as well adjusted as their nondrug-using peers. By and large, the heavier the use of alcohol and other drugs by young people, the more likely they are to be doing poorly in school, to be withdrawn from peer-group activities, to have strained relationships with their parents, and to be engaging in delinquent behavior (Barnes & Welte, 1986; Brook, Gordon, Brook, & Brook, 1989; Kovach & Glickman, 1986; Shedler & Block, 1990).

Consistent with the implications of drug abuse for psychological disorder, a substantial percentage of young people who self-medicate themselves with drugs or become drug dependent demonstrate **comorbidity**, which consists of having some condition in addition to their drug problem that needs to be recognized and treated in its own right. The comorbid disorders found most frequently among drug-abusing adolescents involve either antisocial conduct or affective distress, especially depression, which we describe in Chapter 13. Research studies suggest that more than half of adolescents being treated for substance abuse in residential settings are likely to demonstrate affective or conduct disorders, and that drug-dependent adolescents are three times more likely than young people in general to be significantly depressed (Belfer, 1993; Deykin, Buka, & Zeena, 1992; Stowell & Estroff, 1992).

There is also considerable evidence that youthful drug abuse has substantial negative implications for the future. Longitudinal studies indicate that adult drug use is largely continuous with and predictable from adolescent drug use. Among adults with substance abuse disorders, 50% are found to have become drug dependent by age 21 in the case of alcohol and by age 18 in the case of other addictive substances (Burke, Burke, Regier, & Rae, 1990). Furthermore, the earlier the age at which adolescents begin using drugs and the more heavily they become involved with them, the more likely they are to use or abuse drugs as adults (Kandel, Davies, Karus, & Yamaguchi, 1986; Schuckit & Russell, 1983).

FACTORS ASSOCIATED WITH DRUG USE

Certain personal, social, and family factors are associated with how frequently adolescents use drugs and with the likelihood of their beginning to use them in the first place. These factors exert different kinds of influences at the four stages of drug use we have just described, and addictive drug use appears to be influenced by genetic factors, as well.

Personal, Social, and Family Factors

Numerous studies have yielded some consistent but not particularly surprising information about personal characteristics that are associated with adolescent drug use. These include a high degree of openness to experience, tolerance of deviance, sensation seeking, impulsiveness, unconventionality, and rebelliousness, on the one hand, and a low degree of social inhibition, interest in achievement, and involvement with religion, on the other hand. Thus the more impulsive, unconventional, and sensation seeking adolescents are, the more likely they are to use drugs and the more likely they are to progress to more serious stages of drug use. Conversely, cautious, dependent, conforming, socially inhibited, achievement-oriented, and religious adolescents are relatively unlikely to try drugs or to use them frequently (Boyle, Offord, Racine, & Szatmari, 1992; Brook, Gordon, & Whiteman, 1986; Greening & Dollinger, 1991).

Research has also identified some relationships between the identity status of young people and their use of drugs. Among approximately 13,000 junior and senior high school students in one survey, those who were ideologically identity diffused, as described in Chapter 10, were twice as likely as those who were identity foreclosed to have smoked cigarettes or drunk alcohol; they were three times as likely to have tried marijuana, and five times as likely to have used cocaine (Christopherson, Jones, & Sales, 1988; Jones, 1992). Adolescents in this survey who were in different identity statuses also tended to give different reasons for having used drugs. Those who were identity achieved or in a moratorium were more likely than those who were identity foreclosed or diffused to cite curiosity or peer relationships as their primary reason for trying drugs. According to other survey data, adolescents who expect that alcohol and drugs will help them function better socially or in athletic or intellectual activities are at relatively high risk for progressive drug involvement, whereas those who regard drugs as dangerous to their health are relatively unlikely to try them or to continue using them (Christiansen, Smith, Roehling, & Goldman, 1989; Marlatt et al., 1988; Nucci, Guerra, & Lee, 1991).

Socially, the disposition to use drugs is influenced by the nature of an adolescents' peer relationships. The more their friends use drugs, the closer company they keep with these friends, and the more they value approval by these friends, the more likely young people are to become involved with drugs. Consistent with the general trends in peer conformity in young people noted in Chapter 8, however, adolescents are most susceptible to the influence of drug-taking peers during the junior high school and early high school years when they are making the transition from early to middle adolescence (Brook, Whiteman, Cohen, & Tanaka, 1992; Forney, Forney, & Ripley, 1991; Shilts, 1991).

As for family factors, research findings indicate that parents are likely to influence the drug-taking behavior of their children by the example they set with their own behavior and by the climate they create in their home. Parents who do not use drugs seldom have children who do, whereas the more heavily parents use any particular drug, the more likely their children are to use or abuse the same drug (Chassin, McLaughlin, & Sher, 1988; Johnson & Pandina, 1991; Johnson, Shontz, & Locke, 1984).

Regarding climate in the home, parents who are preoccupied with their own affairs, disinterested in their children, and given to the kinds of authoritarian or permissive discipline we described in Chapter 7 are relatively likely to have adolescent youngsters who become involved with drugs. By contrast, parents who support and communicate actively with their children, set and enforce limits in an authoritative fashion, and conduct family life with a minimum of stress and conflict are relatively unlikely to have offspring who become regular or continuing users of drugs (Baumrind, 1991; Brook et al., 1992; Kafka & London, 1991; Rhodes & Jason, 1990).

Similarly, early adolescents who have not used drugs typically report being more closely involved with their families than those who have tried drugs. Drug users, on the other hand, are more likely than nonusers to describe their families as disorganized, and among older adolescents a relationship has been found between how distant young people are from their families and how often and how much they drink (Martin & Pritchard, 1991; Protinsky & Shilts, 1990).

Judith Brook and her colleagues have found further that these personality, peer, and parental influences on adolescent drug use can operate similarly among culturally diverse groups of young people, including African-American and Hispanic as well as white youth, and can operate independently of each other (Brook, Nomura, & Cohen, 1989; Brook, Whiteman, & Gordon, 1983; Brook, Whiteman, Balka, & Hamburg, 1992). Their findings with respect to the independence of these influences have three important implications:

1. First, the greatest likelihood of trying drugs or using them heavily occurs when all three kinds of drug-taking influence—personality, peer, and parental—coexist to a substantial extent.

2. Second, a particularly strong influence of one kind may be sufficient to foster drug use even when the other kinds of influence are minimal. For example, heavy parental drug taking and a negative climate in the home can lead to drug use in adolescents who are not personally oriented toward drugs and are not being socially influenced in this direction; likewise, a personal attraction to drugs and strong peer pressure can result in drug use even when parents are neither modeling drug use nor neglecting their parental responsibilities.

3. Third, especially positive influences of one kind or another can protect an otherwise high-risk adolescent from becoming involved with drugs. In some studies, for example, close and supportive parent–child relationships have appeared to "inoculate" young people against being attracted to drugs even when they are immersed in a heavily drug-using peer culture (Brook, Brook, Gordon, & Whiteman, 1990; Marston, Jacobs, Singer, & Widaman, 1988).

◆ *Profile*

JUDITH BROOK

Born in Brooklyn, New York, Judith Brook went to Hunter College in Manhattan intending to become a teacher. On graduating from Hunter, she wanted to become a bit further educated herself before taking a teaching job, and she entered the graduate program in developmental psychology at Columbia University. At Columbia she came under the influence of Arthur Jersild, a prominent scholar who was one of the first psychologists to write a basic textbook of adolescent development. Encouraged by Professor Jersild, she decided to forego teaching and devote herself to the study of child and adolescent development.

After she received her doctorate from Columbia in 1967, Dr. Brook was involved in being a mother to her own two sons and was looking for a part-time research position rather than a full-time academic job. A colleague offered her such a position in a research project on drug use if she would design and carry out a study of substance abuse in adolescents. Although she had not previously done any work in this area, she took on the challenge of this opportunity, and thus was born a highly productive career as a contributor to knowledge about drug use in young people.

Over the years Dr. Brook has done research and taught at Columbia, at the Mount Sinai School of Medicine in New York, and at the New York Medical College, where since 1990 she has been Professor of Psychiatry and Behavioral Science. Many of her studies have been conducted in collaboration with her husband, David Brook, a psychiatrist with many research interests similar to hers. These studies have identified many ways in which personality style, family attitudes, and peer-group influences interact to increase or decrease the likelihood of an adolescent abusing drugs. Currently, with support from the National Institute on Drug Abuse, Dr. Brook is examining patterns of drug use among culturally diverse groups, particularly with respect to comparative factors that lead to or protect against problematic drug use among white, Hispanic, and African-American youth. She hopes in the future to extend her research models to adolescents living in other countries as well.

Stage-Related Influences

Kandel and her colleagues noted early in their work that the relative importance of personal, peer, and parental influences on drug taking differs for the three stages of hard liquor, marijuana, and hard drug use (Adler & Kandel, 1981; Kandel, Kessler, & Margulies, 1978). Starting to use hard liquor is determined primarily by parental and peer influences and not very much by personal characteristics. These influences are exerted primarily through modeling effects, so that, more than anything else, adolescents who start to drink hard liquor are imitating the behavior of important people in their lives. Neither the quality of their family relationships nor their parents' attitudes seem to have much impact on this stage of drug use.

Starting to use marijuana is more likely than beginning to drink to involve some of the personal characteristics associated with drug taking, such as being a nonconformist and believing that marijuana is a nonharmful substance. The initiation into marijuana differs further from starting to use alcohol in being influenced more by peers than by parent modeling. What influence parents do exert typically comes less from any example they set than from the attitudes they express. The more strongly parents discourage marijuana use, the less likely their children are to try it; the more permissive they are in this regard, the more likely their children are to start using it. Young people who begin using marijuana are also likely to have been frequent drinkers and to show some of the problems associated with drug use, such as minor delinquencies and relatively poor school performance. They are not especially likely to have serious personality problems, however.

Beginning to use hard drugs is the stage in which serious personality problems are most likely to play a role. Hard drug users will usually have already been heavy or at least regular marijuana users, and they are very often feeling depressed and alienated and having difficulty managing their lives. Because adolescents who start to use hard drugs tend to be withdrawn or cut off from peer-group activities and any rewarding social life, the influence of friends does not have much to do with initiating this stage of drug use. Parental influences, on the other hand, become critical at this stage, especially in relation to the models and the quality of family life parents provide. Parental use of hard liquor, stimulants, and sedatives is an important predictor of adolescent initiation into drugs other than marijuana, and parental rejection and neglect are strongly associated with movement to this stage of drug use.

Genetic Factors in Addiction

In addition to the influence of personal, social, and family experiences on the inclination to drug use, there is some evidence to suggest that genetic factors may contribute to the disposition to become an addictive drug user. Alcoholism, in particular, has been found to run strongly in families, with children of alcoholics being about four times as likely to develop drinking problems as children of nonalcoholic parents (Marlatt et al., 1988). This familial incidence of alcoholism goes far beyond circumstances that could be explained on the basis of shared family experience or modeling.

The most compelling evidence in this regard comes from long-term follow-up studies of adults who were placed for adoption early in life. Alcoholism is much more frequent among adoptees whose biological parents were problem drinkers than among those with no history of heavy drinking in their biological relatives, regardless of whether or not their adoptive parents drink (Bohman, Sigvardsson, & Cloninger, 1981; Cadoret, Troughton, O'Gorman, & Heywood, 1986; Cloninger, Bohman, & Sigvardsson, 1981). Because heavy drinking increases the likelihood that alcohol users will progress to stages of marijuana and hard drug use, any genetic influences on becoming addicted to alcohol can be expected to play a role in how frequently or heavily young persons become involved with these other drugs as well.

On the other hand, genetic studies of substance abuse have so far focused primarily on adults, and there are very few data concerning the heritability of addiction in young people (Rutter et al., 1990). Moreover, the genetic disposition to alcoholism in some cases does not mean that drug addiction is primarily an inherited condition. To the contrary, three other findings leave little doubt that environmental influences play a very important role in the onset of substance abuse: (1) there is, so far, no consistent evidence of preexisting biological differences between people who become drug dependent and those who do not; (2) about half of those adults hospitalized for alcoholism do not have any family history of drinking problems; and (3) genetic influences on excessive drinking appear limited to instances of alcoholism in males that begin in adolescence or early adulthood; genetic influences do not appear very much involved in drinking problems that occur in women or begin later in adulthood (Alford, 1989; McGue, Pickens, & Svikis, 1992; Searles, 1988).

TREATMENT AND PREVENTION

Treatment is seldom necessary for young people who are experimental or social drug users. They either stop taking drugs of their own accord or use drugs infrequently in ways that do not get them into psychological difficulty. Medicinal and addictive use of drugs, on the other hand, typically interferes with normal development and calls for professional intervention.

The treatment of drug-abusing adolescents focuses on the particular personal, social, and family factors associated with an individual young person's drug taking. Various forms of individual and group psychotherapy, family counseling, and community action programs have been developed to help these adolescents improve their coping skills, attach themselves to drug-free models and life styles, find a supportive climate at home, and resolve whatever psychological concerns have contributed to their drug abuse (Davidge & Forman, 1988; Lewis, Piercy, Sprenkle, & Trepper, 1990; Novocek et al., 1991; Weiner, 1992, Chapter 10).

Medicinal drug users who are seeking escape from feelings of anxiety or depression often respond well to treatment programs of this kind that are aimed at easing their tensions and helping them manage difficult situations in their lives more effectively. Addictive drug users, however, like characterological delinquents, are manifesting more of a life style than a reaction to currently troubling circumstances. Hence drug addiction often presents the same kinds of obstacles to effective treatment as characterological delinquency. Addicts, like psychopaths, have difficulty admitting to any psychological problems; typically they deny needing help and resist close or trusting relationships with psychotherapists and counselors. In many cases, only a residential rehabilitation program, in which a therapeutic environment can be provided over an extended period of time, holds any promise for directing addicted young people to a satisfying life style that is not drug dependent (de Leon, 1988; Horan & Straus, 1987; King & Meeks, 1988).

Because the chronic nature of addictive drug use makes it so difficult to modify, most experts in the field believe that the only really effective way of overcoming it is to prevent it from occurring in the first place. With this in mind, enormous resources have been poured into programs of drug education over the past 20 years or so. These programs were based initially on the expectation that adolescents who were informed about the hazards of using drugs would not use them. As sensible as this rationale may seem, no consistent evidence ever emerged that participating in a drug education program deters adolescents from drug use. To the contrary, many investigators found that providing adolescents with information about drugs was producing a boomerang effect that increased rather than decreased their level of drug involvement (Bangert-Drowns, 1988; Fialkov, 1989; Tobler, 1986).

The early efforts at drug education were unsuccessful not because they were ill conceived, but because they were too little and too late. Most adolescents who are going to have drug-related problems have already begun drug use by the time they enter high school; hence, providing factual information about drugs to high school students cannot be expected to accomplish very much. Likewise, scare tactics or moralistic preaching aimed at teenagers, when their value systems have already been largely shaped by family and peer influences, cannot be expected to find receptive ears.

With this in mind, drug education in the schools has gradually been shifted to the lower grades, and focusing on the hazards of using drugs has been replaced by focusing on the benefits of avoiding them. At the same time, contemporary programs of drug-abuse prevention pay special attention to helping young people become sufficiently assertive and decisive to resist social influences that will get them into trouble; that is, to be able to say "No" to drugs. Programs of this kind aimed at junior high and especially elementary school students are showing promise for increasing knowledge about the implications of drug use, generating negative attitudes toward becoming involved with drugs, and reducing the subsequent frequency of drug use (Abbey, Oliansky, Stilianos, & Hohlstein, 1990; Botvin, Baker, Dusenbury, Tortu, & Botvin, 1990; Church, Forehand, Brown, & Holmes, 1990; Johnson et al., 1990).

RUNNING AWAY

In one of America's best-loved stories, Tom Sawyer, depressed after being snubbed by Becky Thatcher, runs into his friend Joe Harper, who complains about having been unfairly punished by his mother, and the two boys decide to run off together with their pal, Huck Finn. In the words of Mark Twain, Tom's thoughts run this way:

> He was gloomy and desperate. He was a forsaken, friendless boy, he said; nobody loved him; when they found out what they had driven him to, perhaps they would be sorry; he had tried to do right and get along, but they would not let him; since nothing would do them but to be rid of him, let it be so. [p. 116]

As for Joe, Twain has him thinking this way about his mother:

> It was plain that she was tired of him and wished him to go; if she felt that way, there was nothing for him to do but succumb; he hoped she would be happy, and never regret having driven her poor boy out into the unfeeling world to suffer and die. [p. 117]

So Tom, Joe, and Huck raft out to a nearby island in the river for a few days of fishing, swimming, and taking it easy. Then, bored and lonely, they come back to town, where they discover that everyone thought they had drowned in the river. Hiding in the back of the church, they listen to their own funeral and hear what they had longed to hear:

As the service proceeded, the clergyman drew such pictures of the graces, the winning ways and the rare promise of the lost lads, that every soul there, thinking he recognized these pictures, felt a pang in remembering that he had persistently blinded himself to them, always before, and had as persistently seen only faults and flaws in the poor boys. [pp. 158–159]

And so, as the preacher breaks into tears under the sway of his eulogy, the boys come out of their hiding place and troop down the aisle, to be welcomed back with hugs and kisses and an anthem of thanks to the Lord.

In this fictitious episode Mark Twain captures the essence of runaway behavior as it existed then and exists today. Running away is delinquent behavior, technically speaking; it is one of those status offenses that break the law by virtue of the person's age, in this case leaving home without parental permission. As a significant problem in its own right, however, with its own varieties, causes, and consequences, running away calls for some discussion separate from our consideration of delinquent behavior in Chapter 11.

VARIETIES OF RUNNING AWAY

Official statistics list 138,155 juveniles as having been arrested for running away in 1990 (Flanagan & Maguire, 1992), and professionals involved in providing social services to youth typically estimate an annual prevalence of 1 million adolescent runaways (Janus, McCormack, Burgess, & Hartman, 1987, Chapter 1; Tomb, 1991). Neither of these numbers means very much, however. With respect to arrests, we have already noted that being arrested is influenced not only by what adolescents do but also by who they are and where they do it. As for social service estimates, such totals do not distinguish among varieties of runaway behavior that have very different consequences, and they do not reflect what is believed to be a substantial frequency of mild runaway behavior that is never reported and hence does not come to the attention of social agencies.

Among adolescents who leave home and stay away without parental permission, some, like Tom Sawyer, enjoy a brief adventure, find some breathing space from a troubling situation, and return to a warm welcome. For others, however, running away means wandering aimlessly and alone, with little hope of being welcomed back, or gravitating to the streets of the big city, with little thought of ever returning. Like delinquency in general, then, runaway behavior ranges widely in frequency and severity from the young person who once or twice stays out late or at a friend's house overnight without parental permission to one who makes a habit of getting on a bus or hitch-hiking out of town to unknown places for extended periods of time.

Most adolescents who are called runaways are young people who did in fact decide to leave their homes. However, about one-fourth of runaway youth who come to the attention of police and social agencies are more accurately called "throwaways"; these are adolescents whose parents have encouraged them to leave home or have forcibly ejected them (Adams, Gullotta, & Clancy, 1985; Kufeldt & Nimmo, 1987; Tomb, 1991). Although both runaways and throwaways typically have strained relationships with their parents, being thrown out of their home tends to have a more traumatic impact on young people and leave a bigger wound to close than leaving voluntarily.

As a further variation in runaway behavior, some adolescents who make their own decision to leave are running *from* a difficult situation at home, whereas others are running *to* some novel or exciting experience. Generally speaking, runaways who are running to something that is anticipated to be pleasant return home sooner and show fewer adverse effects of the experience than those who have run from something unpleasant. Whether the running is to or from, however, research findings indicate that the vast majority of adolescent runaways leave home with the intention of coming back, stay within a 50-mile radius of home, and return within a week. No more than 12 to 15% of adolescent runaways stay away from home for weeks or months at a time or never return at all (Janus et al., 1987, Chapter 2; Sharlin & Mor-Barok, 1992; Tomb, 1991).

CAUSES OF RUNNING AWAY

With few exceptions, the psychological circumstances contributing to runaway behavior are similar for the one-time short-term runaway and the repetitive runaway or stayaway. They involve persistent problems at home and in school and an inability to communicate effectively about these problems with peers, parents, or other adults. With respect to the situation at home, research studies have consistently found that adolescents who run away are likely to be in active conflict with their parents. The parents of these young people have typically been inconsistent or ineffective in managing their children's behavior, and the level of tension in the home has usually been high. Verbal abuse is common, physical and sexual abuse are not infrequent, and constant arguing and complaining leave little time for members of the family to say anything nice to or about each other. The more unpleasant the atmosphere in the home and the less effective the parents are, the more frequently runaway adolescents are likely to leave and the longer they tend to stay away (Adams et al., 1985; Englander, 1984; Janus, Burgess, & McCormack, 1987; Kurtz, Kurtz, & Jarvis, 1991).

These studies have also identified some specific relationships between runaway behavior and the patterns of authoritative, authoritarian, and permissive parental discipline described in Chapter 7. Not surprisingly, parents who have expelled an adolescent from the home are more likely to be authoritarian than either authoritative or permissive in their disciplinary style, and parents who are perceived as being overly restrictive and uncaring (i.e., authoritarian) also outnumber other types of parents in the homes that adolescents run from. Permissive homes are less likely than authoritarian but more likely that authoritative homes to have adolescent runaways, and permissive parents who are perceived as distant, indifferent, and uninvolved are especially likely to foster running to something. With specific respect to abuse, in one study of 149 runaway youth who passed through a shelter over a 3-year period, 73% reported having been physically beaten at home and 51% reported having been subjected to some form of sexual abuse, including 36% who said they had been forced to have sex against their will (Janus et al., 1987, Chapter 1).

These various studies also indicate that young people who run away typically have been having learning and behavior problems in school. Failing grades and special placement have followed them in the classroom, and truancy and suspensions have made them familiar figures in the principal's office. Being a marginal person in school as well as at home, adolescents who run away have come to feel that there is no place for them to be. Their feelings of loneliness and alienation mount over time, and then some event, such as one more dressing-down in school or one more argument or beating at home, serves as a last straw that triggers a decision to take flight.

Finally, with respect to communication, adolescents who run away are usually found to be having considerable difficulty in communicating with other people. Instead of being comfortable members of a peer group, they tend to be on the fringe of peer-group activities and to perceive themselves as personally inadequate and socially irrelevant. Instead of being able to look to adults for the support they lack from their peers, they tend to be as unsuccessful in forming warm relationships with teachers, clergy, a family doctor, or other adults as they are with their parents.

In this context, running away often constitutes both a result of inadequate communication and an effort to cope with the problem by a communication. Like neurotic delinquency, running away can serve as a nonverbal message from young people that they feel unrecognized and unappreciated and that they can no longer tolerate the stresses in their lives. Public attention focuses mainly on dramatic instances of runaway behavior in which young people are determined to stay away and keep their whereabouts secret. Less dramatically but more commonly, adolescents who run away either return of their own accord or leave a clear trail by which their parents can find them and bring them home. Also, as in neurotic delinquency, the act of running away may energize efforts at communication in the family and lead to counseling for school and social problems, both of which can reduce the difficulties that made the running away seem necessary.

CONSEQUENCES OF RUNNING AWAY

The eventual outcome of runaway behavior depends on the circumstances surrounding it. When adolescents leave a home that is relatively stable and peaceful, run to some other place that at the moment seems more interesting or exciting, and return within a few days, there are usually few negative psychological consequences. Although this kind of running away is a maladaptive way of trying to solve problems that is best avoided, it may, like neurotic delinquency, bring problems to a head that would otherwise fester without adequate attention. Mild episodes of running away in a reasonably stable family can lead to some clearing of the air after the wanderer returns and to some constructive family discussion of what the problem is and what needs to be done about it.

In the opinion of most mental health professionals, however, merely returning home is often not sufficient to resolve the family and personal problems that are reflected in even mild episodes of running away (Tomb, 1991). Family counseling may be necessary to turn runaway behavior into a positive learning experience for adolescents and their parents. As the circumstances surrounding runaway behavior become more disruptive, however, family counseling may come too late to avoid a negative outcome. Adolescents who run from stressful and abusive homes usually have more difficulty returning to them than those who have run to something, and those who have been thrown out of their homes find it particularly hard to turn this tragedy to any positive advantage. The older adolescent runaways are and the longer they stay away from home, the more remote become the possibilities for reconciliation with their parents and resolution of the problems that induced their running away.

In addition to failing to solve the old problems, runaway adolescents who become stayaways typically encounter a host of new problems. Often homeless, unemployed, and on the streets, they find themselves struggling to find food, shelter, and adequate clothing. They become easy victims of others who choose to prey on them, and they face a high risk of being drawn into drug abuse, prostitution, and other kinds of delinquency. Adolescent runaways in shelters show two to three times the prevalence of drug use and abuse than young people in general, and substance use is more frequent in repeat runaways than in first-time runaways (Fors & Rojek, 1991; Windle, 1989).

There was a time when "running away" had a glamorous ring to it, like joining the circus. Nowadays, for young runaways who stay away from home, there is often a seamy side of homelessness, drug abuse, delinquency, and prostitution on the streets of the big city.

A study of 260 male and 130 female homeless adolescent runaways by McCarthy and Hagen (1992) provides a good illustration of how running away can turn sour. Among these young people, 80% reported having used marijuana, 55% had used hallucinogens, and 43% had used cocaine or crack. Over 40% of them had stolen items worth more than $50, and 47% had stolen food. Thirty percent had been involved in prostitution, and 46% had been jailed on at least one occasion. In another study by Rotheram-Borus (1993) of 576 predominantly African-American and Hispanic runaways, one-third had previously made at least one suicide attempt.

Given such circumstances, trying to help runaway adolescents return home to their families, even when it seems possible to do so eventually, is often not where intervention needs to begin. McCarthy and Hagen argued on the basis of their research that other priorities may come first, because what homeless runaways need at the moment is less likely to be better family relationships than food, work, shelter, social support, and protection from harm.

ATTEMPTING AND COMMITTING SUICIDE

Difficulties in dealing with the developmental tasks of adolescence give many young people fleeting thoughts about harming themselves. In the wake of bitter disappointments, they think or say to others, "I wish I were dead." In the aftermath of being criticized or rejected, they fantasize as Tom Sawyer did about how they will get even by committing suicide and

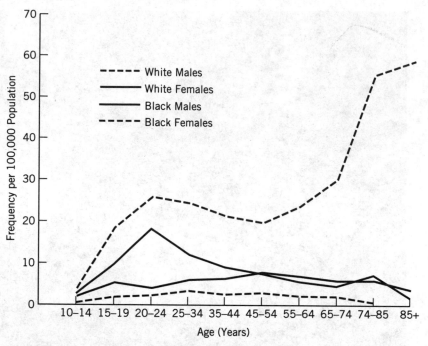

Figure 12.2 Suicide rates by age, sex, and race in the United States. [*Source*: Based on data from NCHS (1991).]

leaving their parents, teachers, or peers feeling guilty and abandoned. One of Konopka's (1976) female subjects had this to say:

> And whenever I used to fight with my mom I used to get to feeling really depressed and I would think, "Oh, if I wasn't here, I wouldn't have to go through all this." But not seriously, because I am afraid of death (age 15, white, urban). [p. 94]

As in this example, such suicidal thoughts are rarely translated by young people into suicidal acts. Of the 30,407 persons known to have killed themselves in the United States in 1988, 243 were children under 15 and 2,059 were adolescents age 15 to 19 (National Center for Health Statistics [NCHS], 1991). As these data indicate, the suicide rate increases sharply during the teenage years, especially among white males (see Figure 12.2).

Note, however, that the highest suicide rate for white males occurs at age 74–85; for white females, the likelihood of suicide is greatest at age 45–54; and for blacks of both genders suicidal risk peaks at age 25–34. This might seem to suggest that a discussion of suicidal behavior belongs in a book about adults rather than a book about adolescents. However, there are additional aspects of suicidal behavior that identify its relevance to adolescent development.

First, youthful suicide has increased at an alarming rate during the last quarter century. Between 1960 and 1988 the rate of suicide in the total United States population grew by approximately 20%, whereas among 15–19-year-olds it tripled during this same period, from

Suicide attempts are often a distress signal to parents who have been indifferent or oblivious to an adolescent's concerns.

3.6 per 100,000 in 1960 to 11.3 per 100,000 in 1988 (NCHS, 1991). This means that adolescents have become much more likely than before to kill themselves and are accounting for an increased percentage of suicides in the United States. Some social scientists have suggested that this increase in suicide among young people is due to the stresses of modern times and the strains of growing up in an increasingly complex and insecure world; this hypothesis has not yet been confirmed by any empirical evidence, however (Hollinger & Lester, 1991; Weiner, 1992, Chapter 9).

Second, suicide is more frequently a cause of death during middle and late adolescence than at any other time of life. This is due in part to the fact that adolescents generally enjoy good physical health. They no longer contract various childhood diseases, and they are not yet susceptible to many of the chronic illnesses that plague older people. As shown in Table 12.3, suicide was the ninth leading cause of death in the general population in 1988, but the third leading cause among 15–19-year-olds, following accidents and homicide. Death by suicide is four times more common in 15–19-year-olds than fatal heart disease, which is the leading cause of death in the general population, and it is 2.5 times as common as dying from cancer, the second most frequent cause of death overall.

Third, although adolescents are much less likely than adults to commit suicide, they are

Table 12.3 LEADING CAUSES OF DEATH IN THE UNITED STATES

Cause	Ages 15–19		General Population	
	Rate Per 100,000	Rank	Rate Per 100,000	Rank
Accidents	46.7	1	39.5	4
Homicide	11.7	2	9.0	10
Suicide	11.3	3	12.4	7
Cancer	4.4	4	197.3	2
Heart disease	2.8	5	394.4	1
Congenital anomalies	1.3	6	5.2	14
Influenza and pneumonia	0.5	7	31.6	5
Cerebrovascular disease	0.4	8	61.2	3
Asthma	0.4	8	1.9	15
Septicemia	0.3	10	8.5	11
Diabetes	0.2	11	16.4	6

Source: National Center for Health Statistics (1991), *Vital Statistics of the United States: 1988.*

almost as likely as adults to think about suicide and to make suicide attempts. Researchers have questioned large numbers of junior and senior high school students in both rural and urban settings and from both advantaged and inner-city neighborhoods about suicidal ideas and actions (Andrews & Lewinsohn, 1992; Dubow, Lovko, & Kausch, 1990; Friedman, Asnis, Boeck, & DiFiore, 1987; Stiffman, Earls, Robins, & Jung, 1988). Substantial samples of college students have similarly been asked whether they have previously considered or carried out any suicidal behavior (Meehan, Lamb, Saltzman, & O'Carroll, 1992; Westefeld & Furr, 1987). The data from these studies of diverse groups suggest that, in contrast to an actual suicide rate of 1 per 10,000 per year among 15–19-year-olds, as many as 1 in every 3–5 may think about committing suicide and 2 to 7% may make some kind of suicide attempt each year. With respect to lifetime prevalence, these studies suggest that 65 to 75% of all young people think about suicide at least once during their adolescence.

Fourth, once adolescents have begun thinking about harming themselves or have made a suicide attempt, suicidal behavior often becomes a persistent risk. Three studies provide some dramatic evidence in this regard. Among 130 adolescents age 13–18 who were seen in a general hospital emergency room or were admitted to a psychiatric hospital following a suicide attempt, a follow-up study by Spirito, Plummer, Gispert, and Levy (1992) found that 6% had made another suicide attempt within the next month, and 10% had reattempted suicide during the subsequent 3 months.

In a similar study in which young people who had been admitted to a psychiatric hospital were followed up after 6–8 years, 31% of those who had made a suicide attempt at the time of the initial assessment had subsequently made at least one additional attempt; of those who attempted suicide during the follow-up period, 40% had made an attempt prior to their initial hospitalization. Compared to a group of nonpatient young people who were also followed, the suicide attempters were six times more likely to make a suicide attempt during the course of the study (Pfeffer et al., 1991; Pfeffer et al., 1993).

The third study used a specialized research method known as **psychological autopsy**. In a psychological autopsy the previous lives of people who have committed suicide are explored by examining existing records about them, such as school reports, and talking with people who knew them well, especially their parents. The purpose of this type of autopsy is to construct a psychological profile of suicide victims that may shed light on why they took their own lives. In this particular study a review of the psychological history and interviews with the families of 53 13–19-year-olds who had killed themselves revealed that two-thirds of them had previously talked about or attempted suicide (Marttunen, Aro, & Lonnqvist, 1992).

GENDER DIFFERENCES

Among adolescents who consider suicide, boys are four times more likely than girls actually to kill themselves, whereas girls are four times more likely to make a suicide attempt (Garland & Zigler, 1993; Hawton, 1986, Chapter 5; NCHS, 1991). Similarly, among adults, men are three to four times more likely to commit suicide, and women are three to four times more likely to attempt it. Although the reasons for this gender difference remain unknown, it has frequently been attributed to differences in gender-role attitudes and preferences.

Lester (1979), for example, in one of the early formulations of gender differences in suicidal behavior, suggested that people tend to see actual suicide as more "masculine" than attempted suicide, which makes males more likely than females to engage in suicidal behavior only when they intend to complete the act. Attempted suicide, on the other hand, is seen as being "feminine," which makes it more likely to be the suicidal behavior of choice among females than males. If this gender-role hypothesis were correct, then the general trend we have noted earlier toward less distinct gender roles in our society would lead us to expect decreasing gender differences in suicidal behavior over the last generation. To the contrary, however, the precise ratio of male to female suicides among 15–19-year-olds stood at 3.4 to 1 in 1965 and subsequently *increased* to 4.1 to 1 in both 1978 and 1988 (Weiner, 1992, Chapter 9).

Males and females also differ in the methods they use to kill themselves, for reasons that are also uncertain. Adolescent boys who kill themselves use firearms or explosives about 65% of the time and hang themselves in another 20% of cases. Girls who commit suicide also shoot themselves most often (45%), but they are almost as likely to choose between taking poison (20%) or using gas (16%) as they are to shoot themselves. Hanging, the second most common suicidal method among adolescent males, ranks fourth (13%) among females.

When young people make suicide attempts, however, poison is by far the most commonly chosen method, in 80 to 90% of both males and females (Hawton, 1986, Chapter 5; McIntosh, 1992; NCHS, 1991). This difference between preferred methods in actual and attempted suicide corresponds to differences in their lethality. Putting a gun to one's head and pulling the trigger has a high probability of resulting in death and rarely leaves any time to reconsider one's intent. Ingesting some substance, on the other hand, allows for a wide range of nonlethal doses and also typically provides some opportunity between swallowing and dying for a young person to be rescued or to call for help.

UNRAVELING SUICIDAL MOTIVATIONS

Clinical and research studies indicate that suicidal behavior typically occurs as the end result of an unfolding process that brings young people to a point of psychological pain in their lives where they can see no other way open to them for relieving this pain. With few exceptions, this unfolding process involves the following four characteristics:

1. *Family instability.* Suicidal adolescents are much more likely than their peers to have grown up in disrupted, disorganized homes. Sometimes through death or desertion of a parent, sometimes through chronic mental or physical illness in the family, sometimes as a result of parental criminality or alcoholism, sometimes in response to marital disharmony, and sometimes because of having to move many times, these young people have frequently passed into adolescence with little reason to feel that they can rely on their parents for support or on their home as a place of sanctuary.

In one illustrative study of 173 young people age 10–20 who were hospitalized following a suicide attempt, only 10% were found to be experiencing harmonious family relationships at the time of the attempt (Withers & Kaplan, 1987). In another study comparing 14–21-year-old suicide attempters with adolescents who had never made a suicide attempt, the attempters had been experiencing more turmoil in their families going back into their childhood (de Wilde, Kienhorts, Diekstra, & Wolters, 1992).

Other research has consistently confirmed that teenage suicidal behavior is associated with chronic family discord, a chaotic home life, and lack of attachment between parents and their children (Bolger, Downey, Walker, & Steininger, 1989; Campbell, Milling, Laughlin, & Bush, 1993; de Jong, 1992; Kosky, Silburn, & Zubrick, 1990; Paluszny, Davenport, & Kim, 1991). On the other hand, there is evidence that a secure and cohesive family environment can act as a protective factor that reduces the likelihood of suicidal behavior in circumstances that otherwise create a risk for it (King, Raskin, Gdowski, Butkus, & Opipari, 1990).

2. *Escalating distress.* Adolescents who harm or kill themselves are typically suffering from frustrations and disappointments that have left them feeling sad, angry, and hopeless. Much more frequently than their nonsuicidal peers, they have experienced recurrent episodes of depression and repetitive experiences of humiliation and rejection. Usually these types of distress have plagued suicidal young people for many years and then begun to escalate in the months preceding an adolescent's attempting or committing suicide. Research studies have found that, with few exceptions, suicidal behavior occurs not in response to any single event, but only after an accumulation of increasingly undesirable life events (Brown, Overholser, Spirito, & Fritz, 1991; Cole, Protinsky, & Cross, 1992; Garrison, Addy, Jackson, McKeown, & Waller, 1991; Myers, McCauley, Calderon, & Treder, 1991; Rich, Sherman, & Fowler, 1990).

Along with other kinds of distress, suicidal adolescents have typically experienced an escalation in their family problems for at least a few months prior to their attempting or committing suicide. Frequent parental separations have eventuated in a final divorce, for example, or especially serious illness has prevented the parents from earning the family's living, or a particularly wrenching move to a new school or community has occurred (Brent et al., 1993; de Wilde et al., 1992).

In addition, the months preceding youthful suicidal behavior have usually brought a sharp increase in parent–child conflict. Often the parents have become highly critical of their child during this period and have imposed rigid limits on his or her behavior. The adolescent has in turn usually complained bitterly about the parents' attitudes and controls, and angry confrontation has become commonplace. Almost always the adolescent has come away the loser in these confrontations and has grown to feel powerless to influence his or her destiny.

3. *Dissolving social relationships.* Feeling alienated from uncaring or overcontrolling parents, suicidal adolescents have typically sought a close relationship with some other relative, with a teacher, or with a boyfriend or girlfriend. Because of their desperate need for such a relationship, however, presuicidal adolescents cannot tolerate the relationship's being disrupted. Hence the recent lives of suicidal adolescents are often marked either by failure to establish contacts with people outside their home or by the dissolution of such desperately needed relationships, as when a relative dies, a teacher moves away, or a boyfriend or girlfriend no longer wants a steady relationship.

Findings reported by Woznica and Shapiro (1990) suggest that suicidal adolescents are especially likely to feel *expendable* in their interpersonal relationships. Feeling expendable means thinking that you are not really valued for yourself in your family or among your friends, but only for the role you play in meeting their needs. Among a group of young people being seen in psychotherapy at a teenage health clinic, Woznica and Shapiro found a significant association between the extent of suicidality shown by these patients and the extent to which they felt they were unwanted or were a burden on their family.

Research findings confirm not only that suicidal adolescents lack supportive social networks, but also that close ties to family and friends, like a secure family environment, can counteract suicidal tendencies that may be provoked by stressful experiences (King et al., 1990; Spirito, Brown, Overholser, & Fritz, 1989). In an illustrative study by Cantor (1976), female college students who had thought about suicide often and students who had made one or more attempts both showed strong needs to be close to people and to be nurtured by them, combined with limited ability to tolerate frustration of these needs. However, those who had just thought about suicide had been successful in satisfying these needs in their interpersonal relationships, whereas those who had attempted suicide had been unable to reach out and establish supportive relationships with others.

On occasion, the news media draw considerable attention to instances in which two or more adolescents have killed themselves or made suicide attempts in a group. Suicide pacts make good stories, and Romeo and Juliet, the star-crossed lovers who kill themselves rather than face the prospect of living without each other, have through Shakespeare's talent made a firm impression on the public mind. Such couple or group suicidal behavior may appear to suggest that close interpersonal relationships can sometimes contribute to rather than help avert self-harmful acts. However, multiple suicide behavior should not be taken to signify a supportive social network. Among young people who act suicidally together, and who are at that moment in a sense supporting each other, each individual is very likely to be feeling estranged from his or her parents, from other people in whom to confide, and from rewarding and nurturant group memberships.

4. *Unsuccessful problem-solving efforts.* In addition to failing to find or hold onto supportive relationships, suicidal adolescents have usually progressed without success through a series of increasingly desperate attempts to resolve their escalating problems. Often they have begun with reasonable efforts to iron out their differences with their parents or to find support and stability elsewhere. Proving unsuccessful, these efforts have given way to more dramatic attempts to convey distress and bring about changing circumstances—including underachievement, truancy, delinquent behavior, and running away. When neither reason nor milder provocations have improved their situation, suicidal young people have decided that harming themselves is their last hope for making some impact on their family and friends:

> See, I really didn't want to die. I just wanted to get into the hospital so they would all be worried about me and so that they would go, "Oh my God, they haven't been treating the poor child right, look what we have done." (Age 17, white, urban). [Konopka, 1976, p. 95]

Research with both high school and college students has confirmed that those who think about or attempt suicide typically have fewer problem-solving skills than their nonsuicidal peers. Especially when they are trying to cope with interpersonal difficulties, suicidal young people are inclined to generate relatively few alternative possibilities for finding solutions; they tend to opt for wishful thinking instead of constructive problem solving; and they are prone to begin feeling hopeless about being able to overcome their difficulties (Dixon, Heppner, & Anderson, 1991; Rotheram-Borus, Trautman, Dopkins, & Shrout, 1990).

With respect to other adjustment problems on the way to suicide behavior, research studies have also documented an increased risk of suicidal behavior in young people who have already turned to delinquency or substance abuse in an effort to ease the pain of unmanageable problems (Adcock, Nagy, & Simpson, 1991; Marttunen et al., 1992; Pfeffer et al., 1993; Windle, Miller-Tutzauer, & Domenico, 1992). Presuicidal adolescents who do not show behavior problems have typically become increasingly depressed, withdrawn, and reclusive in the months prior to their harming themselves. Only rarely will young people who are progressing toward suicide fail to show either emotional or behavioral difficulties that can readily be recognized by anyone who pays close attention to them (Lewinsohn, Rohde, & Seeley, 1993; Marttunen, Aro, Henrikkson, & Lonnqvist, 1991; Rao, Weissman, Martin, & Hammond, 1993; Smith, 1992).

Lonely, alienated young people from disrupted or disorganized homes who have already failed in numerous efforts to resolve mounting problems thus constitute a high-risk group for suicidal behavior. As in the decision to run away, some specific event usually proves to be the "last straw" that precipitates a suicidal act, such as losing one more argument at home or one more close friend at school. Although such precipitating events are often mentioned by adolescents as their main reason for attempting suicide, they almost always turn out to have been just the spark to the tinder box.

Of utmost importance in the unfolding process that leads young people to attempt suicide is their need to communicate their concerns, particularly to their parents, and to bring about a change in how they are being treated by others. For this reason, attempted suicide has for many years been referred to as a cry for help (Farberow & Shneidman, 1961). Research findings reflect in many ways the underlying motivation of suicidal adolescents to lay a heavy message on their parents and other people. These teenagers typically feel that their parents are unaware of or indifferent to their problems; their attempts are usually made at home, often while their parents are there, or in some public place; and their parents commonly have little understanding of what has been bothering their child or what has precipitated his or her suicide attempt (Weiner, 1992, Chapter 9).

As might be expected, whether adolescents repeat suicide attempts depends on the reaction they get. When parents react to suicidal behavior by recognizing their youngster's difficulties and offering to help with or at least talk about the problems, they usually forestall another suicide attempt. On the other hand, parents who show little reaction to a suicide attempt, who do not see it as any reason for changing their behavior, or—even worse—who respond with anger or ridicule rather than with sympathetic understanding set the stage for further and more serious attempts.

TREATMENT

An overriding consideration in treating adolescents who have made a suicide attempt is that every such attempt must be taken seriously. Even the mildest attempt is intended to communicate problems for which no solution seems available, and an unresponsive environment often prompts further, increasingly dangerous self-destructive actions. When suicidal youngsters come to professional attention, the treatment usually assumes that some unappreciated distress and some breakdown in interpersonal relationships have contributed to their behavior. Therapists focus first on opening up lines of communication between these adolescents and those around them and then try to help them share together in understanding the motives underlying the self-destructive behavior (Berman & Jobes, 1991, Chapter 5; Hendin, 1991; Pfeffer, 1989; Weiner, 1992, Chapter 9).

Suicidal adolescents have frequently become convinced that they are cut off from the affection, nurturance, and support of others. Therapists can begin to alter this conviction by being at least one interested and concerned person, eager to listen and understand. Subsequent to the establishment of lines of communication with a suicidal adolescent, and thereby having reduced the immediate risk of further attempts, therapists extend this communication to his or her family. Discussions with the parents or sessions with the entire family are used to help the parents recognize and respond to their youngster's problems more than they have been and to encourage the suicidal adolescent to find ways of communicating with his or her parents with words rather than actions.

The treatment of suicidal young people is thus governed by the expectation that the more they encounter warm concern and attempts to understand their behavior, the less likely they are to consider suicide attempts in the future. Once the initial risk of self-destructive behavior has diminished and family members are communicating with each other, attention can be turned to helping them resolve the long-standing conflicts that initiated the suicidal sequence in the first place. The more progress a family can make in changing maladaptive ways of operating, the more the risk of adolescent suicidal behavior will be reduced.

In recent years numerous community-based programs have been instituted in an effort to prevent suicidal behavior from occurring. Notable among these programs are telephone hotlines, which young people who are concerned about harming themselves can call at any time of night or day to talk about their situation with a trained counselor, and educational programs to help adults who are around young people a lot to become more aware of the early warning signs of suicidal risk and of how to get troubled young people into professional care. To date, however, such community programs have not been consistently effective in reducing youthful suicide behavior, and they appear to require improved methods before they will make a difference (Felner, Adan, & Silverman, 1992; Garland & Zigler, 1993).

ADJUSTING TO CHRONIC ILLNESS AND PHYSICAL DISABILITY

How adolescents look and how they feel physically exert a powerful influence on how they view themselves and are viewed by others. Those who are strong, healthy, graceful, athletic, and good looking tend to think well of themselves and to enjoy the admiration of their family and friends. For them the adolescent developmental tasks of adapting to bodily changes and forming new kinds of social relationships are welcome challenges they meet with aplomb. Those who are weak, sickly, awkward, inept, and unattractive must often live instead with distaste for themselves, disappointment by their parents, and disinterest from their peers. For them the goals of feeling comfortable with their bodies and gratified by their friendships can seem difficult to reach or even beyond their grasp.

Chronic illness and physical disability are particularly important in this regard because they affect an estimated 10 to 14% of young people and pose serious and potentially permanent threats to a person's self-esteem and social adjustment (Eiser, Havermans, Pancer, & Eiser, 1992; Lavigne & Faier-Routman, 1992; Pruzinsky & Cash, 1990). Moreover, because of differences in the kinds of support systems that are available to people of different ages, being chronically ill or physically disabled constitutes an especially significant hazard to psychological well-being during the adolescent years. Professionals concerned with rehabilitation have noted for many years that programs of education and training for the disabled are targeted more for younger children and adults than they are for adolescents, and furthermore that both elementary school children and adults are more tolerant than junior and senior high school students of companions who are "different" (Berenberg, 1976; Schowalter, 1977).

To elaborate on this last point, children prior to puberty often regard a peer with an affliction as a special person whose condition intrigues them and whose needs for assistance and sympathy they are eager to help meet. It is among elementary school children that everyone wants to try using the crutches or the motorized wheelchair of an injured or crippled classmate; it is in the lower grades that teachers find ready volunteers to do special favors for disabled students who cannot fully care for themselves.

Young people do not automatically become less kind or less willing to help a friend in need when they enter adolescence and experience their pubescent growth changes. However, their normal developmental concerns about suffering bodily harm or disfigurement begin to make it difficult for them to interact comfortably with classmates who have suffered such misfortune. It is as if even seeing disabled adolescents around, let alone taking a supportive interest in their condition, brings home a frightening message concerning their own vulnerability: "Something like this could happen to me!" Hence adolescents often prefer to keep disabled, enfeebled, or scarred peers out of sight and out of mind. Likewise, as if to reassure themselves of their own physical adequacy and attractiveness, teenagers may even go out of their way to poke fun at people who make a strange appearance (Blum & Geber, 1992; Eiser, 1990; Fritz, 1992).

Adults usually outgrow such aversion or cruelty toward disabled persons as part of developing a secure sense of their own identity. Exceptions can certainly be found, especially in cultures past and present that have been obsessed with physical perfection, and stigma and discrimination still abound, especially among individuals whose own lack of satisfaction with themselves leads them to depreciate others. Such aberrations aside, however, adults are generally sympathetic toward chronically ill and disabled persons and supportive of efforts to make their lives easier.

In our own contemporary society, encouragement to hire the handicapped and legal requirements for handicapped-accessible structures (buildings, bathrooms, buses, etc.) are two highly visible illustrations of such supportive efforts. Chronically ill and physically disabled adolescents must frequently pass a distressing middle ground between the supportive attitudes of child and adult peers, however. As Berenberg (1976) eloquently described it some years ago, "The sympathetic understanding obtained so easily during childhood and the mature compassionate understanding that can be expected in adult life are little consolation now. So adolescence is a time for many a physically handicapped boy or girl to cry in their pillows" (p. 279).

DEVELOPMENTAL CONCERNS IN TWO ILLUSTRATIVE CONDITIONS: CEREBRAL PALSY AND DIABETES

Generally speaking, children who have been born with a disability or acquired it early in life are better prepared to cope with the developmental tasks of adolescence than are those who become disabled as teenagers. Whatever the frustrations of trying to become a self-reliant and socially successful adult in the face of limitations dating from early childhood, they are less traumatic than having to face unexpected incapacity or deformity beginning in adolescence. Especially when young people have already experienced part of their adolescence with a gratifying sense of what they can accomplish with their physical capacities intact, a debilitating illness or a disfiguring injury can have a devastating effect on self-esteem, sociability, and ability to plan constructively for the future.

For those young people who have grown up with a chronic illness or physical disability, the normal cognitive and physical maturation that occurs during adolescence increases their personal capacities but also creates some new problems for them. Because of the typical adolescent pursuit of autonomy and independence that we described in Chapter 7, the limitations imposed by being ill or disabled may become more difficult to accept than they were before. Being unable to be self-reliant poses more of a threat to normal developmental processes in adolescence than during childhood, and research studies confirm that being chronically ill has a greater psychological impact on teenagers than on younger children (Eiser et al., 1992).

These and other developmental problems of disabled young people were monitored a number of years ago in a very interesting study by Minde (1978), who evaluated 34 children with cerebral palsy when they entered kindergarten or first grade and again when they were age 10–14. **Cerebral palsy** is a neurological disorder caused by damage to the brain at birth or in early childhood. It is estimated to occur in 1–2 of every 1,000 births, and it results in muscle weakness or paralysis, poor coordination, and jerky or odd undulating movements over which the person has no control. Victims of cerebral palsy may be too crippled to take care of their own needs, and many are also mentally retarded. Some, however, have normal or above average intelligence, are able to get about with the aid of crutches or a wheelchair, and can participate in a regular high school classroom. Even then, difficulties in controlling the movements of their limbs and facial muscles may burden them with the social handicaps of looking strange and not being able to speak clearly (Blum & Geber, 1992; Taft, 1987; Williams, Pleak, & Hanesian, 1991).

The cerebral palsied children that Minde studied had progressed fairly well in a special elementary school program. However, their cognitive maturation at puberty brought increased realization that their disability was permanent and that there was little hope for future improvement. This painful realization was discouraging these adolescents from giving much thought to the kind of person they would like to be or what they would like to do with their lives.

Minde also found that adolescence was a time when the parents and siblings of many of these disabled children begin to withdraw from them emotionally. The parents in his study were finding it increasingly difficult to contemplate their youngster's limited future, and the siblings were becoming more likely to express any resentment they felt in relation to the demands that their disabled sibling had made and was still making on their family's attention and resources. As one further difficulty, Minde found that many of these cerebral palsied children were limited in developing adolescent social relationships not only because of their physical disability, but also because most of their previous peer relationships had been limited to interactions with other disabled children with whom they had shared special class programs.

These problems faced by children with cerebral palsy as they enter adolescence are fairly representative of the psychological hazards that await all children who grow up with serious physical disabilities. Other kinds of special problems may confront young people who develop a chronic illness, of which diabetes is an important example. **Diabetes** is a genetically transmitted condition in which insufficient insulin in the body prevents normal metabolism of carbohydrates. This metabolic dysfunction leads to an excess of sugar in the bloodstream and causes the person to become unusually thirsty, to urinate frequently, to lose weight, and to feel weak and lethargic. A profound and continuing imbalance of sugar in the system can eventually result in a person's falling into a coma and dying.

Diabetes is estimated to occur in 1 to 2% of the population and is the sixth leading cause of death in the United States. Although diabetes is primarily an adult illness, it sometimes begins during the developmental years, and it is the 11th leading cause of death among 15–19-year-olds (NCHS, 1991). Approximately 1 in 800 adolescents is diabetic, a prevalence equal to all types of cancer combined. When diabetes begins in childhood or adolescence, it may contribute to numerous health complications later in life, including obesity, hypertension, poor circulation, heart disease, kidney disease, and eye problems. Most such complications can be prevented or at least minimized by good medical care, however, so that diabetics can look forward to a reasonably healthy life provided that they follow a strict treatment program. The main features of such programs are dietary restriction of sugar intake combined in many cases with regular doses of insulin that may be injected under the skin (Fort & Lifshitz, 1992; Golden & Gray, 1992; Johnson, 1988).

Clinical studies of diabetic adolescents have identified two significant psychosocial problems that often result from this illness (Johnson, 1980). First, having to inject themselves with insulin on a daily basis subjects these young people to a physically painful, psychologically threatening, and socially embarrassing process. Second, because diabetes is hereditary and can produce health complications in later life, diabetic young people are likely to wonder whether they should marry and have children and whether they can make ambitious long-range plans with any hope of being able to carry them out. They can be reassured, however, that the manner in which diabetes is transmitted carries only a slight risk of their having diabetic children so long as they avoid marrying someone with a family history of the illness. Furthermore, with continuing treatment their prospects for a full and active life justify their planning in every possible way to exercise their talents and enjoy themselves in the years ahead.

MAKING THE BEST OF ILLNESS AND DISABILITY

As a consequence of their diminished capacities, reduced social attractiveness, deflated self-esteem, and uncertain future prospects, adolescents with a chronic illness or physical disability are generally found to be more susceptible than their unaffected peers to developing various kinds of psychological disorders and adjustment difficulties. Adjustment difficulties are especially likely in young people who are seriously handicapped by their illness or disability and often include inadequate attention to making plans for the future (Blum & Geber, 1992; Coupey, 1992b; Eiser, 1990). In addition, for those who must be hospitalized, separation from their family and friends and being out of school often lead to loneliness, concerns about being out of the mainstream of peer-group activities, and pessimism with respect to being able to pick up the threads of their lives again (Battle, Kreisberg, O'Mahoney, & Chitwood, 1989; Mrazek, 1991; Sexson & Madan-Swain, 1993).

At the same time, many chronically ill or disabled young people show remarkable resilience and considerable capacity to look on the brighter side of their lives. Many get along well with their parents and peers, anticipate marrying and having a family, and plan effectively for completing their education and pursuing other life goals. Prospects for such successful coping are improved when these young people enjoy strong support from their family and friends, have a network of peer relationships that includes teenagers who are not disabled, and maintain a perception of themselves as not being handicapped (Blum & Geber, 1992; Wallander, Varni, Babani, Banis, & Wilcox, 1989). In this last regard, studies of adolescents who are diabetic or have survived treatment for cancer have revealed that being able to make the best of their circumstances and avoid psychological maladjustment is enhanced among those ill youngsters who are successfully denying the full implications of their condition (Friedman & Mulhern, 1992; Johnson, 1988; Stern, Norman, & Zevon, 1993).

This finding may seem surprising, inasmuch as good adjustment ordinarily hinges on being able and willing to perceive one's experience realistically. Getting people with behavior problems to face squarely the full extent of their difficulties, without any denial, is in fact often one of the first steps in treating them effectively. However, chronic illness and physical disability are not ordinary situations, and there are times of overwhelming stress in people's lives when meticulous attention to reality does more harm than good.

Among adolescent diabetics and cancer patients, those who dwell on the possibility of later health complications and recurrent illness are being realistic, but they also tend to feel frightened and gloomy and to put themselves at risk for psychological maladjustment. By contrast, those who recognize that such unpalatable outcomes are possible but who firmly expect to be among the fortunate few who escape them are being somewhat unrealistic, because there can be no guarantee that they will; yet their denial gains them some peace of mind and some reason to plan for the future, which in turn helps them avoid emotional or behavioral problems. There is even evidence to suggest that whether adolescents adjust well to illness or disability depends more on their capacity for this kind of **adaptive denial** than on how physically impaired they are. For this reason, clinicians often recommend promoting such denial during the treatment of chronically ill and disabled adolescents (Koocher & O'Malley, 1981).

COPING WITH DEATH AND DYING

For many years in psychology the experience of death and dying was among a group of taboo topics (Feifel, 1963). Like suicidal behavior, child abuse, and sex crimes, it was too distasteful for "nice" people to talk about, and was certainly not a fit topic for parents to discuss with their children or teachers to place before their students. We have come a long way in contemporary times in recognizing that people should be informed about unpleasant human events, no matter how upsetting they may be, in order to act as responsible citizens when such events threaten their community and in order to cope with them adequately should they touch their lives. Death and dying darken everyone's doorstep, and understanding their psychological impact can be as important to good adjustment as enjoying the occasions that enrich one's life.

Largely due to the contributions of Elisabeth Kübler-Ross, beginning with a book entitled *On Death and Dying* (1969), dealing with life's end has gained a visible place in the teaching of psychology and in the training of mental health workers. Kübler-Ross, a psychiatrist, originated a program of psychotherapy for terminally ill hospital patients designed to help them prepare for death with the support of an interested and empathic professional therapist. Many of her own colleagues objected to this program, because they considered it cruel to discuss death with the dying and because they felt that limited resources for providing psychotherapy should be reserved for people with substantial life opportunities ahead of them. Kübler-Ross nevertheless succeeded in humanizing the dying process and establishing the propriety of attempting to ease the mental anguish of any person in distress, no matter how many or few days remain in his or her life (Kimmel, 1990, Chapter 10).

With respect to understanding adolescence, increasing attention is being paid to particular problems that young people face if their parents or a friend dies or if they themselves become fatally ill or injured. Regarding the first of these, there is a link familiar to most people between losing a loved one and experiencing a period of depression. Beyond this general reaction, adolescents have some developmentally unique sensitivities to the death of one or both their parents.

We described in Chapter 7 how adolescents progress toward autonomy and self-reliance by sometimes asserting independence from their parents and at other times turning dependently to them for help and advice, especially when in their insistence on acting independently they have taken on more than they can handle. Although this process can take place equally well in a one-parent as in a two-parent family, both parents become important to it if both are involved with their youngster, even if they are not particularly devoted to his or her upbringing.

When a parent dies, adolescent children lose both someone they were working to separate themselves from and someone they still counted on for support in times of need. The parental loss deprives them of both the benchmark and the back-up that foster striking out on one's own. Losing both parents or an only parent through illness or an accident can be more traumatic than losing one of two parents, but any parental loss is likely to set back at least for a time a young person's progress toward learning self-reliance and forming an independent identity. Even when there is a surviving parent in the home, he or she is rarely able to fill the gap in an adolescent's life left by the death of the other parent. Surviving parents have their own mourning to do, and they have to plan for how the family will continue to function without the contribution of the deceased parent. No matter how capable a surviving parent is, then, and no matter how close a bond he or she has to an adolescent child, there will be a period of time when he or she cannot possibly be both mother and father to the young person.

Clinical and research studies have identified several ways in which adolescents may respond to this kind of crisis in their lives (Balk, 1991; Lewis, Lewis, & Schonfeld, 1991; Sahler, 1992; Wessel, 1992). Often they reach out toward other parental figures, such as an aunt, uncle, teacher, or older sibling, and look to them for some of the support and guidance that the lost parent had provided. They may even seek out parental figures to argue and disagree with, as a means of continuing to assert their autonomy. Because these can be helpful ways of overcoming developmental arrest following a parent's death, people who can fill this role in a bereaved young person's life should in most cases be encouraged to do so.

There are also times when adolescents find it more painful than they can bear to think and feel realistically about a parent's death. Then, as younger children often do, they may harbor fantasies that the deceased parent did not really die or is not gone forever. Like a bad dream, being told of his or her death, going to the funeral, and seeing the family in mourning will all pass with the dawning of a new day, and the parent will return. Sometimes such periods of wishful thinking are accompanied by the kind of denial that helps adolescents live with chronic illness. Then, instead of suffering consciously with their painful sense of loss, they throw themselves into their customary activities with a show a cheerfulness and enthusiasm that leads others to wonder if they really cared about the lost parent or are showing sufficient respect for his or her memory. Such efforts to go about their business as usual need to be understood as an adaptive means of easing the pain of loss. Like relationships with new parental figures, they should in most cases be encouraged rather than criticized.

Whatever ways adolescents respond to the death of a parent, they usually need more time than adults to get over such a loss. In a two-parent family this means that a surviving parent may be ready to form new love relationships and consider remarriage before his or her adolescent youngster can understand or accept such behavior as being loyal and faithful to the deceased parent. Hence another special strain may be added to an adolescent's development when the death of a parent brings a stepparent into his or her life, as we discussed in Chapter 7. Families in this situation need to be sensitive to possible conflicts between a parent's adaptive interest in remarrying and an adolescent's disapproval of his or her doing so.

When ill or injured adolescents are confronted with the likelihood of their own death, their stage of development also creates special kinds of stress. Young children have only a limited sense of the meaning of death, especially with respect to its permanence (Sahler, 1992). Children are rarely told that someone who has died has ceased to exist; instead, the dead person has "gone away" or is "with God." On television and at the movies they see that the actor who is killed one week shows up again, hale and hearty, the next week. By adolescence, the maturation of formal cognitive operations allows young people to begin grasping the concept of death with an adult perspective. If their own death is imminent, they know full well that it will put a final end to their lives and with it all of their hopes and dreams. None of the pleasures they had imagined will be theirs to enjoy, and none of the accomplishments they had anticipated will be theirs to realize.

Adults facing this finality of death, especially when they have enjoyed a long and full life, can often ease the pain of their mortality with comforting knowledge of what they have been and done. Terminally ill or injured adolescents can find little such solace with which to mute the call of death. They have only just begun to become people in their own right, just begun to plan for lives not yet led, when fate intervenes to deny them their adulthood. Because they understand the meaning of death more than children and feel more cheated by it than adults, adolescents frequently find the prospect of dying even more stressful than those older and younger than they.

CHAPTER SUMMARY

1. The incidence and prevalence of adolescent drug use vary widely by age and for individual drugs. Adolescent involvement with drugs has been decreasing gradually since the late 1970s, and *drug abuse*, in which heavy use of drugs becomes addictive and physically or psychologically harmful, is infrequent.

2. Drug taking is instigated by a variety of personal, peer-group, and family influences that can operate either independently or in combination. The particular influences that are most important in sustaining drug use vary with age and the kinds of drugs being taken.

3. An estimated 1 million adolescents run away from home each year for varying lengths of time. Running away is caused by persistent problems at home and in school that cannot be communicated effectively to others. Often its purpose is to deliver a nonverbal appeal for less stress and better communication. Young people who run away and stay away without hope for or interest in returning to their families are at high risk for serious adjustment difficulties.

4. Although infrequent, youthful suicide has increased at an alarming pace and is the third leading cause of death among 15–19-year-olds. Suicidal behavior, including nonfatal suicide attempts, typically occurs as the end result of an unfolding process involving long-standing family discord, escalating distress, dissolving social relationships, and unsuccessful efforts to find other solutions. Like neurotic delinquency and running away, suicide attempts are communications that can be called a cry for help.

5. Treatment of these several problems seeks to resolve the particular concerns that have led to them in the individual case and to improve the adolescent's coping capacities. A wide range of individual, group, and family therapy approaches is used for this purpose, along with numerous educational, skill training, and community action methods of intervention.

6. Adolescents with a chronic illness or physical disability may have special difficulties coping with developmental tasks. The death of friends and relatives, especially a parent, also demands special coping skills. In such circumstances there are times when being able to deny painful aspects of reality, at least temporarily, serves an adaptive purpose.

KEY WORDS

adaptive denial	diabetes	medicinal drug use	stepping-stone hypothesis
addictive drug use	drug abuse	psychological autopsy	
cerebral palsy	experimental drug use	social drug use	withdrawal symptoms
comorbidity	hard drug	soft drug	

REVIEW QUESTIONS

USING AND ABUSING DRUGS

1. What is the significance of distinguishing between the *incidence* of drug use and the *prevalence* of drug use?

2. Discuss the implications of the stepping-stone hypothesis of drug use formulated by Kandel.

3. How do experimental, social, medicinal, and addictive drug taking relate to distinguishing between *drug use* and *drug abuse*?

4. Describe the kinds of personal, social, and family influences that are likely to contribute to drug use among adolescents. What are some implications of the apparent fact that these influences can operate independently of each other?

5. What kinds of research findings suggest that genetic factors may contribute to alcoholism in some cases?

6. Why is drug addiction difficult to treat?

7. How do drug prevention programs that appear to work differ from programs that usually fail?

RUNNING AWAY

8. With respect to the implications of problem behavior in adolescents, what is the significance of distinguishing between runaways and throwaways?

9. How are authoritative, authoritarian, and permissive patterns of parental discipline likely to be related to runaway behavior?

10. Why have many mental health professionals concluded that simply returning home is not the solution to problems associated with running away?

ATTEMPTING AND COMMITTING SUICIDE

11. List four reasons why suicidal behavior is an important topic to consider in studying adolescent development.

12. What have research findings shown concerning how and why adolescent females and males differ in their likelihood of attempting or committing suicide?

13. Discuss the key elements of the unfolding psychological process that typically precedes suicidal behavior and accounts for adolescents' motivations to harm themselves.

ADJUSTING TO CHRONIC ILLNESS AND PHYSICAL DISABILITY

14. Why is adolescence often a more difficult time psychologically than childhood for young people with a chronic illness or physical disability?

COPING WITH DEATH AND DYING

15. What are some of the ways in which adolescents tend to respond to one of their parents dying?

Chapter 13

◆

Psychological Disturbances

◆

SCHIZOPHRENIA
FUNCTIONING IMPAIRMENTS IN SCHIZOPHRENIC DISORDER
Information From Follow-Back Studies / Information From High-Risk Studies
ORIGINS OF SCHIZOPHRENIA
Genetic Influences / Experiential Influences / The Diathesis-Stress Theory
OUTCOME
TREATMENT

AFFECTIVE DISORDER
CHARACTERISTICS OF AFFECTIVE DISORDER
CAUSES OF AFFECTIVE DISORDER
Genetic Dispositions / Stressful Life Events
OUTCOME AND TREATMENT

EATING DISORDERS: OBESITY, ANOREXIA NERVOSA, AND BULIMIA
THE NATURE AND CONSEQUENCES OF BEING OBESE
CAUSES OF OBESITY
TREATING OBESE ADOLESCENTS
BEHAVIOR PATTERNS IN ANOREXIA NERVOSA AND BULIMIA
UNRAVELING THE MYSTERY OF ANOREXIA NERVOSA AND BULIMIA
TREATMENT FOR ANOREXIA NERVOSA AND BULIMIA

WORKING WITH ADOLESCENTS

CHAPTER SUMMARY
KEY WORDS
REVIEW QUESTIONS

In concluding our discussion of identity formation in Chapter 10, we stressed the continuity that exists between adolescent and adult development. Many personality characteristics remain fairly stable from adolescence to adulthood, and people generally show the same level of adjustment relative to their peers as they mature. Unusually stressful experiences can cause previously well-adjusted people to become emotionally upset or behave inappropriately, and various kinds of good fortune or professional intervention can help psychologically troubled people overcome their difficulties. By and large, however, adolescents who are getting along well will continue to do so as adults, whereas those who are adjusting less comfortably than their peers to being an adolescent are likely to adjust less comfortably to being an adult (Weiner, 1992, Chapter 1).

This type of continuity extends not only across the years, as people grow into maturity, but also across normal and abnormal development. Among people who develop abnormally, including even those who become seriously disturbed, behavior is governed by the same kinds of cognitive and emotional processes that govern normal development and behavior. However, instead of thinking, feeling, and acting the way most other people do, disturbed individuals display some maladaptive exaggeration of normal characteristics.

As an illustration, good adjustment is fostered by having a moderate amount of self-control. If people exercise too much self-control, they become maladaptively rigid and inhibited; if they exercise too little self-control, they become maladaptively impulsive and unstable. From this **continuity perspective**, normal and abnormal behaviors involve *qualitatively similar* traits, with maladjusted individuals simply having *quantitatively more or less* than an optimum amount of some of these traits.

Because of the continuity that exists between normal and abnormal development, normal life experience cannot be fully understood and appreciated without considering how normal processes can become exaggerated into psychological disturbance. Although extensive coverage of this topic belongs in books devoted to psychopathology, we want to conclude our presentation of adolescent psychology by discussing three types of disturbance that have particular significance for teenage development.

Among the many different forms that psychopathology can take, the two that have been most widely discussed and extensively studied are *schizophrenia* and *affective disorder*. Both of these conditions commonly begin during the late adolescent years, and we describe them in the first two sections of the chapter. In the third section we look at three *eating disorders* that cause problems for some teenagers: *obesity, anorexia nervosa*, and *bulimia*. The chapter concludes with some final comments on working with troubled adolescents.

SCHIZOPHRENIA

By virtue of its prevalence and severity, schizophrenia is a major public health problem. Out of every 100 people, 1 or 2 are likely to suffer an episode of schizophrenic disturbance sometime during their lives, and during any 1-month period 0.7% of adults in the United States are likely to demonstrate schizophrenia (Keith, Regier, & Rae, 1991). From 25 to 40% of patients admitted to various kinds of psychiatric facilities are diagnosed as schizophrenic. As for its severity, schizophrenia is a disabling condition that often runs a chronic or recurrent course. Among patients discharged from hospitals after being treated for schizophrenia, only 25% recover sufficiently to lead normal lives. Another 50% of patients hospitalized for schizophrenia improve and may be discharged from the hospital but are likely to suffer lingering symptoms or occasional relapses, and the remaining 25% remain permanently hospitalized or socially incapacitated (National Institute of Mental Health, 1985; Eaton et al., 1992; Keith, Regier, Rae, & Matthews, 1992; Ram, Bromet, Eaton, & Schwartz, 1992).

Schizophrenia is an important topic in adolescent psychology because most forms of this disturbance begin during late adolescence and early adulthood. About one-third of people who become schizophrenic experience their first episode of breakdown before age 20 and over 70% before age 25 (Keith et al., 1992; Lewis, 1989). A notable frequency of teenagers seen by mental health professionals have already developed schizophrenic disorder. Schizophrenia is diagnosed in 25 to 30% of all adolescents admitted to public mental hospitals, and approximately 15% of schizophrenic patients being treated in private psychiatric hospitals are under age 18 (Rosenstein, Milazzo-Sayre, & Manderscheid, 1989; Tyano & Apter, 1992; Weiner, 1992, Chapter 3). Among adolescents who are destined to become schizophrenic in their 20s, moreover, the prelude to the disorder affects their lives in ways that are important to recognize and understand.

FUNCTIONING IMPAIRMENTS IN SCHIZOPHRENIC DISORDER

Schizophrenia consists of a serious breakdown in a person's cognitive, interpersonal, and integrative capacities. As indicated in Box 13.1, these types of incapacity lead to several kinds of functioning impairment that define the nature of this condition. Schizophrenic people have difficulty thinking and talking clearly and coherently; they jump to unreasonable conclusions on the basis of insufficient or irrelevant evidence; they form unrealistic impressions of themselves and of their surroundings and show poor judgment in anticipating the consequences of their actions; they cannot easily make or keep friends and often alienate or offend people they are trying to impress and attract; and they frequently become distressed by their own thoughts and feelings and incapable of behaving in socially acceptable ways.

None of the functioning impairments listed in Box 13.1 is unique to schizophrenia. However, when they occur together and persist over an extended period of time, they define the presence of a schizophrenic disorder (Andreasen, 1988; Andreasen & Flaum, 1991; Arieti, 1974, Chapter 5; Weiner, 1992, Chapter 3).

Along with beginning to experience these kinds of difficulties, young people who are developing a schizophrenic disorder often show two patterns of maladjustment that clinicians refer to as *precursors* of schizophrenia. One of these is a **schizoid pattern** marked by shy, sensitive, seclusive behavior and a shut-in personality style in which emotions and interests are turned inward rather than directed toward other people. The other is a **stormy pattern** involving restlessness, difficulty concentrating, and a history of family conflict, stealing, running away, truancy, and school failure.

Not all preschizophrenic adolescents go through a schizoid or stormy period, and neither pattern always leads to schizophrenia. However, both of these developmental variations are frequently found in people who subsequently become schizophrenic. This information has emerged from two lines of research into the life histories of disturbed people, *follow-back studies* and *high-risk studies*.

♦ **BOX 13.1 INCAPACITY AND IMPAIRMENT IN SCHIZOPHRENIA**

Type of Incapacity	Related Impairments
Cognitive	1. Disconnected thinking
	2. Illogical reasoning
	3. Peculiar patterns of concept and language formation
	4. Inaccurate or distorted perceptions of oneself and one's environment
Interpersonal	5. Poor social skills
	6. Withdrawal from people
Integrative	7. Blunted or inappropriate emotional reactions
	8. Inability to suppress anxiety-provoking thoughts
	9. Inadequate control over aggressive, antisocial, and self-destructive impulses

Information From Follow-Back Studies

In **follow-back studies** of psychopathology, early clinic or school records of disturbed adults are examined for childhood indications of unusual behavior that preceded their beginning to show any obvious disturbance. In one of the first studies of this kind, Barthell and Holmes (1968) counted the number of pictures of a group of adult schizophrenics that had appeared in their high school yearbooks when they were graduating seniors. There were significantly fewer pictures of these preschizophrenic adolescents in their yearbook than there were of a comparison group of their classmates, which can be taken to indicate a lack of involvement in peer-group activities on their part prior to their becoming overtly disturbed. Consistent with this finding, subsequent life history studies have revealed a relatively high incidence of social isolation, weak friendship patterns, and disengagement from peer-group activities among adolescents who later became schizophrenic (Lewine, Watt, Prentky, & Fryer, 1980; Silberman & Tassone, 1985).

Follow-back studies of what adult schizophrenics were like as children and adolescents have also documented an unusual frequency of negativistic and antisocial behavior prior to the onset of any clear-cut psychopathology. Especially when young people have been described as acting selfishly and aggressively not just toward strangers but toward their family and friends as well, the likelihood of their becoming schizophrenic is much greater than when they were described as cooperative, considerate, and well behaved (Watt & Lubensky, 1976).

Information From High-Risk Studies

As an alternative to the older follow-back studies, most contemporary developmental psychologists favor longitudinal research in which the antecedents of adult behavior are observed directly in children while they are growing up instead of inferred indirectly from old records. However, the relatively small percentage of young people who ever develop a particular disorder makes longitudinal research on psychopathology difficult to conduct. For example, because schizophrenia occurs in just 1–2 people per 100, a group of 1,000 chil-

Physical or emotional withdrawal from others may be an early sign of emerging schizophrenia in a disturbed adolescent.

dren would have to be assessed longitudinally, at enormous cost, to end up with a research sample of 10–20 who eventually became schizophrenic.

Efforts to address this problem led to the design of **high-risk studies**, in which the subjects are children and adolescents who have disturbed parents and who are consequently relatively likely to become disturbed themselves (Garmezy, 1974). Children with a schizophrenic parent are about 15 times more likely than children in general to develop schizophrenia as adolescents or adults, as we elaborate shortly. Being a high-risk group of subjects, then, such children greatly reduce the logistical problem of studying how and why schizophrenia develops: Only 50–100 rather than 1,000 subjects will have to be followed to end with 10 subjects whose life history data will say something about precursors of the disorder.

Risk research was pioneered by Mednick and Schulsinger, who began in the early 1960s to follow 207 normally functioning Danish children with a schizophrenic parent (Mednick,

Parnas, & Schulsinger, 1987). As the subjects in this and subsequent high-risk studies have grown into late adolescence and early adulthood, many more than the ordinary population rate have become schizophrenic or developed other serious psychological difficulties. In particular, adolescents with a schizophrenic parent are significantly more likely than adolescents without a family history of schizophrenia to show such cognitive and interpersonal impairments as disordered thinking and poor social skills (Dworkin et al., 1991; Weintraub, 1987).

Direct observations of such already schizophrenic and possibly preschizophrenic young people while they are growing up have largely confirmed what was suggested by follow-back studies about likely precursors of the disorder. Some of them do become increasingly withdrawn as they mature from childhood into adolescence (the schizoid pattern), whereas others become increasingly aggressive (the stormy pattern). Why some children destined to become schizophrenic grow more withdrawn and others more aggressive during adolescence is not yet known, however. Both the earlier follow-back findings and some of the more recent high-risk data suggest that there may be a gender difference in this regard, with preschizophrenic girls likely to become more reclusive as adolescents and preschizophrenic boys more likely to become aggressive (Kendler, Gruenberg, & Strauss, 1982; Wallace, 1984).

ORIGINS OF SCHIZOPHRENIA

The origins of schizophrenia are not yet fully understood. However, most clinicians and researchers believe that it is caused by an interacting combination of genetic and experiential influences. Genetic characteristics transmitted by parents to their children dispose certain people to develop this disorder, and stressful life experiences foster the emergence of the disorder in people who are constitutionally vulnerable to it. This interaction view is known as the **diathesis-stress theory** of schizophrenia.

Genetic Influences

It is a well-established fact that schizophrenia runs in families. The more closely two people are related, the more likely they are to be *concordant* for schizophrenia, which means that if one has the disorder the other will also. Figure 13.1 shows the average familial concordance for schizophrenia reported in a large number of systematic studies involving almost 10,000 relatives of schizophrenic persons. Compared to its prevalence of 1 to 2% in the general population, any close biological relationship to a schizophrenic person can be seen to increase substantially the likelihood of also being schizophrenic, up to just under 45% for identical twins.

These data point strongly to genetic influences in the transmission of schizophrenia. Family studies suggest further that a neurointegrative defect is the probable inherited characteristic that creates a constitutional vulnerability to becoming schizophrenic. Long before they become psychologically disturbed, children who are at risk for becoming schizophrenic by virtue of having a schizophrenic parent are more likely than other children to show neuromotor abnormalities, delayed perceptual-motor development, a heightened sensitivity to stimulation, and a low tolerance for stress (Asarnow, 1989; Marcus et al., 1987).

At the same time, however, familial concordance for schizophrenia can be interpreted from a psychosocial as well as a genetic perspective. Perhaps the children of schizophrenic parents are at risk for becoming schizophrenic because disturbed adults rear their children in

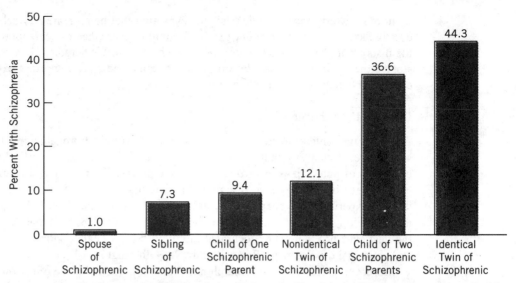

Figure 13.1   Frequency of schizophrenia in relatives of schizophrenics. [*Source:* Data summarized by McGue and Gottesman, 1989.]

a disorganized fashion, and two schizophrenic parents more so than one. Likewise, perhaps the elevated concordance for schizophrenia among siblings and twins results from their being reared in a more similar social-learning environment than people who are unrelated to each other.

Although the shared-environment explanation of familial concordance in schizophrenia seems reasonable, any strictly experiential explanation of the origins of this disorder has been contradicted by data from **cross-fostering** research. In the cross-fostering method, comparisons are made among children who are born to either normal or disturbed parents and then, because of adoption or foster-home placement, are reared by a second set of either normal or disturbed parents. This method distinguishes fairly clearly between hereditary and environmental influences. If heredity is more important, then children born to schizophrenic parents should have an elevated frequency of schizophrenia regardless of whether they are reared by their biological parents or by psychologically normal adoptive parents; if the environment is more important, children born to schizophrenic parents but reared by normal parents should not be any more likely than the general population to become schizophrenic.

Cross-fostering studies have produced two basic results: (1) among children placed for adoption early in life, those whose biological mothers have a history of schizophrenia are much more likely to develop schizophrenia themselves than adopted-away children born to psychologically healthy parents; and (2) adoptees who become schizophrenic are much more likely than nonschizophrenic adoptees to have schizophrenic persons among their biological relatives, but no more likely to have schizophrenic persons among their adoptive relatives (Kessler, 1980; Kety, 1988; Lowing, Mirsky, & Pereira, 1983). As an additional relevant finding, identical twins who are reared apart, in completely different environments, are found to be just as highly concordant for schizophrenia as identical twins reared in the same household (Farber, 1981, Chapter 6).

In other words, there is little basis for expecting that being reared by schizophrenic parents is likely by itself to account for the familial concordance of schizophrenia or to cause the disorder in the absence of a genetic disposition to it. Yet heredity does not tell the whole story either of how this disorder originates, because there are important experiential influences in the diathesis-stress interaction.

Experiential Influences

Although the familial incidence figures we have cited reflect probable genetic influences in schizophrenia, they also indicate that about 55% of the identical twins of schizophrenics and over 60% of people born to two schizophrenic parents do *not* become schizophrenic. This gap between being at genetic risk for schizophrenia and actually developing it means that the life experiences of people with similar or identical genes have a bearing on which of them develop schizophrenia. Some researchers have even suggested that the genetic data are the best evidence there is to document the importance of experiential influences on normal and abnormal development (Reiss, Plomin, & Hetherington, 1991).

Moreover, cross-fostering research has found that the incidence of serious psychopathology in adopted-away children born to schizophrenic mothers increases when there is psychological disturbance in their adoptive family as well. The highest rates of schizophrenia are associated with exposure to both genetic risk (that is, having a schizophrenic parent) and a disturbed child-rearing environment; conversely, being reared in a psychologically healthy adoptive family appears to be a protective factor that reduces the likelihood of at-risk children becoming schizophrenic (Asarnow, 1989).

With respect to the kinds of experiential influence that can contribute to schizophrenia, a high frequency of deviant patterns of interaction has been found in the families of young people who are schizophrenic or apparently becoming so. The most extensive research in this area has been conducted by Michael Goldstein and his colleagues, who for many years have been collecting information on adolescents and their parents who have been referred for psychological help. The main research method used in these studies has been direct observation of how family members communicate with each other while working on tasks together and discussing problems of mutual interest (Asarnow, Goldstein, & Ben-Meir, 1988; Doane, West, Goldstein, Rodnick & Jones, 1981; Goldstein, 1987a).

What Goldstein and his coworkers found was that parents whose adolescent children subsequently progressed toward a schizophrenic disorder interacted with their children in some distinctly deviant ways. They often expressed themselves in unclear or confusing language, frequently lost track of what they were saying, tended to avoid direct eye contact, and seldom seemed truly engaged in interpersonal exchange. Moreover, when they did convey some clear and direct message, it often carried a negative emotional tone of criticism, intrusiveness (presuming to know what the adolescent was thinking or feeling), or guilt induction ("You're causing our family a lot of trouble").

Social learning formulations of schizophrenia suggest that children who are reared by parents who communicate in such confusing and critical ways are susceptible to schizophrenia because they find it difficult to grasp a firm sense of reality, to feel certain about what they should think and how they should feel, and to relate comfortably to other people. Instead, influenced by disorganized and detached parents, they tend to learn schizophrenic ways of adapting to their world, including disordered thinking and interpersonal withdrawal (Goldstein, 1987b; Shapiro, 1981, Chapter 8).

♦ *Profile*

MICHAEL GOLDSTEIN

Michael Goldstein grew up in Brooklyn, New York, and then began moving West—first to attend the University of Iowa, where he received his bachelor's degree, then to Washington State University for a master's degree, and next to the University of Washington in Seattle, where he completed a doctorate in clinical psychology in 1957. Having decided to pursue an academic career, he took a position as an Instructor in the Psychology Department at the University of California at Los Angeles. He has remained at UCLA throughout his career, since 1971 as Professor of Psychology.

Dr. Goldstein had first become interested in psychology as a high school student, when he heard a series of lectures about personality and how it develops. As a college student interested in working with people, however, he was initially turned off by the biological focus of the psychology courses he took and decided to major in speech pathology. While working in the world-renowned speech therapy clinic at the University of Iowa, he was so impressed with the contributions of a consulting psychologist to understanding patient problems that his wish to be a psychologist was rekindled.

From the early days of his career, Dr. Goldstein focused his research on the origins of psychological disorders, with particular emphasis on the role of family relationship factors in the development of schizophrenia. He was a pioneer in designing laboratory methods of studying relationships between adolescents and their parents and in identifying how deviant patterns of communication in the family can increase the risk of psychological disorder in young people. Of particular importance has been his longitudinal work on how certain kinds of events in adolescence can lead to successful or unsuccessful adaptation in adulthood.

Along with the research contributions for which he is being recognized here, Dr. Goldstein also devoted himself over the years to clinical work with disturbed adolescents and their families and to the teaching of psychology to young people. For 36 years he has taught courses in abnormal psychology to undergraduate students and participated in training graduate students in clinical psychology. Perhaps above all, he is noted for his emphasis on the family as a system that can influence each of its members for better or worse.

The author of several books and more than 160 articles, Dr. Goldstein has been a consultant on schizophrenia to the World Health Organization and has received awards for his work from the American Family Therapy Association and the American Association for Marriage and Family Therapy. He is currently engaged in clinical research studies designed to extend his conceptions of family influences and the benefits of family treatment from schizophrenia to affective disorder as well.

Current findings suggest that these patterns of deviant family communication are not unique to the lives of preschizophrenic young people, but may instead constitute a general type of experiential stress associated with susceptibility to other disorders as well (Miklowitz et al., 1991; Thompson, Asarnow, Goldstein, & Miklowitz, 1990). Nevertheless, the data concerning schizophrenia are clear in two respects: First, the more deviant the parental communication is in a family, the more likely the children in that family are to develop a schizophrenic disorder; second, the more parents continue to communicate with a son or daughter in this fashion after schizophrenia develops, the more serious the disorder is likely to become and the longer it is likely to persist.

The Diathesis-Stress Theory

What has been learned so far about the origins of schizophrenia makes it unlikely that either genetic or experiential influences account entirely for this disorder. To recapitulate our discussion, genetic factors cannot be ruled out, especially in light of the cross-fostering data, but most people with a family history of schizophrenia do not become schizophrenic, including 85 to 90% of persons with a schizophrenic parent or sibling. Similarly with respect to social learning, the kinds of deviant family interactions that are associated with schizophrenia in some cases produce no disorder, or may produce different disorders in other cases. Among the subjects in Goldstein's studies, for example, all of the young people who showed evidence of becoming schizophrenic came from families with a high level of deviant communication and negative affective expression, but most of those whose families showed these patterns did not appear to be preschizophrenic.

These findings compel the conclusion that schizophrenia is most likely to result from some combination of genetic predisposing influences and psychosocial precipitating influences. This interaction view, which as we noted earlier is known as the *diathesis-stress* theory, is currently the most widely endorsed view of what causes schizophrenia (Gottesman, 1991; Tienari et al., 1987). This theory postulates that certain genetic and experiential influences are both necessary for schizophrenic disorder to develop, but that neither is sufficient by itself. The stronger the genetic predisposition (*diathesis*) to the disturbance, the more likely it is to arise in response to even minimal psychosocial stress. Persons with little or no predisposition to schizophrenia, on the other hand, are likely to cope adequately with family disorganization and environmental pressures, even when they are severe, and to develop other forms of psychopathology should they become disturbed.

OUTCOME

Generally speaking, the earlier in life a serious psychological disorder begins, the more likely it will be to persist. Among adults who are hospitalized for schizophrenia, as we have already mentioned, about 25% recover, 50% improve but suffer lingering symptoms or occasional relapses, and the remaining 25% make little or no progress and remain permanently hospitalized or, if discharged, socially incapacitated. When adolescents are admitted to a hospital with schizophrenia, they are about as likely as adults to recover (25%). However, fewer of them achieve partial recovery with a period of improvement (only 25%), and more of them require continuing residential care (50%) (Weiner, 1992, Chapter 3; Westermeyer, 1993).

Although these outcome data confirm how serious a disorder schizophrenia is, they also demonstrate that it is not a hopeless condition ending inevitably in institutionalization.

Three-quarters of the adults and half of the adolescents who are hospitalized for schizophrenia return home at least partially recovered. Schizophrenic persons who can be treated entirely on an outpatient basis, without ever having to be hospitalized, probably have even less unfavorable long-term prospects than this. There are as yet no reliable data concerning the long-term course and future adjustment of nonhospitalized schizophrenic adolescents or adults. However, there is evidence that schizophrenics who have never been hospitalized are less likely to require hospital care in the future than those who have already had at least one admission to an inpatient facility (Engelhardt, Rosen, Feldman, Engelhardt, & Cohen, 1982).

Numerous follow-up studies have identified several other circumstances that predict outcome in both adolescent and adult schizophrenics (Breier, Schreiber, Dyer, & Pickar, 1991; Grossman, Harrow, Goldberg, & Fichtner, 1991; Haas & Sweeney, 1992; McGlashan, 1988a; Werry & McClellan, 1992):

1. With respect to the age factor already noted, people who enter a hospital with schizophrenia at age 15–19 are twice as likely to remain continuously hospitalized as those who first receive inpatient care at age 20–29. The earlier in adolescence a young person becomes overtly schizophrenic, the more likely he or she is to suffer persistent or recurrent psychological impairment.

2. The more serious a schizophrenic disturbance has become, as indicated by how much the person's functioning is impaired, the less favorable the outcome is likely to be. Additionally, with respect to the symptoms that are present, schizophrenic adolescents who are initially confused, disorganized, and emotionally upset are generally more likely to improve or recover than those who appear calm and collected and show little affect. Calm, collected, and unemotional schizophrenic adolescents are likely to have developed a tolerance for the symptoms of their disorder that increases the risk of its persisting in a chronic form.

3. When schizophrenia begins suddenly in response to apparent precipitating events, the outcome is more favorable than when it emerges gradually in the absence of obvious and recent stressful circumstances.

4. The more adequately people have adjusted in school, work, and social situations before becoming schizophrenic, the better their prospects are for recovery. The outlook is especially favorable when a schizophrenic person has been able to maintain reasonably good social relationships and appropriate emotional reactions despite his or her difficulties in thinking. Many clinicians regard **premorbid course**, which consists of one's life history of adjustment prior to the onset of some disorder, as the most reliable of all available clues to a schizophrenic person's probable future course.

5. Family disturbance and disorganization, to the extent that they prevent parents from providing an understanding and supportive environment, contribute to an unfavorable outcome in schizophrenic disorder. In contrast, parental support in the home can be very helpful in preventing or minimizing relapse in recovering schizophrenics. Among schizophrenic persons discharged from hospital care, the quality of their family environment is a better predictor of their needing rehospitalization than how disturbed they are.

6. The more opportunities there are to implement an appropriate treatment program, and the more able and willing the schizophrenic person is to enter and complete this program, the better the long-term outcome for at least partial recovery. An early positive response to treatment is particularly likely to indicate a favorable **prognosis**, which is a technical term for expectations or predictions of how a matter is likely to turn out. Although needing to stay in the hospital for a long time does not eliminate possibilities for eventual improvement or recovery, an initial lack of treatment response frequently calls for a "guarded" prognosis, one in which a hopeful picture of the future cannot be painted with confidence.

TREATMENT

Schizophrenia is typically treated with a combination of psychotherapy and medication. Psychotherapy with schizophrenic adolescents focuses on helping them develop or reestablish effective ties with reality and with other people. To this end, the therapist seeks primarily to foster capacities for engaged, trusting, and mutual interpersonal relatedness and to correct the distorted impressions that schizophrenic people have of themselves, their environment, and the consequences of their actions (Karon & Vandenbos, 1981; Weiner, 1992, Chapter 3).

The goals of psychotherapy with schizophrenic adolescents can often be achieved in group or family sessions as well as in individual treatment. Discussions among a group of disturbed adolescents or between a schizophrenic person and members of his or her family provide real-life situations in which therapists can observe patients interacting with important people in their lives. These interactions can help to identify faulty reality testing and poor social skills in action and thereby facilitate working on ways to improve them (Anderson, Reiss, & Hogarty, 1986; Morris, 1985; Mosher & Keith, 1980).

Various antipsychotic drugs have proved effective in treating schizophrenic disturbance. These antipsychotic drugs are commonly referred to as **neuroleptics**, and they include substances marketed under such trade names as Clozaril, Haldol, Mellaril, Thorazine, Trilafon, and Stelazine. For schizophrenic patients who are anxious, agitated, or out of control, neuroleptic medications have a calming effect that reduces their disruptive symptoms and increases their accessibility to psychotherapy (see Box 13.2). Antipsychotic drugs are as effective with adolescents as with adults who are actively schizophrenic. In treating schizophrenic adolescents, however, care must be taken to avoid excessive reliance on medication to curb their disturbed behavior at the expense of adequate attention to their needs for improved social and cognitive skills. Most authorities recommend conservative use of drugs with younger people to promote progress in a multifaceted treatment program aimed at fostering social adjustment rather than to serve as the sole or primary agent for eliminating disorder (Campbell, 1985; Gadow, 1991; Green, 1991; Wyatt, 1991).

Clinicians usually prefer to work with disturbed adolescents outside of a hospital or other residential setting, if possible. Hospitalization is a disruptive event that removes young people from their normal home and school surroundings, threatens their self-esteem, and often fosters negative reactions in their parents, teachers, and friends. Yet residential care is sometimes necessary to provide adequate treatment for serious psychological disorders, and schizophrenia is the most likely of all adolescent disturbances to require hospitalization.

Whatever the particular characteristics of a hospital setting, schizophrenic adolescents benefit most when it provides a treatment program tailored to their needs. At their best, such programs are staffed by people who are trained and committed to working with disturbed adolescents; who administer multiple treatments including individual and group psychotherapy, family counseling, and drug therapy as necessary; and who provide a supportive, pro-

◆ BOX 13.2 BIOCHEMICAL PERSPECTIVES ON SCHIZOPHRENIA AND AFFECTIVE DISORDER

Some important biochemical theories about the nature and causes of schizophrenia and affective disorder revolve around the action of **neurotransmitters**, which are chemical substances in the brain that carry messages in the form of electrical impulses from one nerve cell to another. The kinds of medication that relieve symptoms of schizophrenia and affective disorder have been found to alter the amount of various neurotransmitters in the brain, which has led to theories concerning the role of excessive or insufficient neurotransmitter activity in causing these disorders.

With respect to schizophrenia, for example, considerable attention has been paid to the neurotransmitter *dopamine*, which is blocked or reduced in amount by neuroleptic medications, and the *dopamine hypothesis* attributes schizophrenia to an excess of this substance in the brain. With regard to affective disorder, the neurotransmitter *serotonin* has been identified as a general regulator of neurochemical systems in the brain, and the *serotonin hypothesis* proposes that an insufficient amount of this substance makes people susceptible to the extreme and fluctuating moods that characterize affective disorder. Consistent with this hypothesis, many antidepressant medications produce an increase in serotonin levels.

Although logical and compelling, neither the dopamine hypothesis nor the serotonin hypothesis has been documented in clinical studies, probably because both hypotheses are oversimplified. The biochemistry of the brain is extremely complex, and there are a large number of neurotransmitters other than these two that appear to interact with each other and influence each other's effects. As a consequence, not all schizophrenics show excessive dopamine, not all people with affective disorder show insufficient serotonin, and some medications produce symptomatic improvement in these conditions without altering the amounts of these neurotransmitters.

Moreover, the measured level of these substances has not proved helpful in predicting the course of disturbance among patients or how they will respond to treatment. Most authorities concur that no one type of chemical imbalance common to either of these conditions has yet been identified and that no known biological marker is as yet adequate for diagnosing them. Further biological research on the origins of these conditions will have to address these issues and also determine whether any chemical imbalances that are found constitute a vulnerability to disorder that preceded onset of the condition or are instead a consequence or manifestation of the disorder.

Sources: Davis, Kahn, Ko, and Davison (1991); Delgado, Price, Henninger, and Charney (1992); Szymanski, Kane, and Liberman (1991).

tective, and encouraging environment around the clock. Provision must also be made in such programs for adolescents to continue their education and to participate in social and recreational activities in order to promote a smooth return to their school and peer-group environments after discharge (Hendren & Berlin, 1991; Lyman, Prentice-Dunn, & Gabel, 1989; Siegel, Radojevic, & Whitmont, 1992).

AFFECTIVE DISORDER

Most people know moments of gloom and discouragement at times when disappointment crosses their path. Losing a loved one or good friend, failing to achieve a desired goal, and becoming physically ill or incapacitated are among common events that leave people feeling sad and subdued. This response to tribulation is generally described as "feeling depressed" or having depressive symptoms. Depressive symptoms ordinarily fade in a few days' or

Disappointment causes most people to experience moments of depression from time to time.

weeks' time, as saddened and subdued people gradually accommodate to the occasion of their distress and reach out for new relationships and revised aspirations.

When depressive symptoms persist for several weeks or longer and interfere with everyday activities, they become a pathological condition known as **unipolar affective disorder**. In some cases, the persistent or recurrent episodes of **depression** that mark this condition alternate with episodes of **mania**, which is an exaggerated degree of elation, optimism, enthusiasm, and self-confidence persisting out of proportion to actual events that could account for a person's feeling so happy. Disturbed people who experience both depressive and manic episodes have a condition called **bipolar affective disorder**; an older and still frequently heard term for this condition is **manic-depressive disorder** (Paykell, 1992, Part 1). In addition to unipolar disorder and bipolar disorder, two other standard terms for describing varieties of affective disorder are **dysthymia**, which refers to a disposition to recurrent but mild episodes of depression, and **cyclothymia**, which refers to a disposition to alternating episodes of depression and mania in mild forms.

Although affective disorders do not occur nearly as often as the common experience of depressive symptoms, they are nevertheless a prominent pattern of psychopathology, especially in the unipolar form. During any 1-month period, 5.5% of adults in the United States are likely to demonstrate significant depression, and 9.1% will experience an episode of depressive disorder sometime during their lives. For manic episodes, the 1-month prevalence among persons aged 18 and above in the United States is 0.4%, and the lifetime frequency is 0.8% (Smith & Weissman, 1992; Weissman, Bruce, Leaf, Floria, & Holzer, 1991).

Numerous studies have assessed the frequency of depressive symptoms in adolescents using a variety of questionnaires and self-report measures. Because of the many different methods used in these studies, the results have ranged from 20 to 50% of high school students who report a substantial number of depressive symptoms; on the average, 35% of adolescents report having experienced depressed mood in the previous 6 months (Ehrenberg, Cox, & Koopman, 1990; Petersen et al., 1993; Roberts, Andrews, Lewinsohn, & Hops, 1990). Such self-reports seldom provide a reliable basis for estimating the frequency of depressive disorder among young people, however. When depressive disorder has been carefully assessed with clinical methods in community samples of high school students, the results show just about the same frequency of depressive disorder as is found in adults. At any one point in time, 7 to 8% of high school students are significantly depressed and about 9%, despite their youth, have already experienced an episode of depressive disorder during their lifetime (Kashani et al., 1987; Petersen et al., 1993; Whitaker et al., 1990).

The prevalence of mania has not yet been examined systematically in adolescents. Nevertheless, the importance of bipolar affective disorder as a developmental problem for young people has been demonstrated by evidence that this condition frequently begins during the adolescent years. Survey data indicate that 50% of adults with bipolar affective disorder experienced the first onset of their disturbance before they turned age 20 (Burke et al., 1990). Similarly, among adults with depressive disorders at some point in their lives, 25% first became depressed before age 18, and 50% before age 25 (Sorenson, Rutter, & Anashensel, 1991). Hence, like schizophrenia, affective disorder very often has its first detectable beginnings during the adolescent years.

Adolescence is also a time when gender differences begin to appear in the frequency with which depression occurs. Prior to puberty, boys and girls are equally likely to display features of depression and mania. During adolescence the gender distribution of mania remains about even, but depression becomes much more common in females than in males. High school girls in general report significantly more numerous depressive symptoms than boys (Allgood-Merten, Lewinsohn, & Hops, 1990; Petersen et al., 1993). Among those young people who develop an affective disorder, bipolar disturbance is about equally frequent in boys and girls, but unipolar disorder is more frequent in the girls (Angold 1988; Gillberg, Wahlstrom, Forsman, Hellgren, & Gillberg, 1986).

This gender difference in susceptibility to depression has not yet been explained adequately. Some researchers have suggested that it derives from depressing experiences that females encounter in relation to elements of their traditional gender role in our society, especially low social status, discrimination in achievement-related situations, and lack of choice in planning their lives (Chevron, Quinlan, & Blatt, 1978; Weissman & Klerman, 1979). Others have attributed the vulnerability of girls to becoming depressed to their growing up amid messages from their culture and their family that proper feminine behavior consists of silencing themselves, that is, keeping their feelings to themselves, playing a subordinate role, and taking responsibility for problems without complaining (Jack, 1991).

As one more possibility, Gore et al. (1993) proposed that the combination of the typical challenges adolescents face in resolving interpersonal issues (which we described in Chapter 8) with the typically greater investment of girls than boys in interpersonal matters (which we described in Chapter 10) makes girls more vulnerable to the disappointments that lead people to feel depressed.

These possibilities merit consideration in light of our earlier discussions of gender differences in identity formation, underachievement, delinquent behavior, and suicidal behavior (see Chapters 10, 11, and 12). With respect to identity formation, research has suggested that males and females do begin in late childhood and early adolescence to form a gender-role identity involving different ways of resolving conflict. Males, according to these findings, start preferring to resolve conflict through external channels of expression, which is known as **acting out**; females, by contrast, develop a preference for dealing with conflict internally, which is called **acting in**. Such differences in identity formation might contribute to the higher likelihood of males engaging in delinquent behavior and of females becoming depressed, and this might also be one of those gender differences that could be expected to diminish as societal attitudes toward gender roles change.

For both adolescents and adults, there is evidence to indicate that males are more inclined than females to respond to interpersonal conflict by blaming or attacking someone else, whereas females are more likely to respond by directing aggressive thoughts or actions toward themselves (Cramer, 1988; Cramer & Carter, 1978). Researchers have also found that depression in adolescence is more likely to be associated with disobedience and misbehavior in boys than in girls, whereas in girls depression is more likely than in boys to be associated with such inward-focused symptoms as feeling sad and unworthy (Gjerde, Block, & Block, 1988; Smucker, Craighead, Craighead, & Green, 1986).

An especially interesting study in this regard was conducted by Block, Gjerde, and Block (1991), who followed 46 girls and 42 boys from age 3 to age 18 and assessed them on seven different occasions with a battery of personality and cognitive tests. Those youngsters who at age 18 were showing depressive tendencies had begun as early as age 7 to show gender differences: the boys who subsequently demonstrated depression were relatively aggressive, self-aggrandizing, and undercontrolled when they were assessed at ages 7, 11, and 14; the subsequently depressed girls were relatively overconforming, self-blaming, and overcontrolled from age 7 on. Generally speaking, then, girls who are destined to become depressed in late adolescence are as children more likely than boys to be passive, to devalue themselves, and to keep unhappiness inside, whereas predepressed boys are more likely than girls to be active, to think well of themselves, and to blame others for their problems. These gender differences are reminiscent of the tendencies we noted in Chapter 10 for girls to attribute success to fortunate external circumstances and failure to their own shortcomings, whereas boys tend to attribute success to their ability and hard work and failure to bad luck.

CHARACTERISTICS OF AFFECTIVE DISORDER

The observable characteristics of depression and mania derive from maladaptive changes in a person's mood, attitudes, energy level, and physical status; these maladaptive changes define the nature of **affective disorder** (Costello, 1993; Weiner, 1992, Chapter 4). With respect to deviant mood, which is the predominant feature of this disorder, pathologically depressed individuals become persistently sad and tearful, disinterested in people and activities they previously enjoyed, and unable to take pleasure in what should be happy events. Mania, by contrast, is characterized by persistent cheerfulness, enormous enthusiasm, and excessive pleasure that other people experience as inappropriate and overly intense and that often lead to painful consequences not anticipated by the manic individual.

In their *attitudes*, people with affective disorder tend to view themselves, the world, and their future in either very negative or very positive terms. Those who are depressed regard themselves as inadequate and unworthy, the world as rotten and uncaring, and the future as gloomy and beyond their capacity to influence. Those who are manic have an inflated sense of their own worth and unrealistically high expectations. In sharp contrast to depressed people, manic individuals anticipate being admired by anyone they meet and succeeding in everything they do. Whereas the low self-esteem, hopelessness, and helplessness that mark depression discourage people from trying to do anything, the grandiosity and optimism that accompany mania fuel ambitious plans and determined but frequently poorly planned efforts to carry them out.

Mental and physical *energy level* is depleted by depressive episodes, which leave people lethargic and unable to concentrate. Like a windup toy that is running down, depressed individuals move slowly, talk slowly, and think slowly. This phenomenon, known as **psychomotor retardation**, makes it difficult for depressed people to get their bodies to move and their minds to function. Because of their low energy level, individuals who are depressed are likely to perform poorly on cognitive and motor tasks that require sustained attention and effort even though their basic skills in these areas have not been impaired.

Manic individuals, by contrast, appear to have vast stores of energy at their disposal, even more than they can harness effectively. Their speech pours out rapidly, sometimes with words stumbling over each other more quickly than they can be pronounced clearly (known as **pressure of speech**), and their thoughts flow in such quick succession that new ideas take over before previous ones have been brought to closure (known as **flight of ideas**). People who are manic move quickly, but with haste rather than deliberate speed, and they take off in so many directions at once that they often become disorganized and end up wasting more effort than they use constructively.

Regarding their *physical status*, people with an affective disorder often show disturbed patterns of sleeping and eating. Those who are depressed tend to fall asleep slowly, sleep fitfully, and awaken early, before they are rested. Their appetite may become much smaller or larger than usual, causing them to lose or gain a great deal of weight. They also tend to feel poor physically, to worry excessively about their health and bodily functions, and to experience an unusual number of aches, pains, and other somatic complaints for which there is no clear organic basis.

People in manic episodes present a contrasting picture of robust good health. They sleep soundly, eat heartily but not too much, regard themselves as being in great shape, and rarely complain of any physical symptom—even when they become seriously ill and should be worried enough to seek medical care.

Although these various manifestations of affective disorder have been identified mainly in studies of adults, each of the four dimensions of depression and mania has been demonstrated to characterize young people as well. Considerable evidence indicates that the disturbances in mood, attitudes, energy level, and physical status associated with affective disorder can be identified and measured as reliably in adolescents as in adults (Carey, Finch, &

Carey, 1991; Kovacs, 1989; McCauley, Carlson, & Calderon, 1991; McCauley, Mitchell, Burke, & Moss, 1988; Ryan et al., 1987). Clinicians and researchers have accordingly come to agree that only minor modifications of the criteria used with adults are necessary to identify these conditions in young people (Clark & Mokros, 1993; Goodyer, 1992; Reynolds, 1992; Strober, McCracken, & Hanna, 1989).

At the same time, the developmental concerns of young people often color affective disorder in unique ways, especially during depressive episodes. Because adolescents are struggling to establish their adequacy and self-reliance, they are often reluctant to admit any negative attitudes toward themselves or any doubts about being a competent person. This makes them less likely than adults to display the gloom, self-criticism, and feelings of helplessness and hopelessness that commonly characterize depression.

Instead, adolescents who become depressed often work hard to ward off feeling sad or discouraged. As observed in numerous clinical reports, they sometimes try to keep busy to avoid feeling depressed, which leads to their becoming restless, constantly in need of stimulation, and easily bored; sometimes depressed adolescents withdraw from social and achievement-related situations, which minimizes possible experiences of rejection or failure but results in their becoming reclusive and underachieving; and sometimes they engage in disruptive or delinquent behavior that keeps them busy and stimulated and may even bolster their self-esteem, but also compounds their adjustment difficulties (Carlson & Kashani, 1988; Kendall et al., 1989; Strober et al., 1989; Weiner, 1992, Chapter 4). The expression of underlying depression through problem behavior is consistent with our description in Chapter 11 of how delinquent acts can occur as a consequence of unresolved psychological conflict.

As adolescents mature, they become increasingly capable of thinking about themselves critically and sharing self-doubts with other people. They accordingly become more likely to resemble adults in the way that they manifest depressive episodes. In some cases, however, older adolescents may still express depression indirectly, sometimes through such maladaptive behavior as suicide attempts and drug abuse. The more depressed young people become, the more likely they are to think about or attempt suicide (Kovacs, Goldston, & Gatsonis, 1993; Petersen et al., 1993; Ryan et al., 1987; Sheras, 1992), and adolescents with depressive disorder are three to four times more likely than their nondepressed peers to abuse alcohol and other addictive substances (Fleming & Offord, 1990; Rohde, Lewinsohn, & Seeley, 1991; Ryan, 1989).

CAUSES OF AFFECTIVE DISORDER

Like schizophrenia, affective disorder most probably results from the combined influence of genetic dispositions (*diathesis*) and unpleasant life experiences (*stress*). The relative influence of these two causes varies with the specific nature of the affective disorder.

Genetic Dispositions

Research data on familial patterns of affective disorder parallel the findings in schizophrenia. Identical twins show about a 65% concordance for affective disorder in various studies, compared to just a 14% concordance among nonidentical twins (Nurnberger & Gershon, 1992; Wesner & Winokur, 1990). The concordance rate for identical twins remains high even when they are reared apart and therefore have relatively little experience in common (Farber, 1981, Chapters 6 and 8).

Parents and siblings are just about as concordant for affective disorder as nonidentical twins, compared to whom they have similar genetic relatedness but usually much less experience in common. Compared to the approximate 10% lifetime risk for an episode of bipolar disorder or unipolar depressive disorder in the general population and the 65% risk among identical twins, the risk among other first-degree relatives of persons with an affective disorder falls in the 10 to 20% range (Plomin, 1989; Ryan, 1989). Finally, children whose mothers have an affective disorder and are placed for adoption soon after birth are much more likely to become affectively disordered than adopted-away offspring of nondisturbed mothers; similarly, the biological parents of individuals who develop affective disorder are more likely to be affectively disordered themselves than either the biological or adoptive parents of normal children, regardless of whether the disordered offspring are reared by their biological parents or in an adoptive home (Cadoret, 1978; Wender et al., 1986).

As in schizophrenia, affective disorder runs in families in ways that cannot be explained solely on the basis of shared experience or other psychosocial influences. Available evidence also indicates that the probable genetic influences in affective disorder operate separately from those that contribute to schizophrenia. The relatives of schizophrenic persons do not show any elevated frequency of affective disorder, and the relatives of people with affective disorder are no more likely to become schizophrenic than people in general (Nurnberger & Gershon, 1992; Strober et al., 1989).

Two other interesting features of familial concordance in affective disorder have been discovered. First, the genetic vulnerability to affective disorder is greater among relatives of persons with the bipolar than the unipolar form of the disorder. Numerous researchers have reported that parents with a bipolar condition are more likely to transmit a disposition to affective disorder to their offspring than parents with a unipolar condition (Andreasen et al., 1987; Kutcher & Marton, 1991). Such findings suggest that bipolar disorder has a stronger hereditary component than unipolar affective disorder, which is less heritable and more likely to be influenced by experiential factors.

Second, familial incidence also relates to the age at which affective disorders first appear and whether they recur. Among people who become significantly depressed, those with depressed parents are likely to experience their first episode of depression at an earlier age than those whose parents have no history of depression. Among depressed offspring of depressed parents, moreover, those whose parents had their first depressive episode before age 20 are eight times more likely to have become depressed as adolescents themselves than those whose parents had an adult onset of the condition (Rutter et al., 1990; Weissman et al., 1987). As for bipolar disorders, the risk of having this condition themselves is four times greater among the parents and siblings of bipolar adolescents than among the first-degree relatives of persons who first become bipolar as adults (Strober, Hanna, & McCracken, 1989). Hence, there is reason to believe that affective disorder appearing during the developmental years involves a greater genetic liability than affective disorder with adult onset.

Genetic influences aside, the familial concordance data indicate that 35% of the identical twins of persons with affective disorder and 85% of the nonidentical twins and other first-degree relatives of depressed and bipolar patients avoid becoming affectively disturbed. Hence, life experiences also determine whether people develop this disorder, regardless of how strongly they may be genetically predisposed to it. Studies of depressed adolescents and adults confirm that they are more likely than nondepressed individuals to have experienced stressful events in the recent past (Goodyer, 1992; Rubin, Rubenstein, Stechler, & Heeren, 1992; Shrout et al., 1989; Stiffman, Cheuh, & Earls, 1992).

Stressful Life Events

The kind of stressful event that most often precipitates a depressive disorder is the experience of loss. As we have already noted, depression in response to loss is especially likely to occur when someone who is loved dies, moves away, or breaks off a relationship. Other experiences of loss that commonly contribute to depressive reactions include having treasured possessions damaged or stolen, having some ambition thwarted, and having one's bodily functions disrupted by illness, physical disability, disfigurement, or even normal biological changes. Among adolescents, for example, being spurned by a boyfriend or girlfriend, losing out in some competition, or having to wear braces on their teeth can deprive young people, respectively, of a valued personal relationship, a highly desired success, or a gratifying sense of having a well-formed body and making an attractive appearance.

As most of us know from our own experience, however, people differ in the types of loss experience that are likely to cause them to become depressed. Individuals who place more importance on how well they are getting along socially than on how much they are able to achieve are distressed more by interpersonal losses or disappointments than by lack of accomplishment, for example; people who are primarily achievement oriented rather than socially oriented are more likely to become upset in relation to unsuccessful striving than because of interpersonal difficulties (Hammen, Ellicott, Gitlin, & Jamison, 1989). Interestingly, this relationship between personality orientation and the types of events that influence symptom formation is found in people with unipolar but not bipolar affective disorder (Hammen et al., 1989; Hammen, 1991). This finding is consistent with the likely possibility mentioned earlier that unipolar affective disorder is less genetically influenced and more experientially determined than bipolar disorder.

People differ not only with respect to the types of loss experiences that trouble them most, but also in how much loss they can tolerate. What seem to be equivalent losses may cause one person to become deeply depressed whereas another person takes them in stride without becoming unduly upset. Such individual differences in sensitivity to loss appear determined largely by two kinds of developmental events, the experience of *parental deprivation* and the emergence of a *negative attributional personality style*.

Parental deprivation consists of diminished opportunity that young people have for contact with one or both of their parents as a result of death, separation, or rejection. As we discussed in Chapter 7, the psychological impact of an absent or disinterested parent varies considerably in relation to numerous aspects of an individual family situation. Generally speaking, however, parental deprivation during the developmental years is a painful loss experience that interferes with developing a sense of security and appears to heighten a young person's subsequent sensitivity to loss, criticism, and disappointment; similarly, the less supportive their parents are, the more likely adolescents are to develop depressive symptoms (Armsden, McCauley, Greenberg, & Burke, 1990; Barrera & Garrison-Jones, 1992; Blatt & Homann, 1992; Roy, 1988; Tennant, 1988).

A **negative attributional personality** style consists of a tendency to attribute bad experiences to shortcomings within oneself that are relatively permanent. The authoritarian child-rearing practices we described in Chapter 7 appear particularly likely to cause young people to feel helpless and unworthy when things go wrong in their lives and to blame themselves for their problems. Generally speaking, the more inclined people are to this kind of self-blaming negative attributional style, the more prone they are to becoming depressed in the face of frustrating or disappointing circumstances (Alloy, Lipman, & Abramson, 1992; Gottlib, 1992; Haaga, Dyck, & Ernst, 1991; Hammen, 1990; Koestner, Zuroff, & Powers, 1991).

Nevertheless, just as most people with depressed family members do *not* develop major depressive disorder themselves, most depressed people have *not* experienced early loss events, and many have not tended to think badly of themselves prior to becoming depressed. Hence, even though both genetic and experiential influences apparently contribute to a depressive diathesis, affective disorder probably originates in the same fashion as schizophrenia: Complex patterns of interaction link heredity, early experience, and current stress into a chain of events that causes the condition to occur.

Experiential factors that dispose people to bipolar affective disorder and precipitate episodes of mania have not yet been studied as extensively as those associated with unipolar depression. Nevertheless, there is good reason to believe that stressful experiences of loss precipitate manic as well as depressive reactions and that parental deprivation and a negative attributional style are disposing factors in both bipolar and unipolar forms of affective disorder. One reasonable hypothesis suggests that stressful experiences of loss are involved in all forms of affective disorder and that mania appears largely as an effort to ward off depression subsequent to loss. From this perspective, manic-depressive individuals will slip into depression at times when they are unable to muster or sustain manic behavior patterns (Davenport & Adland, 1988; Post et al., 1989).

Two lines of evidence are consistent with such a possibility. First, there are clinical reports of manic attacks precipitated by object loss and of manic patients who have suffered childhood experiences of loss similar to those that increase the likelihood of subsequent depressive episodes (Aleksandrowicz, 1980; Carpenter & Stephens, 1980). Second, follow-up studies indicate that only 10 to 20% of people with a major depressive disorder also develop episodes of mania, whereas manic individuals almost always have a history of periodic depressive episodes as well (Coryell & Winokur, 1992; Strober & Carlson, 1982).

OUTCOME AND TREATMENT

Most people recover from episodes of depression and mania, and many show **spontaneous remission,** which involves improvement even without treatment. On the other hand, affective disorder often occurs as a lifetime susceptibility to recurring episodes of disorder. Among adults who are hospitalized with depression, approximately 50% are likely to recover within 1 year after the onset of their symptoms and another 25 to 30% within the second year. This leaves about 20 to 25% who are found to show persistent symptoms up to 5 years after they first became disturbed, and clinical studies indicate further that almost half of adults who experience a first episode of depression can be expected to have a second episode at some point (Coryell, Endicott, & Keller, 1990; Keitner, Ryan, Miller, & Norman, 1992; Lewinsohn, Zeiss, & Duncan, 1989). The outlook in mania is a little less favorable, with 35% of adults discharged from hospital care following a manic episode showing poor outcome over the next 2 years (Harrow, Goldberg, Grossman, & Meltzer, 1990).

Young people who develop an affective disorder are especially prone to recurrent difficulties. Most adolescents will recover from an initial episode of depression for which they are referred for treatment, but two-thirds can be expected to become depressed again while they are still in their teens, and 20% are likely to give evidence of bipolar disorder before they reach adulthood (Kovacs, 1989). Among nonpatient adolescents, as well, tendencies to experience maladaptive mood states show considerable continuity from adolescence to adulthood. Follow-up studies of high school students who reported depressive symptoms showed that they were more likely than the general population also to report such symptoms as young adults in their mid-20s (Kandel & Davies, 1986).

In a particularly informative study by Fleming, Boyle, and Offord (1993), 552 13–16-year-olds who were identified in a community survey as having depressive disorder were followed up 4 years later. At age 17–20, 25% of these young people still demonstrated a depressed condition, 50% had dropped out of school, and almost one-third had been in trouble with the police.

Even so, the outlook in affective disorder is more favorable than in schizophrenia. In one long-term study involving several hundred hospitalized patients, 50% of those with manic episodes and 61% of those with depressive episodes subsequently adjusted well when they returned to their community, compared to only 20% of those with schizophrenia. Poor long-term adjustment was found in 54% of these schizophrenics but in only 21% of the manic and 30% of the depressed patients (Tsuang, Woolson, & Fleming, 1979).

With respect to adolescents, even though symptoms of depression may often persist or recur, recovery from depressive episodes severe enough to require hospitalization is very likely to occur. In one study of 58 adolescents hospitalized for depression, 90% were recovered 2 years after their admission (Strober, Lampert, Schmidt, & Morrell, 1993). Ample time and treatment must be allowed for such recovery from severe depression to occur, however. Only 30% of the young people in this study had fully recovered within the first 5 months of their hospital admission, and half of those who recovered required more than 7 months to do so.

As in schizophrenia, however, the outcome of affective disorder becomes less favorable when it begins early and is so incapacitating as to require hospital care. Generally speaking, the younger adolescents are when they have a first episode, the more disturbed they are likely to be and the greater their likelihood of relapse following recovery; the older they are at the time of an initial manic or depressive episode and the less incapacitating their disorder, the better their prospects are for recovery and subsequent good adjustment without relapse.

Prospects for avoiding relapse are also improved when depressed adolescents return from the hospital to a home in which there is a reasonably calm and stable, as opposed to disruptive and intense, emotional climate. Finally, adolescents hospitalized with a unipolar depressive disorder have better prospects for full recovery than those with severe bipolar disorder, many of whom are likely to suffer continuing susceptibility to further episodes (Asarnow, Goldstein, Tompson, & Guthrie, 1993; Belsher & Costello, 1988; McGlashan, 1988b).

Even when spontaneous remission can be expected—which is the case for most affectively disturbed adolescents who do not have to be hospitalized—appropriate treatment can help to shorten episodes of depression or mania. The main ingredients of this treatment are certain approaches in psychotherapy and specific kinds of medication.

Psychotherapy with affectively disordered adolescents focuses on (1) helping them come to grips effectively with the circumstances that are causing them to experience a sense of loss, (2) helping them recognize maladaptive ways in which they may be attempting to ward off depressing thoughts or feelings, and (3) helping them improve their social competence and problem-solving skills (Nezu, Nezu, & Perri, 1989; Oster & Caro, 1990; Paykel, 1992, Part 3; Weiner, 1992, Chapter 4). In addition, through conversations with parents, teachers, and other significant adults in young people's lives, psychotherapists can sometimes bring about changes in how adolescents are being treated at home, in school, and in the community. To the extent that such changes diminish disappointments and frustrations, they can help affectively disturbed youngsters feel better and recover more quickly.

Various antidepressant medications are also beneficial in treating adults with depressive disorder. Approximately 70% of depressed patients improve in response to medication, and, on the average, depressed patients treated solely with appropriate drugs show the same kinds of improvements in their moods and attitudes as patients treated with various forms of psychotherapy (Paykel, 1992, Part 3; Robinson, Berman, & Niemeyer, 1990). With respect to maintaining symptomatic improvement and preventing relapse, moreover, combining medication with psychotherapy often proves more effective than using either alone (Hollon, Spoden, & Chastek, 1986; Simons, Murphy, Levine, & Wetzel, 1986).

Among numerous **antidepressants** used for this purpose, some commonly prescribed substances are sold under the trade names of Elavil, Nardil, Prozac, Tofranil, Wellbutrin, and Zoloft. Opinion is divided concerning the utility of antidepressant medications in young people, however. Available evidence so far has not demonstrated the effectiveness of drugs in treating adolescent depression, and some clinicians recommend deferring their use until other treatment methods have been tried without success (Ambrosini, Bianchi, Rabinovich, & Elia, 1993; Pliszka, 1991; Ryan & Puig-Antich, 1987). Other clinicians encourage early use of drugs in treatment, however, despite uncertainty about their effects, as a way of minimizing acute distress and thereby helping adolescents become involved in other aspects of a treatment program. Although they do not eliminate depression, these drugs may lead to improved behavior that leads other people to respond more positively to the young person (Green, 1991; Kaminer, Seifer, & Mastrian, 1992; Rancurello, 1986).

For adolescents who are experiencing episodes of mania, treatment is often facilitated by a drug called Lithium. Lithium affects people by stabilizing their moods, which helps to curb manic behavior, and it is just as effective in treating adolescents as adults who have a bipolar affective disorder. As in the case of successful drug treatment of depression, however, Lithium treatment of mania works best in sustaining improvement and avoiding relapse when it is combined with adequate psychological intervention (Strober, Morrell, Lampert, & Burroughs, 1990).

EATING DISORDERS: OBESITY, ANOREXIA NERVOSA, AND BULIMIA

Schizophrenia and affective disorders are primarily psychological disturbances. Even though they may be accompanied by certain biochemical and neurophysiological abnormalities, and even though they can cause such biological problems as energy depletion and insomnia, these disorders consist chiefly of deviant patterns of cognitive and emotional expression. Certain other conditions that consist chiefly of biological abnormalities are substantially influenced by psychological concerns that contribute to their onset and influence the course that they take. These conditions are frequently referred to as **psychosomatic** or **psychophysiological disorders**.

Psychosomatic disorders affect many different systems of the body and lead to conditions that most people have had occasion to observe in a friend or relative. These include pathological involvement of the respiratory system in *asthma*; involvement of the gastrointestinal system in *stomach ulcers* or *ulcerative colitis*; involvement of the cardiovascular system in *hypertension* (high blood pressure); and involvement of the musculoskeletal system in *tics* or *tension headaches*. In each of these psychophysiological conditions, worries and mood states of the individual play a role in causing bodily dysfunctions to begin and to pass through various cycles of recovery and relapse.

Young people as well as adults are susceptible to a broad range of psychosomatic disorders that interfere with their leading normal lives, physically and psychosocially (Kager, Arndt, & Kenny, 1992; Werry, 1986). Extended discussion of these disorders would be outside the focus of this book. However, to illustrate the impact that psychosomatic disorders can have on the transition from childhood to adulthood, we will look at three disorders of eating that often bring adolescents to the joint attention of physicians and mental health specialists: *obesity*, *anorexia nervosa*, and *bulimia*.

Like schizophrenia and affective disorders, these eating disorders constitute a type of psychopathology that often begins during the teenage years and has special significance for adolescent development. In these conditions, however, deviant patterns of behavior (eating activity) define the chief feature of the disorder, and the effects of the condition are apparent not only in how people think and feel, but also in how they look and how their bodies function.

THE NATURE AND CONSEQUENCES OF BEING OBESE

Obesity is a condition of abnormal fatness or overweight that is defined in one of two ways: either by weighing 20% or more than is normal for a person's age, height, and gender, or by having a percentage of body fat greater than 25% for males or 30% for females. Obesity is estimated to occur in 10 to 25% of adolescents in the United States, which makes it a very common problem. And it is a serious problem, because obesity can undermine a person's physical health and psychological well-being. Young people who are markedly overweight are more susceptible as adults to diabetes, heart disease, high blood pressure, and various other illnesses than are adolescents of average weight (Arden, 1992; Boeck, 1992; Perri, Nezu, & Viegener, 1992, Chapter 1).

Obesity by itself can be a physically handicapping condition because it prevents people from moving about easily and participating in many kinds of activities. Even such everyday events as climbing a flight of stairs, getting into a seat in a movie theater or on a bus, or passing through a narrow doorway can be painfully challenging to obese people.

There is a story that William Howard Taft, while President of the United States and weighing well over 300 pounds, had to endure the humiliation of requiring several aides to pull him out of the White House bathtub, in which he had become stuck. As an example closer to adolescence, consider the physical and psychological plight of this teenager:

J——, an obese 13-year-old boy, was excluded from his school, despite being well-behaved and doing adequate academic work, because he was officially labeled a "fire hazard." School officials, in consultation with the fire department, had decided that he took up so much space in the stairway and moved so slowly that he constituted a "dangerous obstacle" to rapid evacuation of the school in case of fire.

Being too fat to participate comfortably in peer-group activities can undermine an adolescent's sense of well-being.

In addition to suffering adult assaults on their self-esteem (How must it feel to be labeled a "dangerous obstacle"?), obese adolescents have to contend with a peer-group environment that places special value on having a sound and attractive body. Being enormously fat—not just on the plump side, which is a normal variation, but obese, which is an illness—often subjects adolescents to a steady stream of ridicule and rejection from their classmates. Obese adolescents are at risk for being avoided and disliked by their peers and excluded from peer-group activities, especially dating. Together with their problems in peer relationships, excessively fat young people may face problems at home with parents or siblings who regard their obesity as an embarrassment to the family and constantly harp on their unattractive appearance. Although some obese young people find ways of weathering this psychological storm successfully, others are found to react with understandable feelings of inadequacy, oversensitivity to criticism, withdrawal from social interactions, and distaste for their own bodies (Arden, 1992; Foreyt & Cousins, 1987; Perri et al., 1992, Chapter 1).

On the other hand, the potential psychological hazards of being obese are neither uniform nor inevitable. In the first place, there are several moderating variables that affect how obese young people feel about themselves and are regarded by their peers. Generally speaking, the less obese they are, the more they are able to accomplish, and the more attractive their appearance is despite their being markedly overweight, the less likely they are to suffer serious social or psychological consequences. Facial attractiveness has been found to be especially important in this regard (Jarvie, Lahey, Graziano, & Framer, 1983).

Second, some research with early adolescents has suggested that, even at this age of especially heightened concern about bodily development, appearance by itself is only a small factor in determining popularity. When they observed social behavior among 12- and 13-year-olds, Baum and Forehand (1984) found that those who were moderately or extremely overweight were more likely than their normal-weight peers to get involved in teasing, fighting, cheating, and other negative interactions, on both the giving and receiving ends. Nevertheless, when the subjects in this study were asked to name classmates with whom they would or would not like to work on a project, the overweight adolescents proved on the average to be no less popular with their classmates than normal-weight adolescents.

CAUSES OF OBESITY

People become overweight and eventually obese as a result of taking in more calories than their body uses. This imbalance typically occurs when people eat too much and eat too many high-calorie foods, such as sweets. Contrary to common opinion, research findings indicate that obese people are not necessarily likely to eat larger meals or to eat more rapidly than nonobese people; they are, however, more likely than nonobese people to consume large amounts of high-calorie foods (Perri et al., 1992, Chapter 2). For many obese people, moreover, eating helps them meet some internal psychological needs, and they are consequently likely to spend more time eating than other people, especially in the form of constant snacking and nibbling between meal times. Overeating in this respect resembles an addiction. Most individuals who become and remain markedly overweight would prescribe a leaner diet for themselves if they could, but they cannot. Like addicts who can no longer choose whether to use drugs or alcohol, they have an uncontrollable compulsion to eat. As one obese girl explained it, "I just feel anxious if I don't have something in my mouth all the time, and I always keep stuff around, in my pockets or my locker, just in case."

Although overeating is almost certain to cause overweight, some people become obese without ingesting an unusual number of calories. In these cases two other contributing factors in obesity are usually at work. First, obese people tend to be less active than other people. Because they expend relatively little energy, they tend to put on and retain weight even when they eat normally. Second, the body's ability to metabolize caloric intake is often impaired in obese individuals. Metabolic differences among people in the rate at which their bodies use energy account for the fact that some people are able to eat heartily and remain lean, whereas others gain weight despite a sparse diet.

Neither eating too much of the wrong foods, getting too little exercise, or having an underactive metabolism is ever the only reason why people become obese. Instead, these determinants of obesity combine in various proportions to cause weight problems in the individual case (Linscheid, Tarnowski, & Richmond, 1988; Lucas, 1991; Perri et al., 1992, Chapter 1). There is also good reason to believe that familial factors contribute to individual risk for becoming obese. Studies of adoptees indicate that young people reared apart from their families of origin resemble their biological parents more than their adoptive parents in their weight (Stunkard et al., 1986). Research findings indicate that obesity occurs in 70 to 80% of young people who have two obese parents and in 40 to 50% of those with one obese parent, but in fewer than 10% of offspring when neither parent is obese (Boeck, 1992; Epstein & Cluss, 1986; Linscheid, 1992). Figure 13.2 shows the concordance rate for obesity among various pairs of relatives. Like the familial incidence data for schizophrenia and affective disorders, these frequencies for obesity confirm a direct relationship between genetic similarity and sharing the disorder.

How much of the familial incidence of obesity is due to heredity and how much to the psychological impact of obese parents on their children is not yet known. What is certain is that being markedly overweight, like so many of the other dysfunctional conditions we have discussed, runs in families. However, despite the obvious genetic influence reflected in Figure 13.2, heredity accounts for only 10% of the variation in weight among family members (Linscheid et al., 1988). As for parental impact, obese parents obviously provide overweight models for their children to follow. In addition, home observation studies indicate that parents who have both obese and nonobese children more frequently encourage their obese children to eat than they do their nonobese children (Foreyt & Cousins, 1987). On the other hand, the concordance for obesity among identical twins remains just as high when they have been separated and reared apart as when they are reared together (Boeck, 1992). These kinds of findings demonstrate the complexity of determining in any individual case the proportion of interacting factors that have led to excessive weight.

With respect to the addictive nature of overeating in some people, very powerful psychological influences are obviously at work to cause people to become addicted to a life style that keeps them obese. We can suggest two such possible influences, one related to developmental concerns about sexuality and the other related to fears of powerlessness. In the first instance, obesity, by making a young person unattractive, may serve to minimize social overtures and thereby spare him or her from having to deal with dating and physical intimacy. Especially when adolescents begin to put on excessive weight at or soon after puberty, the possibility exists that intense interpersonal anxieties and sexual aversions are overriding more normal social interests and sustaining obesity despite its many negative consequences. Fagan and Anderson (1990) referred to this motivation for obesity as an effort, through excess fat, to achieve a body that is "sexually neutral." Not uncommonly, in fact, obese women

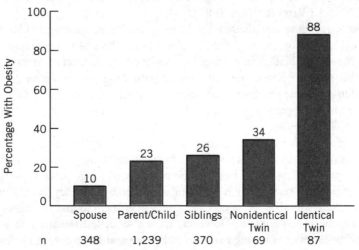

Figure 13.2 Frequency of obesity in relatives of obese persons. [*Source:* Data summarized by Perri, Nezu, and Viegenar, 1992, Chapter 2.]

will report having gained a large amount of weight in order to make themselves essentially nonsexual in appearance and thereby diminish the likelihood that any male would make a sexual overture to them (Hall, Tice, Beresford, Wooley, & Hall, 1988).

In the second instance, people may form an unrealistic association in their minds between size and power. For them, being a big person comes to mean being strong and influential—literally "carrying a lot of weight." For adolescents who feel weak and helpless in the face of developmental challenges, large size can be a reassuring way of having a commanding presence that causes other people to take notice and stand aside. Consistent with these two possibilities, obese people may become increasingly anxious should they begin to reduce, either because they fear becoming more attractive or because they fear becoming less powerful as a result of losing weight.

TREATING OBESE ADOLESCENTS

Weight relative to expectation for one's age, height, and gender remains fairly stable from adolescence to adulthood. This means that lean adolescents usually become lean adults and overweight adolescents tend to become overweight adults. Consequently, obesity that becomes established during the adolescent years often persists or recurs throughout a person's life. About 75 to 80% of obese adolescents become obese adults, and fewer than 10% of young people who remain obese through their adolescence are likely to succeed in losing weight later in their lives (Arden, 1992; Boeck, 1992).

Many different approaches have been used in attempting to treat obesity. These include helping markedly overweight people understand and resolve fears they may have of losing weight and thereby becoming more attractive or less powerful; educating them in proper nutrition, a sensible diet, and healthy eating habits; encouraging them to become more active and follow a regular exercise schedule; training them in improved methods of monitoring and controlling their own behavior, especially in relation to eating and exercise; and working with their families and other people involved in their lives to promote environmental encouragement and rewards for losing weight (Agras, 1987; Linscheid et al., 1988; Perry et al., 1992, Part II; Varni & Banis, 1985).

Neither psychotherapy, dietary guidance, exercise programs, self-help training, family counseling, or reinforcement schedules alone holds the key to successful treatment of obesity. Used in combination in a carefully designed, multifaceted treatment approach, they may be able to help obese adolescents lose weight. However, as we have already noted, obesity is often a chronic condition that persists or recurs despite intensive treatment, and adolescents with obese parents are especially likely to respond slowly in a treatment program (Epstein & Cluss, 1986).

As one perspective on the difficulty of treating obesity successfully, Garner and Wooley (1991) raised the question of whether the effort is worth the result. In developing their argument, they pointed first to the fact that the majority of participants in weight reduction programs, even of the very best kind, regain whatever weight they lose. Next, they acknowledged that the health risks of being overweight may seem to justify intervention efforts even when their success is limited. However, they also called attention to adverse affects on health and well-being of having one's weight go up and down during cycles of weight reduction and relapse. They concluded by raising the interesting question of whether maintaining a high but stable weight may be physically safer and more psychologically comforting in the

---

♦ **BOX 13.3   CRITERIA USED TO IDENTIFY ANOREXIA NERVOSA**

1. Weight loss of 15% or more of a person's original body weight or, among young people who are still growing, weighing only 85% or less of the expected weight for their age, height, and gender.

2. Intense and unreasonable fear of gaining weight or becoming fat, even though being underweight.

3. A disturbed sense of their body's weight, size, shape, or condition that prevents anorexic people from per-

ceiving realistically that they are malnourished or ill.

4. In females, the absence of at least three consecutive menstrual cycles that would otherwise be expected to occur—a condition known as **amenorrhea**.

Source: Based on American Psychiatric Association, *Diagnostic and Statistical Manual of Mental Disorders*, 1987.

---

long run than a widely fluctuating weight or even weight reduction. This seems to be an interesting question for future research to address.

BEHAVIOR PATTERNS IN ANOREXIA NERVOSA AND BULIMIA

Anorexia nervosa is a life-threatening condition of extreme underweight in which people are literally starving themselves. Box 13.3 lists the criteria that are most commonly used by mental health specialists to identify this condition.

With respect to their body image, people with anorexia nervosa sincerely believe that they look the way they should; if anything, they worry about still being too fat, even when their self-starvation has reduced them to skin and bones. They regard themselves as being in good health, despite emaciation that is apparent to everyone but themselves. They ignore or misinterpret bodily sensations that would tell them they are hungry, and they consequently have little appetite even when they are starving. What they want most from other people is not to be helped, but to be left alone. Two landmark books on anorexia nervosa that captured some of these features of the disorder in their vivid title and subtitle were *Starving to Death in a Sea of Objects* by John Sours (1980) and *Let Me Be* by A. H. Crisp (1980).

Systematic criteria for identifying anorexia nervosa have been in place for only a short time, and the prevalence of this condition has not yet been determined in large community samples. Preliminary estimates suggest that somewhere between 2 and 10 in every 1,000 young people age 12–18 may have the disorder at any point in time (Kinder, 1991; Whitaker et al., 1990).

Two facts about the occurrence of anorexia nervosa have become well established, however. First, it appears primarily in females, who constitute approximately 90% of all cases. Second, it very often begins during the adolescent years. The peak periods of onset for anorexia nervosa are in early adolescence, soon after puberty, and again around age 18, as young people are preparing to leave home or go off to college. It may continue to make its first appearance up to age 25, but rarely after this; onset occurs before age 20 in 50% of all cases and before age 25 in 75% (Caspar, 1992; Coupey, 1992a; Kinder, 1991; Lucas, 1991).

Anorexic people achieve their state of extreme underweight by behaving in just the opposite way from people who become obese; they restrict their food intake dramatically, and they expend enormous amounts of energy in industrious pursuits. By eating almost nothing,

♦ BOX 13.4 CRITERIA USED TO IDENTIFY BULIMIA

1. Recurrent episodes of **binge eating**, which consist of rapid consumption of a large amount of food in a limited period of time.

2. A feeling of lack of control over the eating behavior during eating binges.

3. Regularly engaging in either self-induced vomiting, use of laxatives, strict dieting, fasting, or vigorous exercise to prevent weight gain.

4. Averaging at least two binge-eating episodes per week for a period of 3 months or more.

5. Persistent excessive concern with the size, shape, or weight of their body.

Source: Based on American Psychiatric Association, *Diagnostic and Statistical Manual of Mental Disorders,* 1987.

working hard on their studies and various hobbies, and often keeping strictly to a demanding schedule of physical exercise, anorexic young people keep their weight constantly going down. As we have already noted, the distorted body sense that characterizes this condition often sustains anorexics' dissatisfaction with whatever amount of weight they have lost. They continue to feel that they are too heavy and must reduce even further, and they become very upset if the scale tells them they have gained a few pounds. Then they may take such drastic steps as using laxatives or inducing vomiting after they eat in order to prevent their food intake from adding to their weight.

These features of anorexia nervosa identify why it is a life-threatening condition. The longer it persists, the more likely it is to cause death from starvation. Short of death, the malnourishment that results from anorexia impairs many bodily functions. In addition to becoming amenorrheic, anorexics are also likely to suffer from stomachaches, constipation, intolerance to cold, and low blood pressure, and in advanced stages of the disorder they may become too weak to carry on everyday activities and may require bed care. Specialists estimate that 5 to 18% of anorexic patients eventually die as a direct or indirect result of their condition (Coupey, 1992a; Linscheid et al., 1988; Thompson & Gans, 1985).

Bulimia is an eating disorder in which people cannot control recurrent urges to gorge themselves with food. The criteria commonly used to identify this condition are shown in Box 13.4.

About 40 to 50% of anorexics are also bulimic and alternate their customary pattern of food avoidance with episodes of binge eating (Coupey, 1992a; Garner, 1993; Walsh, 1993). Bulimia can also occur as a condition in its own right in persons who never diet to the point of becoming seriously underweight. Bulimics regard their gorging as abnormal and are usually disgusted with themselves for not being able to stop it. Although taking in large amounts of food may gratify some psychological needs they have, as in the case of obese people with a food addiction, they typically use laxatives or induce vomiting after each eating episode to get rid of the food they hate themselves for having ingested. Because they also alternate their eating binges with periods of normal eating or dieting, bulimics tend to maintain fairly normal weight and avoid becoming obese (Halmi, 1987; Herzog, Keller, Lavori, & Bradburn, 1991; Muuss, 1986).

Like anorexia, bulimia occurs about 90% of the time in females and is associated with being excessively concerned about the size, shape, and weight of one's body. Common to both conditions are excessive concerns about eating too much and unwarranted convictions that parts of their body are or are likely to become big, fat, and ugly (Cooper & Fairburn, 1992; Horne, Van Vactor, & Emerson, 1991; Striegel-Moore, Silberstein, & Rodin, 1986). Also like anorexia, bulimia frequently begins in adolescence, most commonly between the ages of 15 and 18. Frequency studies of this condition indicate that approximately 1 to 3.5% of late adolescent and young adult females are likely be bulimic at any one time (Drewnowski, Yee, & Krahn, 1988; Fairburn & Beglia, 1990; Whitaker et al., 1990).

UNRAVELING THE MYSTERY OF ANOREXIA NERVOSA AND BULIMIA

Anorexia nervosa can easily lay claim to being one of the most difficult disorders to understand from a commonsense point of view. Why people would jeopardize their health by starving themselves has been and remains somewhat of a mystery. Nevertheless, clinical and research studies involving psychological, sociological, and biological ways of looking at the problem have each produced some potentially fruitful hypotheses concerning it.

From a psychological perspective, work with anorexic patients has identified two kinds of concerns that appear to motivate this self-destructive condition: an unreasonable fear of fatness and an excessive fear of losing self-control. An unreasonable fear of being fat or even of average weight leads people with anorexia nervosa to pursue thinness at any cost.

Adolescents with anorexia nervosa have a strong aversion to food and resist efforts to get them to eat.

They feel comfortable only when they are taking off weight, and having fat on their bodies fills them with a dread that is more painful to bear than the effects of starvation.

At the same time, an excessive fear of losing self-control leads anorexic people to impose the strictest possible discipline on themselves and their bodies, and the satisfaction they derive from self-denial sustains their determination to keep fasting. When episodes of bulimia occur in the face of such fears, they signify both a risk of adding dreaded pounds and a terrifying loss of control. This helps to explain why anorexic and bulimic people take such drastic steps as inducing vomiting when they have overeaten, or think they have, as a way of undoing the ingestion of food and reestablishing control over themselves.

Conceiving of anorexic behavior as motivated by such specific fears raises the question of how these fears originate. Many of the clinicians who pioneered in studying this condition suggested that fears of fatness in adolescent girls derive from anxieties about developing physically shapely bodies and becoming sexually attractive women (Bruch, 1976; Sours, 1979). Being anorexic does minimize femininity, at least in the physical sense, because it arrests menstruation, prevents or reduces breast development, and produces a gaunt, unappealing, asexual appearance. Consistent with these notions, contemporary theory and research tend to confirm a reluctance to mature and a lack of age-appropriate romantic and sexual interests in anorexic girls, most of whom will say that they are too busy with things that are more important to them such as schoolwork, sports activities, or other hobbies to think about boys or go out on dates (Fagan & Anderson, 1990; Halmi, 1987; Romeo, 1984). Bulimics also show evidence of being more fearful than people in general of becoming involved in intimate personal relationships (Pruitt, Kappius, & Gorman, 1992).

With respect to fears of losing control, there is evidence that adolescents who become anorexic have usually grown up as well-behaved but rigid, cautious, overconforming, perfectionistic children (Caspar, 1992; Coupey, 1992a; Harris & Phelps, 1987). Typically, their lives have been dominated by overcontrolling parents who have given them little opportunity to make decisions for themselves or gain confidence in managing their own affairs. As a result, these young people enter adolescence ill prepared to cope with developmental demands for increased self-reliance; much more than most of their peers, they are susceptible to feeling inadequate and fearing loss of control when they find themselves in situations that call for independent action.

Consistent with this likely contribution of inadequate independence training to making an adolescent vulnerable to anorexia nervosa, the drastic dieting that marks this condition typically begins at times when young people are expected to strike out more on their own and with less parental support than before. Two times when such shifting expectations commonly occur are when adolescents are entering junior and senior high school and when they are beginning college. This helps to account for the two peak periods of onset for this condition that we noted earlier, one in early adolescence and the second around age 18. These situations of change, in which more self-directed behavior is demanded than potentially anorexic young people feel capable of delivering, are likely to generate fears of losing control and behaving improperly, which in turn elicit maladaptive efforts to establish self-control through self-starvation.

As for sociological influences on anorexia, many authorities have called attention to the contemporary enthronement of slimness as the essence of beauty, especially in females (Agras & Kirkley, 1986; Gordon, 1990; Hsu, 1989; Linscheid et al., 1988). The notion that thinner is better shows up in numerous studies of the attitudes of young people toward weight and dieting. Among elementary school students, even as early as the fourth grade, girls are more likely than boys to show concerns about being or becoming overweight and to express a wish to be thinner than their perceived body image (Thelen, Powell, Lawrence, & Kuhnert, 1992). By early adolescence, certain cultural ideals are likely to be well established: Girls in grades 7–12 are much more likely than boys to be dissatisfied with their bodies and to want to be thinner; boys are much more likely than girls to be satisfied with their bodies and to want, if anything, to be more muscular (Phelps, Johnston, Jimenez, & Wilczenski, 1993).

Table 13.1 shows the results of a survey of several hundred ninth-grade students in which a substantial proportion of the girls, but not the boys, reported that they either had been or currently were on a diet.

In a related study of interest involving 182 11–18-year-old girls, only 4% were overweight by usual standards, but 40% said they felt they weighed too much; in a similar survey of 385 12–14-year-old girls, 19% were in fact overweight, but 78% said they wished they weighed less (Davies & Furnham, 1986; Eisele, Hertsgaard, & Light, 1986). This focus on slimness, as influenced by social attitudes, poses a significant risk for the development of abnormal food restriction; among 751 high school cheerleaders, as one case in point, Lundholm and Litrell (1986) found a direct relationship between how badly they wanted to be thin and how likely they were to report abnormal eating patterns and unhealthy weight control behavior.

Finally, biochemical studies have suggested that, once anorexia begins, it may sustain itself through hormonal changes in the body. In particular, severe weight loss may trigger hormonal abnormalities that lead to further disruption of eating patterns. There is also some evidence that anorexic individuals may have a pituitary defect that prevents their body from retaining water and thereby makes it difficult for them to gain weight even when they want to (Herzog & Copeland, 1985).

As for the origins of bulimia, this condition, as we have noted, is closely linked to anorexia through distorted body perceptions and excessive concerns about controlling weight and food intake. Consequently, many of the same factors that make young people susceptible to anorexia are also found in the developmental history and life experiences of those who become bulimic (Crowther, Tennenbaum, Hobfoll, & Stephens, 1992; Herzog et al., 1991). Research with bulimic young women, much of which has been done with college students, has provided further elaboration of two aspects of the onset of this disorder.

Table 13.1 **DIETING IN NINTH-GRADE STUDENTS**

	Percent Saying "Yes"	
Question	Girls (n = 256)	Boys (n = 248)
Are you currently on a weight loss diet?	25.8	2.4
Have you tried to lose weight before?	73.4	18.9

Source: Leon, Perry, Mangelsdorf, and Tell (1989), reprinted with permission of Plenum Publishing Corp.

First, with respect to family relationships, a close attachment to parents who have not fostered much autonomy in their children is associated with increased likelihood of developing an eating disorder in general and bulimia in particular when late adolescents separate from their parents by going off to college (Kenny & Hart, 1992). Second, the specific susceptibility to developing binge eating, as opposed to a strictly anorexic eating disorder, may derive from long-standing tendencies to use food and eating as ways of warding off anxiety or depression (Rosen & Leitenberg, 1985).

TREATMENT FOR ANOREXIA NERVOSA AND BULIMIA

Treatment for anorexia nervosa involves combined efforts to promote normal eating habits and weight gain, to correct distorted body perceptions, and to identify unrealistic fears and maladaptive patterns of family interaction that are contributing to the disorder. Individual psychotherapy, behavioral training programs, nutritional guidance, and family counseling all play a necessary part in these efforts. Without doubt, however, none of these treatment methods is by itself adequate to produce recovery. Psychotherapy can help anorexics understand their fears and revise their perception of their body, but better eating habits and weight gain do not automatically follow; behavior therapy can improve poor eating habits and add weight, but such improvements rarely last unless they are accompanied by increased self-knowledge and a more accurate self-image; and the beneficial effects of both psychotherapy and behavior therapy are likely to be for naught in the absence of an understanding and supportive family system.

In describing these requirements of adequate treatment for anorexia nervosa, most authorities agree that a hospital-based program is usually necessary, at least initially, in order to make an impact on this very serious illness (Agras, 1987; Garner & Garfinkel, 1985; Linscheid et al., 1988; Powers, 1990). Among anorexic patients treated in hospital programs, about two-thirds recover or at least improve, although they may be vulnerable to recurrences of the condition. The other one-third remain chronically ill, despite treatment, and are at high risk for eventually dying from complications of their self-induced starvation (Coupey, 1992a; Lucas, 1991; Thompson & Gans, 1985).

Treatment for bulimia similarly calls for a broadly based, multifaceted program that combines individual, group, and family methods. Behavioral training and the use of antidepressant medication have proved particularly helpful in relieving the symptoms of bulimia. Like anorexia, however, bulimia is often a chronic condition in which recovery proceeds slowly and perhaps as many as 50% of those who recover experience relapses (Fairburn, 1985; Garner & Garner, 1992; Herzog et al., 1991).

WORKING WITH ADOLESCENTS

In this chapter and in Chapters 11 and 12 we have examined numerous developmental problems and abnormalities that may appear during the adolescent years. As we indicated in introducing these topics, adolescent development cannot be fully understood without being familiar with the nature and consequences of such potential difficulties in growing up. On the other hand, the frequently dramatic nature of deviant behavior often attracts attention out of proportion to its frequency. This can be confirmed by looking through almost any daily newspaper.

How much space is devoted to adolescents who are in some kind of trouble, and how much to adolescents who are getting along well or distinguishing themselves in positive ways?

We have discussed specific problems of adolescence in 3 of the 13 chapters of this book. This is close to the right proportion, because approximately 20% of adolescents get into adjustment difficulties that moderately or severely impair their school or social functioning (Weiner, 1992, Chapter 1). On the other hand, many individual kinds of difficulties occur far less frequently than is often supposed on the basis of how much we hear about them and how much psychological damage they can cause when they do occur.

To begin with academic underachievement, we discussed the missed opportunities of adolescents who fail to finish high school despite having adequate ability to do so. Yet most young people do graduate from high school, and about half go on for some form of further education. About 4% of 10–17-year-olds appear in juvenile court each year, but this means that 96% do not. Most high school students have drunk alcohol and many have tried marijuana, but only 24.5% of 12–17-year-olds report having used alcohol in the past month, and fewer than 3% of high school seniors report daily use of marijuana, which means that 97% do not. The fact that an estimated 1 in every 1,000 adolescents makes a suicide attempt each year means that 99.9% do not.

Turning to psychological disturbance, the 1 to 2% lifetime prevalence of schizophrenia means that 98 to 99% of people do not develop this disorder. Many adolescents experience occasional depressed moods and 9% have had an episode of depressive disorder, but more than 90% are free from significant affective disturbance at any point in time. With respect to eating disorders, the rough estimates that 10 to 25% of American adolescents are markedly overweight and that as many as 1% show features of anorexia nervosa mean that 75 to 90% are not obese and 99% or more are not anorexic.

Chronic illness and physical disability can be especially troubling impediments to psychological well-being during adolescence, but teenagers are less likely than either younger children or adults to suffer serious physical illness. This is reflected in the fact that the three leading causes of death among 15–19-year-olds are accidents, homicide, and suicide (see Table 12.4). As for dealing with death in the family, the percentage of young people who lose a parent by death before age 18 is estimated at 5% (Berlinksky & Biller, 1982), which means that 95% do not experience this type of deprivation.

For the vast majority of adolescents, in other words, the problems and pitfalls covered in Chapters 11 and 12 do not seriously affect their lives, and the psychological disturbances discussed in the present chapter rarely occur. Instead, most young people grow to maturity in a healthy and adaptive manner—developing physically (Chapter 3), maturing cognitively (Chapters 4 and 5), individuating within their families (Chapter 7), expanding their social world (Chapter 8), dealing with sex and sexuality (Chapter 9), forming an identity (Chapter 10), and preparing themselves for adult participation in the community. They do so with a broad range of personal styles, through periods of trial and tribulation, and with varying levels of success and failure—but without serious psychological difficulty.

What about periods of trial and tribulation, however, and what about those young people who do develop more psychological problems than they can handle by themselves? The answer is this: Because adolescence is a time of so much development and so many new opportunities, it is an age of considerable capacity for change and unusual openness to the intervention of people who work with adolescents, including teachers, counselors, clergy, youth group leaders, and mental health professionals.

Compared to younger children, adolescents are more capable of looking at and evaluating their own behavior. They are more capable of thinking for themselves, sharing their feelings with others, and understanding how other people think and feel. And they are more capable of looking ahead to the future and concerning themselves in the present with making improvements that will benefit them later. Compared to adults, adolescents are less set in their ways and less decided on how they want to lead their lives. They are less likely to have restricted their future options by missing out on certain kinds of interpersonal experiences or failing to prepare themselves for particular kinds of educational or vocational opportunities, and they are less likely to have taken on commitments or obligations that limit their freedom to choose among alternative new possibilities.

For these reasons, working with adolescents to help them resolve psychological concerns can be a fruitful and rewarding endeavor. Professionals who understand adolescent behavior and have been adequately trained in methods for involving young people in a counseling or psychotherapy relationship can frequently make a big difference in a young person's life. In turn, adolescents who need professional help are generally likely to profit considerably from it in a relatively short period of time.

CHAPTER SUMMARY

1. Normal and abnormal development exist on a continuum, with maladjusted individuals having more or less than an optimum amount of certain traits.

2. *Schizophrenia* is a seriously disabling disorder that occurs in 1 to 2% of the population and disrupts a person's ability to think clearly, reason logically, perceive experience realistically, and maintain comfortable interpersonal relationships. Most forms of this disturbance begin during the late adolescent and early adult years.

3. Although the origins of schizophrenia are not fully understood, it most probably results from some combination of genetic predisposing factors and psychosocial precipitating factors. This interaction view is called the *diathesis-stress model*.

4. *Affective disorder* involves a persistent and maladaptive state of elevated or depressed mood, positive or negative attitudes, high or low energy level, and good or bad feelings about one's physical status. About 7 to 8% of high school students are likely to be significantly depressed at any one point in time, and affective disorder, like schizophrenia, often has its first beginnings during the adolescent years.

5. Like schizophrenia, affective disorder most probably results from the combined influence of genetic predispositions (diathesis) and unpleasant life experiences (stress). Experiences of loss appear particularly likely to sensitize people to becoming depressed and to developing episodes of mania as well.

6. *Obesity*, *anorexia nervosa*, and *bulimia* are three eating disorders that are likely to bring adolescents to professional attention. Becoming and remaining markedly overweight is determined by a variety of factors that vary in the individual case. Anorexia nervosa is a condition of extreme underweight in which people are literally starving themselves. This condition appears primarily in females, often begins during the adolescent years, and involves an unreasonable fear of fatness and an excessive fear of losing self-control. About 40 to 50% of anorexics also show bulimia, which consists of alternating dieting with episodes of binge eating and may occur as a condition in its own right. Bulimia shares many characteristics and causes in common with anorexia and is also especially likely to begin during adolescence.

8. Because they are more mature than children but not yet as set in their ways as adults or as limited in their possibilities for directing their lives in new ways, adolescents with psychological problems tend to be highly responsive to counseling and psychotherapy. This means that adequately trained professionals can often be very helpful to the approximately 20% of young people who get into major adjustment difficulties.

KEY WORDS

acting in

acting out

affective disorder

amenorrhea

anorexia nervosa

antidepressants

binge eating

bipolar affective disorder

bulimia

continuity perspective

cross-fostering

cyclothymia

depression

diathesis-stress theory

dysthymia

flight of ideas

follow-back studies

high-risk studies

mania

manic-depressive disorder

negative attributional personality style

neuroleptics

neurotransmitters

obesity

parental deprivation

premorbid course

pressure of speech

prognosis

psychophysiological disorders

psychomotor retardation

psychosomatic

schizoid pattern

schizophrenia

spontaneous remission

stormy pattern

unipolar affective disorder

REVIEW QUESTIONS

SCHIZOPHRENIA

1. What features of schizophrenia make it an important topic to consider in adolescent psychology?
2. Describe the types of cognitive, interpersonal, and integrative functioning impairments that schizophrenia is likely to produce.
3. What have follow-back and high-risk research studies revealed about personality patterns that are likely to precede schizophrenic breakdown?
4. Why have most researchers concluded that schizophrenia is caused by some interaction between genetic factors that produce a constitutional vulnerability to the disorder and stressful life experiences that foster its emergence?
5. How are age of onset and premorbid course likely to influence the outcome of a schizophrenic breakdown?

6. Why do most authorities recommend conservative use of drugs in treating adolescents with schizophrenia?

AFFECTIVE DISORDER

7. Discuss the possible reasons why adolescent girls are more likely than boys to experience episodes of depression.
8. Describe the major differences between depressed and manic individuals in their mood, attitudes, energy level, and physical status.
9. What kinds of evidence demonstrate the role of genetic dispositions in the origin of affective disorders?
10. How are parental deprivation and a negative attributional personality style likely to contribute to a susceptibility to becoming depressed?
11. Among adolescents who have an episode of

affective disorder, what factors improve their prospects for full recovery?

EATING DISORDERS: OBESITY, ANOREXIA NERVOSA, AND BULIMIA

12. What are some of the potential physical and psychological hazards of being obese in adolescence?

13. Discuss the role that eating patterns, activity level, metabolic rate, and family influences are likely to play in causing obesity.

14. On what basis have some researchers questioned whether efforts to treat obesity are worth the result?

15. How are the behaviors and concerns associated with being anorexic similar to and different from those associated with being bulimic?

16. What are some possible reasons why adolescents with eating disorders become fearful of losing control?

Glossary

◆

Academic underachievement A gap between capacity and performance in school in which students receive lower grades than they are intellectually capable of earning.

Accommodation Modifying existing mental structures as a result of experience.

Acne Inflammation of hair follicles and skin glands, often leading to pimples; it may occur on the face, upper back, and chest.

Acquired immune deficiency syndrome (AIDS) A chronic disease that causes the body to become susceptible to several unusual and potentially fatal infections.

Acting in An inclination to deal with psychological conflict internally; that is, by thinking or feeling in certain ways.

Acting out A tendency to resolve psychological conflict through external channels of expression; that is, by behaving in certain ways.

Acute school phobia A reluctance or refusal to go to school that appears suddenly in children who have not previously shown adjustment difficulties but are anxious about being separated from their parents.

Adaptive denial An avoidance of recognizing fully the limitations associated with being ill or disabled that serves adaptive purposes by allowing the person to function more effectively and enjoy life more fully.

Addictive drug use Habituation to one or more drugs on which the person becomes dependent to feel good physically or mentally.

Adolescence The period of life between childhood and adulthood, roughly corresponding to the teenage years; it comes from a Latin word that means to grow up or to grow into maturity.

Adolescent growth spurt Rate of growth in height increases dramatically during early adolescence; it begins about 2 years earlier in girls than in boys.

Adolescent turmoil Stormy and unpredictable behavior during the teenage years that resembles psychological disorder; once believed to be a common and normal feature of growing up, it has been demonstrated to be an infrequent development that identifies adjustment difficulties.

Affective disorder A form of psychopathology consisting of persistent and maladaptive changes in a person's mood, attitudes, energy level, and physical status; the forms in which this disorder appears include *unipolar affective disorder, bipolar affective disorder, dysthymia,* and *cyclothymia.*

Age composition The relative number of persons from different age groups within the population.

Age-specific Effects of population characteristics that apply to a specific age group, such as having been born during a period of high birth rate.

Alternative schools Specialized schools with programs for specific types of students that are available as alternatives to mainstream schools.

Altruism Being concerned about the welfare of other people and prepared to help them even at the expense of self-sacrifice.

Ambivalence An emotional state involving mixed feelings, some positive and some negative, toward the same person or situation.

Amenorrhea Absence of menstruation in females who have had their menarche.

Androgens The group of sex hormones that is higher in men than in women; testosterone is one important form of androgen.

Androgyny The incorporation of both traditionally feminine and traditionally masculine features into one's gender-role identity.

Anorexia nervosa An eating disorder characterized by extreme underweight, food avoidance, and a disturbed body sense that prevents people from perceiving that they are malnourished.

Antidepressants A technical term for medications used in the treatment of depressive disorder, including substances marketed under such trade names as Elavil, Nardil, Prozac, Tofranil, Wellbutrin, and Zoloft.

Antisocial personality A personality disorder characterized by an underdeveloped conscience and an inability to identify with other people; used synonymously with *psychopathic personality*.

Asceticism A psychological *defense mechanism* that involves minimizing anxiety by turning away from temptations and denying oneself the normal pleasures of human life.

Assimilation Incorporating experience into existing mental structures.

Attention deficit hyperactivity disorder (ADHD) A developmental disorder characterized by an age-inappropriate extent of inattentiveness, impulsiveness, emotionality, and hyperactivity.

Authoritarian parenting A parental style characterized by attention and concern without much warmth and support, inappropriate demands and unreasonable punishments, and firm control based on power-assertion discipline.

Authoritative parenting A parental style characterized by caring and warmth, appropriate demands and reasonable punishments, and firm control based on *inductive discipline*.

Autonomy Freedom to decide for oneself how to think, feel, and act.

B-love Maslow's concept of love for the other person that permits the other to grow as a being.

Bicultural competence Repertoire of skills and knowledge for interacting with individuals in different cultures.

Binge eating Rapid consumption of a large amount of food in a limited period of time.

Biological age A scale of development based on maturation of the physical body. It is a better measure of the beginning of adolescence than is chronological age.

Biopsychosocial model View that considers the interaction of biological, psychological, and social influences.

Bipolar affective disorder A form of affective disorder manifest in alternating episodes of depression and mania.

Bisexual Sexual interest in both men and women, either concurrently or sequentially; some men and women identify with the bisexual community and adopt this term as a positive label for themselves.

Bulimia An eating disorder characterized by recurrent episodes of binge eating.

Cerebral palsy A neurological disorder in which damage to the brain produces motor difficulties and often mental retardation as well.

Characterological delinquency Illegal behavior that reflects an essentially asocial personality orientation; usually associated with psychopathic personality.

Chronic school phobia A lingering inability to attend school that develops gradually in adolescents who already have a history of adjustment problems and encounter unpleasant experiences in school.

Chronological age A person's actual age, in years and months, measured from his or her time of birth.

Chumships Close relationships formed by many preadolescents with just one other person, usually of the same age and gender, with whom they spend most of their time and share many features of their lives in an exclusive fashion.

Chunking The process of combining complex bits of data into meaningful patterns to increase memory capacity.

Circular relationship A relationship between two events in which changes in either one produce changes in the other that in turn produce more changes in the first one; a "vicious circle" is a common expression for one type of circular relationship.

Cliques Small social groups that include only certain individuals based on similarity in age, sex, neighborhood, interests, and social status; members of cliques spend much of their time together, understand and appreciate each other more than anyone outside the clique, and regard the clique as their primary base of interaction with other people.

Cognition The way humans think about and know things.

Cognitive processes Mental processes involved in thinking and knowing, such as paying attention to particular stimuli, recalling previous experiences from memory, solving problems, and understanding the physical and social world, including oneself.

Cohort In developmental research, a group of people born at about the same time. Because they grow older together, members of a cohort experience similar historical changes that may differ from those experienced by members of other cohorts.

Comorbidity Having two or more types of psychological disorder at the same time; this term is used most commonly to describe the cooccurrence of a drug abuse problem with some emotional or behavior problem that also needs to be diagnosed and treated.

Comprehensive high schools Secondary schools that offer both academic courses to prepare students for college, vocational courses designed to prepare students for work, and general studies program for students whose goals are not clear.

Concrete operations Ability to perform mental actions on objects that are physically present, on thoughts about such objects, and the results of previous experience with the physical world. The *operations* are called "concrete" because they involve objects; they do not involve reasoning about hypothetical or future possibilities.

Conditioning An important form of learning that occurs when a reinforcement is linked to a specific behavior.

Conformity Doing what other people do, or what you think they want or expect you to do, in order to make a favorable impression.

Contextualism A model of development that takes a broad and complex view of the effects of the social environmental context on adolescent life.

Continuity perspective The view that normal and abnormal behaviors involve *qualitatively similar* traits, with maladjusted individuals having *quantitatively more or less* than an optimum amount of some of these traits.

Continuous growth A term used to designate smooth and adaptive progress in personality development through adolescence into young adulthood.

Cross-fostering A research method for distinguishing between hereditary and environmental influences in which the subjects are children born to either normal or disturbed parents but, as a result of adoption or foster-home placement, reared by other either normal or disturbed parents.

Cross-sectional studies Develop-

mental research utilizing a strategy in which persons representing a cross-section of different ages are studied at one point in time.

Crowds Groups of young people who are affiliated not necessarily with each other but with the reputation they have; members of crowds may not actually spend time together, but they are identified as sharing some particular set of attitudes or interests.

Cyclothymia A disposition to alternating episodes of depression and mania in mild form.

D-love Maslow's concept of love for another to make up for a deficiency within oneself; it is selfish love, a need for love.

Date rape One partner on a date exerts control and power over the other to force compliance with some sexual experience that is not voluntary.

Defense mechanisms When people are confronted with threatening situations or anxiety-provoking impulses, they call upon various psychological processes to reduce their level of distress; examples include repression, denial, and projection.

Deidealization A process in which childhood tendencies to regard one's parents as all-knowing and all-powerful give way in adolescence to more realistic perceptions of them as imperfect people.

Depression A psychological state involving sadness, negative attitudes, low energy level, and a sense of ill health that are out of proportion to actual circumstances.

Developmental stake A way of referring to the fact that adolescents and their parents have somewhat different perspectives concerning teenage maturation.

Developmental tasks Specific knowledge, skills, attitudes, or functions that individuals are expected to acquire or develop at particular points in their lives. They result from a combination of personal effort, physical maturation, and social pressure.

Diabetes A genetically transmitted condition in which insufficient insulin in the body prevents normal metabolism of carbohydrates.

Dialectical interaction Tension between two or more opposing forces results in a new synthesis that reflects, not the sum of the forces, but a resolution of them in a way that is different from the original separate forces.

Dialectical thinking Ability to analyze conflict between interacting forces that are always changing, and to seek a synthesis. Riegel suggested that dialectical thinking includes but transcends formal operational thinking.

Diathesis-stress theory An interaction view that certain conditions most probably result from some combination of genetic predisposing factors and psychosocial precipitating factors.

Direct effects model The idea that changes in hormone levels during *puberty* have a direct effect on the adolescent's behavior, personality, or adjustment.

Distancing hypothesis An expectation that pubertal maturation results in young people becoming more distant from their parents than they were as children, in the form of less emotional attachment to parents, more frequent disagreements with them, and less willingness to submit to their authority.

Domain The content area of specialization in which an individual has acquired *expertise*.

Drug abuse Heavy use of drugs that has grave psychological implications; drug abuse typically involves patterns of *medicinal* and *addictive* drug use, which differ from patterns of *experimental* and *social* drug use that usually do not constitute drug abuse.

Dual-earner families Families in which both parents live in the home but are gainfully employed outside of it on a full- or part-time basis.

Dual identity Ability to integrate one's conception of oneself as a member of more than one important social group; e.g., one's ethnic, racial, or religious culture and also the larger culture.

Dyslexia An inability to read at grade level despite adequate intelligence and reading instruction.

Dysthymia A disposition to recurrent but mild episodes of depression.

Ecology The interrelationship between the environment in which an organism lives and the organism itself. The school, family, and peer group are important aspects of the adolescent's social ecology.

Egocentrism Failure to distinguish between one's own point of view and that of another person; it is not the same as "selfish."

Empirical methods Research approach utilizing observation, inquiry about one's experience, and carefully designed experiments to produce data that may be quantitative (i.e., numerical or able to be structured into categories) or qualitative.

Empty nest reaction Sadness that some parents experience when all of their children have grown up and moved out of the family home.

Epigenesis Sequential unfolding of stages in human development in which developments during one stage become building blocks on which later stages depend.

Estrogens A group of sex hormones that is higher in women than in men.

Ethic of care Moral judgments based on a recognition of interconnected human relationships in which each person has a responsibility for others and cares for their welfare.

Experimental drug use Taking mild drugs once or a few times and then stopping using them.

Expertise Systematic knowledge about a particular topic such as auto mechanics, chess, or mathematics in which one's skill allows efficient perception, procedure, and response.

Fears of failure Concerns about doing poorly that lead people to set unrealistically high goals and then work only halfheartedly toward them.

Fears of success Concerns about doing well that lead people to set limited goals that are easily within their grasp, work hard enough to attain them, and then make little further effort.

Flight of ideas A characteristic of mania in which thoughts flow in such quick succession that new ideas take over before previous ones have been brought to closure.

Follicle stimulating hormone (FSH) One of the gonadotropic hormones produced by the pituitary gland. In females it acts on the ovaries to stimulate development of the ova and production of estrogens; in males it acts on the testes to stimulate production of sperm.

Follow-back studies A research method in which past records are examined for possible antecedents of currently observed behavior.

Formal operations Ability to perform mental actions that are effective and flexible even when dealing with hypothetical and abstract ideas; also an ability to imagine possibilities in a situation and to compensate mentally for changes in reality.

Friendships Special relationships between two people who care for each other and share important parts of their lives.

Gay men Some men who are sexually attracted to men identify as a part of the gay community and adopt this term as a positive label for themselves.

Gender intensification Refers to the fact that distinctions between what constitutes femininity and what constitutes masculinity begin to crystallize following puberty.

Gender-role socialization Teaching or learning the behaviors that make up the gender roles associated with being a male or female.

Generation gap A mythical notion that the prevailing pattern of relationships between the adolescent and adult generations consists of poor communication and adolescent rejection of adult values.

Generational transmission The occurrence in children of behavior patterns similar to those shown by their parents; many factors can contribute to generational transmission, including genetic, modeling, and social learning influences.

Gonadotropic hormones Substances produced by the pituitary gland that control the release of sex hormones from the gonads; they include *follicle stimulating hormone (FSH)* and *luteinizing hormone (LH)*.

Hard drugs A term sometimes used to refer to drugs that have more powerful effects than marijuana, a *soft drug*; the main types of hard drugs are stimulants, sedatives, hallucinogens, cocaine, and heroin.

Height spurt The period of rapid increase in height resulting from puberty (see *adolescent growth spurt*).

Hidden delinquency Delinquent acts that are not detected and are therefore not included in official delinquency statistics.

High-risk studies A research method in which children with a relatively high likelihood of becoming disturbed, usually as determined on the basis of a family history of disturbance, are followed longitudinally to determine whether and under what circumstances they become disturbed themselves.

Homosexuality Sexual attraction to persons of the same gender.

Hormones Chemical substances that send a powerful and highly specialized message to particular cells and tissues in the body. They are produced by endocrine glands and are carried to the target cells by blood vessels.

Human immunodeficiency virus (HIV) The virus transmitted from an infected person through specific bodily fluids and associated with *acquired immune deficiency syndrome (AIDS)*, a serious disease of the immune system.

Hypersexuality Preoccupation with sexual thoughts and behavior leading to markedly sexualized conduct and an unusually high level of sexual activity.

Hyposexuality Fear and avoidance of sexuality leading to sexual unresponsiveness and inactivity.

Identity achievement A state of reasonably firm commitment to a set of goals, values, and beliefs arrived at after a period of active uncertainty concerning alternative possibilities.

Identity confusion Difficulty forming an identity that fits one's personal characteristics and environment, leading to uncertainty about oneself and one's future possibilities.

Identity diffusion The apparent absence of any firm commitments to goals, values, and beliefs or of any current effort to form them.

Identity foreclosure A premature termination of the process of identity formation involving commitment to the goals and beliefs of others without the person's having considered alternative possibilities on his or her own terms.

Identity formation The process by which people arrive at their sense of identity.

Identity moratorium An ongoing process of identity formation in which the person is considering and beginning to make commitments to goals and beliefs but has not yet achieved a clear and satisfying self-definition.

Identity status A discrete step along the way to forming a sense of identity; the identity statuses most commonly seen are *diffusion*, *foreclosure*, *moratorium*, and *achievement*.

Ideological stance The set of values and beliefs that guide one's actions.

Imaginary audience Belief that other people are preoccupied with one's appearance and behavior; a form of *egocentrism* noted during adolescence.

Incestuous relationships Sexual involvement between members of the same immediate family.

Individuation A process in which adolescents become capable of separating themselves from their parents and thinking for themselves, while at the same time continuing to participate as family members and collaborate with their parents in resolving issues in their lives.

Inductive discipline Discipline that consists of explaining the purpose of rules to be followed and then being willing to consider changing these rules.

Indulgent parenting A form of permissive parenting in which parents care about their children and are warmly supportive of them, but offer little or no constructive criticism.

Information processing The cognitive activity that individuals engage in when dealing with tasks in daily life. It includes attending to the flow of information from various inputs (e.g., vision, hearing, touch), transforming it into a meaningful code, comparing it with other information stored in memory, and then emitting an output such as a verbal response or a memory for later use.

Initiation rites Public celebration of the transition from childhood to adulthood in some cultures.

Intellectualization A psychological *defense mechanism* that involves thinking about ideas, taking up causes, and debating ethical and moral issues in a manner that avoids or at least minimizes their specific psychological importance or threatening nature to the individual.

Interaction Combination of changes or influences that mutually affect the outcome. The result is not necessarily the simple addition of one influence to another; instead, the result is likely to be different from the sum of the parts.

Interdependence A characteristic of interpersonal relationships in which people share responsibility for meeting each other's needs.

Interpersonal stance The gender orientation that influences one's forms of acquaintanceship and intimacy with males and females.

Intimacy In psychological terms, refers to a relationship between people who share their innermost thoughts and feelings and know each other well.

Joint custody An arrangement following divorce in which children live part of the time with their mothers and part of the time with their fathers.

Junior high school Secondary school that contains grades 7 and 8 in some school systems and grades 7–9 in others.

Latent functions Implicit effects that result from the actual characteristics of social institutions but are not intentional goals.

Lesbians Some women who are sexually attracted to women identify as a part of the lesbian community and adopt this term as a positive label for themselves.

Loneliness A distressing, unpleasant experience of having your social relationships fall short of your needs for companionship or intimacy.

Longitudinal studies Research utilizing a strategy in which the same persons are studied periodically over several years.

Long-term memory Store of information that is remembered after a few minutes or that can be recalled at a later time.

Lust dynamism Sullivan's concept that refers to a pattern of recurring sexual tension involving the genitals.

Luteinizing hormone (LH) One of the gonadotropic hormones produced by the pituitary gland. In females it acts on the ovaries to stimulate ovulation and production of progestins; in males it acts on the testes to stimulate production of *androgens* and also sperm.

Magnet schools Secondary schools that concentrate on specific programs such as the arts, business, or science that attract students from a wide area.

Mania A psychological state involving elation, positive attitudes, high energy level, and a sense of well-being that are out of proportion to actual circumstances.

Manic-depressive disorder A term for bipolar affective disorder that refers to alternating episodes of mania and depression.

Manifest functions Goals of social institutions that are explicitly acknowledged.

Mapping Cognitive skill that involves recognizing a relationship between objects or events.

Masturbation Self-stimulation of the genitals.

Mediated effects model The idea that hormonal and physical changes of *puberty* affect the nature of the adolescents' interactions with others and thus have only indirect effects on behavior, personality, or adjustment.

Medicinal drug use Taking drugs to relieve anxiety or tension or to enjoy a drug experience for its own sake.

Menarche First menstrual period a female experiences.

Metacognition Cognition about cognition; it involves monitoring, reflecting upon, and critiquing one's thoughts.

Middle school Secondary school with grades 6–8 or 7 and 8.

Midlife transition A period during the middle years of life when many adults evaluate their past and present and prepare for their remaining years.

Mini-rites Simple events that signify the attainment of some group membership or level of privilege, such as an initiation ceremony or being awarded a driver's license.

Moral development Progression in cognitive level of thinking about moral issues.

Moratorium Period of delay or pause in development. It is a typical aspect of the search for a sense of identity (see *identity moratorium*).

Mutuality Refers to a relationship in which people treat each other with equality and reciprocity, which means that they are fair with each other and try to be helpful to each other whenever help is needed.

Negative attributional personality style A tendency to attribute bad experiences to shortcomings within oneself that are relatively permanent.

Neglectful parenting A form of permissive parenting in which parents are largely indifferent to their children and disengaged from child-rearing responsibilities.

Neuroleptics A technical term for antipsychotic medications, which include substances marketed under such trade names as Clozaril, Haldol, Mellaril, Stelazine, Thorazine, and Trilafon.

Neurotic delinquency Illegal acts committed as an individual effort to communicate some specific unmet psychological needs.

Neurotransmitters Chemical substances in the brain that carry messages in the form of electrical impulses from one nerve cell to another; two neurotransmitters that have been studied extensively in biochemical research on psychological disorders are *dopamine* and *serotonin*.

Obesity An eating disorder characterized by a condition of abnormal fatness or overweight.

Observational learning Acquiring skills and behavior by watching and imitating various models.

Occupational stance The set of educational and career goals that direct one's efforts in work.

One-parent households Households in which children are living with just one parent, either mother or father; children may be living in a one-parent household even though they are part of a two-parent family, with a divorced or separated parent who lives elsewhere.

Operation Actions that a person performs mentally that form a coherent and reversible system.

Organizational core The idea that cognitive development functions as a central process that affects all areas of thinking, regardless of the content of the topic.

Parental deprivation Diminished opportunity for contact with one or both parents as a result of rejection, separation, or death.

Passive-aggressive behavior Purposeful inactivity by which people express anger and resentment that they cannot bring themselves to show openly.

Passive-aggressive underachievement A form of school learning difficulty determined by anger toward parents, concerns about rivalry, and a passive-aggressive behavioral style.

Permissive parenting A parental style characterized by minimal control, few requirements or restrictions, and premature granting of independence in decision making.

Personal fable Belief in one's immortal, special, and unique existence; a form of *egocentrism* noted during adolescence.

Perspective taking The ability to recognize how other people feel and understand why they view situations as they do.

Popularity The extent to which people are well liked in the groups to which they belong.

Power assertion discipline Discipline that consists of setting forth rules to be followed in an arbitrary fashion that is not open to discussion.

Precocious puberty The occurrence of physical and hormonal changes of puberty much earlier than the average age.

Premorbid course A person's life history prior to the onset of some disorder.

Pressure of speech A characteristic of mania in which speech pours out rapidly, sometimes with words stumbling over each other more quickly than they can be pronounced clearly.

Progestins One group of sex hormones that is higher in women than in men; progesterone is one important form of progestin.

Prognosis A technical term for expectations or predictions of how a matter is likely to turn out, such as the course and outcome of a psychological disorder.

Psychological autopsy A research method in which the previous history of someone who has committed suicide is examined and people who knew the person well are interviewed to create a psychological profile of the suicide victim.

Psychomotor retardation A fre-
quent manifestation of depressive disorder in which people move, talk, and think more slowly than they would normally.

Psychopathic personality A personality disorder characterized by an underdeveloped conscience and an inability to identify with other people; used synonymously with *antisocial personality*.

Psychophysiological disorders Pathological conditions consisting chiefly of biological abnormalities, but substantially influenced by psychological concerns; used synonymously with *psychosomatic disorders*.

Psychosomatic disorders Pathological conditions consisting chiefly of biological abnormalities, but substantially influenced by psychological concerns; used synonymously with *psychophysiological disorders*.

Pubertal status The level of a young person's physical maturity as reflected in bodily changes during late childhood and early adolescence.

Puberty The process of becoming physically and sexually mature and developing adult characteristics of one's gender.

Pygmalion effect Based on the legend of a sculptor named Pygmalion, this term is sometimes used to describe situations in which a person's behavior appears to have been determined by what others have expected of him or her; in schools the Pygmalion effect refers to the influence that teachers' expectations may have on their students' performance.

Reconstituted families Families created by remarriage, following divorce or death of a parent, in which children live with one or more step-parents and step-siblings.

Regression Using a psychologically less mature mode of functioning—such as coping styles that worked successfully earlier in life—when confronted with situations that are difficult to handle.

Relational viewpoint Perspective on human development that emphasizes the importance of dynamic interaction between individuals and attending to the feelings of others.

Relativism A transitional phase of cognitive development in which the adolescent appears to be unsure of the solution to a problem although enough information is available to make a decision.

Romantic love A type of love that combines intimacy and passion.

Romantic myth A concept of love based on a cultural myth such as the Tristan and Isolde legend in which ideal love is one that is prevented from being consummated except in the eternity of death.

Sample A manageable portion of the population that is being studied; ideally, this group is similar to the total population in important ways.

Schizoid pattern A pattern of maladjustment marked by shy, sensitive, seclusive behavior and a "shut-in" personality style in which emotions and interests are turned inward rather than directed toward other people; many young people who subsequently become schizophrenic show either this premorbid pattern or a *stormy* pattern.

Schizophrenia A serious breakdown in a person's cognitive, interpersonal, and integrative capacities that disrupts the ability to think clearly, reason logically, perceive reality accurately, enjoy relationships with other people, and exert self-control.

School phobia A reluctance or refusal to go to school because of intense anxiety experienced in the school setting.

Secondary schools Junior high, middle school, or high school, which contain the grades following primary school.

Self The term that describes our unique individuality and consists of identifiable characteristics that can be seen by others in generally similar ways to those in which one sees oneself.

Self-concept The group of ideas and feelings one has about oneself.

Self-esteem The emotional evaluation one has of oneself, ranging from high self-esteem (positive evaluation) to low self-esteem (negative evaluation).

Self-fulfilling prophecy Predictions that come to pass in part because people who expect certain things to happen act in ways that cause them to happen.

Sense of identity An integrated view of one's talents, beliefs, and impact on other people; it includes being reasonably sure of what kind of person you are and what you want to do with your life.

Separation-individuation Blos' concept that adolescents typically feel uneasy about separating themselves from their parents and becoming self-reliant individuals in their own right.

Sequential studies Research utilizing a strategy that combines *cross-sectional* and *longitudinal* research models to distinguish between effects of age, historical time, and *cohort*.

Sexual abuse Any inappropriate sexualized behavior involving a minor child or adolescent, as defined by law.

Sexually transmitted diseases (STDs) Diseases caused by bacteria, viruses, and other organisms that one may be exposed to during sexual contact.

Short-term memory Temporary storage of information that has just been input and can be recalled.

Shyness A pattern of social anxiety and interpersonal inhibition arising in situations that raise the prospect of being evaluated by others.

Social age A measure of social maturity based on expectations about the roles and responsibilities for persons of different ages in a particular society. It is a better measure of the end of adolescence than is chronological age.

Social cognition Thinking and knowledge about people and their activities, including oneself, social relations, and social institutions.

Social drug use Taking drugs infrequently and mainly as a way of participating in peer-group activities.

Socialized delinquency Illegal behavior associated with membership in a subculture that endorses antisocial standards of conduct.

Soft drug A term sometimes used to refer to marijuana as a way of distinguishing its relatively mild effects from the more powerful effects of *hard drugs*.

Spermarche The first production of sperm in males. The first ejaculation of semen, the fluid transporting the sperm, may occur during sleep and is known as a "wet dream"; it may also occur through masturbation or sexual contact.

Spontaneous remission Recovery from disturbance without treatment.

States Situationally determined aspects of how a person is reacting to a specific set of circumstances; to be distinguished from traits.

Status offenses Acts that are illegal by virtue of the youthfulness of the person committing them, such as running away.

Stepping-stone hypothesis A way of referring to the evidence that use of hard drugs is usually preceded by use of mild or soft drugs; soft drug use does not necessarily lead to hard drug use, but it does appear to be a necessary step along the way.

Stormy pattern A pattern of maladjustment involving restlessness, difficulty concentrating, and a history of family conflict, stealing, running away, truancy, and school failure; many young people who subsequently become schizophrenic show either this premorbid pattern or a *schizoid* pattern.

Strategic interactions In interpersonal relationships, ways in which people behave toward each other when they are trying to convey, conceal, or obtain information through indirect means.

Surgent growth A term used to designate adaptive but irregular progress in personality development during adolescence.

Testing the limits Actions intended to see how much one can get away with or to provoke others to set restrictions that will provide guidance and control.

Testosterone Chemical substance produced by the testes that is one of the group of sex *hormones* known as *androgens*.

Traits Persistent tendencies of people to respond to their experiences in certain characteristic ways, whatever the circumstances; to be distinguished from *states*.

Transition A period of change, growth, and disequilibrium that serves as a kind of bridge between one relatively stable point in life and another relatively stable, but different, point.

Transitional relationship A relationship based on erotic attraction that aids the young person's development during the period between the emergence of sexual feelings and the beginning of a mutually supportive loving relationship.

Truancy Skipping school to spend time in ways the person finds more enjoyable.

Tumultuous growth A term used to designate adolescent personality development marked by inner unrest and overt behavior problems.

Unipolar affective disorder A form of affective disorder manifest in episodes of depression.

Universal Refers to a phenomenon that is widespread, occurring in many different societies and over many generations..

Withdrawal symptoms Physical or psychological distress experienced by people who are deprived of drugs to which they have become addicted.

References

Abbey, A., Oliansky, D., Stilianos, K., & Hohlstein, L. A. (1990). Substance abuse prevention for second graders: Are they too young to benefit? *Journal of Applied Developmental Psychology, 11*, 149–162.

Adams, G. R. (1983). Social competence during adolescence: Social sensitivity, locus of control, empathy, and peer popularity. *Journal of Youth and Adolescence, 8*, 125–138.

Adams, G. R. (1992). Introduction and overview. In G. R. Adams, T. P. Gullotta, & R. Montemayor (Eds.), *Adolescent identity formation* (pp. 1–8). Newbury Park, CA: Sage.

Adams, G. R., Abraham, K. G., & Markstrom, C. A. (1987). The relations among identity development, self-consciousness, and self-focusing during middle and late adolescence. *Developmental Psychology, 23*, 292–297.

Adams, G. R., Day, T., Dyk, P. H., Frede, E., & Rogers, D. R. B. (1992). On the dialectics of pubescence and psychosocial development. *Journal of Early Adolescence, 12*, 348–365.

Adams, G. R., Gullotta, T., & Clancy, M. A. (1985). Homeless adolescents: A descriptive study of similarities and differences between runaways and throwaways. *Adolescence, 20*, 715–724.

Adams, G. R., Gullotta, T. P., & Markstrom-Adams, C. (1994). *Adolescent life experiences* (3rd ed.). Pacific Grove, CA: Brooks/Cole.

Adams, G. R., Gullotta, T. P., & Montemayor, R. (Eds.) (1992). *Adolescent identity formation*. Newbury Park, CA: Sage.

Adams, G. R., & Jones, R. M. (1983). Female adolescents' identity development: Age comparisons and perceived child-rearing experience. *Developmental Psychology, 19*, 249–256.

Adams, G. R., Openshaw, D. K., Bennion, L., Mills, T., & Noble, S. (1988). Loneliness in late adolescence: A social skills training study. *Journal of Adolescent Research, 3*, 81–96.

Adams, G. R., Ryan, J. H., Hoffman, J. J., Dobson, W. R., & Nielson, E. C. (1984). Ego identity status, conformity behavior, and personality in late adolescence. *Journal of Personality and Social Psychology, 47*, 1091–1104.

Adams, P. L., Milner, J. R., & Schrepf, N. A. (1984). *Fatherless children*. New York: Wiley.

Adcock, A. G., Nagy, S., & Simpson, J. A. (1991). Selected risk factors in adolescent suicide attempts. *Adolescence, 26*, 817–828.

Adegoke, A. A. (1993). The experience of spermarche (the age of onset of sperm emission) among selected adolescent boys in Nigeria. *Journal of Youth and Adolescence, 22*, 201–209.

Adelson, J. (1971). The political imagination of the young adolescent. *Daedalus, 100*, 1013–1050.

Adelson, J., & Doehrman, M. J. (1980). The psychodynamic approach to adolescence. In J. Adelson (Ed.), *Handbook of adolescent psychology* (pp. 99–116). New York: Wiley.

Adler, I., & Kandel, D. B. (1981). Cross-cultural perspectives on developmental stages in adolescent drug use. *Journal of Studies on Alcohol, 42*, 701–715.

Agras, W. S. (1987). *Eating disorders*. New York: Pergamon.

Agras, W. S., & Kirkley, B. G. (1986). Bulimia: Theories of etiology. In K. D. Brownell & J. Foreyt (Eds.), *Handbook of eating disorders* (pp. 369–378). New York: Basic Books.

Akhtar, S. (1984). The syndrome of identity diffusion. *American Journal of Psychiatry, 141*, 1381–1385.

Alden, L., & Cappe, R. (1986). Interpersonal process training for shy clients. In W. H. Jones, J. M. Cheek, & S. R. Biggs (Eds.), *Shyness* (pp. 343–355). New York: Plenum.

Aleksandrowicz, D. R. (1980). Psychoanalytic studies of mania. In R. H. Belmaker & H. M. van Praag (Eds.), *Mania: An evolving concept* (pp. 309–322). New York: Spectrum.

Alford, G. S. (1989). Psychoactive substance use disorders. In L. K. G. Hsu & M. Hersen (Eds.), *Recent developments in adolescent psychiatry* (pp. 310–333). New York: Wiley.

Allen, L. S., & Gorski, R. A. (1992). Sexual orientation and the size of the anterior commissure in the human brain. *Proceedings of the National Academy of Sciences, USA, 89,* 7199–7202.

Allgood-Merton, B., Lewinsohn, P. M., & Hops, H. (1990). Sex differences and adolescent depression. *Journal of Abnormal Psychology, 99,* 55–63.

Allison, P. D., & Furstenberg, F. F. (1989). How marital dissolution affects children: Variations by age and sex. *Developmental Psychology, 25,* 504–549.

Allison, M. D., & Sabatelli, R. M. (1988). Differentiation and individuation as mediators of identity and intimacy in adolescence. *Journal of Adolescent Research, 3,* 1–16.

Alloy, L. B., Lipman, A. J., & Abramson, L. Y. (1992). Attributional style as a vulnerability factor for depression: Validation by past history of mood disorders. *Cognitive Therapy and Research, 16,* 391–407.

Alsaker, F. D., & Olweus, D. (1992). Stability of global self-evaluations in early adolescence: A cohort longitudinal study. *Journal of Research on Adolescence, 2,* 123–145.

Amato, P. R. (1989). Family processes and the competence of adolescents and primary school children. *Journal of Youth and Adolescence, 18,* 39–54.

Amato, P. R., & Keith, B. (1991). Parental divorce and the well-being of children: A meta-analysis. *Psychological Bulletin, 110,* 26–46.

Ambrosini, P. J., Bianchi, M. D., Rabinovich, H., & Elia, J. (1993). Antidepressant treatments in children and adolescents: I. Affective disorders. *Journal of the American Academy of Child and Adolescent Psychiatry, 32,* 1–6.

American Psychological Association. (1985). *Violence on television.* Washington, DC: APA Board of Social and Ethical Responsibility for Psychology. (Cited in Huston et al., 1992.)

Ames, C. (1992). Classrooms: Goals, structures, and student motivation. *Journal of Educational Psychology, 84,* 261–271.

Ammerman, R. T., & Hersen, M. (1990). Issues in the assessment and treatment of family violence. In R. T. Ammerman & M. Hersen (Eds.), *Treatment of family violence* (pp. 3–16). New York: Wiley.

Ammerman, R. T., & Hersen, M. (1992). Current issues in the assessment of family violence. In R. T.

Ammerman & M. Hersen (Eds.), *Assessment of family violence* (pp. 3–11). New York: Wiley.

Anderson, C. M., Reiss, D. J., & Hogarty, G. E. (1986). *Schizophrenia and the family.* New York: Guilford.

Anderson, E. R., Hetherington, E. M., & Clingempeel, W. G. (1989). Transformations in family relations at puberty: Effects of family context. *Journal of Early Adolescence, 9,* 310–334.

Anderson-Kulman, R. E., & Paludi, M. A. (1986). Working mothers and the family context: Predicting positive coping. *Journal of Vocational Behavior, 28,* 241–253.

Andreasen, N. C. (1988). Clinical phenomenology. *Schizophrenia Bulletin, 14,* 345–363.

Andreasen, N. C., & Flaum, M. (1991). Schizophrenia: The characteristic symptoms. *Schizophrenia Bulletin, 17,* 27–50.

Andreasen, N. C., Rice, J., Endicott, J., Coryell, W., Grove, W. M., & Reich, T. (1987). Familial rates of affective disorder. *Archives of General Psychiatry, 44,* 461–469.

Andrews, J. A., & Lewinsohn, P. M. (1992). Suicidal attempts among older adolescents: Prevalence and co-occurrence with psychiatric disorders. *Journal of the American Academy of Child and Adolescent Psychiatry, 31,* 655–662.

Angold, A. (1988). Childhood and adolescent depression: II. Research in clinical populations. *British Journal of Psychiatry, 153,* 476–492.

Apter, A., Galatzer, A., Beth-Halachmi, N., & Laron, Z. (1981). Self-image in adolescents with delayed puberty and growth retardation. *Journal of Youth and Adolescence, 10,* 501–505.

Apter, D., & Vihko, R. (1977). Serum pregnenolone, progesterone, 17-hydroxyprogesterone, testosterone and 5-alpha-dihydrotestosterone during female puberty. *Journal of Clinical Endocrinology and Metabolism, 45,* 1039–1048.

Arbuthnot, J., Gordon, D. A., & Jurkovic, G. J. (1987). Personality. In H. C. Quay (Ed.), *Handbook of juvenile delinquency* (pp. 139–183). New York: Wiley.

Arden, M. R. (1992). Obesity. In E. R. McAnarney, R. E. Kreipe, D. P. Orr, & G. D. Comerci (Eds.), *Textbook of adolescent medicine* (pp. 547–553). Philadelphia: Saunders.

Arditti, J. A. (1992). Differences between fathers with joint custody and non-custodial fathers. *American Journal of Orthopsychiatry, 62,* 186–195.

Arieti, S. (1974). *Interpretation of schizophrenia* (2nd ed.). New York: Basic Books.

Arkin, R. M., & Baumgardner, A. H. (1985). Self-handicapping. In J. H. Harvey & G. Weary (Eds.), *Attribution: Basic issues and applications* (pp. 169–202). London: Academic.

Arkin, R. M., Lake, E. A., & Baumgardner, A. H. (1986). Shyness and self-presentation. In W. H. Jones, J. M. Cheek, & S. R. Biggs (Eds.), *Shyness* (pp. 189–203). New York: Plenum.

Armistead, L., Wierson, M., Forehand, R., & Frame, C. (1992). Psychopathology in incarcerated juvenile delinquents: Does it extend beyond externalizing problems? *Adolescence, 27,* 309–314.

Armsden, G. C., McCauley, E., Greenberg, M. T., & Burke, P. M. (1990). Parent and peer attachment in early adolescent depression. *Journal of Abnormal Child Psychology, 18,* 683–697.

Arnett, J. (1991a). Adolescents and heavy metal music: From the mouths of metalheads. *Youth & Society, 23,* 76–98.

Arnett, J. (1991b). Heavy metal music and reckless behavior among adolescents. *Journal of Youth and Adolescence, 20,* 573–592.

Aro, H. M., & Palosaari, U. K. (1992). Parental divorce, adolescence, and transition to young adulthood: A follow-up study. *American Journal of Orthopsychiatry, 62,* 421–429.

Asarnow, J. R. (1988). Children at risk for schizophrenia: Converging lines of evidence. *Schizophrenia Bulletin, 14,* 613–631.

Asarnow, J. R., Goldstein, M. J., & Ben-Meir, S. (1988). Parental communication deviance in childhood onset schizophrenia spectrum and depressive disorders. *Journal of Child Psychology and Psychiatry, 29,* 825–838.

Asarnow, J. R., Goldstein, M. J., Tompson, M., & Guthrie, D. (1993). One-year outcomes of depressive disorders in child psychiatric in-patients: Evaluation of the prognostic power of a brief measure of expressed emotion. *Journal of Child Psychology and Psychiatry, 34,* 129–137.

Asendorpf, J. (1986). Shyness in middle and late childhood. In W. H. Jones, J. M. Cheek, & S. R. Biggs (Eds.), *Shyness* (pp. 91–103). New York: Plenum.

Asher, S. R. (1990). Recent advances in the study of peer rejection. In S. R. Asher & J. D. Coie (Eds.), *Peer rejection in childhood* (pp. 3–14). New York: Cambridge University Press.

Asher, S. R., Parkhurst, J. F., Hymel, S., & Williams, G. A. (1990). Peer rejection and loneliness in childhood. In S. R. Asher & J. D. Coie (Eds.), *Peer rejection in childhood* (pp. 253–273). New York: Cambridge University Press.

Asher, S. R., & Wheeler, V. A. (1985). Children's loneliness: A comparison of rejected and neglected peer status. *Journal of Consulting and Clinical Psychology, 53,* 500–505.

Atkinson, L., Quarrington, B., & Cyr, J. J. (1985). School refusal: The heterogeneity of a concept. *American Journal of Orthopsychiatry, 55,* 83–111.

Axelsson, A., & Lindgren, F. (1981). Hearing in classical musicians. *Acta Oto-Laryngologica, Supplement 377,* 1–74.

Azar, S. T., & Wolfe, D. A. (1989). Child abuse and neglect. In E. J. Mash & R. A. Barkley (Eds.), *Treatment of childhood disorders* (pp. 451–489). New York: Guilford.

Bachman, J. G., Johnston, L. D., & O'Malley, P. M. (1987). *Monitoring the future: Questionnaire responses from the nation's high school seniors, 1986.* Ann Arbor, MI: Institute for Social Research. (Cited in Mortimer et al., 1992b.)

Bachman, J. G., O'Malley, P. M., & Johnston, J. (1979). *Adolescence to adulthood: Change and stability in the lives of young men.* Ann Arbor, MI: Institute for Social Research.

Bailey, J. M., & Benishay, D. S. (1993). Familial aggregation of female sexual orientation. *American Journal of Psychiatry, 150,* 272–277.

Bailey, J. M., & Pillard, R. C. (1991). A genetic study of male sexual orientation. *Archives of General Psychiatry, 48,* 1089–1096.

Bailey, J. M., Pillard, R. C., Neale, M. C., & Agyei, Y. (1993). Heritable factors influence sexual orientation in women. *Archives of General Psychiatry, 50,* 217–223.

Balk, D. E. (1991). Death and adolescent bereavement: Current research and future directions. *Journal of Adolescent Research, 6,* 7–27.

Baly, I. (1989). Career and vocational development of black youth. In R. L. Jones (Ed.), *Black adolescents* (pp. 249–265). Berkeley, CA: Sage.

Bandura, A. (1969a). Social-learning theory of identificatory processes. In D. A. Goslin & D. C. Glass (Eds.), *Handbook of socialization theory and research* (pp. 213–262). Chicago: Rand McNally.

Bandura, A. (1969b). *Principles of behavior modification.* New York: Holt, Rinehart, & Winston.

Bandura, A. (1973). *Aggression: A social learning analysis.* Englewood Cliffs, NJ: Prentice-Hall.

Bandura, A. (1976). Social learning analysis of aggression. In E. Ribes-Inesta & A. Bandura (Eds.),

Analysis of delinquency and aggression (pp. 203–232). Hillsdale, NJ: Erlbaum.

Bandura, A. (1977). *Social learning theory.* Englewood Cliffs, NJ: Prentice-Hall.

Bandura, A. (1986). *Social foundations of thought and action: A social cognitive theory.* Englewood Cliffs, NJ: Prentice Hall.

Bangert-Drowns, R. L. (1988). The effects of school-based substance abuse education: A meta-analysis. *Journal of Drug Education, 18,* 243–264.

Barber, B. L., & Eccles, J. S. (1992). Long-term influence of divorce and single parenting on adolescent family- and work-related values, behaviors, and aspirations. *Psychological Bulletin, 111,* 108–126.

Bardin, C. W., & Paulsen, C. A. (1981). The testes. In R. H. Williams (Ed.), *Textbook of endocrinology* (6th ed., pp. 293–354). Philadelphia: W. B. Saunders.

Barkley, R. A., Anastopoulos, A. D., Guevremont, D. C., & Fletcher, K. E. (1991). Adolescents with ADHD: Patterns of behavioral adjustment, academic functioning, and treatment utilization. *Journal of the American Academy of Child and Adolescent Psychiatry, 30,* 752–761.

Barkley, R. A., Anastopoulos, A. D., Guevremont, D. C., & Fletcher, K. E. (1992). Adolescents with attention deficit hyperactivity disorder: Mother–adolescent interactions, family beliefs and conflicts, and maternal psychopathology. *Journal of Abnormal Child Psychology, 20,* 263–288.

Barnes, G. M., & Welte, J. W. (1986). Adolescent alcohol abuse: Subgroup differences and relationships to other problem behaviors. *Journal of Adolescent Research, 1,* 79–94.

Barrera, M., & Garrison-Jones, C. (1992). Family and peer social support as specific correlates of adolescent depressive symptoms. *Journal of Abnormal Child Psychology, 20,* 1–16.

Barringer, F. (1993, June 2). School hallways as a gauntlet of sexual taunts. *New York Times,* B-7.

Barsalou, L. W. (1992). *Cognitive psychology: An overview for cognitive scientists.* Hillsdale, NJ: Erlbaum.

Barth, R. P. (1986). *Social and cognitive treatment of children and adolescents.* San Francisco: Jossey-Bass.

Barthell, C. N., & Holmes, D. S. (1968). High school yearbooks: A nonreactive measure of social isolation in graduates who later became schizophrenic. *Journal of Abnormal Psychology, 73,* 313–316.

Bartle, S. E., Anderson, S. A., & Sabatelli, R. M. (1989). A model of parenting style, adolescent individuation and adolescent self-esteem: Preliminary findings. *Journal of Adolescent Research, 4,* 283–298.

Baruch, G. K., & Barnett, R. C. (1987). Role quality and psychological well-being. In F. J. Crosby (Ed.), *Spouse, parent, worker: On gender and multiple roles* (pp. 91–108). New Haven, CT: Yale University Press.

Basseches, M. (1980). Dialectical schemata: A framework for the empirical study of the development of dialectical thinking. *Human Development, 21,* 400–421.

Battle, C. U., Kreisberg, R. V., O'Mahoney, K., & Chitwood, D. L. (1989). Ethical and developmental considerations in caring for hospitalized adolescents. *Journal of Adolescent Health Care, 10,* 479–489.

Baum, C. G., & Forehand, R. L. (1984). Social factors associated with adolescent obesity. *Journal of Pediatric Psychology, 73,* 293–302.

Baumrind, D. (1968). Authoritative vs. authoritarian parental control. *Adolescence, 3,* 255–272.

Baumrind, D. (1971). Current patterns of parental authority. *Genetic Psychology Monographs, 4*(1, Pt. 2).

Baumrind, D. (1991). The influence of parenting style on adolescent competence and substance use. *Journal of Early Adolescence, 11,* 56–95.

Bayer, R. (1981). *Homosexuality and American psychiatry: The politics of diagnosis.* New York: Basic Books.

Belfer, M. L. (1993). Substance abuse with psychiatric illness in children and adolescents: Definitions and terminology. *American Journal of Orthopsychiatry, 63,* 70–79.

Bell, A. P., Weinberg, M. S., & Hammersmith, S. K. (1981). *Sexual preference: Its development in men and women.* Bloomington: Indiana University Press.

Bell, D., Feraios, A., & Bryan, T. (1990). Adolescent males' knowledge and attitudes about AIDS in the context of their social world. *Journal of Applied Social Psychology, 20,* 424–448.

Belsher, B., & Costello, C. G. (1988). Relapse after recovery from unipolar depression: A critical review. *Psychological Bulletin, 104,* 84–96.

Bem, S. L. (1974). The measurement of psychological androgyny. *Journal of Consulting and Clinical Psychology, 42,* 155–162.

Bem, S. L. (1975). Sex role adaptability: One consequence of psychological androgyny. *Journal of Personality and Social Psychology, 31,* 634–643.

Bem, S. L., & Lenney, E. (1976). Sex typing and the avoidance of cross-sex behavior. *Journal of Personality and Social Psychology, 33,* 48–54.

Bengtson, V., & Kuypers, J. A. (1971). Generational differences and the development of stake. *International Journal of Aging and Human Development, 2,* 249–259.

Benson, M. J., Harris, P. B., & Rogers, C. S. (1992). Identity consequences of attachment to mothers and fathers among late adolescents. *Journal of Research on Adolescence, 2,* 187–204.

Berenberg, W. (1976). The adolescent with physical handicaps. In J. R. Gallagher, F. P. Heald, & D. C. Garrell (Eds.), *Medical care of the adolescent* (3rd ed., pp. 279–282). New York: Appleton-Century-Crofts.

Berg, I. (1991). School avoidance, school phobia, and truancy. In M. Lewis (Ed.), *Child and adolescent psychiatry* (pp. 1092–1098). Baltimore, MD: Williams & Wilkins.

Berg, I., & Jackson, A. (1985). Teenage school refusers grow up: A follow-up study of 168 subjects, ten years on average after inpatient treatment. *British Journal of Psychiatry, 147,* 366–370.

Berg-Cross, L., Kidd, F., & Carr, P. (1990). Cohesion, affect, and self-disclosure in African-American families. *Journal of Family Psychology, 4,* 235–250.

Berlinsky, E. B., & Biller, H. B. (1982). *Parental death and psychological development.* Lexington, MA: Lexington Books.

Berman, A. L., & Jobes, D. A. (1991). *Adolescent suicide: Assessment and intervention.* Washington, DC: American Psychological Association.

Bernardo, D. H., Shehan, C. L., & Leslie, G. R. (1987). A residue of tradition: Jobs, careers, and spouses' time in housework. *Journal of Marriage and the Family, 49,* 381–390.

Berndt, T. J. (1982). The features and effects of friendship in early adolescence. *Child Development, 53,* 1447–1460.

Berndt, T. J. (1989). Obtaining support from friends during childhood and adolescence. In D. Belle (Ed.), *Children's social networks and social supports* (pp. 308–331). New York: Wiley.

Berndt, T. J. (1992). Friendship and friends' influence in adolescence. *Current Directions in Psychological Science, 1,* 156–159.

Berndt, T. J., & Das, R. (1987). Effects of popularity and friendship on perceptions of the personality and social behavior of peers. *Journal of Early Adolescence, 7,* 429–439.

Berndt, T. J., Hawkins, J. A., & Hoyle, S. G. (1986). Changes in friendship during a school year: Effects on children's and adolescents' impressions of friendship and sharing with friends. *Child Development, 57,* 1284–1297.

Berndt, T. J., & Hoyle, S. G. (1985). Stability and change in childhood and adolescent friendships. *Developmental Psychology, 21,* 1007–1015.

Berndt, T. J., & Perry, T. B. (1990). Distinctive features and effects of early adolescent friendships. In R. Montemayor, G. R. Adams, & T. P. Gullotta (Eds.), *From childhood to adolescence* (pp. 269–287). Newbury Park, CA: Sage.

Berndt, T. J., & Savin-Williams, R. C. (1992). Peer relationships and friendships. In P. H. Tolan & B. J. Cohler (Eds.), *Clinical research and practice with adolescents* (pp. 203–219). New York: Wiley.

Bernstein, G. A. (1991). Comorbidity and severity of anxiety and depressive disorders in a clinic sample. *Journal of the American Academy of Child and Adolescent Psychiatry, 30,* 43–50.

Bernstein, G. A., & Borchardt, C. M. (1991). Anxiety disorders of childhood and adolescence: A critical review. *Journal of the American Academy of Child and Adolescent Psychiatry, 30,* 519–532.

Bernstein, G. A., Svingen, P. H., & Garfinkel, B. D. (1990). School phobia: Patterns of family functioning. *Journal of the American Academy of Child and Adolescent Psychiatry, 29,* 24–30.

Berscheid, E. (1988). Some comments on love's anatomy: Or, whatever happened to old-fashioned lust? In R. J. Sternberg & M. L. Barnes (Eds.), *The psychology of love* (pp. 359–374). New Haven, CT: Yale University Press.

Berti, A. E. (1988). The development of political understanding in children between 6–15 years old. *Human Relations, 41,* 437–446.

Berzonsky, M. D. (1989). Identity style: Conceptualization and measurement. *Journal of Adolescent Research, 4,* 268–282.

Berzonsky, M. D. (1992). A process perspective on identity and stress management. In G. R. Adams, T. P. Gullotta, & R. Montemayor (Eds.), *Adolescent identity formation* (pp. 193–215). Newbury Park, CA: Sage.

Berzonsky, M. D., & Barclay, C. R. (1981). Formal reasoning and identity formation: A reconceptualization. In J. A. Meacham and N. R. Santilli (Eds.), *Social development in youth: Structure and content* (pp. 64–87). Basel: S. Karger.

Berzonsky, M. D., Rice, K. G., & Neimeyer, G. J. (1990). Identity status and self-construct systems: Process x structure. *Journal of Adolescence, 13,* 251–263.

Bierman, K. L. (1987). The clinical significance and

assessment of poor peer relationships: Peer neglect versus peer rejection. *Journal of Developmental and Behavioral Pediatrics, 8,* 233–240.

Bierman, K. L. (1989). Improving the peer relationships of rejected children. In B. B. Lahey & A. E. Kazdin (Eds.), *Advances in clinical child psychology* (Vol. 12, pp. 53–84). New York: Plenum.

Biernat, M. (1991). Gender stereotypes and the relationship between masculinity and femininity: A developmental analysis. *Journal of Personality and Social Psychology, 61,* 351–365.

Bigelow, B. J. (1977). Children's friendship expectations: A cognitive-developmental study. *Child Development, 48,* 246–253.

Binder, A. (1988). Juvenile delinquency. *Annual Review of Psychology, 39,* 253–282.

Birren, J. E., & Renner, V. J. (1977). Research on the psychology of aging: principles and experimentation. In J. E. Birren & K. W. Schaie (Eds.), *Handbook of the psychology of aging* (pp. 3–38). New York: Van Nostrand Reinhold.

Blagg, N. R., & Yule, W. (1984). The behavioural treatment of school refusal: A comparative study. *Behavior Research and Therapy, 22,* 119–127.

Blain, M. D., Thompson, J. M., & Whiffen, W. E. (1993). Attachment and perceived social support in late adolescence. *Journal of Adolescent Research, 8,* 226–241.

Blanchard-Fields, F. (1986). Reasoning on social dilemmas varying in emotional saliency: An adult developmental perspective. *Psychology and Aging, 1,* 325–332.

Blanchard-Fields, F., Coon, R. C., & Mathews, R. C. (1986). Inferencing and television: A developmental study. *Journal of Youth and Adolescence, 15,* 453–459.

Blasi, A., & Hoeffel, E. C. (1974). Adolescence and formal operations. *Human Development, 17,* 344–363.

Blatt, S. J., Hart, B., Quinlan, D. M., Leadbetter, B., & Auerbach, J. (1993). Interpersonal and self-critical dysphoria and behavioral problems in adolescents. *Journal of Youth and Adolescence, 22,* 253–270.

Blatt, S. J., & Homann, E. (1992). Parent–child interactions in the etiology of dependent and self-critical depression. *Clinical Psychology Review, 12,* 47–92.

Bleich, S., Zillmann, D., & Weaver, J. (1991). Enjoyment and consumption of defiant rock music as a function of adolescent rebelliousness. *Journal of Broadcasting & Electronic Media, 35,* 351–366.

Block, J., Gjerde, P. F., & Block, J. H. (1991). Personality antecedents of depressive tendencies in 18-year-olds: A prospective study. *Journal of Personality and Social Psychology, 60,* 726–738.

Blos, P. (1962). *On adolescence: A psychoanalytic interpretation.* New York: Free Press.

Blos, P. (1967). The second individuation process of adolescence. *Psychoanalytic Study of the Child, 22,* 162–188.

Blos, P. (1970). *The young adolescent.* New York: Free Press.

Blos, P. (1983). The contribution of psychoanalysis to the psychotherapy of adolescents. In M. Sugar (Ed.), *Adolescent psychiatry* (Vol. 11, pp. 104–124). Chicago: University of Chicago Press.

Blosser, B. J. (1988). Ethnic differences in children's media use. *Journal of Broadcasting & Electronic Media, 32,* 453–470.

Blum, H. M., Boyle, M. H., & Offord, D. R. (1988). Single-parent families: Child psychiatric disorder and school performance. *Journal of the American Academy of Child and Adolescent Psychiatry, 27,* 214–219.

Blum, R. W., & Geber, G. (1992). Chronically ill youth. In E. R. McAnarney, R. E. Kreipe, D. P. Orr, & G. D. Comerci (Eds.), *Textbook of adolescent medicine* (pp. 222–228). Philadelphia: Saunders.

Blumstein, P. W., & Schwartz, P. (1977). Bisexuality: Some social psychological issues. *Journal of Social Issues, 33,* 30–45.

Blustein, D. L., Devenis, L. E., & Kidney, B. A. (1989). Relationship between the identity formation process and career development. *Journal of Counseling Psychology, 36,* 196–202.

Blustein, D. L., & Phillips, S. D. (1990). Relation between ego identity statuses and decision-making styles. *Journal of Counseling Psychology, 37,* 160–168.

Blyth, D. A., & Simmons, R. G. (1983). The adjustment of early adolescents to school transitions. *Journal of Early Adolescence, 3,* 105–120.

Boeck, M. A. (1992). Obesity. In S. B. Friedman, M. Fisher, & S. K. Schonberg (Eds.), *Comprehensive adolescent health care* (pp. 238–249). St. Louis, MO: Quality Medical Publishing.

Bohman, M., Sigvardsson, S., & Cloninger, R. C. (1981). Maternal inheritance of alcohol abuse: Cross-fostering analysis of adopted women. *Archives of General Psychiatry, 38,* 965–969.

Bolger, N., Downey, G., Walker, E., & Steininger, P. (1989). The onset of suicidal ideation in childhood and adolescence. *Journal of Youth and Adolescence, 18,* 175–190.

Borrine, M. L., Handal, P. J., Brown, N. Y., & Searight, H. R. (1991). Family conflict and adolescent adjustment in intact, divorced, and blended families. *Journal of Consulting and Clinical Psychology, 59,* 753–755.

Boston Women's Health Collective. (1979). *Our bodies, our selves.* New York: Simon and Schuster.

Botvin, G. J., Baker, E., Dusenbury, L., Tortu, S., & Botvin, E. M. (1990). Preventing adolescent drug abuse through a multimodal cognitive-behavioral approach: Results of a 3-year study. *Journal of Consulting and Clinical Psychology, 58,* 437–446.

Bourne, E. (1978). The state of research on ego identity: A review and appraisal. Part I. *Journal of Youth and Adolescence, 7,* 223–251.

Boxer, A. M., Cohler, B. J., Herdt, G., & Irvin, F. (1993). Gay and lesbian youth. In P. H. Tolan & B. J. Cohler (Eds.), *Handbook of clinical research and practice with adolescents* (pp. 249–280). New York: Wiley.

Boyer, E. L. (1983). *High school: A report on secondary education in America.* The Carnegie Foundation for the Advancement of Teaching. New York: Harper & Row.

Boyes, M., & Chandler, M. J. (1992). Cognitive development, epistemic doubt, and identity formation in adolescence. *Journal of Youth and Adolescence, 21,* 277–304.

Boyle, M. H., Offord, D. R., Racine, Y. A., & Szatmari, P. (1992). Predicting substance use in late adolescence: Results from the Ontario Child Health Study follow-up. *American Journal of Psychiatry, 149,* 761–767.

Bransford, J. D., & Stein, B. S. (1984). *The IDEAL problem solver: A guide for improving thinking, learning, and creativity.* New York: Freeman.

Braun, C. M., & Giroux, J. (1989). Arcade video games: Proxemic, cognitive and content analysis. *Journal of Leisure Research, 21,* 92–105.

Breese, R. W. (1978). The application of Piagetian theory to sexuality: A preliminary exploration. *Adolescence, 13,* 269–278.

Breier, A., Kelsoe, J. R., Kirwin, P. D., Beller, W. A., Wolkowitz, O. M., & Pickar, D. (1988). Early parental loss and development of adult psychopathology. *Archives of General Psychiatry, 45,* 987–993.

Breier, A., Schrieber, J. L., Dyer, J., & Pickar, D. (1991). National Institute of Mental Health study of chronic schizophrenia. *Archives of General Psychiatry, 48,* 239–246.

Brent, D. A., Kolko, D. J., Wartella, M. E., Boylan, M. B., Moritz, G., Baugher, M., & Zelenak, J. P. (1993). Adolescent psychiatric inpatients' risk of suicide attempts at 6-month follow-up. *Journal of the American Academy of Child and Adolescent Psychiatry, 32,* 95–105.

Briere, J. N. (1992). *Child abuse trauma.* Newbury Park, CA: Sage.

Briggs, S. R., Cheek, J. M., & Jones, W. H. (1986). Introduction. In W. H. Jones, J. M. Cheek, & S. R. Biggs (Eds.), *Shyness* (pp. 1–14). New York: Plenum.

Brody, N. (1988). *Personality: In search of individuality.* San Diego, CA: Academic Press.

Bronfenbrenner, U. (1977). Toward an experimental ecology of human development. *American Psychologist, 32,* 513–531.

Bronson, W. C. (1972). The role of enduring orientations to the environment in personality development. *Genetic Psychology Monographs, 87,* 3–80.

Bronstein, P. (1988). Father–child interaction. In P. Bronstein & C. P. Cowan (Eds.), *Fatherhood today* (pp. 107–124). New York: Wiley.

Brook, J. S., Brook, D. W., Gordon, A. S., & Whiteman, M. (1990). The psychosocial etiology of adolescent drug use: A family interactional approach. *Genetic, Social, and General Psychology Monographs, 116,* 111–267.

Brook, J. S., Gordon, A. S., Brook, A., & Brook, D. W. (1989). The consequences of marijuana use on intrapersonal and interpersonal functioning in black and white adolescents. *Genetic, Social, and General Psychology Monographs, 111,* 317–330.

Brook, J. S., Gordon, A. S., & Whiteman, M. (1986). Stability of personality during adolescence and its relationship to stage of drug use. *Genetic, Social, & General Psychology Monographs, 115,* 221–241.

Brook, J. S., Nomura, C., & Cohen, P. (1989). A network of influences on adolescent drug involvement: Neighborhood, school, peer, and family. *Genetic, Social, & General Psychology Monographs, 115,* 125–145.

Brook, J. S., Whiteman, M., Balka, E. B., & Hamburg, B. A. (1992). African-American and Puerto-Rican drug use: Personality, familial, and other environmental risk factors. *Genetic, Social, and General Psychology Monographs, 118,* 417–438.

Brook, J. S., Whiteman, M., Cohen, P., & Tanaka, J. S. (1992). Childhood precursors of adolescent drug use: A longitudinal analysis. *Genetic, Social, and General Psychology Monographs, 118,* 195–213.

Brook, J. S., Whiteman, M., & Gordon, A. S. (1983). Stages of drug use in adolescence: Personality, peer, and family correlates. *Developmental Psychology, 19,* 269–277.

Brooks-Gunn, J. (1988). Antecedents and consequences of variations in girls' maturational timing. In M. D.

Levine & E. R. McAnarney (Eds.), *Early adolescent transitions* (pp. 101–121). Lexington, MA: Lexington Books.

Brooks-Gunn, J., & Furstenberg, F. F., Jr. (1989). Adolescent sexual behavior. *American Psychologist, 44,* 249–257.

Brooks-Gunn, J., & Furstenberg, F. F., Jr. (1990). Coming of age in the era of AIDS: Puberty, sexuality, and contraception. *The Milbank Quarterly, 68* (Suppl. 1), 59–84.

Brooks-Gunn, J., & Warren, M. (1988). The psychological significance of secondary sexual characteristics in nine-to-eleven-year-old girls. *Child Development, 59,* 1061–1069.

Brophy, J. (1986). Teacher influences on academic achievement. *American Psychologist, 41,* 1069–1077.

Brown, A., & Finkelhor, D. (1986). The impact of child sexual abuse: A review of the research. *Psychological Bulletin, 99,* 66–77.

Brown, B. B. (1989). The role of peer groups in adolescents' adjustment to secondary school. In T. J. Berndt & G. W. Ladd (Eds.), *Peer relationships in child development* (pp. 188–215). New York: Wiley.

Brown, B. B. (1990). Peer groups and peer cultures. In S. S. Feldman & G. R. Elliott (Eds.), *At the threshold: The developing adolescent* (pp. 171–196). Cambridge, MA: Harvard University Press.

Brown, B. B., Clasen, D. R., & Eicher, S. A. (1986). Perceptions of peer pressure, peer conformity dispositions, and self-reported behavior among adolescents. *Developmental Psychology, 22,* 521–530.

Brown, J. K. (1963). Adolescent initiation rites among preliterate peoples. In R. E. Grinder (Ed.), *Studies in adolescence* (pp. 75–85). New York: Macmillan.

Brown, L. K., Overholser, J., Spirito, A., & Fritz, G. K. (1991). The correlates of planning in adolescent suicide attempts. *Journal of the American Academy of Child and Adolescent Psychiatry, 30,* 95–99.

Bruch, H. (1976). Anorexia nervosa in adolescence. In J. R. Gallagher, F. P. Heald, & D. C. Garrell (Eds.), *Medical care of the adolescent* (3rd ed., pp. 251–259). New York: Appleton-Century-Crofts.

Bruer, J. T. (1993). The mind's journey from novice to expert. *American Educator, 17,* 6–15, 38–46.

Bryant, B. K. (1992). Conflict resolution strategies in relation to children's peer relations. *Developmental Psychology, 13,* 35–50.

Buchanan, C. M., Maccoby, E. E., & Dornbusch, S. M. (1991). Caught between parents: Adolescents'

experience in divorced homes. *Child Development, 62,* 1008–1029.

Buchanan, C. M., Maccoby, E. E., & Dornbusch, S. M. (1992). Adolescents and their families after divorce: Three residential arrangements. *Journal of Research on Adolescence, 2,* 261–291.

Buis, J. M., & Thompson, D. N. (1989). Imaginary audience and personal fable: A brief review. *Adolescence, 24,* 773–781.

Bukowski, W. M., & Hoza, B. (1989). Popularity and friendship: Issues in theory, measurement, and outcome. In T. J. Berndt & G. W. Ladd (Eds.), *Peer relationships in child development* (pp. 15–45). New York: Wiley.

Bukowski, W. M., & Newcomb, A. F. (1984). Stability and determinants of sociometric status and friendship choice: A longitudinal perspective. *Developmental Psychology, 20,* 941–951.

Burke, K. C., Burke, J. D., Regier, D. A., & Rae, D. S. (1990). Age at onset of selected mental disorders in five community populations. *Archives of General Psychiatry, 47,* 511–518.

Byrne, D., Kelley, K., & Fisher, W. A. (1993). Unwanted teenage pregnancies: Incidence, interpretation, and intervention. *Applied & Preventive Psychology, 2,* 101–113.

Cadoret, R. J. (1978). Evidence for genetic inheritance of primary affective disorder in adoptees. *American Journal of Psychiatry, 135,* 463–466.

Cadoret, R. J., Troughton, T. W., O'Gorman, T. W., & Heywood, E. (1986). An adoption study of genetic and environmental factors in drug abuse. *Archives of General Psychiatry, 43,* 1131–1136.

Cairns, R. B., Cairns, B. D., Neckerman, H. J., Ferguson, L. L., & Gariepy, J. (1989). Growth and aggression: 1. Childhood to early adolescence. *Developmental Psychology, 25,* 320–330.

Calderone, M. S. (1983). Childhood sexuality: Approaching the prevention of sexual disease. In G. W. Albee, S. Gordon, & H. Leitenberg (Eds.), *Promoting sexual responsibility and preventing sexual problems* (pp. 333–344). Hanover, NH: University Press of New England.

Cameron, J. L. (1990). Factors controlling the onset of puberty in primates. In J. Bancroft & J. M. Reinisch (Eds.), *Adolescence and puberty* (pp. 9–28). New York: Oxford University Press.

Campbell, E., Adams, G. R., & Dobson, W. R. (1984). Familial correlates of identity formation in late adolescence: A study of the predictive utility of connectedness and individuality in family relations. *Journal of Youth and Adolescence, 13,* 509–524.

Campbell, M. (1985). Schizophrenic disorders and pervasive developmental disorders/autism. In J. M. Wiener (Ed.), *Diagnosis and psychopharmacology of childhood and adolescent disorders* (pp. 113–150). New York: Wiley.

Campbell, N. B., Milling, L., Laughlin, A., & Bush, E. (1993). The psychosocial climate of families with suicidal preadolescent children. *American Journal of Orthopsychiatry, 63,* 142–145.

Cantor, P. (1976). Personality characteristics found among youthful suicide attempters. *Journal of Abnormal Psychology, 85,* 324–329.

Cappell, C., & Heiner, R. B. (1990). The intergenerational transmission of family aggression. *Journal of Family Violence, 5,* 135–152.

Carey, T. C., Finch, A. J., & Carey, M. P. (1991). Relation between differential emotions and depression in emotionally disturbed children and adolescents. *Journal of Consulting and Clinical Psychology, 59,* 594–597.

Carlson, G. A., & Kashani, J. H. (1988). Phenomenology of major depression from childhood through adulthood: Analysis of three studies. *American Journal of Psychiatry, 145,* 1222–1225.

Carpenter, W. T., & Stephens, J. H. (1980). The diagnosis of mania. In R. H. Belmaker & H. M. van Praag (Eds.), *Mania: An evolving concept* (pp. 7–24). New York: Spectrum.

Carr, M., Borkowski, J. G., & Maxwell, S. E. (1991). Motivational components of underachievement. *Developmental Psychology, 27,* 108–118.

Carroll, J. L., & Rest, J. R. (1982). Moral development. In B. B. Wolman (Ed.), *Handbook of developmental psychology* (pp. 434–451). Englewood Cliffs, NJ: Prentice-Hall.

Case, R. (1985). *Intellectual development: Birth to adulthood.* New York: Academic Press.

Case, R. (1991). *The mind's staircase.* Hillsdale, NJ: Erlbaum.

Caspar, R. C. (1992). Risk factors for the development of eating disorders. In S. C. Feinstein (Ed.), *Adolescent psychiatry* (pp. 91–103). Chicago: University of Chicago Press.

Caspi, A., Elder, G. H., & Bem, D. J. (1987). Moving against the world: Life-course patterns of explosive children. *Developmental Psychology, 23,* 308–313.

Caspi, A., Elder, G. H., & Bem, D. J. (1988). Moving away from the world: Life-course patterns of shy

children. *Developmental Psychology, 24,* 824–831.

Caspi, A., & Moffitt, T. E. (1991). Individual differences are accentuated during periods of social change: The sample case of girls at puberty. *Journal of Personality and Social Psychology, 61,* 157–168.

Celis, W., III. (1993, April 28). 10 years after scathing report, schools show uneven progress. *New York Times,* A19.

Cella, D. F., DeWolfe, A. S., & Fitzgibbon, M. (1987). Ego identity status, identification, and decision-making style in late adolescents. *Adolescence, 22,* 849–861.

Chamberlain, D. B. (1989). Babies remember pain. *Pre- and Peri-Natal Psychology Journal, 3,* 297–310.

Chan, C. S. (1993). Cultural/gender factors in sexual activity among Asian American adolescents. *Focus, 7,* 9. (Published by the Society for the Psychological Study of Ethnic Minority Issues, a division of the American Psychological Association.)

Chandler, M. J., & Boutilier, R. G. (1992). The development of dynamic system reasoning. *Human Development, 35,* 121–137.

Chandler, M. J., & Boyes, M. C. (1982). Social-cognitive development. In B. B. Wolman (Ed.), *Handbook of developmental psychology* (pp. 387–402). Englewood Cliffs, NJ: Prentice-Hall.

Chandler, M. J., Boyes, M., & Ball, L. (1990). Relativism and stations of epistemic doubt. *Journal of Experimental Child Psychology, 50,* 370–395.

Chandler, M. J., & Helm, D. (1980). Knowing the sort of help that is really needed. (Unpublished paper cited in Chandler & Boyes, 1982.)

Chase, W. G., & Simon, H. A. (1973). Perception in chess. *Cognitive Psychology, 4,* 55–81.

Chase, W. G., & Ericsson, K. A. (1981). Skilled memory. In J. R. Anderson (Ed.), *Cognitive skills and their acquisition* (pp. 141–189). Hillsdale, NJ: Erlbaum.

Chassin, L., McLaughlin, L. M., & Sher, K. J. (1988). Self-awareness theory, family history of alcoholism, and adolescent alcohol involvement. *Journal of Abnormal Psychology, 97,* 206–217.

Cheek, J. M., Carpentieri, A. M., Smith, T. G., Rierdan, J., & Koff, E. (1986). In W. H. Jones, J. M. Cheek, & S. R. Biggs (Eds.), *Shyness* (pp. 105–115). New York: Plenum.

Cherry, D. C. (1953). Some experiments on the recognition of speech, with one and with two ears. *Journal of the Acoustical Society of America, 25,* 975–979.

Chevron, E. S., Quinlan, D. M., & Blatt, S. J. (1978). Sex roles and gender differences in the experience of depression. *Journal of Abnormal Psychology, 87,* 680–683.

Chiles, J. A., Miller, M. L., & Cox, G. B. (1980). Depression in an adolescent delinquent population. *Archives of General Psychiatry, 37,* 1179–1184.

Chilman, C. S. (1983). *Adolescent sexuality in a changing American society* (2nd ed.). New York: Wiley.

Chiu, L. (1990). A comparison of moral reasoning in American and Chinese school children. *International Journal of Adolescence and Youth, 2,* 185–198.

Chodorow, N. (1974). Family structure and feminine personality. In M. Z. Rosaldo & L. Lamphere (Eds.), *Women, culture and society.* Stanford, CA: Stanford University Press.

Christiansen, B. A., Smith, G. T., Roehling, P. V., & Goldman, M. S. (1989). Using alcohol expectancies to predict adolescent drinking behavior after one year. *Journal of Consulting and Clinical Psychology, 57,* 93–99.

Christensen-Szalanski, J. J., Boyce, W. T., Harrell, H., & Gardner, M. M. (1987). Circumcision and informed consent: Is more information always better? *Medical Care, 25,* 856–867.

Christoff, K. A. (1985). Social skills and social problem-solving training for shy young adolescents. *Behavior Therapy, 16,* 468–477.

Christopherson, B. B., Jones, R. M., & Sales, A. P. (1988). Diversity in reported motivations for substance use as a function of ego-identity development. *Journal of Adolescent Research, 3,* 141–152.

Church, P., Forehand, R., Brown, C., & Holmes, T. (1990). Prevention of drug abuse: Examination of the effectiveness of a program with elementary school children. *Behavior Therapy, 21,* 339–347.

Cillissen, A. H., Van IJzendoorn, H. W., Van Lieshout, C. F., & Hartup, W. W. (1992). Heterogeneity among peer-rejected boys: Subtypes and stabilities. *Child Development, 63,* 893–905.

Clark, C. M. (1992). Deviant adolescent subcultures: Assessment strategies and clinical interventions. *Adolescence, 27,* 283–293.

Clark, D. C., & Mokros, H. B. (1993). Depression and suicidal behavior. In P. H. Tolan & B. J. Cohler (Eds.), *Handbook of clinical research and practice with adolescents* (pp. 333–358). New York: Wiley.

Clark, M. L. (1989). Friendship and peer relations of black adolescents. In R. L. Jones (Ed.), *Black adolescents* (pp. 175–204). Berkeley, CA: Cobb & Henry.

Clark, M. L., & Bittle, M. L. (1992). Friendship expectations and the evaluation of present friendships in middle childhood and early adolescence. *Child Study Journal, 22,* 115–135.

Clark, R. M. (1983). *Family life and school achievement: Why poor black children succeed or fail.* Chicago: University of Chicago Press.

Clark-Lempers, D. S., Lempers, J. D., & Ho, C. (1991). Early, middle, and late adolescents'perceptions of their relationships with significant others. *Journal of Adolescent Research, 6,* 296–315.

Clasen, D. R., & Brown, B. B. (1985). The multidimensionality of peer pressure in adolescence. *Journal of Youth and Adolescence, 14,* 451–468.

Clausen, J. A. (1975). The social meaning of differential physical and sexual maturation. In S. E. Dragastin & G. H. Elder, Jr. (Eds.), *Adolescence in the life cycle* (pp. 25–47). New York: Halsted.

Clemens, S. L. (1876/1958). *The Adventures of Tom Sawyer.* New York: Dodd, Mead & Co.

Cloninger, R. C., Bohman, M., & Sigvardsson, S. (1981). Inheritance of alcohol abuse: Cross-fostering analysis of adult men. *Archives of General Psychiatry, 38,* 861–868.

Coates, T. J. (1992). Forward. In R. J. DiClemente (Ed.), *Adolescents and AIDS: A generation in jeopardy* (pp. vii–ix). Newbury Park, CA: Sage.

Cohn, L. D., Millstein, S. G., Irwin, C. E., Adler, N. E., Kegeles, S. M., Dolcini, P., & Stone, G. (1988). A comparison of two measures of egocentrism. *Journal of Personality Assessment, 52,* 212–222.

Coie, J. D., Belding, M., & Underwood, M. (1988). Aggression and peer rejection in childhood. In B. B. Lahey & A. E. Kazdin (Eds.), *Advances in clinical child psychology* (Vol. 11, pp. 124–158). New York: Plenum.

Coie, J. D., Dodge, K. A., & Kupersmidt, J. B. (1990). Peer group behavior and social status. In S. R. Asher & J. D. Coie (Eds.), *Peer rejection in childhood* (pp. 17–59). New York: Cambridge University Press.

Cole, D. E., Protinsky, H. O., & Cross, L. H. (1992). An empirical investigation of adolescent suicidal ideation. *Adolescence, 27,* 813–818.

Coleman, J. S., Hoffer, T., & Kilgore, S. (1982). *High school achievement: Public, Catholic, and private schools compared.* New York: Basic Books.

Collins, W. A. (1990). Parent–child relationships in the transition to adolescence: Continuity and change in interaction, affect, and cognition. In R. Montemayor, G. R. Adams, & T. P. Gullotta (Eds.), *From childhood to adolescence* (pp. 85–106). Newbury Park, CA: Sage.

Comite, F., Cutler, G. B., Jr., Rivier, J., Vale, W. W., Loriaux, D. L., & Crowley, W. F., Jr. (1981). Short-term treatment of idiopathic precocious puberty with a long-acting analogue of luteinizing hormone-releasing hormone. A preliminary report. *New England Journal of Medicine, 305*, 1546–1550.

Condry, S. (1987). Therapy implementation problems in a residence for delinquents. *Journal of Applied Developmental Psychology, 8*, 259–272.

Conger, J. J. (1975). Proceedings of the American Psychological Association, Incorporated, for the Year 1974: Minutes of the Annual Meeting of the Council of Representatives. *American Psychologist, 30*, 620–651.

Conoway, L. P., & Hansen, D. J. (1989). Social behavior of physically abused and neglected children: A critical review. *Clinical Psychology Review, 9*, 627–652.

Constantine, L. L. (1987). Adolescent process and family organization: A model of development as a function of family paradigm. *Journal of Adolescent Research, 2*, 349–366.

Consumer Reports. (1989, March). Readers report on condoms. p. 138.

Cooney, E. W., & Selman, R. L. (1978). Children's use of social conceptions: Toward a dynamic model of social cognition. In W. Damon (Ed.), *Social cognition* (pp. 23–44). San Francisco: Jossey-Bass.

Cooper, M. J., & Fairburn, C. G. (1992). Thoughts about eating, weight and shape in anorexia nervosa and bulimia nervosa. *Behaviour Research and Therapy, 30*, 501–511.

Cooper, C. R., & Grotevant, H. D. (1987). Gender issues in the interface of family experience and adolescents' friendships and dating identity. *Journal of Youth and Adolescence, 16*, 247–264.

Coryell, W., Endicott, J., & Keller, M. (1990). Outcome of patients with chronic affective disorder: A five-year follow-up. *American Journal of Psychiatry, 147*, 1627–1633.

Coryell, W., & Winokur, G. (1992). Course and outcome. In E. S. Paykel (Ed.), *Handbook of affective disorders* (2nd ed., pp. 89–108). New York: Guilford.

Cosse, W. J. (1992). Who's who and what's what? The effects of gender on development in adolescence. In B. R. Wainrib (Ed.), *Gender issues across the life cycle* (pp. 5–16). New York: Springer.

Costanzo, P. R., & Shaw, M. E. (1966). Conformity as a function of age level. *Child Development, 37*, 967–975.

Costello, C. G. (Ed.) (1993). *Symptoms of depression.* New York: Wiley.

Coté, J. E. (1992). Was Mead wrong about coming of age in Samoa? An analysis of the Mead/Freeman controversy for scholars of adolescence and human development. *Journal of Youth and Adolescence, 21*, 499–527.

Coupey, S. M. (1992a). Anorexia nervosa. In S. B. Friedman, M. Fisher, & S. K. Schonberg (Eds.), *Comprehensive adolescent health care* (pp. 217–231). St. Louis, MO: Quality Medical Publishing.

Coupey, S. M. (1992b). Chronic illness. In S. B. Friedman, M. Fisher, & S. K. Schonberg (Eds.), *Comprehensive adolescent health care* (pp. 119–128). St. Louis, MO: Quality Medical Publishing.

Covell, K., & Abramovitch, R. (1988). Children's understanding of maternal anger: Age and source of anger differences. *Merrill-Palmer Quarterly, 34*, 353–368.

Craig, M. E. (1990). Coercive sexuality in dating relationships: A situational model. *Clinical Psychology Review, 10*, 395–423.

Crain, W. C. (1992). *Theories of development* (3rd ed.). Englewood Cliffs, NJ: Prentice-Hall.

Crain, W. C., & Crain, E. F. (1974). The growth of political ideas and their expression among young activists. *Journal of Youth and Adolescence, 3*, 105–133.

Cramer, P. (1988). The Defense Mechanism Inventory: A review of research and discussion of the scales. *Journal of Personality Assessment, 52*, 142–164.

Cramer, P., & Carter, T. (1978). The relationship between sexual identification and the use of defense mechanisms. *Journal of Personality Assessment, 42*, 63–73.

Cranston, K. (1991). HIV education for gay, lesbian, and bisexual youth: Personal risk, personal power, and the community of conscience. *Journal of Homosexuality, 22*, 247–259.

Crisp, A. H. (1980). *Anorexia nervosa: Let me be.* New York: Grune & Stratton.

Crowther, J. H., Tennenbaum, D. L., Hobfoll, S. E., & Stephens, M. P. (Eds.) (1992). *The etiology of bulimia nervosa.* Washington, DC: Hemisphere.

Csikszentmihalyi, M., & Larson, R. (1984). *Being adolescent: Conflict and growth in the teenage years.* New York: Basic Books.

Cunliffe, T. (1992). Arresting youth crime: A review of social skills training with young offenders. *Adolescence, 27*, 891–900.

Cusick, P. A. (1973). *Inside high school: The student's world.* New York: Holt, Rinehart & Winston.

Cutrona, C. E. (1982). Transition to college: Loneliness and the process of social adjustment. In L. A. Peplau & D. Perlman (Eds.), *Loneliness: A sourcebook of theory, research, and therapy* (pp. 291–309). New York: Wiley.

Cvetkovich, G. (1975). On the psychology of adolescent use of contraception. *Journal of Sex Research, 11,* 256–270.

D'Augelli, A. R., & Bingham, C. R. (1993). Interventions to prevent HIV infections in young adolescents. In R. Lerner (Ed.), *Early adolescence: Perspectives on research, policy, and intervention* (pp. 353–368). Hillsdale, NJ: Erlbaum.

Damon, W., & Hart, D. (1988). *Self understanding in childhood and adolescence.* New York: Cambridge University Press.

Danenberg, M. A., Loos-Cosgrove, M., & LoVerde, M. (1987). Temporary hearing loss and rock music. *Language, Speech, and Hearing Services in Schools, 18,* 267–274.

Darling, C. A., Davidson, J. K., Sr., & Passarello, L. C. (1992). The mystique of first intercourse among college youth: The role of partners, contraceptive practices, and psychological reactions. *Journal of Youth and Adolescence, 21,* 97–117.

Davenport, Y. B., & Adland, M. L. (1988). Management of manic episodes. In J. F. Clarkin, G. L. Haas, & I. D. Glick (Eds.), *Affective disorders and the family* (pp. 173–195). New York: Guilford.

Davidge, A. M., & Forman, S. G. (1988). Psychological treatment of adolescent substance abusers: A review. *Children and Youth Services Review, 10,* 43–53.

Davies, E., & Furnham, A. (1986). The dieting and body shape concerns of adolescent females. *Journal of Child Psychology & Psychiatry, 27,* 417–428.

Davis, K. L., Kahn, R. S., & Davison, M. (1991). Dopamine and schizophrenia: A review and reconceptualization. *American Journal of Psychiatry, 148,* 1474–1486.

Davis, M. H., & Kraus, L. A. (1989). Social contact, loneliness, and mass media use: A test of two hypotheses. *Journal of Applied Social Psychology, 19,* 1100–1124.

Davis, S. M., & Harris, M. B. (1982). Sexual knowledge, sexual interests, and sources of sexual information of

rural and urban adolescents from three cultures. *Adolescence, 17,* 471–492.

Deaux, K. (1985). Sex and gender. *Annual Review of Psychology, 36,* 49–81.

de Jong, M. L. (1992). Attachment, individuation, and risk of suicide in late adolescence. *Journal of Youth and Adolescence, 21,* 357–374.

de Leon, G. (1988). The therapeutic community perspective and approach for adolescent substance abusers. In S. C. Feinstein (Ed.), *Adolescent psychiatry* (Vol. 15, pp. 535–556). Chicago: University of Chicago Press.

Delgado, P. L., Price, L. H., Henninger, G. R., & Charney, D. S. Neurochemistry. (1992). In E. S. Paykel (Ed.), *Handbook of affective disorders* (2nd ed., pp. 219–254). New York: Guilford.

Dellarosa, D. (1988). A history of thinking. In R. J. Sternberg & E. E. Smith (Eds.), *The psychology of human thought* (pp. 1–18). New York: Cambridge University Press.

della Silva, P. C., & Dusek, J. B. (1984). Sex role orientation and resolution of Eriksonian crises during the late adolescent years. *Journal of Personality and Social Psychology, 47,* 204–212.

Dembo, M. H., & Lundel, B. (1979). Factors affecting adolescent contraception practices: Implications for sex education. *Adolescence, 14,* 657–664.

Demetriou, A., Efklides, A., Papadaki, M., Papantoniou, G., & Economou, A. (1993). Structure and development of causal-experimental thought: From early adolescence to youth. *Developmental Psychology, 29,* 480–497.

DeParle, J. (1992, November 26). Teaching high school students how to work. *New York Times,* A1, D15.

Deutsch, H. (1967). *Selected problems of adolescence.* New York: International Universities Press.

Deutsch, L. J., & Erickson, M. T. (1989). Early life events as discriminators of socialized and undersocialized delinquents. *Journal of Abnormal Child Psychology, 17,* 541–551.

de Wilde, E. J., Kienhorts, I., Diekstra, R., & Wolters, W. (1992). The relationship between adolescent suicidal behavior and life events in childhood and adolescence. *American Journal of Psychiatry, 149,* 45–51.

Deykin, E. Y., Buka, S. L., & Zeena, T. H. (1992). Depressive illness among chemically dependent adolescents. *American Journal of Psychiatry, 149,* 1341–1347.

Diaz, R. M., & Berndt, T. J. (1982). Children's knowledge

of a best friend: Fact or fancy? *Developmental Psychology, 18*, 787–794.

Dickson, L. R., Heffron, W. M., & Parker, C. (1990). Children from disrupted and adoptive homes on an inpatient unit. *American Journal of Orthopsychiatry, 60*, 594–602.

DiClemente, R. J. (Ed.) (1992a). *Adolescents and AIDS: A generation in jeopardy.* Newbury Park, CA: Sage.

DiClemente, R. J. (1992b). Psychosocial determinants of condom use among adolescents. In R. J. DiClemente (Ed.), *Adolescents and AIDS: A generation in jeopardy* (pp. 34–51). Newbury Park, CA: Sage.

DiClemente, R. J. (1993). Confronting the challenge of AIDS among adolescents: Directions for future research. *Journal of Adolescent Research, 8*, 156–166.

Dishion, T. J., Patterson, G. R., Stoolmiller, M., & Skinner, M. L. (1991). Family, school, and behavioral antecedents to early adolescent involvement with antisocial peers. *Developmental Psychology, 27*, 172–180.

Dixon, W. A., Heppner, P. P., & Anderson, W. (1991). Problem-solving appraisals, stress, hopelessness, and suicidal ideation in a college population. *Journal of Counseling Psychology, 38*, 51–56.

Doane, J. A., West, K. L., Goldstein, M. J., Rodnick, E. H., & Jones, J. E. (1981). Parental communication deviance and affective style: Predictors of subsequent schizophrenic disorders in vulnerable adolescents. *Archives of General Psychiatry, 38*, 679–685.

Dodge, K. A., & Feldman, E. (1990). Issues in social cognition and sociometric status. In S. R. Asher & J. D. Coie (Eds.), *Peer rejection in childhood* (pp. 119–155). New York: Cambridge University Press.

Dorn, L. D., Susman, E. J., Nottelmann, E. D., Inoff-Germain, G., & Chrousos, G. P. (1990). Perceptions of puberty: Adolescent, parent, and health care personnel. *Developmental Psychology, 26*, 322–329.

Dornbusch, S. M., Carlsmith, J. M., Bushwall, S. J., Ritter, P. L., Leiderman, H., Hastorf, A. H., & Gross, R. T. (1985). Single parents, extended households, and the control of adolescents. *Child Development, 56*, 326–341.

Dornbusch, S. M., Carlsmith, J. M., Gross, R. T., Martin, J. A., Jennings, D., Rosenberg, A., & Duke, P. (1981). Sexual development, age, and dating: A comparison of biological and social influences upon one set of behaviors. *Child Development, 52*, 179–185.

Dornbusch, S. M., Ritter, P. L., Mont-Reynaud, R., & Chien, Z. (1990). Family decision making and academic performance in a diverse high school population. *Journal of Adolescent Research, 5*, 143–160.

Douvan, E., & Adelson, J. (1966). *The adolescent experience.* New York: Wiley.

Doyle, A. B. (1973). Listening to distraction: A developmental study of selective attention. *Journal of Experimental Child Psychology, 15*, 100–115.

Drewnowski, A., Yee, D. K., & Krahn, D. D. (1988). Bulimia in college women: Incidence and recovery rates. *American Journal of Psychiatry, 145*, 753–755.

Dreyer, P. H. (1982). Sexuality during adolescence. In B. B. Wolman (Ed.), *Handbook of developmental psychology* (pp. 559–601). Englewood Cliffs, NJ: Prentice-Hall.

DuBois, D. L., Felner, R. D., Brand, S., Adan, A. M., & Evans, E. G. (1992). A prospective study of life stress, social support, and adaptation in early adolescence. *Child Development, 63*, 542–557.

DuBois, D. L., & Hirsch, B. J. (1990). School and neighborhood friendship patterns of black and whites in early adolescence. *Child Development, 61*, 524–536.

Dubow, E. F., Lovko, K. R., & Kausch, D. F. (1990). Demographic differences in adolescents' health concerns and perceptions of helping agents. *Journal of Clinical Child Psychology, 19*, 44–54.

Dunphy, D. C. (1963). The social structure of urban adolescent groups. *Sociometry, 26*, 230–246.

Durbin, D. L., Darling, N., Steinberg, L., & Brown, B. B. (1993). Parenting style and peer group membership among European-American adolescents. *Journal of Research on Adolescence, 3*, 87–100.

Durlak, J. A. (1992). School problems of children. In C. E. Walker & M. C. Roberts (Eds.), *Handbook of clinical child psychology* (2nd ed., pp. 497–510). New York: Wiley.

Dutton, D., & Aron, A. (1974). Some evidence for heightened sexual attraction under conditions of high anxiety. *Journal of Personality and Social Psychology, 30*, 510–517.

Dworkin, R. H., Bernstein, G., Kaplansky, L. M., Lipsitz, J. D., Rinaldi, A., Slater, S. L., Cornblatt, B. A., & Erlenmeyer-Kimling, L. (1991). Social competence and positive and negative symptoms: A longitudinal study of children and adolescents at risk for schizophrenia and affective disorder. *American Journal of Psychiatry, 148*, 1182–1188.

Dyk, P. H., & Adams, G. R. (1990). Identity and intimacy: An initial investigation of three theoretical models using cross-lag panel correlations. *Journal of Youth and Adolescence, 19*, 91–110.

Easterlin, R. A. (1980). *Birth and fortune: The impact of numbers on personal welfare.* New York: Basic Books.

Eaton, W. W., Mortensen, P. B., Herrman, H., Freeman, H., Bilder, W., Burgess, P., & Wooff, K. (1992). Long-term course of hospitalization for schizophrenia: Part I. Risk for rehospitalization. *Schizophrenia Bulletin, 18,* 217–228.

Eccles, J. S., Lord, S., & Midgley, C. (1991). What are we doing to early adolescents? The impact of educational contexts on early adolescents. *American Journal of Education, 99,* 521–542.

Eccles, J. S., Midgley, C., Wigfield, A., Buchanan, C. M., Reuman, D., Flanagan, C., & MacIver, D. (1993). Development during adolescence: The impact of stage-environment fit on young adolescent's experiences in schools and in families. *American Psychologist, 48,* 90–101.

Eckenrode, J., Laird, M., & Doris, J. (1993). School performance and disciplinary problems among abused and neglected children. *Developmental Psychology, 29,* 53–62.

Eckert, P. (1989). *Jocks and burnouts: Social categories and identity in the high school.* New York: Teachers College Press.

Ehrenberg, M. F., Cox, D. N., & Koopman, R. F. (1990). The prevalence of depression among high school students. *Adolescence, 25,* 905–912.

Ehrhardt, A. A., & Meyer-Bahlburg, H. F. L. (1975). Psychological correlates of abnormal pubertal development. In J. Bierich (Ed.), *Disorders of puberty. Clinics in endocrinology and metabolism,* Vol. 4, No. 1. Philadelphia: Saunders.

Eichorn, D. H. (1973). The Berkeley longitudinal studies: Continuities and correlates of behaviour. *Canadian Journal of Behavioral Science, 5,* 197–320.

Eichorn, D. H. (1975). Asynchronizations in adolescent development. In S. Dragastin & G. H. Elder, Jr. (Eds.), *Adolescence in the life cycle: Psychological change and the social context* (pp. 81–96). New York: Halsted.

Eisele, J., Hertsgaard, D., & Light, H. K. (1986). Factors related to eating disorders in young adolescent girls. *Adolescence, 21,* 283–290.

Eisenstadt, S. N. (1956). *From generation to generation.* Glencoe, IL: Free Press.

Eiser, C., Havermans, T., Pancer, M., & Eiser, R. (1992). Adjustment to chronic disease in relation to age and gender: Mothers' and fathers' reports of their childrens' behavior. *Journal of Pediatric Psychology, 17,* 261–275.

Eisser, C. (1990). Psychological effects of chronic disease. *Journal of Child Psychology and Psychiatry, 31,* 85–98.

Eissler, K. R. (1958). Notes on problems of technique in the psychoanalytic treatment of adolescents. *Psychoanalytic Study of the Child, 13,* 223–254.

Ekstein, R. (1968). Impulse—acting out—purpose: Psychotic adolescents and their quest for goals. *International Journal of Psycho-Analysis, 49,* 347–352.

Elder, G. H., Jr. (1980). Adolescence in historical perspective. In J. Adelson (Ed.), *Handbook of adolescent psychology* (pp. 3–46). New York: Wiley.

Elkind, D. (1967). Egocentrism in adolescence. *Child Development, 38,* 1025–1034.

Elkind, D. (1974). *Children and adolescents: Interpretive essays on Jean Piaget* (2nd ed.). New York: Oxford University Press.

Elkind, D. (1978). Understanding the young adolescent. *Adolescence, 13,* 127–134.

Elkind, D. (1980). Strategic interactions in early adolescence. In J. Adelson (Ed.), *Handbook of adolescent psychology* (pp. 432–444). New York: Wiley.

Elkind, D. (1985). Egocentrism redux. *Developmental Review, 5,* 218–226.

Elkind, D., & Bowen, R. (1979). Imaginary audience behavior in children and adolescents. *Developmental Psychology, 15,* 38–44.

Elliott, D. S., Huizinga, D., & Ageton, S. S. (1985). *Explaining delinquency and drug use.* Beverly Hills, CA: Sage.

Elliott, D. S., Huizinga, D., & Menard, S. (1989). *Multiple problem youth: Delinquency, substance abuse, and mental health problems.* New York: Springer.

Elmen, J., & Offer, D. (1992). Normality, turmoil, and adolescence. In P. H. Tolan & B. J. Cohler (Eds.), *Handbook of clinical research and practice with adolescents* (pp. 5–19). New York: Wiley.

Emery, R. E. (1988). *Marriage, divorce, and children's adjustment.* Newbury Park, CA: Sage.

Empey, L. T. (1982). *American delinquency: Its meaning and construction* (rev. ed.). Homewood, IL: Dorsey.

Engelhardt, D. M., Rosen, B., Feldman, J., Engelhardt, J. Z., & Cohen, P. (1982). A 15-year followup of 646 schizophrenic outpatients. *Schizophrenia Bulletin, 8,* 493–503.

Englander, S. W. (1984). Some self-reported correlates of runaway behavior in adolescent females. *Journal of Consulting and Clinical Psychology, 52,* 484–485.

English, A. (1992). Expanding access to HIV services for

adolescents: Legal and ethical issues. In R. J. DiClemente (Ed.), *Adolescents and AIDS: A generation in jeopardy* (pp. 262–283). Newbury Park, CA: Sage.

Entwisle, D. R. (1990). Schools and the adolescent. In S. S. Feldman & G. R. Elliott (Eds.), *At the threshold: The developing adolescent* (pp. 197–224). Cambridge, MA: Harvard University Press.

Epstein, J. L. (1989). The selection of friends. In T. J. Berndt & G. W. Ladd (Eds.), *Peer relationships in child development* (pp. 158–187). New York: Wiley.

Epstein, L. H., & Cluss, P. A. (1986). Behavioral genetics of childhood obesity. *Behavior Therapy, 17*, 324–334.

Erikson, E. H. (1956). The problem of ego identity. *Journal of the American Psychoanalytic Association, 4*, 56–121.

Erikson, E. H. (1959). Identity and the life cycle. *Psychological Issues, 1*, 1–171.

Erikson, E. H. (1963). *Childhood and society* (2nd ed.). New York: Norton.

Erikson, E. H. (1968). *Identity: Youth and crisis.* New York: Norton.

Erikson, E. H. (1976). Reflections on Dr. Borg's life cycle. *Daedalus, 105,* 1–28.

Everson, M. D., Hunter, W. A., Runyon, D. K., Edelsohn, G. A., & Coulter, M. L. (1989). Maternal support following disclosure of incest. *American Journal of Orthopsychiatry, 59*, 197–207.

Exner, J. E., & Weiner, I. B. (1982). *The Rorschach: A comprehensive system.* Vol. 3. *Assessment of children and adolescents.* New York: Wiley.

Fagan, P. J., & Andersen, A. E. (1990). Sexuality and eating disorders in adolescence. In M. Sugar (Ed.), *Atypical adolescence and sexuality* (pp. 108–126). New York: Norton.

Fairburn, C. G. (1985). Cognitive-behavioral treatment for bulimia. In D. M. Garner & P. E. Garfinkel (Eds.), *Handbook of psychotherapy for anorexia nervosa and bulimia* (pp. 213–239). New York: Guilford.

Fairburn, C. G., & Beglia, S. J. (1990). Studies in the epidemiology of bulimia nervosa. *American Journal of Psychiatry, 147*, 401–408.

Farber, S. L. (1981). *Identical twins reared apart.* New York: Basic Books.

Farberow, N. L., & Shneidman, E. S. (Eds.) (1961). *The cry for help.* New York: McGraw-Hill.

Farnworth, M. (1984). Family structure, family attributes, and delinquency in a sample of low-income, minority males and females. *Journal of Youth and Adolescence, 13*, 349–364.

Farrington, D. P. (1983). Offending from 10 to 25 years of age. In K. T. Van Dusen & S. A. Mednick (Eds.), *Prospective studies of crime and delinquency* (pp. 7–37). Boston: Kluwer-Nijhoff.

Farrington, D. P. (1986). The sociocultural context of childhood disorders. In H. C. Quay & J. W. Werry (Eds.), *Psychopathological disorders of childhood* (pp. 391–422). New York: Wiley.

Farrington, D. P. (1987). Epidemiology. In H. C. Quay (Ed.), *Handbook of juvenile delinquency* (pp. 33–61). New York: Wiley.

Featherstone, D. R., Cundick, B. P., & Jensen, L. C. (1992). Differences in school behavior and achievement between children from intact, reconstituted, and single-parent families. *Adolescence, 27*, 1–12.

Feehan, M., McGee, R., Stanton, W. R., & Silva, P. A. (1991). Strict and inconsistent discipline in childhood: Consequences for adolescent mental health. *British Journal of Clinical Psychology, 30*, 325–331.

Fehrman, P. G., Keith, T. Z., & Reimers, T. M. (1987). Home influence on school learning: Direct and indirect effects of parental involvement on high school grades. *Journal of Educational Research, 80*, 323–337.

Feifel, H. (1963). Death. In N. L. Farberow (Ed.), *Taboo topics* (pp. 8–21). New York: Atherton.

Felner, R. D., Adan, A. M., & Silverman, M. M. (1992). Risk assessment and prevention of youth suicide in school and educational contexts. In R. W. Maris, A. L. Berman, J. T. Maltsberger, & R. I. Yufit (Eds.), *Assessment and prediction of suicide* (pp. 420–447). New York: Guilford.

Feltey, K. M., Ainslie, J. J., & Geib, A. (1991). Sexual coercion attitudes among high school students: The influence of gender and rape education. *Youth & Society, 23*, 229–250.

Fenichel, O. (1945). *The psychoanalytic theory of neurosis.* New York: Norton.

Fennelly, K. (1993). Sexual activity and childbearing among Hispanic adolescents in the United States. In R. Lerner (Ed.), *Early adolescence: Perspectives on research, policy, and intervention* (pp. 335–352). Hillsdale, NJ: Erlbaum.

Fialkov, M. J. (1989). Substance use disorders. In C. G. Last & M. Hersen (Eds.), *Child psychiatric diagnosis* (pp. 356–387). New York: Wiley.

Fine, M. A., Donnelly, B. W., & Voydanoff, P. (1991). The relation between adolescents' perceptions of their family lives and their adjustment in stepfather families. *Journal of Adolescent Research, 6,* 423–436.

Finkelhor, D. (1990). Early and long-term effects of child sexual abuse: An update. *Professional Psychology, 21,* 325–330.

Finkelhor, D., Hotaling, G., Lewis, I. A., & Smith, C. (1990). Sexual abuse in a national survey of adult men and women: Prevalence characteristics and risk factors. *Child Abuse and Neglect, 14,* 19–28.

Fischer, J. L. (1981). Transitions in relationship styles from adolescence to young adulthood. *Journal of Youth and Adolescence, 10,* 11–24.

Fiske, S. T. (1993). Social cognition and social perception. *Annual Review of Psychology, 44,* 155–194.

Flaherty, L. T. (1982). To love and/or to work: The ideological dilemma of young women. In S. C. Feinstein (Ed.), *Adolescent psychiatry* (Vol. X, pp. 41–51). Chicago: University of Chicago Press.

Flanagan, T. J., & Jamieson, K. M. (1988). *Sourcebook of criminal justice statistics—1987.* Washington, DC: U. S. Department of Justice.

Flanagan, T. J., & Maguire, K. (Eds.) (1992). *Sourcebook of criminal justice statistics—1991.* Washington, DC: U. S. Department of Justice.

Flavell, J. H. (1985). *Cognitive development* (2nd ed.). Englewood Cliffs, NJ: Prentice-Hall.

Fleisher, S. J., Berkovitz, I. H., Briones, L., Lovetro, K., & Morhar, N. (1987). Antisocial behavior, school performance, and reactions to loss: The value of group counseling and communication skills training. *Adolescent Psychiatry, 14,* 546–555.

Fleming, J. E., Boyle, M. H., & Offord, D. R. (1993). The outcome of adolescent depression in the Ontario Child Health Study follow-up. *Journal of the American Academy of Child and Adolescent Psychiatry, 32,* 28–33.

Fleming, J. E., & Offord, D. R. (1990). Epidemiology of childhood depressive disorders: A critical review. *Journal of the American Academy of Child and Adolescent Psychiatry, 29,* 571–580.

Folberg, J. (1991). Custody overview. In J. Folberg (Ed.), *Joint custody and shared parenting* (2nd ed., pp. 3–10). New York: Guilford.

Forehand, R., Wierson, M., Thomas, A. M., Armistead, L., Kempton, T., & Neighbors, B. (1991). The role of family stressors and parent relationships on adolescent functioning. *Journal of the American Academy of Child and Adolescent Psychiatry, 30,* 316–322.

Forehand, R., Wierson, M., Thomas, A. M., Fauber, R., Armistead, L., Kempton, T., & Long, N. (1991). A short-term longitudinal examination of young adolescent functioning following divorce: The role of family factors. *Journal of Abnormal Child Psychology, 19,* 97–111.

Foreyt, J. P., & Cousins, J. H. (1987). Obesity. In M. Hersen & V. B. Van Hasselt (Eds.), *Behavior therapy with children and adolescents* (pp. 485–511). New York: Wiley.

Forney, M. A., Forney, P. D., & Ripley, W. K. (1991). Alcohol use among black adolescents: Parental and peer influences. *Journal of Alcohol and Drug Education, 36,* 36–46.

Forrest, J. D., & Singh, S. (1990). The sexual and reproductive behavior of American women, 1982–1988. *Family Planning Perspectives, 22,* 206–214.

Fors, S., & Rojek, D. G. (1991). A comparison of drug involvement between runaways and school youths. *Journal of Drug Education, 21,* 13–25.

Fort, P., & Lifshitz, F. (1992). Insulin-dependent diabetes mellitus. In S. B. Friedman, M. Fisher, & S. K. Schonberg (Eds.), *Comprehensive adolescent health care* (pp. 152–164). St. Louis, MO: Quality Medical Publishing.

Francoeur, R. T. (1982). *Becoming a sexual person.* New York: Wiley.

Frantz, A. G. (1981). The breasts. In R. H. Williams (Ed.), *Textbook of endocrinology* (6th ed., pp. 400–411). Philadelphia: W. B. Saunders.

Freud, A. (1936/1946). *The ego and the mechanisms of defense.* New York: International Universities Press.

Freud, A. (1958). Adolescence. *Psychoanalytic Study of the Child, 13,* 255–278.

Freud, S. (1905/1953). Three essays on the theory of sexuality. *Standard Edition* (Vol. VII, pp. 135–243). London: Hogarth.

Friedman, A. G., & Mulhern, R. K. (1992). Psychological aspects of childhood cancer. In B. B. Lahey & A. E. Kazdin (Eds.), *Advances in clinical child psychology* (Vol. 14, pp. 165–189). New York: Plenum.

Friedman, J. M. H., Asnis, G. M., Boeck, M., & DiFiore, J. (1987). Prevalence of specific suicidal behaviors in a high school sample. *American Journal of Psychiatry, 144,* 1203–1206.

Frisch, R. E. (1974). Critical weight at menarche,

initiation of the adolescent growth spurt, and control of puberty. In M. M. Grumbach, G. D. Grave, & F. E. Mayer (Eds.), *Control of the onset of puberty.* New York: Wiley.

Frisch, R. E., Gotz-Welbergen, A. V., McArthur, J. W., Albright, T., Witschi, J., Bullen, B., Birnholz, J., Reed, R. B., & Hermann, H. (1981). Delayed menarche and amenorrhea of college athletes in relation to age of onset of training. *Journal of the American Medical Association, 246,* 1559–1563.

Fritz, G. K. (1992). Chronic illness and psychological health. In E. R. McAnarney, R. E. Kreipe, D. P. Orr, & G. D. Comerci (Eds.), *Textbook of adolescent medicine* (pp. 1133–1137). Philadelphia: Saunders.

Frost, A. K., & Pakiz, B. (1990). The effects of marital disruption on adolescents: Time as a dynamic. *American Journal of Orthopsychiatry, 60,* 544–555.

Fry, P. S., & Scher, A. (1984). The effects of father absence on children's achievement motivation, ego-strength, and locus-of-control orientation: A five-year longitudinal assessment. *British Journal of Developmental Psychology, 2,* 167–178.

Furman, W., & Buhrmester, D. (1992). Age and sex differences in perception of networks of personal relationships. *Child Development, 63,* 103–115.

Furman, W., & Gavin, L. A. (1989). Peers' influence on adjustment and development: A view from the intervention literature. In T. J. Berndt & G. W. Ladd (Eds.), *Peer relationships in child development* (pp. 319–340). New York: Wiley.

Furstenberg, F. F., Jr., Brooks-Gunn, J., & Morgan, S. P. (1987). *Adolescent mothers in later life.* New York: Cambridge University Press.

Gaddis, A., & Brooks-Gunn, J. (1985). The male experience of pubertal change. *Journal of Youth and Adolescence, 14,* 61–69.

Gadow, K. D. (1991). Clinical issues and child and adolescent psychopharmacology. *Journal of Consulting and Clinical Psychology, 59,* 842–852.

Gagnon, J. H. (1973). Scripts and the coordination of sexual conduct. *Nebraska Symposium on Motivation, 21,* 27–59.

Gamble, T. J., & Zigler, E. (1986). Effects of infant day care: Another look at the evidence. *American Journal of Orthopsychiatry, 56,* 26–42.

Gamoran, A., & Nystrand, M. (1991). Background and instructional effects on achievement in eighth-grade English and social studies. *Journal of Research on Adolescence, 1,* 277–300.

Ganong, L. H., & Coleman, M. (1984). The effects of remarriage on children: A review of the empirical literature. *Family Relations, 33,* 389–406.

Gardner, G. A. (1991). Joint custody is not for everyone. In J. Folberg (Ed.), *Joint custody and shared parenting* (2nd ed., pp. 88–96). New York: Guilford.

Gardner, K. E., & LaBrecque, S. V. (1986). Effects of maternal employment on sex role orientation of adolescents. *Adolescence, 21,* 875–885.

Gargiulo, J., Attie, I., Brooks-Gunn, J., & Warren, M. P. (1987). Girls' dating behavior as a function of social context and maturation. *Developmental Psychology, 23,* 730–737.

Garland, A. F., & Zigler, E. (1993). Adolescent suicide prevention: Current research and social policy implications. *American Psychologist, 48,* 169–182.

Garmezy, N. (1974). Children at risk: The search for the antecedents of schizophrenia: Parts 1 and 2. *Schizophrenia Bulletin, 1,* Nos. 8 (14–90) and 9 (55–125).

Garner, D. M., & Garfinkel, P. E. (Eds.) (1985). *Handbook of psychotherapy for anorexia nervosa and bulimia.* New York: Guilford.

Garner, D. M., & Garner, M. V. (1992). Treatment of eating disorders in adolescents. In C. E. Walker & M. C. Roberts (Eds.), *Handbook of clinical child psychology* (2nd ed., pp. 623–642). New York: Wiley.

Garner, D. M., & Wooley, S. C. (1991). Confronting the failure of behavioral and dietary treatments for obesity. *Clinical Psychology Review, 11,* 729–780.

Garnets, L. D., Herek, G. M., & Levy, B. (1990). Violence and victimization of lesbians and gay men: Mental health consequences. *Journal of Interpersonal Violence, 5,* 366–383.

Garnets, L. D., & Kimmel, D. C. (1991). Lesbian and gay male dimensions in the psychological study of human diversity. In J. Goodchilds (Ed.), *Psychological perspectives on human diversity in America* (pp. 143–192). Washington, DC: American Psychological Association.

Garnets, L. D., & Kimmel, D. C. (Eds.). (1993). *Psychological perspectives on lesbian and gay male experiences.* New York: Columbia University Press.

Garrison, C. Z., Addy, C. L., Jackson, K. L., McKeown, R. E., & Waller, J. L. (1991). A longitudinal study of suicidal ideation in young adolescents. *Journal of the American Academy of Child and Adolescent Psychiatry, 30,* 597–603.

Gary, R. (1964). *The ski bum.* New York: Harper & Row.

Gavin, L. A., & Furman, W. (1989). Age differences in

adolescents' perceptions of their peer group. *Developmental Psychology, 25*, 827–834.

Geffner, R., & Pagelow, M. D. (1990). Victims of spouse abuse. In R. T. Ammerman & M. Hersen (Eds.), *Treatment of family violence* (pp. 113–135). New York: Wiley.

Gibbs, J. T. (1989). Black adolescents and youth: An update on an endangered species. In R. L. Jones (Ed.), *Black adolescents* (pp. 3–27). Berkeley, CA: Cobb & Henry.

Gibbs, J. T. (1990). Black American adolescents. In J. T. Gibbs & L. N. Huang (Eds.), *Children of color: Psychological interventions with minority youth* (pp. 179–223). San Francisco: Jossey-Bass.

Gibbs, J. T., & Huang, L. N. (1990). *Children of color: Psychological interventions with minority youth.* San Francisco: Jossey-Bass.

Gibson, P. (1989). *Gay male and lesbian youth suicide. Report of the Secretary's Task Force on Youth Suicide,* pp. 3-110–3-142. Washington, DC: U.S. Department of Health & Human Services. (Publication No. (ADM) 89-1623.)

Gifford, V., & Dean, M. M. (1990). Differences in extracurricular activity participation, achievement, and attitudes toward school between ninth-grade students attending junior high school and those attending senior high school. *Adolescence, 25*, 799–802.

Gillberg, C., Wahlstrom, J., Forsman, A., Hellgren, L., & Gillberg, I. C. (1986). Teenage psychoses: Epidemiology, classification and reduced optimality in the pre-, peri-, and neonatal periods. *Journal of Child Psychology and Psychiatry, 27*, 87–98.

Gilligan, C. (1982). *In a different voice: Psychological theory and women's development.* Cambridge, MA: Harvard University Press.

Gilligan, C. (1987). Adolescent development reconsidered. In C. E. Irwin, Jr. (Ed.), *Adolescent social behavior and health* (pp. 63–92). San Francisco: Jossey-Bass.

Gilligan, C., & Attanucci, J. (1985). Two moral orientations: Implications for developmental theory and assessment. Unpublished paper, Center for the Study of Gender, Education, and Human Development, Harvard Graduate School of Education. (Cited in Gilligan, 1987.)

Ginsburg, H. P., & Opper, S. (1988). *Piaget's theory of intellectual development* (3rd ed.). Englewood Cliffs, NJ: Prentice-Hall.

Giovacchini, P. L. (1978). The borderline aspects of adolescence and the borderline state. In S. C. Feinstein & P. L. Giovacchini (Eds.), *Adolescent psychiatry* (Vol. 6, pp. 320–338). Chicago: University of Chicago Press.

Gjerde, P. F., Block, J., & Block, J. H. (1988). Depressive symptoms and personality during late adolescence: Gender differences in the externalization-internalization of symptom expression. *Journal of Abnormal Psychology, 97*, 475–486.

Glass, C. R., & Shea, C. A. (1986). Cognitive therapy for shyness and social anxiety. In W. H. Jones, J. M. Cheek, & S. R. Biggs (Eds.), *Shyness* (pp. 315–327). New York: Plenum.

Glick, P. (1989). Remarried families, stepfamilies, stepchildren: A brief demographic profile. *Family Relations, 38*, 24–27.

Goethals, G. W., & Klos, D. S. (1976). *Experiencing youth: First-person accounts* (2nd ed.). Boston: Little, Brown.

Goffman, E. (1969). *Strategic interactions.* Philadelphia: University of Pennsylvania Press.

Gold, M. (1987). Social ecology. In H. C. Quay (Ed.), *Handbook of juvenile delinquency* (pp. 62–105). New York: Wiley.

Gold, M., & Yanof, D. S. (1985). Mothers, daughters, and girlfriends. *Journal of Personality and Social Psychology, 49*, 654–659.

Golden, M. P., & Gray, D. L. (1992). Diabetes mellitus. In E. R. McAnarney, R. E. Kreipe, D. P. Orr, & G. D. Comerci (Eds.), *Textbook of adolescent medicine* (pp. 525–535). Philadelphia: Saunders.

Goldstein, J. (1991). In whose best interest? In J. Folberg (Ed.), *Joint custody and shared parenting* (2nd ed., pp. 16–28). New York: Guilford.

Goldstein, J., Freud, A., & Solnit, A. J. (1973). *Beyond the best interests of the child.* New York: Free Press.

Goldstein, M. J. (1987a). The UCLA high-risk project. *Schizophrenia Bulletin, 13*, 505–514.

Goldstein, M. J. (1987b). Psychosocial issues. *Schizophrenia Bulletin, 13*, 157–172.

Golombek, H., & Marton, P. (1992). Adolescents over time: A longitudinal study of personality development. In S. C. Feinstein (Ed.), *Adolescent Psychiatry* (Vol. 18, pp. 213–284). Chicago: University of Chicago Press.

Gonsiorek, J. C. (1988). Mental health issues of gay and lesbian adolescents. *Journal of Adolescent Health Care, 9*, 114–122.

González, E. R. (1982). For puberty that comes too soon, new treatment highly effective. *Journal of the American Medical Association, 248*, 1149–1155.

Good, T. L., & Weinstein, R. S. (1986). Schools make a

difference: Evidence, criticisms, and new directions. *American Psychologist, 41,* 1090–1097.

Goodenow, C. (1993). Classroom belonging among early adolescent students: Relationships to motivation and achievement. *Journal of Early Adolescence, 13,* 21–43.

Goodyer, I. M. (1992). Depression in childhood and adolescence. In E. S. Paykel (Ed.), *Handbook of affective disorders* (2nd ed., pp. 585–600). New York: Guilford.

Gordon, R. A. (1990). *Anorexia and bulimia: Anatomy of a social epidemic.* Oxford, England: Blackwell.

Gore, S., Aseltine, R. H., & Colten, M. E. (1993). Gender, social-relational involvement, and depression. *Journal of Research on Adolescence, 3,* 101–125.

Gorrell, J., & Shaw, E. L. (1988). Upper elementary and high school students' attitudes toward gender-typed occupations. *Journal of Adolescent Research, 3,* 189–199.

Goswick, R. A., & Jones, W. H. (1982). Components of loneliness during adolescence. *Journal of Youth and Adolescence, 11,* 373–383.

Gottesman, I. I. (1991). *Schizophrenia genesis: The origins of madness.* San Francisco: Freeman.

Gottlib, I. H. (1992). Interpersonal and cognitive aspects of depression. *Current Directions in Psychological Science, 1,* 149–154.

Gottlieb, D., & Heinsohn, A. L. (1973). Sociology and youth. *Sociological Quarterly, 14,* 249–270.

Gottschalk, R., Davidson, W. S., Gensheimer, L. K., & Mayer, J. P. (1987). Community-based intervention. In H. C. Quay (Ed.), *Handbook of juvenile delinquency* (pp. 266–298). New York: Wiley.

Gray, W. M. (1990). Formal operational thought. In W. F. Overton (Ed.), *Reasoning, necessity, and logic: Developmental perspectives* (pp. 227–253). Hillsdale, NJ: Erlbaum.

Graystone, A. D., de Luca, R. V., & Boyes, D. A. (1992). Self-esteem, anxiety, and loneliness in preadolescent girls who have experienced sexual abuse. *Child Psychiatry and Human Development, 22,* 277–286.

Green, A. H. (1991). Child sexual abuse and incest. In M. Lewis (Ed.), *Child and adolescent psychiatry* (pp. 1019–1029). Baltimore, MD: Williams & Wilkins.

Green, D. L. (1990). High school student employment in social context: Adolescents' perceptions of the role of part-time work. *Adolescence, 25,* 425–434.

Green, W. H. (1991). *Child and adolescent clinical psychopharmacology.* Baltimore, MD: Williams & Wilkins.

Greenbaum, P. E., Prange, M. E., Friedman, R. M., &

Silver, S. E. (1991). Substance abuse prevalence and comorbidity with other psychiatric disorders among adolescents with severe emotional disturbances. *Journal of the American Academy of Child and Adolescent Psychiatry, 30,* 575–583.

Greene, A. L., & Grimsley, M. D. (1990). Age and gender differences in adolescents' preferences for parental advice: Mum's the word. *Journal of Adolescent Research, 5,* 396–413.

Greenfield, P. M., Bruzzone, L., Koyamatsu, K., Satuloff, W., Nixon, K., Brodie, M., & Kingsdale, D. (1987). What is rock music doing to the minds of our youth? A first experimental look at the effects of rock music lyrics and music videos. *Journal of Early Adolescence, 7,* 315–329.

Greening, L., & Dollinger, S. J. (1991). Adolescent smoking and perceived invulnerability to smoking-related causes of death. *Journal of Pediatric Psychology, 16,* 687–699.

Greeson, L. E. (1991). Recognition and ratings of television music videos: Age, gender, and sociocultural effects. *Journal of Applied Social Psychology, 21,* 1908–1920.

Greif, E. B., & Ulman, K. J. (1982). The psychological impact of menarche on early adolescent females: A review of the literature. *Child Development, 53,* 1413–1430.

Grinnell, G. B. (1923). *The Cheyenne Indians, their history and ways of life,* Vol. 1. New Haven: Yale University Press.

Grossman, L. S., Harrow, M., Goldberg, J. F., & Fichtner, C. G. (1991). Outcome of schizoaffective disorder at two long-term follow-ups: Comparisons with outcome of schizophrenia and affective disorders. *American Journal of Psychiatry, 148,* 1359–1365.

Grotevant, H. D. (1992). Assigned and chosen identity components: A process perspective on their integration. In G. R. Adams, T. P. Gullotta, & R. Montemayor (Eds.), *Adolescent identity formation* (pp. 73–90). Newbury Park, CA: Sage.

Grotevant, H. D., & Adams, G. R. (1984). Development of an objective measure to assess ego identity in adolescence: Validation and replication. *Journal of Youth and Adolescence, 13,* 419–438.

Grotevant, H. D., & Cooper, C. R. (1986). Individuation in family relationships: A perspective on individual differences in the development of identity and role-taking skill in adolescence. *Human Development, 29,* 82–100.

Grotevant, H. D., & Thorbecke, W. L. (1982). Sex

difference in styles of occupational identity formation in late adolescence. *Developmental Psychology, 18,* 396–405.

Grotjahn, M. (1956). A letter by Sigmund Freud with recollection of his adolescence. *Journal of the American Psychoanalytic Association, 4,* 644–645, 649–650.

Grove, K. J. (1990). Identity development in interracial, Asian/white late adolescents: Must it be so problematic? *Journal of Youth and Adolescence, 20,* 617–628.

Grumbach, M. M., Roth, J. C., Kaplan, S. L., & Kelch, R. P. (1974). Hypothalamic-pituitary regulation of puberty in man: Evidence and concepts derived from clinical research. In M. M. Grumbach, G. D. Grave, & F. E. Mayer (Eds.), *Control of the onset of puberty* (pp. 118–127). New York: Wiley.

Gump, P. V. (1980). The school as a social situation. *Annual Review of Psychology, 31,* 553–582.

Gustafson, S. B., Sattin, H., & Magnusson, D. (1992). Aspects of the development of a career versus homemaking orientation among females: The longitudinal influence of educational motivation and peers. *Journal of Research on Adolescence, 2,* 241–259.

Haaga, D. A., Dyck, M. J., & Ernst, D. (1991). Empirical status of cognitive theory of depression. *Psychological Bulletin, 110,* 215–236.

Haan, N., & Day, D. (1974). A longitudinal study of change and sameness in personality development: Adolescence to later adulthood. *International Journal of Aging and Human Development, 5,* 11–39.

Haas, G. L., & Sweeney, J. A. (1992). Premorbid and onset features of first-episode schizophrenia. *Schizophrenia Bulletin, 18,* 373–386.

Haddad, J. D., Barocas, R., & Hollenbeck, A. R. (1991). Family organization and parent attitudes of children with conduct disorder. *Journal of Clinical Child Psychology, 20,* 152–161.

Halderman, D. C. (1991). Sexual orientation conversion therapy for gay men and lesbians: A scientific examination. In J. C. Gonsiorek & J. D. Weinrich (Eds.), *Homosexuality: Research implications for public policy* (pp. 149–160). Newbury Park, CA: Sage.

Hall, G. S. (1904). *Adolescence: Its psychology and its relations to physiology, anthropology, sociology, sex, crime, religion, and education.* Vols. I and II. New York: D. Appleton.

Hall, R. C., Tice, L., Beresford, T. P., Wooley, B., & Hall,

A. K. (1988). Sexual abuse in patients with anorexia nervosa and bulimia. *Psychosomatics, 30,* 73–79.

Halmi, K. A. (1987). Anorexia nervosa and bulimia. In V. B. Van Hasselt & M. Hersen (Eds.), *Handbook of adolescent psychology* (pp. 265–287). New York: Pergamon.

Hamer, D. H., Hu, S., Magnuson, V. L., Hu, N., & Pattatucci, A. M. L. (1993). A linkage between DNA markers on the X chromosome and male sexual orientation. *Science, 261,* 321–327.

Hamilton, S. F. (1990). *Apprenticeship for adulthood.* New York: Free Press.

Hammen, C. (1990). Cognitive approaches to depression in children. In B. B. Lahey & A. E. Kazdin (Eds.), *Advances in clinical child psychology* (Vol. 13, pp. 139–173). New York: Plenum.

Hammen, C. (1991). Generation of stress in the course of unipolar depression. *Journal of Abnormal Psychology, 100,* 555–561.

Hammen, C., Ellicott, A., Gitlin, M., & Jamison, K. R. (1989). Sociotropy/autonomy and vulnerability to specific life events in patients with unipolar depression and bipolar disorders. *Journal of Abnormal Psychology, 98,* 154–160.

Hammond, W. R., & Yung, B. (1993). Psychology's role in the public health response to assaultive violence among young African-American men. *American Psychologist, 48,* 142–154.

Hansen, D. J., Conaway, L. P., & Christopher, J. S. (1990). Victims of child physical abuse. In R. T. Ammerman & M. Hersen (Eds.), *Treatment of family violence* (pp. 17–49). New York: Wiley.

Hansen, D. J., & Warner, J. E. (1992). Child physical abuse and neglect. In R. T. Ammerman & M. Hersen (Eds.), *Assessment of family violence* (pp. 123–147). New York: Wiley.

Harpur, T. J., Hare, R. D., & Hakstian, A. R. (1989). Two-factor conceptualization of psychopathy: Construct validity and assessment implications. *Psychological Assessment, 1,* 6–17.

Harris, F. C., & Phelps, C. F. (1987). Anorexia and bulimia. In M. Hersen & V. B. Van Hasselt (Eds.), *Behavior therapy with children and adolescents* (pp. 465–484). New York: Wiley.

Harrison, G. A., Weiner, J. S., Tanner, J. M., & Barnicot, N. A. (1964). *Human biology.* New York: Oxford University Press.

Harrow, M., Goldberg, J. F., Grossman, L. S., & Meltzer, H. Y. (1990). Outcome in manic disorders: A naturalistic follow-up study. *Archives of General Psychiatry, 47,* 665–671.

Hart, J. (1981). Theoretical explanations in practice. In J. Hart & D. Richardson (Eds.), *The theory and practice of homosexuality* (pp. 38–67). Boston: Routledge & Kegan Paul.

Harter, S. (1990a). Processes underlying adolescent self-concept formation. In R. Montemayor, G. R. Adams, & T. P. Gullotta (Eds.), *From childhood to adolescence* (pp. 205–239). Newbury, CA: Sage.

Harter, S. (1990b). Self and identity development. In S. S. Feldman & G. R. Elliott (Eds.), *At the threshold: The developing adolescent* (pp. 352–387). Cambridge, MA: Harvard University Press.

Hartup, W. E., & Sancilio, M. F. (1986). Children's friendships. In E. Schopler & G. B. Mesibov (Eds.), *Social behavior in autism* (pp. 61–80). New York: Plenum.

Hartup, W. W. (1989a). Social relationships and their developmental significance. *American Psychologist, 44,* 120–126.

Hartup, W. W. (1989b). Behavioral manifestations of children's friendships. In T. J. Berndt & G. W. Ladd (Eds.), *Peer relationships in child development* (pp. 46–70). New York: Wiley.

Hatano, Y. (1993). Sexual activities of Japanese youth. *Journal of Sex Education and Therapy, 19,* 131–144.

Hatfield, E. (1988). Passionate and companionate love. In R. J. Sternberg & M. L. Barnes (Eds.), *The psychology of love* (pp. 191–217). New Haven, CT: Yale University Press.

Hau, K., & Lew, W. J. (1989). Moral development of Chinese students in Hong Kong. *International Journal of Psychology, 24,* 561–569.

Hauck, W. E., Martens, M., & Wetzel, M. (1986). Shyness, group dependence and self-concept: Attributes of the imaginary audience. *Adolescence, 21,* 529–534.

Haugaard, J. J. (1992). Epidemiology and family violence involving children. In R. T. Ammerman & M. Hersen (Eds.), *Assessment of family violence* (pp. 89–120). New York: Wiley.

Haugaard, J. J., & Reppucci, N. D. (1988). *The sexual abuse of children.* San Francisco: Jossey-Bass.

Hauser, S. T. (1991). *Adolescents and their families.* New York: Free Press.

Hauser, S. T., Borman, R., Jacobson, A. M., & Powers, S. I. (1991). Understanding family contexts of adolescent coping: A study of parental ego development and adolescent coping strategies. *Journal of Early Adolescence, 11,* 96–124.

Havighurst, R. J. (1972). *Developmental tasks and education* (3rd ed.). New York: McKay.

Haviland, J. M., & Kramer, D. A. (1991). Affect-cognition relationships in adolescent diaries: The case of Anne Frank. *Human Development, 34,* 143–159.

Hawton, K. (1986). *Suicide and attempted suicide among children and adolescents.* Beverly Hills, CA: Sage.

Healy, J. M., Jr., Malley, J. E., & Stewart, A. J. (1990). Children and their fathers after parental separation. *American Journal of Orthopsychiatry, 60,* 531–543.

Hecht, M. L., Collier, M. J., & Ribeau, S. A. (1993). *African American communication: Ethnic identity and cultural interpretation.* Newbury Park, CA: Sage.

Hendin, H. (1991). Psychodynamics of suicide, with particular reference to the young. *American Journal of Psychiatry, 148,* 1150–1158.

Hendren, R. L., & Berlin, I. N. (Eds.) (1991). *Psychiatric inpatient care of children and adolescents.* New York: Wiley.

Hendrick, S. S., & Hendrick, C. (1992). *Romantic love.* Newbury Park, CA: Sage.

Henggeler, S. W., Melton, G. B., & Smith, L. A. (1992). Family preservation using multisystemic therapy: An effective alternative to incarcerating serious juvenile offenders. *Journal of Consulting and Clinical Psychology, 60,* 935–961.

Herdt, G. (Ed.). (1989). *Gay and lesbian youth.* New York: Haworth.

Herdt, G. (1990). Developmental discontinuities and sexual orientation across cultures. In D. P. McWhirter, S. A. Sanders, & J. M. Reinisch (Eds.), *Homosexuality/heterosexuality: Concepts of sexual orientation* (pp. 208–236). New York: Oxford University Press.

Hernandez, D. J. (1988). Demographic trends and the living arrangements of children. In E. M. Hetherington & J. Arasteh (Eds.), *Impact of divorce, single parenting, and step-parenting on children* (pp. 3–22). Hillsdale, NJ: Erlbaum.

Hersov, L. A. (1990). School refusal: An overview. In C. Chiland & J. G. Young (Eds.), *Why children reject school* (pp. 16–44). New Haven, CT: Yale University Press.

Herzog, D. B., & Copeland, P. M. (1985). Eating disorders. *New England Journal of Medicine, 313,* 295–303.

Herzog, D. B., Keller, M. B., Lavori, P. W., & Bradburn, I. S. (1991). Bulimia nervosa in adolescence. *Journal of*

Developmental and Behavioral Pediatrics, *12*, 191–195.

Hetherington, E. M. (1972). Effects of father absence on personality development in adolescent daughters. *Developmental Psychology*, *7*, 313–326.

Hetherington, E. M. (1989). Coping with family transitions: Winners, losers, and survivors. *Child Development*, *60*, 1014.

Hetherington, E. M. (1991). Families, lies, and videotapes. *Journal of Research on Adolescence*, *1*, 323–348.

Hetherington, E. M., Cox, M., & Cox, R. (1982). Effects of divorce on parents and children. In M. E. Lamb (Ed.), *Nontraditional families: Parenting and child development* (pp. 233–288). Hillsdale, NJ: Erlbaum.

Hightower, E. (1990). Adolescent interpersonal and familial precursors of positive mental health at midlife. *Journal of Youth and Adolescence*, *19*, 257–276.

Hill, J. P. (1987). Research on adolescents and their families: Past and prospect. In C. E. Irwin (Ed.), *Adolescent social behavior and health* (pp. 13–31). San Francisco: Jossey-Bass.

Hill, J. P., & Holmbeck, G. N. (1987). Disagreements about rules in families with seventh-grade girls and boys. *Journal of Youth and Adolescence*, *16*, 221–246.

Hill, J. P., Holmbeck, G. N., Marlow, L., Green, T. M., & Lynch, M. E. (1986). Menarcheal status and parent–child relations in families of seventh-grade girls. *Journal of Youth and Adolescence*, *14*, 301–316.

Hingson, R., & Strunin, L. (1992). Monitoring adolescents' response to the AIDS epidemic: Changes in knowledge, attitudes, beliefs, and behaviors. In R. J. DiClemente (Ed.), *Adolescents and AIDS: A generation in jeopardy* (pp. 17–33). Newbury Park, CA: Sage.

Hinshaw, S. P. (1992). Externalizing behavior problems and academic underachievement in childhood and adolescence: Causal relationships and underlying mechanisms. *Psychological Bulletin*, *111*, 127–155.

Hodges, W. F. (1991). *Interventions for children of divorce* (2nd ed.). New York: Wiley.

Hoffman, A. R., & Crowley, W. F., Jr. (1982). Induction of puberty in men by long-term pulsatile administration of low-dose gonadotropin-releasing hormone. *New England Journal of Medicine*, *307*, 1237–1241.

Hoffman, L. W. (1984). Work, family, and the socialization of the child. In R. D. Parke (Ed.), *Review of child development research* (Vol. 7, pp. 223–281). Chicago: University of Chicago Press.

Hoffman, M. L. (1980). Moral development in adolescence. In J. Adelson (Ed.), *Handbook of adolescent psychology* (pp. 295–343). New York: Wiley.

Holbrook, M. B., & Schindler, R. M. (1989). Some exploratory findings on the development of musical tastes. *Journal of Consumer Research*, *16*, 119–124.

Holland, A., & Andre, T. (1987). Participation in extracurricular activities in secondary school: What is known, what needs to be known? *Review of Educational Research*, *57*, 437–466.

Hollinger, P. C., & Lester, D. (1991). Suicide, homicide, and demographic shifts: An epidemiologic study of regional and national trends. *Journal of Nervous and Mental Disease*, *179*, 574–575.

Hollon, S. D., Spoden, F., & Chastek, J. (1986). Unipolar depression. In M. Hersen (Ed.), *Pharmacological and behavioral treatment: An integrative approach* (pp. 199–239). New York: Wiley.

Holmbeck, G. N., Crossman, R. E., Wandrei, M. L., & Gasiewski, E. (1994). Cognitive development, egocentrism, self-esteem, and adolescent contraceptive knowledge, attitudes, and behavior. *Journal of Youth and Adolescence*, *23*, 169–193.

Holzman, P. S. (1970). *Psychoanalysis and psychopathology*. New York: McGraw-Hill.

Hooker, E. (1957). The adjustment of the male overt homosexual. *Journal of Projective Techniques*, *21*, 18–31.

Hopwood, N. J., Kelch, R. P., Hale, P. M., Mendes, T. M., Foster, C. M., & Beitins, I. Z. (1990). The onset of human puberty: Biological and environmental factors. In J. Bancroft & J. M. Reinisch (Eds.), *Adolescence and puberty* (pp. 29–49). New York: Oxford University Press.

Horan, J. J., & Straus, L. K. (1987). Substance abuse. In M. Hersen & V. B. Van Hasselt (Eds.), *Behavior therapy with children and adolescents* (pp. 440–464). New York: Wiley.

Horne, R. L., Van Vactor, J. C., & Emerson, S. (1991). Disturbed body image in patients with eating disorders. *American Journal of Psychiatry*, *148*, 211–215.

Howes, C. (1990). Social status and friendship from kindergarten to third grade. *Journal of Applied Developmental Psychology*, *11*, 321–330.

Hsu, L. K. G. (1989). The gender gap in eating disorders: Why are the eating disorders more common among women? *Clinical Psychology Review*, *9*, 393–407.

Hudson, L. M., & Gray, W. M. (1986). Formal operations, the imaginary audience and the personal fable. *Adolescence*, *21*, 751–765.

Hunt, E. (1989). Cognitive science: Definition, status, and

questions. *Annual Review of Psychology, 40*, 603–629.

Hunter, F. T. (1985). Adolescents' perceptions of discussions with parents and friends. *Developmental Psychology, 21*, 433–440.

Hunter, J. (1990). Violence against lesbian and gay male youths. *Journal of Interpersonal Violence, 5*, 295–300.

Hunter, J., & Schaecher, R. (1987). Stresses on lesbian and gay adolescents in schools. *Social Work in Education, 9*, 180–190.

Huston, A. C. (1985). The development of sex typing: Themes from recent research. *Developmental Review, 5*, 1–17.

Huston, A. C., & Alvarez, M. M. (1990). The socialization context of gender role development in early adolescence. In R. Montemayor, G. R. Adams, & T. P. Gullotta (Eds.), *From childhood to adolescence* (pp. 156–179). Newbury Park, CA: Sage.

Huston, A. C., Donnerstein, D., Fairchild, H., Feshbach, N. D., Katz, P. A., Murray, J. P., Rubinstein, E. A., Wilcox, B. L., & Zuckerman, D. (1992). *Big world, small screen: The role of television in American society.* Lincoln: University of Nebraska Press.

Hymel, S., Wagner, E., & Butler, L. J. (1990). Reputational bias: View from the peer group. In S. R. Asher & J. D. Coie (Eds.), *Peer rejection in childhood* (pp. 156–186). New York: Cambridge University Press.

Ickes, W. (1993). Traditional gender roles: Do they make, and then break, our relationships? *Journal of Social Issues, 49*(3), 71–85.

Inclán, J. E., & Herron, D. G. (1990). Puerto Rican adolescents. In J. T. Gibbs & L. N. Huang (Eds.), *Children of color: Psychological interventions with minority youth* (pp. 251–277). San Francisco: Jossey-Bass.

Inderbitzen-Pisaruk, H., Clark, M. L., & Solano, C. H. (1992). Correlates of loneliness in midadolescence. *Journal of Youth and Adolescence, 21*, 151–168.

Inderbitzen-Pisaruk, H., & Foster, S. L. (1990). Adolescent friendship and peer acceptance: Implications for social skills training. *Clinical Psychology Review, 10*, 425–439.

Inhelder, B., & Piaget, J. (1958). *The growth of logical thinking from childhood to adolescence.* (Translated by Anne Parsons & Stanley Milgram). New York: Basic Books.

Irion, J. C., Coon, R. C., & Blanchard-Fields, F. (1988). The influence of divorce on coping in adolescence. *Journal of Youth and Adolescence, 17*, 135–146.

Ishiyama, F. I. (1984). Shyness: Anxious social sensitivity and self-isolating tendency. *Adolescence, 19*, 903–911.

Jack, D. J. (1991). *Silencing the self: Women and depression.* Cambridge, MA: Harvard University Press.

Jacklin, C. N. (1989). Female and male: Issues of gender. *American Psychologist, 44*, 127–133.

Jackson, R. H., & Sikora, D. (1992). Parenting: The child in the context of the family. In C. E. Walker & M. C. Roberts (Eds.), *Handbook of clinical child psychology* (2nd ed., pp. 727–747). New York: Wiley.

Jacobs, J. W. (1983). Treatment of divorcing fathers: Social and psychotherapeutic considerations. *American Journal of Psychiatry, 140*, 1294–1299.

Jaffe, P. G., Sudermann, M., & Reitzel, D. (1992). Child witnesses of marital violence. In R. T. Ammerman & M. Hersen (Eds.), *Assessment of family violence* (pp. 313–331). New York: Wiley.

Jahnke, H. C., & Blanchard-Fields, F. (1993). A test of two models of adolescent egocentrism. *Journal of Youth and Adolescence, 22*, 313–326.

Janus, M., Burgess, A. W., & McCormack, A. (1987). Histories of sexual abuse in adolescent male runaways. *Adolescence, 22*, 405–417.

Janus, M., McCormack, A., Burgess, A. W., & Hartman, C. (1987). *Adolescent runaways.* Lexington, MA: Heath.

Janus, S. S., & Janus, C. L. (1993). *The Janus report on sexual behavior.* New York: Wiley.

Jaquish, G. A., & Savin-Williams, R. C. (1981). Biological and ecological factors in the expression of adolescent self-esteem. *Journal of Youth and Adolescence, 10*, 473–485.

Jarvie, G. J., Lahey, B. B., Graziano, W., & Framer, E. (1983). Childhood obesity and social stigma: What we know and what we don't know. *Developmental Review, 3*, 237–273.

Jemmott, L. S., & Jemmott, J. B., III. (1990). Sexual knowledge, attitudes, and risky sexual behavior among inner-city black male adolescents. *Journal of Adolescent Research, 5*, 346–369.

Jensen, J. M., & Howard, M. O. (1990). Skill deficits, skills training, and delinquency. *Children and Youth Services Review, 12*, 213–228.

Jessor, R., Donovan, J. E., & Costa, F. M. (1991). *Beyond adolescence.* New York: Cambridge University Press.

Johnson, B. M., Shulman, S., & Collins, W. A. (1991). Systemic patterns of parenting as reported by adolescents: Developmental differences and implications for psychosocial outcomes. *Journal of Adolescent Research, 6*, 235–252.

Johnson, C. A., Pents, M. A., Wever, M. D., Dwyer, J. H., Baer, N., MacKinnon, D. P., Hansen, W. B., & Flay, B. R. (1990). Relative effectiveness of comprehensive community programming for drug abuse prevention with high-risk and low-risk adolescents. *Journal of Consulting and Clinical Psychology, 58,* 447–456.

Johnson, G. M., Shontz, F. C., & Locke, T. P. (1984). Relationships between adolescent drug use and parental drug behaviors. *Adolescence, 19,* 295–299.

Johnson, J. H., & Fennell, E. B. (1992). Aggressive, antisocial, and delinquent behavior in childhood and adolescence. In C. E. Walker & M. C. Roberts (Eds.), *Handbook of clinical child psychology* (2nd ed., pp. 341–358). New York: Wiley.

Johnson, S. (1983). Facts about precocious puberty. Mimeographed document available from Office of Research Reporting, NICHD, NIH, Room 2A32, Building 31, 9000 Rockville Pike, Bethesda, MD 20205.

Johnson, S. A., & Green, V. (1993). Female adolescent contraceptive decision making and risk taking. *Adolescence, 28,* 81–96.

Johnson, S. B. (1980). Psychosocial factors in juvenile diabetes: A review. *Journal of Behavioral Medicine, 3,* 95–116.

Johnson, S. B. (1988). Diabetes mellitus in childhood. In D. K. Routh (Ed.), *Handbook of pediatric psychology* (pp. 9–31). New York: Guilford.

Johnson, V., & Pandina, R. J. (1991). Effects of the family environment on adolescent substance use, delinquency, and coping styles. *American Journal of Drug and Alcohol Abuse, 17,* 71–88.

Johnston, J. R., Gonzalez, R., & Campbell, L. E. G. (1987). Ongoing postdivorce conflict and child disturbance. *Journal of Abnormal Child Psychology, 15,* 493–509.

Johnston, J. R., Kline, M., & Tschann, J. M. (1991). Ongoing post-divorce conflict in families contesting custody: Do joint custody and frequent access help? In J. Folberg (Ed.), *Joint custody and shared parenting* (2nd ed., pp. 177–184). New York: Guilford.

Johnston, L. D., O'Malley, P. M., & Bachman, J. G. (1989). *Drug use, drinking, and smoking: National survey results from high school, college, and young adult populations, 1975–1988.* Washington, DC: National Institute on Drug Abuse.

Jones, R. L. (Ed.). (1989). *Black adolescents.* Berkeley, CA: Cobb & Henry.

Jones, R. M. (1992). Ego identity and adolescent problem behavior. In G. R. Adams, T. P. Gullotta, &

R. Montemayor (Eds.), *Adolescent identity formation* (pp. 216–233). Newbury Park, CA: Sage.

Jones, W. H., & Carpenter, B. N. (1986). Shyness, social behavior, and relationships. In W. H. Jones, J. M. Cheek, & S. R. Biggs (Eds.), *Shyness* (pp. 227–283). New York: Plenum.

Jordan, J. V., Kaplan, A. G., Miller, J. B., Stiver, I. P., & Surrey, J. L. (Eds.). (1991). *Women's growth in connection: Writings from the Stone Center.* New York: Guilford.

Josephs, R. A., Markus, H. R., & Tafarodi, R. W. (1992). Gender and self-esteem. *Journal of Personality and Social Psychology, 63,* 391–402.

Josselson, R. (1987). *Finding herself: Pathways to identity development in women.* San Francisco: Jossey-Bass.

Josselson, R. (1989). Identity formation in adolescence: Implications for young adulthood. In S. C. Feinstein (Ed.), *Adolescent psychiatry* (Vol. 16, pp. 142–154). Chicago: University of Chicago Press.

Josselson, R., Greenberger, E., & McConochie, D. (1977a). Phenomenological aspects of psychosocial maturity in adolescence. Part I. Boys. *Journal of Youth and Adolescence, 6,* 22–55.

Josselson, R., Greenberger, E., & McConochie, D. (1977b). Phenomenological aspects of psychosocial maturity in adolescence. Part II. Girls. *Journal of Youth and Adolescence, 6,* 145–167.

Juhasz, A. M., & Sonnenshein-Schneider, M. (1987). Adolescent sexuality: Values, morality and decision making. *Adolescence, 22,* 579–590.

Junod, H. A. (1927). The life of a South African tribe. London: Macmillan. (Cited by J. W. M. Whiting, R. C. Kluckhohn, & A. Anthony, The function of male initiation ceremonies at puberty. *Readings in social psychology,* E. E. Maccoby, T. M. Newcomb, & E. L. Hartley (Eds.). New York: Henry Holt and Co., 1958, p. 360.)

Juvonen, J. (1991). Deviance, perceived responsibility, and negative peer reactions. *Developmental Psychology, 27,* 672–681.

Kafka, R. R., & London, P. (1991). Communication in relationships and adolescent substance use: The influence of parents and friends. *Adolescence, 26,* 587–598.

Kagan, J., & Moss. H. A. (1962). *From birth to maturity.* New York: Wiley.

Kagan, J., & Reznick, J. S. (1986). Shyness and temperament. In W. H. Jones, J. M. Cheek, & S. R. Biggs (Eds.), *Shyness* (pp. 81–90). New York: Plenum.

Kagan, J., Snidman, N., & Arcus, D. M. (1992). Initial reactions to unfamiliarity. *Current Directions in Psychological Science, 1,* 171–174.

Kager, V. A., Arndt, E. K., & Kenny, T. (1982). Psychosomatic problems of children. In C. E. Walker & M. C. Roberts (Eds.), *Handbook of clinical child psychology* (2nd ed., pp. 303–317). New York: Wiley.

Kalter, N. (1987). Long-term effects of divorce on children: A developmental vulnerability model. *American Journal of Orthopsychiatry, 57,* 587–600.

Kaminer, Y., Seifer, R., & Mastrian, A. (1992). Observational measurement of symptoms responsive to treatment of major depressive disorder in children and adolescents. *Journal of Nervous and Mental Disease, 180,* 639–643.

Kandel, D. B. (1975). Stages in adolescent involvement in drug use. *Science, 190,* 912–914.

Kandel, D. B., & Davies, M. (1986). Adult sequelae of adolescent depressive symptoms. *Archives of General Psychiatry, 43,* 255–262.

Kandel, D. B., Davies, M., Karus, D., & Yamaguchi, K. (1986). The consequences in young adulthood of adolescent drug involvement. *Archives of General Psychiatry, 43,* 746–754.

Kandel, D. B., & Faust, R. (1975). Sequence and stages in patterns of adolescent drug use. *Archives of General Psychiatry, 32,* 923–932.

Kandel, D. B., Kessler, R. C., & Margulies, R. Z. (1978). Antecedents of adolescent initiation into stages of drug use: A developmental analysis. *Journal of Youth and Adolescence, 7,* 13–40.

Kaplan, E. H. (1991). Adolescents, age fifteen to eighteen: A psychoanalytic developmental view. In S. I. Greenspan & G. H. Pollock (Eds.), *The course of life* (Vol. IV, pp. 201–233). New York: International Universities Press.

Kaplan, S. J. (1991). Physical abuse and neglect. In M. Lewis (Ed.), *Child and adolescent psychiatry* (pp. 1010–1018). Baltimore, MD: Williams & Wilkins.

Karon, B. P., & Vandenbos, G. R. (1981). *Psychotherapy of schizophrenia.* New York: Aronson.

Kasen, S., Johnson, J., & Cohen, P. (1990). The impact of school emotional climate on student psychopathology. *Journal of Abnormal Child Psychology, 18,* 165–177.

Kashani, J. H., Carlson, G. A., Beck, N. C., Hoeper, E. W., Corcoran, C. M., McAllister, J. A., Fallahi, C., Rosenberg, T. K., & Reid, J. C. (1987). Depression, depressive symptoms, and depressed mood among a community sample of adolescents. *American Journal of Psychiatry, 146,* 871–875.

Kashani, J. H., Daniel, A. E., Dandoy, A. C., & Holcomb, W. R. (1992). Family violence: Impact on children. *Journal of the American Academy of Child and Adolescent Psychiatry, 31,* 181–189.

Katz, M. B. (1975). *The people of Hamilton, Canada West: Family and class in a mid-nineteeth-century city.* Cambridge, MA: Harvard University Press.

Keating, D. P. (1980). Thinking processes in adolescence. In J. Adelson (Ed.), *Handbook of adolescent psychology* (pp. 211–246). New York: Wiley.

Keating, D. P. (1990). Adolescent thinking. In S. S. Feldman & G. R. Elliott (Eds.), *At the threshold: The developing adolescent* (pp. 54–89). Cambridge, MA: Harvard University Press.

Keith, S. J., Regier, D. A., & Rae, D. S. (1991). Schizophrenic disorder. In L. N. Robins & D. A. Regier (Eds.), *Psychiatric disorders in America: The epidemiologic catchment area study* (pp. 33–52). New York: Free Press.

Keith, S. J., Regier, D. A., Rae, D. S., & Matthews, S. (1992). The prevalence of schizophrenia: Analysis of demographic features, symptom patterns, and course. In A. Z. Schwartzberg (Ed.), *International Annals of Adolescent Psychiatry* (Vol. 2, pp. 260–284). Chicago: University of Chicago Press.

Keitner, G. I., Ryan, C. E., Miller, I. W., & Norman, W. H. (1992). Recovery and major depression: Factors associated with twelve-month outcome. *American Journal of Psychiatry, 149,* 93–99.

Keller, M., & Wood, P. (1989). Development of friendship reasoning: A study of interindividual differences in intraindividual change. *Developmental Psychology, 25,* 820–826.

Kelly, J. A., & Hanson, D. J. (1987). Social interactions and adjustment. In V. B. Van Hesselt & M. Hersen (Eds.), *Handbook of adolescent psychology* (pp. 131–146). New York: Pergamon.

Kelly, J. G. (1979). The high school: Students and social contexts—An ecological perspective. In J. G. Kelly (Ed.), *Adolescent boys in high school: A psychological study of coping and adaptation* (pp. 3–13). Hillsdale, NJ: Erlbaum.

Kendall, P. C., Cantwell, D. P., & Kazdin, A. E. (1989). Depression in children and adolescents: Assessment issues and recommendations. *Cognitive Therapy and Research, 13,* 109–146.

Kendall-Tackett, K. A., Williams, L. M., & Finkelhor, D. (1993). Impact of sexual abuse on children: A review and synthesis of recent empirical studies. *Psychological Bulletin, 113,* 164–180.

Kendler, K. S., Gruenberg, A. M., & Strauss, J. S. (1982). An independent analysis of the Copenhagen sample of the Danish adoption study of schizophrenia. *Archives of General Psychiatry*, *39*, 1257–1261.

Kennedy, J. H. (1990). Determinants of peer social status: Contributions of physical appearance, reputation, and behavior. *Journal of Youth and Adolescence, 19,* 233–244.

Kenniston, K. (1965). *The uncommitted: Alienated youth in American society.* New York: Harcourt.

Kenny, M. E., & Hart, K. (1992). Relationship between parental attachment and eating disorders in an inpatient and a college sample. *Journal of Counseling Psychology, 39,* 521–526.

Kessler, S. (1980). The genetics of schizophrenia: A review. *Schizophrenia Bulletin, 6,* 404–416.

Kety, S. S. (1988). Schizophrenic illness in the families of schizophrenic adoptees: Findings from the Danish national sample. *Schizophrenia Bulletin, 14,* 217–222.

Kiell, N. (1964). *The universal experience of adolescence.* New York: International Universities Press.

Kielwasser, A. P., & Wolf, M. A. (1992). Mainstream television, adolescent homosexuality, and significant silence. *Critical Studies in Mass Communication, 9,* 350–373.

Kilpatrick, A. C. (1992). *Long-range effects of child and adolescent sexual experiences: Myths, mores, menaces.* Hillsdale, NJ: Erlbaum.

Kimmel, D. C. (1990). *Adulthood and aging: An interdisciplinary, developmental view* (3rd ed.). New York: Wiley.

Kinder, B. N. (1991). Eating disorders (anorexia nervosa and bulimia nervosa). In M. Hersen & S. M. Turner (Eds.), *Adult psychopathology and diagnosis* (2nd ed., pp. 392–409). New York: Wiley.

King, A. C., Raskin, A., Gdowski, C. L., Butkus, M., & Opipari, L. (1990). Psychosocial factors associated with urban adolescent female suicide attempts. *Journal of the American Academy of Child and Adolescent Psychiatry, 29,* 289–294.

King, H. E. (1992). The reactions of children to divorce. In C. E. Walker & M. C. Roberts (Eds.), *Handbook of clinical child psychology* (2nd ed., pp. 1009–1023). New York: Wiley.

King, J. W., & Meeks, J. E. (1988). Hospital programs for psychiatrically disturbed, drug-abusing adolescents. In S. C. Feinstein (Ed.), *Adolescent psychiatry* (Vol. 15, pp. 522–534). Chicago: University of Chicago Press.

Kirby, D. (1992). School-based prevention programs: Design, evaluation, and effectiveness. In R. J. DiClemente (Ed.), *Adolescents and AIDS: A generation in jeopardy* (pp. 159–180). Newbury Park, CA: Sage.

Kiser, L. J., Heston, J., Millsap, P. A., & Pruitt, D. B. (1991). Physical and sexual abuse in childhood: Relationship with post-traumatic stress disorder. *Journal of the American Academy of Child and Adolescent Psychiatry, 30,* 776–783.

Koestner, R., Zuroff, D. C., & Powers, T. A. (1991). Family origins of adolescent self-criticism and its continuity into adulthood. *Journal of Abnormal Psychology, 100,* 191–197.

Kohlberg, L. (1958). The development of modes of thinking and choices in years 10 to 16. Unpublished Ph.D. dissertation, University of Chicago.

Kohlberg, L. (1966). A cognitive-developmental analysis of children's sex-role concepts and attitudes. In E. E. Maccoby (Ed.), *The development of sex differences* (pp. 82–173). Stanford, CA: Stanford University Press.

Kohlberg, L. (1981). *Essays on moral development. Vol. 1. The philosophy of moral development.* New York: Harper & Row.

Kohlberg, L. (1984). *The psychology of moral development: The nature and validity of moral stages.* San Francisco: Harper & Row.

Konopka, G. (1976). *Young girls: A portrait of adolescence.* Englewood Cliffs, NJ: Prentice-Hall.

Koocher, G. P., & O'Malley, J. E. (1981). *The Damocles syndrome: Psychosocial consequences of surviving childhood cancer.* New York: McGraw-Hill.

Kosky, R., Silburn, S., & Zubrick, S. R. (1990). Are children and adolescents who have suicidal thoughts different from those who attempt suicide? *Journal of Nervous and Mental Disease, 178,* 38–43.

Kovach, J. A., & Glickman, N. W. (1986). Levels and psychosocial correlates of adolescent drug use. *Journal of Youth and Adolescence, 15,* 61–77.

Kovacs, M. (1989). Affective disorders in children and adolescents. *American Psychologist, 44,* 209–215.

Kovacs, M., Goldston, D., & Gatsonis, C. (1993). Suicidal behaviors and childhood-onset depressive disorder: A longitudinal investigation. *Journal of the American Academy of Child and Adolescent Psychiatry, 32,* 8–20.

Kramer, D. A., & Melchior, J. (1990). Gender, role conflict, and the development of relativistic and dialectical thinking. *Sex Roles, 23,* 553–575.

Kramer, D. A., & Woodruff, D. S. (1986). Relativistic and dialectical thought in three adult age-groups. *Human Development, 29,* 280–290.

Kubey, R., & Larson, R. (1990). The use and experience of the new video media among children and young adolescents. *Communication Research, 17*, 107–130.

Kübler-Ross, E. (1969). *On death and dying.* New York: Macmillan.

Kufeldt, K., & Nimmo, M. (1987). Youth on the street: Abuse and neglect in the eighties. *Child Abuse and Neglect, 11*, 531–543.

Kuhn, D. (1986, May). Coordinating theory and evidence in reasoning. Invited address presented at the Sixteenth Annual Symposium of The Jean Piaget Society, Philadelphia. (Cited in Gray, 1990.)

Kupersmidt, J. B., & Coie, J. D. (1990). Preadolescent peer status, aggression, and school adjustment as predictors of externalizing problems in adolescence. *Child Development, 61*, 1350–1362.

Kupersmidt, J. B., Coie, J. D., & Dodge, K. A. (1990). The role of poor peer relationships in the development of disorder. In S. R. Asher & J. D. Coie (Eds.), *Peer rejection in childhood* (pp. 274–305). New York: Cambridge University Press.

Kurdek, L. A., & Sinclair, R. J. (1988). Adjustment of young adolescents in two-parent nuclear, stepfather, and mother-custody families. *Journal of Consulting and Clinical Psychology, 56*, 91–96.

Kurtz, P. D., Kurtz, G. L., & Jarvis, S. V. (1991). Problems of maltreated runaway youth. *Adolescence, 26*, 543–555.

Kutcher, S., & Marton, P. (1991). Affective disorders in first-degree relatives of adolescent onset bipolars, unipolars, and normal controls. *Journal of the American Academy of Child and Adolescent Psychiatry, 30*, 75–78.

Ladd, G. W. (1990). Having friends, keeping friends, making friends, and being liked by peers in the classroom: Predictors of children's early school adjustment? *Child Development, 61*, 1081–1100.

Ladd, G. W., & Asher, S. R. (1985). Social skill training and children's peer relations. In L. L'Abate & M. A. Milan (Eds.), *Handbook of social skills training and research* (pp. 219–244). New York: Wiley.

LaFromboise, T. D., & Low, K. G. (1990). American Indian children and adolescents. In J. T. Gibbs & L. N. Huang (Eds.), *Children of color: Psychological interventions with minority youth* (pp. 114–147). San Francisco: Jossey-Bass.

Lamb, M. E. (1982). Maternal employment and child development: A review. In M. E. Lamb (Ed.), *Nontraditional families: Parenting and child development* (pp. 45–70). Hillsdale, NJ: Erlbaum.

Lamb, M. E. (1986). The changing roles of fathers. In M. E. Lamb (Ed.), *The father's role: Applied perspectives* (pp. 3–28). New York: Wiley.

Lamb, M. E., & Sternberg, K. J. (1990). Do we really know how day care affects children? *Journal of Applied Developmental Psychology, 11*, 351–379.

Lambert, B. G., & Mounce, N. B. (1987). Career planning. In V. B. Van Hasselt & M. Hersen (Eds.), *Handbook of adolescent psychology* (pp. 458–470). New York: Pergamon.

Lamborn, S. D., Mounts, N. S., Steinberg, L., & Dornbusch, S. M. (1991). Patterns of competence and adjustment among adolescents from authoritative, authoritarian, indulgent, and neglectful families. *Child Development, 62*, 1049–1065.

Lancelotta, G. X., & Vaughn, S. (1989). Relation between types of aggression and sociometric status: Peer and teacher perceptions. *Journal of Educational Psychology, 81*, 86–90.

Landerman, R., George, L. K., & Blazer, D. G. (1991). Adult vulnerability for psychiatric disorders: Interactive effects of negative childhood experiences and recent stress. *Journal of Nervous and Mental Disease, 179*, 656–663.

Lapsley, D. K. (1985). Elkind on egocentrism. *Developmental Review, 5*, 227–236.

Lapsley, D. K. (1990). Continuity and discontinuity in adolescent social cognitive development. In R. Montemayor, G. R. Adams, & T. P. Gullotta (Eds.), *From childhood to adolescence: A transitional period?* (pp. 183–204). Newbury Park, CA: Sage.

Lapsley, D. K., FitzGerald, D. P., Rice, K. G., & Jackson, S. (1989). Separation-individuation and the "new look" at the imaginary audience and personal fable: A test of an integrative model. *Journal of Adolescent Research, 4*, 483–505.

Lapsley, D. K., Jackson, S., Rice, K., & Shadid, G. E. (1988). Self-monitoring and the "new look" at the imaginary audience and personal fable: An ego-developmental analysis. *Journal of Adolescent Research, 3*, 17–31.

Lapsley, D. K., Milstead, M., Quintana, S., Flannery, D., & Buss, R. (1986). Adolescent egocentrism and formal operations: Tests of a theoretical assumption. *Developmental Psychology, 22*, 800–807.

Lapsley, D. K., & Murphy, M. N. (1985). Another look at the theoretical assumptions of adolescent egocentrism. *Developmental Review, 5*, 201–217.

Laron, Z., Arad, J., Gurewitz, R., Grunebaum, M., & Dickerman, Z. (1980). Age at first conscious ejaculation: A milestone in male puberty. *Helevetica Paediatrica Acta, 5,* 13–20.

Larson, R. (1990). The solitary side of life: An examination of the time people spend alone from childhood to old age. *Developmental Review, 10,* 155–183.

Larson, R., Csikszentmihalyi, M., & Graef, R. (1982). Time alone in daily experience: Loneliness or renewal? In L. A. Peplau & D. Perlman (Eds.), *Loneliness: A sourcebook of theory, research, and therapy* (pp. 40–53). New York: Wiley.

Larson, R., & Kleiber, D. (1993). Daily experience of adolescents. In P. H. Tolan & B. J. Cohler (Eds.), *Handbook of clinical research and practice with adolescents* (pp. 125–145). New York: Wiley.

Larson, R., Kubey, R., & Colletti, J. (1989). Changing channels: Early adolescent media choices and shifting investments in family and friends. *Journal of Youth and Adolescence, 18,* 583–599.

Larson, R., & Richards, M. H. (1989). Introduction: The changing life space of early adolescence. *Journal of Youth and Adolescence, 18,* 501–509.

Last, C. G. (1992). Anxiety disorders in childhood and adolescence. In W. M. Reynolds (Ed.), *Internalizing disorders in children and adolescents* (pp. 61–106). New York: Wiley.

Last, C. G., & Strauss, C. C. (1990). School refusal in anxiety-disordered children and adolescents. *Journal of the American Academy of Child and Adolescent Psychiatry, 29,* 31–35.

Lauer, R. H. (1973). *Perspectives in social change.* Boston: Allyn & Bacon.

Lavigne, J. V., & Faier-Routman, J. (1992). Psychological adjustment to pediatric physical disorders: A meta-analytic review. *Journal of Pediatric Psychology, 17,* 133–157.

Leary, M. R. (1986). Affective and behavioral components of shyness. In W. H. Jones, J. M. Cheek, & S. R. Biggs (Eds.), *Shyness* (pp. 27–38). New York: Plenum.

Leary, W. E. (1993, May 11). Female condom approved for market. *New York Times,* C-5.

Lebra, T. S. (1976). *Japanese patterns of behavior.* Honolulu: University of Hawaii Press.

Lee, J. A. (1973/1977). *The colors of love: An exploration of the ways of loving.* New York: Bantam. (Originally published by New Press, Don Mills, Ontario, Canada, 1973.)

Lee, J. A. (1988). Love-styles. In R. J. Sternberg & M. L. Barnes (Eds.), *The psychology of love* (pp. 38–67). New Haven, CT: Yale University Press.

Lee, M. M. C., Chang, K. S. F., & Chan, M. M. C. (1963). Sexual maturation of Chinese girls in Hong Kong. *Pediatrics, 32,* 389–398.

Lee, P. A. (1980). Normal ages of pubertal events among American males and females. *Journal of Adolescent Health Care, 1,* 26–29.

Lempers, J. D., & Clark-Lempers, D. S. (1992). Young, middle, and late adolescents' comparisons of the functional importance of five significant relationships. *Journal of Youth and Adolescence, 21,* 53–96.

Lempers, J. D., & Clark-Lempers, D. S. (1993). A functional comparison of same-sex and opposite-sex friendships during adolescence. *Journal of Adolescent Research, 8,* 89–108.

Lempers, J. D., Clark-Lempers, D. S., & Simons, R. L. (1989). Economic hardship, parenting, and distress. *Child Development, 60,* 25–39.

Leon, G. R., Perry, C. L., Mangelsdorf, C., & Tell, G. J. (1989). Adolescent nutritional and psychological patterns and risk for the development of an eating disorder. *Journal of Youth and Adolescence, 18,* 273–282.

Leone, C. M., & Richards, M. H. (1989). Classwork and homework in early adolescence: The ecology of achievement. *Journal of Youth and Adolescence, 18,* 531–548.

Lerner, J. V., Hertzog, C., Hooker, K. A., & Hassibi, M. (1988). A longitudinal study of negative emotional states and adjustment from early childhood through adolescence. *Child Development, 59,* 356–366.

Lerner, R. M. (1991). Changing organism-context relations as the basic process of development: A developmental contextual perspective. *Developmental Psychology, 27,* 27–32.

Lerner, R. M. (1993). Early adolescence: Toward an agenda for the integration of research, policy, and intervention. In R. M. Lerner (Ed.), *Early adolescence: Perspectives on research, policy, and intervention* (pp. 1–13). Hillsdale, NJ: Erlbaum.

Lerner, R. M., Iwawaki, S., Chihara, T., & Sorell, G. T. (1980). Self-concept, self-esteem, and body attitudes among Japanese male and female adolescents. *Child Development, 51,* 847–855.

Lerner, R. M., & Spanier, G. B. (1980). *Adolescent development: A life-span perspective.* New York: McGraw-Hill.

Lester, D. (1979). Sex differences in suicidal behavior. In

E. S. Gomberg & V. Franks (Eds.), *Gender and disordered behavior* (pp. 287–300). New York: Brunner/Mazel.

Leung, J., & Leung, K. (1992). Life satisfaction, self-concept, and relationships with parents in adolescence. *Journal of Youth and Adolescence, 21*, 653–666.

LeVay, S. (1991). A difference in hypothalamic structure between heterosexual and homosexual men. *Science, 253*, 1034–1037.

Lever, J. (1976). Sex differences in games children play. *Social Problems, 23*, 478–487.

Levinson, D. J. (1978). *The seasons of a man's life.* New York: Knopf.

Levy, B. (1993). *In love and in danger: A teen's guide to breaking free of abusive relationships.* Seattle, WA: Seal Press.

Levy, R. I. (1983). The attack on Mead. *Science, 220*, 829–832.

Lewin, K. (1948). *Resolving social conflict.* New York: Harper.

Lewine, R. R., Watt, N. F., Prentky, R. A., & Fryer, J. H. (1980). Childhood social competence in functionally disordered psychiatric patients and in normals. *Journal of Abnormal Psychology, 89*, 132–138.

Lewinsohn, P. M., Rohde, P., & Seeley, J. R. (1993). Psychosocial characteristics of adolescents with a history of suicide attempts. *Journal of the American Academy of Child and Adolescent Psychiatry, 32*, 60–68.

Lewinsohn, P. M., Zeiss, A. M., & Duncan, E. M. (1989). Probability of relapse after recovery from an episode of depression. *Journal of Abnormal Psychology, 98*, 107–116.

Lewis, M., Lewis, D. O., & Schonfeld, D. J. (1991). Dying and death in childhood and adolescence. In M. Lewis (Ed.), *Child and adolescent psychiatry* (pp. 1051–1059). Baltimore, MD: Williams & Wilkins.

Lewis, M. S. (1989). Age incidence and schizophrenia: II. Beyond age incidence. *Schizophrenia Bulletin, 15*, 75–80.

Lewis, R. A., Piercy, F. P., Sprenkle, D. H., & Trepper, T. S. (1990). Family-based interventions for helping drug-abusing adolescents. *Journal of Adolescent Research, 5*, 82–95.

Lin, C. A., & Atkin, D. J. (1989). Parental mediation and rulemaking for adolescent use of television and VCRs. *Journal of Broadcasting & Electronic Media, 33*, 53–67.

Lindeke, L., Iverson, S., Fisch, R. (1986). Neonatal circumcision: A social and medical dilemma. *Maternal Child Nursing Journal, 15*, 31–37.

Linscheid, T. R. (1992). Eating problems in children. In C. E. Walker & M. C. Roberts (Eds.), *Handbook of clinical child psychology* (2nd ed., pp. 451–473). New York: Wiley.

Linscheid, T. R., Tarnowski, K. J., & Richmond, D. A. (1988). Behavioral approaches to anorexia nervosa, bulimia, and obesity. In D. K. Routh (Ed.), *Handbook of pediatric psychology* (pp. 332–362). New York: Guilford.

Litovsky, V. G., & Dusek, J. B. (1985). Perceptions of child rearing and self-concept during the early adolescent years. *Journal of Youth and Adolescence, 14*, 373–388.

Livesley, W. J., & Bromley, D. B. (1973). *Person perception in childhood and adolescence.* London: Wiley.

Locke, J. (1690/1959). *An essay concerning human understanding.* New York: Dover.

Loeber, R. (1990). Development and risk factors of juvenile antisocial behavior and delinquency. *Clinical Psychology Review, 10*, 1–41.

Loewen, J. W. (1988). Visitation fatherhood. In P. Bronstein & C. P. Cowan (Eds.), *Fatherhood today* (pp. 195–213). New York: Wiley.

Loewenstein, G., & Furstenberg, F. (1991). Is teenage sexual behavior rational? *Journal of Applied Social Psychology, 21*, 957–986.

Long, N., Forehand, R., Fauber, R., & Brody, G. H. (1987). Self-perceived and independently observed competence of young adolescents as a function of parental marital conflict and recent divorce. *Journal of Abnormal Child Psychology, 15*, 15–27.

Looft, W. R. (1972). Egocentrism and social interaction across the life span. *Psychological Bulletin, 78*, 73–92.

Lovko, A. M., & Ullman, D. G. (1989). Research on the adjustment of latchkey children: Role of background/demographic and latchkey situation variables. *Journal of Clinical Child Psychology, 18*, 16–24.

Lowery, S., & De Fleur, M. L. (1983). *Milestones in mass communication research: Media effects.* New York: Longman.

Lowing, P. A., Mirsky, A. F., & Pereira, R. (1983). The inheritance of schizophrenia spectrum disorders: A reanalysis of the Danish adoptee study data. *American Journal of Psychiatry, 140*, 1167–1171.

Lowman, R. L. (1991). *The clinical practice of career*

assessment. Washington, DC: American Psychological Association.

Lowney, J. (1984). The Wall Gang: A study of interpersonal process and deviance among twenty-three middle-class youths. *Adolescence, 19*, 527–538.

Lucas, A. R. (1991). Eating disorders. In M. Lewis (Ed.), *Child and adolescent psychiatry* (pp. 573–583). Baltimore, MD: Williams & Wilkins.

Lucas, M. S., & Epperson, D. L. (1991). Types of vocational indecision: A replication and refinement. *Journal of Counseling Psychology, 38*, 382–388.

Luepnitz, D. A. (1991). A comparison of maternal, paternal, and joint custody: Understanding the varieties of post-divorce family life. In J. Folberg (Ed.), *Joint custody and shared parenting* (2nd ed., pp. 105–113). New York: Guilford.

Lukesch, H. (1988). Mass media use, deviant behavior and delinquency. *Communications, 14*, 53–64.

Lull, J. (1992). Popular music and communication: An introduction. In J. Lull (Ed.), *Popular music and communication* (2nd ed., pp. 1–32). Newbury Park, CA: Sage.

Lundberg-Love, P. K. (1990). Adult survivors of incest. In R. T. Ammerman & M. Hersen (Eds.), *Treatment of family violence* (pp. 211–240). New York: Wiley.

Lundholm, J. K., & Litrell, J. M. (1986). Desire for thinness among high school cheerleaders: Relationship to disordered eating and weight control behaviors. *Adolescence, 21*, 573–579.

Lutes, C. J. (1981). Early marriage and identity foreclosure. *Adolescence, 16*, 809–815.

Lyman, R. D., Prentice-Dunn, S., & Gabel, S. (Eds.) (1992). *Residential and inpatient treatment of children and adolescents*. New York: Plenum.

Lyon, J., Henggeler, S., & Hall, J. A. (1992). The family relations, peer relations, and criminal activities of Caucasian and Hispanic-American gang members. *Journal of Abnormal Child Psychology, 20*, 439–450.

Maccoby, E. E., Depner, C. E., & Mnookin, R. H. (1988). Custody of children following divorce. In E. M. Hetherington & J. D. Aresteh (Eds.), *Impact of divorce, single parenting, and stepparenting* (pp. 91–114). Hillsdale, NJ: Erlbaum.

Maccoby, E. E., & Martin, J. (1983). Socialization in the context of the family: Parent–child interactions. In E. M. Hetherington (Ed.) & P. H. Mussen (Series Ed.), *Handbook of child psychology* (Vol. 4, pp. 1–101). New York: Wiley.

Magnusson, D., Stattin, H., & Allen, V. L. (1985).

Biological maturation and social development: A longitudinal study of some adjustment processes from mid-adolescence to adulthood. *Journal of Youth and Adolescence, 14*, 267–283.

Mallory, M. E. (1989). Q-sort definition of ego identity status. *Journal of Youth and Adolescence, 18*, 399–412.

Malyon, A. K. (1981). The homosexual adolescent: Developmental issues and social bias. *Child Welfare, 60*, 321–330.

Manaster, G. J., Chan, J. C., & Safady, R. (1992). Mexican-American migrant students' academic success: Sociological and psychological acculturation. *Adolescence, 27*, 123–126.

Mannarino, A. P. (1976). Friendship patterns and altruistic behavior in preadolescent males. *Developmental Psychology, 12*, 555–556.

Marcia, J. E. (1966). Development and validation of ego-identity statuses. *Journal of Personality and Social Psychology, 3*, 551–558.

Marcia, J. E. (1980). Identity in adolescence. In J. Adelson (Ed.), *Handbook of adolescent psychology* (pp. 159–187). New York: Wiley.

Marcus, I. M. (1991). The influence of family dynamics on adolescent learning disorders. In S. I. Greenspan & G. H. Pollock (Eds.), *The course of life. Vol IV. Adolescence* (pp. 253–282). New York: International Universities Press.

Marcus, J., Hans, S. L., Nagler, S., Auerbach, J. G., Mirsky, A. F., & Aubrey, A. (1987). Review of the NIMH Israeli kibbutz-city study and the Jerusalem infant development study. *Schizophrenia Bulletin, 13*, 425–438.

Mark, A. (1988). Metaphoric lyrics as a bridge to the adolescent's world. *Adolescence, 23*, 313–323.

Markstrom, C. A., & Mullis, R. L. (1986). Ethnic differences in the imaginary audience. *Journal of Adolescent Research, 1*, 289–301.

Markstrom-Adams, C. (1992). A consideration of intervening factors in adolescent identity formation. In G. R. Adams, T. P. Gullotta, & R. Montemayor (Eds.), *Adolescent identity formation* (pp. 173–192). Newbury Park, CA: Sage.

Marlatt, G. A., Baer, J. S., Donovan, D. M., & Kivlahan, D. R. (1988). Addictive behavior: Etiology and treatment. *Annual Review of Psychology, 39*, 223–252.

Marohn, R. C. (1993). Residential services. In P. H. Tolan & B. J. Cohler (Eds.), *Handbook of clinical research and practice with adolescents* (pp. 453–466). New York: Wiley.

Marsh, H. W. (1987). The big-fish–little-pond effect on

academic self-concept. *Journal of Educational Psychology, 79,* 280–295.

Marsh, H. W. (1992). Extracurricular activities: Beneficial extension of the traditional curriculum or subversion of academic goals? *Journal of Educational Psychology, 84,* 553–561.

Marshall, E. (1983). A controversy on Samoa comes of age. *Science, 219,* 1042–1045.

Marshall, W. A., & Tanner, J. M. (1969). Variations in pattern of pubertal changes in girls. *Archives of Disease in Childhood, 44,* 291–303.

Marshall, W. A., & Tanner, J. M. (1970). Variations in the pattern of pubertal changes in boys. *Archives of Disease in Childhood, 45,* 13–23.

Marsiglio, W. (1988). Adolescent male sexuality and heterosexual masculinity: A conceptual model and review. *Journal of Adolescent Research, 3,* 285–303.

Marston, A. R., Jacobs, D. F., Singer, R. D., & Widaman, K. F. (1988). Adolescents who apparently are invulnerable to drug, alcohol, and nicotine use. *Adolescence, 23,* 593–598.

Martin, A. D. (1982). Learning to hide: The socialization of the gay adolescent. In S. C. Feinstein, J. G. Looney, A. Z. Schwartzberg, & A. D. Sorosky (Eds.), *Adolescent psychiatry* (Vol. 10, pp. 52–65). Chicago: University of Chicago Press.

Martin, M. J., & Pritchard, M. E. (1991). Factors associated with alcohol use in later adolescence. *Journal of Studies on Alcohol, 52,* 5–9.

Marttunen, M. J., Aro, H. M., Henriksson, M. M., & Lonnqvist, J. K. (1991). Mental disorders in adolescent suicide. *Archives of General Psychiatry, 48,* 834–839.

Marttunen, M. J., Aro, H. M., & Lonnqvist, J. K. (1992). Adolescent suicide: Endpoint of long-term difficulties. *Journal of the American Academy of Child and Adolescent Psychiatry, 31,* 649–654.

Maslow, A. (1955). Deficiency motivation and growth motivation. In M. R. Jones (Ed.), *Nebraska symposium on motivation* (pp. 1–30). Lincoln, NE: University of Nebraska Press.

Masters, W. H., & Johnson, V. E. (1979). *Homosexuality in perspective.* Boston: Little, Brown.

Matter, R. M. (1982). Elkind's theory of adolescent egocentrism as expressed in selected characters of M. E. Kerr. *Adolescence, 17,* 657–666.

McAdams, D. P., Lester, R. M., Brand, P. A., McNamara, W. J., & Lensky, D. B. (1988). Are women more intimate than men? Do men fear intimacy? *Journal of Personality Assessment, 52,* 397–409.

McCall, R. B., Evahn, C., & Kratzer, L. (1992). *High school underachievers: What do they achieve as adults?* Newbury Park, CA: Sage.

McCarthy, B., & Hagan, J. (1992). Surviving on the street: The experiences of homeless youth. *Journal of Adolescent Research, 7,* 412–430.

McCauley, E., Carlson, G. A., & Calderon, R. (1991). The role of somatic complaints in the diagnosis of depression in children and adolescents. *Journal of the American Academy of Child and Adolescent Psychiatry, 30,* 631–635.

McCauley, E., Mitchell, J. R., Burke, P., & Moss, S. (1988). Cognitive attributes of depression in children and adolescents. *Journal of Consulting and Clinical Psychology, 56,* 903–908.

McClelland, D. (1979). *Power: The inner experience.* New York: Irvington.

McClelland, K. A. (1982). Adolescent subculture in the schools. In T. M. Field, A. Huston, H. C. Quay, L. Troll, & G. E. Finley (Eds.), *Review of human development* (pp. 395–417). New York: Wiley.

McGlashan, T. H. (1988a). A selective review of recent North American long-term followup studies of schizophrenia. *Schizophrenia Bulletin, 14,* 515–542.

McGlashan, T. H. (1988b). Adolescent versus adult onset of mania. *American Journal of Psychiatry, 145,* 221–223.

McGue, M., & Gottesman, I. I. (1989). Genetic linkage in schizophrenia: Perspectives from genetic epidemiology. *Schizophrenia Bulletin, 15,* 453–464.

McGue, M., Pickens, R. W., & Svikis, D. S. (1992). Sex and age effects on the inheritance of alcohol problems. A twin study. *Journal of Abnormal Psychology, 101,* 3–17.

McGuire, K. D., & Weisz, J. R. (1982). Social cognition and behavior correlates of preadolescent chumship. *Child Development, 53,* 1478–1484.

McIntosh, J. L. (1992). Methods of suicide. In R. W. Maris, A. L. Berman, J. T. Maltsberger, & R. I. Yufit (Eds.), *Assessment and prediction of suicide* (pp. 381–397). New York: Guilford.

McLeer, S. V., Deblinger, E., Henry, D., & Orvaschel, H. (1992). Sexually abused children at high risk for post-traumatic stress disorder. *Journal of the American Academy of Child and Adolescent Psychiatry, 31,* 875–879.

Mead, M. (1928/1961). *Coming of age in Samoa.* New York: Morrow.

Mead, M. (1949). *Male and female.* New York: Morrow.

Mead, M. (1970). *Culture and commitment: A study of the generation gap.* Garden City, NY: Doubleday.

Mead, M. (1978). *Culture and commitment: The new relationships between the generations in the 1970s* (rev. ed.). New York: Columbia University Press.

Mednick, S. A., Parnas, J., & Schulsinger, F. (1987). The Copenhagen high-risk project, 1962–1986. *Schizophrenia Bulletin, 13*, 485–496.

Meehan, P. J., Lamb, J. A., Saltzman, L. E., & O'Carroll, P. W. (1992). Attempted suicide among young adults: Progress toward a meaningful estimate of prevalence. *American Journal of Psychiatry, 149*, 41–44.

Meeks, J. E., & Cahill, A. J. (1988). Therapy of adolescents with severe behavior problems. In S. C. Feinstein (Ed.), *Adolescent Psychiatry* (Vol. 15, pp. 475–486). Chicago: University of Chicago Press.

Melchert, T., & Burnett, K. F. (1990). Attitudes, knowledge, and sexual behavior of high-risk adolescents: Implications for counseling and sexuality education. *Journal of Counseling and Development, 68*, 293–298.

Melnick, M. J., Sabo, D. F., & Vanfossen, B. (1992). Educational effects of interscholastic athletic participation on African-American and Hispanic youth. *Adolescence, 27*, 295–308.

Meloy, J. R. (1988). *The psychopathic mind.* Northvale, NJ: Aronson.

Mercer, R. T., Nichols, E. G., & Dole, G. C. (1989). *Transitions in a woman's life: Major life events in developmental context.* New York: Springer.

Meyer-Bahlburg, H. F. L., Ehrhardt, A. A., Bell, J. J., Cohen, S. F., Healey, J. M., Feldman, J. F., Morishima, A., Baker, S. W., & New, M. I. (1985). Idiopathic precocious puberty in girls: Psychosexual development. *Journal of Youth and Adolescence, 14*, 339–353.

Miklowitz, D. J., Velligan, D. I., Goldstein, M. J., Nuechterlein, K. H., Gitlin, M. J., Ranlett, G., & Doane, J. A. (1991). Communication deviance in families of schizophrenic and manic patients. *Journal of Abnormal Psychology, 100*, 163–173.

Miller, A. (1949). *The death of a salesman.* New York: Viking.

Miller, B. C., & Fox, G. L. (1987). Theories of adolescent heterosexual behavior. *Journal of Adolescent Research, 2*, 269–282.

Miller, B. C., & Paikoff, R. L. (1992). Comparing adolescent pregnancy prevention programs: Methods and results. In B. C. Miller, J. J. Card, R. L. Paikoff, & J. L. Peterson (Eds.), *Preventing adolescent pregnancy: Model programs and evaluations* (pp. 265–284). Newbury Park, CA: Sage.

Miller, G. E., & Prinz, R. J. (1990). Enhancement of social learning family interventions for childhood conduct disorder. *Psychological Bulletin, 108*, 291–307.

Miller, J. B. (1981/1991). The development of women's sense of self. In J. V. Jordan, A. G. Kaplan, J. B. Miller, I.P. Stiver, & J. L. Surrey (Eds.), *Women's growth in connection* (pp. 11–26). New York: Guilford.

Miller, J. B. (1982/1991). The construction of anger in women and men. In J. V. Jordan, A. G. Kaplan, J. B. Miller, I. P. Stiver, & J. L. Surrey (Eds.), *Women's growth in connection* (pp. 181–196). New York: Guilford.

Miller, K. E. (1990). Adolescents' same-sex and opposite-sex peer relations: Sex differences in popularity, perceived social competence, and social cognitive skills. *Journal of Adolescent Research, 5*, 222–241.

Miller, P. H., & Weiss, M. G. (1981). Children's attention allocation, understanding of attention, and performance on the incidental learning task. *Child Development, 52*, 1183–1190.

Mills, C. J., & Noyes, H. L. (1984). Patterns and correlates of initial and subsequent drug use among adolescents. *Journal of Consulting and Clinical Psychology, 52*, 231–243.

Minde, K. (1978). Coping styles of 34 adolescents with cerebral palsy. *American Journal of Psychiatry, 135*, 1335–1349.

Modell, J., & Goodman, M. (1990). Historical perspectives. In S. S. Feldman & G. R. Elliott (Eds.), *At the threshold: The developing adolescent* (pp. 93–122). Cambridge, MA: Harvard University Press.

Moffitt, T. E., & Henry, B. (1989). Neuropsychological assessment of executive functioning in self-reported delinquents. *Development and Psychopathology, 1*, 105–118.

Mohr, P. H., Sprinthall, N. A., & Gerler, E. R. (1987). Moral reasoning in early adolescence: Implications for drug abuse prevention. *School Counselor, 35*, 120–127.

Money, J. (1980). *Love and love sickness: The science of sex, gender difference, and pair-bonding.* Baltimore: Johns Hopkins University Press.

Money, J. (1987). Sin, sickness, or status? Homosexual gender identity and psychoneuroendocrinology. *American Psychologist, 42*, 384–399.

Money, J., & Ehrhardt, A. A. (1972). *Man and woman, boy and girl: Differentiation and dimorphism of gender identity from conception to maturity.* Baltimore: Johns Hopkins University Press.

Money, J., & Lamacz, M. (1987). Genital examination and exposure experienced as nosocomial sexual abuse in childhood. *Journal of Nervous and Mental Disease, 175*, 713–721.

Money, J., & Walker, P. A. (1971). Psychosexual development, maternalism, nonpromiscuity, and body image in 15 females with precocious puberty. *Archives of Sexual Behavior, 1*, 45–60.

Monge, R. H. (1973). Developmental trends in factors of adolescent self-concept. *Developmental Psychology, 8*, 382–393.

Montemayor, R. (1986). Family variation in parent–adolescent storm and stress. *Journal of Adolescent Research, 1*, 15–31.

Montemayor, R., & Flannery, D. J. (1989). A naturalistic study of the involvement of children and adolescents with their mothers and friends: Developmental differences in expressive behavior. *Journal of Adolescent Research, 4*, 3–14.

Moore, K. A., & Stief, T. M. (1991). Changes in marriage and fertility behavior: Behavior versus attitudes of young adults. *Youth & Society, 22*, 362–386.

Moran, J. R., & Corley, M. D. (1991). Sources of sexual information and sexual attitudes and behaviors of Anglo and Hispanic adolescent males. *Adolescence, 26*, 857–864.

Morris, J. (1985). The treatment of adolescent psychosis: An integrated perspective. In M. P. Mirkin & S. L. Koman (Eds.), *Handbook of adolescents and family therapy* (pp. 295–307). New York: Gardner Press.

Morrison, P., & Masten, A. S. (1991). Peer reputation in middle childhood as a predictor of adaptation in adolescence: A seven-year follow-up. *Child Development, 62*, 991–1007.

Morrison, R. F., & Adams, J. (Eds.) (1991). *Contemporary career development issues.* Hillsdale, NJ: Erlbaum.

Mortimer, J. T., Finch, M., Shanahan, M., & Ryu, S. (1992a). Adolescent work history and behavioral adjustment. *Journal of Research on Adolescence, 2*, 59–80.

Mortimer, J. T., Finch, M., Shanahan, M., & Ryu, S. (1992b). Work experience, mental health, and behavioral adjustment in adolescence. *Journal of Research on Adolescence, 2*, 25–57.

Mosher, L. R., & Keith, S. J. (1980). Psychosocial treatment: Individual, group, family, and community approaches. *Schizophrenia Bulletin, 6*, 10–41.

Mrazek, D. A. (1991). Dying and death in childhood and adolescence. In M. Lewis (Ed.), *Child and adolescent psychiatry* (pp. 1041–1050). Baltimore, MD: Williams & Wilkins.

Mulholland, D. J., Watt, N. F., Philpott, A., & Sarlin, N. (1991). Academic performance in children of divorce: Psychological resilience and vulnerability. *Psychiatry, 54*, 268–280.

Mullis, R. L., & Markstron, C. A. (1986). An analysis of the imaginary audience scale. *Journal of Early Adolescence, 6*, 305–314.

Mulvey, E. P., & LaRosa, J. F. (1986). Delinquency cessation and adolescent development: Preliminary data. *American Journal of Orthopsychiatry, 56*, 212–224.

Murphy, B. C. (1991). Educating mental health professionals about gay and lesbian issues. *Journal of Homosexuality, 22*, 229–246.

Murstein, B. I., Chalpin, M. J., Heard, K. V., & Vyse, S. A. (1989). Sexual behavior, drugs, and relationship patterns on a college campus over thirteen years. *Adolescence, 24*, 125–139.

Mussen, P. (1987). Longitudinal study of the life span. In N. Eisenberg (Ed.), *Contemporary topics in developmental psychology* (pp. 375–393). New York: Wiley.

Muuss, R. E. (1982). *Theories of adolescence* (4th ed.). New York: Random House.

Muuss, R. E. (1986). Adolescent eating disorder: Bulimia. *Adolescence, 20*, 525–536.

Myers, K., McCauley, E., Calderon, R., & Treder, R. (1991). The 3-year longitudinal course of suicidality and predictive factors for subsequent suicidality in youths with major depressive disorder. *Journal of the American Academy of Child and Adolescent Psychiatry, 30*, 804–810.

National Center for Health Statistics. (1989). Annual summary of births, marriages, divorces, and deaths: United States, 1988. *Monthly Statistical Report, 37.* Hyattsville, MD: Public Health Service.

National Center for Health Statistics. (1991). *Vital statistics of the United States, 1988: Vol. 2. Mortality.* Hyattsville, MD: Author.

National Commission on AIDS. (1993). *Behavioral and social sciences and the HIV/AIDS epidemic.* Washington, DC: Author.

National Institute of Mental Health. (1985). *Mental health, United States.* Washington, DC: U. S. Department of Health and Human Services.

National Institute on Drug Abuse. (1991). *National household survey of drug abuse: Population estimates 1990.* Rockville, MD: Author.

Neimark, E. D. (1982). Adolescent thought: Transition to formal operations. In B. B. Wolman (Ed.), *Handbook of developmental psychology* (pp. 485–502). Englewood Cliffs, NJ: Prentice-Hall.

Neimeyer, G. J., & Heesacker, M. (1992). Vocational development: Assessment and intervention in adolescent career choice. In C. E. Walker & M. C. Roberts (Eds.), *Handbook of clinical child psychology* (2nd ed., pp. 661–676). New York: Wiley.

Nelson, K. E. (1990). Family-based services for juvenile offenders. *Children and Youth Services Review, 12*, 193–212.

Nesselroade, J. R., & Baltes, P. B. (1974). Adolescent personality development and historical change: 1970–1972. *Monographs of the Society for Research in Child Development, 39* (Whole No. 154), 1–80.

Neugarten, B. L. (1968). Adult personality: Toward a psychology of the life cycle. In B. L. Neugarten (Ed.), *Middle age and aging* (pp. 137–147). Chicago: University of Chicago Press.

New York Times. (1992, December 17). Medicaid widening the use of implant for birth control, pp. A1, B21.

Newcomb, A. F., Bukowski, W. M., & Pattee, L. (1993). Children's peer relations: A meta-analytic review of popular, rejected, neglected, controversial, and average sociometric status. *Psychological Bulletin, 113*, 99–128.

Newcomb, M. D., & Bentler, P. M. (1989). Substance use and abuse among children and teenagers. *American Psychologist, 44*, 242–248.

Newman, B. M. (1989). The changing nature of the parent adolescent relationship from early to late adolescence. *Adolescence, 24*, 915–924.

Nezu, A. M., Nezu, C. M., & Perri, M. G. (1989). *Problem-solving therapy for depression.* New York: Wiley.

Noblit, G. W., & Collins, T. W. (1980). Cultural degradation and minority student adaptations: The school experience and minority adjustment contingencies. In M. Sugar (Ed.), *Responding to adolescent needs* (pp. 73–87). New York: SP Medical & Scientific Books.

Noller, P., & Callan, V. J. (1990). Adolescents' perceptions of the nature of their communications with parents. *Journal of Youth and Adolescence, 19*, 349–361.

Noshpitz, J. D. (1991). Disturbances in early adolescent development. In S. I. Greenspan & G. H. Pollock (Eds.), *The course of life.* Vol. IV. *Adolescence* (pp. 119–180). New York: International Universities Press.

Nottelmann, E. D., Inoff-Germain, G., Susman, E. J., & Chrousos, G. P. (1990). Hormones and behavior at puberty. In J. Bancroft & J. M. Reinisch (Eds.), *Adolescence and puberty* (pp. 88–123). New York: Oxford University Press.

Novacek, J., Raskin, R., & Hogan, R. (1991). Why do adolescents use drugs? Age, sex, and user differences. *Journal of Youth and Adolescence, 20*, 475–492.

Nucci, L., Guerra, N., & Lee, J. (1991). Adolescent judgments of the personal, prudential, and normative aspects of drug usage. *Developmental Psychology, 27*, 841–848.

Nurnberger, J. I., Jr., & Gershon, E. S. (1992). Genetics. In E. S. Paykell (Ed.), *Handbook of affective disorders* (2nd ed., pp. 131–148). New York: Guilford.

O'Leary, K. D., & Smith, D. A. (1991). Marital interactions. *Annual Review of Psychology, 42*, 191–212.

O'Malley, J. E., Foster, D., Koocher, G., & Slavin, L. (1980). Visible physical impairment and psychological adjustment among pediatric cancer patients. *American Journal of Psychiatry, 137*, 94–96.

O'Malley, J. E., Koocher, G., Foster, D., & Slavin, L. (1979). Psychiatric sequelae of surviving childhood cancer. *American Journal of Orthopsychiatry, 49*, 608–616.

Odell, W. D. (1979). The physiology of puberty: Disorders of the pubertal process. In L. J. DeGroot, et al. (Eds.), *Endocrinology* (Vol. 3, pp. 1363–1379). New York: Grune & Stratton.

Offer, D. (1969). *The psychological world of the teen-ager.* New York: Basic Books.

Offer, D. (1991). Adolescent development: A normative perspective. In S. I. Greenspan & G. H. Pollock (Eds.), *The course of life. Vol. IV. Adolescence* (pp. 181–199). New York: International Universities Press.

Offer, D., & Boxer, A. M. (1991). Normal adolescent development: Empirical research findings. In M. Lewis (Ed.), *Child and adolescent psychiatry* (pp. 266–278). Baltimore, MD: Williams & Wilkins.

Offer, D., Howard, K. I., Schonert, K. A., & Ostrov, E. (1991). To whom do adolescents turn for help? Differences between disturbed and nondisturbed adolescents. *Journal of the American Academy of Child and Adolescent Psychiatry, 30*, 623–630.

Offer, D., & Offer, J. B. (1975). *From teenage to young manhood.* New York: Basic Books.

Offer, D., Ostrov, E., & Howard, K. I. (1981). *The*

adolescent: A psychological self-portrait. New York: Basic Books.

Offer, D., Ostrov, E., Howard, K. I., & Atkinson, R. (1992). A study of quietly disturbed and normal adolescents in ten countries. In A. Z. Schwartzberg (Ed.), *International Annals of Adolescent Psychiatry* (Vol. 2, pp. 285–297). Chicago: University of Chicago Press.

Offer, D., & Schonert-Reichl, K. A. (1992). Debunking the myths of adolescence: Findings from recent research. *Journal of the American Academy of Child and Adolescent Psychiatry, 31,* 1003–1014.

Olsen, J., Weed, S., Daly, D., & Jensen, L. (1992). The effects of abstinence sex education programs on virgin versus nonvirgin students. *Journal of Research and Development in Education, 25,* 69–75.

Oster, G. D., & Caro, J. E. (1990). *Understanding and treating depressed adolescents and their families.* New York: Wiley.

Paikoff, R. L., & Brooks-Gunn, J. (1991). Do parent–child relationships change during puberty? *Psychological Bulletin, 110,* 47–66.

Paluszny, M., Davenport, C., & Kim, W. J. (1991). Suicide attempts and ideation: Adolescents evaluated on a pediatric ward. *Adolescence, 26,* 209–215.

Papini, D. R., Micka, J. C., & Barnett, J. K. (1989). Perceptions of intrapsychic and extrapsychic functioning as bases of adolescent ego identity status. *Journal of Adolescent Research, 4,* 462–482.

Papini, D. R., Roggman, L. A., & Anderson, J. (1991). Early-adolescent perceptions of attachment to mother and father: A test of emotional-distancing and buffering hypotheses. *Journal of Early Adolescence, 11,* 258–275.

Papini, D. R., & Sebby, R. A. (1987). Adolescent pubertal status and affective family relationships: A multivariate assessment. *Journal of Youth and Adolescence, 16,* 1–15.

Parish, T. S., & Dostal, J. W. (1980). Evaluations of self and parent figures by children from intact, divorced, and reconstituted families. *Journal of Youth and Adolescence, 9,* 347–352.

Parker, F. (1981). Skin and hormones. In R. H. Williams (Ed.), *Textbook of endocrinology* (6th ed., pp. 1080–1098). Philadelphia: W. B. Saunders.

Parker, J. G., & Asher, S. R. (1987). Peer relations and later personal adjustment: Are low-accepted children at risk? *Psychological Bulletin, 102,* 357–389.

Parker, H., & Parker, S. (1986). Father-daughter sexual abuse: An emerging perspective. *American Journal of Orthopsychiatry, 56,* 531–549.

Parkhurst, J. T., & Asher, S. R. (1992). Peer rejection in middle school: Subgroup differences in behavior, loneliness, and interpersonal concerns. *Developmental Psychology, 28,* 231–241.

Paroski, P. A., Jr. (1987). Health care delivery and the concerns of gay and lesbian adolescents. *Journal of Adolescent Health Care, 8,* 188–192.

Patterson, G. R., Capaldi, D., & Bank, L. (1991). An early starter model for predicting delinquency. In D. J. Pepler & K. H. Rubin (Eds.), *The development and treatment of childhood aggression* (pp. 139–169). Hillsdale, NJ: Erlbaum.

Patterson, S. J., Sochting, I., & Marcia, J. E. (1992). The inner space and beyond: Women and identity. In G. R. Adams, T. P. Gullotta, & R. Montemayor (Eds.), *Adolescent identity formation* (pp. 9–24). Newbury Park, CA: Sage.

Paul, E. L., & White, K. M. (1990). The development of intimate relationships in late adolescence. *Adolescence, 25,* 375–400.

Paulson, S. E., Hill, J. P., & Holmbeck, G. N. (1991). Distinguishing between perceived closeness and parental warmth in families with seventh-grade boys and girls. *Journal of Early Adolescence, 11,* 276–293.

Paykell, E. S. (Ed.) (1992). *Handbook of affective disorders* (2nd ed.). New York: Guilford.

Pearl, R., Bryan, T., & Herzog, A. (1990). Resisting or acquiescing to peer pressure to engage in misconduct: Adolescent's expectations of probable consequences. *Journal of Youth and Adolescence, 19,* 43–56.

Pellegrini, D. S. (1986). Variability in children's level of reasoning about friendship. *Journal of Applied Developmental Psychology, 7,* 341–354.

Peplau, L. A., & Cochran, S. D. (1990). A relationship perspective on homosexuality. In D. P. McWhirter, S. A. Sanders, & J. M. Reinisch (Eds.), *Homosexuality/heterosexuality: Concepts of sexual orientation* (pp. 321–349). New York: Oxford University Press.

Peplau, L. A., & Perlman, D. (1982). Perspectives on loneliness. In L. A. Peplau & D. Perlman (Eds.), *Loneliness: A source book of current theory, research, and therapy* (pp. 1–20). New York: Wiley.

Perri, M. G., Nezu, A. M., & Viegener, B. J. (1992). *Improving the long-term management of obesity.* New York: Wiley.

Pesce, R. C., & Harding, C. G. (1986). Imaginary audience behavior and its relationship to operational thought and social experience. *Journal of Early Adolescence, 6*, 83–94.

Pestrak, V. A., & Martin, D. (1985). Cognitive development and aspects of adolescent sexuality. *Adolescence, 20*, 981–987.

Petersen, A. C. (1983). Menarche: Meaning of measures and measuring meaning. In S. Golub (Ed.), *Menarche* (pp. 63–76). New York: Heath.

Petersen, A. C. (1988). Adolescent development. *Annual Review of Psychology, 39*, 583–697.

Petersen, A. C. (1992). Creating adolescents: The role of context and process in developmental trajectories. *Journal of Research on Adolescence, 3*, 1–18.

Petersen, A. C., Compas, B. E., Brooks-Gunn, J., Stemmler, M., Ey, S., & Grant, K. E. (1993). Depression in adolescence. *American Psychologist, 48*, 155–168.

Petersen, A. C., & Taylor, B. (1980). The biological approach to adolescence: Biological change and psychological adaptation. In J. Adelson (Ed.), *Handbook of adolescent psychology* (pp. 117–155). New York: Wiley.

Peterson, C. C., & Murphy, L. (1990). Adolescents' thoughts and feelings about AIDS in relation to cognitive maturity. *Journal of Adolescence, 13*, 185–187.

Peterson, G. W., & Leigh, G. K. (1990). The family and social competence in adolescence. In T. P. Gullotta, G. R. Adams, & R. Montemayor (Eds.), *Developing social competency in adolescence* (pp. 97–138). Newbury Park, CA: Sage.

Peterson, K. L., & Roscoe, B. (1991). Imaginary audience behavior in older adolescent females. *Adolescence, 26*, 195–200.

Pfeffer, C. R. (1989). Suicide. In L. K. G. Hsu & M. Hersen (Eds.), *Recent developments in adolescent psychiatry* (pp. 116–134). New York: Wiley.

Pfeffer, C. R., Klerman, G. L., Hurt, S. W., Kakuma, T., Peskin, J. R., & Siefker, C. A. (1993). Suicidal children grown up: Rates and psychosocial risk factors for suicide attempts during follow-up. *Journal of the American Academy of Child and Adolescent Psychiatry, 32*, 106–113.

Pfeffer, C. R., Klerman, G. L., Hurt, S. W., Lesser, M., Peskin, J. R., & Siefker, C. A. (1991). Suicidal children grown up: Demographic and clinical risk factors for adolescent suicide attempts. *Journal of the American Academy of Child and Adolescent Psychiatry, 30*, 609–616.

Phelps, L., Johnston, L. S., Jimenez, D.P., & Wilczenski,

F. L. (1993). Figure preference, body dissatisfaction, and body distortion in adolescence. *Journal of Adolescent Research, 8*, 297–310.

Phinney, J. S. (1990). Ethnic identity in adolescents and adults: Review of research. *Psychological Bulletin, 108*, 499–514.

Phinney, J. S., & Alipuria, L. L. (1990). Ethnic identity in college students from four ethnic groups. *Journal of Adolescence, 13*, 171–183.

Phinney, J. S., & Rosenthal, D. A. (1992). Ethnic identity in adolescence: Process, context, and outcome. In G. R. Adams, T. P. Gullotta, & R. Montemayor (Eds.), *Adolescent identity formation* (pp. 145–172). Newbury Park, CA: Sage.

Piaget, J. (1962). *Comments on Vygotsky's critical remarks concerning the language and thought of the child, and judgment and reasoning in the child. Attachment to L. S. Vygotsky, Thought and language.* Cambridge, MA: MIT Press.

Piaget, J. (1972). Intellectual evolution from adolescence to adulthood. *Human Development, 15*, 1–12.

Piaget, J., & Inhelder, B. (1969). *The psychology of the child.* New York: Basic Books.

Pillard, R. C. (1990). The Kinsey scale: Is it familial? In D. P. McWhirter, S. A. Sanders, & J. M. Reinisch (Eds.), *Homosexuality/heterosexuality: Concepts of sexual orientation* (pp. 88–100). New York: Oxford University Press.

Pillard, R. C., & Weinrich, J. D. (1986). Evidence of familial nature of male homosexuality. *Archives of General Psychiatry, 43*, 808–812.

Pleck, J. H., Sonenstein, F. L., & Ku, L. C. (1991). Adolescent males' condom use: Relationships between perceived cost-benefits and consistency. *Journal of Marriage and the Family, 53*, 733–745.

Pleck, J. H., Sonenstein, F. L., & Ku, L. C. (1993). Masculinity ideology: Its impact on adolescent males' heterosexual relationships. *Journal of Social Issues, 49*, 11–29.

Pliszka, S. R. (1991). Antidepressants in the treatment of child and adolescent psychopathology. *Journal of Clinical Child Psychology, 20*, 313–320.

Plomin, R. (1989). Environment and genes. *American Psychologist, 44*, 105–111.

Pokay, P., & Blumenfeld, P. C. (1990). Predicting achievement early and late in the semester: The role of motivation and use of learning strategies. *Journal of Educational Psychology, 82*, 41–50.

Polit, D. F., White, C. M., & Morton, T. D. (1990). Child sexual abuse and premarital intercourse among high-risk adolescents. *Journal of Adolescent Health Care, 11*, 231–234.

Poole, M. E., & Evans, G. T. (1989). Adolescent's self-perceptions of competence in life skill areas. *Journal of Youth and Adolescence, 18*, 147–174.

Post, R. M., Rubinow, D. R., Uhde, T. W., Roy-Byrne, P. P., Linnoila, M., Rosoff, A., & Cowdry, R. (1989). Dysphoric mania. *Archives of General Psychiatry, 46*, 353–358.

Power, T. G., & Shanks, J. A. (1989). Parents as socializers: Maternal and paternal views. *Journal of Youth and Adolescence, 18*, 203–230.

Powers, S. I., Hauser, S. T., & Kilner, L. (1989). Adolescent mental health. *American Psychologist, 44*, 200–208.

Powers, P. S. (1990). Anorexia nervosa: Evaluation and treatment. *Comprehensive Therapy, 16*, 24–34.

Prager, K. J. (1986). Identity development, age, and college experience in women. *Journal of Genetic Psychology, 147*, 31–36.

Prange, M. E., Greenbaum, P. E., Silver, S. E., Friedman, R. M., Kutach, K., & Duchnowski, A. J. (1992). Family functioning and psychopathology among adolescents with severe emotional disturbance. *Journal of Abnormal Child Psychology, 20*, 83–102.

Price, R. (1953). *Droodles*. New York: Simon & Schuster.

Protinsky, H., & Shilts, L. (1990). Adolescent substance use and family cohesion. *Family Therapy, 17*, 173–175.

Protinsky, H., & Wilkerson, J. (1986). Ego identity, egocentrism, and formal operations. *Adolescence, 21*, 461–466.

Pruitt, J. A., Kappius, R. E., & Gorman, P. W. (1992). Bulimia and fear of intimacy. *Journal of Clinical Psychology, 48*, 472–476.

Pruzinsky, T., & Cash, T. F. (1990). Medical interventions for the enhancement of adolescents' physical appearance: Implications for social competence. In T. P. Gullotta, G. R. Adams, & R. Montemayor (Eds.), *Developing social competency in adolescence* (pp. 220–242). Newbury Park, CA: Sage.

Putallaz, M., & Wasserman, A. (1990). Children's entry behavior. In S. R. Asher & J. D. Coie (Eds.), *Peer rejection in childhood* (pp. 60–89). New York: Cambridge University Press.

Quay, H. C. (1987). Patterns of delinquent behavior. In H. C. Quay (Ed.), *Handbook of juvenile delinquency* (pp. 118–138). New York: Wiley.

Quay, H. C., Routh, D. K., & Shapiro, S. K. (1987). Psychopathology of childhood. *Annual Review of Psychology, 38*, 491–532.

Quintana, S. M., & Lapsley, D. K. (1990). Rapprochement in late adolescent separation-individuation: A structural equations approach. *Journal of Adolescence, 13*, 371–385.

Radin, N. (1981). The role of the father in cognitive, academic, and intellectual development. In M. E. Lamb (Ed.), *The role of the father in child development* (2nd ed., pp. 379–428). New York: Wiley.

Raffaelli, M., & Duckett, E. (1989). "We were just talking . . .": Conversations in early adolescence. *Journal of Youth and Adolescence, 18*, 567–582.

Raja, S. N., McGee, R., & Stanton, W. R. (1992). Perceived attachment to parents and peers and psychological well-being in adolescence. *Journal of Youth and Adolescence, 21*, 471–485.

Ram, R., Bromet, E. J., Eaton, C. P., & Schwartz, J. E. (1992). The natural course of schizophrenia: A review of first admission studies. *Schizophrenia Bulletin, 18*, 185–208.

Ramirez, O. (1990). Mexican American children and adolescents. In J. T. Gibbs & L. N. Huang (Eds.), *Children of color: Psychological interventions with minority youth* (pp. 224–250). San Francisco: Jossey-Bass.

Rancurello, M. (1986). Antidepressants in children: Indications, benefits, and limitations. *American Journal of Psychotherapy, 40*, 377–392.

Rao, U., Weissman, M. M., Martin, J. A., & Hammond, R. W. (1993). Childhood depression and risk of suicide: A preliminary report of a longitudinal study. *Journal of the American Academy of Child and Adolescent Psychiatry, 32*, 21–27.

Raphael, B., Cubis, J., Dunne, M., & Lewin, T. (1990). The impact of parental loss on adolescents' psychosocial characteristics. *Adolescence, 25*, 689–700.

Raphael, R. (1988). *The men from the boys: Rites of passage in male America*. Lincoln: University of Nebraska Press.

Ravenscroft, K. (1974). Normal family regression at adolescence. *American Journal of Psychiatry, 131*, 31–35.

Rebok, G. W. (1987). *Life-span cognitive development*. New York: Holt, Reinhart and Winston.

Reichlin, S. (1981). Neuroendocrinology. In R. H. Williams (Ed.), *Textbook of endocrinology* (6th ed., pp. 589–645). Philadelphia: W. B. Saunders.

Reid, W. J., & Crisafulli, A. (1990). Marital discord and child behavior problems: A meta-analysis. *Journal of Abnormal Child Psychology, 18*, 105–117.

Reis, H. T., Senchak, M., & Solomon, B. (1985). Sex

differences in the intimacy of social interaction: Further examination of potential explanations. *Journal of Personality and Social Psychology, 48*, 1204–1217.

Reiss, D., Oliveri, M. E., & Curd, K. (1983). Family paradigm and adolescent social behavior. In H. Grotevant & C. Cooper (Eds.), *New directions for child development* (pp. 77–92). San Francisco, CA: Jossey-Bass.

Reiss, D., Plomin, R., & Hetherington, E. M. (1991). Genetics and psychiatry: An unheralded window on the environment. *American Journal of Psychiatry, 148*, 283–291.

Remafedi, G., Farrow, J. A., & Deisher, R. W. (1991). Risk factors for attempted suicide in gay and bisexual youth. *Pediatrics, 87*, 869–875.

Reyes, O., & Jason, L. A. (1993). Pilot study examining factors associated with academic success for Hispanic high school students. *Journal of Youth and Adolescence, 22*, 57–72.

Reynolds, W. M. (1992). Depression in children and adolescents. In W. M. Reynolds (Ed.), *Internalizing disorders in children and adolescents* (pp. 149–253). New York: Wiley.

Rhodes, J. E., & Jason, L. A. (1990). A social stress model of substance abuse. *Journal of Consulting and Clinical Psychology, 58*, 395–401.

Rich, C. L., Sherman, M., & Fowler, R. C. (1990). San Diego Suicide Study: The adolescents. *Adolescence, 25*, 855–865.

Richards, M. H., Abell, S., & Petersen, A. C. (1993). Biological development. In P. H. Tolan & B. J. Cohler (Eds.), *Handbook of clinical research and practice with adolescents* (pp. 21–44). New York: Wiley.

Richards, M. H., Boxer, A. M., Petersen, A. C., & Albrecht, R. (1990). Relation of weight to body image in pubertal girls and boys from two communities. *Developmental Psychology, 26*, 313–321.

Richards, M. H., & Larson, R. (1989). The life space and socialization of the self: Sex differences in the young adolescent. *Journal of Youth and Adolescence, 18*, 617–626.

Richards, M. P. M., Bernal, J. F., & Brackbill, Y. (1976). Early behavioral differences: Gender or circumcision. *Developmental Psychobiology, 9*, 89–95.

Richards, P., Berk, R. A., & Forster, B. (1979). *Crime as play: Delinquency in a middle class suburb.* Cambridge, MA: Balinger.

Riegel, K. F. (1973). Dialectic operations: The final period of cognitive development. *Human Development, 16*, 371–381.

Riegel, K. F. (1976). The dialectics of human development. *American Psychologist, 31*, 689–700.

Riegel, K. F. (1977). The dialectics of time. In N. Datan & H. W. Reese (Eds.), *Life-span developmental psychology: Dialectical perspectives on experimental research* (pp. 4–45). New York: Academic Press.

Rierdan, J., Koff, E., & Stubbs, M. L. (1989). Timing of menarche, preparation, and initial menstrual experience: Replication and further analyses in a prospective study. *Journal of Youth and Adolescence, 18*, 413–426.

Rinzler, C. E. (1979, October 11). Adolescence poses a hurdle for adults. *New York Times*, pp. C1, C12.

Roberts, R. E., Andrews, J. A., Lewinsohn, P. M., & Hops, H. (1990). Assessment of depression in adolescents using the Center for Epidemiologic Studies Depression Scale. *Psychological Assessment, 2*, 122–128.

Robertson, P., & Schachter, J. (1981). Failure to identify venereal disease in a lesbian population. *Sexually Transmitted Diseases, 8*, 75–76.

Robins, L. N., & Price, R. K. (1991). Adult disorders predicted by childhood conduct problems: Results from the NIMH epidemiologic catchment area project. *Psychiatry, 54*, 116–132.

Robinson, L. A., Berman, J. S., & Niemeyer, R. A. (1990). Psychotherapy for the treatment of depression: A comprehensive review of controlled outcome research. *Psychological Bulletin, 108*, 30–49.

Rodgers, W. L., & Bachman, J. G. (1988). *The subjective well-being of young adults: Trends and relationships.* Ann Arbor: Institute for Social Research.

Roe, K. (1983). *Mass media and adolescent schooling: Conflict or co-existence?* Stockholm: Almqvist & Wiksell.

Roe, K. (1987). The school and music in adolescent socialization. In J. Lull (Ed.), *Popular music and communication* (pp. 212–230). Newbury Park, CA: Sage.

Rofes, E. (1989). Opening up the classroom closet: Responding to the educational needs of gay and lesbian youth. *Harvard Educational Review, 59*, 444–453.

Rohde, P., Lewinsohn, P. M., & Seeley, J. R. (1991). Comorbidity of unipolar depression: II. Comorbidity with other mental disorders in adolescents and adults. *Journal of Abnormal Psychology, 100*, 214–222.

Roman, M., & Haddad, W. (1978). *The disposable parent: The case for joint custody.* New York: Holt, Rinehart & Winston.

Romeo, F. F. (1984). Adolescence, sexual conflict, and anorexia nervosa. *Adolescence, 19*, 551–555.

Roscoe, B., Diana, M. S., & Brooks, R. H. (1987). Early, middle, and late adolescents' views on dating and factors influencing partner selection. *Adolescence, 22,* 59–68.

Rose, R. M., & Sachar, E. (1981). Psychoendocrinology. In R. H. Williams (Ed.), *Textbook of endocrinology* (6th ed., pp. 646–671). Philadelphia: W. B. Saunders.

Rosen, J. C., & Leitenberg, H. (1985). Exposure plus response prevention treatment of bulimia. In D. M. Garner & P. E. Garfinkel (Eds.), *Handbook of psychotherapy for anorexia nervosa and bulimia* (pp. 193–209). New York: Guilford.

Rosenbaum, J. E. (1991). Are adolescent problems caused by school or society? *Journal of Youth and Adolescence, 20,* 301–322.

Rosenbaum, J. L., & Prinsky, L. (1991). The presumption of influence: Recent responses to popular music subcultures. *Crime & Delinquency, 37,* 528–535.

Rosenstein, M. J., Milazzo-Sayre, L. J., & Manderscheid, R. W. (1989). Care of persons with schizophrenia: A statistical profile. *Schizophrenia Bulletin, 15,* 45–58.

Rosenthal, R., & Jacobsen, L. (1968). *Pygmalion in the classroom.* New York: Holt.

Ross, G. T., & Vande Wiele, R. L. (1981). The ovaries and the breasts. In R. H. Williams (Ed.), *Textbook of endocrinology* (6th ed., pp. 355–400). Philadelphia: W. B. Saunders.

Rotenberg, K. J., & Whitney, P. (1992). Loneliness and disclosure processes in preadolescence. *Merrill-Palmer Quarterly, 38,* 401–416.

Rothenberg, A. (1990). Creativity in adolescence. *Psychiatric Clinics of North America, 13,* 415–434.

Rotheram-Borus, M. J. (1990). Adolescents' reference-group choices, self-esteem, and adjustment. *Journal of Personality and Social Psychology, 59,* 1075–1081.

Rotheram-Borus, M. J. (1993). Suicidal behavior and risk factors among runaway youths. *American Journal of Psychiatry, 150,* 103–107.

Rotheram-Borus, M. J., Trautman, P. D., Dopkins, S. C., & Shrout, P. E. (1990). Cognitive style and pleasant activities among female adolescent suicide attempters. *Journal of Consulting and Clinical Psychology, 58,* 554–561.

Rothschild, N., & Morgan, M. (1987). Cohesion and control: Adolescents' relationships with parents as mediators of television. *Journal of Early Adolescence, 7,* 299–314.

Rougemont, D. de. (1956). *Love in the Western world.* New York: Pantheon.

Rousseau, J. J. (1762/1911). *Emile.* London: J. M. Dent. (Translation by B. Foxley.)

Roy, A. (1988). Early parental loss and depression. In F. Flach (Ed.), *Affective disorders* (pp. 19–28). New York: Norton.

Rozendal, F. G. (1983). Halos vs. stigmas: Long-term effects of parent's death or divorce on college students' concepts of the family. *Adolescence, 18,* 947–955.

Rubin, C., Rubenstein, J. L., Stechler, G., & Heeren, T. (1992). Depressive affect in "normal" adolescents: Relationship to life stress, family, and friends. *American Journal of Orthopsychiatry, 62,* 430–441.

Rubin, K. H., LeMare, L. J., & Lollis, S. (1990). Social withdrawal in childhood: Developmental pathways to peer rejection. In S. R. Asher & J. D. Coie (Eds.), *Peer rejection in childhood* (pp. 217–249). New York: Cambridge University Press.

Rubin, Z. (1982). Children without friends. In L. A. Peplau & D. Perlman (Eds.), *Loneliness: A sourcebook of theory, research and therapy* (pp. 255–268). New York: Wiley.

Ruble, D. N. (1984). Sex-role development. In M. H. Bornstein & M. E. Lamb (Eds.), *Developmental psychology* (pp. 325–371). Hillsdale, NJ: Erlbaum.

Ruble, D. N., & Brooks-Gunn, J. (1982). The experience of menarche. *Child Development, 53,* 1557–1566.

Russell, D., Cutrona, C. E., Rose, J., & Yurko, K. (1984). Social and emotional loneliness: An examination of Weiss's typology of loneliness. *Journal of Personality and Social Psychology, 46,* 1313–1321.

Rutter, M. (1989). Pathways from childhood to adult life. *Journal of Child Psychology and Psychiatry, 30,* 23–51.

Rutter, M., Graham, P., Chadwick, O. F. D., & Yule, W. (1976). Adolescent turmoil: Fact or fiction? *Journal of Child Psychology and Psychiatry, 17,* 35–56.

Rutter, M., Macdonald, H., Le Couteur, A., Harrington, R., Bolton, R., & Bailey, A. (1990). Genetic factors in child psychiatric disorders: II. Empirical findings. *Journal of Child Psychology and Psychiatry, 31,* 39–83.

Ryan, N. D. (1989). Major depression. In C. G. Last & M. Hersen (Eds.), *Handbook of child psychiatric diagnosis* (pp. 317–329). New York: Wiley.

Ryan, N. D., & Puig-Antich, J. (1987). Pharmacological treatment of adolescent psychiatric disorder. *Journal of Adolescent Health Care, 8,* 137–142.

Ryan, N. D., Puig-Antich, J., Ambrosini, P., Rabinovich, H., Robinson, D., Nelson, B., Iyengar, S., & Twomey, J.

(1987). The clinical picture of major depression in children and adolescents. *Archives of General Psychiatry, 44*, 854–861.

Sahler, O. J. (1992). Grief and bereavement. In E. R. McAnarney, R. E. Kreipe, D. P. Orr, & G. D. Comerci (Eds.), *Textbook of adolescent medicine* (pp. 1105–1112). Philadelphia: Saunders.

Sales, B., Manber, R., & Rohman, L. (1992). Social science research and child-custody decision making. *Applied and Preventive Psychology, 1*, 23–40.

Salinger, J. D. (1945). *The catcher in the rye.* New York: Random House.

Samet, N., & Kelly, E. W. (1987). The relationship of steady dating to self-esteem and sex-role identity among adolescents. *Adolescence, 22*, 231–245.

Sandberg, D. E., Ehrhardt, A. A., Ince, S. E., & Meyer-Bahlburg, H. (1991). Gender differences in children's and adolescents' career aspirations: A follow-up study. *Journal of Adolescent Research, 6*, 371–386.

Sanders, S. A., & Reinisch, J. M. (1990). Biological and social influences on the endocrinology of puberty: Some additional considerations. In J. Bancroft & J. M. Reinisch (Eds.), *Adolescence and puberty* (pp. 50–62). New York: Oxford University Press.

Sang, B. E. (1992, October). Alexandra Symmond's contributions to feminist psychology: From a Horneyan perspective. Paper presented at the Feminist Therapy Institute Annual Conference, Lincoln City, OR.

Santrock, J. W., Sitterle, K. A., & Warshak, R. A. (1988). Parent-child relationships in stepfather families. In P. Bronstein & C. P. Cowan (Eds.), *Fatherhood today* (pp. 144–165). New York: Wiley.

Santrock, J. W., & Warshak, R. A. (1986). Development, relationships, and legal/clinical considerations in father-custody families. In M. E. Lamb (Ed.), *The father's role* (pp. 135–163). New York: Wiley.

Sarrel, L. J., & Sarrel, P. M. (1979). *Sexual unfolding: Sexual development and sex therapies in late adolescence.* Boston: Little, Brown.

Sarrel, L. J., & Sarrel, P. M. (1981). Sexual unfolding. *Journal of Adolescent Health Care, 2*, 93–99.

Savin-Williams, R. C. (Ed.). (1990). *Gay and lesbian youth: Expressions of identity.* New York: Hemisphere.

Savin-Williams, R. C., & Small, S. A. (1986). The timing of puberty and its relationship to adolescent and parent perceptions of family interactions. *Developmental Psychology, 22*, 342–347.

Scarr, S. (1984). *Mother care/other care.* New York: Basic Books.

Scarr, D., Phillips, D., & McCartney, K. (1989). Working

mothers and their families. *American Psychologist, 44*, 1402–1409.

Schaefer, E. S. (1959). A circumplex model for maternal behavior. *Journal of Abnormal and Social Psychology, 59*, 226–235.

Schaie, K. W. (1977). Quasi-experimental research designs in the psychology of aging. In J. E. Birren & K. W. Schaie (Eds.), *Handbook of the psychology of aging* (pp. 39–58). New York: Van Nostrand Reinhold.

Scheinfeld, D. R. (1983). Family relationships and school achievement among boys of lower-income urban black families. *American Journal of Orthopsychiatry, 53*, 127–143.

Schiedel, D. G., & Marcia, J. E. (1985). Ego identity, intimacy, sex role orientation, and gender. *Developmental Psychology, 21*, 149–160.

Schlegel, A., & Barry, H., III. (1991). *Adolescence: An anthropological inquiry.* New York: Free Press.

Schneider, D. J. (1991). Social cognition. *Annual Review of Psychology, 42*, 527–561.

Schowalter, J. E. (1977). Psychological reactions to physical illness and hospitalization in adolescence. *Journal of the American Academy of Child Psychiatry, 16*, 500–516.

Schuckit, M. A., & Russell, J. W. (1983). Clinical importance of age at first drink in a group of young men. *American Journal of Psychiatry, 140*, 1221–1223.

Schulenberg, J., Goldstein, A. E., & Vondracek, F. W. (1991). Gender differences in adolescents' career interests: Beyond main effects. *Journal of Research on Adolescence, 1*, 37–61.

Searles, J. S. (1988). The role of genetics in the pathogenesis of alcoholism. *Journal of Abnormal Psychology, 97*, 153–167.

Sebald, H. (1989). Adolescents' peer orientation: Changes in the support system during the past three decades. *Adolescence, 24*, 937–946.

Selman, R. L. (1980). *The growth of interpersonal understanding.* New York: Academic Press.

Selman, R. L., Jaquette, D., & Lavin, D. R. (1977). Interpersonal awareness in children: Toward an integration of developmental and clinical child psychology. *American Journal of Orthopsychiatry, 47*, 264–274.

Selman, R. L., & Selman, A. P. (1979, October). Children's ideas about friendship: A new theory. *Psychology Today, 13*, 71–80, 114.

Serna, L. A., Schumaker, J. B., Hazel, J. S., & Sheldon, J. B. (1986). Teaching reciprocal social skills to parents and their delinquent adolescents. *Journal of Clinical Child Psychology*, *15*, 64–77.

Sexson, S. B., & Madan-Swain, A. (1993). School reentry for the child with chronic illness. *Journal of Learning Disabilities*, *26*, 115–125.

Sexton, M. A., & Geffen, G. (1979). Development of three strategies of attention in dichotic monitoring. *Developmental Psychology*, *15*, 299–310.

Shain, L., & Farber, B. A. (1989). Female identity development and self-reflection in late adolescence. *Adolescence*, *24*, 381–392.

Shantz, C. U. (1983). Social cognition. In P. H. Mussen (Ed.), *Handbook of child psychology* (Vol. 3, pp. 495–555). New York: Wiley.

Shapiro, S. A. (1981). *Contemporary theories of schizophrenia*. New York: McGraw-Hill.

Sharlin, S. A., & Mor-Barak, M. (1992). Runaway girls in distress: Motivation, background, and personality. *Adolescence*, *27*, 387–405.

Shedler, J., & Block, J. (1990). Adolescent drug use and psychological health. *American Psychologist*, *45*, 612–630.

Sheras, P. L. (1992). Depression and suicide in adolescence. In C. E. Walker & M. C. Roberts (Eds.), *Handbook of child clinical psychology* (2nd ed., pp. 587–606). New York: Wiley.

Sherman, S. J., Judd, C. M., & Park, B. (1989). Social cognition. *Annual Review of Psychology*, *40*, 281–326.

Shilts, L. (1991). The relationship of early adolescent substance abuse to extracurricular activities, peer influence, and personal attitudes. *Adolescence*, *26*, 613–617.

Shimahara, N. K. (1983). Polarized socialization in an urban high school. *Anthropology and Education Quarterly*, *14*, 109–130.

Shore, M. F., & Massimo, J. L. (1979). Fifteen years after treatment: A follow-up study of comprehensive vocationally oriented psychotherapy. *American Journal of Orthopsychiatry*, *49*, 240–245.

Shrout, P. E., Link, B. G., Dohrenwend, B. P., Skodol, A. E., Stueve, A., & Mirotznik, J. (1989). Characterizing life events as risk factors for depression: The role of fateful loss events. *Journal of Abnormal Psychology*, *98*, 460–467.

Siegel, L. I., Radojevic, A., & Whitmont, S. (1992). Residential treatment for severely disturbed adolescents. In A. Z. Schwartzberg (Ed.), *International annals of adolescent psychiatry* (Vol. 2, pp. 204–220). Chicago: University of Chicago Press.

Siegel, O. (1982). Personality development in adolescence. In B. B. Wolman (Ed.), *Handbook of developmental psychology* (pp. 537–548). Englewood Cliffs, NJ: Prentice-Hall.

Siegler, R. S. (1989). Mechanisms of cognitive development. *Annual Review of Psychology, 40,* 353–379.

Silbereisen, R. K., Petersen, A. C., Albrecht, H. T., & Kracke, B. (1989). Maturational timing and the development of problem behavior: Longitudinal studies in adolescence. *Journal of Early Adolescence*, *9*, 247–268.

Silberman, E. K., & Tassone, E. P. (1985). The Israeli high-risk study: Statistical overview and discussion. *Schizophrenia Bulletin*, *11*, 138–145.

Silverberg, S. B., & Steinberg, L. (1987). Adolescent autonomy, parent–adolescent conflict, and parental well-being. *Journal of Youth and Adolescence*, *16*, 293–312.

Silverberg, S. B., & Steinberg, L. (1990). Psychological well-being of parents with early adolescent children. *Developmental Psychology, 26,* 658–666.

Simmons, R. G., Black, A., & Zhou, Y. (1991). African-American versus white children and the transition into junior high school. *American Journal of Education*, *99*, 481–520.

Simmons, R. G., & Blyth, D. A. (1987). *Moving into adolescence: The impact of pubertal change and school context*. Hawthorn, NY: Aldine de Gruyter.

Simons, A. D., Murphy, D. E., Levine, J. L., & Wetzel, R. D. (1986). Cognitive therapy and pharmacotherapy for depression. *Archives of General Psychiatry*, *43*, 43–48.

Simons, R. L., Robertson, J. F., & Downs, W. R. (1989). The nature of the association between parental rejection and delinquent behavior. *Journal of Youth and Adolescence*, *18*, 297–319.

Simons, R. L., Whitbeck, L. B., Conger, R. D., & Wu, C. (1991). Intergenerational transmission of harsh parenting. *Developmental Psychology*, *27*, 159–171.

Skoe, E. E., & Gooden, A. (1993). Ethic of care and real-life moral dilemma content in male and female early adolescents. *Journal of Early Adolescence*, *13*, 154–167.

Slaney, R. B. (1988). The assessment of career decision making. In W. B. Walsh & S. H. Osipow (Eds.), *Career decision making* (pp. 33–76). Hillsdale, NJ: Erlbaum.

Slater, B. R. (1988). Essential issues in working with lesbian and gay male youths. *Professional Psychology: Research and Practice*, *19*, 226–235.

Slugoski, B. R., Marcia, J. E., & Koopman, R. F. (1984). Cognitive and social interactional characteristics of ego identity statuses in college males. *Journal of Personality and Social Psychology, 47*, 646–661.

Small, S. A., Eastman, G., & Cornelius, S. (1988). Adolescent autonomy and parental stress. *Journal of Youth and Adolescence, 17*, 377–392.

Smetana, J. G. (1988). Adolescents' and parents' conceptions of parental authority. *Child Development, 59*, 321–335.

Smetana, J. G. (1993). Conceptions of parental authority in divorced and married mothers and their adolescents. *Journal of Research on Adolescence, 3*, 19–39.

Smetana, J. G., Yau, J., & Hanson, S. (1991). Conflict resolution in families with adolescents. *Journal of Research on Adolescence, 1*, 189–206.

Smith, A. L., & Weissman, M. M. (1992). Epidemiology. In E. S. Paykel (Ed.), *Handbook of affective disorders* (2nd ed., pp. 111–129). New York: Guilford.

Smith, E. A. (1989). A biosocial model of adolescent sexual behavior. In G. R. Adams, R. Montemayor, & T. P. Gullotta (Eds.) *Biology of adolescent behavior and development* (pp. 143–167). Newbury Park, CA: Sage.

Smith, K. (1992). Suicidal behavior in children and adolescents. In W. M. Reynolds (Ed.), *Internalizing disorders in children and adolescents* (pp. 255–282). New York: Wiley.

Smith, L. B., Sera, M., & Gattuso, B. (1988). The development of thinking. In R. J. Sternberg & E. E. Smith (Eds.), *The psychology of human thought* (pp. 366–391). New York: Cambridge University Press.

Smith, M. A., & Jenkins, J. M. (1991). The effects of marital disharmony on prepubertal children. *Journal of Abnormal Child Psychology, 19*, 625–644.

Smollar, J., & Youniss, J. (1989). Transformations in adolescents' perceptions of parents. *International Journal of Behavioral Development, 12*, 71–84.

Smucker, M. R., Craighead, W. E., Craighead, L. W., & Green, B. J. (1986). Normative and reliability data for the Children's Depression Inventory. *Journal of Abnormal Child Psychology, 14*, 25–40.

Snyder, J., & Patterson, G. (1987). Family interaction and delinquent behavior. In H. C. Quay (Ed.), *Handbook of juvenile delinquency* (pp. 216–243). New York: Wiley.

Sobocinski, M. R. (1990). Ethical principles in the counseling of gay and lesbian adolescents: Issues of autonomy, competence, and confidentiality. *Professional Psychology, 21*, 240–247.

Sommer, B. (1985). What's different about truants: A comparison study of eighth-graders. *Journal of Youth and Adolescence, 14*, 411–422.

Sonenstein, F. L., Pleck, J. H., & Ku, L. C. (1991). Levels of sexual activity among adolescent males in the United States. *Family Planning Perspectives, 23*, 162–167.

Sorensen, R. C. (1973). *Adolescent sexuality in contemporary America: Personal values and sexual behavior ages 13–19*. New York: World.

Sorenson, S. B., Rutter, C. M., & Anashensel, C. S. (1991). Depression in the community: An investigation into age of onset. *Journal of Consulting and Clinical Psychology, 59*, 541–546.

Sours, J. A. (1979). The primary anorexia nervosa syndrome. In J. D. Noshpitz (Ed.), *Basic handbook of child psychiatry* (Vol. II, pp. 568–580). New York: Basic Books.

Sours, J. A. (1980). *Starving to death in a sea of objects: The anorexia nervosa syndrome*. New York: Aronson.

Southworth, S., & Schwarz, J. C. (1987). Post-divorce contact, relationship with father, and heterosexual trust in female college students. *American Journal of Orthopsychiatry, 57*, 371–382.

Spencer, M. B. (1988). Self-concept development. *New Directions for Child Development, 42*, 59–72.

Spencer, M. B., & Dornbusch, S. M. (1990). Challenges in studying minority youth. In S. S. Feldman & G. R. Elliott (Eds.), *At the threshold: The developing adolescent* (pp. 123–146). Cambridge, MA: Harvard University Press.

Spencer, M. B., & Markstrom-Adams, C. (1990). Identity processes among racial and ethnic minority children in America. *Child Development, 61*, 290–310.

Spirito, A., Brown, L., Overholser, J., & Fritz, G. (1989). Attempted suicide in adolescence: A review and critique of the literature. *Clinical Psychology Review, 9*, 335–363.

Spirito, A., Plummer, B., Gispert, M., & Levy, S. (1992). Adolescent suicide attempts: Outcomes at follow-up. *American Journal of Orthopsychiatry, 62*, 464–468.

Spokane, A. R. (1991). *Career intervention*. Englewood Cliffs, NJ: Prentice-Hall.

Stattin, H., & Magnusson, D. (1989). The role of early aggressive behavior in the frequency, seriousness, and types of later crime. *Journal of Consulting and Clinical Psychology, 57*, 710–718.

Stattin, H., & Magnusson, D. (1990). *Pubertal maturation in female development*. Hillsdale, NJ: Erlbaum.

Steinberg, L. (1981). Transformations in family relations at puberty. *Developmental Psychology, 17*, 833–840.

Steinberg, L. (1986). Latchkey children and susceptibility to peer pressure: An ecological analysis. *Developmental Psychology, 22,* 433–439.

Steinberg, L. (1987a). Impact of puberty on family relations: Effects of pubertal status and pubertal timing. *Developmental Psychology, 23,* 451–460.

Steinberg, L. (1987b). Recent research on the family at adolescence: The extent and nature of sex differences. *Journal of Youth and Adolescence, 16,* 191–198.

Steinberg, L. (1987c). Single parents, stepparents, and the susceptibility of adolescents to peer pressure. *Child Development, 58,* 269–275.

Steinberg, L. (1988). Reciprocal relation between parent–child distance and pubertal maturation. *Developmental Psychology, 24,* 122–128.

Steinberg, L. (1989). Pubertal maturation and parent–adolescent distance: An evolutionary perspective. In G. R. Adams, R. Montemayor, & T. P. Gullotta (Eds.), *Biology of adolescent behavior and development* (pp. 71–97). Newbury Park, CA: Sage.

Steinberg, L. (1990). Autonomy, conflict, and harmony in the family relationship. In S. S. Feldman & G. R. Elliott (Eds.), *At the threshold: The developing adolescent* (pp. 255–276). Cambridge, MA: Harvard University Press.

Steinberg, L., & Dornbusch, S. M. (1991). Negative correlates of part-time employment during adolescence: Replication and elaboration. *Developmental Psychology, 27,* 304–313.

Steinberg, L., Dornbusch, S. M., & Brown, B. B. (1992). Ethnic differences in adolescent achievement: An ecological perspective. *American Psychologist, 47,* 723–729.

Steinberg, L., Elman, J. D., & Mounts, N. S. (1989). Authoritative parenting, psychosocial maturity, and academic success among adolescents. *Child Development, 60,* 1424–1436.

Steinberg, L., Greenberger, E., Garduque, L., Ruggiero, M., & Vaux, A. (1982). Effects of working on adolescent development. *Developmental Psychology, 18,* 385–395.

Steinberg, L., Lamborn, S. D., Dornbusch, S. M., & Darling, N. (1992). Impact of parenting practices on adolescent achievement: Authoritative parenting, school involvement, and encouragement to succeed. *Child Development, 63,* 1266–1281.

Steinberg, L., Mounts, N. S., Lamborn, S. D., & Dornbusch, S. M. (1991). Authoritative parenting and adolescent adjustment across varied ecological niches. *Journal of Research on Adolescence, 1,* 19–36.

Steinberg, L., & Silverberg, S. B. (1986). The vicissitudes of autonomy in early adolescence. *Child Development, 57,* 841–851.

Stern, D., Stone, J. R., Hopkins, C., McMillion, M. (1990). Quality of students' work experience and orientation toward work. *Youth and Society, 22,* 263–282.

Stern, L. (1990). Conceptions of separation and connection in female adolescents. In C. Gilligan, N. P. Lyons, & T. J. Hanmer (Eds.), *Making connections* (pp. 73–87). Cambridge, MA: Harvard University Press.

Stern, M., Norman, S. L., & Zevon, M. A. (1993). Adolescents with cancer: Self-image and perceived social support as indexes of adaptation. *Journal of Adolescent Research, 8,* 124–142.

Stern, M., Northman, J. E., & Van Slyck, M. R. (1984). Father absence and adolescent "problem behaviors": Alcohol consumption, drug use and sexual activity. *Adolescence, 19,* 301–312.

Sternberg, R. J. (1986a). *Intelligence applied: Understanding and increasing your intellectual skills.* San Diego, CA: Harcourt, Brace, Jovanovich.

Sternberg, R. J. (1986b). A triangular theory of love. *Psychological Review, 93,* 119–135.

Sternberg, R. J. (1988a). Triangulating love. In R. J. Sternberg & M. L. Barnes (Eds.), *The psychology of love* (pp. 119–138). New Haven, CT: Yale University Press.

Sternberg, R. J. (1988b). *The triarchic mind: A new theory of human intelligence.* New York: Viking.

Sternberg, R. J. (1990). *Metaphors of mind: Conceptions of the nature of intelligence.* New York: Cambridge University Press.

Sternberg, R. J., & Rifkin, B. (1979). The development of analogical reasoning processes. *Journal of Experimental Child Psychology, 27,* 195–232.

Stevens, D. P., & Truss, C. V. (1985). Stability and change in adult personality over 12 and 20 years. *Developmental Psychology, 21,* 568–584.

Stiffman, A. R., Cheuh, H., & Earls, F. (1992). Predictive modeling of change in depressive disorder and counts of depressive symptoms in urban youths. *Journal of Research in Adolescence, 2,* 295–316.

Stiffman, A. R., Earls, F., Robins, L. N., & Jung, K. G. (1988). Problems and help seeking in high-risk adolescent patients of health clinics. *Journal of Adolescent Health Care, 9,* 305–309.

Stipek, D. J., & Gralinski, J. H. (1991). Gender differences in children's achievement-related beliefs and emotional responses to success and failure in mathematics. *Journal of Educational Psychology, 83,* 361–371.

Stone, M. H. (1993). Long-term outcome in personality disorders. *British Journal of Psychiatry, 162,* 299–313.

Stowell, R. J. A., & Estroff, T. W. (1992). Psychiatric disorders in substance abusing adolescent inpatients: A pilot study. *Journal of the American Academy of Child and Adolescent Psychiatry, 31,* 1036–1040.

Striegel-Moore, R. H., Silberstein, L. R., & Rodin, J. (1986). Toward an understanding of risk factors for bulimia. *American Psychologist, 41,* 246–263.

Strober, M. (1986). Psychopathology in adolescence revisited. *Clinical Psychology Review, 6,* 199–209.

Strober, M., & Carlson, G. (1982). Bipolar illness in adolescents with major depression. *Archives of General Psychiatry, 39,* 549–555.

Strober, M., Hanna, G., & McCracken, J. (1989). Bipolar disorder. In C. G. Last & M. Hersen (Eds.), *Handbook of child psychiatric diagnosis* (pp. 299–316). New York: Wiley.

Strober, M., Lampert, C., Schmidt, S., & Morrell, W. (1993). The course of major depressive disorder in adolescents: I. Recovery and risk of manic switching in a follow-up of psychotic and nonpsychotic subtypes. *Journal of the American Academy of Child and Adolescent Psychiatry, 32,* 32–42.

Strober, M., McCracken, J., & Hanna, G. (1989). Affective disorders. In L. K. G. Hsu & M. Hersen (Eds.), *Recent developments in adolescent psychiatry* (pp. 201–232). New York: Wiley.

Strober, M., Morrell, W., Lampert, C., & Burroughs, J. L. (1990). Relapse following discontinuation of lithium maintenance therapy in adolescents with bipolar I illness: A naturalistic study. *American Journal of Psychiatry, 147,* 457–461.

Stubbs, M. L., Rierdan, J., & Koff, E. (1989). Developmental differences in menstrual attitudes. *Journal of Early Adolescence, 9,* 480–498.

Stunkard, A. J., Sorensen, T. I., Hanis, C., Teasdale, T. W., Chakbraborty, R., Schull, W. J., & Schulsinger, F. (1986). An adoption study of human obesity. *New England Journal of Medicine, 314,* 193–198.

Styne, D. M. (1988). The physiology of normal and delayed puberty. In M. D. Levine & E. R. McAnarney, Eds., *Early adolescent transitions* (pp. 79–100). Lexington, MA: Lexington Books.

Sullivan, H. S. (1953). *The interpersonal theory of psychiatry.* New York: Norton.

Sun, S.-W., & Lull, J. (1986). The adolescent audience for music videos and why they watch. *Journal of Communication, 36,* 115–125.

Sung, B. L. (1979). *Transplanted Chinese children.* Washington, DC: Department of Health, Education, and Welfare. (ERIC Document Reproduction Service No. ED 182-040).

Sung, B. L. (1985). Bicultural conflicts in Chinese immigrant children. *Journal of Comparative Family Studies, 16,* 255–270.

Surrey, J. L. (1983/1991). The self-in-relation: A theory of women's development. In J. V. Jordan, A. G. Kaplan, J. B. Miller, I. P. Stiver, & J. L. Surrey (Eds.), *Women's growth in connection* (pp. 51–66). New York: Guilford.

Swaab, D. F., & Hofman, M. A. (1990). An enlarged suprachiasmatic nucleus in homosexual men. *Brain Research, 537,* 141–148.

Swann, W. B., Jr. (1984). Quest for accuracy in person perception: A matter of pragmatics. *Psychological Review, 91,* 457–477.

Swedo, S. E., & Offer, D. (1989). The pediatrician's concept of the normal adolescent. *Journal of Adolescent Health Care, 12,* 6–10.

Szymanski, S., Kane, J. M., & Liberman, J. A. (1991). A selective review of biological markers in schizophrenia. *Schizophrenia Bulletin, 17,* 99–112.

Taft, L. T. (1987). Cerebral palsy. In R. A. Hoekelman, S. Blatman, N. M. Nelson, S. B. Friedman, & H. M. Seidel (Eds.), *Primary pediatric care* (pp. 1183–1186). St. Louis, MO: Mosby.

Tanner, J. M. (1962). *Growth at adolescence.* Oxford: Blackwell Scientific Publications.

Tanner, J. M. (1971). Sequence, tempo, and individual variation in the growth and development of boys and girls aged twelve to sixteen. *Daedalus, 100,* 907–930.

Tanner, J. M. (1978). *Education and physical growth* (2nd ed.). New York: International Universities Press.

Tavris, C. (1978). 40,000 men tell about their sexual behavior, their fantasies, their ideal women and their wives. *Redbook,* February, p. 113.

Taylor, A. R. (1989). Predictors of peer rejection in early elementary grades: Roles of problem behavior, academic achievement, and teacher preference. *Journal of Clinical Child Psychology, 18,* 360–365.

Taylor, L., & Adelman, H. S. (1990). School avoidance behavior: Motivational bases and implications for intervention. *Child Psychiatry and Human Development, 20,* 219–233.

Taylor, M. C., Boss, M. W., Bedard, R., & Thibault, C. J. (1990). Variables related to the transition of youth from school to work. *Canadian Journal of Counseling, 24,* 153–164.

Taylor, R. L. (1989). Black youth, role models and the social construction of identity. In R. L. Jones (Ed.), *Black adolescents* (pp. 155–174). Berkeley, CA: Cobb & Henry.

Tennant, C. (1988). Parental loss in childhood. *Archives of General Psychiatry, 45,* 1045–1050.

Tharinger, D. (1990). Impact of child sexual abuse on developing sexuality. *Professional Psychology, 21,* 331–337.

Thelen, M. H., Powell, A. L., Lawrence, C., & Kuhnert, M. E. (1992). Eating and body image concerns among children. *Journal of Clinical Child Psychology, 21,* 41–46.

Thompson, M. C., Asarnow, J. R., Goldstein, M. J., & Miklovitz, D. J. (1990). Thought disorder and communication problems in children with schizophrenia spectrum and depressive disorders and their parents. *Journal of Clinical Child Psychology, 19,* 159–168.

Thompson, M. G., & Gans, M. T. (1985). Do anorexics and bulimics get well? In S. W. Emmett (Ed.), *Theory and treatment of anorexia nervosa and bulimia* (pp. 291–303). New York: Brunner/Mazel.

Tienari, P., Sorri, A., Lahti, I., Naarala, M., Wahlber, K., Moring, J. P., & Wynne, L. C. (1987). Genetic and psychosocial factors in schizophrenia: The Finnish adoptive study. *Schizophrenia Bulletin, 13,* 477–484.

Tittle, C. K. (1986). Gender research and education. *American Psychologist, 41,* 1161–1168.

Tobler, N. S. (1986). Meta-analysis of 143 adolescent drug prevention programs: Quantitative outcome results of program participants compared to a control or comparison group. *Journal of Drug Issues, 16,* 537–568.

Todd, D. M. (1979). Contrasting adaptations to the social environment of a high school. In J. G. Kelly (Ed.), *Adolescent boys in high school: A psychological study of coping and adaptation* (pp. 177–186). New York: Erlbaum.

Tolan, P. H. (1987). Implications of age of onset for delinquency risk. *Journal of Abnormal Child Psychology, 15,* 47–66.

Tolan, P. H., & Loeber, R. (1993). Antisocial behavior. In P. H. Tolan & B. J. Cohler (Eds.), *Handbook of clinical research and practice with adolescents* (pp. 307–331). New York: Wiley.

Tolson, J. M., & Urberg, K. A. (1993). Similarity between adolescent best friends. *Journal of Adolescent Research, 8,* 274–288.

Tomb, D. A. (1991). The runaway adolescent. In M. Lewis (Ed.), *Child and adolescent psychiatry* (pp. 1066–1071). Baltimore, MD: Williams & Wilkins.

Tomlinson-Keasey, C., & Eisert, D. C. (1981). From a 'structure d'ensemble' to separate organizations for cognitive and affective development. In J. A. Meacham & N. R. Santilli (Eds.), *Social development in youth: Structure and content* (pp. 1–19). Basel: S. Karger.

Torney-Purta, J. (1989). Political cognition and its restructuring in young people. *Human Development, 32,* 14–23.

Tsuang, M. T., Woolson, R. F., & Fleming, J. A. (1979). Long-term outcome of major psychoses. *Archives of General Psychiatry, 36,* 1295–1301.

Tubman, J. G., Lerner, R. M., Lerner, J. V., & von Eye, A. (1992). Temperament and adjustment in young adulthood: A 15-year longitudinal analysis. *American Journal of Orthopsychiatry, 62,* 564–574.

Tucker, L. A. (1987). Television, teenagers, and health. *Journal of Youth and Adolescence, 16,* 415–425.

Turing, A. M. (1936). On computable numbers, with an application to the Entscheidungs problem. *Proceedings of the London Mathematical Society, Ser. 2, 42,* 230–265.

Turing, A. M. (1963). Computing machinery and intelligence. In E. A. Feigenbaum & J. Feldman (Eds.), *Computers and thought* (pp. 11–35). New York: McGraw-Hill.

Tyano, S., & Apter, A. (1992). Adolescent psychosis: An eight-year follow-up. In A. Z. Schwartzberg (Ed.), *International Annals of Adolescent Psychiatry* (Vol. 2, pp. 317–324). Chicago: University of Chicago Press.

Tyrer, P., & Tyrer, S. (1974). School refusal, truancy, and adult neurotic illness. *Psychological Medicine, 4.* 416–421.

Tzuriel, D. (1984). Sex role typing and ego identity in Israeli, Oriental, and Western adolescents. *Journal of Personality and Social Psychology, 46,* 440–457.

U. S. Bureau of the Census. (1988). *Statistical abstract of the United States: 1988* (108th ed.). Washington, DC: U.S. Government Printing Office.

U. S. Bureau of the Census. (1992). *Statistical abstract of the United States: 1992* (112th ed.). Washington, DC: U. S. Government Printing Office

U. S. Department of Labor. (1987). *Employment and earnings,* 34(10). Washington, DC: U. S. Government Printing Office.

Udry, J. R. (1990). Hormonal and social determinants of adolescent sexual initiation. In J. Bancroft & J. M. Reinisch (Eds.), *Adolescence and puberty* (pp. 70–87). New York: Oxford University Press.

Udry, J. R., Billy, J. O. G., Morris, N. M., Groff, T. R., & Raj, M. H. (1985). Serum androgenic hormones motivate sexual behavior in boys. *Fertility and Sterility, 43*, 90–94.

Udry, J. R., Talbert, L., & Morris, N. M. (1986). Biosocial foundations for adolescent female sexuality. *Demography, 23*, 217–230.

Underwood, L. E., & Van Wyk, J. J. (1981). Hormones in normal and aberrant growth. In R. H. Williams (Ed.), *Textbook of endocrinology* (6th ed., pp. 11–49). Philadelphia: W. B. Saunders.

Urberg, K. A. (1992). Locus of peer influence: Social crowd and best friend. *Journal of Youth and Adolescence, 21*, 439–450.

Uribe, V., & Harbeck, K. M. (1991). Addressing the needs of lesbian, gay, and bisexual youth: The origins of PROJECT 10 and school-based intervention. *Journal of Homosexuality, 22*, 9–28.

Ursano, R. J., Wetzler, H. P., Slusarcick, A., & Gemelli, R. J. (1987). Preadolescent friendships recalled by the young adult. *Journal of Nervous and Mental Disease, 175*, 686–687.

Uttal, D. H., & Perlmutter, M. (1989). Toward a broader conceptualization of development: The role of gains and losses across the life span. *Developmental Review, 9*, 101–132.

Vaillant, G. E. (1978). Natural history of male psychological health: VI. Correlates of successful marriage and fatherhood. *American Journal of Psychiatry, 135*, 653–659.

Van Kammen, W. B., Loeber, R., Stouthamer-Loeber, M. (1991). Substance use and its relationship to conduct problems and delinquency in young boys. *Journal of Youth and Adolescence, 20*, 399–414.

Varni, J. W., & Banis, H. T. (1985). Behavior therapy techniques applied to eating, exercise, and diet modification in childhood obesity. *Journal of Developmental and Behavioral Pediatrics, 6*, 367–372.

Veneziano, C., & Veneziano, O. (1992). A typology of family social environments for institutional juvenile delinquents: Implications for research and treatment. *Journal of Youth and Adolescence, 21*, 593–608.

Verhulst, F. C., & van der Ende, J. (1992). Six-year stability of parent-reported problem behavior in an epidemiological sample. *Journal of Abnormal Child Psychology, 20*, 595–610.

Villee, D. B. (1975). *Human endocrinology: A developmental approach.* Philadelphia: W. B. Saunders Company.

Visher, E., & Visher, J. (1988). *Old loyalties, new ties: Therapeutic strategies with stepfamilies.* New York: Brunner/Mazel.

Visher, J. S., & Visher, E. B. (1982). Stepfamilies and stepparenting. In F. Walsh (Ed.), *Normal family processes* (pp. 331–353). New York: Guilford.

Volling, B. L., & Belsky, J. (1992). Infant, father, and marital antecedents of infant-father attachment security in dual-earner and single-earner families. *International Journal of Behavioral Development, 15*, 83–100.

Vondracek, F. W., Hostetler, M., Schulenberg, J. E., & Shimizu, K. (1990). Dimensions of career indecision. *Journal of Counseling Psychology, 37*, 98–106.

Wagner, J. A. (1976). A study of the relationship between formal operations and ego identity in adolescence. Unpublished Ph.D. dissertation, SUNY at Buffalo.

Wagner, J. A. (1987). Formal operations and ego identity in adolescence. *Adolescence, 22*, 23–35.

Wakil, S. P., Siddique, C. M., & Wakil, F. A. (1981). Between two cultures: A study in socialization of children of immigrants. *Journal of Marriage and the Family, 43*, 929–940.

Waldhauser, F., Boepple, P. A., Schemper, M., Mansfield, M. J., & Crowley, W. F., Jr. (1991). Serum melatonin in central precocious puberty is lower than in age-matched prepubertal children. *Journal of Clinical Endocrinology and Metabolism, 73*, 793–796.

Waldhauser, F., Weissenbacher, G., Frisch, H., Zeitlhuber, U., Waldhauser, M., & Wurtman, R. J. (1984). Fall in nocturnal serum melatonin during prepuberty and pubescence. *The Lancet, I*, 362–365.

Walker, L. J. (1989). A longitudinal study of moral reasoning. *Child Development, 60*, 157–166.

Walker, L. J., & Taylor, J. H. (1991). Family interactions and the development of moral reasoning. *Child Development, 62*, 264–283.

Wallace, C. J. (1984). Community and interpersonal functioning in the course of schizophrenic disorder. *Schizophrenia Bulletin, 10*, 233–257.

Wallander, J. L., Varni, J. W., Babani, L., Banis, H. T., & Wilcox, K. T. (1989). Family resources as resistance factors for psychological maladjustment in chronically ill and handicapped children. *Journal of Pediatric Psychology, 14*, 157–174.

Wallerstein, J. S. (1987). Children of divorce: Report of a

ten-year follow-up of early latency children. *American Journal of Orthopsychiatry, 57*, 199–211.

Wallerstein, J. S., & Corbin, S. B. (1991). The child and the vicissitudes of divorce. In M. Lewis (Ed.), *Child and adolescent psychiatry* (pp. 1108–1118). Baltimore, MD: Williams & Wilkins.

Wallerstein, J. S. & Kelly, J. B. (1980). *Surviving the breakup: How children and parents cope with divorce.* New York: Basic Books.

Walsh, T. B. (1993). Binge eating in bulimia nervosa. In C. G. Fairburn & G. T. Wilson (Eds.), *Binge eating* (pp. 37–49). New York: Guilford.

Ward, J. V. (1990). Racial identity formation and transformation. In C. Gilligan, N. P. Lyons, & T. J. Hanmer (Eds.), *Making connections* (pp. 215–232). Cambridge, MA: Harvard University Press.

Warren, M. P. (1980). The effects of exercise on pubertal progression and reproductive function in girls. *Journal of Clinical Endocrinology and Metabolism, 51*, 1150–1157.

Waterman, A. L. (1982). Identity development from adolescence to adulthood: An extension of theory and a review of research. *Developmental Psychology, 18*, 341–358.

Watkins, W. G., & Bentovim, A. (1992). The sexual abuse of male children and adolescents: A review of current research. *Journal of Child Psychology & Psychiatry, 33*, 197–248.

Watt, N. F., & Lubensky, A. W. (1976). Childhood roots of schizophrenia. *Journal of Consulting and Clinical Psychology, 44*, 363–375.

Weinberg, S. K. (1955). *Incest behavior.* New York: Citadel.

Weiner, I. B. (1963). On incest: A survey. *Excerpta Criminologica, 4*, 137–155.

Weiner, I. B. (1985). Clinical contributions to the developmental psychology of adolescence. *Genetic Psychology Monographs, 111*, 195–204.

Weiner, I. B. (1992). *Psychological disturbance in adolescence* (2nd ed.). New York: Wiley.

Weinraub, M., & Wolf, B. M. (1983). Effects of stress and social supports on mother–child interactions in single- and two-parent families. *Child Development, 54*, 1297–1311.

Weinrich, J. D. (1987). *Sexual landscapes: Why we are what we are, why we love whom we love.* New York: Scribners.

Weintraub, S. (1987). Risk factors in schizophrenia: The Stony Brook high-risk project. *Schizophrenia Bulletin, 13*, 439–450.

Weiss, R. S. (1973). *Loneliness: The experience of emotional and social isolation.* Cambridge, MA: MIT Press.

Weissman, M. M., Bruce, M. L., Leaf, P. J., Floria, L. P., & Holzer, C. (1991). Affective disorders. In L. N. Robins & D. A. Regier (Eds.), *Psychiatric disorders in America: The epidemiological catchment area study* (pp. 53–80). New York: Guilford.

Weissman, M. M., Gammon, D., John, K., Merikangas, K. R., Watner, V., Prusoff, B. A., & Sholomskas, D. (1987). Children of depressed parents. *Archives of General Psychiatry, 44*, 847–853.

Weissman, M. M., & Klerman, G. L. (1979). Sex differences and the epidemiology of depression. In E. S. Gomberg & V. Franks (Eds.), *Gender and disordered behavior* (pp. 381–425). New York: Brunner/Mazel.

Weissman, S. H., Cohen, R. S., Boxer, A. M., & Cohler, B. J. (1989). Parenthood experience and the adolescent's transition to young adulthood: Self psychological perspectives. In S. C. Feinstein (Ed.), *Adolescent psychiatry* (Vol. 16, pp. 155–174). Chicago: University of Chicago Press.

Wender, P. H., Kety, S. S., Rosenthal, D., Schulsinger, F., Ortmann, J., & Lunde, I. (1986). Psychiatric disorders in the biological and adoptive families of adopted individuals with affective disorders. *Archives of General Psychiatry, 43*, 923–929.

Wentzel, K. R. (1989). Adolescent classroom goals, standards for performance, and academic achievement: An interactionist perspective. *Journal of Educational Psychology, 81*, 131–142.

Wentzel, K. R. (1992). Motivation and achievement in early adolescence: The role of multiple classroom goals. *Journal of Early Adolescence, 13*, 4–20.

Wentzel, K. R., & Feldman, S. S. (1993). Parental predictors of boys' self-restraint and motivation to achieve at school: A longitudinal study. *Journal of Early Adolescence, 13*, 183–203.

Werry, J. S. (1986). Physical illness, symptoms, and allied disorders. In H. C. Quay & J. S. Werry (Eds.), *Psychopathological disorders of childhood* (3rd ed., pp. 232–293). New York: Wiley.

Werry, J. S., & McClellan, J. M. (1992). Predicting outcome in child and adolescent (early onset) schizophrenia and bipolar disorder. *Journal of the American Academy of Child and Adolescent Psychiatry, 31*, 147–150.

Wesner, R. B., & Winokur, G. (1990). Genetics of affective disorders. In B. B. Wolman & G. Stricker

(Eds.), *Depressive disorders* (pp. 125–146). New York: Wiley.

Wessel, M. A. (1992). Mourning. In S. B. Friedman, M. Fisher, & S. K. Schonberg (Eds.), *Comprehensive adolescent health care* (pp. 662–664). St. Louis, MO: Quality Medical Publishing.

Westefeld, J. S., & Furr, S. R. (1987). Suicide and depression among college students. *Professional Psychology, 18,* 119–123.

Westermeyer, J. F. (1993). Schizophrenia. In P. H. Tolan & B. J. Cohler (Eds.), *Handbook of clinical research and practice with adolescents* (pp. 359–385). New York: Wiley.

Westney, O. E., Jenkins, R. R., Butts, J. D., & Williams, I. (1984). Sexual development and behavior in black preadolescents. *Adolescence, 19,* 557–568.

Wetzel, J. R. (1987). *American youth: A statistical snapshot.* Washington, DC: William T. Grant Foundation.

Whipple, E. E., & Webster-Stratton, C. (1991). The role of parental stress in physically abusive families. *Child Abuse and Neglect, 15,* 279–291.

Whitaker, A., Johnson, J., Shaffer, D., Rapoport, J. L., Kalikow, K., Walsh, B. T., Davies, M., Braiman, S., & Dolinsky, A. (1990). Uncommon troubles in young people. *Archives of General Psychiatry, 47,* 487–496.

White, K. R. (1982). The relation between socioeconomic status and academic achievement. *Psychological Bulletin, 91,* 461–481.

White, S. D., & DeBlassie, R. R. (1992). Adolescent sexual behavior. *Adolescence, 27,* 183–191.

White, W. J. (1992). The postschool adjustment of persons with learning disabilities: Current status and future projections. *Journal of Learning Disabilities, 25,* 448–456.

Wierson, M., Forehand, R., Fauber, R., & McCombs, A. (1989). Buffering young male adolescents against negative parental divorce influences: The role of good parent–adolescent relations. *Child Study Journal, 19,* 101–115.

Wilks, J. (1986). The relative importance of parents and friends in adolescent decision making. *Journal of Youth and Adolescence, 15,* 323–334.

Williams, D. T., Pleak, R. R., & Hanesian, H. (1991). Neurological disorders. In M. Lewis (Ed.), *Child and adolescent psychiatry* (pp. 629–646). Baltimore, MD: Williams & Wilkins.

Williamson, J. M., Borduin, C. M., & Howe, B. A. (1991). The ecology of adolescent maltreatment: A multilevel examination of adolescent physical abuse, sexual abuse, and neglect. *Journal of Consulting and Clinical Psychology, 59,* 449–457.

Williamson, M. L., & Williamson, P. S. (1988). Women's preferences for penile circumcision in sexual partners. *Journal of Sex Education and Therapy, 14,* 8–12.

Windle, M. (1989). Substance use and abuse among adolescent runaways: A four-year follow-up study. *Journal of Youth and Adolescence, 18,* 331–344.

Windle, M., Miller-Tutzauer, C., & Domenico, D. (1992). Alcohol use, suicidal behavior, and risky activities among adolesents. *Journal of Research on Adolescence, 2,* 317–330.

Winer, G. A., & McGlone, C. (1993). On the uncertainty of conservation: Responses to misleading conservation questions. *Developmental Psychology, 29,* 760–769.

Withers, L. E., & Kaplan, D. W. (1987). Adolescents who attempt suicide: A retrospective clinical chart review of hospitalized patients. *Professional Psychology, 18,* 391–393.

Wolfe, D. A. (1985). Child-abusive parents: An empirical review and analysis. *Psychological Bulletin, 97,* 462–483.

Wood, J., Chapin, K., & Hannah, M. E. (1988). Family environment and its relationship to underachievement. *Adolescence, 23,* 283–290.

Wood, W., Wong, F. Y., Chachere, J. G. (1991). Effects of media violence on viewers' aggression in unconstrained social interaction. *Psychological Bulletin, 109,* 371–383.

Woods, P. (1979). *The divided school.* London: Routledge and Kegan Paul.

Woznica, J. G., & Shapiro, J. R. (1990). An analysis of adolescent suicide attempts. *Journal of Pediatric Psychology, 15,* 789–796.

Wyatt, J. W. (1991). Neuroleptics and the natural course of schizophrenia. *Schizophrenia Bulletin, 17,* 325–351.

Wyshak, G., & Frisch, R. E. (1982). Evidence for a secular trend in age of menarche. The *New England Journal of Medicine, 306,* 1033–1035.

Yamaguchi, K., & Kandel, D. B. (1984). Patterns of drug use from adolescence to young adulthood: III. Prediction of progression. *American Journal of Public Health, 74,* 673–681.

Young, F. W. (1962). The function of male initiation ceremonies: A cross-cultural test of an alternate hypothesis. *American Journal of Sociology, 67,* 379–396.

Young, H. B., & Ferguson, L. R. (1981). *Puberty to manhood in Italy and America.* New York: Academic Press.

Young, R. A. (1983). Career development of adolescents: An ecological perspective. *Journal of Youth and Adolescence, 12,* 401–418.

Youniss, J., & Ketterlinus, R. D. (1987). Communication and connectedness in mother- and father-adolescent relationships. *Journal of Youth and Adolescence, 16,* 265–280.

Youniss, J., & Smollar, J. (1985). Adolescent relations with mothers, fathers, and friends. Chicago: University of Chicago Press.

Youniss, J., & Smollar, J. (1989). Adolescents' interpersonal relationships in social context. In T. J. Berndt & G. W. Ladd (Eds.), *Peer relationships in child development* (pp. 300–316). New York: Wiley.

Zabin, L. S. (1992). School-linked reproductive health services: The Johns Hopkins program. In B. C. Miller, J. J. Card, R. L. Paikoff, & J. L. Peterson (Eds.), *Preventing adolescent pregnancy: Model programs and evaluations* (pp. 156–184). Newbury Park, CA: Sage.

Zabin, L. S., & Hayward, S. C. (1993). *Adolescent sexual behavior and childbearing.* Newbury Park, CA: Sage.

Zaslow, M. J. (1989). Sex differences in children's response to parental divorce: 2. Samples, variables, ages, and sources. *American Journal of Orthopsychiatry, 59,* 118–140.

Zeidler, D. L. (1985). Hierarchical relationships among formal cognitive structures and their relationship to principled moral reasoning. *Journal of Research in Science Teaching, 22,* 461–471.

Zimbardo, P. G. (1986). The Stanford shyness project. In W. H. Jones, J. M. Cheek, & S. R. Biggs (Eds.), *Shyness* (pp. 17–25). New York: Plenum.

Zimbardo, P. G., & Radl, S. L. (1981). *The shy child.* New York: McGraw-Hill.

Zimet, G. D., Hillier, S. A., Anglin, T. M., Ellick, E. M., Krowchuk, D. P., & Williams, P. (1991). Knowing someone with AIDS: The impact on adolescents. *Journal of Pediatric Psychology, 16,* 287–294.

Zimiles, H., & Lee, V. E. (1991). Adolescent family structure and educational progress. *Developmental Psychology, 27,* 314–320.

✦ *Photo Credits*

Chapter 1 Opener: David Hurn/Magnum Photos, Inc. Page 5: David Hurn/Magnum Photos Inc. Page 8: Lewis Hines/Bettmann Archive. Page 13: Paul Fusco/Magnum Photos, Inc. Page 14: courtesy of University of Michigan. Page 20: Phaneuf Gurdziel/The Picture Cube.

Chapter 2 Opener: Richard Hutchings/Photo Researchers. Page 33: Donna Jernigan/Monkmeyer Press Photo. Page 38: Bettmann Archive. Page 42: Jean-Claude Lejeune. Page 50: Randy Matusow/Monkmeyer Press Photo. Page 53: Jean-Claude Lejeune/Stock, Boston.

Chapter 3 Opener: Rick Kopstein/Monkmeyer Press Photo. Page 62: Fred Dubs. Page 67: Paul Conklin/ Monkmeyer Press Photo. Figure. 3.7: J.M. Tanner, Growth at Adolescence. Oxford: Blackwell Scientific Publications, Ltd., 1962, Figures 13 and 14. Reprinted with permission. Page 80: Rick Kopstein/Monkmeyer Press Photo. Figure. 3.9: J.M. Tanner, Growth at Adolescence. Oxford: Blackwell Scientific Publications, Ltd., 1962, plate 6, facing p. 33. Reprinted with permission. Figure. 3.10: J.M. Tanner, Growth at Adolescence. Oxford: Blackwell Scientific Publications, Ltd., 1962, plate 7, facing p. 37. Reprinted with permission. Figure. 3.11: J.M. Tanner, Growth at Adolescence. Oxford: Blackwell Scientific Publications, Ltd., 1962, plate 3, facing p. 32. Reprinted with permission. Page 92: Randy Matusow/Monkmeyer Press Photo.

Chapter 4 Opener: George Zimbel/Monkmeyer Press Photo. Page 114: Bettmann Archive. Figure 4.4: courtesy William C. Crain. Page 121: Grant LeDuc/Stock, Boston. Page 127: Polly Brown/Actuality. Page 134: Charles Gatewood/Stock, Boston. Page 138: reprinted by permission of United Features Syndicate, Inc.

Chapter 5 Opener: Ancil Nance/AllStock, Inc. Page 156: Misha Erwitt/Magnum Photos, Inc. Page 163: HGSE. Page 67: Christopher Morris/Black Star.

Chapter 6 Opener: Eli Reed/Magnum Photos, Inc. Page 186: Danny Lyon/Magnum Photos, Inc. Page 200: Joan Liftin/Actuality Inc. Page 208: Alan Carey/The Image Works. Page 216: courtesy Vera Paster. Page 218: Polly Brown/Actuality Inc.

Chapter 7 Opener: LeDuc/Monkmeyer Press Photo. Page 225: Arlene Collins/Monkmeyer Press Photo. Page 246: courtesy Diana Baumrind. Page 259 (top): Skip Brown. Page 259 (bottom): Lawrence Migdale/Photo Researchers. Page 262: Blair Seitz/Photo Researchers.

Chapter 8 Opener: Deborah Yale/Monkmeyer Press Photo. Page 285: courtesy Thomas Berndt. Page 296: Shirley Zeiberg/Photo Researchers. Page 300: Jean-Claude Lejeune. Page 310: John Coletti/Stock, Boston. Page 313: Polly Brown/Actuality Inc.

Chapter 9 Opener: Richard Renaldi. Page 338: Bob Krist/Black Star. Page 348: Paul Fusco/Magnum Photos, Inc. Page 350: Steve Goldberg/Monkmeyer Press Photo. Page 358: Bettmann Archive. Page 380: Courtesy CDC.

Chapter 10 Opener: Inge Morath/Magnum Photos, Inc. Page 388: courtesy Clarke-Stewart. Page 391: Alan Dorow/Actuality. Page 408: Dennis Brack/Black Star. Page 414: Eve Arnold/Magnum Photos, Inc. Page 438: Polly Brown/Actuality.

Chapter 11 Opener: Paul Conklin/Monkmeyer Press Photo. Page 438: Shackman/Monkmeyer Press Photo. Page 444: Glassman/The Image Works. Page 452: Bruce Davidson/Magnum Photos, Inc. Page 454: courtesy Herbert C. Quay.

Chapter 12 Opener: Arthur Tress/Photo Researchers. Page 475: Richard Hutchings/Photo Researchers. Page 480: courtesy Judith Brook. Page 487: Dorothy Littell/Stock, Boston. Page 489: William Therryman/The Picture Cube.

Chapter 13 Opener: Leonard Freed/Magnum Photos, Inc. Page 509: Antman/The Image Works. Page 513: courtesy Michael Goldstein. Page 518: Lionel Delevingne/Stock, Boston. Page 529: Joseph Szabo/Photo Researchers. Page 535: Arlene Collins/Monkmeyer Press Photo.

◆ Subject Index

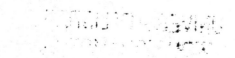